SECRET CODES

2007 VOLUME 1

BLOCKBUSTER®

S0-AVD-442

PLAYSTATION® 3

Games List

CALL OF DUTY 3

ALL CHAPTERS & BONUS CONTENT
At the Chapter Select screen, hold Select and press Right, Right, Left, Left, ⬤, ⬤.

MARVEL ULTIMATE ALLIANCE

UNLOCK ALL SKINS
At the Team menu, press Up, Down, Left, Right, Left, Right, START.

UNLOCKS ALL HERO POWERS
At the Team menu, press Left, Right, Up, Down, Up, Down, START.

ALL HEROES TO LEVEL 99
At the Team menu, press Up, Left, Up, Left, Down, Right, Down, Right, START.

UNLOCK ALL HEROES
At the Team menu, press Up, Up, Down, Down, Left, Left, Left, START.

UNLOCK DAREDEVIL
At the Team menu, press Left, Left, Right, Right, Up, Down, Up, Down, START.

UNLOCK SILVER SURFER
At the Team menu, press Down, Left, Left, Up, Right, Up, Down, Left, START.

GOD MODE
During gameplay, press Up, Down, Up, Down, Up, Left, Down, Right, START.

TOUCH OF DEATH
During gameplay, press Left, Right, Down, Down, Right, Left, START.

SUPER SPEED
During gameplay, press Up, Left, Up, Right, Down, Right, START.

FILL MOMENTUM
During gameplay, press Left, Right, Right, Left, Up, Down, Down, Up, START.

UNLOCK ALL COMICS
At the Review menu, press Left, Right, Right, Left, Up, Up, Right, START.

UNLOCK ALL CONCEPT ART
At the Review menu, press Down, Down, Down, Right, Right, Left, Down, START.

UNLOCK ALL CINEMATICS
At the Review menu, press Up, Left, Left, Up, Right, Right, Up, START.

UNLOCK ALL LOAD SCREENS
At the Review menu, press Up, Down, Right, Left, Up, Up Down, START.

UNLOCK ALL COURSES
At the Comic Missions menu, press Up, Right, Left, Down, Up, Right, Left, Down, START.

RESISTANCE: FALL OF MAN

HARD DIFFICULTY
Complete the game on Medium difficulty.

SUPERHUMAN DIFFICULTY
Complete the game on Hard difficulty.

SKILL POINTS
You can access the Skill Points and Rewards menus during gameplay by pressing START to access the Pause Menu, then selecting EXTRAS.

ENEMIES

NAME	LEVEL ACQUIRED	DESCRIPTION
Hybrid	The Gauntlet	After defeating first set of Hybrids.
Leaper	A Lone Survivor	After defeating first few Leapers.
Crawler	A Lone Survivor	After the cinematic and FPNICS.
Menial	Fate Worse Than Death	After the first room.
Cocoon	Conversion	At the third checkpoint.
Carrier	Fate Worse Than Death	At the window when you first see the Carriers.
Howler	Path of Least Resistance	After defeating the Howlers at the end of the level.
Steelhead	Cathedral	After defeating the first two Steelheads in the church.
Titan	Conduits	After defeating the Titan at the beginning of Conduits.
Slipskull	No Way Out	After defeating all three Slipskulls in the burrower room.
Leaper Pod	No Way Out or 61	After finding the Leaper Pods for the first time.
Gray Jack	Angel	After the cryo room.
Hardfang	Evacuation	After defeating the first Hardfang in the cafeteria.
Roller	Into the Depths	After defeating the Rollers in the room with the tunnel in the floor.
Widowmaker	Ice and Iron	After defeating the first Widowmaker.
Hybrid 2.0	Angel's Lair	After the first wave of Hybrids in the node.
Angel	Angel's Lair	After defeating the first Angel on the bridge.

VEHICLES

NAME	LEVEL ACQUIRED	DESCRIPTION
Hawk	The Gauntlet	Player automatically starts with this.
Kingfisher	Path of Least Resistance	At the start of the level.
Sabertooth	A Lone Survivor	After getting inside the tank.
Dropship	Hunted Down	After spotting a Dropship in the parking lot area.
Stalker	Outgunned	After spotting the first one in Outgunned.
Burrower	No Way Out	After spotting the first one in No Way Out.
Lynx	Common Ground	After getting inside the Lynx.
Goliath	Giant Slayer	After spotting the first one.

WEAPONS—1ST PLAYTHROUGH

NAME	LEVEL ACQUIRED	DESCRIPTION
M5A2 Carbine	The Gauntlet	Automatically unlocked at start of the game.
Frag Grenade	The Gauntlet	Automatically unlocked at start of the game.
Bullseye	The Gauntlet	In the alleyway after checkpoint 2.
Shotgun	Fate Worse Than Death or 32 or 40	Fate Worse Than Death: Behind the stairs in the outdoor area. Hunted Down: Behind the bar. Hunted Down: In the docks area. Path of Least Resistance: Forced here on the stairs between hill 1 and 2.
Auger	Cathedral	After defeating the first two advanced Hybrids.
Fareye	Conduits	After defeating the large Hybrid and reaching checkpoint 1.
Hailstorm	Search and Rescue	After leaving the first area.
Sapper	A Disturbing Discovery	At the back of the first mech factory.
LAARK	In a Darker Place	On the ground in the first room.
Bullseye Mark 2	Angel's Lair	After leaving the first room and going into the node.

WEAPONS—2ND PLAYTHROUGH

NAME	LEVEL ACQUIRED	DESCRIPTION
Reapers	The Gauntlet	Inside the house at the bottom of the hill.
Backlash Grenade	Cathedral	After crossing alley just past the cathedral; it's the first room on the left.
Arc Charger	No Way Out	At the end of the long hallway prior to the burrower.
L11-Dragon	Evacuation	Before the first elevator leading to the hangar.
Splitter	A Desperate Gambit	At checkpoint 1, near the big windows.

LOCATIONS

NAME	LEVEL ACQUIRED	DESCRIPTION
York	The Gauntlet	Unlocked at the start of the level.
Grimsby	Fate Worse Than Death	Unlocked at the start of the level.
Manchester	Path of Least Resistance	Unlocked at the start of the level.
Nottingham	Into the Fire	Unlocked at the start of the level.
Cheshire	No Way Out	Unlocked at the start of the level.
Somerset	Search and Rescue	Unlocked at the start of the level.
Bristol	Devil at the Door	Unlocked at the start of the level.
Bracknell	Into the Depths	Unlocked at the start of the level.
London	A Desperate Gambit	Unlocked at the start of the level.
Thames	Burning Bridges	Unlocked at the start of the level.
Tower	Angel's Lair	Unlocked at the start of the level.

REWARDS

NAME	HOW TO UNLOCK
Concept Art Pack 1	10 points
Concept Art Pack 2	20 points
The Mighty Wrench - Gives allies wrench	40 points
Flip Levels	70 points
Clank Backpacks	100 points
MP Mechanic Skin	126 points
MP Soldier Skin	Beat game on Superhuman mode
MP Soldier head skin	Beat game on Superhuman mode and collect all Skill Points
Movie player	Beat game once

TONY HAWK'S PROJECT 8

SPONSOR ITEMS

As you progress through Career mode and move up the rankings, you gain sponsors and each comes with its own Create-a-skater item.

RANK REQUIRED	CAS ITEM UNLOCKED
Rank 040	Adio Kenny V2 Shoes
Rank 050	Quiksilver_Hoody_3
Rank 060	Birdhouse Tony Hawk Deck
Rank 080	Vans No Skool Gothic Shoes
Rank 100	Volcom Scallero Jacket
Rank 110	eS Square One Shoes
Rank 120	Almost Watch What You Say Deck
Rank 140	DVS Adage Shoe
Rank 150	Element Illuminate Deck
Rank 160	Etnies Sheckler White Lavender Shoes
Complete Skateshop Goal	Stereo Soundwave Deck

SKATERS

All of the skaters, except for Tony Hawk, must be unlocked by completing challenges in the Career Mode. They are useable in Free Skate and 2 Player modes.

SKATER	HOW TO UNLOCK
Tony Hawk	Always Unlocked
Lyn-z Adams Hawkins	Complete Pro Challenge
Bob Burquist	Complete Pro Challenge
Dustin Dollin	Complete Pro Challenge
Nyjah Huston	Complete Pro Challenge
Bam Margera	Complete Pro Challenge
Rodney Mullen	Complete Pro Challenge
Paul Rodriguez	Complete Pro Challenge
Ryan Sheckler	Complete Pro Challenge
Daewon Song	Complete Pro Challenge
Mike Vallely	Complete Pro Challenge
Stevie Willams	Complete Pro Challenge

SKATER	HOW TO UNLOCK
Travis Barker	Complete Pro Challenge
Kevin Staab	Complete Pro Challenge
Zombie	Complete Pro Challenge
Christiaian Hosoi	Rank #1
Jason Lee	Complete Final Tony Hawk Goal
Photographer	Unlock Shops
Security Guard	Unlock School
Bum	Unlock Car Factory
Beaver Mascot	Unlock High School
Real Estate Agent	Unlock Downtown
Filmer	Unlock High School
Skate Jam Kid	Rank #4
Dad	Rank #1
Colonel	All Gaps
Nerd	Complete School Spirit Goal

CHEAT CODES

Select Cheat Codes from the Options and enter the following codes. In game you can access some codes from the Options menu.

CHEAT CODE	RESULTS
plus44	Unlocks Travis Barker
hohohosoi	Unlocks Christian Hosoi
notmono	Unlocks Jason Lee
mixitup	Unlocks Kevin Staab
strangefellows	Unlocks Dad & Skater Jam Kid
themedia	Unlocks Photog Girl & Filmer
militarymen	Unlocks Colonel & Security Guard
jammypack	Unlocks Always Special
balancegalore	Unlocks Perfect Rail
frontandback	Unlocks Perect Manual
shellshock	Unlocks Unlimited Focus
shescaresme	Unlocks Big Realtor
birdhouse	Unlocks Inkblot deck
allthebest	Full stats
needaride	All decks unlocked and free, except for Inkblot Deck and Gamestop Deck
yougotitall	All specials unlocked and in player's special list and set as owned in skate shop
wearelosers	Unlocks Nerd and a Bum
manineedadate	Unlocks Beaver Mascot
suckstobedead	Unlocks Officer Dick
HATEDANDPROUD	Unlocks the Vans item

PLAYSTATION® 2

Games List

24: THE GAME

SECURITY CLEARANCE MENU

At the Main menu, hold L1 + L2 + R1 + R2 until the Security Clearance screen appears. Now you can enter the following codes.

Highlight the character you want to change. Hold ✖ and press Left or Right to change it, then release ✖. After entering the code, press ⬤.

INVULNERABLE
Enter 66BAUER at the
Security Clearance screen.

INFINITE AMMO
Enter 62ALMEIDA at the
Security Clearance screen.

ALL MISSIONS
Enter 72DESSLER at the
Security Clearance screen.

ALL BONUSES
Enter 54PALMER at the Security Clearance screen.

50 CENT: BULLETPROOF

BULLETPROOF CHEAT
Pause the game and select Codes from the Options menu. Enter ny'sfinestyo to become invincible.

ALL WEAPONS
Pause the game and select Codes from the Options menu. Enter gotthemrachets.

INFINITE AMMO
Pause the game and select Codes from the Options menu. Enter grizzspecial.

MIKE MODE
Pause the game and select Codes from the Options menu. Enter the hub is broken. This gives you better guns.

BLOODHOUND COUNTERKILL
Pause the game and select Codes from the Options menu. Enter gunrunner.

EMPTY'N CLIPS COUNTERKILL
Pause the game and select Codes from the Options menu. Enter workout.

GUILLOTINE COUNTERKILL
Pause the game and select Codes from the Options menu. Enter gettingdropped.

G'D UP COUNTERKILL
Pause the game and select Codes from the Options menu. Enter gooddieyoung.

WANKSTA COUNTERKILL
Pause the game and select Codes from the Options menu. Enter aintgotnothin.

TRACK ACTION 26
Pause the game and select Codes from the Options menu. Enter orangejuice.

ALL MUSIC
Pause the game and select Codes from the Options menu. Enter graballthat50.

BULLETPROOF EXCLUSIVES
Pause the game and select Codes from the Options menu. Enter 50bpexclusives. This unlocks the following music tracks: "I'm A Rider," "Maybe We Crazy," and "Pimp Pt2."

UNLOCK SO SEDUCTIVE SONG
Pause the game and select Codes from the Options menu. Enter killa1.

ALL MOVIES
Pause the game and select Codes from the Options menu. Enter HookMeUp50.

SO SEDUCTIVE VIDEO
Pause the game and select Codes from the Options menu. Enter yayoshome.

MY BUDDY VIDEO
Pause the game and select Codes from the Options menu. Enter sayhellotomylittlefriend.

AEON FLUX

BOMBER JACKET OUTFIT
Select Enter Cheat from the Extras menu and enter JULIET ALPHA CHARLIE KILO ECHO TANGO. Find the outfit under Outfits in the Extras menu.

FAME OUTFIT
Select Enter Cheat from the Extras menu and enter GOLF ROMEO ALPHA YANKEE. Find the outfit under Outfits in the Extras menu.

ALTERNATE OUTFITS
Select Enter Cheat from the Extras menu and enter CHARLIE LIMA OSCAR TANGO HOTEL ECHO SIERRA. Find the outfits under Outfits in the Extras menu. These outfits include the following: Freya, Monican Freya, Hostess Judy, Una, and Fashion Una.

MRS. GOODCHILD OUTFIT

Select Enter Cheat from the Extras menu and enter WHISKEY HOTEL INDIA TANGO ECHO. Find the outfit under Outfits in the Extras menu.

REVELATION OUTFIT

Select Enter Cheat from the Extras menu and enter ALPHA ROMEO MIKE SIERRA. Find the outfit under Outfits in the Extras

SEEDS OUTFIT

Select Enter Cheat from the Extras menu and enter MIKE OSCAR VICTOR INDIA ECHO. Find the outfit under Outfits in the Extras menu.

WAR OUTFIT

Select Enter Cheat from the Extras menu and enter BRAVO LIMA UNIFORM ROMEO. Find the outfit under Outfits in the Extras menu.

ALL REPLAY EPISODES

Select Enter Cheat from the Extras menu and enter BRAVO ALPHA YANKEE OSCAR UNIFORM. Select Replay Episode from the Extras menu.

ALL SLIDESHOWS

Select Enter Cheat from the Extras menu and enter PAPA INDIA XRAY ECHO SIERRA. Select Slideshows from the Extras menu.

ACTION MOVIE CHEAT

Select Enter Cheat from the Extras menu and enter BRAVO ALPHA GOLF MIKE ALPHA NOVEMBER or UNIFORM KILO GOLF ALPHA MIKE ECHO ROMEO. Pause the game and select Cheats to access the code.

GOD MODE CHEAT
Select Enter Cheat from the Extras menu and enter TANGO ROMEO INDIA ROMEO OSCAR XRAY.
Pause the game and select Cheats to access the code.

FREE FATALITIES CHEAT
Select Enter Cheat from the Extras menu and enter CHARLIE UNIFORM TANGO INDIA OSCAR
NOVEMBER ECHO. Pause the game and select Cheats to access the code.

ONE-STRIKE KILLS CHEAT
Select Enter Cheat from the Extras menu and enter BRAVO UNIFORM CHARLIE KILO FOXTROT
SIERRA TANGO. Pause the game and select Cheats to access the code.

RESTORE HEALTH CHEAT
Select Enter Cheat from the Extras menu and enter HOTEL ECHO ALPHA LIMA MIKE ECHO.
Pause the game and select Cheats to access the code.

UNLIMITED AMMO CHEAT
Select Enter Cheat from the Extras menu and enter FOXTROT UNIFORM GOLF. Pause the game
and select Cheats to access the code.

UNLIMITED HEALTH CHEAT
Select Enter Cheat from the Extras menu and enter CHARLIE LIMA OSCAR NOVEMBER ECHO.
Pause the game and select Cheats to access the code.

UNLIMITED POWER STRIKES CHEAT
Select Enter Cheat from the Extras menu and enter LIMA CHARLIE VICTOR GOLF. Pause the
game and select Cheats to access the code.

AIRFORCE DELTA STRIKE

SELF DESTRUCT
Pause the game and press Up, Up, Down, Down, Left, Right, Left, Right, ✖, ●.

REFILL HP AND MISSILES
Pause the game and press Up, Up, Down, Down, Left, Right, Left, Right, L3, R3.

ALIAS

LEVEL SELECT
Complete the game, then press L1 + R1 at the new game screen.

AIRFORCE DELTA STRIKE

SELF DESTRUCT
Pause the game and press Up, Up, Down, Down, Left, Right, Left, Right, ✖, ●.

REFILL HP AND MISSILES
Pause the game and press Up, Up, Down, Down, Left, Right, Left, Right, L3, R3.

ALIAS

LEVEL SELECT
Complete the game, then press L1 + R1 at the new game screen.

ALIEN HOMINID

ALL LEVELS,
MINI-GAMES & HATS
Select Player 1 Setup or Player 2 Setup and
change the name to ROYGBIV.

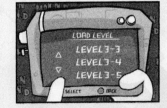

HATS FOR 2-PLAYER GAME

Go to the Options and rename your alien one of the following: Abe, april, behemoth, cletus, dandy, Goodman, grrl, princess, superfly.

ALIENS VS. PREDATOR: EXTINCTION

CHEATS

Pause the game and press R1, R1, L1, R1, L1, L1, R1, L1, R1, R1, L1, R1, L1, L1, R1, L1. This will unlock a Cheat option in the Options.

AMERICAN CHOPPER

UNLOCK EVERYTHING

During a game, press R1, R2, L2, L1, R2, L3, R3.

AMPLITUDE

BLUR

During a game, press R3 (x4), L3 (x4), then R3.

MONKEY NOTES

During a game, press L3 (x4), R3 (x4), then L3. Quit the game and go back into the song to see the effect. Re-enter the code to disable it.

RANDOM NOTE PLACEMENT

During a game, press ✕, ✕, Left, Left, R3, R3, Right, Right. Quit the game and go back into the song to see the effect. Re-enter the code to disable it.

CHANGE SHAPE OF TRACK LAYOUT

During the game, press L3 (x3), R3 (x3), L3, R3, and L3. Quit the game and go back into the song to see the effect. Enter it once for a tunnel appearance and a second time for a Tempest-style look. Enter the code a third time to disable it.

AND 1 STREETBALL

GLOBAL UNLOCK

Select Cheat Codes from the Options menu and enter △, △, ✕, ✕, ■, ◯, ■, ◯.
This unlocks all Bonus Stuff

ALL BREAKDOWNS

Select Cheat Codes from the Options menu and enter ✕, ✕, ◯, ■, ■, △, △, △.

WARDROBE UNLOCK

Select Cheat Codes from the Options menu and enter ✕, △, ◯, ✕, ■, △, △, ◯.

ALL BLACKTOPS
Select Cheat Codes from the Options menu
and enter ●, ✕, ✕, ■, ■, ▲, ●, ✕.

CHATTERBOX UNLOCK
Select Cheat Codes from the Options menu
and enter ▲, ■, ●, ■, ▲, ✕, ■, ▲.

SIDE GAMES
Select Cheat Codes from the Options menu
and enter ●, ■, ▲, ✕, ✕, ●, ●, ■.

DJ GREEN LANTERN
Select Cheat Codes from the Options menu
and enter ●, ●, ▲, ✕, ■, ✕, ▲, ●.

PLAY AS FLASH
Select Cheat Codes from the Options menu
and enter ▲, ✕, ✕, ●, ▲, ▲, ●, ■.

PLAY AS SHANE
Select Cheat Codes from the Options menu
and enter ■, ✕, ▲, ✕, ▲, ●, ▲, ✕.

PLAY AS SKIP TO MY LOU
Select Cheat Codes from the Options menu and enter ●, ✕, ●, ■, ▲, ✕, ●, ■.

HAMILTONS
Select Cheat Codes from the Options menu
and enter ●, ▲, ■, ■, ▲, ●, ✕, ●.
This gives you $1,000,000.

ALWAYS ON FIRE
Select Cheat Codes from the Options menu
and enter ■, ✕, ✕, ▲, ■, ✕, ■, ●.

IBALL MOVES
Select Cheat Codes from the Options menu and enter ✕, ▲, ✕, ●, ■, ●, ✕, ■.

LIKE WATER
Select Cheat Codes from the Options menu and enter ■, ✕, ●, ■, ✕, ●, ▲, ▲.

THE OG WAY
Select Cheat Codes from the Options menu and enter ▲, ●, ■, ■, ●, ▲, ✕, ■.

SHOT TIMING TEXT
Select Cheat Codes from the Options menu and enter ▲, ■, ●, ●, ■, ■, ●, ▲.

APE ESCAPE 3

SECRET PASSWORDS
At the Title screen, press L1 + R1 + L2 + R2. Now you can enter the following codes.

DARK MASTER ON THE LOOSE!
Enter blackout at the Secret Password screen.

MOVIE 28 AND 2 CINEMA FILES
Enter 2 snakes at the Secret Password screen.

SHIMMY ON THE LOOSE!
Enter 2nd man at the Secret Password screen.

MONKEY AS SPIKE
Enter krops at the Secret Password screen.

BLUE PIPOTRON
Enter coolblue at the Secret Password screen.

RED PIPOTRON
Enter redmon at the Secret Password screen.

YELLOW PIPOTRON
Enter yellowy at the Secret Password screen.

SAL-1000 MONKEY
Enter grobyc at the Secret Password screen.

SAL-3000 MONKEY
Enter SAL3000 at the Secret Password screen.

APE ESCAPE: PUMPED & PRIMED

ALL GADGETS
Complete Story Mode. At the mode select, hold R1 + L1 + R2 + L2 to access the password screen. Enter Go Wild!.

DISABLE ALL GADGETS CHEAT
Complete Story Mode. At the mode select, hold R1 + L1 + R2 + L2 to access the password screen. Enter Limited!.

NORMAL DIFFICULTY
Complete Story Mode. At the mode select, hold R1 + L1 + R2 + L2 to access the password screen. Enter NORMAL!.

HARD DIFFICULTY
Complete Story Mode. At the mode select, hold R1 + L1 + R2 + L2 to access the password screen. Enter HARD!.

ATV OFFROAD FURY 3

UNLOCK EVERYTHING, EXCEPT THE FURY BIKE
Select Player Profile from the Options menu. Then select Enter Cheat and enter !SLACKER!. This will not unlock the Fury.

ALL ATVS IN TRAINING
Select Player Profile from the Options menu. Then select Enter Cheat and enter NOSKILLS.

ALL RIDER GEAR
Select Player Profile from the Options menu. Then select Enter Cheat and enter FITS.

$1500
Select Player Profile from the Options menu. Then select Enter Cheat and enter +foodstamps+.

MUSIC VIDEOS
Select Player Profile from the Options menu. Then select Enter Cheat and enter ROCKNROLL.

ATV QUAD POWER RACING 2

UNLOCK EVERYTHING
Name your profile GOLDRUSH or GOLDDUST. You will receive confirmation that the cheat has been enabled.

UNLOCK TRACKS
Name your profile ROADKILL. You will receive confirmation that the cheat has been enabled.

UNLOCK VEHICLES
Name your profile GENERALLEE. You will receive confirmation that the cheat has been enabled.

UNLOCK RIDERS
Name your profile BUBBA. You will receive confirmation that the cheat has been enabled.

UNLOCK TRICKS
Name your profile FIDDLERSELBO. You will receive confirmation that the cheat has been enabled.

UNLOCK CHALLENGES
Name your profile DOUBLEBARREL. You will receive confirmation that the cheat has been enabled.

UNLOCK CHAMP
Name your profile REDROOSTER. You will receive confirmation that the cheat has been enabled.

MAX STATS
Name your profile GINGHAM. You will receive confirmation that the cheat has been enabled.

AVATAR: THE LAST AIRBENDER

ALL TREASURE MAPS
Select Code Entry from the Extras menu and enter 37437.

1-HIT DISHONOR
Select Code Entry from the Extras menu and enter 54641.

DOUBLE DAMAGE
Select Code Entry from the Extras menu and enter 34743.

UNLIMITED COPPER
Select Code Entry from the Extras menu and enter 23637.

UNLIMITED CHI
Select Code Entry from the Extras menu and enter 24463.

UNLIMITED HEALTH
Select Code Entry from the Extras menu and enter 94677.

NEVERENDING STEALTH
Select Code Entry from the Extras menu and enter 53467.

CHARACTER CONCEPT ART GALLERY
Select Code Entry from the Extras menu and enter 97831.

BACKYARD WRESTLING 2: THERE GOES THE NEIGHBORHOOD

ALL BONUSES
At the Main menu, hold L1 and press ✕, ■, ▲, ●, ✕, ■, ▲, ●.

CHEAT MODE
At the Main menu, hold L1 and press ✕, ▲, ✕, ▲, ✕.

BRATZ: FOREVER DIAMONDZ

1000 BLINGZ
While in the Bratz Office, use the Cheat computer to enter SIZZLN.

2000 BLINGZ
While in the Bratz Office, use the Cheat computer to enter FLAUNT.

PET TREATS
While in the Bratz Office, use the Cheat computer to enter TREATZ.

GIFT SET A
While in the Bratz Office, use the Cheat computer to enter STYLIN.

GIFT SET B
While in the Bratz Office, use the Cheat computer to enter SKATIN.

GIFT SET C
While in the Bratz Office, use the Cheat computer to enter JEWELZ.

GIFT SET E
While in the Bratz Office, use the Cheat computer to enter DIMNDZ.

BRATZ: ROCK ANGELZ

CAMERON CHANGED
While in the Bratz Office, use the Cheat computer to ENTER STYLIN.

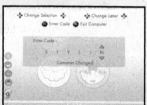

CHLOE CHANGED
While in the Bratz Office, use the Cheat computer to enter SPARKLE, FASHION, STRUT or FLAIR.

DYLAN CHANGED
While in the Bratz Office, use the Cheat computer to enter MEYGEN.

JADE CHANGED
While in the Bratz Office, use the Cheat computer to enter FUNKALISH, SLAMMIN or HOT.

LONDON BOY CHANGED
While in the Bratz Office, use the Cheat computer to enter BLINGZ.

PARIS BOY CHANGED
While in the Bratz Office, use the Cheat computer to enter ROCKIN.

SASHA CHANGED
While in the Bratz Office, use the Cheat computer to enter FUNKY, SCORCHIN, PRETTY or MODEL

YASMIN CHANGED
While in the Bratz Office, use the Cheat computer to enter COOL, CRAZY or SASSY.

RECEIVE 1000 BLINGZ
While in the Bratz Office, use the Cheat computer to enter YASMIN.

RECEIVE 2000 BLINGZ
While in the Bratz Office, use the Cheat computer to enter PHOEBE.

RECEIVE 2100 BLINGZ
While in the Bratz Office, use the Cheat computer to enter DANCIN.

RECEIVE 3000 BLINGZ
While in the Bratz Office, use the Cheat computer to enter WAYFAB.

RECEIVE 6000 BLINGZ
While in the Bratz Office, use the Cheat
computer to enter HOTTIE.

UNLOCKED RINGTONE 12
While in the Bratz Office, use the Cheat
computer to enter BLAZIN.

UNLOCKED RINGTONE 15
While in the Bratz Office, use the Cheat
computer to enter FIANNA.

UNLOCKED RINGTONE 16
While in the Bratz Office, use the Cheat computer to enter ANGELZ.

BUTT UGLY MARTIANS: ZOOM OR DOOM

ALL RACERS
During a game, hold L1 + R1 and press ▲, ●, ✖, ●.

CABELA'S DANGEROUS HUNTS 2

DOUBLE HEALTH
Select Codes and enter Eye, Bolt, Skull, Hand, Boot.

HEALTH REGENERATES FASTER
Select Codes and enter Skull, Eye, Boot, Bolt, Hand.

DOUBLE DAMAGE
Select Codes and enter Hand, Boot, Skull, Eye, Bolt.

INFINITE AMMO
Select Codes and enter Bolt, Hand, Eye, Boot, Skull.

CABELA'S DEER HUNT 2005 SEASON

GPS
At the Equipment menu, press ▲, ●, ●, R1, R2, ✖.

CALL OF DUTY: FINEST HOUR

ALL LEVELS
Players may unlock all the levels in the game by progressing to the Level Select
screen and pressing the following key combination:
    While holding Up on the Controller 2 D-pad, On Controller 1 press START, SELECT, SELECT, ●.

CALL OF DUTY 2: BIG RED ONE

UNLOCK ALL CHAPTERS
At the Chapter Select screen, hold R1 + L1
and press Up, Up, Down, Down, Left, Left,
Right, Right, ●, Right, ●, Right, ●.

CALL OF DUTY 3

ALL CHAPTERS & BONUS CONTENT
At the Chapter Select screen, hold Select and press Right, Right, Left, Left, ●, ●.

CAPCOM CLASSICS COLLECTION

ALL LOCKS OPENED
At the Title screen, press L1, R1, Up on Right Analog Stick, Down on Right Analog Stick, L1, R1, Up on Left Analog Stick, Down on Left Analog Stick, L1, R1, Up, Down.

CARS

UNLOCK EVERYTHING
Select Cheat Codes from the Options menu and enter IF900HP.

ALL CHARACTERS
Select Cheat Codes from the Options menu and enter YAYCARS.

ALL CHARACTER SKINS
Select Cheat Codes from the Options menu and enter R4MONE.

ALL MINI-GAMES & COURSES
Select Cheat Codes from the Options menu and enter MATTL66.

MATER'S COUNTDOWN CLEAN-UP MINI-GAME & MATER'S SPEEDY CIRCUIT
Select Cheat Codes from the Options menu and enter TRGTEXC.

FAST START
Select Cheat Codes from the Options menu and enter IMSPEED.

INFINITE BOOST
Select Cheat Codes from the Options menu and enter VROOOOM.

ART
Select Cheat Codes from the Options menu
and enter CONC3PT.

VIDEOS
Select Cheat Codes from the Options menu
and enter WATCHIT.

CHAMPIONS OF NORRATH: REALMS OF EVERQUEST

LEVEL 20 CHARACTER
During a game, press and hold L1 + R2 +
⚠ + R3. This makes your character level
20 with 75,000 coins and 999 skill points.
This does not increase your character's
main attributes.

CHICKEN LITTLE

INVINCIBILITY
Select Cheat Codes from the Extras menu and enter Baseball, Baseball, Baseball, Shirt.

BIG FEET
Select Cheat Codes from the Extras menu and enter Hat, Glove, Glove, Hat.

BIG HAIR
Select Cheat Codes from the Extras menu and enter Baseball, Bat, Bat, Baseball.

BIG HEAD
Select Cheat Codes from the Extras menu and enter Hat, Helmet, Helmet, Hat.

PAPER PANTS
Select Cheat Codes from the Extras menu and enter Bat, Bat, Hat, Hat.

SUNGLASSES
Select Cheat Codes from the Extras menu and enter Glove, Glove, Helmet, Helmet.

UNDERWEAR
Select Cheat Codes from the Extras menu and enter Hat, Hat, Shirt, Shirt.

THE CHRONICLES OF NARNIA: THE LION, THE WITCH AND THE WARDROBE

ENABLE CHEATS
At the Title screen, press ❌ and hold L1 + R1, then press Down, Down, Right, Up. The
text should turn green when entered correctly. Now you can enter the following codes.

LEVEL SELECT
At the wardrobe, hold L1 and press Up, Up, Right, Right, Up, Right, Down.

ALL BONUS LEVELS
At the Bonus Drawer, hold L1 and press Down, Down, Right, Right, Down, Right, Up.

LEVEL SKIP
During gameplay, hold L1 and press Down, Left, Down, Left, Down, Right, Down, Right, Up.

INVINCIBILITY
During gameplay, hold L1 and press Down, Up, Down, Right, Right.

RESTORE HEALTH
During gameplay, hold L1 and press Down, Left, Left, Right.

10,000 COINS
During gameplay, hold L1 and press Down, Left, Right, Down, Down.

ALL ABILITIES
During gameplay, hold L1 and press Down, Left, Right, Left, Up.

FILL COMBO METER
During gameplay, hold L1 and press Up, Up, Right, Up.

COMMANDOS STRIKE FORCE

MISSION SELECT
Enter TRUCO as a profile name.

CONFLICT: GLOBAL TERROR

CHEAT OPTION
At the Main menu, press L1, R1, L1, R1, ●, ●, ●, ●.

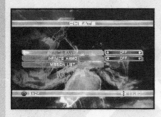

CONFLICT: VIETNAM

CHEAT MENU
At the Main menu, press L1, R1, L1, R1, ■, ▲, ●, ▲, ■, ●. Access the Cheats by selecting Options from the Pause menu. Select Cheats for infinite saves, infinite ammo, mission list and mission skip.

CONFLICT ZONE

INVINCIBLE UNITS
Pause the game and press Right, Left, Right, Right, ✖.

MONEY CHEAT
Pause the game and press ✖, Left, Right, Up, Left.

100 POPULATION
Pause the game and press ✖, Right, Right, Left, Up.

FAST BUILDING
Pause the game and press ✖, Down, Down, Up, Left, Right.

MISSIONS IN REPLAY MODE
Pause the game and press ✖, Up, Up, Left, Right, Left.

VIEW ENTIRE MAP
Pause the game and press ✖, Left, Right, Right, Left.

CONSTANTINE

BIG DEMON HEADS
Press SELECT to get to the Journal and press R2, Left, Right, Left, Left, Right, Left, R2.

BIG WEAPON
Press SELECT to get to the Journal and press Left, ⬤, ⬤, ⬤, ⬤, ⬤, ⬤.

INFINITE SOUL ENERGY
Press SELECT to get to the Journal and press Left, Right, Right, Left, Left, Right, Right, Left, ⬤, ⬤.

RAPID FIRE SHOTGUN
Press SELECT to get to the Journal and press L2, Left, R2, Left, ⬤, ⬤, ⬤, ⬤.

SHOOT LARGE FIREBALLS
Press SELECT to get to the Journal and press ⬤, ⬤, ⬤, Left, Right, Right, Left, Left, Right.

EXPLOSIVE HOLY BOMBS
Press SELECT to get to the Journal and press Right, Left, ⬤, ⬤, ⬤, ⬤, Left, Right.

CRASH TAG TEAM RACING

FASTER VEHICLES
At the Main menu, hold L1 + R1 and press ⬤, ⬤, ▲, ▲.

ONE-HIT KO
At the Main menu, hold L1 + R1 and press ✖, ⬤, ⬤, ✖.

DISABLE HUD
At the Main menu, hold L1 + R1 and press ✖, ⬛, ▲, ⬤.

CHICKEN HEADS
At the Main menu, hold L1 + R1 and press ✖, ⬤, ⬤, ⬛

JAPANESE CRASH
At the Main menu, hold L1 + R1 and press ⬛, ⬤, ⬛, ⬤.

DRIVE A BLOCK VEHICLE
At the Main menu, hold L1 + R1 and press ⬤, ⬤, ▲, ⬛.

THE DA VINCI CODE

GOD MODE
Select Codes from the Options menu and enter VITRUVIAN MAN.

EXTRA HEALTH
Select Codes from the Options menu and enter SACRED FEMININE.

MISSION SELECT
Select Codes from the Options menu and enter CLOS LUCE 1519.

1-HIT FIST KILL
Select Codes from the Options menu and enter PHILLIPS EXETER.

1-HIT WEAPON KILL
Select Codes from the Options menu and enter ROYAL HOLLOWAY.

ALL VISUAL DATABASE
Select Codes from the Options menu and enter APOCRYPHA.

ALL VISUAL DATABASE & CONCEPT ART
Select Codes from the Options menu and enter ET IN ARCADIA EGO.

DEF JAM: FIGHT FOR NY

Select Cheats from the Extras menu and
enter the following:

100 REWARD POINTS
Enter NEWJACK, THESOURCE, CROOKLYN,
DUCKETS, or GETSTUFF. You can enter each
code only once.

**UNLOCK SONG:
"AFTERHOURS" BY NYNE**
Enter LOYALTY.

**UNLOCK SONG: "ANYTHING
GOES" BY C-N-N**
Enter MILITAIN.

**UNLOCK SONG: "BUST" BY
OUTKAST**
Enter BIGBOI.

**UNLOCK SONG: "BLINDSIDE"
BY BAXTER**
Enter CHOPPER.

**UNLOCK SONG: "COMP" BY
COMP**
Enter CHOCOCITY.

**UNLOCK SONG: "DRAGON
HOUSE" BY CHIANG**
Enter AKIRA.

**UNLOCK SONG: "GET IT NOW"
BY BLESS**
Enter PLATINUMB.

**UNLOCK SONG: "KOTO" BY
CHIANG**
Enter GHOSTSHELL.

**UNLOCK SONG: "LIL' BRO" BY
RIC-A-CHE**
Enter GONBETRUBL.

**UNLOCK SONG: "MAN UP" BY
STICKY FINGAZ**
Enter KIRKJONES.

**UNLOCK SONG: "MOVE!" BY
PUBLIC ENEMY**
Enter RESPECT.

**UNLOCK SONG: "O. G.
ORIGINAL GANGSTER" BY
ICE T**
Enter POWER.

**UNLOCK SONG: "POPPA
LARGE" BY ULTRAMAGNETIC
MC'S**
Enter ULTRAMAG.

**UNLOCK SONG: "SIEZE THE
DAY" BY BLESS**
Enter SIEZE.

**UNLOCK SONG: "TAKE A LOOK
AT MY LIFE" BY FAT JOE**
Enter CARTAGENA.

**UNLOCK SONG: "WALK WITH
ME" BY JOE BUDDEN**
Enter PUMP.

DESTROY ALL HUMANS!

AMMO-A-PLENTY
Pause the game, press and hold L2 and press Left, ●, R2, Right, R1, ●. This gives you unlimited ammo.

BULLETPROOF CRYPTO
Pause the game, press and hold L2 and press ●, ●, Left, Left, ●, ●. This makes you invincible.

DEEP THINKER
Pause the game, press and hold L2 and press R1, R2, ●, Right, R2, ●. This gives you unlimited Concentration.

AWARE LIKE A FOX
Pause the game, press and hold L2 and press Right, ●, R2, R1, Right, R2. This maxes out the alert meter.

NOBODY LOVES YOU
Pause the game, press and hold L2 and press R2, Right, R2, R1, ●, Right. This resets the alert meter.

FOUND KEY TO ORTHOPOX'S LAB
On the Mothership, press and hold L2 and press ●, ●, Left, Left, ●, ●. This gives you access to the Upgrades at Pox's Lab.

MMMM BRAINS!
On the Mothership, press and hold L2 and press R1, R1, R2, R2, Left, Right, Left, Right, R2, R1. This gives you extra DNA.

DESTROY ALL HUMANS! 2

SALAD DAYS WITH POX & CRYPTO
Pause the game and select Archives. Then press and hold L3 and press ✕, ●, ▲, ●, ●, ●, ▲, ✕, ✕.

DOG'S LIFE

CHEAT MENU
During a game, press ● (Bark), ● (Bark), ● (Bark), hold ● (Growl), hold ● (Growl), hold ● (Growl), Left, Right, Down (Fart).

DRAGON BALL Z: SAGAS

PENDULUM ROOMS
Select Options from the Main menu and press Up, Down, Up, Down, Left, Right, Left, Right, Select, Start, Select, Start, ●, ●, ●, ●, ✕, ✕, Start. When entered correctly, the message "Pendulum Rooms Unlocked" will appear on-screen. This unlocks the Pendulum mode, all Extras, all Sagas, and all Upgrades.

INVINCIBILITY
Pause the game, select Controller and press Down, ✕, Select, Start, Right, ●, Left, ●, Up, ▲.

ALL UPGRADES
Pause the game, select Controller and press Up, Left, Down, Right, Select, Start, ●, ✕, ●, ▲.

DROME RACERS

INSTANT WIN
At the Main menu, press Left, Right, Left, Right, Up, Down, Up, Down, ●, ▲, ●. Press L3 during a race to win.

ALL TRACKS
At the Main menu, press Left, Right, Left, Right, Up, Down, Up, Down, ▲, ▲, ✕.

PURPLE RAIN
At the Main menu, press Left, Right, Left, Right, Up, Down, Up, Down, Up, Down, ● (x3).

WIREFRAME MODE
At the Main menu, press Left, Right, Left, Right, Up, Down, Up, Down, ●, ●, ✕.

DT RACER

FERRARI
At the Main menu, press Up, Down, Down, R1, L1, Left, Up, Up.

DUEL MASTERS

ALL LOCATIONS
At the Map screen, hold R3 and press ● (x3).

4 OF EVERY CARD & UNLOCK CHUCK IN ARCADE MODE
At the Deck Building screen, hold R3 and press L1, L1, L1.

PLAYER 1 LOSES SHIELD
During a duel, hold R3 and press ▲, ●, ✕. Release R3.

PLAYER 2 LOSES SHIELD
During a duel, hold R3 and press ▲, ●, ✕. Release R3.

PLAYER 1 GAINS SHIELD
During a duel, hold R3 and press ✕, ●, ▲. Release R3.

PLAYER 2 GAINS SHIELD
During a duel, hold R3 and press ✕, ●, ▲. Release R3.

PLAYER 1 WINS
During a duel, hold R3 and press L1, R1, L1.

PLAYER 2 WINS
During a duel, hold R3 and press R1, L1, R1.

TURN OFF DECK OUTS
During a duel, hold R3 and press ● (x3).

EA SPORTS ARENA FOOTBALL

BIG BALL
At the line of scrimmage, press L1 + ▲, Up, Up.

SMALL BALL
At the line of scrimmage, press L1 + ▲, Down, Down.

NORMAL SIZE BALL
At the line of scrimmage, press L1 + ▲, Up, Down.

MAX STATS IN QUICK PLAY
Load a profile with the name IronMen. This will maximize all players' stats in Quick Play.

EPHEMERAL FANTASIA

ALL NOTES IN MIDDLE BAR
Select Pattimo from Items. Press L2 (x3), L1, L1, Right (x3), ● before selecting your song.

NOTES MOVE FASTER & FURTHER APART
Select Pattimo from Items. Press L2, L1, Right, ●, ● before selecting your song.

NOTES MOVE EVEN FASTER & FURTHER APART
Select Pattimo from Items. Press L2, L1, Right, ●, ●, L2, L1, Right, ●, ● before selecting
your song.

NOTES DISAPPEAR BEFORE HITTING TOP BAR
Select Pattimo from Items. Press L2, Right, L1, Right, L2, L1 before selecting your song.

NOTES IN DIFFERENT PLACES
Select Pattimo from Items. Press Right, L1, L1, L2, L1, ● before selecting your song.

FANTASTIC 4

BARGE ARENA & STAN LEE INTERVIEW #1
At the Main menu, press ●, ●, ●, Down, Down, ●, Up.

INFINITE COSMIC POWER
At the Main menu, press Up, ●, ●, ●, Left, Right, ●.

BONUS LEVEL
At the Main menu, press Right, Right, ●, ●, Left, Up, Down.

FIFA STREET 2

ALL VENUES
At the Main menu, hold L1 + ▲ and press
Left, Up, Up, Right, Down, Down, Right,
Down.

FIGHT NIGHT ROUND 3

ALL VENUES
Select Create Champ and change the first name to NEWVIEW.

FLATOUT

ALL CARS, CLASSES & RACES
Create a new profile with the name GIVEALL.

$40,000
Create a new profile with the name GIVECASH.

EJECT YOURSELF FROM CAR
Create a new profile with the name RAGDOLL. Use the Gear Up button to throw yourself from the car without hitting anything.

FLATOUT 2

ALL CARS & 1,000,000 CREDITS
Select Enter Code from the Extras menu and enter GIEVEPIX.

1,000,000 CREDITS
Select Enter Code from the Extras menu and enter GIVECASH.

PIMPSTER CAR
Select Enter Code from the Extras menu and enter RUTTO.

FLATMOBILE CAR
Select Enter Code from the Extras menu and enter WOTKINS.

MOB CAR
Select Enter Code from the Extras menu and enter BIGTRUCK.

SCHOOL BUS
Select Enter Code from the Extras menu and enter GIEVCARPLZ.

ROCKET CAR
Select Enter Code from the Extras menu and enter KALJAKOPPA.

TRUCK
Select Enter Code from the Extras menu and enter ELPUEBLO.

FROGGER: ANCIENT SHADOW

LEVEL SELECT
For the following codes, choose Secret Code and enter the appropriate code to unlock the levels.

LEVEL	ENTER
Level 4-1	Berry, Lily, Lumpy, Lily
Level 4-2	Finnius, Frogger, Frogger, Wani
Level 5-1	Lily, Lily, Wani, Wani
Level 5-2	Frogger, Berry, Finnius, Frogger
Level 6-1	Lily, Wani, Lily, Wani
Level 6-2	Frogger, Lily, Lily, Lily
Level 6-3	Frogger, Frogger, Frogger, Berry
Level 7-1	Lily, Lily, Wani, Lumpy
Level 7-2	Lily, Frogger, Frogger, Lumpy

UNLOCK LETTERS
To unlock the various letter, choose Secret Code and enter the following codes.

LETTER	ENTER
Hyacinth Letter	Lumpy, Frogger, Frogger, Berry
Cosmos Letter	Berry, Lumpy, Frogger, Lumpy
Rose Letter	Wani, Lily, Wani, Frogger
Pansy Letter	Lumpy, Berry, Lumpy, Finnius

UNLOCK WIGS
To unlock the various wigs, choose Secret Code and enter the following codes.

WIG	ENTER
Lobster Wig	Finnius, Wani, Lumpy, Frogger
Bird Nest Wig	Lily, Lily, Lily, Lily
Sail Boat Wig	Lumpy, Lumpy, Lumpy, Lumpy
Skull Wig	Frogger, Lumpy, Lily, Frogger

DEVELOPER PICTURE 1
Select Secret Code and enter Wani, Frogger, Wani, Frogger.

DEVELOPER PICTURE 2
Select Secret Code and enter Berry, Berry, Berry, Wani.

UNLOCK ARTWORK

To unlock the various artwork pieces, choose Secret Code and enter the following codes.

ART NAME	ENTER
Programmer Art 1	Wani, Wani, Wani, Wani
Programmer Art 2	Lumpy, Frogger, Berry, Lily
Programmer Art 3	Wani, Frogger, Lily, Finnius
Additional Art 1	Frogger, Frogger, Frogger, Frogger
Additional Art 2	Finnius, Finnius, Finnius, Finnius
Additional Art 3	Berry, Berry, Berry, Berry

FULL SPECTRUM WARRIOR

INFINITE AMMO
Select Cheat Codes from the Extra Content menu and enter MERCENARIES.

BIG HEAD MODE
Select Cheat Codes from the Extra Content menu and enter NICKWEST.

US ARMY VERSION
Select Cheat Codes from the Extra Content menu and enter HA2P1PY9TUR5TLE.

AUTHENTIC MODE
Select Cheat Codes from the Extra Content menu and enter SWEDISHARMY.

FULL SPECTRUM WARRIOR: TEN HAMMERS

ALL LEVELS IN SINGLE PLAYER
Select Cheats from the Bonus Material menu and enter FULLSPECTRUMPWNAGE. Select Restart from the Play menu to access the levels.

FUTURE TACTICS: THE UPRISING

LEVEL SKIP
At the Game Select screen, press L1, ●, R1, R1, R2, ●, L1, R1, R2.

UNLIMITED TURNS AND MOVEMENT
During a game, press Up, Up, Down, Down, Left, Right, Left, Left, R1, L1.

BIG HEADS
During a game, press Up, Left, Down, Left, Down, Up, Up, Left.

DISCO MODE
During a game, press L1, Left, L1, Left, R1, Right, R1, Right.

LOW GRAVITY
During a game, press Up (x6), Down, Right, Up.

GODZILLA: SAVE THE EARTH

CHEAT MENU
At the Main menu, press and hold L2, ●, R2 in order, then let go of ●, R2, L2 in order. Now you can enter the following cheats.

ALL CITIES
Enter 659996.

ALL MONSTERS
Enter 525955.

UNLOCK CHALLENGES
Enter 975013.

HEALTH REGENERATES
Enter 536117.

ENERGY DOES NOT REGENERATE
Enter 122574.

INDESTRUCTIBLE BUILDINGS
Enter 812304.

100,000 POINTS
Enter 532459.

150,000 POINTS
Enter 667596.

200,000 POINTS
Enter 750330.

PLAYER 1: 4X DAMAGE
Enter 259565.

PLAYER 1: INFINITE ENERGY
Enter 819342.

PLAYER 1: INVISIBLE
Enter 531470.

PLAYER 1: INVULNERABLE
Enter 338592.

PLAYER 2: 4X DAMAGE
Enter 927281.

PLAYER 2: INFINITE ENERGY
Enter 324511.

PLAYER 2: INVISIBLE
Enter 118699.

PLAYER 2: INVULNERABLE
Enter 259333.

PLAYER 3: 4X DAMAGE
Enter 500494.

PLAYER 3: INFINITE ENERGY
Enter 651417.

PLAYER 3: INVISIBLE
Enter 507215.

PLAYER 3: INVULNERABLE
Enter 953598.

PLAYER 4: 4X DAMAGE
Enter 988551.

PLAYER 4: INFINITE ENERGY
Enter 456719.

PLAYER 4: INVISIBLE
Enter 198690.

PLAYER 4: INVULNERABLE
Enter 485542.

GALLERY
Enter 294206.

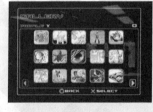

GODZILLA FINAL WARS
Enter 409014.

GOLDENEYE: ROGUE AGENT

FULL HEALTH AND ARMOR
Pause the game and press R1, R1, R2, L2, R2, R1, L1, R2.

FULLY CHARGE EYE POWER
Pause the game and press L1, R1, L1, L2, L2, R2, R1, L2.

ALL EYE POWERS
Pause the game and press L1, L1, R2, R2, R1, R2, L1, L2.

ALL LEVELS
At the Extra screen, press Down, Right, Down, Right, Up, Down, Up, Left.

ALL SKINS IN MULTIPLAYER
At the Extra screen, press Down, Left, Up, Left, Right, Down, Left, Up

NO EYE POWERS IN MULTIPLAYER
At the Extra screen, press Up, Up, Down, Left, Right, Right, Left, Down.

PAINTBALL
At the Extra screen, press Right, Left, Right, Left, Down, Down, Up, Up.

ONE-LIFE MODE
At the Extra screen, press Left, Down, Up, Right, Up, Right, Left, Down.

GRADIUS V

You can use one of these for each level completed.

DOUBLE SHOT POWER
After the first boss, pause the game and press Up, Up, Down, Down, Left, Right, Left, Right, L2, R2.

LASER POWER
After the first boss, pause the game and press Up, Up, Down, Down, Left, Right, Left, Right, L1, R1.

GRAFFITI KINGDOM

PLAY AS FAKE PASTEL IN VS BOSSES
After completing the game, select VS Mode. Then hold L2 + R1 while selecting VS Bosses.

PLAY AS FAKE PIXEL IN VS BOSSES
After completing the game, select VS Mode. Then hold L1 + L2 while selecting VS Bosses.

PLAY AS PASTEL IN VS BOSSES
After completing the game, select VS Mode. Then hold L1 + R1 while selecting VS Bosses.

PLAY AS PIXEL IN VS BOSSES
After completing the game, select VS Mode. Then hold L1 + R2 while selecting VS Bosses.

FAKE PASTEL VS PASTEL IN 2-PLAYER TOURNAMENT
After completing the game, select VS Mode. Then hold L1 + L2 + R1 while selecting 2 Player Tournament.

FAKE PASTEL VS PIXEL IN 2-PLAYER TOURNAMENT
After completing the game, select VS Mode. Then hold L2 + R1 while selecting 2 Player Tournament.

FAKE PIXEL VS FAKE PASTEL IN 2-PLAYER TOURNAMENT
After completing the game, select VS Mode. Then hold L2 + R2 while selecting 2 Player Tournament.

FAKE PIXEL VS PIXEL IN 2-PLAYER TOURNAMENT
After completing the game, select VS Mode. Then hold L1 + L2 while selecting 2 Player Tournament.

PASTEL VS FAKE PASTEL IN 2-PLAYER TOURNAMENT
After completing the game, select VS Mode. Then hold L1 + R1 while selecting 2 Player Tournament.

PASTEL VS FAKE PIXEL IN 2-PLAYER TOURNAMENT
After completing the game, select VS Mode. Then hold R1 + R2 while selecting 2 Player Tournament.

PIXEL VS FAKE PIXEL IN 2-PLAYER TOURNAMENT
After completing the game, select VS Mode. Then hold L1 + R2 while selecting 2 Player Tournament.

GRAND THEFT AUTO III

BETTER VEHICLE HANDLING
Press R1, L1, R2, L1, Left, R1, R1, ▲ while out of your vehicle. This code makes all vehicles handle better. When activated, press L3 to cause the suspension to hop!

VEHICLE HEALTH CHEAT
Press R2, R2, L1, R1, Left, Down, Right, Up, Left, Down, Right, Up while in your a vehicle. The car will still look damaged, but it will stop smoking and reach its 100% health status.

EXPLODE ALL VEHICLES
Press L2, R2, L1, R1, L2, R2, ▲, ■, ●, ▲, L2, L1.

RHINO
Press ● (x6), R1, L2, L1, ▲, ●, ▲.

INVISIBLE CAR CHASSIS
Press L1, L1, ■, R2, ▲, L1, ▲.

FLYING VEHICLES
Press Right, R2, ●, R1, L2, Down, L1 R1.

FOGGY
Press L1, L2, R1, R2, R2, R1, L2, ✕.

CLOUDY
Press L1, L2, R1, R2, R2, R1, L2, ■.

RAIN
Press L1, L2, R1, R2, R2, R1, L2, ●.

NORMAL WEATHER
Press L1, L2, R1, R2, R2, R1, L2, ▲.

PEDESTRIANS RIOT
Press Down, Up, Left, Up, ✕, R1, R2, L2, L1. Please note that this code is irreversible, so do NOT enter the code and save your game!

PEDESTRIANS OUT TO GET YOU
Press Down, Up, Left, Up, ✕, R1, R2, L1, L2. Please note that this code is irreversible, so do NOT enter the code and save your game!

PEDESTRIANS PACKING HEAT
Press R2, R1, ▲, ✕, L2, L1, Up, Down. Please note that this code is irreversible, so do NOT enter the code and save your game!

WANTED LEVEL UP
Press R2, R2, L1, R2, Left, Right, Left, Right, Left to increase your Wanted Level by two stars each time you enter it.

WANTED LEVEL DOWN
Press R2, R2, L1, R2, Up, Down, Up, Down, Up, Down to decrease your Wanted Level to nothing.

WEAPON CHEAT
Press R2, R2, L1, R2, Left, Down, Right, Up, Left, Down, Right, Up. Continue to enter the code until you reach the maximum ammo capacity of 9999 (for each weapon). When a weapon reaches its maximum ammo capacity, its ammunition supply becomes infinite.

CHANGE CHARACTER MODEL
Press Right, Down, Left, Up, L1, L2, Up, Left, Down, Right. Please note that this code is irreversible, so do NOT enter the code and save your game!

HEALTH CHEAT
Press R2, R2, L1, R1, Left, Down, Right, Up, Left, Down, Right, Up.

ARMOR CHEAT
Press R2, R2, L1, L2, Left, Down, Right, Up, Left, Down, Right, Up.

MONEY CHEAT ($250,000)
Press R2, R2, L1, L1, Left, Down, Right, Up, Left, Down, Right, Up.

INCREASED GORE FACTOR
Press ■, L1, ●, Down, L1, R1, ▲, Right, L1, ✕ to make victims lose body parts.

SLOW-MOTION GAMEPLAY
Press ▲, Up, Right, Down, ■, R1, R2. Enter this cheat three times for even more slowdown.

FAST-MOTION GAMEPLAY
Press ▲, Up, Right, Down, ■, L1, L2. Enter this cheat three times for even faster gameplay.

SPEED UP TIME
Press ● (x3), ■ (x5), L1, ▲, ●, ▲. Enter this cheat a second time to return to "normal" time.

GRAND THEFT AUTO: LIBERTY CITY STORIES

$250,000
During a game, press L1, R1, ▲, L1, R1, ●, L1, R1.

FULL HEALTH
During a game, press L1, R1, ✕, L1, R1, ■, L1, R1.

FULL ARMOR
During a game, press L1, R1, ●, L1, R1, ✕, L1, R1.

WEAPON SET 1
During a game, press Up, ■, ■, Down, Left, ●, ●, Right.

WEAPON SET 2
During a game, press Up, ●, ●, Down, Left, ●, ●, Right.

WEAPON SET 3
During a game, press Up, ✕, ✕, Down, Left, ✕, ✕, Right.

CHROME PLATED CARS
During a game, press ▲, R1, L1, Down, Down, R1, R1, ▲.

BLACK CARS
During a game, press ●, ●, R1, ▲, ▲, L1, ■, ■.

WHITE CARS
During a game, press ✕, ✕, R1, ●, ●, L1, ▲, ▲.

CARS DRIVE ON WATER
During a game, press ●, ✕, Down, ●, ✕, Up, L1, L1.

PERFECT TRACTION
During a game, press L1, Up, Left, R1, ▲, ●, Down, ✕.

CHANGE BIKE TIRE SIZE
During a game, press ●, Right, ✕, Up, Right, ✕, L1, ■.

AGGRESSIVE DRIVERS
During a game, press ■, ■, R1, ✕, ✕, L1, ●, ●.

ALL GREEN LIGHTS
During a game, press ▲, ▲, R1, ■, ■, L1, ✕, ✕.

DESTROY ALL CARS
During a game, press L1, L1, Left, L1, L1, Right, ✕, ■.

RAISE MEDIA ATTENTION
During a game, press L1, Up, Right, R1, ▲, ■, Down, X.

RAISE WANTED LEVEL
During a game, press L1, R1, ■, L1, R1, ▲, L1, R1.

NEVER WANTED
During a game, press L1, L1, ▲, R1, R1, ✕, ■, ●.

CHANGE OUTFIT
During a game, press L1, L1, Left, L1, L1, Right, ■, ▲.

BOBBLE HEAD WORLD
During a game, press Down, Down, Down, ●, ●, ✕, L1, R1.

PEOPLE ATTACK YOU
During a game, press L1, L1, R1, L1, L1, R1, Up, ▲.

PEOPLE FOLLOW YOU
During a game, press Down, Down, Down, ▲, ▲, ●, L1, R1.

PEOPLE HAVE WEAPONS
During a game, press R1, R1, L1, R1, R1, L1, Right, ●.

PEOPLE RIOT
During a game, press L1, L1, R1, L1, L1, R1, Left, ■.

SPAWN RHINO
During a game, press L1, L1, Left, L1, L1, Right, ▲, ●.

SPAWN TRASHMASTER
During a game, press ▲, ●, Down, ▲, ●, Up, L1, L1.

FASTER CLOCK
During a game, press L1, L1, Left, L1, L1, Right, ●, ✕.

FASTER GAMEPLAY
During a game, press R1, R1, L1, R1, R1, L1, Down, ✕.

SLOWER GAMEPLAY
During a game, press R1, ▲, ✕, R1, ■, ●, Left, Right.

CLEAR WEATHER
During a game, press Up, Down, ●, Up, Down, ■, L1, R1.

FOGGY WEATHER
During a game, press Up, Down, ▲, Up, Down, ✖, L1, R1.

OVERCAST WEATHER
During a game, press Up, Down, ✖, Up, Down, ▲, L1, R1.

RAINY WEATHER
During a game, press Up, Down, ●, Up, Down, ●, L1, R1.

SUNNY WEATHER
During a game, press L1, L1, ●, R1, R1, ●, ▲, ✖.

UPSIDE DOWN
During a game, press Down, Down, Down, ✖, X, ●, R1, L1.

UPSIDE DOWN
During a game, press ✖, ✖, ✖, Down, Down, Right, L1, R1.

RIGHT SIDE UP
During a game, press ▲, ▲, ▲, Up, Up, Right, L1, R1.

COMMIT SUICIDE
During a game, press L1, Down, Left, R1, ✖, ●, Up, ▲.

GAME CREDITS
During a game, press L1, R1, L1, R1, Up, Down, L1, R1.

GRAND THEFT AUTO: SAN ANDREAS

During a game, enter the following cheats:

FULL HEALTH, FULL ARMOR & $250,000
Press R1, R2, L1, ✖, Left, Down, Right, Up, Left, Down, Right, Up.

INFINITE LUNG CAPACITY
Press Down, Left, L1, Down, Down, R2, Down, L2, Down.

0 FAT & 0 MUSCLE
Press ▲, Up, Up, Left, Right, ●, ●, Right.

MAXIMUM MUSCLES
Press ▲, Up, Up, Left, Right, ●, ●, Left.

MAXIMUM FAT
Press ▲, Up, Up, Left, Right, ●, ●, Down.

BIG JUMPS
Press Up, Up, ▲, ▲, Up, Up, Left, Right, ●, R2, R2.

BIG BUNNY HOPS ON BMX
Press ▲, ●, ●, ●, ●, ●, ●, L1, L2, L2, R1, R2.

SUICIDE
Press Right, L2, Down, R1, Left, Left, R1, L1, L2, L1.

FASTER GAMEPLAY
Press ▲, Up, Right, Down, L2, L1, ●.

SLOWER GAMEPLAY
Press ▲, Up, Right, Down, ●, R2, R1.

FASTER TIME
Press ●, ●, L1, ●, L1, ●, ●, ●, L1, ▲, ●, ▲.

BLACK CARS
Press ●, L2, Up, R1, Left, ✖, R1, L1, Left, ●.

PINK CARS
Press ●, L1, Down, L2, Left, ✖, R1, L1, Right, ●.

FAST CARS
Press Up, L1, R1, Up, Right, Up, ✖, L2, ✖, L1.

TAXIS HAVE NITROUS & HOP WITH L3
Press Up, ✖, ▲, ✖, ▲, ✖, ●, R2, Right.

INVISIBLE VEHICLES
Press ▲, L1, ▲, R2, ●, L1, L1.

INVINCIBLE VEHICLE
Press L1, L2, L2, Up, Down, Down, Up, R1, R2, R2.

DRIVE-BY WHILE DRIVING
Press Up, Up, ●, L2, Right, ✖, R1, Down, R2, ●.

GREEN STOPLIGHTS
Press Right, R1, Up, L2, L2, Left, R1, L1, R1, R1.

AGGRESSIVE TRAFFIC
Press R2, ●, R1, L2, Left, R1, L1, R2, L2.

LESS TRAFFIC
Press ✖, Down, Up, R2, Down, ▲, L1, ▲, Left.

FASTER CARS
Press Right, R1, Up, L2, L2, Left, R1, L1, R1, R1.

BETTER CAR HANDLING
Press ▲, R1, R1, Left, R1, L1, R2, L1.

CARS FLOAT
Press Right, R2, ●, R1, L2, ■, R1, R2.

CARS FLY
Press Up, Down, L1, R1, L1, Right, Left, L1, Left.

ALL CARS EXPLODE
Press R2, L2, R1, L1, L2, R2, ■, ▲, ●, ▲, L2, L1.

FLYING BOATS
Press R2, ●, Up, L1, Right, R1, Right, Up, ■, ▲.

PEDESTRIANS ATTACK YOU
Press Down, Up, Up, Up, ✖, R2, R1, L2, L2.

PEDESTRIANS ATTACK EACH OTHER
Press Down, Left, Up, Left, ✖, R2, R1, L2, L1.

PEDESTRIANS CARRY WEAPONS
Press R2, R1, ✖, ▲, ✖, ▲, Up, Down.

ELVISES EVERYWHERE
Press L1, ●, ▲, L1, L1, ■, L2, Up, Down, Left.

CJ IS A CLOWN, CIVILIANS IN FAST FOOD APPAREL & MORE!
Press ▲, ▲, L1, ■, ■, ●, ■, Down, ●.

PEOPLE IN SWIMSUITS
Press Up, Up, Down, Down, ■, ●, L1, R1, ▲, Down.

GANGS
Press L2, Up, R1, R1, Left, R1, R1, R2, Right, Down.

REDUCE WANTED LEVEL
Press R1, R1, ●, R2, Up, Down, Up, Down, Up, Down.

RAISE WANTED LEVEL
Press R1, R1, ●, R2, Left, Right, Left, Right, Left, Right.

CLEAR WEATHER
Press R2, ✖, L1, L1, L2 (x3), ▲.

SUNNY WEATHER
Press R2, ✖, L1, L1, L2 (x3), Down.

FOGGY WEATHER
Press R2, ✖, L1, L1, L2 (x3), ✖.

CLOUDY WEATHER
Press R2, ✖, L1, L1, L2 (x3), ■.

RAINY WEATHER
Press R2, ✖, L1, L1, L2 (x3), ●.

WEAPON SET 1
Press R1, R2, L1, R2, Left, Down, Right, Up, Left, Down, Right, Up.

WEAPON SET 2
Press R1, R2, L1, R2, Left, Down, Right, Up, Left, Down, Down, Left.

WEAPON SET 3
Press R1, R2, L1, R2, Left, Down, Right, Up, Left, Down, Down, Down.

PARACHUTE
Press Left, Right, L1, L2, R1, R2, Up, Down, Right, L1.

JETPACK
Press L1, L2, R1, R2, Up, Down, Left, Right, L1, L2, R1, R2, Up, Down, Left, Right.

BLOODRING BANGER
Press Down, R1, ●, L2, L2, ✖, R1, L1, Left, Left.

CADDY
Press ●, L1, Up, R1, L2, ✖, R1, L1, ●, ✖.

DOZER
Press R2, L1, L1, Right, Right, Up, Up, ✖, L1, Left.

HOTRING RACER 1
Press R1, ●, R2, Right, L1, L2, ✖, ✖, ■, R1.

HOTRING RACER 2
Press R2, L1, ●, Right, L1, R1, Right, Up, ●, R2.

HYDRA
Press △, △, ■, ◉, ✕, L1, L1, Down, Up.

MONSTER
Press Right, Up, R1, R1, R1, Down, △, △, ✕, ◉, L1, L1.

QUADBIKE
Press Left, Left, Down, Down, Up, Up, ■, ◉, △, R1, R2.

RANCHER
Press Up, Right, Right, L1, Right, Up, ■, L2.

RHINO
Press ◉, ◉, L1, ◉, ◉, ◉, L1, L2, R1, △, ◉, △.

ROMERO
Press Down, R2, Down, R1, L2, Left, R1, L1, Left, Right.

STRETCH
Press R2, Up, L2, Left, Left, R1, L1, ◉, Right.

STUNTPLANE
Press ◉, Up, L1, L2, Down, R1, L1, L1, Left, Left, ✕, △.

TRASHMASTER
Press ◉, R1, ◉, R1, Left, Left, R1, L1, ◉, Right.

VORTEX
Press △, △, ■, ◉, ◉, ✕, L1, L2, Down, Down.

SUPER JUMP ON BICYCLE WITHOUT CHEAT CODE
With a Tec-9, MP5, or Micro MP5 equipped, hop on a bicycle. Tap ◉ quickly after bunny hopping L1.

GRAND THEFT AUTO: VICE CITY

Enter the following cheats during a game. Some of these cheats may affect your gameplay. Don't save your progress, unless you are sure you want the code to stay in effect.

HEALTH CHEAT
Press R1, R2, L1, ◉, Left, Down, Right, Up, Left, Down, Right, Up.

ARMOR CHEAT
Press R1, R2, L1, ✕, Left, Down, Right, Up, Left, Down, Right, Up.

LOW GRAVITY
Press Right, R2, ◉, R1, L2, Down, L1, R1.

BETTER DRIVING
Press △, R1, R1, Left, R1, L1, R2, L1. Press L3 to jump.

SUICIDE
Press Right, L2, Down, R1, Left, Left, R1, L1, L2, L1.

WANTED LEVEL UP 2
Press R1, R1, ◉, R2, Left, Right, Left, Right, Left, Right.

WANTED LEVEL DOWN 2
Press R1, R1, ◉, R2, Up, Down, Up, Down, Up, Down.

SLOW MOTION
Press △, Up, Right, Down, ■, R2, R1.

SPEED UP TIME
Press ◉, ◉, L1, ■, L1, ■, ■, ■, L1, △, ◉, △.

BLACK CARS
Press ◉, L2, Up, R1, Left, ✕, R1, L1, Left, ◉.

PINK CARS
Press ◉, L1, Down, L2, Left, ✕, R1, L1, Right, ◉.

CHANGE WHEELS
Press R1, ✕, △, Right, R2, ■, Up, Down, ■.

CAR SPEED X2
Press R1, R2, L1, L1, Left, Down, Right, Up, Left, Down, Right, Up.

CARS FLOAT
Press Right, R2, ●, R1, L2, ●, R1, R2.

ALL CARS EXPLODE
Press R2, L2, R1, L1, L2, R2, ●, ▲, ●,
▲, L2, L1.

ROBOCOPS
Press ●, L1, Down, L2, Left, ✖, R1, L1,
Right, ✖.

CARS DON'T STOP
Press R2, ●, R1, L2, Left, R1, L1, R2, L2.

PEDESTRIANS RIOT
Press Down, Left, Up, Left, ✖, R2, R1, L2, L1.

PEDESTRIANS ATTACK
Press Down, Up (x3), ✖, R2, R1, L2, L2.

ARMED PEDESTRIANS
Press R2, R1, ✖, ▲, ✖, ▲, Up, Down.

WOMEN WITH GUNS
Press Right, L1, ●, L2, Left, ✖, R1, L1, L1, ✖.

WOMEN FOLLOW YOU
Press ●, ✖, L1, L1, R2, ✖, ✖, ●, ▲.

MEDIA LEVEL METER
Press R2, ●, Up, L1, Right, R1, Right, Up,
●, ▲.

The following codes provide one
weapon for each weapon class:

WEAPONS SET 1
Press R2, R2, R1, R2, L1, R2, Left, Down,
Right, Up, Left Down, Right, Up.

WEAPONS SET 2
Press R1, R2, L1, R2, Left, Down, Right, Up,
Left, Down, Down, Left.

WEAPONS SET 3
Press R1, R2, L1, R2, Left, Down, Right, Up,
Left, Down, Down, Down.

CLEAR WEATHER
Press R2, ✖, L1, L1, L2, L2, L2, Down.

SUNNY
Press R2, ✖, L1, L1, L2 (x3), ▲.

OVERCAST
Press R2, ✖, L1, L1, L2 (x3), ●.

RAIN
Press R2, ✖, L1, L1, L2 (x3), ●.

FOG
Press R2, ✖, L1, L1, L2 (x3), ✖.

RED LEATHER
Press Right, Right, Left, Up, L1, L2, Left, Up,
Down, Right.

CANDY SUXXX
Press ●, R2, Down, R1, Left, Right, R1,
L1, ✖, L2.

HILARY KING
Press R1, ●, R2, L1, Right, R1, L1, ✖, R2.

KEN ROSENBERG
Press Right, L1, Up, L2, L1, Right, R1, L1,
✖, R1.

LANCE VANCE
Press ●, L2, Left, ✖, R1, L1, ✖, L1.

LOVE FIST 1
Press Down, L1, Down, L2, Left, ✖, R1,
L1, ✖, ✖.

LOVE FIST 2
Press R1, L2, R2, L1, Right, R2, Left, ✖,
●, L1.

MERCEDES
Press R2, L1, Up, L1, Right, R1, Right, Up,
●, ▲.

PHIL CASSADY
Press Right, R1, Up, R2, L1, Right, R1, L1,
Right, ●.

RICARDO DIAZ
Press L1, L2, R1, R2, Down, L1, R2, L2.

SONNY FORELLI
Press ●, L1, ●, L2, Left, ✖, R1, L1, ✖, ✖.

BLOODRING BANGER
Press Up, Right, Right, L1, Right, Up, ●, L2.

BLOODRING BANGER
Press Down, R1, ●, L2, L2, ✖, R1, L1,
Left, Left.

CADDY
Press ●, L1, Up, R1, L2, ✖, R1, L1, ●, ✖.

HOTRING RACER
Press R2, L1, ●, Right, L1, R1, Right, Up,
●, R2.

HOTRING RACER
Press R1, ●, R2, Right, L1, L2, ✖, ✖,
●, R1.

LOVE FIST LIMO
Press R2, Up, L2, Left, Left, R1, L1, ●, Right.

RHINO TANK
Press ●, ●, L1, ● (x3), L1, L2, R1, ▲, ●, ▲.

ROMERO'S HEARSE
Press Down, R2, Down, R1, L2, Left, R1, L1, Left, Right.

SABRE TURBO
Press Right, L2, Down, L2, L2, ✖, R1, L1, ●, Left.

TRASHMASTER
Press ●, R1, ●, R1, Left, Left, R1, L1, ●, Right.

GRAN TURISMO 4

EXTRA TRACKS FOR ARCADE MODE
Play through the indicated number of days to unlock the corresponding track in Arcade Mode.

DAYS	UNLOCKS
15	Deep Forest Raceway
29	Opera Paris
43	Fuji Speedway 80s
57	Special Stage Route 5
71	Suzuka Circuit
85	Twin Ring Motegi Road Course East Short
99	Grand Valley Speedway
113	Hong Kong
127	Suzuka Circuit West Course
141	Fuji Speedway 2005 GT
155	Ice Arena
169	Apricot Hill Raceway
183	Cote d Azur
197	Tahiti Maze
211	Twin Ring Motegi Road Course
225	George V Paris
239	Cathedral Rocks Trail I
253	Costa di Amalfi
267	Circuit de la Sarthe 1
281	Autumn Ring
309	Chamonix
309	Infineon Raceway Stock Car Course
323	Fuji Speedway 2005 F
337	Tsukuba Circuit Wet
351	Circuit de la Sarthe 2 (not chicaned)

GROWLANSER GENERATIONS

ALL ARMOR, GEMS & MAX MONEY
At the World Map, press Up, Right, L2, L2, Down, R2, R2 Up, Down, R2, L2, Right, Left, ●, ●, ●.

GUITAR HERO

UNLOCK ALL CHEATS
At the Main menu, press Yellow, Orange, Blue, Blue, Orange, Yellow, Yellow.

GUITAR HERO GUITAR CHEAT
At the Main menu, press Blue, Orange, Yellow, Blue, Blue.

CROWD METER CHEAT
At the Main menu, press Yellow, Blue, Orange, Orange, Blue, Blue, Yellow, Orange.

MONKEY HEAD CROWD
At the Main menu, press Blue, Orange, Yellow, Yellow, Yellow, Blue, Orange.

SKULL HEAD CROWD
At the Main menu, press Orange, Yellow, Blue, Blue, Orange, Yellow, Blue, Blue.

AIR GUITAR CHEAT
At the Main menu, press Orange, Orange, Blue, Yellow, Orange.

NO VENUE CHEAT
At the Main menu, press Blue, Yellow, Orange, Blue, Yellow, Orange.

GUITAR HERO II

AIR GUITAR
At the Main menu, press Yellow, Yellow, Blue, Orange, Yellow, Blue.

EYEBALL HEAD CROWD
At the Main menu, press Blue, Orange, Yellow, Orange, Yellow, Orange, Blue.

MONKEY HEAD CROWD
At the Main menu, press Orange, Blue, Yellow, Yellow, Orange, Blue, Yellow, Yellow.

FLAMING HEAD
At the Main menu, press Orange, Yellow, Orange, Orange, Yellow, Orange, Yellow, Yellow.

HORSE HEAD
At the Main menu, press Blue, Orange, Orange, Blue, Orange, Orange, Blue, Orange, Orange, Blue.

HYPER SPEED DEACTIVATE
At the Main menu, press Orange, Blue, Orange, Yellow, Orange, Blue, Orange, Yellow.

PERFORMANCE MODE
At the Main menu, press Yellow, Yellow, Blue, Yellow, Yellow, Orange, Yellow, Yellow.

.HACK//G.U. VOL. 1//REBIRTH

VOL.2 PREVIEW
On the desktop, hold R1 + R2 and press ●, ▲, ●, ▲. Release R1 and R2. Hold L1 + L2 and press Right, Up, Right, Up. Release L1 and L2 and press R3 + L3.

HEROES OF THE PACIFIC

The following cheats will disable game saving.

CHEAT MENU
At the Main menu, press L1, R2, L2, R3, R1, L3.

PLANES AND MISSIONS
At the Main menu, press Up on Right Analog Stick , Down on Right Analog Stick , Left, R2, L1, Right on Right Analog Stick.

UPGRADE PLANES
At the Main menu, press L1, Left on Right Analog Stick, R2, Right on Right Analog Stick, Right, Down.

JAPANESE
At the Main menu, press ●, R2, L1, L2, Left, Up.

HIGH ROLLERS CASINO

CHEAT MODE
Enter your name as SAM and change the gender to Female.

HITMAN: CONTRACTS

ALL LEVELS
At the Main menu, press ●, ▲, ●, Left, Up, Right, L2, R2.

COMPLETE LEVEL
During a game, press R2, L2, Up, Down, ✕, L3, ●, ✕, ●, ●, ✕.

HITMAN 2: SILENT ASSASSIN

LEVEL SELECT
At the Main menu, press R2, L2, Up, Down, ●, ▲, ●.

COMPLETE LEVEL
During a game, press R2, L2, Up, Down, ✕, L3, ●, ✕, ●, ✕.

ALL WEAPONS

During a game, press R2, L2, Up, Down, ✖, Up, ⬛, ✖.

INVINCIBILTY

During a game, press R2, L2, Up, Down, ✖, R2, L2, R1, L1.

FULL HEAL

During a game, press R2, L2, Up, Down, ✖, Up, Down.

TOGGLE LETHAL CHARGE

During a game, press R2, L2, Up, Down, ✖, R1, R1.

GRAVITY

During a game, press R2, L2, Up, Down, ✖, L2, L2.

SLOW MOTION

During a game, press R2, L2, Up, Down, ✖, Up, L2.

MEGAFORCE

During a game, press R2, L2, Up, Down, ✖, R2, R2.

TOGGLE BOMB MODE

During a game, press R2, L2, Up, Down, ✖, Up, L1.

TOGGLE PUNCH MODE

During a game, press R2, L2, Up, Down, ✖, Up, Up.

TOGGLE NAILGUN MODE

During a game, press R2, L2, Up, Down, ✖, L1, L1.

HOT SHOTS GOLF FORE!

Select Password from the Options menu and enter the following codes to enable these cheats.

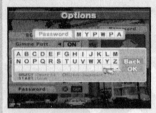

ALL CHARACTERS IN VS MODE
Enter REZTWS.

PRICE REDUCTION SALE IN SHOP
Enter MKJEFQ.

ALOHA BEACH RESORT COURSE IN SHOP
Enter XSREHD.

BAGPIPE CLASSIC COURSE IN SHOP
Enter CRCNHZ.

BLUE LAGOON C.C. COURSE IN SHOP
Enter WVRJQS.

DAY DREAM G.C. IN SHOP
Enter OQUTNA.

MINI-GOLF 2 G.C. IN SHOP
Enter RVMIRU.

SILKROAD CLASSIC COURSE IN SHOP
Enter ZKOGJM.

UNITED FOREST G.C. IN SHOP
Enter UIWHLZ.

WESTERN VALLEY COUNTRY CLUB COURSE IN SHOP
Enter LIBTFL.

WILD GREEN C.C. COURSE IN SHOP
Enter YZLOXE.

CAPSULE 01 IN SHOP
Enter WXAFSJ.

CAPSULE 2 IN SHOP
Enter OEINLK.

CAPSULE 3 IN SHOP
Enter WFKVTG.

CAPSULE 4 IN SHOP
Enter FCAVDO.

CAPSULE 5 IN SHOP
Enter YYPOKK.

CAPSULE 6 IN SHOP
Enter GDQDOF.

CAPSULE 7 IN SHOP
Enter HHXKPV.

CAPSULE 8 IN SHOP
Enter UOKXPS.

CAPSULE 9 IN SHOP
Enter LMIRYD.

CAPSULE 10 IN SHOP
Enter MJLJEQ.

CAPSULE 11 IN SHOP
Enter MHNCQI.

LOWER TOURNEY STAGE
Enter XKWGFZ.

CADDIE CLANK IN SHOP
Enter XCQGWJ.

CADDIE DAXTER IN SHOP
Enter WSIKIN.

CADDIE KAYLA IN SHOP
Enter MZIMEL.

CADDIE KAZ IN SHOP
Enter LNNZJV.

CADDIE MOCHI IN SHOP
Enter MYPWPA.

CADDIE SIMON IN SHOP
Enter WRHZNB.

CADDIE SOPHIE IN SHOP
Enter UTWIVQ.

BEGINNER'S BALL IN SHOP
Enter YFQJJI.

BIR AIR BALL IN SHOP
Enter CRCGKR.

INFINITY BALL IN SHOP
Enter DJXBRG.

PIN HOLE BALL IN SHOP
Enter VZLSGP.

SIDESPIN BALL IN SHOP
Enter JAYQRK.

TURBO SPIN BALL IN SHOP
Enter XNETOK.

100T HAMMER CLUB (B-CLASS) IN SHOP
Enter NFSNHR.

UPGRADE 100T HAMMER CLUB (A-CLASS) IN SHOP
Enter BVLHSI.

UPGRADE 100T HAMMER CLUB (S-CLASS) IN SHOP
Enter MCSRUK.

BIG AIR CLUB (B-CLASS) IN SHOP
Enter DLJMFZ.

UPGRADE BIG AIR CLUB (A-CLASS) IN SHOP
Enter TOSXUJ.

UPGRADE BIG AIR CLUB (S-CLASS) IN SHOP
Enter JIDTQI.

INFINITY CLUB IN SHOP
Enter RZTQGV.

UPGRADE INFINITY CLUB (A-CLASS) IN SHOP
Enter WTGFOR.

UPGRADE INFINITY CLUB (S-CLASS) IN SHOP
Enter EIPCUL.

PIN HOLE CLUB (B-CLASS) IN SHOP
Enter DGHFRP.

UPGRADE PIN HOLE CLUB (A-CLASS) IN SHOP
Enter TTIMHT.

UPGRADE PIN HOLE CLUB (S-CLASS) IN SHOP
Enter RBXVEL.

UPGRADE TURBO SPIN CLUB (A-CLASS) IN SHOP
Enter NIWKWP.

UPGRADE TURBO SPIN CLUB (S-CLASS) IN SHOP
Enter DTIZAB.

EXTRA POSE CAM IN SHOP
Enter UEROOK.

EXTRA SWING CAM IN SHOP
Enter RJIFQS.

EXTRA VIDEO IN SHOP
Enter DPYHIU.

HECKLETS IN SHOP
Enter DIXWFE.

HSG CD/VOICE IN SHOP
Enter UITUGF.

HSG CD/MUSIC IN SHOP
Enter PAJXLI.

HSG RULES IN SHOP
Enter FKDHDS.

LANDING GRID IN SHOP
Enter MQTIMV.

REPLAY CAM A IN SHOP
Enter PVJEMF.

REPLAY CAM B IN SHOP
Enter EKENCR.

REPLAY CAM C IN SHOP
Enter ZUHHAC.

MENU CHARACTER BRAD IN SHOP
Enter ZKJSIO.

MENU CHARACTER PHOEBE IN SHOP
Enter LWVLCB.

MENU CHARACTER RENEE IN SHOP
Enter AVIQXS.

WALLPAPER SET 2 IN SHOP
Enter RODDHQ.

MIKE'S COSTUME IN SHOP
Enter YKCFEZ.

LIN'S COSTUME IN SHOP
Enter BBLSKQ.

MEL'S COSTUME IN SHOP
Enter ARFLCR.

PHOEBE'S COSTUME IN SHOP
Enter GJBCHY.

ICE AGE 2: THE MELTDOWN

INFINITE PEBBLES
Pause the game and press Down, Down, Left, Up, Up, Right, Up, Down. ICE AGE 2: THE MELTDOWN

INFINITE PEBBLES
Pause the game and press Down, Down, Left, Up, Up, Right, Up, Down.

INFINITE ENERGY
Pause the game and press Down, Left, Right, Down, Down, Right, Left, Down.

INFINITE HEALTH
Pause the game and press Up, Right, Down, Up, Left, Down, Right, Left.

IHRA DRAG RACING: SPORTSMAN EDITION

$999,999
Select Season and enter Loaded as your profile name.

ROCKET CARS
Select Season and enter HotRodz as your profile name.

ALL BONUSES
Select Season and enter IWantIt as your profile name.

ALL ITEMS IN TROPHY ROOM
Select Season and enter FilMeUp as your profile name.

THE INCREDIBLES: RISE OF THE UNDERMINER

Pause the game, select Secrets, and enter the following.

BIG HEADS FOR MR. INCREDIBLE AND FROZONE
Enter EGOPROBLEM.

MR. INCREDIBLE GAINS 1000 EXPERIENCE POINTS
Enter MRIPROF.

FROZONE GAINS 1000 EXPERIENCE POINTS
Enter FROZPROF.

MR. INCREDIBLE GAINS A SUPER-MOVE
Enter MRIBOOM.

FROZONE GAINS A SUPER-MOVE
Enter FROZBOOM.

GAME CREDITS
Enter ROLLCALL.

REDUCE DAMAGE
Enter THISISTOOEASY. Cuts damage done to enemies in half, doubles damage done to the Supers, no health recovery, and Experience Points are halved.

DOUBLE DAMAGE
Enter THISISTOOHARD. Doubles damage done to enemies, halves damage done to the Supers, doubles amount of health recovery and Experience Points.

GALLERY ITEMS
Enter SHOWME.

DOUBLE EXP
Enter MAXIMILLION.

IN THE GROOVE

ALL SONGS
At the Main menu, press Up, Right, Up, Right, Left, Down, Left, Down, Up, Right, Down, Left, Up, Left, Down, Right.

JAK X: COMBAT RACING

DAXTER
Play for five hours to unlock Daxter in the Secrets Shop for 50,000 Orbs.

KIERA
Defeat the game.

KLEVER
Defeat Beachfront Drive Circuit Race

RAZER
Defeat Northern Tour Ciruit Race

SIG
Defeat Spargus City Death Race

UR-86
Defeat Kras City Qualifier

JAK
Make sure you have a Jak and Daxter save file on your memory card. Select Scan for Secret Characters from the Secrets Shop.

JAK II
Make sure you have a Jak II save file on your memory card. Select Scan for Secret Characters from the Secrets Shop.

JAK 3
Make sure you have a Jak 3 save file on your memory card. Select Scan for Secret Characters from the Secrets Shop.

RATCHET
Make sure you have a Ratchet: Deadlocked save file on your memory card. Select Scan for Secret Characters from the Secrets Shop.

HERO MODE
Complete the game with 100%. You can now purchase it for 50,000 Orbs at the Secret Shop.

DAXTERMOBILE, KAEDEN, OSMO, TARYN & XIMON
With Daxter in your PSP, connect it to the PS2. Scan for Secrets in the Secrets Shop.

JAWS UNLEASHED

LEVEL SELECT
Start a new game with shaaark as your profile name.

1,000,000 UPGRADE POINTS
Start a new game with blooood as your profile name.

JUICED

ARCADE/CUSTOM MODE UNLOCKED
Select Cheats from the Extras menu and enter PINT.

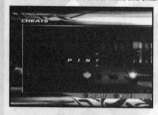 

JUSTICE LEAGUE HEROES

UNLOCK EVERYTHING
Pause the game, hold L1 + R1 + L2 + R2 and press Down, Left, Up, Right.

UNLIMITED ENERGY
Pause the game, hold L1 + R1 + L2 + R2 and press Down, Down, Right, Right, Up, Up, Left, Left.

KARAOKE REVOLUTION VOLUME 2

ALL SONGS
At the Title screen, press ●, ▲, Down, Left, Up, Right, L2, R2, Start.

ALL CHARACTERS
At the Title screen, press Up, ●, Right, ●, ●, Left, ●, Up, L3, R3.

ALL COSTUMES
At the Title screen, press Up, ●, Left, ●, ●, Down, ●, Right, R3, L3.

ALL VENUES
At the Title screen, press ●, ▲, Right, Up, Left, Down, R2, L2, Start.

GAME INFORMER T-SHIRT FOR ANGELA
At the Title screen, press Down, L3(x2), R3(x2), ●, Right, ●, L3, R3.

GAMEPRO T-SHIRT
At the Title screen, press Down, R3, Up, R3, L3, Down, L3, Up, Down, ●.

GAME STAR T-SHIRT
At the Title screen, press Up, R3, Right, R3(x2), Left, R3, Down, ●, ●.

HARMONIX T-SHIRT FOR ISHANI
At the Title screen, press L3, ●, Up, ●, ●, L3, Down, Down, R3.

KONAMI T-SHIRT FOR DWAYNE
At the Title screen, press Right, R3, Right, R3, ●, Right, ●, ●, Down, Left.

PSM T-SHIRT FOR DEVRON
At the Title screen, press Left, Right, Left, L3, R3, Down, Up, Up, ●, ●.

BANANA MICROPHONE
Select Cheat Collection from the Extras menu (or enter them during a game), then press L1, L1, R2, R2, Right, Down, ●, Left, Up, ●.

DWAYNE DOLL MICROPHONE
Select Cheat Collection from the Extras menu (or enter them during a game), then press ●, R2, ●, L1, R1, L2, ●, Up, ●, ●.

TOOTHBRUSH MICROPHONE
Select Cheat Collection from the Extras menu (or enter them during a game), then press R1, L1, R2, L2, Right, Left, Down, Up, ●, ●.

BIG HEAD CHARACTER
Select Cheat Collection from the Extras menu (or enter them during a game), then press Down (x3), Up, R1, L2, R2, L1, ●, ●.

SMALL HEAD CHARACTER
Select Cheat Collection from the Extras menu (or enter them during a game), then press Right, Right, Up, Up, L2, L2, R2, R1, L1.

BIG EYE CHARACTER
Select Cheat Collection from the Extras menu (or enter them during a game), then press ● (x4), ●, Down, Down, R2, L2, R1.

GLASS CHARACTER
Select Cheat Collection from the Extras menu (or enter them during a game), then press ●, ●, ●, R2, R2, L2, Down, Right, Right, Up.

OIL SLICK CHARACTER
Select Cheat Collection from the Extras menu (or enter them during a game), then press L2, R2, L2, R2, ●, Down, ●, Up, Left, Right.

MERCURY CHARACTER
Select Cheat Collection from the Extras menu (or enter them during a game), then press ●, L1, R2, Up, Up, Left, Left, ●, ●, R1.

WRAITH CHARACTER
Select Cheat Collection from the Extras menu (or enter them during a game), then press R2, Left, R1, Right, Up, Up, ●, ●, Down, L2.

TOUGH CROWD
Select Cheat Collection from the Extras menu, then press Right, Up, ● (x3), R2, R1, R1, L2, Down.

PIRATE CROWD
Select Cheat Collection from the Extras menu, then press ●, ●, Left, Left, R2, L1, R2, R1, ●, L2.

ROBOT CROWD
Select Cheat Collection from the Extras menu, then press ●, ●, Right, Right, R2, R1, R1, R2, ●, R2.

ZOMBIE CROWD
Select Cheat Collection from the Extras menu, then press Left, L1, L2, ●, ●, L2, L2, L1, Left, Left.

KARAOKE REVOLUTION VOLUME 3

BANANA MICROPHONE
Score gold at each venue in Showtime mode. At the Extras menu, press Down, Up, Left, Right, ●, ●, ●, ● at Cheat Collection 1.

BIG EYED CHARACTER
Score gold at each venue in Showtime mode. At the Extras menu, press ●, ●, ●, ●, Down, Left, Left, Down at Cheat Collection 1.

DWAYNE DOLL MICROPHONE
Score gold at each venue in Showtime mode. At the Extras menu, press ●, ●, R3, ●, Up, Down, Right, Left at Cheat Collection 1.

TOOTHBRUSH MICROPHONE
Score gold at each venue in Showtime mode. At the Extras menu, press L2, L2, ●, ●, Down, Up, Left, L3 at Cheat Collection 1.

BIG HEAD CHARACTER
Score gold at each venue in Showtime mode. At the Extras menu, press ●, ●, ●, ●, Up, Right, Down, Left at Cheat Collection 2.

FISH MICROPHONE
Score gold at each venue in Showtime mode. At the Extras menu, press ●, Down, Up, Left, ●, ●, L2, L1 at Cheat Collection 2.

MERCURY CHARACTER
Score gold at each venue in Showtime mode. At the Extras menu, press Down, Down, Right, Left, Right, Left, ●, ● at Cheat Collection 2.

WRAITH CHARACTER
Score gold at each venue in Showtime mode. At the Extras menu, press L2, L2, Right, Right, ●, ●, R1, R1 at Cheat Collection 2.

GLASS CHARACTER
Score gold at each venue in Showtime mode. At the Extras menu, press Down, L2, R1, R2, L1, ●, ●, ● at Cheat Collection 3.

ICE CREAM MICROPHONE
Score gold at each venue in Showtime mode. At the Extras menu, press ●, ●, ●, ●, R2, L2, R1, L1 at Cheat Collection 3.

OIL SLICK CHARACTER
Score gold at each venue in Showtime mode. At the Extras menu, press L3, L3, R2, R1, L2, L1, Down, Up at Cheat Collection 3.

SMALL HEAD CHARACTER
Score gold at each venue in Showtime mode. At the Extras menu, press ●, R2, L2, R1, L1, Down, Down, Up at Cheat Collection 3.

ALIEN CROWD
Score gold at each venue in Showtime mode. At the Extras menu, press Up, Up, Down, ●, ●, L2, R2, ● at Cheat Collection 4.

PIRATE CROWD
Score gold at each venue in Showtime mode. At the Extras menu, press Down, L2, L2, R2, R2, ●, ●, ● at Cheat Collection 4.

ROBOT CROWD
Score gold at each venue in Showtime mode. At the Extras menu, press L3, Down, Down, R1, ●, ●, ●, ● at Cheat Collection 4.

TOUGH AUDIO CROWD
Score gold at each venue in Showtime mode. At the Extras menu, press ●, L1, L2, R1, R2, Right, Right, Down at Cheat Collection 4.

ZOMBIE CROWD
Score gold at each venue in Showtime mode. At the Extras menu, press ●, ●, ●, ●, Up, Right, Right, Up at Cheat Collection 4.

KATAMARI DAMACY

COMETS
Finish a "Make a Star" level under a certain time to earn a comet.

LEVEL	FINISH WITHIN
Make a Star 1	1 minute
Make a Star 2	3 minutes
Make a Star 3	4 minutes
Make a Star 4	6 minutes
Make a Star 5	8 minutes
Make a Star 6	8 minutes
Make a Star 7	8 minutes
Make a Star 8	12 minutes
Make a Star 9	15 minutes
Make the Moon	20 minutes

KILLZONE

ALL LEVELS AND CHARACTERS
Start a new game and enter Shooterman as your name.

BIG HEAD ENEMIES
At the Main menu, hold L1 and press ◉, ▣, ✕, ◉, ◉.

ALL MOVIES
At the Main menu, hold L1 and press ◉, ▣, ▲, ◉, ▣.

BETTER WEAPONS
At the Main menu, hold L1 and press ◉, ▲, ◉, ▲, ✕.

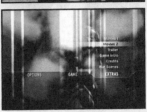

KYA: DARK LINEAGE

BONUS GALLERY
At the Main menu, press ▲, Up, ◉, Right, Down, Down, ▣, Left.

RESTORE LIFE
Pause the game and press L1, R2, L2, R1, Up, Up, Left, ▣, Right, ◉, START.

SHRINK JAMGUT
Pause the game and press R2, R2, ◉, R2, L2, L2, Left, L2, ▲.

L.A. RUSH

$5,000
During a game, press Up, Down, Left, Right, ◉, Left, R2, Up.

DISABLE POLICE
During a game, press Up, Down, Left, Right, R2, ▣, Right, R1, Left.

UNLIMITED N20
During a game, press Up, Down, Left, Right, ▣, Up, Down, ◉, Up.

FAST TRAFFIC
During a game, press Up, Down, Left, Right, ▣, Right, ◉, Left.

ALL CARS IN GARAGE PIMPED
During a game, press Up, Down, Left, Right, ◉, ▣, R2, R1, Up, Down, Left, Right.

NO CATCH UP
Use C-VHARD as a profile name.

LEGACY OF KAIN: BLOOD OMEN 2

BEGIN GAME WITH SOUL REAVER AND IRON ARMOR
At the Main menu, press L1, R1, L2, R2, ■, ●, ▲.

REFILL BLOOD
Press L2 to access the Map screen, then press Up, Right, ■, ●, Up, Down, Right, Left.

REFILL MAGIC
Press L2 to access the Map screen, then press Right (x2), ■, ●, Up, Down, Right, Left.

EXTRA MOVIE
At the Main menu press Up, Up, Down, Right, Left.

LEGACY OF KAIN: DEFIANCE

INVINCIBILITY
Pause the game and press Up, Down, Right, Down, R1, R2, Down, ▲, L1.

ALL POWER-UPS
Pause the game and press Left, Left, Up, Up, L1, R2, ●, Down, ▲.

ALL COMBO MOVES
Pause the game and press Right, Down, Up, Down, Down, R1, ▲, ●, Down.

FULL HEALTH, TK, AND REAVER CHARGE
Pause the game and press Left, Right, Left, Right, R1, L1, ●, ▲, Down.

UNLIMITED REAVER CHARGE AND BALANCE EMBLEM
Pause the game and press Down, Down, Up, Left, R1, R2, Down, ▲, ●.

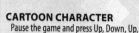

ALL DARK CHRONICLES
Pause the game and press R1, Down, R2, L1, Right, R2, ▲, Down, L1.

ALL BONUSES
Pause the game and press R2, Down, L2, R1, Left, L2, Down, L1, ▲.

TUBE REAVER
Pause the game and press Up, Down, Left, Right, R2, L2, ▲, Down, ●.

CARTOON CHARACTER
Pause the game and press Up, Down, Up, Down, R1, R2, Down, ●, ▲

WIREFRAME
Pause the game and press L1, Down, L1, Up, R1, L2, L1, Down, ▲.

NO TEXTURES
Pause the game and press L1, Down, R2, Right, R2, Up, ▲, L1, Down.

LEGO STAR WARS: THE VIDEO GAME

Pause the game and select Extras to toggle these cheats on and off.

INVINCIBILITY
At Dexter's Diner, select Enter Code and enter 4PR28U.

BIG BLASTERS
At Dexter's Diner, select Enter Code and enter IG72X4.

CLASSIC BLASTERS
At Dexter's Diner, select Enter Code and enter L449HD.

SILLY BLASTERS
At Dexter's Diner, select Enter Code and enter NR37W1.

BRUSHES
At Dexter's Diner, select Enter Code and enter SHRUB1.

TEA CUPS
At Dexter's Diner, select Enter Code and enter PUCEAT.

MINIKIT DETECTOR
At Dexter's Diner, select Enter Code and enter LD116B.

MOUSTACHES
At Dexter's Diner, select Enter Code and enter RP924W.

PURPLE
At Depxter's Diner, select Enter Code and enter YD77GC.

SILHOUETTES
At Dexter's Diner, select Enter Code and enter MS999Q.

The following codes make each character available for purchase from Dexter's Diner.

BATTLE DROID
At Dexter's Diner, select Enter Code and enter 987UYR.

BATTLE DROID (COMMANDER)
At Dexter's Diner, select Enter Code and enter EN11K5.

BATTLE DROID (GEONOSIS)
At Dexter's Diner, select Enter Code and enter LK42U6.

BATTLE DROID (SECURITY)
At Dexter's Diner, select Enter Code and enter KF999A.

BOBA FETT
At Dexter's Diner, select Enter Code and enter LA811Y.

CLONE
At Dexter's Diner, select Enter Code and enter F8B4L6.

CLONE (EPISODE III)
At Dexter's Diner, select Enter Code and enter ER33JN.

CLONE (EPISODE III, PILOT)
At Dexter's Diner, select Enter Code and enter BHU72T.

CLONE (EPISODE III, SWAMP)
At Dexter's Diner, select Enter Code and enter N3T6P8.

CLONE (EPISODE III, WALKER)
At Dexter's Diner, select Enter Code and enter RS6E25.

COUNT DOOKU
At Dexter's Diner, select Enter Code and enter 14PGMN.

DARTH MAUL
At Dexter's Diner, select Enter Code and enter H35TUX.

DARTH SIDIOUS
At Dexter's Diner, select Enter Code and enter A32CAM.

DISGUISED CLONE
At Dexter's Diner, select Enter Code and enter VR832U.

DROIDEKA
At Dexter's Diner, select Enter Code and enter DH382U.

GENERAL GRIEVOUS
At Dexter's Diner, select Enter Code and enter SF321Y.

GEONOSIAN
At Dexter's Diner, select Enter Code and enter 19D7NB.

GRIEVOUS' BODYGUARD
At Dexter's Diner, select Enter Code and enter ZTY392.

GONK DROID
At Dexter's Diner, select Enter Code and enter U63B2A.

JANGO FETT
At Dexter's Diner, select Enter Code and enter PL47NH.

KI-ADI MUNDI
At Dexter's Diner, select Enter Code and enter DP55MV.

KIT FISTO
At Dexter's Diner, select Enter Code and enter CBR954.

LUMINARA
At Dexter's Diner, select Enter Code and enter A725X4.

MACE WINDU (EPISODE III)
At Dexter's Diner, select Enter Code and enter MS952L.

PADMÉ
At Dexter's Diner, select Enter Code and enter 92UJ7D.

PK DROID
At Dexter's Diner, select Enter Code and enter R840JU.

PRINCESS LEIA
At Dexter's Diner, select Enter Code and enter BEQ82H.

REBEL TROOPER
At Dexter's Diner, select Enter Code and enter L54YUK.

ROYAL GUARD
At Dexter's Diner, select Enter Code and enter PP43JX.

SHAAK TI
At Dexter's Diner, select Enter Code and enter EUW862.

SUPER BATTLE DROID
At Dexter's Diner, select Enter Code and enter XZNR21.

LEGO STAR WARS II: THE ORIGINAL TRILOGY

BEACH TROOPER
At Mos Eisley Canteena, select Enter Code and enter UCK868. You must still select Characters and purchase this character for 20,000 studs.

BEN KENOBI (GHOST)
At Mos Eisley Canteena, select Enter Code and enter BEN917. You must still select Characters and purchase this character for 1,100,000 studs.

BESPIN GUARD
At Mos Eisley Canteena, select Enter Code and enter VHY832. You must still select Characters and purchase this character for 15,000 studs.

BIB FORTUNA
At Mos Eisley Canteena, select Enter Code and enter WTY721. You must still select Characters and purchase this character for 16,000 studs.

BOBA FETT
At Mos Eisley Canteena, select Enter Code and enter HLP221. You must still select Characters and purchase this character for 175,000 studs.

DEATH STAR TROOPER
At Mos Eisley Canteena, select Enter Code and enter BNC332. You must still select Characters and purchase this character for 19,000 studs.

EWOK
At Mos Eisley Canteena, select Enter Code and enter TTT289. You must still select Characters and purchase this character for 34,000 studs.

GAMORREAN GUARD
At Mos Eisley Canteena, select Enter Code and enter YZF999. You must still select Characters and purchase this character for 40,000 studs.

GONK DROID
At Mos Eisley Canteena, select Enter Code and enter NFX582. You must still select Characters and purchase this character for 1,550 studs.

GRAND MOFF TARKIN
At Mos Eisley Canteena, select Enter Code and enter SMG219. You must still select Characters and purchase this character for 38,000 studs.

GREEDO
At Mos Eisley Canteena, select Enter Code and enter NAH118. You must still select Characters and purchase this character for 60,000 studs.

HAN SOLO (HOOD)
At Mos Eisley Canteena, select Enter Code and enter YWM840. You must still select Characters and purchase this character for 20,000 studs.

IG-88
At Mos Eisley Canteena, select Enter Code and enter NXL973. You must still select Characters and purchase this character for 20,000 studs.

IMPERIAL GUARD
At Mos Eisley Canteena, select Enter Code and enter MMM111. You must still select Characters and purchase this character for 45,000 studs.

IMPERIAL OFFICER
At Mos Eisley Canteena, select Enter Code and enter BBV889. You must still select Characters and purchase this character for 28,000 studs.

IMPERIAL SHUTTLE PILOT
At Mos Eisley Canteena, select Enter Code and enter VAP664. You must still select Characters and purchase this character for 29,000 studs.

IMPERIAL SPY
At Mos Eisley Canteena, select Enter Code and enter CVT125. You must still select Characters and purchase this character for 13,500 studs.

JAWA
At Mos Eisley Canteena, select Enter Code and enter JAW499. You must still select Characters and purchase this character for 24,000 studs.

LOBOT
At Mos Eisley Canteena, select Enter Code and enter UUB319. You must still select Characters and purchase this character for 11,000 studs.

PALACE GUARD
At Mos Eisley Canteena, select Enter Code and enter SGE549. You must still select Characters and purchase this character for 14,000 studs.

REBEL PILOT
At Mos Eisley Canteena, select Enter Code and enter CYG336. You must still select Characters and purchase this character for 15,000 studs.

REBEL TROOPER (HOTH)
At Mos Eisley Canteena, select Enter Code and enter EKU849. You must still select Characters and purchase this character for 16,000 studs.

SANDTROOPER
At Mos Eisley Canteena, select Enter Code and enter YDV451. You must still select Characters and purchase this character for 14,000 studs.

SKIFF GUARD
At Mos Eisley Canteena, select Enter Code and enter GBU888. You must still select Characters and purchase this character for 12,000 studs.

SNOWTROOPER
At Mos Eisley Canteena, select Enter Code and enter NYU989. You must still select Characters and purchase this character for 16,000 studs.

STORMTROOPER
At Mos Eisley Canteena, select Enter Code and enter PTR345. You must still select Characters and purchase this character for 10,000 studs.

THE EMPEROR
At Mos Eisley Canteena, select Enter Code and enter HHY382. You must still select Characters and purchase this character for 275,000 studs.

TIE FIGHTER
At Mos Eisley Canteena, select Enter Code and enter HDY739. You must still select Characters and purchase this item for 60,000 studs.

TIE FIGHTER PILOT
At Mos Eisley Canteena, select Enter Code and enter NNZ316. You must still select Characters and purchase this character for 21,000 studs.

TIE INTERCEPTOR
At Mos Eisley Canteena, select Enter Code and enter QYA828. You must still select Characters and purchase this item for 40,000 studs.

TUSKEN RAIDER
At Mos Eisley Canteena, select Enter Code and enter PEJ821. You must still select Characters and purchase this character for 23,000 studs.

UGNAUGHT
At Mos Eisley Canteena, select Enter Code and enter UGN694. You must still select Characters and purchase this character for 36,000 studs.

LOONEY TUNES SPACE RACE

ALL BONUSES
Select Cheats from the Options menu and enter MADAESAN.

NO GAG CRATES
Select Cheats from the Options menu and enter ENGARDE.

INFINITE TURBO
Select Cheats from the Options menu and enter KABOOM.

ALL TOURNAMENTS & ACME EVENTS
Select Cheats from the Options menu and enter TRUTHOR.

ALL GALLERIA ITEMS
Select Cheats from the Options menu and enter ALLMINE.

MIRROR MODE
Select Cheats from the Options menu and enter ITIS2LAFF.

MARVIN THE MARTIAN
Select Cheats from the Options menu and enter Q32.

PORKY PIG
Select Cheats from the Options menu and enter 20LBHAM.

THE KING
Select Cheats from the Options menu and enter KOTIM.

ASTEROID BELT TRACK
Select Cheats from the Options menu and enter WHATISUI.

NEBULA TRACK
Select Cheats from the Options menu and enter CLOSEIT.

PLANET ACME 2 TRACK
Select Cheats from the Options menu and enter HLORALPH.

PYRAMIDS OF MARS 2 TRACK
Select Cheats from the Options menu and enter TORGO.

WILD WEST QUADRANT 2 TRACK
Select Cheats from the Options menu and enter GULLIBLE.

GALACTORAMA PARK 2 STAGE
Select Cheats from the Options menu and enter 124ADIME.

NORTH POLE STAR 2 STAGE
Select Cheats from the Options menu and enter PLANETX.

THE LORD OF THE RINGS: THE RETURN OF THE KING

SHARE EXPERIENCE IN COOPERATIVE MODE
Pause the game, press and hold L1 + L2 + R1 + R2, then press Down, ✖ (x3).

SHARE HEALTH IN COOPERATIVE MODE
Pause the game, press and hold L1 + L2 + R1 + R2, then press ▲, Up, ●, ●.

INFINITE CONTINUES
Pause the game, press and hold L1 + L2 + R1 + R2, then press ●, ●, Up, ●.

UNLIMITED RESPAWNS IN COOPERATIVE MODE
Pause the game, press and hold L1 + L2 + R1 + R2, then press ●, ●, Up, ●.

1,000 EXPERIENCE, ARAGORN
Pause the game, press and hold L1 + L2 + R1 + R2, then press Up, ●, ▲, ✖.

LEVEL 2 SKILLS, ARAGORN
Pause the game, press and hold L1 + L2 + R1 + R2, then press ●, ▲, ✖, ▲.

LEVEL 4 SKILLS, ARAGORN
Pause the game, press and hold L1 + L2 + R1 + R2, then press Down, ■, ●, ■.

LEVEL 6 SKILLS, ARAGORN
Pause the game, press and hold L1 + L2 + R1 + R2, then press ●, ▲, ■, ■.

LEVEL 8 SKILLS, ARAGORN
Pause the game, press and hold L1 + L2 + R1 + R2, then press Up, ■, ▲, Up.

RESTORE MISSILES, ARAGORN
Pause the game, press and hold L1 + L2 + R1 + R2, then press ▲, ■, ■, ▲.

3-HIT COMBO, ARAGORN
Pause the game, press and hold L1 + L2 + R1 + R2, then press ■, Down, ●, Up.

4-HIT COMBO, ARAGORN
Pause the game, press and hold L1 + L2 + R1 + R2, then press Up, ■, ▲, Down.

1,000 EXPERIENCE, FARAMIR
Pause the game, press and hold L1 + L2 + R1 + R2, then press ■, ▲, Up, ■.

LEVEL 2 SKILLS, FARAMIR
Pause the game, press and hold L1 + L2 + R1 + R2, then press ✖, ■, ✖, Down.

LEVEL 4 SKILLS, FARAMIR
Pause the game, press and hold L1 + L2 + R1 + R2, then press ✖, ✖, ■, ■.

LEVEL 6 SKILLS, FARAMIR
Pause the game, press and hold L1 + L2 + R1 + R2, then press ▲, ✖, Down, ●.

LEVEL 8 SKILLS, FARAMIR
Pause the game, press and hold L1 + L2 + R1 + R2, then press ●, Down (x3).

RESTORE MISSILES, FARAMIR
Pause the game, press and hold L1 + L2 + R1 + R2, then press ▲, Up, ✖, ✖.

3-HIT COMBO, FARAMIR
Pause the game, press and hold L1 + L2 + R1 + R2, then press ■, ▲, Up, ▲.

4-HIT COMBO, FARAMIR
Pause the game, press and hold L1 + L2 + R1 + R2, then press ✖, ■, Up, ✖.

1,000 EXPERIENCE, FRODO
Pause the game, press and hold L1 + L2 + R1 + R2, then press Down, ▲, Up, Down.

LEVEL 2 SKILLS, FRODO
Pause the game, press and hold L1 + L2 + R1 + R2, then press ▲, Up, Down, ●.

LEVEL 4 SKILLS, FRODO
Pause the game, press and hold L1 + L2 + R1 + R2, then press ▲, Up, ●, Down.

LEVEL 6 SKILLS, FRODO
Pause the game, press and hold L1 + L2 + R1 + R2, then press Down, Down, ✖, ▲.

LEVEL 8 SKILLS, FRODO
Pause the game, press and hold L1 + L2 + R1 + R2, then press ●, ●, Down, Down.

RESTORE MISSILES, FRODO
Pause the game, press and hold L1 + L2 + R1 + R2, then press ▲ (x3), ●.

3-HIT COMBO, FRODO
Pause the game, press and hold L1 + L2 + R1 + R2, then press ■, Down, ▲, ■.

4-HIT COMBO, FRODO
Pause the game, press and hold L1 + L2 + R1 + R2, then press Down, ■, Down, ●.

1,000 EXPERIENCE, GANDALF
Pause the game, press and hold L1 + L2 + R1 + R2, then press ●, ▲, Up, Down.

LEVEL 2 SKILLS, GANDALF
Pause the game, press and hold L1 + L2 + R1 + R2, then press Down, ▲, ✖, ▲.

LEVEL 4 SKILLS, GANDALF
Pause the game, press and hold L1 + L2 + R1 + R2, then press ▲, Up, ■, ✖.

LEVEL 6 SKILLS, GANDALF
Pause the game, press and hold L1 + L2 + R1 + R2, then press ▲, ▲, ✖, Up.

LEVEL 8 SKILLS, GANDALF
Pause the game, press and hold L1 + L2 + R1 + R2, then press ◉, ◉, Down, Down.

RESTORE MISSILES, GANDALF
Pause the game, press and hold L1 + L2 + R1 + R2, then press ▲, Down, ✖, ◉.

3-HIT COMBO, GANDALF
Pause the game, press and hold L1 + L2 + R1 + R2, then press Down, ✖, ▲, Down.

4-HIT COMBO, GANDALF
Pause the game, press and hold L1 + L2 + R1 + R2, then press Down, ▲, Up, ◉.

1,000 EXPERIENCE, GIMLI
Pause the game, press and hold L1 + L2 + R1 + R2, then press ◉, ◉, ▲, ✖.

LEVEL 2 SKILLS, GIMLI
Pause the game, press and hold L1 + L2 + R1 + R2, then press Up, ◉, ◉, ◉.

LEVEL 4 SKILLS, GIMLI
Pause the game, press and hold L1 + L2 + R1 + R2, then press ▲, ◉, Down, Up.

LEVEL 6 SKILLS, GIMLI
Pause the game, press and hold L1 + L2 + R1 + R2, then press Down, ▲, Down ◉.

LEVEL 8 SKILLS, GIMLI
Pause the game, press and hold L1 + L2 + R1 + R2, then press ✖, ◉, Down, ◉.

RESTORE MISSILES, GIMLI
Pause the game, press and hold L1 + L2 + R1 + R2, then press ◉ (x3), ✖.

3-HIT COMBO, GIMLI
Pause the game, press and hold L1 + L2 + R1 + R2, then press Up, ◉, ◉, ◉.

4-HIT COMBO, GIMLI
Pause the game, press and hold L1 + L2 + R1 + R2, then press ▲, ◉, Up, ✖.

1,000 EXPERIENCE, LEGOLAS
Pause the game, press and hold L1 + L2 + R1 + R2, then press ✖, ▲, Up, ✖.

LEVEL 2 SKILLS, LEGOLAS
Pause the game, press and hold L1 + L2 + R1 + R2, then press ◉, ◉, ◉, ◉.

LEVEL 4 SKILLS, LEGOLAS
Pause the game, press and hold L1 + L2 + R1 + R2, then press Down, Down, ✖, ✖.

LEVEL 6 SKILLS, LEGOLAS
Pause the game, press and hold L1 + L2 + R1 + R2, then press Down, ◉, Up, Down.

LEVEL 8 SKILLS, LEGOLAS
Pause the game, press and hold L1 + L2 + R1 + R2, then press ◉, Up, Up, Down.

RESTORE MISSILES, LEGOLAS
Pause the game, press and hold L1 + L2 + R1 + R2, then press ▲ (x3), Down.

3-HIT COMBO, LEGOLAS
Pause the game, press and hold L1 + L2 + R1 + R2, then press ◉, ▲, ▲, ◉.

4-HIT COMBO, LEGOLAS
Pause the game, press and hold L1 + L2 + R1 + R2, then press ✖, ◉, ▲, ◉.

1,000 EXPERIENCE, MERRY
Pause the game, press and hold L1 + L2 + R1 + R2, then press Down, Down, ◉, ✖.

LEVEL 2 SKILLS, MERRY
Pause the game, press and hold L1 + L2 + R1 + R2, then press Down, Down, ◉, ◉.

LEVEL 4 SKILLS, MERRY
Pause the game, press and hold L1 + L2 + R1 + R2, then press ◉, ✖, ◉, Down.

LEVEL 6 SKILLS, MERRY
Pause the game, press and hold L1 + L2 + R1 + R2, then press Down, Down, ◉, ▲.

LEVEL 8 SKILLS, MERRY
Pause the game, press and hold L1 + L2 + R1 + R2, then press Down, ▲, ✖, ◉.

RESTORE MISSILES, MERRY
Pause the game, press and hold L1 + L2 + R1 + R2, then press ◉, ◉, ◉, ▲.

3-HIT COMBO, MERRY
Pause the game, press and hold L1 + L2 + R1 + R2, then press ▲, ✕, Up, ▲.

4-HIT COMBO, MERRY
Pause the game, press and hold L1 + L2 + R1 + R2, then press ▲, ✕, ■, ■.

1,000 EXPERIENCE, PIPPIN
Pause the game, press and hold L1 + L2 + R1 + R2, then press ▲, ✕, ■, ✕.

LEVEL 2 SKILLS, PIPPIN
Pause the game, press and hold L1 + L2 + R1 + R2, then press Down, ✕, Down, Up.

LEVEL 4 SKILLS, PIPPIN
Pause the game, press and hold L1 + L2 + R1 + R2, then press ✕, Down (x3).

LEVEL 6 SKILLS, PIPPIN
Pause the game, press and hold L1 + L2 + R1 + R2, then press ●, ▲, ●, ▲.

LEVEL 8 SKILLS, PIPPIN
Pause the game, press and hold L1 + L2 + R1 + R2, then press ■, Up, Up, ●.

RESTORE MISSILES, PIPPIN
Pause the game, press and hold L1 + L2 + R1 + R2, then press Up, ●, Down, ■.

3-HIT COMBO, PIPPIN
Pause the game, press and hold L1 + L2 + R1 + R2, then press Up, Up, ■, ●.

4-HIT COMBO, PIPPIN
Pause the game, press and hold L1 + L2 + R1 + R2, then press ✕, ✕, Down, ●.

1,000 EXPERIENCE, SAM
Pause the game, press and hold L1 + L2 + R1 + R2, then press ▲, ✕, Down, ✕.

LEVEL 2 SKILLS, SAM
Pause the game, press and hold L1 + L2 + R1 + R2, then press ●, ✕, ●, ▲.

LEVEL 4 SKILLS, SAM
Pause the game, press and hold L1 + L2 + R1 + R2, then press Up, Down, ■, ✕.

LEVEL 6 SKILLS, SAM
Pause the game, press and hold L1 + L2 + R1 + R2, then press Down, Down, Up, Up.

LEVEL 8 SKILLS, SAM
Pause the game, press and hold L1 + L2 + R1 + R2, then press ●, ●, ▲, ▲.

RESTORE MISSILES, SAM
Pause the game, press and hold L1 + L2 + R1 + R2, then press ✕, ✕, ●, ✕.

3-HIT COMBO, SAM
Pause the game, press and hold L1 + L2 + R1 + R2, then press ■, ✕, ●, ■.

4-HIT COMBO, SAM
Pause the game, press and hold L1 + L2 + R1 + R2, then press Up, Down, ▲, ▲.

ALL INTERVIEWS
Pause the game, press and hold L1 + L2 + R1 + R2, then press ✕, ■, ✕, Up.

You must defeat the game to unlock the following codes.

PERFECT MODE
Pause the game, press and hold L1 + L2 + R1 + R2, then press ●, Down, ▲, ✕.

ALL ATTACK UPGRADES
Pause the game, press and hold L1 + L2 + R1 + R2, then press Up, Down, ▲, ■.

INVINCIBILITY
Pause the game, press and hold L1 + L2 + R1 + R2, then press ■, ●, ■, Up.

FULL HEALTH
Pause the game, press and hold L1 + L2 + R1 + R2, then press ■, ■, ●, ●.

UNLIMITED MISSILE WEAPONS
Pause the game, press and hold L1 + L2 + R1 + R2, then press ■, ■, Down, ●.

ALWAYS DEVASTATING
Pause the game, press and hold L1 + L2 + R1 + R2, then press ▲, Up, ▲, Down.

TARGET INDICATOR
Pause the game, press and hold L1 + L2 + R1 + R2, then press Down, ●, Up, ■.

THE LORD OF THE RINGS: THE TWO TOWERS

HEALTH
Pause the game, press and hold R1 + R2 + L1 + L2, then press ▲, Down, ✖, Up.

ARROWS
Pause the game, press and hold L1 + L2 + R1 + R2, then press ✖, Down, ▲, Up.

1000 EXPERIENCE POINTS
Pause the game, press and hold R1 + R2 + L1 + L2, then press ✖, Down.

LEVEL 2 SKILLS
Pause the game, press and hold R1 + R2 + L1 + L2, then press ●, Right, ●, Right.

LEVEL 4 SKILLS
Pause the game, press and hold R1 + R2 + L1 + L2, then press ▲, Up, ▲, Up.

LEVEL 6 SKILLS
Pause the game, press and hold R1 + R2 + L1 + L2, then press ●, Left, ●, Left.

LEVEL 8 SKILLS
Pause the game, press and hold R1 + R2 + L1 + L2, then press ✖, ✖, Down, Down.

MADDEN NFL 06

MADDEN CARDS
Select Madden Cards from My Madden. Then select Madden Codes and enter the following:

PASSWORD	CARD	PASSWORD	CARD
6W5J6Z	#1 Rex Grossman Gold	7T3V5K	#28 Anquan Boldin Gold
6X7W20	#2 Thomas Jones Gold	7T6B5N	#29 Larry Fitzgerald Gold
6Y5Z6H	#3 Brian Urlacher Gold	7U4M9B	#30 Bertrand Berry Gold
6Z9X5Y	#4 Olin Kreutz Gold	7U6B3L	#31 LaDainian Tomlinson Gold
7A7Z2G	#5 Tommie Harris Gold	8Q2J2R	#55 Donovan McNabb Bronze
7C6U4H	#6 Carson Palmer Gold	8Q2J2X	#55 Donovan McNabb Gold
7D1B2H	#7 Chad Johnson Gold		
7D1X8K	#8 Rudi Johnson Gold		
7D5W8J	#9 Brian Simmons Gold		
7D8S6J	#10 J.P. Losman Gold		
7E3G7Y	#11 Willis McGahee Gold		
7F5B2Y	#12 Eric Moulds Gold		
7H3B2Y	#13 Takeo Spikes Gold		
7H9E8L	#14 Lawyer Milloy Gold		
7J3Y7F	#15 Jake Plummer Gold	8V9Y3X	#62 Michael Vick Gold
7J8F4J	#16 Ashley Lelie Gold	8X2Y9G	#64 Alge Crumpler Gold
7K5C8V	#17 Al Wilson Gold	2W4P9T	#188 First and Fifteen Bronze
7L8C2W	#18 Champ Bailey Gold	2W4P9G	#188 First and Fifteen Silver
1A2D9F	#19 John Lynch Gold	2Y7L8B	#189 First and Five Bronze
701J3F	#20 D.J. Williams Gold		
7P5G3N	#21 Lee Suggs Gold		
7Q2E45	#22 Kellen Winslow Jr. Gold		
7Q6F4G	#23 Simeon Rice Gold		
7Q6X4L	#24 Derrick Brooks Gold		
7R7V2E	#25 Ronde Barber Gold		
7S4C4D	#26 Anthony McFarland Gold		
7T1G2Y	#27 Michael Clayton Gold		

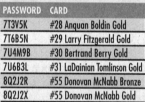

PASSWORD	CARD
2Z2F4H	#190 Unforced Errors Bronze
2Z2F4G	#190 Unforced Errors Silver
3D3Q3P	#191 Extra Credit Bronze

PASSWORD	CARD
3D8X6Z	#191 Extra Credit Gold
3D8X6T	#192 Tight Fit Bronze
3E9R4V	#193 5th Down Bronze

PASSWORD	CARD
3E9R4I	#193 5th Down Silver
3F9G4J	#194 3rd Down Bronze
3F9G4O	#194 3rd Down Silver
3H3U7T	#194 3rd Down Gold

PASSWORD	CARD
3H3U7F	#195 Human Plow Bronze

PASSWORD	CARD
3H8M5U	#196 Super Dive Bronze
3J3S9Y	#197 Da Boot Bronze

PASSWORD	CARD
3J3S9E	#197 Da Boot Silver
3T4E3Y	#208 Pocket Protectors Gold
3X1V2H	#210 QB on Target Gold
4D1V2Y	#217 Ouch Gold
4F9D2B	#220 Super Bowl XL Gold
4F9D2H	#221 Super Bowl XLI Gold
4I1V6T	#222 Super Bowl XLII Gold
4F3D7E	#223 Super Bowl XLIII Gold
4I1V6K	#224 Aloha Stadium Gold

MADDEN NFL 07

#199 GOLD LAME DUCK CHEAT CARD
In My Madden, select Madden Codes from Madden Cards. Enter 5LAWOO.

#200 GOLD MISTAKE FREE CHEAT CARD
In My Madden, select Madden Codes from Madden Cards. Enter XL7SP1.

#210 GOLD QB ON TARGET CHEAT CARD
In My Madden, select Madden Codes from Madden Cards. Enter WROA0R.

MAJOR LEAGUE BASEBALL 2K5

ALL CHEATS
Create a new profile with the name Ima Cheater.

ALL CLASSIC TEAMS
Create a new profile with the name Old Timers.

ALL EXTRAS
Create a new profile with the name Gimme Goods.

MAJOR LEAGUE BASEBALL 2K6

UNLOCK EVERYTHING
Select Enter Cheat Code from the My 2K6 menu and enter Derek Jeter.

TOPPS 2K STARS
Select Enter Cheat Code from the My 2K6 menu and enter Dream Team.

SUPER WALL CLIMB
Select Enter Cheat Code from the My 2K6 menu and enter Last Chance. Enable the cheats by selecting My Cheats or selecting Cheat Codes from the Options screen in-game.

SUPER PITCHES
Select Enter Cheat Code from the My 2K6 menu and enter Unhittable. Enable the cheats by selecting My Cheats or selecting Cheat Codes from the Options screen in-game.

ROCKET ARMS
Select Enter Cheat Code from the My 2K6 menu and enter Gotcha. Enable the cheats by selecting My Cheats or selecting Cheat Codes from the Options screen in-game.

BOUNCY BALL
Select Enter Cheat Code from the My 2K6 menu and enter Crazy Hops. Enable the cheats by selecting My Cheats or selecting Cheat Codes from the Options screen in-game.

MARC ECKO'S GETTING UP: CONTENTS UNDER PRESSURE

ALL LEVELS
Select Codes from the Options menu and enter IPULATOR.

INFINITE HEALTH
Select Codes from the Options screen and enter MARCUSECKOS.

MAX HEALTH
Select Codes from the Options screen and enter BABYLONTRUST.

INFINITE SKILLS
Select Codes from the Options screen and enter FLIPTHESCRIPT. Max Skills
Select Codes from the Options screen and enter VANCEDALLISTER.

ALL COMBAT UPGRADES
Select Codes from the Options menu and enter DOGTAGS.

ALL CHARACTERS IN VERSUS MODE
Select Codes from the Options menu and enter STATEYOURNAME.

ALL VERSUS ARENAS
Select Codes from the Options menu and enter WORKBITCH.

ALL ART
Select Codes from the Options menu and enter SIRULLY.

ALL BLACK BOOK
Select Codes from the Options menu and enter SHARDSOFGLASS.

ALL IPOD
Select Codes from the Options menu and enter GRANDMACELIA.

ALL LEGENDS
Select Codes from the Options menu and enter NINESIX.

ALL MOVIES
Select Codes from the Options menu and enter DEXTERCROWLEY.

MARVEL NEMESIS: RISE OF THE IMPERFECTS

UNLOCK ALL FANTASTIC FOUR COMICS
Select Cheats from the Options menu and enter SAVAGELAND.

**UNLOCKS ALL TOMORROW
PEOPLE COMICS**
Select Cheats from the Options menu and
enter NZONE.

ELEKTRA BONUS CARD
Select Cheats from the Options menu and
enter THEHAND.

SOLARA BONUS CARD
Select Cheats from the Options menu and
enter REIKO.

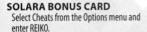

STORM BONUS CARD
Select Cheats from the Options menu and
enter MONROE.

MARVEL ULTIMATE ALLIANCE

UNLOCK ALL SKINS
At the Team Menu, press Up, Down, Left, Right, Left, Right, Start.

UNLOCKS ALL HERO POWERS
At the Team Menu, press Left, Right, Up, Down, Up, Down, Start.

ALL HEROES TO LEVEL 99
At the Team Menu, press Up, Left, Up, Left, Down, Right, Down, Right, Start.

UNLOCK ALL HEROES
At the Team Menu, press Up, Up, Down, Down, Left, Left, Left, Start.

UNLOCK DAREDEVIL
At the Team Menu, press Left, Left, Right, Right, Up, Down, Up, Down, Start.

UNLOCK SILVER SURFER
At the Team Menu, press Down, Left, Left, Up, Right, Up, Down, Left, Start.

GOD MODE
During gameplay, press Up, Down, Up, Down, Up, Left, Down, Right, Start.

TOUCH OF DEATH
During gameplay, press Left, Right, Down, Down, Right, Left, Start.

SUPER SPEED
During gameplay, press Up, Left, Up, Right, Down, Right, Start.

FILL MOMENTUM
During gameplay, press Left, Right, Right, Left, Up, Down, Down, Up, Start.

UNLOCK ALL COMICS
At the Review menu, press Left, Right, Right, Left, Up, Up, Right, Start.

UNLOCK ALL CONCEPT ART
At the Review menu, press Down, Down, Down, Right, Right, Left, Down, Start.

UNLOCK ALL MOVIES
At the Review menu, press Up, Left, Left, Up, Right, Right, Up, Start.

UNLOCK ALL LOAD SCREENS
At the Review menu, press Up, Down, Right, Left, Up, Up Down, Start.

UNLOCK ALL COURSES
At the Comic Missions menu, press Up, Right, Left, Down, Up, Right, Left, Down, Start.

MASTERS OF THE UNIVERSE HE-MAN: DEFENDER OF GRAYSKULL

INVULNERABILITY
Select Cheats from the Options menu and enter Right, ●, Up, Left, ❌.

UNLIMITED GRAYSKULL POWER
Select Cheats from the Options menu and enter Down, Right, ❌, ●, Down.

DOUBLE DAMAGE
Select Cheats from the Options menu and enter ●, Right, ❌, Up, ❌.

ALL LEVELS
Select Cheats from the Options menu and enter ❌, Left, Up, ●, Down.

MAX PAYNE 2: THE FALL OF MAX PAYNE

ALL GAME MODES AND CHAPTERS
During a game, press ▣ (x3), ❌, Left, Right, Left, Right, ▣ (x3), ❌, Left, Right, Left, Right. Return to the Main menu and select New Game.

MEDAL OF HONOR: EUROPEAN ASSAULT

Pause the game, hold L1 + R1 and press ●, ●, Left, ▲, ●, ❌. You can now enter the following codes.

DISABLE SHELLSHOCK
Press L2, R1, L2, L1, ▲, ▲.

FULL ADRENALINE METER
Press L1, R2, R1, Up, ▲, ●.

HIDE HUD
Press ●, Down, ●, Up, ▲, ●.

KILL NEMESIS
Press Down, L2, L1, R1, Up, ▣.

PICKUP OSS DOCUMENT
Press Up, ❌, R2, R1, Up, ▣.

SUICIDE (SINGLE PLAYER ONLY)
Press ❌, ▲, ●, Right, ▲, ●.

UNLIMITED AMMO
Press L2, L1, ▣, L2, L1, R1.

MEDAL OF HONOR: RISING SUN

Select Password from options and enter the following. Select the Bonus option to enable cheats.

ALL MISSIONS
Enter BUTTERFLY.

UNLIMITED AMMUNITION
Enter GOBY.

ACHILLES HEAD MODE
Enter MANDARIN.

BULLET SHIELD MODE
Enter TANG.

PERFECTIONIST
Enter HOGFISH.

RUBBER GRENADE MODE
Enter DAMSEL.

SILVER BULLET MODE
Enter TILEFISH.

SNIPE-O-RAMA MODE
Enter PUFFER.

INVISIBLE SOLDIERS
Enter TRIGGER.

MEN WITH HATS
Enter SEAHORSE.

ALL REPLAY ITEMS
Enter GARIBALDI.

MEGA MAN X8

PLAY AS ALIA
At the Title screen, press Down, R1, Up, L1, ●, ✖, ▲, ●.

PLAY AS LAYER
At the Title screen, press ●, ●, Right, ✖, R1.

BATTLE CUTMAN
At the Title screen, press Left, ●, Up, ▲, Down, ✖, Right, ●, L1, R1, L2, R2.

SIGMA BLADE
At the Title screen, press L3, L3, R3, L3, R3, L3, L3, R3, L3, L3, R3.

BLACK ZERO
At the Title screen, press L1, L1, R1, R1, L1, L1, L1, L1.

PALLETE
At the Title screen, press R1, ✖, Left, ●, ●.

ULTIMATE ARMOR X
At the Title screen, press Left, Left, Left, Right, Right, Right, Left, Left, Left, Left, Right, Right, Right, Right.

WHITE AXL
At the Title screen, press L2, L2, L2, R2, R2, R2, L2, L2, L2, R2.

MEGA MAN X COLLECTION

Mega Man X4

BLACK ZERO
At the Character Select screen, highlight Zero, hold R1 and press Right (x6). Then release R1, hold ● and press Start. Continue holding ● until the game starts.

ULTIMATE ARMOR FOR MEGA MAN X
At the Character Select screen, highlight Mega Man X, press ●, ●, Left (x6), hold L1 + R2 and press Start. Continue holding L1 + R2 until the game starts. Complete the level, then find

Mega Man X5

BLACK ZERO
At the Character Select screen, highlight Zero and press Down, Down, Up (x9).

ULTIMATE ARMOR FOR MEGA MAN X
At the Character Select screen, highlight Mega Man X and press Up, Up, Down (x9).

Mega Man X6

BLACK ZERO
At the Main menu, highlight Game Start and press L1, L1, L1, R2.

ULTIMATE ARMOR FOR MEGA MAN X
At the Main menu, highlight Game Start and press Left, Left, Left, Right.

MIDNIGHT CLUB 3: DUB EDITION REMIX

ALL CITIES & RACES IN ARCADE MODE
Select Cheat Codes from the Options menu and enter urbansprawl, roadtrip or crosscountry.

NO DAMAGE
Select Cheat Codes from the Options menu and enter ontheroad.

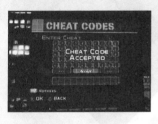

ARGO SPECIAL MOVE
Select Cheat Codes from the Options menu and enter dfens.

ROAR SPECIAL MOVE
Select Cheat Codes from the Options menu and enter Rjnr.

ZONE SPECIAL MOVE
Select Cheat Codes from the Options menu and enter allin.

ADD $1 TO CAREER MONEY
Select Cheat Codes from the Options menu and enter kubmir.

SUBTRACT $1 OF CAREER MONEY
Select Cheat Codes from the Options menu and enter rimbuk.

BUNNY HEAD
Select Cheat Codes from the Options menu and enter getheadl.

CHROME HEAD
Select Cheat Codes from the Options menu and enter haveyouseenthisboy.

FLAMING HEAD
Select Cheat Codes from the Options menu and enter trythisathome.

SNOWMAN HEAD
Select Cheat Codes from the Options menu and enter getheadm.

PUMPKIN HEAD
Select Cheat Codes from the Options menu and enter getheadk.

YELLOW SMILE HEAD
Select Cheat Codes from the Options menu and enter getheadj.

HYDRO THUNDER

ALL TRACKS & BOATS

Get a high score and enter ?PB as your initials.

OFFROAD THUNDER

CLIFFHANGER TRACK

Select Rally and press Right at the Choose Track screen to bring up the Secret Code option. Press Right, Up, Left, to unlock the Cliffhanger track.

CHIEFTAIN & GENERAL VEHICLES

Select Rally and press Right at the Choose Machine screen to bring up the Secret Code option. Press Left (x3) to unlock Chieftain. Press Left (x3) again to unlock General.

DUST DEVIL & SILVER STREAK VEHICLES

Select Rally and press Right at the Choose Machine screen to bring up the Secret Code option. Press Left, Up, Right to unlock Dust Devil. Press Left, Up, Right again to unlock Silver Streak.

HYENA & BAD OMEN VEHICLES

Select Rally and press Right at the Choose Machine screen to bring up the Secret Code option. Press Right (x3) to unlock Hyena. Press Right (x3) again to unlock Bad Omen.

WILDCAT & THRASHER VEHICLES

Select Rally and press Right at the Choose Machine screen to bring up the Secret Code option. Press Up (x3) to unlock Wildcat. Press Up (x3) again to unlock Thrashe

SAN FRANCISCO: RUSH 2049

ACTIVATE CHEAT MENU

At the Main menu, highlight Options and press L1 + R1 + ● + ●. Now you can enter the following cheats.

ALL CARS

At the Cheat menu, highlight All Cars and press ⊗, ⊗, ●, ●, L1, L1. Hold R1 and press ●. Release R1, hold L1 and press ⊗.

ALL TRACKS

At the Cheat menu, highlight All Tracks, hold ✖ + ● and press R1. Release ✖ and ●. Hold ● + ● and press L1. Release ● and ●. Press ✖, ✖, ●, ●, hold L1 + R1 and press ●.

ALL PARTS

At the Cheat menu, highlight All Parts, hold ● and press ●, ✖, L1, R1. Release ●, hold ● and press ✖. Release ● and press ●, ●.

RESURRECT IN PLACE

At the Cheat menu, highlight Resurrect in Place and press R1, R1, L1, L1, ✖, ●, ●.

FRAME SCALE

At the Cheat menu, highlight Frame Scale hold L1 and press ✖, ✖, ●. Release L1, hold R1 and press ✖, ✖, ●.

TIRE SCALING

At the Cheat menu, highlight Tire Scaling press and press ●, ●, ✖, ●, ●, ✖. Hold R1 and press ✖.

FOG COLOR

At the Cheat menu, highlight Fog Color hold L1 and press ●, release L1, hold ✖ and press ●, release ✖, hold ● and press ●, release ●, hold R1 and press ●.

CAR COLLISIONS

At the Cheat menu, highlight Car Collisions hold L1 + R1 and press ●, ●, ✖. Release L1 and R1 and press ●, ●, ✖.

CONE MINES

At the Cheat menu, highlight Cone Mines hold ● and press R1, L1. Release ● and press ●. Hold ✖ and press ●. Release ✖ and press ●.

CAR MINES

At the Cheat menu, highlight Car Mines, hold L1 + R1 + ● and press ✖, ●. Release L1, R1 and ●. Press ✖, ●.

TRACK ORIENTATION

At the Cheat menu, highlight Track Orientation hold L1 + R1 and press ●. Release L1 and R1 and press ✖, ●, ●. Hold L1 + R1 and press ●.

AUTO ABORT

At the Cheat menu, highlight Auto Abort and press ✖, L1, ●, R1, ●. Hold L1 + R1 and press ✖, ●.

SUPER SPEED

At the Cheat menu, highlight Super Speed hold ● + R1 and press L1. Release ● and R1. Hold ✖ and press ●. Release ✖ and press ✖, ✖, ✖.

INVINCIBLE

At the Cheat menu, highlight Invincible hold L1 + ● and press ●, ✖. Release L1 + ●. Hold R1 and press ✖, ●, ●.

INVISIBLE CAR

At the Cheat menu, highlight Invisible Car hold L1 and press ●. Release L1. Hold R1 and press ●. Release R1 and press ✖. Hold L1 + R1 and press ●. Release L1 and R1 and press ●, ●, ●.

INVISIBLE TRACK

At the Cheat menu, highlight Invisible Track press R1, L1, ●, ●, ✖, ✖, ●, ●. Hold L1 + R1 and press ✖.

BRAKES

At the Cheat menu, highlight Brakes press ●, ●, ●. Hold L1 + ● + ✖ and press R1.

SUPER TIRES

At the Cheat menu, highlight Super Tires hold R1 and press ●, ●, ●. Release R1. Hold L1 and press ✖, ✖, ●.

MASS

At the Cheat menu, highlight Mass hold ✖ and press ●, ●, ●. Release ✖ and press L1, R1.

PLAYSTATION® 2

SUICIDE MODE
At the Cheat menu, highlight Suicide Mode hold ⊙ and press R1, L1, R1, L1. Release ⊙. Hold ⊙ and press R1, L1, R1, L1.

BATTLE PAINT SHOP
At the Cheat menu, highlight Battle Paint Shop hold ✕ and press L1, R1, L1, R1. Release ✕ and press ⊙, ⊙, ⊙.

DEMOLITION BATTLE
At the Cheat menu, highlight Demolition Battle hold L1 + ✕ and press ⊙, ⊙. Release L1 and ✕. Hold R1 + ✕ and press ⊙, ⊙.

RANDOM WEAPONS
At the Cheat menu, highlight Random Weapons hold L1 + ✕ and press ⊙, ⊙. Release L1 and ✕. Hold R1 + ✕ and press ⊙, ⊙.

MIKE TYSON HEAVYWEIGHT BOXING

PLATINUM UNLOCK
At the Title screen press ⊙, ⊙, L2, R2. This unlocks all Modes, all Boxers, and all Arenas.

BIG HEAD MODE
At the Title screen press ⊙, ⊙, Up, Down.

SMALL HEAD MODE
At the Title screen press ⊙, ⊙, Down, Up.

2-D MODE
At the Title screen press Down, Up, ⊙, ⊙.

SUPER MUTANT MODE
At the Title screen press ⊙, Left, Up, ▲.

CUSTOM BOXER TEXTURES
At the Title screen press L1, R1, ✕, ✕, ▲, ✕.

UNLOCK CODIES CREDITS
At the Title screen press ✕, ▲, ⊙, ⊙.

MINORITY REPORT

Select Cheats from the Special menu and enter the following:

INVINCIBILITY
Enter LRGARMS.

LEVEL WARP ALL
Enter PASSKEY.

LEVEL SKIP
Enter QUITER.

ALL COMBOS
Enter NINJA.

ALL WEAPONS
Enter STRAPPED.

INFINITE AMMO
Enter MRJUAREZ.

SUPER DAMAGE
Enter SPINACH.

HEALTH
Enter BUTTERUP.

Select Alternate Heroes from the Special menu to find the following:

CLOWN HERO
Enter SCARYCLOWN.

CONVICT HERO
Enter JAILBREAK.

GI JOHN HERO
Enter GNRLINFANTRY.

LIZARD HERO
Enter HISSSS.

MOSELEY HERO
Enter HAIRLOSS.

NARA HERO
Enter WEIGHTGAIN.

NIKKI HERO
Enter BIGLIPS.

ROBOT HERO
Enter MRROBOTO.

SUPER JOHN HERO
Enter SUPERJOHN.

ZOMBIE HERO
Enter IAMSODEAD.

FREE AIM
Enter FPSSTYLE.

PAIN ARENAS
Enter MAXIMUMHURT.

ARMOR
Enter STEELUP.

BASEBALL BAT
Enter SLUGGER.

RAG DOLL
Enter CLUMSY.

SLOMO BUTTON
Enter SLIZOMIZO.

BOUNCY MEN
Enter BOUNZMEN.

WRECK THE JOINT
Enter CLUTZ.

DRAMATIC FINISH
Enter STYLIN.

ENDING
Enter WIMP.

CONCEPT ART
Enter SKETCHPAD.

ALL MOVIES
Enter DIRECTOR.

DO NOT SELECT
Enter DONOTSEL.

MISSION: IMPOSSIBLE—OPERATION SURMA

LEVEL SELECT
Select Profiles, highlight Jasmine Curry, then press and hold L1 + R1 + ▲ + ●.

MISTER MOSQUITO

KANEYO MOSQUITO
At the Character Select screen, press and hold L1 and press Up, Right, Left, Down, ●, ●, R1, R1, R1.

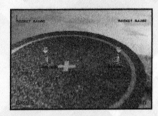

KENICHI MOSQUITO
After entering the Kaneyo Mosquito code, hold L2 and press Up, Right, Left, Down, ●, ●, R2, R2, R2 at the Character Select screen.

2-PLAYER MINI GAME
Turn on the system and hold START + SELECT on controller two.

MLB '06: THE SHOW

ALL TEAMS
At the Main menu, press Left, Right, Right, Down, Down, Left, Up, Up.

ALL PLAYERS
At the Main menu, press Left, Up, Left, Right, Down, Right, Left, Up.

ALL UNIFORMS
At the Main menu, press Up, Down, Right, Left, Down, Right, Down, Up.

ALL STADIUMS
At the Main menu, press Down, Up, Left, Right, Up, Right, Up, Down.

BIG BALL
Pause the game and press Up, Right, Down, Left, Right, Down, Left, Up.

MAX PITCH
Pause the game and press Right, Right, Up, Up, Down, Down, Left, Left Break.

MAX PITCH SPEED
Pause the game and press Up, Up, Left, Right, Left, Right, Up, Up.

RUN FASTER
Pause the game and press Left, Left, Left, Up, Right, Right, Right, Down.

RUN SLOWER
Pause the game and press Right, Right, Right, Up, Left, Left, Left, Down.

MLB SLUGFEST 2006

ATLANTIS
Hit a homer in AT&T Park.

COLISEUM
Hit a homer in Fenway Park.

EMPIRE
Hit a homer in Yankee Stadium.

FORBIDDEN CITY
Hit homer in PetCo Park.

MONUMENT STADIUM
Hit homer in Citizens Bank Park.

ROCKET PARK
Hit a homer in Minute Maid Park.

TEAM BOBBLE HEAD
Hit 10 homers in one game.

TEAM CASEY
Hit a triple in Wrigley Field.

TEAM DOLPHINS
Hit a homer in Atlantis.

TEAM EAGLES
Walk three times in one game.

TEAM EVIL CLOWNS
Hit a homer in Empire Park with the Yankees.

TEAM GLADIATOR
Hit homer in The Coliseum.

TEAM HORSE
Steal five bases in one game.

TEAM LIONS
Hit a homer with the Tigers in Comerica Park.

TEAM MARTIANS
Hit a triple in Rocket Park.

TEAM MINOTAUR
Hit a homer in The Forbidden City.

TEAM PINTO
Hit an inside-the-park homer in Busch Stadium.

TEAM RODEO CLOWN
Perform a double play.

MLB SLUGFEST: LOADED

CHEATS

At the Match-Up screen, press ●, ▲, and ● to enter the following codes, then press the appropriate direction. For example, for 16" Softball press ● (x2), ▲ (x4), ● (x2), then press Down.

CODE	ENTER
Bone Bat	0-0-1 Up
Blade Bat	0-0-2 Up
Ice Bat	0-0-3 Up
Log Bat	0-0-4 Up
Spike Bat	0-0-5 Up
Whiffle Bat	0-0-4 Right
Max Batting	3-0-0 Left
Max Power	0-3-0 Left
Max Speed	0-0-3 Left
Unlimited Turbo	4-4-4 Down
Extra Time After Plays	1-2-3 Left
Little League Mode	1-0-1 Down
16" Softball	2-4-2 Down
Rubber Bball	2-4-2 Up
Tiny Head	2-0-0 Left
Big Head	2-0-0 Right
Alien Team	2-3-1 Down
Bobblehead Team	1-3-3 Down
Casey Team	2-3-3 Down
Dolphin Team	1-0-2 Down

CODE	ENTER
Dwarf Team	1-0-3 Down
Eagle Team	2-1-2 Right
Evil Clown Team	2-1-1 Down
Gladiator Team	1-1-3 Down
Horse Team	2-1-1 Right
Lion Team	2-2-0 Right
Minotaur Team	1-1-0 Down
Napalitano Team	2-3-2 Down
Olshan Team	2-2-2 Down
Pinto Team	2-1-0 Right
Rivera Team	2-2-2 Up
Rodeo Clown Team	1-3-2 Down
Scorpion Team	1-1-2 Down
Terry Fitzgerald Team	3-3-3 Right
Todd McFarlane Team	2-2-2 Right
Atlantis Stadium	3-2-1 Left
Coliseum Stadium	3-3-3 Up
Empire Park Stadium	3-2-1 Right
Forbidden City Stadium	3-3-3 Left
Midway Park Stadium	3-2-1 Down
Monument Stadium	3-3-3 Down
Rocket Park Stadium	3-2-1 Up

MORTAL KOMBAT: ARMAGEDDON

BLAZE CHARACTER
While in The Krypt, select the "?" and press ⬤, ⬛, Left, L1, Left, ⬤.

DAEGON CHARACTER
While in The Krypt, select the "?" and press R1, L1, ⬤, Down, Down, ⬛.

MEAT CHARACTER
While in The Krypt, select the "?" and press
Up, ⬛, ⬛, ⬤, ⬤, Up.

TAVEN CHARACTER
While in The Krypt, select the "?" and press
L2, Left, R1, Up, ⬤, Down.

DRAHMIN'S ALTERNATE
COSTUME
While in The Krypt, select the "?" and press
L2, Right, ✖, R2, Up, Up.

FROST'S ALTERNATE
COSTUME
While in The Krypt, select the "?" and press
Down, R2, R1, L1, ⬤, L2.

NITARA'S ALTERNATE
COSTUME
While in The Krypt, select the "?" and press
Down, L1, Up, L1, L1, Right.

SHANG TSUNG'S ALTERNATE COSTUME
While in The Krypt, select the "?" and press L1, Left, Up, ⬤, Up, L2.

FALLING CLIFFS ARENA
While in The Krypt, select the "?" and press R2, ⬤, ⬛, ❌, ⬤, 🔺.

KRIMSON FOREST ARENA
While in The Krypt, select the "?" and press ⬤, L1, Up, ⬛, ⬤, Down.

NETHERSHIP INTERIOR ARENA
While in The Krypt, select the "?" and press R1, Left, Left, Down, L1, ⬛.

THE PYRAMID OF ARGUS ARENA
While in The Krypt, select the "?" and press R1, L1, ⬛, ❌, R2, Up.

REIKO'S WAR ROOM ARENA
While in The Krypt, select the "?" and press R2, 🔺, R1, Up, ❌, ❌.

SHINNOK'S SPIRE ARENA
While in The Krypt, select the "?" and press Left, Left, ⬤, Up, 🔺, L2.

ARMAGEDDON PROMO MOVIE
While in The Krypt, select the "?" and press Up, Up, Down, Up, L1, ❌.

CYRAX FATALITY BLOOPER MOVIE
While in The Krypt, select the "?" and press Right, L1, R2, Down, Up, L1.

MOTOR GAMEPLAY MOVIE
While in The Krypt, select the "?" and press 🔺, Up, R2, L1, R1, R2.

BLAZE BOSS SKETCH KONCEPT ART
While in The Krypt, select the "?" and press L1, 🔺, L2, L2, R1, ⬛.

COLOR STUDY FOR OPENING MOVIE 3 KONCEPT ART
While in The Krypt, select the "?" and press 🔺, Left, Left, ❌, Down, ⬤.

FIREWELL SKETCH 3 KONCEPT ART
While in The Krypt, select the "?" and press Up, ⬛, R1, L2, ⬤, L1.

GAUNTLET TRAP SKETCH KONCEPT ART
While in The Krypt, select the "?" and press ⬤, R2, 🔺, Down, ⬤, Left.

HERO SKETCHES 1 KONCEPT ART
While in The Krypt, select the "?" and press Up, ❌, R2, Down, L2, ❌

MILEENA'S CAR SKETCH KONCEPT ART
While in The Krypt, select the "?" and press R2, Right, Up, R1, 🔺, Up.

SCORPION THROW SKETCH KONCEPT ART
While in The Krypt, select the "?" and press L1, Left, Up, ⬤, R2, L1.

SEKTOR'S 2-HAND PULSE BLADE SKETCH KONCEPT ART
While in The Krypt, select the "?" and press R2, L1, Left, ❌, Up, R1.

ARMORY FIGHT TUNE
While in The Krypt, select the "?" and press ❌, ⬛, Left, 🔺, ⬛, ❌.

LIN KUEI PALACE TUNE
While in The Krypt, select the "?" and press L2, Left, ⬤, ❌, R2, Right.

PYRAMID OF ARGUS TUNE
While in The Krypt, select the "?" and press Down, Left, R2, L2, Up, L1.

TEKUNIN WARSHIP TUNE
While in The Krypt, select the "?" and press Up, ⬤, L1, R1, R1, ❌.

Ultimate Mortal Kombat 3

The following codes are for the Armageddon emulation of UMK3 from the Premium Edition.

RANDOM SELECT
At the Fighter Select screen, press Up + Start.

PLAY AS HUMAN SMOKE
Select Smoke and hold High Punch + High Kick + Block + Run + Away until the match starts.

KOMBAT CODES
You must enter the following codes at the VS screen before a match. Use Low Punch, Block and Low Kick to enter the following codes. The first three numbers are entered by player 1 and the last three by player 2. For example, for Dark Kombat player 1 presses Low Punch (x6), Block (x8), Low Kick (x8) and player 2 presses Low Punch (x4), Block (x2), Low Kick (x2). You may also hold Up and press a button to count down. If you need to enter a 7, you can hold Up and press the button three times.

CODE	ENTER
Dark Kombat	688 422
Explosive Kombat (2V2)	277 277
Explosive Kombat, No Throws (2V2)	022 220
Fast Uppercut	788 322
Galaga Before Match	642 468
Infinite Run/Combo time	466 466
No Blocking	020 020
No Power Bar	987 123
No Sound Kombat	300 300
P1 Half Life	033 000
P1 Low Life	707 000
P2 Half Life	000 033
P2 Low Life	000 707
Psycho Kombat	985 125
Random Kombat 1	460 460
Random Kombat 2	444 444
Stage Select: Bell Tower	091 190
Stage Select: Bridge	077 022
Stage Select: Graveyard	666 333
Stage Select: Jade's Desert	330 033
Stage Select: Khan's Kave	004 700
Stage Select: Khan's Tower	880 220
Stage Select: Kombat Temple	600 040
Stage Select: Noob's Lair	050 050
Stage Select: Pit 3	820 028
Stage Select: River Kombat	002 003
Stage Select: Rooftop	343 343
Stage Select: Scorpion's Hell (Netherrealm)	666 444
Stage Select: Soul Chamber	123 904
Stage Select: Street	079 035
Stage Select: Subway	880 088
Throwing Disabled	100 100
Winner of R1 Fights Motaro	969 141
Winner of R1 Fights Noob Saibot	769 342
Winner of R1 Fights Shao Khan	033 564
Winner of R1 Fights Smoke	205 205

CLASIC SUB-ZERO
After the continue screen, you will see an Enter the Ultimate Kombat Kode screen. Enter 81835 81835 with the High Punch, High Kick, Low Punch, Low Kick and Block buttons on both controllers.

ERMAC
After the continue screen, you will see an Enter the Ultimate Kombat Kode screen. Enter 12344 44321 with the High Punch, High Kick, Low Punch, Low Kick and Block buttons on both controllers.

MILEENA
After the continue screen, you will see an Enter the Ultimate Kombat Kode screen. Enter 22264 22264 with the High Punch, High Kick, Low Punch, Low Kick and Block buttons on both controllers.

MOTOCROSS MANIA 3

ALL TRACKS
At the Main menu, press Up, Left, Down, Right, Up, Left, Down, Left, Left, ⬤.

ALL RIDERS & BIKES
At the Main menu, press Up, Left, Down, Right, Up, Left, Down, Up, ⬤.

ALL BIKE UPGRADES
At the Main menu, press Up, Left, Down, Right, Up, Down, Down, Left, Down, ⬤.

ALL WEAPONS & ARMOR
At the Main menu, press Up, Left, Down, Right, Up, Left, Down, Left, Down, ⬤.

FREESTYLE
At the Main menu, press Up, Left, Down, Right, Up, Left, Down, Left, Left, ⬤. Go into another menu and back out to access Freestyle.

MTX: MOTOTRAX

FASTER BIKE
Select Cheats from the Options menu and enter jih345.

ALL TRACKS
Select Cheats from the Options menu and enter BA7H.

MAXIMUM AIR
Select Cheats from the Options menu and enter BFB0020.

SKY CAMERA
Select Cheats from the Options menu and enter HIC.

BUTTERFINGER GEAR
Select Cheats from the Options menu and enter B77393.

LEFT FIELD GEAR
Select Cheats from the Options menu and enter 12345.

SOBE GEAR
Select Cheats from the Options menu and enter 50B3.

OFFICER DICK
Select Cheats from the Options menu and enter BADG3.

NOKIA TRICKBOT
Select Cheats from the Options menu and enter HA79000.

SPEED DEMON
Select Cheats from the Options menu and enter 773H999.

SLIPKNOT MAGGOT
Select Cheats from the Options menu and enter 86657457.

SLIPKNOT FMV
Select Cheats from the Options menu and enter 23F7IC5.

ALL FMVS
Select Cheats from the Options menu and enter 23F7ICS.

MVP 06 NCAA BASEBALL

ALL CHALLENGE ITEMS
In Dynasty Mode, create a player with the name Dee Jay Randall.

LEVEL 1 CHALLENGE ITEMS
In Dynasty Mode, create a player with the name Peter Trenouth.

ALL LEVEL 2 CHALLENGE ITEMS
In Dynasty Mode, create a player with the name Trey Smith.

ALL LEVEL 3 CHALLENGE ITEMS
In Dynasty Mode, create a player with the name Chris Chung.

ALL LEVEL 4 CHALLENGE ITEMS
In Dynasty Mode, create a player with the name Federico Rahal.

BIG BAT
In Dynasty Mode, create a player with the name Chris Deas.

SHORT PLAYER WITH BIG BAT
In Dynasty Mode, create a player with the name Alan Blouin.

THICK BAT
In Dynasty Mode, create a player with the name Melissa Shim.

LARGE PLAYER WITH THIN BAT
In Dynasty Mode, create a player with the name Neale Genereux.

SHORT PLAYER WITH THIN BAT
In Dynasty Mode, create a player with the name Julia Kwan.

SUPER HITTER
In Dynasty Mode, create a player with the name Tim Regel.

MVP BASEBALL 2005

ALL STADIUMS, PLAYERS, UNIFORMS AND REWARDS
Create a player named Katie Roy.

RED SOX ST. PATRICK'S DAY UNIFORM
Create a player named Neverlose Sight.

BAD HITTER WITH THIN BAT
Create a player named Erik Kiss.

GOOD HITTER WITH BIG BAT
Create a player named Isaiah Paterson, Jacob Paterson, or Keegan Paterson.

BIGGER BODY
Create a player named Kenny Lee.

MX UNLEASHED

Select Cheat Codes from the Options menu, then highlight the desired cheat and press ● to access a keyboard. Then enter the following codes:

SUPERCROSS TRACKS
Enter STUpERCROSS.

NATIONAL TRACKS
Enter ECONATION.

FREESTYLE TRACKS
Enter BUSTBIG.

PRO PHYSICS
Enter SWAPPIN.

EXPERT AI
Enter OBTGOFAST.

MACHINES
Enter MINIGAMES.

50CC BIKES
Enter SQUIRRELDOG.

500CC BIKES
Enter BIGDOGS.

CAREER COMPLETION
Enter CLAPPEDOUT.

AI BOWLING
Enter WRECKINGBALL.

MX VS. ATV UNLEASHED

UNLOCK EVERYTHING
Select Cheat Codes from the Options menu and enter TOOLAZY.

1,000,000 POINTS
Select Cheat Codes from the Options menu and enter BROKEASAJOKE. After entering the code, press Done multiple times for more points.

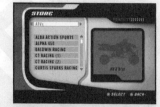

ALL PRO RIDERS
Select Cheat Codes from the Options menu and enter WANNABE.

ALL GEAR
Select Cheat Codes from the Options menu and enter WARDROBE.

50CC BIKE CLASS
Select Cheat Codes from the Options menu and enter MINIMOTO.

ALL MACHINES
Select Cheat Codes from the Options menu and enter LEADFOOT.

ALL FREESTYLE TRACKS
Select Cheat Codes from the Options menu and enter HUCKIT.

NARC

ALL DRUGS
During a game, press R1, L1, R1, L1, R1, L1, L3.

ALL WEAPONS
During a game, press R1, L1, R1, L1, R1, L1, R3.

INVINCIBILITY
During a game, press R1, L1, R1, L1, R1, L1, ✖.

SHOW HIDDEN STASHES
During a game, press R1, L1, R1, L1, R1, L1, Left.

UNLIMITED AMMO FOR CURRENT WEAPON
During a game, press R1, L1, R1, L1, R1, L1, Down.

THE REFINERY
During a game, press R1, L1, R1, L1, R1, L1, ●.

NASCAR 2005: CHASE FOR THE CUP

DALE EARNHARDT
At the Edit Driver screen, enter The Intimidator as your name.

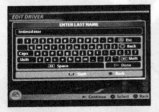

$10,000,000
At the Edit Driver screen, enter Walmart NASCAR as your name.

10,000,000 FANS
At the Edit Driver screen, enter MakeMe Famous as your name.

2,000,000 PRESTIGE POINTS
At the Edit Driver screen, enter You TheMan as your name.

EXCLUSIVE TRACK
At the Edit Driver screen, enter Walmart Exclusive as your name.

ALL BONUSES
At the Edit Driver screen, enter Open Sesame as your name.

ALL MR. CLEAN CARS
At the Edit Driver screen, enter Mr.Clean Racing as your name.

MR. CLEAN PIT CREW
At the Edit Driver screen, enter Clean Crew as your name.

DODGE CARS
At the Edit Driver screen, enter Race Dodge as your name.

DODGE TRACKS
At the Edit Driver screen, enter Dodge Stadium as your name.

LEVI STRAUSS CARS
At the Edit Driver screen, enter Levi Stauss153 as your name.

OLD SPICE CARS
At the Edit Driver screen, enter OldSpice Motorsports as your name.

OLD SPICE TRACKS
At the Edit Driver screen, enter OldSpice Venue as your name.

NASCAR 06: TOTAL TEAM CONTROL

UNLOCK EVERYTHING
In Fight to the Top mode, select Edit Driver. Enter Gimme Gimme as the first and last names.

$10,000,000
In Fight to the Top mode, select Edit Driver. Enter Walmart Money as the first and last names.

MAX FAN LEVEL
In Fight to the Top mode, select Edit Driver. Enter Super Star as the first and last names.

MAX PRESTIGE
In Fight to the Top mode, select Edit Driver. Enter MeMyself AndI as the first and last names.

MAX TEAM PRESTIGE
In Fight to the Top mode, select Edit Driver. Enter All ForOne as the first and last names.

WALMART TRACKS & CARS
In Fight to the Top mode, select Edit Driver. Enter Walmart Exclusive as the first and last names.

OLD SPICE TRACKS & CARS
In Fight to the Top mode, select Edit Driver. Enter KeepCool SmellGreat as the first and last names.

DALE EARNHARDT SR.
In Fight to the Top mode, select Edit Driver. Enter The Intimidator as the first and last names.

NASCAR 07

$10,000,000
In Fight to the Top mode, enter your name as GiveMe More.

10,000,000 FANS
In Fight to the Top mode, enter your name as AllBow ToMe.

PRESTIGE LEVEL 10 WITH 2,000,000 POINTS
In Fight to the Top mode, enter your name as Outta MyWay.

100% TEAM PRESTIGE
In Fight to the Top mode, enter your name as MoMoney BlingBling.

ALL CHASE PLATES
In Fight to the Top mode, enter your name as ItsAll ForMe.

OLD SPICE TRACKS & CARS.
In Fight to the Top mode, enter your name as KeepCool SmellGreat.

WALMART TRACK & CARS
In Fight to the Top mode, enter your name as Walmart EveryDay.

NBA '06: FEATURING THE LIFE VOL. 1

CAVALIERS ALTERNATE JERSEY
Select NBA.com from the Trophy Room and enter J8E5RAMI7E.

NUGGETS ALTERNATE JERSEY
Select NBA.com from the Trophy Room and enter 4J52U2N64E.

PISTONS ALTERNATE JERSEY
Select NBA.com from the Trophy Room and enter 7C43H21A8D.

CELTICS ALTERNATE JERSEY
Select NBA.com from the Trophy Room and enter C83A22G93E.

PACERS AWAY JERSEY
Select NBA.com from the Trophy Room and enter D2A7LL2A3S.

PACERS HOME JERSEY
Select NBA.com from the Trophy Room and enter 3E98M2I6LY.

CHICAGO BULLS CLASSIC JERSEY
Select NBA.com from the Trophy Room and enter S60T9E2V9E.

LOS ANGELES CLIPPERS CLASSIC JERSEY
Select NBA.com from the Trophy Room and enter 3W6E2ST1ON.

MEMPHIS GRIZZLIES CLASSIC JERSEY
Select NBA.com from the Trophy Room and enter N76I33A4L2.

NEW CLASSIC JERSEY NETS CLASSIC JERSEY
Select NBA.com from the Trophy Room and enter T73R387HF2.

NEW YORK KNICKS CLASSIC JERSEY
Select NBA.com from the Trophy Room and enter S25LFG33Z4.

ORLANDO MAGIC CLASSIC JERSEY
Select NBA.com from the Trophy Room and enter IX55LD1A9P.

PHOENIX SUNS CLASSIC JERSEY
Select NBA.com from the Trophy Room and enter L76HJY52K6.

SEATTLE SUPERSONICS CLASSIC JERSEY
Select NBA.com from the Trophy Room and enter S27T3E9V1E.

WASHINGTON WIZARDS CLASSIC JERSEY
Select NBA.com from the Trophy Room and enter J44X9YLL3F.

NBA 2K6

CELEBRITY STREET OPTION
Select Codes from the Features menu and enter ballers.

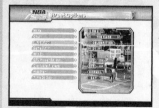

2KSPORTS TEAM
Select Codes from the Features menu and enter 2ksports.

2K6 TEAM
Select Codes from the Features menu and enter nba2k6.

VC TEAM
Select Codes from the Features menu and enter vcteam.

NIKE SHOX MTX SHOES
Select Codes from the Features menu and enter crazylift.

NIKE ZOOM 20-5-5 SHOES
Select Codes from the Features menu and enter lebronsummerkicks.

NIKE ZOOM KOBE 1 SHOES
Select Codes from the Features menu and enter kobe.

NIKE ZOOM LEBRON III ALL-STAR COLORWAY SHOES
Select Codes from the Features menu and enter lb allstar.

NIKE ZOOM LEBRON III BLACK/CRIMSON SHOES
Select Codes from the Features menu and enter lb crimsonblack.

NIKE ZOOM LEBRON III SPECIAL BIRTHDAY EDITION SHOES
Select Codes from the Features menu and enter lb bday.

NIKE ZOOM LEBRON III WHITE/GOLD SHOES

Select Codes from the Features menu and enter lb whitegold.

NIKE UP TEMPO PRO SHOES

Select Codes from the Features menu and enter anklebreakers.

ALTERNATE UNIFORMS

For the following codes, choose Codes from the Features menu and enter the appropriate code.

UNIFORM	ENTER
2006 All-Star	fanfavorites
St. Patrick's Day	gogreen
Bulls Retro	chi retro
Cavaliers Alternate	cle 2nd
Celtics Alternate	bos 2nd
Clippers Retro	lac retro
Grizzlies Retro	mem retro
Heat Retro	mia retro
Hornets Retro	no retro
Kings Alternate	sac 2nd
Knicks Retro	ny retro
Magic Retro	orl retro
Nets Retro	nj retro
Nuggets Alternate	den 2nd
2005-06 Pacers Uniform	31andonly

Pistons Alternate	det 2nd
Rockets Retro	hou retro
Sonics Retro	sea retro
Suns Retro	phx retro
Wizards Retro	was retro

+10 BONUS FOR DEFENSIVE AWARENESS

Find the PowerBar vending machine in The Crib. Choose Enter Code and enter lockdown.

+10 BONUS FOR OFFENSIVE AWARENESS
Find the PowerBar vending machine in The Crib. Choose Enter Code and enter getaclue.

MAX DURABILITY
Find the PowerBar vending machine in The Crib. Choose Enter Code and enter noinjury.

UNLIMITED STAMINA
Find the PowerBar vending machine in The Crib. Choose Enter Code and enter nrgmax.

POWERBAR TATTOO
Find the PowerBar vending machine in The Crib. Choose Enter Code and enter pbink. You can now use it in the game's Create Player feature.

ALL ITEMS IN THE CRIB
Find the PowerBar vending machine in The Crib. Choose Enter Code and enter criball.

NBA 2K7

MAX DURABILITY
Select Codes from the Features menu and enter ironman.

UNLIMITED STAMINA
Select Codes from the Features menu and enter norest.

+10 DEFFENSIVE AWARENESS
Select Codes from the Features menu and enter getstops.

+10 OFFENSIVE AWARENESS
Select Codes from the Features menu and enter inthezone.

TOPPS 2K SPORTS ALL-STARS
Select Codes from the Features menu and enter topps2ksports.

ABA BALL
Select Codes from the Features menu and enter payrespect.

NBA BALLERS

VERSUS SCREEN CHEATS

You can enter the following codes at the Versus screen. The ● button corresponds to the first number in the code, the ▲ is the second number, and the ● button corresponds to the last number. Press the D-pad in any direction to enter the code.

CODE NAME	ENTER
Big Head	1 3 4
Baby Ballers	4 2 3
Kid Ballers	4 3 3
Young Ballers	4 4 3
Paper Ballers	3 5 4
Alternate Gear	1 2 3

Show Shot Percentage	0 1 2
Expanded Move Set	5 1 2
Super Push	3 1 5
Super Block Ability	1 2 4
Great Handles	3 3 2
Unlimited Juice	7 6 3
Super Steals	2 1 5
Perfect Free Throws	3 2 7
Speedy Players	2 1 3
Better Free Throws	3 1 7
Fire Ability	7 2 2
Hotspot Ability	6 2 7
Back-In Ability	1 2 2
2x Juice Replenish	4 3 1
Stunt Ability	3 7 4
Pass 2 Friend Ability	5 3 6
Alley-Oop Ability	7 2 5
Put Back Ability	3 1 3
Legal Goaltending	7 5 6
R2R Mode	0 0 8
Play As Coach	5 6 7

CODE NAME	ENTER
Play As Agent	5 5 7
Play As Secretary	5 4 7
Play As BiznezMan-A	5 3 7
Play As BiznezMan-B	5 2 7
Play As Afro Man	5 1 7

Super Back-Ins	2 3 5
Half House	3 6 7
Random Moves	3 0 0
Pygmy	4 2 5
Tournament Mode	0 1 1

PHRASE-OLOGY CODES/ALTERNATE GEAR

Select Phrase-ology from the Inside Stuff option and enter the following codes to unlock the Alternate Gear for the corresponding player.

PLAYER	PHRASE
Allan Houston	KNICKER BOCKER PLEASE
Allen Iverson	KILLER CROSSOVER
Alonzo Mourning	ZO
Amare Stoudemire	RISING SUN
Antoine Walker	BALL HAWK
Baron Davis	STYLIN' & PROFILIN'
Ben Wallace	RADIO CONTROLLED CARS
Bill Russell	CELTICS DYNASTY
Bill Walton	TOWERS OF POWER
Carmelo Anthony	NEW TO THE GAME
Chris Webber	24 SECONDS
Clyde Drexler	CLYDE THE GLIDE
Darko Milicic	NBA FASTBREAK
Darryl Dawkins	RIM WRECKER
Dejaun Wagner	NBA HANGTIME

PLAYER	PHRASE
Dikembe Mutumbo	IN THE PAINT
Dominique Wilkins	DUNK FEST
Eddie Jones	BALLER UPRISING
Elton Brand	REBOUND
Manu Ginobili	MANU
Gary Payton	GLOVE IS IN LA
George Gervin	THE ICE MAN COMETH
Grant Hill	GONE GOLD WITH IT
Isiah Thomas	TRUE BALLER
Jalen Rose	BRING IT
Jason Kidd	PASS THE ROCK
Jason Terry	BALL ABOVE ALL
Jason Williams	GIVE AND GO
Jerry Stackhouse	STOP DROP AND ROLL
John Stockton	COURT VISION
Julius Irving	ONE ON ONE
Karl Malone	SPECIAL DELIVERY
Kenyon Martin	TO THE HOLE
Kevin Garnett	BOSS HOSS
Kevin McHale	HOLLA BACK
Kobe Bryant	JAPANESE STEAK
Larry Bird	HOOSIER
Latrell Sprewell	SPREE
Lebron James	KING JAMES
Magic Johnson	LAKER LEGENDS
Michael Finley	STUDENT OF THE GAME
Mike Bibby	DREAMS & SCHEMES
Moses Malone	LOST FREESTYLE FILES
Nate "Tiny" Archibald	NATE THE SKATE
Nene Hilario	RAGS TO RICHES
Oscar Robertson	AINT NO THING
Pau Gasol	POW POW POW
Paul Pierce	CELTICS SUPREME
Pete Maravich	PISTOL PETE
Rashard Lewis	FAST FORWARD
Rasheed Wallace	BRING DOWN THE HOUSE
Ray Allen	ALL STAR
Reggie Miller	FROM DOWNTOWN
Richard Hamilton	RIP
Robert Parish	THE CHIEF
Scottie Pippen	PLAYMAKER
Shaquille O'Neal	DIESEL RULES THE PAINT
Shawn Marion	MAKE YOUR MARK
Stephon Marbury	PLATINUM PLAYA
Steve Francis	ANKLE BREAKER
Steve Francis	RISING STAR
Steve Nash	HAIR CANADA
Tim Duncan	MAKE IT TAKE IT
Tony Parker	RUN AND SHOOT
Tracy McGrady	LIVING LIKE A BALLER
Vince Carter	CHECK MY CRIB
Wally Szczerbiak	WORLD
Walt Frazier	PENETRATE AND PERPETRATE

PLAYER	PHRASE
Wes Unseld	OLD SCHOOL
Willis Reed	HALL OF FAME
Wilt Chamberlain	WILT THE STILT
Yao Ming	CENTER OF ATTENTION

CRIBS

Select Phrase-ology from the Inside Stuff option and enter the following to unlock player cribs.

CRIB	PHRASE
Allen Iverson's Recording Studio	THE ANSWER

Karl Malone's Devonshire Estate	ICE HOUSE

Kobe Bryant's Italian Estate	EURO CRIB

Scottie Pippen's Yacht	NICE YACHT

Yao Ming's Childhood Grade School	PREP SCHOOL

OTHER PHRASE-OLOGY CODES

Select Phrase-ology from the Inside Stuff option and enter the following to unlock that bonus.

BONUS	PHRASE
All Players, Alternate Gear, & Cinemas	NBA BALLERS TRUE PLAYA
Special Movie #1	JUICE HOUSE
Special Movie #2	NBA SHOWTIME
Special Movie #3	NBA BALLERS RULES
Special Movie #4	HATCHET MAN
Special Movie #5	SLAM IT
Special Shoe #2	COLD STREAK
Special Shoe #3	LOST YA SHOES

NBA BALLERS: PHENOM

VERSUS SCREEN CHEATS

You can enter the following codes at the Vs screen. The ● button corresponds to the first number in the code, the ▲ is the second number, and the ● button corresponds to the last number. Press the D-pad in any direction to enter the code.

CODE NAME	ENTER
Tournament Mode	0 1 1
Big Head	1 3 4
Baby Ballers	4 2 3
Kid Ballers	4 3 3
2D Ballers	3 5 4
Speedy Players	2 1 3
Unlimited Juice	7 6 3
House Meter Half-Full at Start	3 6 7
Super Block Ability	1-2-4
Show Shot Percentage	0 1 2
Alternate Gear	1 2 3

NBA LIVE 06

EASTERN ALL-STARS 2005-06 AWAY JERSEYS
Select NBA Codes from My NBA Live and enter XCVB5387EQ.

EASTERN ALL-STARS 2005-06 HOME JERSEY
Select NBA Codes from My NBA Live and enter 234SDFGHMO.

WESTERN ALL-STARS 2005-06 AWAY JERSEY
Select NBA Codes from My NBA Live and enter 39N56B679J.

WESTERN ALL-STARS 2005-06 HOME JERSEY
Select NBA Codes from My NBA Live and enter 2J9UWABNP1.

BOSTON CELTICS 2005-06 ALTERNATE JERSEY
Select NBA Codes from My NBA Live and enter 193KSHU88J.

CLEVELAND CAVALIERS 2005-06 ALTERNATE JERSEY
Select NBA Codes from My NBA Live and enter 9922NVDKVT.

DENVER NUGGETS 2005-06 ALTERNATE JERSEYS
Select NBA Codes from My NBA Live and enter XWETJK72FC.

DETROIT PISTONS 2005-06 ALTERNATE JERSEY
Select NBA Codes from My NBA Live and enter JANTWIKBS6.

INDIANA PACERS 2005-06 ALTERNATE AWAY JERSEY
Select NBA Codes from My NBA Live and enter PSDF90PPJN.

INDIANA PACERS 2005-06 ALTERNATE HOME JERSEY
Select NBA Codes from My NBA Live and enter SDF786WSHW.

SACRAMENTO KINGS 2005-06 ALTERNATE JERSEY
Select NBA Codes from My NBA Live and enter 654NNBFDWA.

A3 GARNETT 3
Select NBA Codes from My NBA Live and enter DRI239CZ49.

JORDAN MELO V.5 WHITE & BLUE
Select NBA Codes from My NBA Live and enter 5223WERPII.

JORDAN MELO V.5 WHITE & YELLOW
Select NBA Codes from My NBA Live and enter ZXDR7362Q1.

JORDAN XIV BLACK & RED
Select NBA Codes from My NBA Live and enter 144FVNHM35.

JORDAN XIV WHITE & GREEN
Select NBA Codes from My NBA Live and enter 67YFH9839F.

JORDAN XIV WHITE & RED
Select NBA Codes from My NBA Live and enter 743HFDRAU8.

S. CARTER III LE
Select NBA Codes from My NBA Live and enter JZ3SCARTVY.

T-MAC 5 BLACK
Select NBA Codes from My NBA Live and enter 258SHQW95B.

T-MAC 5 WHITE
Select NBA Codes from My NBA Live and enter HGS83KP234P.

ANSWER DMX 10
Select NBA Codes from My NBA Live and enter RBKAIUSAB7.

ANSWER IX & THE RBK ANSWER IX VIDEO
Select NBA Codes from My NBA Live and enter AI9BUBBA7T.

THE QUESTION & THE MESSAGE FROM ALLEN IVERSON VIDEO
Select NBA Codes from My NBA Live and enter HOYAS3AI6L.

NBA LIVE 07

**ADIDAS ARTILLERY II BLACK
& THE RBK ANSWER 9 VIDEO**
Select NBA Codes from My NBA Live and
enter 99B6356HAN.

ADIDAS ARTILLERY II
Select NBA Codes and enter NTGNFUE87H.

**ADIDAS BTB LOW AND THE
MESSAGE FROM ALLEN
IVERSON VIDEO**
Select NBA Codes and enter 7FB3KS9JQ0.

ADIDAS C-BILLUPS
Select NBA Codes and enter BV6877HB9N.

ADIDAS C-BILLUPS BLACK
Select NBA Codes and enter 85NVLDMWS5.

ADIDAS CAMPUS LT
Select NBA Codes and enter CLT2983NC8.

ADIDAS CRAZY 8
Select NBA Codes and enter CC98KKL814.

ADIDAS EQUIPMENT BBALL
Select NBA Codes and enter 22OIUJKMDR.

ADIDAS GARNETT BOUNCE
Select NBA Codes and enter HYIOUHCAAN.

ADIDAS GARNETT BOUNCE BLACK
Select NBA Codes and enter KDZ2MQL17W.

ADIDAS GIL-ZERO
Select NBA Codes and enter 23DN1PPOG4.

ADIDAS GIL-ZERO BLACK
Select NBA Codes and enter QQQ3JCUYQ7.

ADIDAS GIL-ZERO MID
Select NBA Codes and enter 1GSJC8JWRL.

ADIDAS GIL-ZERO MID BLACK
Select NBA Codes and enter 369V6RVU3G.

ADIDAS STEALTH
Select NBA Codes and enter FE454DFJCC.

ADIDAS T-MAC 6
Select NBA Codes and enter MCJK843NNC.

ADIDAS T-MAC 6 WHITE
Select NBA Codes and enter 84GF7EJG8V.

CHARLOTTE BOBCATS 2006-07 ALTERNATE JERSEY
Select NBA Codes and enter WEDX671H7S.

UTAH JAZZ 2006-07 ALTERNATE JERSEY
Select NBA Codes and enter VCBI89FK83.

NEW JERSEY NETS 2006-07 ALTERNATE JERSEY
Select NBA Codes and enter D4SAA98U5H.

WASHINGTON WIZARDS 2006-07 ALTERNATE JERSEY
Select NBA Codes and enter QV93NLKXQC.

EASTERN ALL-STARS 2006-07 AWAY JERSEY
Select NBA Codes and enter WOCNW4KL7L.

EASTERN ALL-STARS 2006-07 HOME JERSEY
Select NBA Codes and enter 5654ND43N6.

WESTERN ALL-STARS 2006-07 AWAY JERSEY
Select NBA Codes and enter XX93BVL20U.

WESTERN ALL-STARS 2006-07 HOME JERSEY
Select NBA Codes and enter 993NSKL199.

NCAA FOOTBALL 06

IMPACT PLAYERS IN THE ZONE IN PRACTICE
Create a Profile with the name ZoneOut.

PENNANT CODES

Select Pennant Collection from My NCAA. Press Select and enter the following codes.

ENTER	CODE NAME
Sic Em	#16 Baylor
Oskee Wow	#63 Illinois
Fight	#160 Texas Tech
Thanks	#200 First and Fifteen
For	#201 Blink
Registering	#202 Boing
With EA	#204 Butter Fingers
Tiburon	#205 Crossed The Line
EA Sports	#206 Cuffed

Touchdown	#207 Extra Credit
In The Zone	#208 Helium
Turnover	#209 Hurricane
Impact	#210 Instant Freplay
Heisman	#211 Jumbalaya
Game Time	#212 Molasses
Break Free	#213 Nike Free
Hand Picked	#214 Nike Magnigrip
No Sweat	#215 Nike Pro
Light Speed	#216 Nike Speed TD
Elite 11	#219 QB Dud
NCAA	#222 Stiffed
Football	#224 Take Your Time
06	#225 Thread & Needle
Offense	#226 Tough As Nails
Defense	#227 Trip

ENTER	CODE NAME
Blitz	#228 What a Hit!
Sideline	#229 Kicker Hex
Fumble	#273 2004 All-Americans

Roll Tide	#274 All-Alabama
Woopigsooie	#276 All-Arkansas
War Eagle	#277 All-Auburn
Death Valley	#278 All-Clemson
Glory	#279 All-Colorado
Great To Be	#280 All-Florida
Uprising	#281 All-FSU
Hunker Down	#282 All-Georgia
On Iowa	#283 All-Iowa
Victory	#284 All-Kansas State
Geaux Tigers	#285 All-LSU
Raising Cane	#286 All-Miami
Go Blue	#287 All-Michigan

Hail State	#288 All-Mississippi State
Go Big Red	#289 All-Nebraska
Rah Rah	#290 All-North Carolina
Golden Domer	#291 All-Notre Dame
Killer Nuts	#292 All-Ohio State
Boomer	#293 All-Oklahoma
Go Pokes	#294 All-Oklahoma State
Quack Attack	#295 All-Oregeon
We Are	#296 All-Penn State
Lets Go Pitt	#297 All-Pittsburgh
Boiler Up	#298 All-Purdue
Orange Crush	#299 All-Syracuse
Big Orange	#300 All-Tennessee

ENTER	CODE NAME
Hook Em	#301 All-Texas
Gig Em	#302 All-Texas A&M
Mighty	#303 All-UCLA
Fight On	#304 All-USC
Wahoos	#305 All-Virginia
Tech Triumph	#306 All-Virginia Tech
Bow Down	#307 All-Washington
U Rah Rah	#308 All-Wisconsin
Bear Down	#311 Ark Mascot
Red And Gold	#333 ISU Mascot
Rock Chalk	#335 KU Mascot
Go Green	#346 Michigan State Mascot
Rah Rah Rah	#341 Minn Mascot

Hotty Totty	#342 Miss Mascot
Mizzou Rah	#344 Mizzou Mascot
Go Pack	#349 NCSU Mascot
Go Cats	#352 NU Mascot
On On UK	#371 UK Mascot
Go Deacs Go	#382 Wake Mascot
All Hail	#385 WSU Mascot
Hail WV	#386 WVU Mascot

NCAA FOOTBALL 07

#16 BAYLOR
Select Pennant Collection from My NCAA. Press Select and enter Sic Em.

#16 NIKE SPEED TD
Select Pennant Collection from My NCAA. Press Select and enter Light Speed.

#63 ILLINOIS
Select Pennant Collection from My NCAA. Press Select and enter Oskee Wow.

#160 TEXAS TECH
Select Pennant Collection from My NCAA. Press Select and enter Fight.

#200 FIRST AND FIFTEEN
Select Pennant Collection from My NCAA. Press Select and enter Thanks.

#201 BLINK
Select Pennant Collection from My NCAA. Press Select and enter For.

#202 BOING
Select Pennant Collection from My NCAA. Press Select and enter Registering.

#204 BUTTER FINGERS
Select Pennant Collection from My NCAA. Press Select and enter With EA.

#205 CROSSED THE LINE
Select Pennant Collection from My NCAA. Press Select and enter Tiburon.

#206 CUFFED
Select Pennant Collection from My NCAA. Press Select and enter EA Sports.

#207 EXTRA CREDIT
Select Pennant Collection from My NCAA. Press Select and enter Touchdown.

#208 HELIUM
Select Pennant Collection from My NCAA. Press Select and enter In The Zone.

#209 HURRICANE
Select Pennant Collection from My NCAA. Press Select and enter Turnover.

#210 INSTANT FREPLAY
Select Pennant Collection from My NCAA. Press Select and enter Impact.

#211 JUMBALAYA
Select Pennant Collection from My NCAA. Press Select and enter Heisman.

#212 MOLASSES
Select Pennant Collection from My NCAA. Press Select and enter Game Time.

#213 NIKE FREE
Select Pennant Collection from My NCAA. Press Select and enter Break Free.

#214 NIKE MAGNIGRIP
Select Pennant Collection from My NCAA. Press Select and enter Hand Picked.

#215 NIKE PRO
Select Pennant Collection from My NCAA. Press Select and enter No Sweat.

#219 QB DUD
Select Pennant Collection from My NCAA. Press Select and enter Elite 11.

#221 STEEL TOE
Select Pennant Collection from My NCAA. Press Select and enter Gridiron.

#222 STIFFED
Select Pennant Collection from My NCAA. Press Select and enter NCAA.

#223 SUPER DIVE
Select Pennant Collection from My NCAA. Press Select and enter Upset.

#224 TAKE YOUR TIME
Select Pennant Collection from My NCAA. Press Select and enter Football.

#225 THREAD & NEEDLE
Select Pennant Collection from My NCAA. Press Select and enter 06.

#226 TOUGH AS NAILS
Select Pennant Collection from My NCAA. Press Select and enter Offense.

#227 TRIP
Select Pennant Collection from My NCAA. Press Select and enter Defense.

#228 WHAT A HIT
Select Pennant Collection from My NCAA. Press Select and enter Blitz.

#229 KICKER HEX
Select Pennant Collection from My NCAA. Press Select and enter Sideline.

#273 2004 ALL-AMERICANS
Select Pennant Collection from My NCAA. Press Select and enter Fumble.

#274 ALL-ALABAMA
Select Pennant Collection from My NCAA. Press Select and enter Roll Tide.

#276 ALL-ARKANSAS
Select Pennant Collection from My NCAA. Press Select and enter Woopigsooie.

#277 ALL-AUBURN
Select Pennant Collection from My NCAA. Press Select and enter War Eagle.

#278 ALL-CLEMSON
Select Pennant Collection from My NCAA. Press Select and enter Death Valley.

#279 ALL-COLORADO
Select Pennant Collection from My NCAA. Press Select and enter Glory.

#280 ALL-FLORIDA
Select Pennant Collection from My NCAA. Press Select and enter Great To Be.

#281 ALL-FSU
Select Pennant Collection from My NCAA. Press Select and enter Uprising.

#282 ALL-GEORGIA
Select Pennant Collection from My NCAA. Press Select and enter Hunker Down.

#283 ALL-IOWA
Select Pennant Collection from My NCAA. Press Select and enter On Iowa.

#284 ALL-KANSAS STATE
Select Pennant Collection from My NCAA. Press Select and enter Victory.

#285 ALL-LSU
Select Pennant Collection from My NCAA. Press Select and enter Geaux Tigers.

#286 ALL-MIAMI
Select Pennant Collection from My NCAA. Press Select and enter Raising Cane.

#287 ALL-MICHIGAN
Select Pennant Collection from My NCAA. Press Select and enter Go Blue.

#288 ALL-MISSISSIPPI STATE
Select Pennant Collection from My NCAA. Press Select and enter Hail State.

#289 ALL-NEBRASKA
Select Pennant Collection from My NCAA. Press Select and enter Go Big Red.

#290 ALL-NORTH CAROLINA
Select Pennant Collection from My NCAA. Press Select and enter Rah Rah.

#291 ALL-NOTRE DAME
Select Pennant Collection from My NCAA. Press Select and enter Golden Domer.

#292 ALL-OHIO STATE
Select Pennant Collection from My NCAA. Press Select and enter Killer Nuts.

#293 ALL-OKLAHOMA
Select Pennant Collection from My NCAA. Press Select and enter Boomer.

#294 ALL-OKLAHOMA STATE
Select Pennant Collection from My NCAA. Press Select and enter Go Pokes.

#295 ALL-OREGON
Select Pennant Collection from My NCAA. Press Select and enter Quack Attack.

#296 ALL-PENN STATE
Select Pennant Collection from My NCAA. Press Select and enter We Are.

#297 ALL-PITTSBURGH
Select Pennant Collection from My NCAA. Press Select and enter Lets Go Pitt.

#298 ALL-PURDUE
Select Pennant Collection from My NCAA. Press Select and enter Boiler Up.

#299 ALL-SYRACUSE
Select Pennant Collection from My NCAA. Press Select and enter Orange Crush.

#300 ALL-TENNESSEE
Select Pennant Collection from My NCAA. Press Select and enter Big Orange.

#301 ALL-TEXAS
Select Pennant Collection from My NCAA. Press Select and enter Hook Em.

#302 ALL-TEXAS A&M
Select Pennant Collection from My NCAA. Press Select and enter Gig Em.

#303 ALL-UCLA
Select Pennant Collection from My NCAA. Press Select and enter MIGHTY.

#304 ALL-USC
Select Pennant Collection from My NCAA. Press Select and enter Fight On.

#305 ALL-VIRGINIA
Select Pennant Collection from My NCAA. Press Select and enter Wahoos.

#306 ALL-VIRGINIA TECH
Select Pennant Collection from My NCAA. Press Select and enter Tech Triumph.

#307 ALL-WASHINGTON
Select Pennant Collection from My NCAA. Press Select and enter Bow Down.

#308 ALL-WISCONSIN
Select Pennant Collection from My NCAA. Press Select and enter U Rah Rah.

#311 ARK MASCOT
Select Pennant Collection from My NCAA. Press Select and enter Bear Down.

#329 GT MASCOT
Select Pennant Collection from My NCAA. Press Select and enter RamblinWreck.

#333 ISU MASCOT
Select Pennant Collection from My NCAA. Press Select and enter Red And Gold.

#335 KU MASCOT
Select Pennant Collection from My NCAA. Press Select and enter Rock Chalk.

#341 MINN MASCOT
Select Pennant Collection from My NCAA. Press Select and enter Rah Rah Rah.

#344 MIZZOU MASCOT
Select Pennant Collection from My NCAA. Press Select and enter Mizzou Rah.

#346 MSU MASCOT
Select Pennant Collection from My NCAA. Press Select and enter Go Green.

#349 NCSU MASCOT
Select Pennant Collection from My NCAA. Press Select and enter Go Pack.

#352 NU MASCOT
Select Pennant Collection from My NCAA. Press Select and enter Go Cats.

#360 S CAR MASCOT
Select Pennant Collection from My NCAA. Press Select and enter Go Carolina.

#371 UK MASCOT
Select Pennant Collection from My NCAA. Press Select and enter On On UK.

#382 WAKE FOREST
Select Pennant Collection from My NCAA. Press Select and enter Go Deacs Go.

#385 WSU MASCOT
Select Pennant Collection from My NCAA. Press Select and enter All Hail.

#386 WVU MASCOT
Select Pennant Collection from My NCAA. Press Select and enter Hail WV.

NCAA MARCH MADNESS 06

ALL TEAMS
Select My NCAA, then Cheat Codes from the lounge. Enter PSDF9078VT.

AIR JORDAN III SHOES
Select My NCAA, then Cheat Codes from the lounge. Enter 39N56BXC4S.

FIRST AIR JORDANS
Select My NCAA, then Cheat Codes from the lounge. Enter 2J9UWAS44L.

NEED FOR SPEED CARBON

CASTROL CASH
At the main menu, press Down, Up, Left, Down, Right, Up, ●, ▶, ▲. This gives you 10,000 extra cash.

INFINITE CREW CHARGE
At the main menu, press Down, Up, Up, Right, Left, Left, Right, ●.

INFINITE NITROUS
At the main menu, press Left, Up, Left, Down, Left, Down, Right, ●.

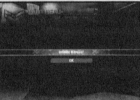

INFINITE SPEEDBREAKER
At the main menu, press Down, Right, Right, Left, Right, Up, Down, ●.

NEED FOR SPEED CARBON LOGO VINYLS
At the main menu, press Right, Up, Down, Up, Down, Left, Right, ●.

NEED FOR SPEED CARBON SPECIAL LOGO VINYLS
At the main menu, press Up, Up, Down, Down, Down, Down, Up, ●.

NEED FOR SPEED MOST WANTED

BURGER KING CHALLENGE
At the Title screen, press Up, Down, Up, Down, Left, Right, Left, Right.

CASTROL SYNTEC VERSION OF THE FORD GT
At the Title screen, press Left, Right, Left, Right, Up, Down, Up, Down.

MARKER IN BACKROOM OF THE ONE-STOP SHOP
At the Title screen, press Up, Up, Down, Down, Left, Right, Up, Down.

NEED FOR SPEED UNDERGROUND 2

ALL CIRCUIT TRACKS
At the Title screen, press Down, R1, R1, R1, R2, R2, R2, ●.

$200 IN CAREER MODE
At the Title screen, press Up, Up, Up, Left, R1, R1, R1, Down.

$1000 IN CAREER MODE
At the Title screen, press Left, Left, Right, ●, ●, Right, L1, R1. This code also unlocks the RX-8 and Skyline in Quick Race.

HUMMER H2 CAPONE
At the Title screen, press Up, Left, Up, Up, Down, Left, Down, Left.

NISSAN SKYLINE
At the Title screen, press Down, Down, L1, L2, L1, L2, L1, Down.

SHINESTREET LEXUS IS300
At the Title screen, press Up, Down, Left, Up, Left, Up, Right, Left.

BEST BUY VINYL
At the Title screen, press Up, Down, Up, Down, Down, Up, Right, Left.

BURGER KING VINYL
At the Title screen, press Up, Up, Up, Up, Down, Up, Up, Left.

UNIQUE VINYL
At the Title screen, press Down, Up, Down, Left, L1, L1, L1, Down.

PERFORMANCE LEVEL 1
At the Title screen, press L1, R1, L1, R1, Left, Left, Right, Up.

PERFORMANCE LEVEL 2
At the Title screen, press R1, R1, L1, R1, Left, Right, Up, Down.

VISUAL LEVEL 1
At the Title screen, press R1, R1, Up, Down, L1, L1, Up, Down.

VISUAL LEVEL 2
At the Title screen, press L1, R1, Up, Down, L1, Up, Up, Down.

NEO CONTRA

19 LIVES
At the Title screen, press Up, Up, Down, Down, L1, R1, L2, R2, L3, R3.

NFL STREET

PASSWORDS
Enter the following as your user ID:

PASSWORD	EFFECT
Travel	All Fields
Classic	NFL Legends
Excellent	X-ecutioner Team
AW9378	Division All-Star Teams

NFL STREET 2

FUMBLE MODE
Enter GreasedPig as a code.

MAX CATCH
Enter MagnetHands as a code.

NO CHAINS MODE
Enter NoChains as a code.

NO FUMBLE MODE
Enter GlueHands as a code.

UNLIMITED TURBO
Enter NozBoost as a code.

EA FIELD
Enter EAField as a code.

AFC EAST ALL-STARS
Enter EAASFSCT as a code.

AFC NORTH ALL-STARS
Enter NAOFRCTH as a code.

AFC SOUTH ALL-STARS
Enter SAOFUCTH as a code.

AFC WEST ALL-STARS
Enter WAEFSCT as a code.

NFC EAST ALL-STARS
Enter NNOFRCTH as a code.

NFC NORTH ALL-STARS
Enter NNAS66784 as a code.

NFC SOUTH ALL-STARS
Enter SNOFUCTH as a code.

NFC WEST ALL-STARS
Enter ENASFSCT as a code.

TEAM REEBOK
Enter Reebok as a code.

TEAM XZIBIT
Enter TeamXzibit as a code.

NHL 2K6

UNLOCK EVERYTHING
Select Manage Profiles from the Options menu. Create a New Profile with the name Turco813.

ONE PIECE: GRAND BATTLE

CHOPPER'S 3RD COSTUME
At the Title screen, hold L1 or L2 and press Left, Right ✖, ⬤, ✖, ⬤.

LUFFY'S 3RD COSTUME
At the Title screen, hold L1 or L2 and press Up, Up, ✖, ⬤, ✖, ✖.

ROBIN'S 3RD COSTUME
At the Title screen, hold L1 or L2 and press Down, Right, ✖, ⬤, ✖, ✖.

SANJI'S 3RD COSTUME
At the Title screen, hold L1 or L2 and press Up, Down, ✖, ⬤, ✖, ⬤.

NAMI'S 3RD COSTUME
At the Title screen, hold L1 or L2 and press Left, Left, ✖, ⬤, ✖.

USOPP'S 3RD COSTUME
At the Title screen, hold L1 or L2 and press Right, Right, ✖, ⬤, ✖, △.

ZORO'S 3RD COSTUME
At the Title screen, hold L1 or L2 and press Down, Down, ✖, ⬤, ✖, △.

ONIMUSHA: DAWN OF DREAMS

HARD MODE
Complete the game on the Normal difficulty setting and select "Hard Mode" from the Title screen. The parameters have been changed to make the game more difficult.

VERY HARD MODE
Complete the game on the Hard difficulty setting to unlock this even more difficult option. Game parameters have been changed to make for a more difficult experience.

EXTRA HARD MODE
Complete the game on the Very Hard difficulty setting to unlock this extremely difficult option. Although the parameters are the same as Very Hard Mode, certain additional functions have been added to make the gameplay more challenging.

SPECIAL COSTUMES

Each of the five playable characters in the game has three bonus outfits to unlock. Two of the three can be unlocked through exceptional play, while the third costume requires the use of cheat codes. Visit the "Special" screen from the Main menu to enter the codes and select the extra costumes.

EXTRA COSTUMES VERSION 1

CHARACTER	COSTUME DESCRIPTION	UNLOCKING CONDITIONS
Soki	Western Knight	Complete all 30 Tests of Valor
Jubei	Gothic Lolita	Complete all 30 Tests of Valor
Ohatsu	Female Bounty Hunter	Complete all 30 Tests of Valor
Roberto	Bullfighter	Complete all 30 Tests of Valor
Tenkai	Man in Mantle	Complete all 30 Tests of Valor

EXTRA COSTUMES VERSION 2

CHARACTER	COSTUME DESCRIPTION	UNLOCKING CONDITIONS
Soki	Host	Earn a Gold Medal in all 30 Tests of Valor
Jubei	Girl Student	Earn a Gold Medal in all 30 Tests of Valor
Ohatsu	Female Office Worker	Earn a Gold Medal in all 30 Tests of Valor
Roberto	Boxer	Earn a Gold Medal in all 30 Tests of Valor
Tenkai	Punk Rocker	Earn a Gold Medal in all 30 Tests of Valor

EXTRA COSTUMES VERSION 3

CHARACTER	COSTUME DESCRIPTION	UNLOCKING CONDITIONS
Soki	Ryu of Street Fighter 2	Left, ▲, R2, R3, ●, R1, R1, Right, Left, L2
Jubei	Cammy of Street Fighter 2	L2, L2, Right, Right, L3, ▲, Left, L1, L2, ●
Ohatsu	Chun-Li of Street Fighter 2	R3, Right, L2, Left, Left, R3, L1, R1, Right, R3
Roberto	Guile of Street Fighter 2	R2, L2, Left, L1, Left, Right, R3, ●, ●, ▲
Tenkai	Ken of Street Fighter 2	L3, L3, R3, R3, R3, Left, R2, L1, ●, Right

EXTRA WEAPONS

Each of the five playable characters has a special weapon that can be unlocked by inputting a specific cheat code. Use the "Special" option from the Main menu to access the "Equipment Change" option and have fun!

EXTRA WEAPONS

CHARACTER	WEAPON	UNLOCKING CONDITIONS
Soki	Steel Pipe	L2, ●, ▲, R1, R1, R3, Left, ●, L1, ▲
Jubei	Racket	L1, R1, Right, L2, ▲, Right, L1, Right, L3, R1
Ohatsu	Piggy Bank	Right, ▲, Left, L3, L1, ●, ▲, R2, ●, R2
Roberto	Boxing Gloves	▲, R3, ▲, Right, R1, L3, ▲, L1, Right, L3
Tenkai	Microphone Stand	R2, R3, ●, Left, Left, Right, L2, Left, R2, Left

ONIMUSHA ARENA

Complete the game on the Normal difficulty setting and select this additional gameplay mode from the "Special" option from the Main menu. Onimusha Arena enables you to fight against a friend using all five playable characters and five main enemy characters.

In Onimusha Arena mode, players square off in a one-on-one battle against one another. The fighters each begin with full HP meters, but no OP or MP. As they suffer damage, their MP meter fills, thereby making a comeback entirely possible. As the fighters lose more HP, their OP gauge fills and Onimusha Mode is available for a brief period.

2-PLAYER MODE
At the Title screen, hold R1 + R2 + L1 + L2 on both controllers and press START on the second controller.

OUTLAW GOLF 2

ALL GOLFERS AND EQUIPMENT
Create a profile with the name I Have No Time.

EASIER TOUR
Create a profile with the name Mr. Chicken 93.

HARDER TOUR
Create a profile with the name Iron Man 93.

OUTLAW TENNIS

UNLOCK EVERYTHING
Create a profile with the name Cut To The Chase. Hold L1 + R1 as you select done and save the profile.

OUTLAW VOLLEYBALL REMIXED

ALL COURTS
Select Exhibition mode, then at the Court Select screen hold L1 and press Up, Down, Up, Down, Left, Left, Right, Right.

BETTER STATS
Select Exhibition mode, then at the Character Select screen hold R1 and press Left, L2, Right, L2.

BIG HEADS
During gameplay, hold L1 and press ●, ✕, ●, ▲.

BIGGER CHEST
During gameplay, hold L1 and press ●, Up, Up, ●, ▲.

THE PIT OF HELL COURT
Select Exhibition mode, then at the Court Select screen hold R1 and press ● (x6), ▲ (x6), L2 (x6).

THE WAREHOUSE COURT
Select Exhibition mode, then at the Court Select screen hold L1 and press Up, ●, ●, ▲, ▲, Down.

BEATING TOKEN
Enter an an exhibition game without any Beating Tokens, then hold L1 and press L2 (x3).

OUTRUN 2006: COAST 2 COAST

100% COMPLETE/UNLOCK EVERYTHING
Edit your license and change the name to ENTIRETY. Select Done, then back out of all menus.

1000000 OUTRUN MILES
Edit your license and change the name to MILESANDMILES. Select Done, then back out of all menus.

OVER THE HEDGE

COMPLETE LEVELS
Pause the game, hold L1 + R1 and press ▲, ●, ▲, ●, ●, ■.

ALL MINI-GAMES
Pause the game, hold L1 + R1 and press
🔺, ⦿, 🔺, 🔺, ◼, ◼.

ALL MOVES
Pause the game, hold L1 + R1 and press
🔺, ⦿, 🔺, ◼, ◼, ⦿.

EXTRA DAMAGE
Pause the game, hold L1 + R1 and press
🔺, ⦿, 🔺, ⦿, 🔺, ◼.

MORE HP FROM FOOD
Pause the game, hold L1 + R1 and 🔺, ⦿, 🔺, ⦿, ◼, 🔺.

ALWAYS POWER PROJECTILE
Pause the game, hold L1 + R1 and press 🔺, ⦿, 🔺, ⦿, ◼, ⦿.

BONUS COMIC 14
Pause the game, hold L1 + R1 and press
🔺, ⦿, ◼, ◼, ⦿, 🔺.

BONUS COMIC 15
Pause the game, hold L1 + R1 and press
🔺, 🔺, ◼, ⦿, ◼, ⦿.

PAC-MAN WORLD 3

ALL LEVELS AND MAZE GAMES
At the Main menu, press Left, Right, Left, Right, ⦿, Up.

SUPER PUNCH
During gameplay, press ❌, L1, R1, ⦿, ⦿, R2.

PETER JACKSON'S KING KONG: THE OFFICIAL GAME OF THE MOVIE

At the Main menu, hold L1 + R1 and press Down, ⦿, Up, ◼, Down, Down, Up, Up.
Release L1 + R1 to get the Cheat option on the menu. The Cheat option will also be
available from the Pause menu.

GOD MODE
Select Cheat and enter 8wonder.

ALL CHAPTERS
Select Cheat and enter KKst0ry.

AMMO 999
Select Cheat and enter KK 999 mun.

MACHINE GUN
Select Cheat and enter KKcapone.

REVOLVER
Select Cheat and enter KKtigun.

SNIPER RIFLE
Select Cheat and enter KKsn1per.

INFINITE SPEARS
Select Cheat and enter lance 1nf.

1-HIT KILLS
Select Cheat and enter GrosBras.

EXTRAS
Select Cheat and enter KKmuseum.

PRINCE OF PERSIA: THE SANDS OF TIME

CLASSIC PRINCE OF PERSIA
Start a new game and while on the balcony, hold L3 and enter ❌, ⬛, ▲, ◉, ▲, ❌, ⬛, ◉.

CLASSIC PASSWORDS

LEVEL	PASSWORD
2	KIEJSC
3	VNNNPC
4	IYVPTC
5	RWSWWC
6	GONWUC
7	DEFNUC
8	SVZMSC
9	DBJRPC
10	MZFYSC
11	BRAYQC
12	UUGTPC
Jafar	LRARUC

PRINCE OF PERSIA: THE TWO THRONES

BABY TOY HAMMER WEAPON
Pause the game and press Left, Left, Right, Right, ◉ ⬛, ⬛, ◉, Up, Down.

CHAINSAW WEAPON
Pause the game and press Up, Up, Down, Down, Left, Right, Left, Right, ◉, ⬛, ◉, ⬛.

SWORDFISH WEAPON
Pause the game and press Up, Down, Up, Down, Left, Right, Left, Right, ◉, ⬛, ◉, ⬛.

TELEPHONE OF SORROW WEAPON
Pause the game and press Left, Right, Left, Right, ◉, ⬛, ◉, ◉, ⬛, ⬛.

PSI-OPS: THE MINDGATE CONSPIRACY

Highlight Extra Content and press R1. Now you can enter the following cheats. Select Mission Select to access the cheats.

CODE NAME	ENTER
All Powers	537893
Bullet Resistant	548975
No Head	987978
Super Psi	456456
Unlimited Ammo	978945
Arcade Mode	05051979
Cooperative Play Mode	07041979
Dark Mode	465486
Survival Extra Mission	7734206
Aura Pool Extra Mission	659785
Bottomless Pit Extra Mission	154897
Bouncy Bouncy Extra Mission	568789
Floor of Death Extra Mission	05120926
Gasoline Extra Mission	9442662
Gearshift Extra Mission	154684
Gnomotron Extra Mission	456878
Panic Room Extra Mission	76635766
Psi Pool Extra Mission	565485
Stoplights Extra Mission	945678
Tip the Idol Extra Mission	428584
TK Alley Extra Mission	090702
Up And Over Extra Mission	020615
Crispy Soldier Skin	454566
Dockworker Skin	364654
Edgar Barrett Skin	497878
Edgar Barret (Training 1) Skin	196001
Edgar Barret (Training 2) Skin	196002
Edgar Barret (Training 3) Skin	196003
Edgar Barret (Training 4) Skin	196004
Edgar Barret (Training 5) Skin	196005
Edgar Barret (Training 6) Skin	196006
The General (Default) Skin	459797
The General (Clown) Skin	431644
Jack Skin	698798
Jov Leonov Skin	468987
Komiko Jones Skin	978798
Labcoat Skin	998789
Marlena Kessler Skin	489788
Marlena Kessler (Bikini) Skin	135454
Marlena Kessler (Leather) Skin	136876
Marlena Kessler (Saranae)	65496873
MP1 Skin	321646
MP2 Skin	698799
MP3 Skin	654659
Nick Scryer (Stealth) Skin	456498
Nick Scryer (Training)Skin	564689
Nick Scryer (Urban) Skin	484646
Nick Scryer (Wasteland) Skin	975466
Sara Blake Skin	135488

CODE NAME	ENTER
Sara Blake (Psi) Skin	468799
Sara Blake (Suicide)	231644
Scorpion Skin	546546
Tonya Skin	678999
UN Soldier Skin	365498
Wei Lu Skin	231324
Wei Lu (Dragon) Skin	978789
Wei Lu (Tranquility) Skin	654654

PSYCHONAUTS

INVINCIBILITY
Hold L1 and R1 and press ◉, R2, ◉, ◉, ▲, L2.

ALL POWERS
Hold L1 and R1 and press ◉, ◉, ▲, R2, L3, ▲.

9999 LIVES
Hold L1 and R1 and press L3, R2, R2, ◉, ✖, R3.

9999 AMMO
Hold L1 and R1 and press R3, ✖, L3, L3, ▲, ◉.

GLOBAL ITEMS
Hold L1 and R1 and press R3, ◉, R2, R2, L3, ▲.

ALL POWERS UPGRADED
Hold L1 and R1 and press L3, R3, L3, R2, ◉, R2.

10K ARROWHEADS
Hold L1 and R1 and press ✖, R3, R3, R2, ▲, ⬟.

CHANGE TEXT
Hold L1 and R1 and press R2, X, L3, R2, R2, ◉.

PUMP IT UP: EXCEED

ARROWS DISAPPEAR
At the Song Select screen, press Up/Left, Up/Right, Down/Left, Down/Right, Center.

ARROW SPEED CHANGES THROUGHOUT SONG
At the Song Select screen, press Up/Left, Up/Right, Up/Left, Up/Right, Up/Left, Up/Right, Up/Left, Up/Right, Center.

DOUBLE SPEED
At the Song Select screen, press Up/Left Up/Right Up/Left Up/Right center 2X speed. Enter this code again to get 3x speed, a third time for 4x speed, and a fourth time to get 8x speed.

DEACTIVATE THE MODIFIERS
At the Song Select screen, press Down/Left, Down/Right, Down/Left, Down/Right, Down/Left, Down/Right.

R-TYPE FINAL

INVINCIBILITY
Pause the game, press and hold L2, then press Right, Right, Left, Right, Left, Left, Right, Left, L1, Up, Up, Down, Down, Up, Down, Up, Down, L1. Re-enter the code to disable it.

99.9% CHARGE DOSE
Pause the game, press and hold L2, then press R2, R2, Left, Right, Up, Down, Right, Left, Up, Down, ▲.

FULL BLUE POWER, MISSILES, & BITS
Pause the game, press and hold L2, then press R2, R2, Left, Right, Up, Down, Right, Left, Up, Down, ◉.

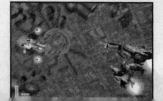

FULL RED POWER, MISSILES, AND BITS
Pause the game, press and hold L2, then press R2, R2, Left, Right, Up, Down, Right, Left, Up, Down, ⬤.

FULL YELLOW POWER, MISSILES, & BITS
Pause the game, press and hold L2, then press R2, R2, Left, Right, Up, Down, Right, Left, Up, Down, ✖.

LADY LOVE SHIP (#3)
At the R Museum, enter 5270 0725 as a password.

STRIDER SHIP (#24)
At the R Museum, enter 2078 0278 as a password.

MR. HELI SHIP (#59)
At the R Museum, enter 1026 2001 as a password.

CURTAIN CALL SHIP (#100)
At the R Museum, enter 1009 9201 as a password.

RAMPAGE: TOTAL DESTRUCTION

ALL MONSTERS
At the Main menu, press R2 + L2 to access the Cheat menu and enter 141421.

INVULNERABLE TO ATTACKS
At the Main menu, press R2 + L2 to access the Cheat menu and enter 986960.

ALL SPECIAL ABILITIES
At the Main menu, press R2 + L2 to access the Cheat menu and enter 011235.

ALL LEVELS
At the Main menu, press R2 + L2 to access the Cheat menu and enter 271828.

CPU VS CPU DEMO
At the Main menu, press R2 + L2 to access the cheat menu and enter 082864.

FAST CPU VS CPU DEMO
At the Main menu, press R2 + L2 to access the cheat menu and enter 874098.

ONE HIT DESTROYS BUILDINGS
At the Main menu, press R2 + L2 to access the Cheat menu and enter 071767.

OPENING MOVIE
At the Main menu, press R2 + L2 to access the Cheat menu and enter 667300.

ENDING MOVIE
At the Main menu, press R2 + L2 to access the Cheat menu and enter 667301.

CREDITS
At the Main menu, press R2 + L2 to access the Cheat menu and enter 667302.

VERSION INFORMATION
At the Main menu, press R2 + L2 to access the Cheat menu and enter 314159.

CLEAR CHEATS
At the Main menu, press R2 + L2 to access the Cheat menu and enter 000000.

RATCHET AND CLANK: UP YOUR ARSENAL

DUEL BLADE LASER SWORD
Pause the game and press ●, ■, ●, ■, Up, Down, Left, Left.

QWARK'S ALTERNATE COSTUME
Start a game of Qwark Vid-Comic and press Up, Up, Down, Down, Left, Right, ●, ●, ■.

PIRATE VS NINJA MINI-GAME
At the Qwark Comics Issue select, press ● to bring up a password screen. Enter _MEGHAN_ as a password.

4-PLAYER BOMB MINI-GAME
At the Qwark Comics Issue select, press ● to bring up a password screen. Enter YING_TZU as a password. Press Start, Select to return to Starship Phoenix.

SLY 2: BAND OF THIEVES DEMO
At the Title screen, hold L1 + L2 + R1 + R2.

Press START button for New Game

RESERVOIR DOGS

UNLIMITED AMMO
Select Cheats from the Extras menu and press R2, L2, ●, L2, ✕, R2.

ALL LEVELS
Select Cheats from the Extras menu and press L2, R2, L2, R2, L1, R1.

ART GALLERY
Select Cheats from the Extras menu and press ●, ✕, L2, R2, ●, ✕.

MOVIE GALLERY
Select Cheats from the Extras menu and press L1, L1, ●, ✕, L1, R1.

RESIDENT EVIL 4

ALTERNATE TITLE SCREEN
Complete the game.

MATILDA
Complete the game.

MERCENARIES
Complete the game.

PROFESSIONAL DIFFICULTY
Complete the game.

SEPERATE WAYS
Complete the game.

ASHLEY'S ARMOR OUTFIT
Defeat Separate Ways

LEON'S GANGSTER OUTFIT
Defeat Separate Ways

RISE OF THE KASAI

INVINCIBLE RAU
At the Title screen, press ■, ●, ✕, ■, ●, ■, ✕, ●, ✕, ■, ●, ✕. Find the Sage at the back of the Inn to activate the cheat.

FULL HEALTH
At the Title screen, press ✕, ✕, ✕, ✕, ■, ■, ■, ■, ●, ●, ●, ●. Find the Sage at the back of the Inn to activate the cheat.

STRONGER OPPONENTS
At the Title screen, press ✕, ●, ■, ●, ✕, ■, ●, ●, ✕, ●, ●, ✕. Find the Sage at the back of the Inn to activate the cheat.

WEAKER OPPONENTS
At the Title screen, press ✕, ●, ●, ■, ✕, ■, ■, ●. Find the Sage at the back of the Inn to activate the cheat.

UNLIMITED ARROWS
At the Title screen, press ✕, ●, ■, ●, ✕, ■, ●, ●, ✕, ■, ●, ✕. Find the Sage at the back of the Inn to activate the cheat.

DISABLE ARENA AI
At the Title screen, press ✕, ●, ●, ●, ✕, ■, ●, ●, ✕, ●, ■, ✕. Find the Sage at the back of the Inn to activate the cheat.

RISE TO HONOR

ALL CHAPTERS
At the Main menu, hold L1 + R1 and press ●, Up, Down, ●.

ROBOTECH: INVASION

INVINCIBILITY
Select Extras from the Options menu and enter supercyc.

UNLIMMITED AMMO
Select Extras from the Options menu and enter trgrhpy.

1-HIT KILLS
Select Extras from the Options menu and enter dustyayres.

ALL LEVELS
Select Extras from the Options menu and enter reclamation.

LANCER'S MULTIPLAYER SKIN
Select Extras from the Options menu and enter yllwfllw.

SCOTT BERNARD'S MULTIPLAYER SKIN
Select Extras from the Options menu and enter ltntcmdr.

RAND'S MULTIPLAYER SKIN
Select Extras from the Options menu and enter kidgloves.

ROOK'S MULTIPLAYER SKIN
Select Extras from the Options menu and enter blueangls.

ROBOTS

BIG HEAD
Pause the game and press Up, Down, Down, Up, Right, Right, Left, Right.

UNLIMITED HEALTH
Pause the game and press Up, Right, Down, Up, Left, Down, Right, Left.

UNLIMITED SCRAP
Pause the game and press Down, Down, Left, Up, Up, Right, Up, Down.

ROGUE OPS

BIG FEET
Pause the game and press Right (x3), Left, Right, Left, Right, Left (x3).

SKELETON
Pause the game and press Left (x3), Right, Left, Right, Left, Right (x3).

BIG GUN
Pause the game and press ● (x4), ●, ●.

UNLIMITED HEALTH
Pause the game and press Left, Right, Right, Left, Left, Right, Right, Left, Left, Right, Right, Left, ●, ●.

UNLIMITED BULLETS
Pause the game and press ●, ●, ●, ●, ●, ●, ●, ●, ●, Left, ●, ●, ●, ●, ●, ●, ●, ●, ●.

UNLIMITED SPY CAM
Pause the game and press Left, Left, Right, Right, R2, R2, L2, L2, ●, ●, ●, ●.

UNLIMITED TOC
Pause the game and press ●, ●, ●, ●, Left, Right, Right, Left, L2, R2, L2.

HALF DAMAGE
Pause the game and press ●, ●, ●, ●, Left, Left, Right, Right, ●, ●, ●, ●.

NO BULLET DAMAGE
Pause the game and press Left, Right, Right, Left, ●, ●, ●, ●.

ONE HIT KILLS
Pause the game and press ●, Left, Right, Right, Left, ●, L2, R2, ●, ●, ●.

EXPLOSIVE CROSSBOW
Pause the game and press Left, Right, Right, Left, ●, ●, L2, R2, ●, ●, Left, Right.

MISSILE CROSSBOW
Pause the game and press Right, Right, Left, Left, L2, L2, R2, R2, ●, ●, ●, ●.

EXPLOSIVE SNIPER
Pause the game and press L2, R2, Right, Right, Left, Left, Right, Right, R2, L2, ●, ●.

MISSILE SNIPER
Pause the game and press ●, Left, Right, L2, R2, Right, ●, R2, R2, L2, Left, Left.

COMPLETE LEVEL
While in the level you want to complete, pause the game and enter the following code that corresponds with that level.

LEVEL	CODE
Bank	R2, L2, ●, ●, Left, R2, Left, Left, ●, ●, ●
Carmen	R2, L2, Right, Left, Left, L2, R2, ● (x3), R2
Forsythe	L2, L2, Right (x3), L2, R2, ●, R2, ●, R2
Installation K	R2, L2, ●, ●, Left, L2, L2, ●, ●, L1, ●
La Casa	R2, L2, Right, Left, Left, L2, R2, ● (x3), R2
Magyar	R2, ●, ●, Left, Left, L2, R2, Right, ●, Right, Right
Mod	R2, L2, Right, R2, Left, ●, R2, ●, Right, Right, Left
Museum	L2, L2, Right (x3), L2, R2, ●, R2, ●, R2
Reliance	R2, L2, Right, Left, R2, L2, Right, ●, ●, ●, ●
Silo	R2, L2, Right, Left, Left, L2, ●, R2, ● (x3)
Training	Left, Right, Right, Left, ●, ●, R2, L2, ●, ●, ●

ROGUE TROOPER

INFINITE HEALTH
At the Extra menu, press Left, Right, Up, Down, L3, ●.

INFINITE SUPPLIES
At the Extra menu, press Select, R1, L1, Select, R3, L1.

LOW GRAVITY RAGDOLL
At the Extra menu, press ●, ●, ●, ●, Up, Down.

EXTREME RAGDOLL
At the Extra menu, press Up, Up, Up, R2, R2, Up.

HIPPY BLOOD
At the Extra menu, press L2, Right, ●, Down, R1, Select.

RUGBY LEAGUE 2

UNLOCK EVERYTHING
Create a player with the name Darren Unlockyer.

BIG HANDS
Create a player with the name Jumbo Mittens.

BIG HEADS
Create a player with the name Planetoid.

SMALL HEADS
Create a player with the name micro noggin.

BIG MUSCLES
Create a player with the name Dale P Pugh.

FAT PLAYERS
Create a player with the name Cakemaster 3000.

SKINNY PLAYERS
Create a player with the name Crash Diet.

TIRE IN BODY
Create a player with the name Junkinthetrunk.

TOGGLE MATRIX KICKING OFF
Create a player with the name There is no spoon.

SAMURAI JACK: THE SHADOW OF AKU

MAXIMUM HEALTH
During a game, hold Left on the Left Analog Stick + Right on the Right Analog Stick and press
✖, ●, ▲, ■.

MAXIMUM ZEN
During a game, hold Left on the Left Analog Stick + Right on the Right Analog Stick and press
●, ✖, ■, ▲.

CRYSTAL SWORD
During a game, press Left on the Left Analog Stick Down + Up on the Right Analog Stick and
press ✖, ●, ■, ▲.

FIRE SWORD
During a game, press Down on the Left Analog Stick + Up on the Right Analog Stick and press
■, ✖, ●, ▲.

LIGHTNING SWORD
During a game, press Down on the Left Analog Stick + Up on the Right Analog Stick and press
●, ✖, ▲, ■.

SAMURAI WESTERN

FULL HEALTH
Pause the game, hold L1 + R1 and press Right, Down, Left, Up.

FULL MASTER MODE
Pause the game, hold L1 + R1 and press Left, Down, Right, Up.

HEALTH DOWN TO 1
Pause the game, hold L2 + R2 and press Down, Up, Right, Left, Down, Up.

MASTER MODE DOWN TO 1
Pause the game, hold L2 + R2 and press Right, Left, Right, Left, Down, Down.

FASTER SHOTS FROM ENEMY
Pause the game, hold L2 + R2 and press Right, Down, Left, Up.

SATURDAY NIGHT SPEEDWAY

UNLOCK EVERYTHING
Start a new career and enter mudeater as your name.

SCALER

FULL HEALTH
Pause the game, select audio from the Options menu, and press R1, L1, R1, L1, ●, ●, ■,
■, R1, ■.

200,000 KLOKKIES
Pause the game, select audio from the Options menu, and press L1, L1, R1, R1, ●, ■, ●.

INFINITE ELECTRIC BOMBS
Pause the game, select audio from the Options menu, and press R1, R1, L1, L1, ●, ●, ■.

SCARFACE: THE WORLD IS YOURS

After entering the following Cheats, highlight the cheat and press A to "DO IT."

MAX AMMO
Pause the game, select Cheats and enter AMMO.

REFILL HEALTH
Pause the game, select Cheats and enter MEDIK.

FILL BALLS METER
Pause the game, select Cheats and enter FPATCH.

KILL TONY
Pause the game, select Cheats and enter KILTONY.

DECREASE COP HEAT
Pause the game, select Cheats and enter FLYSTRT.

INCREASE COP HEAT
Pause the game, select Cheats and enter DONUT.

DECREASE GANG HEAT
Pause the game, select Cheats and enter NOBALLS.

INCREASE GANG HEAT
Pause the game, select Cheats and enter GOBALLS.

REPAIR TONY'S VEHICLE
Pause the game, select Cheats and enter TBURGLR.

SPAWN ARIEL MK III
Pause the game, select Cheats and enter OLDFAST.

SPAWN BACINARI
Pause the game, select Cheats and enter 666999.

SPAWN BODOG STAMPEDE
Pause the game, select Cheats and enter BUMMER.

SPAWN BULLDOZER
Pause the game, select Cheats and enter DOZER.

SPAWN ODIN VH88
Pause the game, select Cheats and enter DUMPER.

BLACK SUIT TONY
Pause the game, select Cheats and enter BLACK.

BLUE PINSTRIPE SUIT TONY WITH SHADES
Pause the game, select Cheats and enter BLUESH.

GRAY SUIT TONY
Pause the game, select Cheats and enter GRAY.

GRAY SUIT TONY WITH SHADES
Pause the game, select Cheats and enter GRAYSH.

HAWAIIAN SHIRT TONY
Pause the game, select Cheats and enter HAWAII.

HAWAIIAN SHIRT TONY WITH SHADES
Pause the game, select Cheats and enter HAWAIIG.

SANDY SHIRT TONY
Pause the game, select Cheats and enter SANDY.

SANDY SHIRT TONY WITH SHADES
Pause the game, select Cheats and enter SANDYSH.

WHITE SUIT TONY
Pause the game, select Cheats and enter WHITE.

WHITE SUIT TONY WITH SHADES
Pause the game, select Cheats and enter WHITESH.

CHANGE TIME OF DAY
Pause the game, select Cheats and enter MARTHA.

TOGGLE LIGHTNING
Pause the game, select Cheats and enter SHAZAAM.

TOGGLE RAIN
Pause the game, select Cheats and enter RAINY.

BREAL "THE WORLD IS YOURS" MUSIC TRACK
Pause the game, select Cheats and enter TUNEME.

SD GUNDAM FORCE: SHOWDOWN!

BAKUNETSUMARU
At Kao Lyn's Laboratory, enter ▲, ◉, ✕, ▲, ◉, ✕, ▲, ◉, ✕, ▲, ◉, ◉.

CAPTAIN GUNDAM
At Kao Lyn's Laboratory, enter ◉, ■, ▲, ▲, ✕, ✕, ▲, ■, ◉, ▲, ■, ✕.

ZERO THE WINGED KNIGHT
At Kao Lyn's Laboratory, enter ▲, ▲, ◉, ◉, ✕, ■, ✕, ■, ◉, ✕, ▲, ◉.

SECRET WEAPONS OVER NORMANDY

ALL PLANES, ENVIRONMENTS, & MISSIONS
At the Main menu, press ■ (x3), ◉ (x3), ▲, ■, then enter R2, R2, L2, L2.

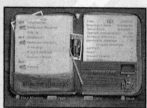

ALL ENVIRONMENTS IN INSTANT ACTION
At the Main menu, press Up, Down, Left, Right, L1, R1, L1, R1.

INVINCIBILITY
At the Main menu, press Up, Down, Left, Right, Left, Left, Right, Right, L1, L1, R1, R1, L2, R2.

UNLIMITED AMMUNITION
At the Main menu, press Up, Right, Down, Left, Up, Right, Down, Left, L1, R1.

BIG HEADS
At the Main menu, press Right, Up, Left, Down, Right, Up, Left, Down, Right, L1, R1, L1, R1.

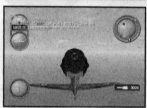

SHAMAN KING: POWER OF SPIRIT

VERSUS MODE
Complete all 20 episodes in Story Mode.

MASKED MERIL IN VERSUS MODE
Press Select on Meril.

MATILDA IN VERSUS MODE
Press Select on Kanna.

MARION FAUNA IN VERSUS MODE
Press Select on Matilda.

ZEKE ASAKURA IN VERSUS MODE
Press Select on Yoh Asakura.

SHARK TALE

REPLACE PEARLS WITH FISH KING COINS
During a level with Pearls, press Select, then hold L1 and press ⊙, ✖, ⊙ (x3), ✖, ⊙, ⊙. Release L1 to enable the cheat.

ATTACK
During a game, press Select, then hold L1 and press ⊙ (x4), ✖, ⊙ (x4). Release L1 to enable the cheat.

CLAMS AND FAME
During a game, press Select, then hold L1 and press ⊙, ⊙, ⊙, ✖, ✖, ⊙, ✖, ⊙, ⊙. Release L1 to enable the cheat.

SHREK 2

BONUS GAMES
Pause the game and select Scrapbook. Press Left, Up, ✖, ⊙, Left, Up, ✖, ⊙, Left, Up, ✖, ⊙, ⊡, ⊙, ⊡, ⊙, ⊡, ⊙. Exit the level and select Bonus to access the games.c

CHAPTER SELECT
Pause the game and select Scrapbook. Press Left, Up, ✖, ⊙, Left, Up, ✖, ⊙, Left, Up, ✖, ⊙, Up, Up, Up, Up, Up. Exit the level and select Chapter Select to change chapters.

FULL HEALTH
Pause the game and select Scrapbook. Press Left, Up, ✖, ⊙, Left, Up, ✖, ⊙, Left, Up, ✖, ⊙, Up, Right, Down, Left, Up.

1,000 COINS
Pause the game and select Scrapbook. Press Left, Up, ✖, ⊙, Left, Up, ✖, ⊙, Left, Up, ✖, ⊙ (x6).

SHREK SUPERSLAM

ALL CHARACTERS AND LEVELS
At the Title screen, press L1, R1, ⊡, ⊙.

ALL CHALLENGES
At the Title screen, press ▲, ▲, ▲, ⊙, ⊙, ⊙, ▲, ⊡, ⊙, ⊡, ⊙, ⊡, ⊡, Up, Down, Left, Right, L1, R1.

ALL STORY MODE CHAPTERS
At the Title screen, press ▲, ⊡, R1, ⊙.

ALL MEDALS & TROPHIES
At the Title screen, press R1, L1, ▲, ●.

SUPER SPEED MODIFIER
At the Title screen, press L1, L1, R1, R1, L1, R1, L1, R1, ●, ●, ▲, ▲.

PIZZA ONE
At the Title screen, press Up, Up, ▲, ▲, Right, Right, ●, ●, Down, Down, L1, R1, Left, Left, ●, ●, L1, R1.

PIZZA TWO
At the Title screen, press ●, ●, ●, ●, Right, Right, Left, Left, L1, L1.

PIZZA THREE
At the Title screen, press Down, Down, Right, ●, Up, ▲, Left, ●, L1, L1.

SLAMMAGEDDON
At the Title screen, press Up, Up, Down, Down, Left, Right, Left, Right, ▲, ●, ●, L1, R1.

THE SIMPSONS: HIT & RUN

Select Options from the Main menu, press and hold L1 + R1, then enter the following:

INVINCIBLE CAR
Press ▲, ✕, ▲, ✕.

RED BRICK CAR
Press ●, ●, ▲, ●.

FAST CARS
Press ●, ●, ●, ●.

FASTER CARS
Press ▲, ▲, ▲, ▲.

ONE-HIT WRECK
Press ▲, ▲, ●, ●.

USE HORN (L3) TO JUMP IN CAR
Press ●, ●, ●, ●.

SHOW SPEED
Press ▲, ▲, ▲, ●.

CHANGE CAMERA
Press ●, ●, ●, ✕.

GRID VIEW
Press ●, ✕, ●, ▲.

TRIPPY
Press ▲, ●, ▲, ●.

CREDITS DIALOG
Press ✕, ●, ●, ▲.

HOLIDAY DECORATED LIVING ROOM
Change the date of the PlayStation 2 to Thanksgiving, Halloween, or Christmas for a new look.

THE SIMPSONS: ROAD RAGE

HIDDEN CHARACTERS
Set the system date to the following to open the secret characters:

DATE	CHARACTER
Jan 1	Happy New Year Krusty the Klown
Oct 31	Happy Halloween Bart
Nov 23, 2006, Nov 22, 2007...	Happy Thanksgiving Marge
Dec 25	Merry Christmas Apu

THE SIMS

At the Main menu, press L1 + R1 + L2 + R2, then enter the following cheats:

PLAY THE SIMS MODE, ALL 2-PLAYER GAMES, OBJECTS AND SKINS
Enter MIDAS, select Get A Life, and start a new game. Join Roxy in the hot tub, pause the game, and quit.

ALL OBJECTS COST 0 SIMOLEANS
Enter FREEALL.

PARTY MOTEL TWO-PLAYER GAME
Enter PARTY M.

PLAY THE SIMS MODE
Enter SIMS.

FIRST PERSON VIEW
Enter FISH EYE. Press ● to toggle the view.

THE SIMS 2: PETS

CHEAT GNOME
During a game, press L1, L1, R1, ✖, ✖, Up.

GIVE SIM PET POINTS
After activating the Cheat Gnome, press
▲, ●, ✖, ■, L1, R1 during a game.

CAT AND DOG CODES
When creating a family, press ■ to Enter Unlock Code. Enter the following for new accessories.

PET	CODE
Bandit Mask Cats	EEGJ2YRQZZAIZ9QHA64
Bandit Mask Dogs	EEGJ2YRQZQARQ9QHA64
Black Dot Cats	EEGJ2YRZQQ1IQ9QHA64
Black Dot Dogs	EEGJ2YRQZZ1IQ9QHA64
Black Smiley Cats	EEGJ2YRQQZ1RQ9QHA64
Black Smiley Dogs	EEGJ2YRZQQARQ9QHA64
Blue Bones Cats	EEGJ2YRQZZARQ9QHA64
Blue Bones Dogs	EEGJ2YRZZZ1IZ9QHA64
Blue Camouflage Cats	EEGJ2YRZZQ1IQ9QHA64
Blue Camouflage Dogs	EEGJ2YRZZZ1RQ9QHA64
Blue Cats	EEGJ2YRQZZAIQ9QHA64
Blue Dogs	EEGJ2YRQQQ1IZ9QHA64
Blue Star Cats	EEGJ2YRQQZ1IZ9QHA64
Blue Star Dogs	EEGJ2YRQZQ1IQ9QHA64
Deep Red Cats	EEGJ2YRQQQAIQ9QHA64
Deep Red Dogs	EEGJ2YRQZQ1RQ9QHA64
Goofy Cats	EEGJ2YRQZQ1IZ9QHA64
Goofy Dogs	EEGJ2YRZZZARQ9QHA64
Green Cats	EEGJ2YRZQQAIZ9QHA64
Green Dogs	EEGJ2YRQZQAIQ9QHA64
Green Flower Cats	EEGJ2YRQZQAIQ9QHA64
Green Flower Dogs	EEGJ2YRQQZZ1R9QHA64
Light Green Cats	EEGJ2YRZZQ1RQ9QHA64
Light Green Dogs	EEGJ2YRZQQ1RQ9QHA64
Navy Hearts Cats	EEGJ2YRQZZ1IQ9QHA64
Navy Hearts Dogs	EEGJ2YRQQZ1IQ9QHA64
Neon Green Cats	EEGJ2YRZZQAIQ9QHA64
Neon Green Dogs	EEGJ2YRZQQAIQ9QHA64
Neon Yellow Cats	EEGJ2YRZZQARQ9QHA64
Neon Yellow Dogs	EEGJ2YRQQQAIZ9QHA64
Orange Diagonal Cats	EEGJ2YRQQZAIQ9QHA64
Orange Diagonal Dogs	EEGJ2YRQZQ1IZ9QHA64

PET	CODE
Panda Cats	EEGJ2YRQZQAIZ9QHA6
Pink Cats	EEGJ2YRQZZ1IZ9QHA64
Pink Dogs	EEGJ2YRZQZ1RQ9QHA64
Pink Vertical Stripe Cats	EEGJ2YRQQQARQ9QHA6
Pink Vertical Stripe Dogs	EEGJ2YRZZZAIQ9QHA64
Purple Cats	EEGJ2YRQQZARQ9QHA6
Purple Dogs	EEGJ2YRQQZAIZ9QHA64
Star Cats	EEGJ2YRZQZARQ9QHA6
Star Dogs	EEGJ2YRZQZAIZ9QHA64
White Paws Cats	EEGJ2YRQQQ1RQ9QHA64
White Paws Dogs	EEGJ2YRZQQ1IZ9QHA64
White Zebra Stripe Cats	EEGJ2YRZZQ1IZ9QHA6
White Zebra Stripe Dogs	EEGJ2YRZZZ1IQ9QHA64
Zebra Stripes Dogs	EEGJ2YRZZQAIZ9QHA64

THE SIMS BUSTIN' OUT

Pause the game, then enter the following codes. You must enter the "Enable Cheats" code first. After entering another code, select the gnome to access it.

ENABLE CHEATS
Press R2, L1, R1, L2, Left, ●. A gnome appears in your yard when the code is entered correctly.

FILL ALL MOTIVES
Press L2, R1, Left, ●, Up.

GIVE MONEY
Press L1, R2, Right, ●, L3. Select the gnome to give money.

UNLOCK ALL LOCATIONS
Press R2, R3, L3, L2, R1, L1.

UNLOCK ALL OBJECTS
Press L2, R2, Up, ▲, L3.

UNLOCK ALL SKINS
Press L1, R2, ✖, ●, Up, Down.

UNLOCK ALL SOCIAL OPTIONS
Press L1, R1, Down, ✖, L3, R3.

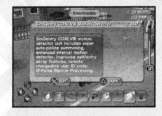

SLY 3: HONOR AMONG THIEVES

TOONAMI PLANE
While flying the regular plane, pause the game and press R1, R1, Right, Down, Down, Right.

SNIPER ELITE

SILENT SNIPER ROUNDS
Enter Stealth as your profile name.

EXPLOSIVE SHOTS
Enter Panzer as your profile name.

EXPLODING RATS
Enter Ratbomb as your profile name. Shooting a rat causes it to explode.

SOCOM 3: U.S. NAVY SEALS

DISPLAY COORDINATES
Pause the game and press ◉, ▲, ◉, ◉, L1, ▲, ◉, ◉, ▲, ◼.

SONIC MEGA COLLECTION PLUS

COMIX ZONE

INVINCIBILITY
Select the jukebox from the options and play the following tracks in order: 3, 12, 17, 2, 2, 10, 2, 7, 7, 11.

STAGE SELECT
Select the jukebox from the options and play the following tracks in order: 14, 15, 18, 5, 13, 1, 3, 18, 15, 6.

DR. ROBOTNIK'S MEAN BEAN MACHINE

EASY PASSWORDS
Continue a game with the following passwords.

LEVEL	PASSWORD
2	Red Bean, Red Bean, Red Bean, Has Bean
3	Clear Bean, Purple Bean, Clear Bean, Green Bean
4	Red Bean, Clear Bean, Has Bean, Yellow Bean
5	Clear Bean, Blue Bean, Blue Bean, Purple Bean
6	Clear Bean, Red Bean, Clear Bean, Purple Bean
7	Purple Bean, Yellow Bean, Red Bean, Blue bean
8	Yellow Bean, Green Bean, Purple Bean, Has Bean
9	Yellow Bean, Purple Bean, Has Bean, Blue Bean
10	Red Bean, Yellow Bean, Clear Bean, Has Bean
11	Green Bean, Purple Bean, Blue Bean, Clear Bean
12	Red Bean, Has Bean, Has Bean, Yellow Bean
13	Yellow Bean, Has Bean, Blue Bean, Blue Bean

NORMAL PASSWORDS

LEVEL	PASSWORD
2	Has Bean, Clear Bean, Yellow Bean, Yellow Bean
3	Blue Bean, Clear Bean, Red Bean, Yellow Bean
4	Yellow Bean, Blue Bean, Clear Bean, Purple Bean
5	Has Bean, Green Bean, Blue Bean, Yellow Bean
6	Green Bean, Purple Bean, Purple Bean, Yellow Bean
7	Purple Bean, Blue Bean, Green Bean, Has Bean
8	Green Bean, Has Bean, Clear Bean, Yellow Bean
9	Blue Bean, Purple Bean, Has Bean, Has Bean
10	Has Bean, Red Bean, Yellow Bean, Clear Bean
11	Clear Bean, Red Bean, Red Bean, Blue Bean
12	Green Bean, Green Bean, Clear Bean, Yellow Bean
13	Purple Bean, Yellow Bean, Has Bean, Clear Bean

HARD PASSWORDS

LEVEL	PASSWORD
2	Green Bean, Clear Bean, Yellow Bean, Yellow Bean
3	Yellow Bean, Clear Bean, Purple Bean, Clear Bean
4	Blue Bean, Green Bean, Clear Bean, Blue Bean
5	Red Bean, Purple Bean, Green Bean, Green Bean
6	Yellow Bean, Yellow Bean, Clear Bean, Green Bean
7	Purple Bean, Clear Bean, Blue Bean, Blue Bean
8	Clear Bean, Yellow Bean, Has Bean, Yellow Bean
9	Purple Bean, Blue Bean, Blue Bean, Green Bean
10	Clear Bean, Green Bean, Red Bean, Yellow Bean
11	Blue Bean, Yellow Bean, Yellow Bean, Has Bean
12	Green Bean, Clear Bean, Clear Bean, Blue bean
13	Has Bean, Clear Bean, Purple Bean, Has Bean

HARDEST PASSWORDS

LEVEL	PASSWORD
2	Blue Bean, Blue Bean, Green Bean, Yellow Bean
3	Green Bean, Yellow Bean, Green Bean, Clear Bean
4	Purple Bean, Purple Bean, Red Bean, Has Bean
5	Green Bean, Red Bean, Purple Bean, Blue Bean
6	Blue Bean, Purple Bean, Green Bean, Yellow Bean
7	Blue Bean, Purple Bean, Green Bean, Has Bean
8	Clear Bean, Purple Bean, Has Bean, Yellow Bean
9	Purple Bean, Green Bean, Has Bean, Clear Bean
10	Green Bean, Blue Bean, Yellow Bean, Has Bean
11	Green Bean, Purple Bean, Has Bean, Red Bean
12	Red Bean, Green Bean, Has Bean, Blue Bean
13	Red Bean, Red Bean, Clear Bean, Yellow Bean

RISTAR

LEVEL SELECT
Enter ILOVEU as a password.

FIGHT ONLY BOSSES
Enter MUSEUM as a password.

TIME ATTACK
Enter DOFEEL as a password.

TONE DEAF SOUNDS
Enter MAGURO as a password.

TRUE SIGHT
Enter MIEMIE as a password.

SUPER HARD
Enter SUPER as a password.

VERY HARD
Enter SUPERB as a password.

CANCEL CODES
Enter XXXXXX as a password.

Sonic the Hedgehog

LEVEL SELECT
At the title screen press Up, Down, Right, Left. Hold ⬤ and press Start.

Sonic the Hedgehog 2

LEVEL SELECT
Select Sound Test from the Options. Play the following in this order: 19, 65, 09, 17. Exit the Options and immediately hold ● and press Start.

SONIC THE HEDGEHOG 3

LEVEL SELECT
While the game is loading, press Up, Up, Down, Down, Up, Up, Up, Up. Scroll down past Competition.

SONIC SPINBALL

ROUND SELECT
At the Options screen, press ●, Down, ✖, Down, ●, Down, ●, ✖, Up, ●, ●, Up, ✖, ●, Up. Then at the Title screen, hold ● and press Start for Round 2. Hold ✖ and press Start for Round 3. Hold ● and press Start for Round 4.

SPARTAN: TOTAL WARRIOR

ALL LEVELS IN SINGLE MISSION REPLAY
At the Main menu, highlight Extras and press Left (x11), Right (x7), ●.

SPIDER-MAN 2

TREYARCH PASSWORD
Start a New Game and enter HCRAYERT as your name. You will start at 44% complete, 201,000 Hero Points, some upgrades, and more.

SPONGEBOB SQUAREPANTS: BATTLE FOR BIKINI BOTTOM

RESTORE HEALTH
Pause the game, hold L1 + L2 + R1 + R2 and press ●, ●, ●, ●, ●, ●, ●, ●, ●, ●, ●, ●, ●.

EXPERT MODE
Pause the game, hold L1 + L2 + R1 + R2 and press ●, ●, ●, ●, ●, ●, ●, ●, ●, ●, ●, ●, ●, ●, ●, ●, ●.

EARN 1,000 SHINY OBJECTS
Pause the game, hold L1 + L2 + R1 + R2 and press ●, ●, ●, ●, ●, ●, ●, ●.

EARN 10 GOLD SPATULAS
Pause the game, hold L1 + L2 + R1 + R2 and press ●, ●, ●, ●, ●, ●, ●, ●.

BUBBLE BOWL POWER-UP
Pause the game, hold L1 + L2 + R1 + R2 and press ●, ●, ●, ●, ●, ●, ●, ●. Press ● to use the power-up.

CRUISE BUBBLE POWER-UP
Pause the game, hold L1 + L2 + R1 + R2
and press ■, ●, ●, ●, ■, ■, ●, ●.
Press L1 to use the power-up.

**INCREASE VALUE OF SHINY
OBJECTS**
Pause the game, hold L1 + L2 + R1 + R2
and press ■, ●, ■, ●, ●, ■, ■, ●,
●, ■, ■, ■, ■, ●, ●, ■.

MODIFIED CRUISE BUBBLE CONTROLS
Pause the game, hold L1 + L2 + R1 + R2 and press ●, ●, ●, ●, ■, ■, ●, ●, ■, ●,
■, ■.

**VILLAGERS GIVE SHINY
OBJECTS WHEN HIT**
Pause the game, hold L1 + L2 + R1 + R2
and press ■, ■, ■, ■, ■, ●, ■, ●,
●, ■, ●, ■.

**VILLAGERS RESTORE HEALTH
WHEN NEAR**
Pause the game, hold L1 + L2 + R1 + R2
and press ■, ■, ■, ■, ■, ●, ■, ●,
●, ●, ■, ■.

NO PANTS
Pause the game, hold L1 + L2 + R1 + R2
and press ●, ●, ●, ●, ■, ■, ●, ■, ●,
■, ■, ●.

BIG PLANKTON
Pause the game, hold L1 + L2 + R1 + R2
and press ■, ■, ■, ■, ●, ■, ■, ●, ■, ●,
●, ●, ●.

SMALL CHARACTERS
Pause the game, hold L1 + L2 + R1 + R2
and press ■, ■, ■, ■, ●, ■, ■, ●,
■, ■, ■, ■.

SMALL VILLAGERS
Pause the game, hold L1 + L2 + R1 + R2
and press ■, ■, ●, ■, ■, ■, ●, ●,
■, ●, ■, ●.

**SPONGEBOB BREAKS APART
WHEN DEFEATED**
Pause the game, hold L1 + L2 + R1 + R2
and press ●, ●, ●, ●, ■, ■, ■, ●, ■, ●,
●, ●, ■.

SPONGEBOB SQUAREPANTS: CREATURE FROM THE KRUSTY KRAB

30,000 EXTRA ZS
Select Cheat Codes from the Extras menu and enter ROCFISH.

PUNK SPONGEBOB IN DIESEL DREAMING
Select Cheat Codes from the Extras menu and enter SPONGE. Select Activate Bonus Items to enable this bonus item.

HOT ROD SKIN IN DIESEL DREAMING
Select Cheat Codes from the Extras menu and enter HOTROD. Select Activate Bonus Items to enable this bonus item.

PATRICK TUX IN STARFISHMAN TO THE RESCUE
Select Cheat Codes from the Extras menu and enter PATRICK. Select Activate Bonus Items to enable this bonus item.

SPONGEBOB PLANKTON IN SUPER-SIZED PATTY
Select Cheat Codes from the Extras menu and enter PANTS. Select Activate Bonus Items to enable this bonus item.

PATRICK LASER COLOR IN ROCKET RODEO
Select Cheat Codes from the Extras menu and enter ROCKET. Select Activate Bonus Items to enable this bonus item.

PATRICK ROCKET SKIN COLOR IN ROCKET RODEO
Select Cheat Codes from the Extras menu and enter SPACE. Select Activate Bonus Items to enable this bonus item.

PLANKTON EYE LASER COLOR IN REVENGE OF THE GIANT PLANKTON MONSTER
Select Cheat Codes from the Extras menu and enter LASER. Select Activate Bonus Items to enable this bonus item.

HOVERCRAFT VEHICLE SKIN IN HYPNOTIC HIGHWAY— PLANKTON
Select Cheat Codes from the Extras menu and enter HOVER. Select Activate Bonus Items to enable this bonus item.

SPONGEBOB SQUAREPANTS: LIGHTS, CAMERA, PANTS!

SILVER STORY MODE
Select Rewards from the Bonuses menu. Then select Codes and enter 486739.

ALL ACTION FIGURES
Select Rewards from the Bonuses menu. Then select Codes and enter 977548.

HOOK, LINE & CHEDDAR GAME
Select Rewards from the Bonuses menu. Then select Codes and enter 893634.

SPONGEBOB SQUAREPANTS: THE MOVIE

SIX HEALTH SLOTS
Pause the game, hold R1 + L1 + R2 + L2 and press ●, ●, ●, ●, ●, ■, ●, ■, ●.

ALL MOVES
Pause the game, hold R1 + L1 + R2 + L2 and press ●, ■, ●, ●, ■, ●, ●, ■, ■.

ALL MOVES TO MACHO
Pause the game, hold R1 + L1 + R2 + L2 and press ●, ■, ●, ■, ●, ●, ●, ■, ●.

DOUBLE MANLINESS POINTS
Pause the game, hold R1 + L1 + R2 + L2 and press ●, ●, ●, ■, ●, ●, ■, ●, ●.

ALL UNKNOWN TASKS
Pause the game, hold R1 + L1 + R2 + L2 and press ●, ■, ●, ●, ●, ●, ●, ■, ■.

SPONGEBOB CAVEMAN
Pause the game, hold R1 + L1 + R2 + L2 and press ■, ■, ■, ■, ●, ■, ■, ■.

SPONGEBOB RIPPED SHORTS
Pause the game, hold R1 + L1 + R2 + L2 and press ■, ■, ■, ●, ■, ●.

PATRICK CAVEMAN
Pause the game, hold R1 + L1 + R2 + L2 and press ■, ■, ■, ■, ●, ■, ●, ●.

PATRICK GOOFY GOOBER
Pause the game, hold R1 + L1 + R2 + L2 and press ■, ■, ■, ●, ●, ■, ●, ■.

SPY HUNTER: NOWHERE TO RUN

SPY HUNTER ARCADE
You must activate the machine when you come across it in the safe house on Level 7 (Cleaning Up).

SPY VS SPY

ALL CLASSIC MAPS
Enter RETROSPY at the password screen.

ALL STORY MODE LEVELS
Enter ANTONIO at the password screen.

ALL LEVELS FOR SINGLE-PLAYER MODERN MODE
Enter PROHIAS at the password screen.

ALL MULTIPLAYER MAPS
Enter MADMAG at the password screen.

ALL OUTFITS
Enter DISGUISE at the password screen.

ALL WEAPONS
Enter WRKBENCH at the password screen.

INVULNERABILITY
Enter ARMOR at the password screen.

SUPER DAMAGE
Enter BIGGUNZ at the password screen.

PERMANENT FAIRY IN MODERN MODE
Enter FAIRY at the password screen.

NO DROPPED ITEMS WHEN KILLED
Enter NODROP at the password screen.

INVISIBLE HUD
Enter BLINK at the password screen.

ALL MOVIES
Enter SPYFLIX at the password screen.

CONCEPT ART
Enter SPYPICS at the password screen.

SSX ON TOUR

NEW THREADS
Select Cheats from the Extras menu and enter FLYTHREADS.

THE WORLD IS YOURS
Select Cheats from the Extras menu and enter BACKSTAGEPASS.

SHOW TIME (ALL MOVIES)
Select Cheats from the Extras menu and enter THEBIGPICTURE.

BLING BLING (INFINITE CASH)
Select Cheats from the Extras menu and enter LOOTSNOOT.

FULL BOOST, FULL TIME
Select Cheats from the Extras menu and enter ZOOMJUICE.

MONSTERS ARE LOOSE (MONSTER TRICKS)
Select Cheats from the Extras menu and enter JACKALOPESTYLE.

SNOWBALL FIGHT
Select Cheats from the Extras menu and enter LETSPARTY.

FEEL THE POWER (STAT BOOST)
Select Cheats from the Extras menu and enter POWERPLAY.

CHARACTERS ARE LOOSE
Select Cheats from the Extras menu and enter ROADIEROUNDUp.

UNLOCK CONRAD
Select Cheats from the Extras menu and enter BIGPARTYTIME.

UNLOCK MITCH KOOBSKI
Select Cheats from the Extras menu and enter MOREFUNTHANONE.

UNLOCK NIGEL
Select Cheats from the Extras menu and enter THREEISACROWD.

UNLOCK SKI PATROL
Select Cheats from the Extras menu and enter FOURSOME.

STAR WARS: BATTLEFRONT

ALL MISSIONS
Select Historical Campaign, then press ●,
●, ●, ● at the Mission Select.

SMALL PEOPLE
Create a profile named Jub Jub.

STAR WARS: BATTLEFRONT II

INFINITE AMMO
Pause the game, hold L2 + R2 and press Up, Down, Left, Down, Down, Left, Down, Down, Left,
Down, Down, Down, Left, Right.

INVINCIBILITY
Pause the game, hold L2 + R2 and press Up, Up, Up, Left, Down, Down, Down, Left, Up, Up,
Up, Left, Right.

NO HUD
Pause the game, hold L2 + R2 and press Up, Up, Up, Up, Left, Up, Up, Down, Left, Down, Up,
Up, Left, Right. Re-enter the code to enable the HUD again.

ALTERNATE SOLDIERS
Pause the game, hold L2 + R2 and press Down, Down, Down, Up, Up, Left, Down, Down,
Down, Down, Down, Left, Up, Up, Up, Left.

ALTERNATE SOUNDS
Pause the game, hold L2 + R2 and press Up, Up, Up, Left, Up, Down, Up, Up, Left, Down, Down,
Down, Left, Up, Down, Down, Left, Right.

FUNNY MESSAGES WHEN REBELS DEFEATED
Pause the game, hold L2 + R2 and press Up, Down, Left, Down, Left, Right.

STAR WARS EPISODE III: REVENGE OF THE SITH

INFINITE FORCE
Select Codes from the Settings menu and enter KAIBURR.

INFINITE HEALTH
Select Codes from the Settings menu and enter XUCPHRA.

QUICK HEALTH & FORCE RESTORATION
Select Codes from the Settings menu and enter BELSAVIS.

ALL STORY, BONUS & CO-OP MISSIONS AND DUELISTS
Select Codes from the Settings menu and enter 021282.

ALL STORY MISSIONS
Select Codes from the Settings menu and enter KORRIBAN.

ALL BONUS MISSIONS
Select Codes from the Settings menu and enter NARSHADDAA.

ALL DUEL ARENAS
Select Codes from the Settings menu and enter TANTIVIEV.

ALL DUELISTS
Select Codes from the Settings menu and enter ZABRAK.

ALL POWERS & MOVES
Select Codes from the Settings menu and enter JAINA.

SUPER LIGHTSABER MODE
Select Codes from the Settings menu and enter SUPERSABERS.

TINY DROID MODE
Select Codes from the Settings menu and enter 071779.

ALL REPLAY MOVIES
Select Codes from the Settings menu and enter COMLINK.

ALL CONCEPT ART
Select Codes from the Settings menu and enter AAYLASECURA.

STOLEN

LEVEL SKIP
At the Title screen, press R1, L1, Start + Down.

99 OF ALL ITEMS
During the game, go to Equipment and press R1, L1, Right.

STREET RACING SYNDICATE

At the Main menu, press Up, Down, Left, Right. This will access the Code Entry screen. Enter the following codes to enable these cheats.

MAZDA RX-8
Enter RENESIS.

TOYOTA SUPRA 3.0L RZ
Enter SICKJZA.

MITSUBISHI ECLIPSE GS-T
Enter IGOTGST.

TOYOTA CELICA GT-S
Enter MYTCGTS.

PAC MAN VINYL
Enter GORETRO.

SUBARU IMPREZA S202 STI
Enter SICKGDB.

FREE CAR REPAIR
Enter FIXITUP. Your first car repair is free.

POLICE CAR
Enter GOTPOPO.

GET WARNING FOR FIRST 3 BUSTS
Enter LETMEGO.

STRIKE FORCE BOWLING

ALL NIGHT ENVIRONMENTS & MARS
Name your bowler !LEVELS!.

THREE HIDDEN CHARACTERS
Name your bowler !BOWLER!.

THE SUFFERING

FULL HEALTH
During a game, press and hold L1 + R1 + ✖ and press Down (x3), R2, Up, Up, Down, Up, R2.

FULL XOMBIUM BOTTLE
During a game, press and hold L1 + R1 + ✖ and press Right, Right, Up, Up, R2, Left, Right, R2, Right, Up, Right, R2.

INCREASE NEGATIVE KARMA
During a game, press and hold L1 + R1 + ✖ and press Left, Left, Down, Up, R2.

OVERCOME INSANITY
During a game, press and hold L1 + R1 + ✖ and press Right (x3), R2, Left, Left, Right, Left, R2.

ALL WEAPONS AND ITEMS
During a game, press and hold L1 + R1 + ✖ and press Down, Up, Down, Left, Right, Left, R2, Up, Left, Down, Right, Up, Right, Down, Left, R2, Down (x3), R2, R2. This code doesn't unlock the Gonzogun.

FULL AMMO FOR CURRENT GUN
During a game, press and hold L1 + R1 + ✖ and press Right, Right, Down, Up, Left, Right, Left, Left, R2.

REFILL RANGED WEAPON AMMO
During a game, press and hold L1 + R1 + ✖ and press Left, Left, Up, Down, Right, Left, Right, Right, R2.

SHOTGUN
During a game, press and hold L1 + R1 + ✖ and press Left (x3), Down (x3).

GONZOGUN
During a game, press and hold L1 + R1 + ✖ and press Left, R2 (x3), Right, Left, Right, Left, Up, R2 (x3), Down, Up, Down, Up, R2.

GRENADES
During a game, press and hold L1 + R1 + ✖ and press Right (x3), Left (x3).

MOLOTOV COCKTAILS
During a game, press and hold L1 + R1 + ✖ and press Down (x3), Up (x3).

BLOODY
During a game, press and hold L1 + R1 + ✖ and press Up, Down, Left, Right.

CLEAN
During a game, press and hold L1 + R1 + ✖ and press Down, Up, Right, Left.

BLACK & WHITE
During a game, press and hold L1 + R1 + ✖ and press Up, R2, Left, R2, Down, R2, Right, R2. Pause the game to disable the code.

TRIPPING THE LIGHT FANTASTIC
During a game, press and hold L1 + R1 + ✖ and press Left, Left, R2, Right, Right, R2, Up, Up, R2, Down, Down, R2.

CLEAN FAMILY PICTURE
During a game, press and hold L1 + R1 + ✖ and press Up, Right, Up, Right, Up, Right, R2.

DIRTY FAMILY PICTURE
During a game, press and hold L1 + R1 + ✖ and press Left, Down, Left, Down, Left, Down, R2.

SUICIDE
During a game, press and hold L1 + R1 + ✖ and press Down (x4).

THE SUFFERING: TIES THAT BIND

SUICIDE
During gameplay, hold L1 + R1 + ⊗ and press Down, Down, Down, Down.

SHOTGUN & AMMO
During gameplay, hold L1 + R1 + ⊗ and press Left, Left, Left, Down, Down, Down.

MOLOTOV COCKTAILS
During gameplay, hold L1 + R1 + ⊗ and press Down, Down, Down, Up, Up, Up.

FULL FLASHLIGHT
During gameplay, hold L1 + R1 + ⊗ and press Up, Left, Down, Right, Up, Right, Down, Left, R2.

FULL AMMO CURRENT WEAPON
During gameplay, hold L1 + R1 + ⊗ and press Right, Right, Down, Up, Left, Right, Left, Left, R2.

FULL AMMO CURRENT THROWN
During gameplay, hold L1 + R1 + ⊗ and press Left, Left, Up, Down, Right, Left, Right, Right, R2.

FULL INSANITY
During gameplay, hold L1 + R1 + ⊗ and press Right, Right, Right, R2, Left, Left, Right, Left, R2.

FULL HEALTH
During gameplay, hold L1 + R1 + ⊗ and press Down, Down, Down, R2, Up, Up, Down, Up, R2.

ARSENAL
During gameplay, hold L1 + R1 + ⊗ and press Down, Right, Up, Left, Down, R2, Left, Left, Right, Right, R2, Down, Up, Left, Right, R2.

INVINCIBILITY
During gameplay, hold L1 + R1 + ⊗ and press Down, Up, Down, Up.

MINUS 50 REP
During gameplay, hold L1 + R1 + ⊗ and press Left, Left, Down, Up.

PLUS 50 REP
During gameplay, hold L1 + R1 + ⊗ and press Up, Up, Right, Up.

FULL BLOOD
During gameplay, hold L1 + R1 + ⊗ and press Up, Down, Left, Right.

ZERO BLOOD
During gameplay, hold L1 + R1 + ⊗ and press Down, Up, Right, Left.

SHRAPNEL
During gameplay, hold L1 + R1 + ⊗ and press Right, Right, Right, Left, Left, Left.

MAX EVIL REP
During gameplay, hold L1 + R1 + ⊗ and press Left, Down, Left, Down, Left, Down, R2.

MAX GOOD REP
During gameplay, hold L1 + R1 + ⊗ and press Up, Right, Up, Right, Up, Right, R2.

FULL BOTTLES
During gameplay, hold L1 + R1 + ⊗ and press Right, Right, Up, Up, R2, Left, Right, R2, Right, Up, Right, R2.

SUPER BAD DUDE
During gameplay, hold L1 + R1 + ⊗ and press Down, Up, Down, Left, Right, Left, R2, Up, Left, Down, Right, Up, Right, Down, Left, R2, Down, Down, Down, R2, R2.

PROJECTOR STATE
During gameplay, hold L1 + R1 + ⊗ and press Up, R2, Left, R2, Down, R2, Right, R2.

DREAM STATE
During gameplay, hold L1 + R1 + ⊗ and press Left, Left, R2, Right, Right, R2, Up, Up, R2, Down, Down, R2.

ALL NOTES
During gameplay, hold L1 + R1 + ⊗ and press Right, Left, Up, Left, R2, Right, Down, Right.

ALL MAPS
During gameplay, hold L1 + R1 + ⊗ and press Left, Right, Down, Right, R2, Left, Up, Left.

SUZUKI TT SUPERBIKES

CHEAT SCREEN
At the Main menu, press R1, R2, L1, L2, R1, R2, L1, L2. Now you can enter the following.

ALL EVENTS
Enter BORN FREE.

RED BULL MAD SUNDAY EVENTS
Enter SUNDAYSUNDAY.

ALL HELMETS
Enter SKID LIDS.

ALL LEATHERS
Enter COLORED HIDE.

ALL BIKES
Enter ROCKETS.

ALL WHEELS
Enter TIRE CITY.

ALL COLLECTION BOOK
Enter COUCH POTATO.

TAITO LEGENDS

EXTRA GAMES
At the Title screen, press L1, R1, R2, L2, Select, Start.

TAK: THE GREAT JUJU CHALLENGE

BONUS SOUND EFFECTS
In Juju's Potions, select Universal Card and enter the following for Bugs, Crystals and Fruits respectively: 20, 17, 5.

BONUS SOUND EFFECTS 2
In Juju's Potions, select Universal Card and enter the following for Bugs, Crystals and Fruits respectively: 50, 84, 92.

BONUS MUSIC TRACK 1
In Juju's Potions, select Universal Card and enter the following for Bugs, Crystals and Fruits respectively: 67, 8, 20.

BONUS MUSIC TRACK 2
In Juju's Potions, select Universal Card and enter the following for Bugs, Crystals and Fruits respectively: 6, 18, 3.

MAGIC PARTICLES
In Juju's Potions, select Universal Card and enter the following for Bugs, Crystals and Fruits respectively: 24, 40, 11.

MORE MAGIC PARTICLES
In Juju's Potions, select Universal Card and enter the following for Bugs, Crystals and Fruits respectively: 48, 57, 57.

VIEW JUJU CONCEPT ART
In Juju's Potions, select Universal Card and enter the following for Bugs, Crystals and Fruits respectively: 33, 22, 28.

VIEW VEHICLE ART
In Juju's Potions, select Universal Card and enter the following for Bugs, Crystals and Fruits respectively: 11, 55, 44.

VIEW WORLD ART
In Juju's Potions, select Universal Card and enter the following for Bugs, Crystals and Fruits respectively: 83, 49, 34.

TEENAGE MUTANT NINJA TURTLES 2: BATTLE NEXUS

PASSWORDS

Select Password from the Options menu and enter the following. Hold L1 while selecting a turtle to get his New Nexus Turtle outfit.

EFFECT	PASSWORD
Challenge Code Abyss	SDSDRLD
Challenge Code Endurance	MRMDRMD
Challenge Code Fatal Blow	LRSRDRD
Challenge Code Lose Shuriken	RLMRDSL
Challenge Code Nightmare	SLSDRDL
Challenge Code Poison	DRSLLSR
Challenge Code Super-Tough	RDSRMRL
Cheat Code All-You-Can-Throw Shuriken	RSRLRSM
Cheat Code Health	DSRDMRM
Cheat Code Mighty Turtle	LSDRRDR
Cheat Code Pizza Paradise	MRLMRMR
Cheat Code Self Recovery	DRMSRLR
Cheat Code Squeaking	MLDSRDM
Cheat Code Super Defense Power	LDRMRLM
Cheat Code Super Offense Power	SDLSRLL
Cheat Code Toddling	SSSMRDD
New Nexus Turtle Outfit for Donatello	DSLRDRM

New Nexus Turtle Outfit for Leonardo	LMRMDRD
New Nexus Turtle Outfit for Michelangelo	MLMRDRM
New Nexus Turtle Outfit for Raphael	RMSRMDR
Playmates added to Bonus Materials	SRMLDDR

TEENAGE MUTANT NINJA TURTLES 3: MUTANT NIGHTMARE

INVINCIBILITY

Select Passwords from the Options menu and enter MDLDSSLR.

HEALTH POWER-UPS BECOME SUSHI

Select Passwords from the Options menu and enter SLLMRSLD.

NO HEALTH POWER-UPS

Select Passwords from the Options menu and enter DMLDMRLD.

ONE HIT DEFEATS TURTLE
Select Passwords from the Options menu and enter LDMSLRDD.

MAX OUGI
Select Passwords from the Options menu and enter RRDMLSDL.

UNLIMITED SHURIKEN
Select Passwords from the Options menu and enter LMDRRMSR.

NO SHURIKEN
Select Passwords from the Options menu and enter LLMSRDMS.

DOUBLE ENEMY ATTACK
Select Passwords from the Options menu and enter MSRLSMML.

DOUBLE ENEMY DEFENSE
Select Passwords from the Options menu and enter SLRMLSSM.

TENCHU: WRATH OF HEAVEN

ALL CHARACTERS
At the Title screen, press L1, R2, L2, R1, Right, Left, L3, R3.

ALL STORY MODE MISSIONS
At the Mission Select screen, press L1, R1, L2, R2, Right, ●, L3, R3.

ALL LAYOUTS
At the Mission Select screen, press R3, L3, R2, L2, R1, L1.

ALL MULTIPLAYER MISSIONS
At the Mission Select screen, press L1, R1, L2, R2, Right, ●, L3, R3.

BONUS RIKIMARU STAGE
At the Title screen, press L1, Up, R1, Down, L2, Right, R2, Left.

HIDDEN LEVEL
At the Title screen, press Up, Down, Right, Left, ✖ (x3).

ALL ITEMS
At the Items screen, press and hold R1 + L1 and press Up, ●, ●, Left, ●, ●, Down, ●, ●, Right, ●, ●.

INCREASE ITEMS
At the Items screen, press and hold R2 + L2 and press ●, ●, ●, Up, Left, Down, Right.

UNLIMITED ITEM CAPACITY
At the Items screen, press and hold L1 + L2 + R1 + R2 and press ● (x3), Up, Left, Down, Right, ●, Up, Right, Down, Left.

REGAIN HEALTH
Pause the game and press Up, Down, Right, Left, ●, ●, ●.

TOGGLE SPECIAL ABILITIES
Pause the game, press and hold L1 + L2, and press Up, Up, Down, Down. Release L1 + L2 and press ●, ●, R1, R2.

ADD 100 POINTS
Pause the game, press and hold L1 + R1, and press Right, Right, Left, Left on controller two.

SCORE AND TIME
Pause the game and press Right, Right, Left, Left on controller two.

TERMINATOR 3: RISE OF THE MACHINES

Select Cheats from the Options menu and enter the following:

EFFECT	CODE
Invincibility	●, ●, ✕, ▲, ✕, ●, ✕, ●
Unlimited Ammunition	✕, ▲, ▲, ▲, ✕, ●, ✕, ■
All Weapons, Future	✕, ✕, ✕, ▲, ●, ●, ■, ✕
All Weapons, Present	●, ●, ▲, ■, ✕, ▲, ▲, ■
Terminator HP's 50 More in Every Fight	▲, ▲, ■, ✕, ●, ▲, ■, ●
T-X HP's 50 More in Every Fight	●, ▲, ■, ▲, ●, ✕, ●, ■
Unlock All Levels	●, ●, ●, ■, ■, ■, ▲, ▲

Unlock All Levels code

CENTIPEDE
Press ●, ●, ●, ■, ■, ■, ▲, ●. You can find it in Special Features/Atari Games menu.

MISSILE COMMAND
Press ●, ●, ●, ■, ■, ■, ✕, ✕.

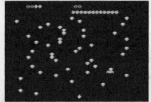

TERMINATOR 3: THE REDEMPTION

LEVEL SELECT
Go to the Credits and press ⊚ + R2 + ▲.

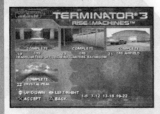

INVINCIBILITY
Go to the Credits and press ⊚ + R2 + R1.

ALL UPGRADES
Go to the Credits and press ⊚ + ▲ + L1.

TIGER WOODS PGA TOUR 06

ALL GOLFERS
Select Password from the Options menu and enter WOOGLIN.

ALL CLUBS
Select Password from the Options menu and enter CLUB11.

LEVEL 2 NIKE ITEMS
Select Password from the Options menu and enter JUSTDOIT.

ALL COURSES

Select Password from the Options menu and enter ITSINTHEHOLE.

TIGER WOODS IN HAT AND TIE

Select Password from the Options menu and enter GOLDENAGE.

TIGER WOODS IN STRIPED PANTS

Select Password from the Options menu and enter TECHNICOLOR.

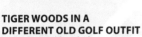

TIGER WOODS IN OLD GOLF OUTFIT

Select Password from the Options menu and enter OLDSKOOL.

TIGER WOODS IN A DIFFERENT OLD GOLF OUTFIT

Select Password from the Options menu and enter THROWBACK.

ARNOLD PALMER

Select Password from the Options menu and enter ARNIESARMY.

BEN HOGAN
Select Password from the Options menu and enter THEHAWK.

JACK NICKLAUS
Select Password from the Options menu and enter GOLDENBEAR.

OLD TOM MORRIS
Select Password from the Options menu and enter FEATHERIE.

TOMMY BLACK
Select Password from the Options menu and enter IDONTHAVEAPROBLEM.

WESLEY ROUNDER
Select Password from the Options menu and enter POCKETPAIR.

TIGER WOODS PGA TOUR 07

NIKE ITEMS
Select the Password option and enter JUSTDOIT.

TIGER WOODS PGA TOUR 2005

Select Passwords from the Options menu and enter the following:

ALL GOLFERS AND COURSES
Enter THEGIANTOYSTER.

ALL COURSES
Enter THEWORLDISYOURS.

THE ROOF IN THE SKILLZONE GAME MODE
Enter NIGHTGOLFER.

JUSTIN TIMBERLAKE
Enter THETENNESSEEKID.

ARNOLD PALMER
Enter THEKING.

BEN HOGAN
Enter PUREGOLF.

SEVE BALLESTEROS
Enter THEMAGICIAN.

JACK NICKLAUS
Enter GOLDENBEAR.

GARY PLAYER
Enter BLACKKNIGHT.

TIFFANY "TIFF" WILLIAMSON
Enter RICHGIRL.

JEB "SHOOTER" MCGRAW
Enter SIXSHOOTER.

HUNTER "STEELHEAD" ELMORE
Enter GREENCOLLAR.

ALASTAIR "CAPTAIN" MCFADDEN
Enter NICESOCKS.

BEV "BOOMER" BUOUCHIER
Enter THEBEEHIVE.

ADRIANA "SUGAR" DULCE
Enter SOSWEET.

APHRODITE PAPADAPOLUS
Enter TEMPTING.

BILLY "BEAR" HIGHTOWER
Enter TOOTALL.

KENDRA "SPIKE" LOVETTE
Enter ENGLISHPUNK.

DION "DOUBLE D" DOUGLAS
Enter DDDOUGLAS.

RAQUEL "ROCKY" ROGERS
Enter DOUBLER.

BUNJIRO "BUD" TANAKA
Enter INTHEFAMILY.

CEASAR "THE EMPEROR" ROSADO
Enter LANDownER.

REGINALD "REG" WEATHERS
Enter REGGIE.

THE HUSTLER
Enter ALTEREGO.

SUNDAY TIGER WOODS
Enter NEWLEGEND.

ADIDAS ITEMS
Enter b

CALLAWAY ITEMS
Enter cgTR78qw.

CLEVELAND ITEMS
Enter CL45etUB.

MAXFLI ITEMS
Enter FDGH597i.

NIKE ITEMS
Enter YJHk342B.

ODYSSEY ITEMS
Enter kjnMR3qv.

PING ITEMS
Enter R453DrTe.

PRECEPT ITEMS
Enter BRi3498Z.

TAG ITEMS
Enter cDsa2fgY.

TOURSTAGE ITEMS
Enter TS345329.

TIM BURTON'S THE NIGHTMARE BEFORE CHRISTMAS: OOGIE'S REVENGE

PUMPKIN JACK AND SANTA JACK COSTUMES
During gameplay, press Down, Up, Right, Left, L3, R3.

TOM AND JERRY IN WAR OF THE WHISKERS

INFINITE LIFE
During a game, press ✖, ●, ✖, ▲, ▲, ■, ●, ▲.

INFINITE AMMUNITION
During a game, press ●, ■, ●, ▲, ✖, ■, ✖, ✖.

ALL ARENAS
During a game, press ▲, ●, ▲, ▲, ✖, ■, ●, ■.

COSTUMES
During a game, press ●, ●, ✖, ■, ●, ▲, ✖, ●.

TOMB RAIDER: LEGEND

You must unlock the following codes in the game before using them.

BULLETPROOF
During gameplay, hold L1 and press ✖, R1, ▲, R1, ●, L2.

DRAIN ENEMY HEALTH
During gameplay, hold L1 and press ■, ●, ✖, L2, R1, ▲.

INFINITE ASSAULT RIFLE AMMO
During gameplay, hold L2 and press ✖, ●, ✖, L1, ■, ▲.

INFINITE GRENADE LAUNCHER AMMO
During gameplay, hold L2 and press L1, ▲, R1, ●, L1, ■.

INFINITE SHOTGUN AMMO
During gameplay, hold L2 and press R1, ●, ■, L1, ■, ✖.

INFINITE SMG AMMO
During gameplay, hold L2 and press ◉, ▲, L1, R1, ✖, ●.

EXCALIBUR
During gameplay, hold L2 and press ▲, ✖, ●, R1, ▲, L1.

ONE-SHOT KILL
During gameplay, hold L1 and press ▲, ✖, ▲, ●, L2, ◉.

NO TEXTURE MODE
During gameplay, hold L1 and press L2, ✖, ◉, ✖, ▲, R1.

TOM CLANCY'S SPLINTER CELL CHAOS THEORY

ALL SOLO LEVELS
At the Solo menu, hold L1 + L2 + R1 + R2
and press ● (x5), ◉ (x5).

ALL COOP LEVELS
At the Coop menu, hold L1 + L2 + R1 + R2
and press ● (x5), ◉ (x5).

TEAM PICTURE
At the Main menu, press R2, ◉ (x5), ●.

TONY HAWK'S AMERICAN WASTELAND

ALWAYS SPECIAL
Select Cheat Codes from the Options menu
and enter uronfire. Pause the game and
select Cheats from the Game Options to
enable the cheat.

PERFECT RAIL
Select Cheat Codes from the Options menu
and enter grindxpert. Pause the game and
select Cheats from the Game Options to
enable the cheat.

PERFECT SKITCH
Select Cheat Codes from the Options menu and enter h!tchar!de. Pause the game and select
Cheats from the Game Options to enable the cheat.

PERFECT MANUAL
Select Cheat Codes from the Options menu and enter 2wheels!. Pause the game and select
Cheats from the Game Options to enable the cheat.

MOON GRAVITY
Select Cheat Codes from the Options menu and enter 2them00n. Pause the game and select
Cheats from the Game Options to enable the cheat.

MAT HOFFMAN
Select Cheat Codes from the Options menu and enter the_condor

JASON ELLIS
Select Cheat Codes from the Options menu and enter sirius-dj.

TONY HAWK'S PROJECT 8

SPONSOR ITEMS
As you progress through Career mode and move up the rankings, you gain sponsors and each comes with its own Create-a-Skater item.

RANK REQUIRED	ITEM UNLOCKED
Rank 040	Adio Kenny V2 Shoes
Rank 050	Quiksilver_Hoody_3
Rank 060	Birdhouse Tony Hawk Deck
Rank 080	Vans No Skool Gothic Shoes
Rank 100	Volcom Scallero Jacket
Rank 110	eS Square One Shoes
Rank 120	Almost Watch What You Say Deck
Rank 140	DVS Adage Shoe
Rank 150	Element Illuminate Deck
Rank 160	Etnies Sheckler White Lavender Shoes
Complete Skateshop Goal	Stereo Soundwave Deck

SKATERS
You must unlock all of the skaters, except for Tony Hawk, by completing challenges in the Career Mode. They are useable in Free Skate and 2-Player modes.

SKATER	HOW TO UNLOCK
Tony Hawk	Always Unlocked
Lyn-z Adams Hawkins	Complete Pro Challenge
Bob Burquist	Complete Pro Challenge
Dustin Dollin	Complete Pro Challenge
Nyjah Huston	Complete Pro Challenge
Bam Margera	Complete Pro Challenge
Rodney Mullen	Complete Pro Challenge
Paul Rodriguez	Complete Pro Challenge
Ryan Sheckler	Complete Pro Challenge
Daewon Song	Complete Pro Challenge
Mike Vallely	Complete Pro Challenge
Stevie Willams	Complete Pro Challenge
Travis Barker	Complete Pro Challenge
Kevin Staab	Complete Pro Challenge
Zombie	Complete Pro Challenge
Christaian Hosoi	Animal Chin Challenge

SKATER	HOW TO UNLOCK
Jason Lee	Complete Final Tony Hawk Goal
Photographer	Unlock Shops
Security Guard	Unlock School
Bum	Unlock Car Factory
Beaver Mascot	Unlock High School
Real Estate Agent	Unlock Downtown
Filmer	Unlock High School
Skate Jam Kid	Rank #4
Dad	Rank #1
Colonel	All Gaps
Nerd	Complete School Spirit Goal

CHEAT CODES

Select Cheat Codes from the Options menu and enter the following codes. You can access some codes in game from the Options menu.

CHEAT CODE	RESULTS
plus44	Unlocks Travis Barker
hohohosoi	Unlocks Christian Hosoi
notmono	Unlocks Jason Lee
mixitup	Unlocks Kevin Staab
strangefellows	Unlocks Dad & Skater Jam Kid
themedia	Unlocks Photog Girl & Filmer
militarymen	Unlocks Colonel & Security Guard
jammypack	Unlocks Always Special
balancegalore	Unlocks Perfect Rail
frontandback	Unlocks Perect Manual
shellshock	Unlocks Unlimited Focus
shescaresme	Unlocks Big Realtor
birdhouse	Unlocks Inkblot deck
allthebest	Full Stats
needaride	All Decks unlocked and free, except for Inkblot Deck and Gamestop Deck
yougotitall	All specials unlocked and in player's special list and set as owned in skate shop
enterandwin	Unlocks bum
wearelosers	Unlocks nerd
manineedadate	Unlocks mascot
suckstobedead	Unlocks zombie
sellsellsell	Unlocks skinny real estate agent
newshound	Unlocks anchor man
badverybad	Unlocks twin

TONY HAWK'S UNDERGROUND

Select Cheat Codes from the Options menu and enter the following codes. Pause the game and select Cheats from the Options menu to toggle the cheats on and off.

PERFECT RAIL
Enter letitslide.

PERFECT MANUAL
Enter keepitsteady.

PERFECT SKITCH
Enter rearrider.

MOON GRAVITY
Enter getitup.

ALL VIDEOS
Enter digivid.

BONUS PRE-MADE SKATERS
Create a skater with the following code to open that skater:

CODE	SKATER
1337	Rulon Raymond
Akira2s	C Surla
Alan Flores	Alan Flores
Alex Garcia	Alex Garcia
Andy Marchel	Andy Marchel
arrr	Captain Cody
Bailey	Bailey
Big Tex	Big Tex
Chauwa Steel	Chauwa Steel
Chris Rausch	Chris Rausch
ChrisP	Chris Peacock
Crom	Eric Grosser
Daddy Mac	Dana MacKenzie
Dan Nelson	Dan Nelson
Dave Stohl	Dave Stohl
DDT	Darren Thorne
deadendroad	Ralph D'Amato
fatass	Brad Bulkley
Frogham	Kendall
Geiger	Jake Geiger
Glycerin	Glycerin
Greenie	Greenie
grjost	grjost
Guilt Ladle	Kevin Mulhall
Hammer	Ted Barber
Henry Ji	Henry Ji
Jason Uyeda	Jason Uyeda
Jeremy Andersen	Jeremy Andersen
Joel Jewett	Joel Jewett
Johnny Ow	Chum
Leedsleedsleeds	Wardy
Marcos Xk8r	Marcos Xk8r
Mike Ward	Mike Ward
moreuberthaned	Mikey Ortai
m'yak	Rock
Noly	Nolan Nelson
Nsjeff	Jeff Morgan
POOPER	Paul Robinson
sik®	sik®
Skillzombie	Skillzombie
Stacey D	Stacey D
tao zheng	Tao Zheng
The Kraken	The Kraken
The Swink	The Swink

CODE	SKATER
Thedoc	Adam Lippmann
Todd Wahoske	Todd Wahoske
Topbloke	Dave Cowling
Tsuenami!	Todd Sue
Woodchuck	Michelle Deyo
Y2KJ	Y2KJ
Yawgurt	Gary Jesdanun
ZiG	Zac Drake

TONY HAWK'S UNDERGROUND 2

Select Cheat Codes from the Game Options and enter the following. For the cheats, pause the game and select Cheats to turn them on.

ALL LEVELS
Enter d3struct.

ALL SKATERS EXCEPT FOR SECRET SKATERS
Enter costars!.

THPS1 TONY HAWK & ALL THUG2 MOVIES
Enter boxoffice.

NATAS KAUPAS
Enter oldskool.

NIGEL BEAVERHAUSEN
Enter sellout.

PHIL MARGERA
Enter aprilsman.

INFINITE RAIL CHEAT
Enter straightedge.

ALWAYS SPECIAL
Enter likepaulie.

SECRETS

REWARDS TABLE

GOAL ACHIEVED	LEVEL UNLOCKED	SKATERS UNLOCKED	MOVIES UNLOCKED
Complete Story Mode on "Easy"	Pro Skater	Shrek, Phil Margera, Peds Group A	World Destruction Tour
Complete Story Mode on "Normal"	Pro Skater	The Hand, Paulie, Peds Group B	World Destruction Tour
Complete Story Mode on "Sick"	Pro Skater	Call of Duty Soldier, Nigel, Peds Group C	World Destruction Tour
Complete Story Mode with 100%	N/A	Peds Group F	Pro Bails 2
Complete Classic Mode on "Normal"	The Triangle	Steve-O, THPS1 Tony, Peds Group D	Pro Bails 1
Complete Classic Mode on "Sick"	The Triangle	Jesse James, Natas Kaupas, Peds Group E	Pro Bails 1
Complete Classic Mode with 100%	N/A	Peds Group G	Neversoft Skates
Get all gaps on all 15 levels	N/A	Peds Group H	Cheat Codes
Complete Boston in Story Mode	N/A	Ben Franklin	N/A
Complete Barcelona in Story Mode	N/A	Bull Fighter	N/A
Complete Berlin in Story Mode	N/A	Graffiti Tagger	N/A
Complete Australia in Story Mode	N/A	Shrimp Vendor	N/A
Complete New Orleans in Story Mode	N/A	Jester	N/A
Complete Skatopia in Story Mode	N/A	Ryan Sheckler	N/A

TOTAL OVERDOSE:
A GUNSLINGER'S TALE IN MEXICO

CHEAT MODE
Hold L1 + R1 + L2 + R2 + L3 + R3 for a few seconds, then you can enter the following codes.

RESTORE HEALTH
Press ✖, ■, ●, ▲.

ALL LOCO MOVES
During a game, hold L1 + L2 + L3 + R1 + R2 + R3 for three seconds. Then press ●, ●, L2, R2.

MAXIMUM HEALTH
During a game, hold L1 + L2 + L3 + R1 + R2 + R3 for three seconds. Then press ✖, ■, ●, ▲.

MAXIMUM OF REWINDINGS
During a game, hold L1 + L2 + L3 + R1 + R2 + R3 for three seconds. Then press R1, R2, L2, ✖.

FREE ALL WEAPONS
During a game, hold L1 + L2 + L3 + R1 + R2 + R3 for three seconds. Then press ▲, L1, R2, ■.

TRANSFORMERS

ALL EXTRAS
Select Extras and press ■, ■, ●, ■, ■, ●, L1, L2.

INVINCIBILITY
Pause the game and press R1, ●, ●, R1, R2, L1, L1, L2.

STEALTH ENEMIES
Pause the game and press Left, Right, Left, R1, R2, R1, Right, Right.

1-HIT KILLS
Pause the game and press ■, ●, ■, ●, L1, L1, L2, L1.

BIG HEAD CHEAT MODE
Press ● (x3), ■, L1 (x3), L2 at the Autobot Headquarters menu.

TURBO CHEAT MODE
Press L1, R2, R2, ■ (x4), L1 at the Autobot Headquarters menu.

UNLIMITED STEALTH
Press Up, Up, Down, Down, L1, L2, L1, L2 at the Autobot Headquarters menu.

UNLIMITED POWERLINK
Press Up, Down, Up, Down, ●, ■, ●, ● at the Autobot Headquarters menu.

DISABLE MINI-CON OVERLOAD
Press R1, R1, L2, R1, R1, L2, ●, ● at the Autobot Headquarters menu.

Enter the following codes at the Difficulty Select screen.

ALASKA LEVEL COMPLETE
Press R1, ●, R1, ■, Left, Left, Right, Left at the Difficulty Select screen.

DEEP AMAZON LEVEL COMPLETE
Press Left, Right, Left, Left, Right, R1, R2, ●.

EARTH LEVEL COMPLETE
Press R2, R1, L1, L2, ■, ●, ■, ● at the Difficulty Select screen.

MID ATLANTIC LEVEL COMPLETE
Press ●, ■, ●, ■, Right, Left, Left, Right at the Difficulty Select screen.

STARSHIP LEVEL COMPLETE
Press Left, Left, Right, ●, ●, Right, Right, Left at the Difficulty Select screen.

AMAZON BOSS FIGHT
Press Left, Left, Right, L1, R2, Left, Left, Right at the Difficulty Select screen.

AMAZON LEVEL COMPLETE
Press L1, L1, L2, ●, ●, ●, R1, R2 at the Difficulty Select screen.

ANARCTICA BOSS FIGHT
Press L1, Left, L2, Right, ●, ●, ●, ● at the Difficulty Select screen.

ANARCTICA LEVEL COMPLETE
Press R1, R1, R2, L2, L1, L1, R1, R1 at the Difficulty Select screen.

MID ATLANTIC BOSS FIGHT
Press L2, Left, Right, Right, Left, L2, L2, L2 at the Difficulty Select screen.

STARSHIP BOSS FIGHT
Press Right, Right, ●, R1, R2, ● Left, Left at the Difficulty Select screen.

TRUE CRIME: NEW YORK CITY

DOUBLE DAMAGE
At the City Map screen, hold L1 + R1 and press ✕, ✕, ●, ✕, ✕, ✕.

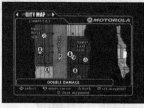

MILLIONAIRE
At the City Map screen, hold L1 + R1 and press ●, ●, ▲, ●, ▲, ●.

SUPER COP
At the City Map screen, hold L1 + R1 and press ▲, ✕, ▲, ✕, ▲, ▲.

ULTRA EASY MODE
At the City Map screen, hold L1 + R1 and press ●, ●, ✕, ✕, ▲, ●.

UNLIMITED AMMO
At the City Map screen, hold L1 + R1 and press ●, ●, ✕, ●, ●, ▲.

UNLIMITED ENDURANCE
At the City Map screen, hold L1 + R1 and press ●, ●, ✕, ●, ✕, ●.

STREET RACES OPEN
At the City Map screen, hold L1 + R1 and press ▲, ▲, ✕, ✕, ▲.

FIGHTS OPEN
At the City Map screen, hold L1 + R1 and press ●, ●, ●, ●, ●.

GHETTO CITY
At the City Map screen, hold L1 + R1 and press ✕, ●, ✕, ●, ▲, ▲, ▲.

ZOMBIEFIED
At the City Map screen, hold L1 + R1 and press ●, ▲, ●, ✕, ●, ✕.

NEW OUTFIT IN PUMA STORE
At the City Map screen, hold L1 + R1 and press ▲, ✕, ●, ■.

RED GONE WILD
At the City Map screen, hold L1 + R1 and press ▲, ✕, ✕, ●, ▲, ■.

ALL MUSIC
At the City Map screen, hold L1 + R1 and press ●, ■, ●, ■.

TWIN CALIBER

UNLIMITED AMMO
During a game, press Right, Right, Up, Right, Down, Down, Right, Up, Right, Down.

INVINCIBILITY
During a game, press Up, Right, Down, Left, Up, Down, Right, Up, Left, Down.

TY THE TASMANIAN TIGER 3: NIGHT OF THE QUINKAN

100,000 OPALS
During a game, press Start, Start, ▲, Start, Start, ▲, ●, ✕, ●, ✕.

ALL 'RANG CHASSIS
During a game, press Start, Start, ▲, Start, Start, ▲, ●, ■, ●, ■.

URBAN CHAOS: RIOT RESPONSE

At the Main menu, press Up, Up, Down, Down, ●, Down, Up, ●. This opens the Cheat screen. Select Add Cheat and enter the following:

ALL LEVELS & EMERGENCIES
Enter KEYTOTHECITY.

TERROR MODE
Enter BURNERSREVENGE.

ASSUALT RIFLE MK. 3 WITH INFINITE SHELLS
Enter ULTIMATEPOWER.

MINI-GUN
Enter MINIFUN.

PISTOL MK. 4
Enter ZEROTOLERANCE.

ENHANCED STUN GUN
Enter FRYINGTIME.

BURNING BULLETS
Enter BURNINGBULLET.

DISCO CHEAT
Enter DANCINGFEET.

HEADLESS CHEAT
Enter KEEPYOURHEAD.

SQUEAKY VOICES
Enter WHATWASTHAT.

THE URBZ: SIMS IN THE CITY

CHEAT GNOME
During a game, press ●, L1, L2, R2, R1.

JUMP AHEAD SIX HOURS
Enter the Cheat Gnome code, then press R2, R3, L3, L2, R1, L2.

ACQUIRE SKILL OBJECT
Enter the Cheat Gnome code, then press L1, R2, Right, ■, L3.

MAX ARTISTIC SKILL
Enter the Cheat Gnome code, then press L3, R3, R1, R2, ◉.

MAX MENTAL SKILL
Enter the Cheat Gnome code, then press L1, R2, ✖, ◉, Up.

MAX PHYSICAL SKILL
Enter the Cheat Gnome code, then press L1, R1, Down, ✖, L3.

ALL SOCIALS
Enter the Cheat Gnome code, then press L2, R2, UP, ▲, L3, ✖.

POWER SOCIALS
Enter the Cheat Gnome code, then press ▲, R2, L1, ✖, ◉.

RAISE MOTIVES
Enter the Cheat Gnome code, then press R2, L1, R1, L2, Left, ◉.

DEVELOPMENT TEAM
Enter the Cheat Gnome code, then press Up, Down, ◉, Up, Down.

ULTIMATE SPIDER-MAN

ALL CHARACTERS
Pause the game and select Controller Setup from the Options menu. Press Right, Down, Right, Down, Left, Up, Left, Right.

ALL COVERS
Pause the game and select Controller Setup from the Options menu. Press Left, Left, Right, Left, Up, Left, Left, Down.

ALL CONCEPT ART
Pause the game and select Controller Setup from the Options menu. Press Down, Down, Down, Up, Down, Up, Left, Left.

ALL LANDMARKS
Pause the game and select Controller Setup from the Options menu. Press Up, Right, Down, Left, Down, Up, Right, Left.

URBAN REIGN

ALL CHARACTERS
At the Title screen, press R1, R2, ✕, Left, Right, ● (x4), L1, ●, ▲, ●.

ALL WEAPONS
At the Title screen, press L1, R1, ✕, X, ●, R1, R1, ▲, ●, ✕, R1.

BONUS WEAPON IN MULTI-PLAYER MODE
At the Title screen, press L2, L2, ✕, ✕, ▲, R1, R1, ●, R1.

CHALLENGE MODE
At the Title screen, press L2, R2, ▲, Right, Left, Up, Up, Left, R2, R2 ,R2, ●.

FREE MODE
At the Title screen, press L1, R1, Left, Left, Left, Left, Left, Left, L2, Up, ▲, ▲, Right.

TWO PLAYERS IN STORY MODE
At the Title screen, press L1, R2, ●, ●, ▲, L2, R1, ●, ▲, ●.

VAN HELSING

BONUS MOVIE 1
During a game, press Up, Down, Up, Down, Left, Left, Right, Right, L1, L3, R3, R1.

BONUS MOVIE 2
During a game, press Up, Right, Down, Left, Up, Left, Down, Right, Up, R1, R2, R3.

BONUS MOVIE 3
During a game, press L1, L2, R2, R1, R2, L2, L1, Up, Up, Down, Down, Select.

BONUS MOVIE 4
During a game, press Select, L3, R3, Select, R3, L3, Select, Left, Left, Up, Right, Right.

BONUS MOVIE 5
During a game, press L2, R2, L1, R1, Select, Select, L1, L1, R2, R2, L3, R3.

BONUS MOVIE 6
During a game, press R2, R1, R2, R1, L1, L2, L1, L2, Left, Right, Select, Select.

BONUS MOVIE 7
During a game, press L3, Left, R3, Right, L2, Up, R2, Down, L1, Left, R1, Right.

VICTORIOUS BOXERS 2: FIGHTING SPRIRT

EXTRA CHARACTERS IN EXHIBITION
Select Password from the Options menu and enter NEL SAZ UMA.

BROCCOMAN IN EXHIBITION MODE
Select Password from the Options menu and enter BRC MAN EXH.

LUNSAKU PAUDY, JUNICHI HOTTA & HIROSHI YAMANAKA
Select Password from the Options menu and enter ALL *ST ARS.

KAMOGAWA, NEKOTA AND HAMA IN EXHIBITION MODE
Select Password from the Options menu and enter MRS AND MAN.

DATE VS. RAMIREZ MATCH IN STORY MODE
Select Password from the Options menu and enter DAT EVS RMZ.

TAKAMURA VS. YAJIMA MATCH IN STORY MODE
Select Password from the Options menu and enter ASA CT3 CLR.

EXTRA STAGES
Select Password from the Options menu and enter DAM ATA MAQ.

THE WARRIORS

100% COMPLETE
During gameplay, press L1, Select, ●, Down, L2, Right.

99 CREDITS IN ARMIES OF THE NIGHT
During the Armies of the Night mini-game, press Up, Up, Down, Down, Left, Right.

$200, FLASH, & SPRAY PAINT
During gameplay, press R1, R2, L1, ✖, Down, L1.

INFINITE HEALTH
During gameplay, press Up, ▲, L3, Select, ✖, L2.

INFINITE RAGE
During gameplay, press ●, ●, ▲, Select, ✖, Left.

INFINITE SPRINT
During gameplay, press Down, ●, left, ✖, L1, Select.

COMPLETE MISSION
During gameplay, press Down, ●, ✖, Select, R1, Left.

BAT
During gameplay, press ●, R2, Down, Down, L1, L1.

UNBREAKABLE BAT
During gameplay, press L3, L3, ●, Up, ●, Select.

BRASS KNUCKLES
During gameplay, press ●, ●, ●, L1, Select, ▲.

KNIFE
During gameplay, press Down, Down, Select, Up, Up, L3.

MACHETE
During gameplay, press L1, ✖, R1, R1, Select, R2.

PIPE
During gameplay, press R2, ●, Select, Up, L1, Right.

STEEL-TOE BOOTS
During gameplay, press R3, R2, R1, L3, L2, L1.

BUM ADVICE UPGRADE
During gameplay, press ●, ●, Down, R2, L2, ●.

COMBAT STAMINA UPGRADE
During gameplay, press ✖, L1, Down, {SQ}, Up, ✖.

FLASH CAPACITY UPGRADE
During gameplay, press L2, X, R2, L1, L1, ●.

FLASH UPGRADE
During gameplay, press Down, Left, Up, Up, ●, Right.

SPRINT STAMINA UPGRADE
During gameplay, press L2, Select, Select, Select, Select, ▲.

CUFF DROPS
During gameplay, press Up, ✖, Up, Select, L3, L1.

CUFF KEY DROPS
During gameplay, press Left, ✖, ✖, R2, L1, Down.

UNCUFF SELF
During gameplay, press ▲, ▲, ▲, Select, ▲, R1.

LOSE THE POLICE
During gameplay, press Up, Select, ✖, ▲, ▲, ●.

HOBO ALLIANCE
During gameplay, press R1, R1, L1, R1, L1, Up.

WEAPONS DEALER
During gameplay, press Right, R1, ●, ✖, Select, ●.

WAY OF THE SAMURAI 2

ALL CHARACTERS
Select Character Customization and highlight Name. Press L1, R2, R1, L2, L1, R2, R1, L2, ●.

MORE STORE ITEMS
At the main map, press L1, R1, L1, R1, R2, R2, ▲.

WITHOUT WARNING

LEVEL SKIP & LEVEL SELECT
At the Main menu, press ●, ▲, ●, L1, Left, Up, Right, R1. Pause the game to access both options.

WORMS 3D

2 BLIMPS
Generate a new landscape with the code igotworms.

3 SUBMARINES
Generate a new landscape with the code CANDY.

TINY ISLAND
Generate a new landscape with the code Smashsumfruit.

X-MEN LEGENDS II: RISE OF APOCALYPSE

ALL CHARACTERS
At the Team Management screen, press Right, Left, Left, Right, Up, Up, Up, Start.

ALL SKINS
At the Team Management screen, press Down, Up, Left, Right, Up, Up, Start

ALL SKILLS
At the Team Management screen, press Left, Right, Left, Right, Down, Up, Start.

LEVEL 99
At the Team Management screen, press Up, Down, Up, Down, Left, Up, Left, Right, Start.

GOD MODE
Pause the game and press Down, Up, Down, Up, Right, Down, Right, Left, Start.

MOVE FASTER
Pause the game and press Up, Up, Up, Down, Up, Down, Start.

UNLIMITED XTREME TOKENS
Pause the game and press Left, Down, Right, Down, Up, Up, Down, Up, Start.

TOUCH OF DEATH
During a game, press Left, Left, Right, Left, Right, Up, Start.

100,000 TECH-BITS
At Forge or Beast's store, press Up, Up, Up, Down, Right, Right, Start.

ALL DANGER ROOM COURSES
At the Danger Room Course menu, press Right, Right, Left, Left, Up, Down, Up, Down, Start.

ALL COMICS

Select Review from the Main menu and press Right, Left, Left, Right, Up, Up, Right, Start.

ALL CINEMATICS

Select Review from the Main menu and press Left, Right, Right, Left, Down, Down, Left, Start.

ALL CONCEPTS

Select Review from the Main menu and press Left, Right, Left, Right, Up, Up, Down, Start.

ALL SCREENS

Select Review from the Main menu and press Right, Left, Right, Left, Up, Up, Down, Start.

X-MEN: THE OFFICIAL GAME

DANGER ROOM ICEMAN

At the Cerebro Files menu, press Right, Right, Left, Left, Down, Up, Down, Up, Start.

DANGER ROOM NIGHTCRAWLER

At the Cerebro Files menu, press Up, Up, Down, Down, Left, Right, Left, Right, Start.

DANGER ROOM WOLVERINE

At the Cerebro Files menu, press Down, Down, Up, Up, Right, Left, Right, Left, Start.

YS: THE ARK OF NAPISHTIM

Enter the cheat codes as follows:

1. Select New Game.

2. Select Cheat to enter the Cheat Room.

3. To activate Cheat Mode, strike the colored crystals in this sequence: Red, Blue, Yellow, Red, Blue, Yellow. The sequence appears at the top left as you strike each crystal.

4. Perform a Downward Thrust strike on the center pedestal to complete the code and activate Cheat Mode.

5. You can now use the same method to enter one of the cheat codes listed below, then exit the Cheat Room.

6. The game selection buttons are now red. Games saved with the Cheat Mode enabled will appear in red.

CLEARFLAG
Hit the crystals in the following order: Red, Red, Red, Red, Blue, Blue, Blue, Blue, Yellow, Yellow, Yellow, Yellow, Blue, Blue, Yellow, Yellow, Red, Red. Turns on all special features normally available only after you've completed the game once—Nightmare Mode, Time Attack, and Red Spirit Monuments. **Note:** When enabled, Red Spirit Monuments appear after you reach Port Rimorge. They allow you to warp between the Rehdan Village and Port Rimorge monuments to save travel time.

OPENING MOVIE WITH ENGLISH VOICE/ENGLISH TEXT
Hit the crystals in the following order: Blue, Blue, Yellow, Red.

OPENING MOVIE WITH ENGLISH VOICE/JAPANESE TEXT
Hit the crystals in the following order: Blue, Blue, Blue, Yellow, Red.

OPENING MOVIE WITH JAPANESE VOICE/ENGLISH TEXT
Hit the crystals in the following order: Blue, Blue, Blue, Blue, Yellow, Red.

OPENING MOVIE WITH JAPANESE VOICE/NO TEXT
Hit the crystals in the following order: Blue, Yellow, Red.

ALTERNATE OPENING MOVIE
Hit the crystals in the following order: Red, Blue, Red.

BEACH MOVIE WITH ENGLISH VOICE/ENGLISH TEXT
Hit the crystals in the following order: Blue, Blue, Red, Yellow

BEACH MOVIE WITH ENGLISH VOICE/JAPANESE TEXT
Hit the crystals in the following order: Blue, Blue, Blue, Red, Yellow.

BEACH MOVIE WITH JAPANESE VOICE/ENGLISH TEXT
Hit the crystals in the following order: Blue, Red, Red, Yellow.

BEACH MOVIE WITH JAPANESE VOICE/JAPANESE TEXT
Hit the crystals in the following order: Blue, Red, Yellow.

ROMUN FLEET ENTRANCE ANIME MOVIE
Hit the crystals in the following order: Blue, Red, Yellow, Red, Red, Yellow, Blue, Blue, Blue.

ROMUN FLEET ENTRANCE CG MOVIE
Hit the crystals in the following order: Blue, Red, Yellow, Red, Red, Yellow, Blue.

ROMUN FLEET DESTROYED ANIME MOVIE
Hit the crystals in the following order: Blue, Red, Yellow, Red, Red, Yellow, Red, Red, Red.

ROMUN FLEET DESTROYED CG MOVIE
Hit the crystals in the following order: Blue, Red, Yellow, Red, Red, Yellow, Red.

NAPISHTIM DESTROYED MOVIE WITH ENGLISH VOICE/ENGLISH TEXT
Hit the crystals in the following order: Blue, Red, Yellow, Red, Red, Blue, Yellow, Yellow.

NAPISHTIM DESTROYED MOVIE WITH ENGLISH VOICE/JAPANESE TEXT
Hit the crystals in the following order: Blue, Red, Yellow, Red, Red, Blue, Yellow, Yellow, Yellow.

NAPISHTIM DESTROYED MOVIE WITH JAPANESE VOICE/ENGLISH TEXT
Hit the crystals in the following order: Blue, Red, Yellow, Red, Red, Blue, Yellow, Yellow, Yellow, Yellow.

NAPISHTIM DESTROYED MOVIE WITH JAPANESE VOICE/JAPANESE TEXT
Hit the crystals in the following order: Blue, Red, Yellow, Red, Red, Blue, Yellow.

OLHA IN BIKINI
Hit the crystals in the following order: Blue, Blue, Blue, Blue, Blue, Yellow, Yellow, Yellow, Red, Blue, Yellow, Yellow, Red, Red, Red.

OLHA DEMO AFTER CLEARING TIME ATTACK ON HARD (JAPANESE)
Hit the crystals in the following order: Red, Red, Red, Red, Red, Blue, Blue, Blue, Yellow, Red, Blue, Blue, Yellow, Yellow, Yellow.

GAME IN JAPANESE
Hit the crystals in the following order: Yellow, Yellow, Red, Blue.

LEVEL 10
Hit the crystals in the following order: Red, Blue, Blue, Red, Red, Blue.

LEVEL 20
Hit the crystals in the following order: Red, Blue, Blue, Red, Red, Blue, Blue.

LEVEL 30
Hit the crystals in the following order: Red, Red, Blue, Blue, Red, Red, Blue, Blue.

LEVEL 40
Hit the crystals in the following order: Red, Red, Blue, Red, Red, Blue, Blue, Yellow.

LEVEL 60
Hit the crystals in the following order: Red, Red, Blue, Blue, Yellow, Yellow, Red, Red, Blue, Blue, Yellow, Yellow.

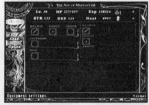

HALF PRICE ITEMS
Hit the crystals in the following order: Yellow, Yellow, Blue, Blue, Red, Red, Red, Yellow, Yellow, Yellow, Red, Red, Blue, Blue.

20 ITEM TOOL MAX INCREASE
Hit the crystals in the following order: Yellow, Yellow, Red, Red, Blue, Blue, Yellow, R.

MAXED OUT BLIRANTE SWORD
Hit the crystals in the following order: Blue, Blue, Yellow, Yellow, Yellow, Red, Blue, Red, Red, Red, Yellow, Yellow.

MAXED OUT LIVART SWORD
Hit the crystals in the following order: Blue, Blue, Blue, Yellow, Yellow, Red, Blue, Red, Red, Yellow, Yellow, Yellow.

MAXED OUT ERICCIL SWORD
Hit the crystals in the following order: Blue, Yellow, Yellow, Red, Red, Red, Blue, Blue, Blue, Red, Red, Yellow.

MAXED OUT ALL 3 SWORDS
Hit the crystals in the following order: Blue, Yellow, Red, Blue, Blue, Red, Red, Red, Yellow, Yellow, Yellow, Blue, Yellow, Red.

ALTERNATE ENDING MOVIES
In the Rehdan Village (Festival at Night): Toksa and Nahrya look toward Adol as he walks by.

At the Entrance of the Village: Isha runs toward the back, then returns.

On the *Tres Mares*: The cat is on the front of the ship.

ENDING CHANGE CRITERIA
Direction Calman is facing: Faces Adol if he has gotten the Gold Locket.
Number of Pikkards: Found all four pikkards and returned them to Emilio.

YU-GI-OH! THE DUELIST OF THE ROSES

PASSWORDS
At the Build Deck screen, press R3 and enter the following passwords:

NUMBER	CARD	PASSWORD
#001	Seiyaryu	2H4D85J7
#019	Meteor Dragon	86985631
#042	Fairy's Gift	NVE7A3EZ
#043	Magician of Faith	GME1S3UM
#057	Left Arm of the Forbidden One	A5CF6HSH
#058	Exodia the Forbidden One	37689434
#146	Swordstalker	AHOPSHEB
#149	Greenkappa	YBJMCD6Z
#152	Tactical Warrior	054TC727
#191	Swordsman from a Foreign Land	CZ81UVGR
#478	Aqua Dragon	JXCB6FU7
#655	Ancient Tree of Enlightenment	EKJHQ109
#502	Barrel Dragon	GTJXSBJ7
#567	Beastking of the Swamps	QXNTQPAX
#291	Birdface	N54T4TY5
#348	Dragon Seeker	81EZCH8B

NUMBER	CARD	PASSWORD
#372	Mystical Capture Chains	N1NDJMQ3
#458	Serpentine Princess	UMQ3WZUZ
#506	Blast Sphere	CZN5GD2X
#510	Robotic Knight	S5S7NKNH
#670	Fairy King Truesdale	YF07QVEZ
#674	Slate Warrior	73153736
#687	Mimicat	69YDQM85
#699	Dark Hole	UMJ10MQB
#702	Harpy's Feather Duster	8HJHQPNP
#732	Change of Heart	SBYDQM8B
#750	Earthshaker	Y34PN1SV
#758	Elf's Light	E5G3NRAD
#765	Horn of the Unicorn	S14FGKQ1
#794	Crush Card	SRA7L5YR
#806	Gravity Bind	0HNFG9WX
#814	Goblin Fan	92886423
#825	Royal Decree	8TETQHE1
#829	Mirror Wall	53297534

ZAPPER

INFINITE LIVES
Pause the game, hold L1 and press Up, Up, Up, Left, Left, Right, Left, Right.

INFINITE SHIELDS
Pause the game, hold L1 and press Up, Down, Up, Left, Right, Down, Up.

PLAYSTATION®
PORTABLE

Games List

APE ESCAPE: ON THE LOOSE

SNOWKIDZ RACING MINI-GAME
Collect 10 Specter Coins.

SPECTER BOXING MINI-GAME
Collect 20 Specter Coins.

EXTRA CHARACTERS IN SPECTER BOXING
Complete Specter Boxing.

JAKE ATTACKS MINI-GAME
Collect 30 Specter Coins.

APE PING PONG MINI-GAME
Collect 40 Specter Coins.

EXTRA CHARACTERS IN APE PING PONG
Complete Ape Ping Pong.

ATV OFFROAD FURY: BLAZIN' TRAILS

UNLOCK EVERYTHING EXCEPT THE FURY BIKE
Select Player Profile from the Options menu. Choose Enter Cheat and enter All Access.

1500 CREDITS
Select Player Profile from the Options menu. Choose Enter Cheat and enter $moneybags$.

ALL RIDER GEAR
Select Player Profile from the Options menu. Choose Enter Cheat and enter Duds.

TIRES
Select Player Profile from the Options menu. Choose Enter Cheat and enter Dubs.

MUSIC VIDEOS
Select Player Profile from the Options menu. Choose Enter Cheat and enter Billboards.

BURNOUT LEGENDS

COP RACER
Earn a Gold in all Pursuit events.

FIRE TRUCK
Earn a Gold in all Crash Events.

GANGSTER BOSS
Earn Gold in all Race events.

CARS

BONUS SPEEDWAY (REVERSED) IN CUSTOM RACE
At the Main menu, hold L and press ✕, ⬤, ▲, ✕, ▲, ⬛.

CRASH TAG TEAM RACING

FASTER VEHICLES
At the Main menu, hold L + R and press ⬤, ⬤, ▲, ▲.

1-HIT KO
At the Main menu, hold L + R and press ✕, ⬤, ⬤, ✕.

DISABLE HUD
At the Main menu, hold L + R and press ✕, ⬛, ▲, ⬤.

CHICKEN HEADS
At the Main menu, hold L + R and press ✕, ⬤, ⬤, ⬛

JAPANESE CRASH
At the Main menu, hold L + R and press ⬛, ⬤, ⬛, ⬤.

DRIVE A BLOCK VEHICLE
At the Main menu, hold L + R and press ⬤, ⬤, ▲, ⬛.

DARKSTALKERS CHRONICLE: THE CHAOS TOWER

EX OPTIONS
At the Main menu, hold L and select Options.

MARIONETTE IN ARCADE MODE
At the Character Select screen, highlight ? and press START (x7), then press P or K.

OBORO BISHAMON IN ALL MODES
At the Character Select screen, highlight

SHADOW IN ARCADE MODE
At the Character Select screen, highlight ? and press START (x5), then press P or K.

DAXTER

THE MATRIX DREAM SEQUENCE
Collect 1 Precursor Orb.

BRAVEHEART DREAM SEQUENCE
Collect 100 Precursor Orbs.

THE LORD OF THE RINGS DREAM SEQUENCE
Collect 200 Precursor Orbs.

INDIANA JONES DREAM SEQUENCE
Collect 300 Precursor Orbs.

THE MATRIX DREAM SEQUENCE 2
Collect 400 Precursor Orbs.

THE LORD OF THE RINGS DREAM SEQUENCE 2
Collect 500 Precursor Orbs.

E3 2005 TRAILER
Collect 600 Precursor Orbs, then pause the game and select Extras from the Secrets menu.

CONCEPT ART
Collect 700 Precursor Orbs, then pause the game and select Extras from the Secrets menu.

INTRO ANIMATIC
Collect 800 Precursor Orbs, then pause the game and select Extras from the Secrets menu.

GAME UNDER CONSTRUCTION
Collect 900 Precursor Orbs, then pause the game and select Extras from the Secrets menu.

BEHIND THE SCENES
Collect 1000 Precursor Orbs, then pause the game and select Extras from the Secrets menu.

PANTS
Earn Gold on The Lord of the Rings Dream Sequence 2, then pause the game and select Cheats from the Secrets menu.

HAT
Earn Gold on the Indiana Jones Dream Sequence, then pause the game and select Cheats from the Secrets menu.

WEBSITE CLUE A
Earn Gold on The Matrix Dream Sequence , then pause the game and select Cheats from the Secrets menu.

WEBSITE CLUE B
Earn Gold on the Braveheart Dream Sequence, then pause the game and select Cheats from the Secrets menu.

WEBSITE CLUE C
Earn Gold on The Lord of the Rings Dream Sequence, then pause the game and select Cheats from the Secrets menu.

WEBSITE CLUE D
Earn Gold on The Matrix Dream Sequence 2, then pause the game and select Cheats from the Secrets menu.

DEATH JR.

CAN'T TOUCH THIS (INVINCIBILITY)
Pause the game, hold L + R and press Up, Up, Down, Down, Left, Left, Right, Right, ⬤, ▲.

INCREASED HEALTH
Pause the game, hold L + R and press Up, Up, Down, Down, ✖, ⬤, ▲, ⬤, ✖, ✖.

WEAPONS UPGRADED (GIVES ALL WEAPONS)
Pause the game, hold L + R and press Up, Up, Down, Down, Left, Right, Left, Right, ✖, ⬤.

AMMO REFILLED
Pause the game, hold L + R and press ▲, ▲, ✖, ✖, ■, ⬤, ■, ⬤, Down, Right.

UNLIMITED AMMO
Pause the game, hold L + R and press ▲, ▲, ✖, ✖, ■, ⬤, ■, ⬤, Right, Down.

MY HEAD FEELS FUNNY (BIG HEAD)
Pause the game, hold L + R and press ▲, ⬤, ✖, ■, ▲, Up, Right, Down, Left, Up. Re-enter the code for normal head size.

GIANT BLADE (BIG SCYTHE)
Pause the game, hold L + R and press ▲, ■, ✖, ⬤, ▲, Up, Left, Down, Right, Up.

FREE SEEP
Pause the game, hold L + R and press Left, Left, Right, Right, Left, Right, Left, Right, ✖, ✖.

A LITTLE MORE HELP (ASSIST EXTENDER)
Pause the game, hold L + R and press Up, Up, Down, Down, ▲, ▲, ✖, ✖, ▲, ▲.

FREE WIDGET
Pause the game, hold L + R and press Right, Up, Down, Up, ▲, Up, Left, ⬤, ▲, Right.

ALL LEVELS & FREE ALL CHARACTERS

Pause the game, hold L + R and press Up (x4), Down (x4), ✕, ✕. Enter a stage and exit back to the museum for the code to take effect.

I'D BUY THAT FOR A DOLLAR (FILL PANDORA ASSIST METER)

Pause the game, hold L + R and press Up, Up, Down, Down, Up, Right, Down, Left, ✕, ✕.

THIS WAS JED'S IDEA (ATTACKS HAVE DIFFERENT NAMES)

Pause the game, hold L + R and press Up, Up, Down, Left, ▲, ▲, ■, ✕, ●, ■.

WEAPON NAMES = NORMAL (WEAPONS HAVE DIFFERENT NAMES)

Pause the game, hold L + R and press Down, Down, Up, Up, Left, Right, Left, Right, ■, ▲.

EYEDOOR SOLIDITY QUESTIONABLE (NO LONGER REQUIRE SOULS)

Pause the game, hold L + R and press Up, Left, Down, Right, Left, ▲, ■, ✕, ●, ■.

BUDDY DECALS (BULLET HOLES BECOME PICTURES)

Pause the game, hold L + R and press Up, Right, Down, Left, Up, ▲, ●, ✕, ■, ▲.

STAGE WARP

Pause the game, hold L + R and enter the following codes to warp to that stage.

STAGE	CODE
Advanced Training	Down, ✕, Down, ✕, Down, ✕, Down, ✕, Down, ■
The Basement	Down, ✕, Down, ✕, Down, ✕, Down, ✕, Up, ▲
Basic Training	Up, ▲, Up, ✕, Down, ✕, Down, ✕, Down, ✕
Big Trouble in Little Downtown	Up, ▲, Down, ✕, Down, ✕, Down, ✕, Down, ✕
Bottom of the Bell Curve	Down, ✕, Down, ✕, Down, ✕, Down, ✕, Down, ▲
The Burger Tram	Down, ✕, Down, ✕, Down, ✕, Up, ▲, Down, ✕
Burn It Down	Down, ✕, Up, ▲, Down, ✕, Down, ✕, Down, ✕
The Corner Store	Down, ✕, Up, ▲, Down, ✕, Down, ✕, Down, ✕
Final Battle	Down, ✕, Down, ✕, Down, ✕, Down, ▲, Up, ✕
Growth Spurt	Down, ✕, Down, ✕, Down, ✕, Down, ✕, Up, ▲
Happy Trails Insanitarium	Down, ✕, Down, ▲, Up, ✕, Down, ✕, Down, ✕
Higher Learning	Down, ✕, Down, ✕, Down, ✕, Down, ▲, Down, ✕
How a Cow Becomes a Steak	Down, ✕, Down, ✕, Down, ▲, Down, ✕, Down, ✕
Inner Madness	Down, ✕, Down, ✕, Up, ▲, Down, ✕, Down, ✕
Into the Box	Down, ✕, Down, ✕, Down, ✕, Up, ▲, Down, ✕
Moving on Up	Down, ▲, Up, ✕, Down, ✕, Down, ✕, Down, ✕
The Museum	Up, ✕, Down ✕, Down, ✕, Down, ✕, Down, ✕
My House	Down, ✕, Down, ✕, Down, ✕, Down, ✕, Down, ✕
Seep's Hood	Down, ▲, Down, ✕, Down, ✕, Down, ✕, Down, ✕
Shock Treatment	Down, ✕, Down, ✕, Down, ▲, Up, ✕, Down, ✕
Udder Madness	Down, ✕, Down, ✕, Up, ▲, Down, ✕, Down, ✕

DEF JAM: FIGHT FOR NY: THE TAKEOVER

100 REWARD POINTS
Select Cheats from the Extras menu and enter REALSTUFF, GOUNDRGRND, THEEMCEE, BULLETPROOF or DASTREETS.

200 REWARD POINTS
Select Cheats from the Extras menu and enter REAL STYLE, SUPER FREAK or DRAGONHOUSE.

300 REWARD POINTS
Select Cheats from the Extras menu and enter NEWYORKCIT.

AFTERHOURS BY NYNE'S BEAT
Select Cheats from the Extras menu and enter LOYALTY.

ANYTHING GOES BY C-N-N
Select Cheats from the Extras menu and enter MILITAIN.

BLINDSIDE BY BAXTER
Select Cheats from the Extras menu and enter CHOPPER.

BUST BY OUTKAST
Select Cheats from the Extras menu and enter BIGBOI.

COMP BY COMP
Select Cheats from the Extras menu and enter CHOCOCITY.

THE DRAGON HOUSE BY MASA MIX
Select Cheats from the Extras menu and enter AKIRA.

GET IT NOW BY BLESS
Select Cheats from the Extras menu and enter PLATINUMB.

KOTO BY CHIANG'S MIX
Select Cheats from the Extras menu and enter GHOSTSHELL.

LIL' BRO BY RIC-A-CHE
Select Cheats from the Extras menu and enter GONBETRUBL.

MAN UP BY STICKY FINGAZ
Select Cheats from the Extras menu and enter KIRKJONES.

MOVE! BY PUBLIC ENEMY
Select Cheats from the Extras menu and enter RESPECT.

O.G. ORIGINAL GANGSTER BY ICE-T
Select Cheats from the Extras menu and enter POWER.

POPPA LARGE BY ULTRAMAGNETIC MC'S
Select Cheats from the Extras menu and enter ULTRAMAG.

SIEZE THE DAY BY BLESS
Select Cheats from the Extras menu and enter SIEZE.

TAKE A LOOK AT MY LIFE BY FAT JOE
Select Cheats from the Extras menu and enter CARTAGENA.

WALK WITH ME BY JOE BUDDEN
Select Cheats from the Extras menu and enter PUMP.

DRAGON BALL Z: SHIN BUDOKAI

MINI-GAME
At the Main menu, press L and then press R to begin the mini-game.

EXIT

SITUATION 8
Complete Situation 1. Then at the Title screen, press L, R, Left, Right, ■, ●, ✖, ▲.

SITUATION 9
Complete Situation 1 and unlock Situation 8. Then at the Title screen, press ▲, Down, ●, Left, ✖, Up, ■, Right.

SITUATION 10
Complete Situation 1 and unlock Situations 8 and 9. Then at the Title screen, press Right, Down, Up, Left, ●, ✖, R, L.

FRANTIX

INVINCIBILITY
At the Level Select screen, hold R + L to access the codes screen. Enter INVINC1. To disable invincibility, enter INVINC0

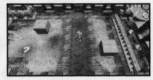

ALL LEVELS
At the Level Select screen, hold R + L to access the codes screen. Enter LVLANY1. The levels will still appear locked, but you can select them. To disable all levels, enter LVLANY0.

FROGGER HELMET CHAOS

MOHAWK WIG
Enter Berry, Lily, Lumpy, Lily as a password.

AFRO WIG
Enter Finnius, Frogger, Frogger, Wani as a password.

SANTA HAT
Enter Lily, Lily, Wani, Wani as a password.

PIRATE HAT
Enter Frogger, Berry, Finnius, Frogger as a password.

BASEBALL CAP
Enter Frogger, Frogger, Frogger, Berry as a password.

CROC HAT
Enter Lily, Lily, Wani, Lumpy as a password.

BUNNY EARS
Enter Lily, Frogger, Frogger, Lumpy as a password.

CAMOUFLAGE COSTUME
Enter Lily, Wani, Lily, Wani as a password.

COWBOY COSTUME
Enter Frogger, Lily, Lily, Lily as a password.

SANTA COSTUME
Play the game for four hours.

PIRATE COSTUME
Play the game for six hours.

PUNK COSTUME
Pause the game and press Up, Up, Down, Down, Left, Right, Left, Right, ▲, ●, Start.

THE GODFATHER: MOB WARS

Each of the following codes will work
once every five minutes.

$1000
Pause the game and press ■, ●, ■,
■, ●, L.

FULL AMMO
Pause the game and press ●, Left, ●,
Right ●, R.

FULL HEALTH
Pause the game and press Left, ●, Right,
●, Right, L.

GRADIUS COLLECTION

ALL WEAPONS & POWER-UPS (EASY DIFFICULTY)
Pause the game and press Up, Up, Down, Down, Left, Right, Left, Right, ✖, ●.

GRAND THEFT AUTO: LIBERTY CITY STORIES

$250,000
During a game, press L, R, ▲, L, R, ●, L, R.

FULL HEALTH
During a game, press L, R, ✖, L, R, ●, L, R.

FULL ARMOR
During a game, press L, R, ●, L, R, ✖, L, R.

WEAPON SET 1
During a game, press Up, ■, ■, Down, Left, ■, ■, Right.

WEAPON SET 2
During a game, press Up, ●, ●, Down, Left, ●, ●, Right.

WEAPON SET 3
During a game, press Up, ✖, X, Down, Left, ✖, X, Right.

CHROME PLATED CARS
During a game, press ▲, R, L, Down, Down, R, R, ▲.

BLACK CARS
During a game, press ●, ●, R, ▲, ▲, L, ■, ■.

WHITE CARS
During a game, press ✖, X, R, ●, ●, L, ▲, ▲.

CARS DRIVE ON WATER
During a game, press ●, ✖, Down, ●, ✖, Up, L, L.

PERFECT TRACTION
During a game, press L, Up, Left, R, ▲, ●, Down, ✖.

CHANGE BICYCLE TIRE SIZE
During a game, press ●, Right, ✖, Up, Right, ✖, L, ■.

AGGRESSIVE DRIVERS
During a game, press ■, ■, R, ✖, X, L, ●, ●.

ALL GREEN LIGHTS
During a game, press ▲, ▲, R, ■, ■, L, ✕, ✕.

DESTROY ALL CARS
During a game, press L, L, Left, L, L, Right, ✕, ■.

RAISE MEDIA ATTENTION
During a game, press L, Up, Right, R, ▲, ■, Down, X.

RAISE WANTED LEVEL
During a game, press L, R, ■, L, R, ▲, L, R.

NEVER WANTED
During a game, press L, L, ▲, R, R, ✕, ■, ●.

CHANGE OUTFIT
During a game, press L, L, Left, L, L, Right, ■, ▲.

BOBBLE HEAD WORLD
During a game, press Down, Down, Down, ●, ●, ✕, L, R.

PEOPLE ATTACK YOU
During a game, press L, L, R, L, L, L, R, Up, ▲.

PEOPLE FOLLOW YOU
During a game, press Down, Down, Down, ▲, ▲, ●, L, R.

PEOPLE HAVE WEAPONS
During a game, press R, R, L, R, R, R, L, Right, ●.

PEOPLE RIOT
During a game, press L, L, R, L, L, R, Left, ■.

SPAWN RHINO
During a game, press L, L, Left, L, L, Right, ▲, ●.

SPAWN TRASHMASTER
During a game, press ▲, ●, Down, ▲, ●, Up, L, L.

FASTER CLOCK
During a game, press L, L, Left, L, L, Right, ●, X.

FASTER GAMEPLAY
During a game, press R, R, L, R, R, L, Down, X.

SLOWER GAMEPLAY
During a game, press R, ▲, ✕, R, ■, ●, Left, Right.

ALL CHARACTERS, CARS, & ENTIRE CITY (MULTIPLAYER)
During a game, press Up (x3), ▲, ▲, ●, L, R.

43 CHARACTERS & 7 GANGS (MULTIPLAYER)
During a game, press Up (x3), ✕, ✕, ■, R, L.

28 CHARACTERS & 4 GANGS (MULTIPLAYER)
During a game, press Up (x3), ●, ●, ✕, L, R.

14 CHARACTERS & 2 GANGS (MULTIPLAYER)
During a game, press Up (x3), ■, ■, ▲, R, L.

CLEAR WEATHER
During a game, press Up, Down, ●, Up, Down, ■, L, R.

FOGGY WEATHER
During a game, press Up, Down, ▲, Up, Down, ✕, L, R.

OVERCAST WEATHER
During a game, press Up, Down, ✕, Up, Down, ▲, L, R.

RAINY WEATHER
During a game, press Up, Down, ■, Up, Down, ●, L, R.

SUNNY WEATHER
During a game, press L, L, ●, R, R, ■, ▲, X.

UPSIDE DOWN
During a game, press Down, Down, Down, ✕, X, ■, R, L.

UPSIDE UP
During a game, press ✕, ✕, ✕, Down, Down, Right, L, R.

RIGHT SIDE UP
During a game, press ▲, ▲, ▲, Up, Up, Right, L, R.

COMMIT SUICIDE
During a game, press L, Down, Left, R, ✕, ●, Up, ▲.

GAME CREDITS
During a game, press L, R, L, R, Up, Down, L, R.

GRAND THEFT AUTO: VICE CITY STORIES

Enter the following cheats during a game.

$250000
Press Up, Down, Left, Right, ✕, ✕, L, R.

ARMOR
Press Up, Down, Left, Right, ●, ●, L, R.

HEALTH
Press Up, Down, Left, Right, ●, ●, L, R.

NEVER WANTED
Press Up, Right, ▲, ▲, Down, Left, ●, ●.

LOWER WANTED LEVEL
Press Up, Right, ▲, ▲, Down, Left, ✕, ✕.

RAISE WANTED LEVEL
Press Up, Right, ●, ●, Down, Left, ●, ●.

WEAPON SET 1
Press Left, Right, ✕, Up, Down, ●, Left, Right.

WEAPON SET 2
Press Left, Right, ●, Up, Down, ▲, Left, Right.

WEAPON SET 3
Press Left, Right, ▲, Up, Down, ●, Left, Right.

SPAWN RHINO
Press Up, L, Down, R, Left, L, Right, R.

SPAWN TRASHMASTER
Press Down, Up, Right, ▲, L, ▲, L, ▲.

BLACK CARS
Press L, R, L, R, Left, ●, Up, ✕.

CHROME CARS
Press Right, Up, Left, Down, ▲, ▲, L, R.

CARS AVOID YOU
Press Up, Up, Right, Left, ▲, ●, ●, ●.

DESTROY ALL CARS
Press L, R, R, Left, Right, ●, Down, R.

GUYS FOLLOW YOU
Press Right, L, Down, L, ●, Up, L, ●.

PERFECT TRACTION
Press Down, Left, Up, L, R, ▲, ●, ✕. Press Down to jump into a car.

PEDESTRIAN GETS INTO YOUR VEHICLE
Press Down, Up, Right, L, L, ●, Up, L.

PEDESTRIANS ATTACK YOU
Press Down, ▲, Up, ✕, L, R, L, R.

PEDESTRIANS HAVE WEAPONS
Press Up, L, Down, R, Left, ●, Right, ▲.

PEDESTRIANS RIOT
Press R, L, L, Down, Left, ⬤, Down, L.

SUICIDE
Press Right, Right, ⬤, ⬤, L, R, Down, ❌.

UPSIDE DOWN 1
Press ⬤, ⬤, ⬤, L, L, R, Left, Right.

UPSIDE DOWN 2
Press Left, Left, Left, R, R, L, Right, Left.

FASTER CLOCK
Press R, L, L, Down, Up, ❌, Down, L.

FASTER GAMEPLAY
Press Left, Left, R, R, Up, ⬤, Down, ❌.

SLOWER GAMEPLAY
Press Left, Left, ⬤, ⬤, Down, Up, ⬤, ❌.

CLEAR WEATHER
Press Left, Down, R, L, Right, Up, Left, ❌.

FOGGY WEATHER
Press Left, Down, ⬤, ❌, Right, Up, Left, L.

OVERCAST WEATHER
Press Left, Down, L, R, Right, Up, Left, ⬤.

RAINY WEATHER
Press Left, Down, L, R, Right, Up, Left, ⬤.

SUNNY WEATHER
Press Left, Down, R, L, Right, Up, Left, ⬤.

GRETZKY NHL

ALL UNLOCKABLES AVAILABLE
At the Gretzky Challenge Unlockables screen, press START, and enter SHOENLOC.

ONE GRETZKY CHALLENGE POINT
At the Gretzky Challenge Unlockables screen, press START, and enter CANADIAN DOLLAR.

BIG BOARDS CHECKING
At the Gretzky Challenge Unlockables
screen, press START, and enter ALL ABOARD.
You can turn this option on by selecting
Unlocked Options when starting a game.

NO SKATER FATIGUE
At the Gretzky Challenge Unlockables
screen, press START, and enter CAFFEINATED. You can turn this option on by selecting Unlocked
Options when starting a game.

PERFECT AIM MODE
At the Gretzky Challenge Unlockables screen, press START, and enter THREAD THE NEEDLE. You
can turn this option on by selecting Unlocked Options when starting a game.

PERFECT SLAP SHOTS
At the Gretzky Challenge Unlockables screen, press START, and enter SLAP THAT PUCK. You can
turn this option on by selecting Unlocked Options when starting a game.

ROBOENFORCER MODEL-44
At the Gretzky Challenge Unlockables screen, press START, and enter ROBO CHECKS.

WAYNE GRETZKY: 1979 EDMONTON OILERS

At the Gretzky Challenge Unlockables screen, press START, and enter UNSTOPPABLE GREATNESS.

WAYNE GRETZKY: 1987 TEAM CANADA

At the Gretzky Challenge Unlockables screen, press START, and enter GLORY DAZE.

WAYNE GRETZKY: 1994 LOS ANGELES KINGS

At the Gretzky Challenge Unlockables screen, press START, and enter WEST COAST WAYNE.

WAYNE GRETZKY: 1999 NEW YORK RANGERS

At the Gretzky Challenge Unlockables screen, press START, and enter A LEGEND ON ICE.

ALTERNATE ANAHEIM MIGHTY DUCKS UNIFORM

At the Gretzky Challenge Unlockables screen, press START, and enter FLYING VEE.

ALTERNATE ATLANTA THRASHERS UNIFORM

At the Gretzky Challenge Unlockables screen, press START, and enter THRASHED TO THE MAX.

ALTERNATE BOSTON BRUINS UNIFORM

At the Gretzky Challenge Unlockables screen, press START, and enter NOMAR STILL RULES.

ALTERNATE BUFFALO SABERS UNIFORM

At the Gretzky Challenge Unlockables screen, press START, and enter IN THE SNOW BELT.

ALTERNATE CALGARY FLAMES UNIFORM

At the Gretzky Challenge Unlockables screen, press START, and enter THREE ALARM BLAZE.

ALTERNATE CHICAGO BLACKHAWKS UNIFORM

At the Gretzky Challenge Unlockables screen, press START, and enter WINDY CITY.

ALTERNATE COLORADO AVALANCHE UNIFORM

At the Gretzky Challenge Unlockables screen, press START, and enter SNOW DRIFTS.

ALTERNATE COLUMBUS BLUE JACKETS UNIFORM

At the Gretzky Challenge Unlockables screen, press START, and enter BLUE SHOES.

ALTERNATE DALLAS STARS UNIFORM

At the Gretzky Challenge Unlockables screen, press START, and enter HOCKEY IN TEXAS.

ALTERNATE EDMONTON OILERS UNIFORM

At the Gretzky Challenge Unlockables screen, press START, and enter PUMPIN OIL.

ALTERNATE FLORIDA PANTHERS UNIFORM

At the Gretzky Challenge Unlockables screen, press START, and enter SOUTH BEACH.

ALTERNATE LOS ANGELES KINGS UNIFORM

At the Gretzky Challenge Unlockables screen, press START, and enter IT IS GOOD TO BE THE KING.

ALTERNATE MINNESOTA WILD UNIFORM

At the Gretzky Challenge Unlockables screen, press START, and enter COLD AS HECK.

ALTERNATE NASHVILLE PREDATORS UNIFORM

At the Gretzky Challenge Unlockables screen, press START, and enter ALIEN VS NASHVILLE.

ALTERNATE NEW YORK ISLANDERS UNIFORM

At the Gretzky Challenge Unlockables screen, press START, and enter LAWNG ISLAND.

ALTERNATE NEW YORK RANGERS UNIFORM

At the Gretzky Challenge Unlockables screen, press START, and enter GREAT WHITE WAY.

ALTERNATE OTTAWA SENATORS UNIFORM

At the Gretzky Challenge Unlockables screen, press START, and enter MAJORITY RULE.

ALTERNATE PHILADELPHIA FLYERS UNIFORM
At the Gretzky Challenge Unlockables screen, press START, and enter FANATICAL.

ALTERNATE SAN JOSE SHARKS UNIFORM
At the Gretzky Challenge Unlockables screen, press START, and enter GET A BIGGER BOAT.

ALTERNATE TORONTO MAPLE LEAFS UNIFORM
At the Gretzky Challenge Unlockables screen, press START, and enter HEY TERRANCE.

ALTERNATE VANCOUVER CANUCKS UNIFORM
At the Gretzky Challenge Unlockables screen, press START, and enter WEST COAST EH.

1910 MONTREAL CANADIENS UNIFORM
At the Gretzky Challenge Unlockables screen, press START, and enter THE HABS.

1924 MONTREAL CANADIENS UNIFORM
At the Gretzky Challenge Unlockables screen, press START, and enter LE HABITANT.

1927 DETROIT RED WINGS UNIFORM
At the Gretzky Challenge Unlockables screen, press START, and enter BEEP BEEP.

1928 BOSTON BRUINS UNIFORM
At the Gretzky Challenge Unlockables screen, press START, and enter WICKED HAAAAAHD.

1929 OTTAWA SENATORS UNIFORM
At the Gretzky Challenge Unlockables screen, press START, and enter THE SENANATOR.

1930 TORONTO MAPLE LEAFS UNIFORM
At the Gretzky Challenge Unlockables screen, press START, and enter NORTH OF THE BORDER.

1967 LOS ANGELES KINGS AWAY UNIFORM
At the Gretzky Challenge Unlockables screen, press START, and enter VOLLEY DOLLY.

1967 PHILADELPHIA FLYERS AWAY UNIFORM
At the Gretzky Challenge Unlockables screen, press START, and enter CHEESESTEAK.

1967 PITTSBURGH PENGUINS AWAY UNIFORM
At the Gretzky Challenge Unlockables screen, press START, and enter POPPIN TALK.

1970 MINNESOTA NORTH STARS UNIFORM
At the Gretzky Challenge Unlockables screen, press START, and enter TWIN STARS.

1975 KANSAS CITY SCOUTS UNIFORM
At the Gretzky Challenge Unlockables screen, press START, and enter YOU LITTLE DEVIL.

1976 NEW YORK RANGERS AWAY UNIFORM
At the Gretzky Challenge Unlockables screen, press START, and enter NEW YORK NEW YORK.

1977 CALGARY FLAMES AWAY UNIFORM
At the Gretzky Challenge Unlockables screen, press START, and enter FLAME ON.

1977 COLORADO ROCKIES UNIFORM
At the Gretzky Challenge Unlockables screen, press START, and enter DEVIL MADE ME DO IT.

1977 VANCOUVER CANUCKS HOME UNIFORM
At the Gretzky Challenge Unlockables screen, press START, and enter GREAT WHITE NORTH.

1977 WASHINGTON CAPITALS AWAY UNIFORM
At the Gretzky Challenge Unlockables screen, press START, and enter CONGRESSIONAL WISDOM.

1978 NEW YORK ISLANDERS AWAY UNIFORM
At the Gretzky Challenge Unlockables screen, press START, and enter ORDWAY MADE ME DO IT.

1979 EDMONTON OILERS AWAY UNIFORM
At the Gretzky Challenge Unlockables screen, press START, and enter A SCARY SIGHT TO THE HOME CROWD.

1979 EDMONTON OILERS HOME UNIFORM
At the Gretzky Challenge Unlockables screen, press START, and enter THREADS OF CHAMPS.

1979 ST. LOUIS BLUES AWAY UNIFORM
At the Gretzky Challenge Unlockables screen, press START, and enter A BLUE NOTE.

1979 ST. LOUIS BLUES HOME UNIFORM
At the Gretzky Challenge Unlockables screen, press START, and enter MARDI GRAS.

1980 QUEBEC NORDIQUES UNIFORM
At the Gretzky Challenge Unlockables screen, press START, and enter FRENCH FOR CANADIAN.

1983 EDMONTON OILERS AWAY UNIFORM
At the Gretzky Challenge Unlockables screen, press START, and enter ALL HAIL WAYNE.

1988 PITTSBURGH PENGUINS AWAY UNIFORM
At the Gretzky Challenge Unlockables screen, press START, and enter STEEL TOWN.

1989 LOS ANGELES KINGS AWAY UNIFORM
At the Gretzky Challenge Unlockables screen, press START, and enter KING GRETZKY.

1989 LOS ANGELES KINGS HOME UNIFORM
At the Gretzky Challenge Unlockables screen, press START, and enter KING WAYNE.

1990 WINNIPEG JETS AWAY UNIFORM
At the Gretzky Challenge Unlockables screen, press START, and enter PORTAGE AND MAIN.

1990 WINNIPEG JETS HOME UNIFORM
At the Gretzky Challenge Unlockables screen, press START, and enter MIDDLE OF CANADA.

1993 SAN JOSE SHARKS AWAY UNIFORM
At the Gretzky Challenge Unlockables screen, press START, and enter SHARK BAIT.

1995 ST. LOUIS BLUES AWAY UNIFORM
At the Gretzky Challenge Unlockables screen, press START, and enter VINTAGE BLUES.

1999 NEW YORK RANGERS HOME UNIFORM
At the Gretzky Challenge Unlockables screen, press START, and enter UPPER WEST SIDE.

GRETZKY NHL '06

UNLOCK EVERYTHING
Select Gretzky Challenge from the Features menu. Choose Unlockables, press Start and enter CONHEOSL.

1 GRETZKY POINT
Select Gretzky Challenge from the Features menu. Choose Unlockables, press Start and enter CULKY NETC.

ALL ALTERNATE UNIFORMS
Select Gretzky Challenge from the Features menu. Choose Unlockables, press Start and enter NNIADOUAMFM.

ALL VINTAGE UNIFORMS
Select Gretzky Challenge from the Features menu. Choose Unlockables, press Start and enter DLEONG ARE.

ALL WAYNE GRETZKYS
Select Gretzky Challenge from the Features menu. Choose Unlockables, press Start and enter TEH ESATGRTE NOES.

BIG BOARDS CHECKING
Select Gretzky Challenge from the Features menu. Choose Unlockables, press Start and enter LAL ABRAOD.

NO SKATER FATIGUE
Select Gretzky Challenge from the Features menu. Choose Unlockables, press Start and enter EFDTAFEACIN.

PERFECT AIM MODE
Select Gretzky Challenge from the Features menu. Choose Unlockables, press Start and enter TADHRE TEH EDNELE.

PERFECT SLAP SHOTS
Select Gretzky Challenge from the Features menu. Choose Unlockables, press Start and enter SAPL TATH CUKP.

BIGGER PLAYERS
Select Gretzky Challenge from the Features menu. Choose Unlockables, press Start and enter ARGLE NI RAGECH.

SMALLER PLAYERS
Select Gretzky Challenge from the Features menu. Choose Unlockables, press Start and enter IGHTMY UOSEM.

ROBOENFORCER MODEL-44
Select Gretzky Challenge from the Features menu. Choose Unlockables, press Start and enter OBOR SKHECC.

STANLEY CUP CHAMPIONSHIP VIDEO
Select Gretzky Challenge from the Features menu. Choose Unlockables, press Start and enter VINIOS FO LYRGO.

HOT SHOTS GOLF: OPEN TEE

UNLOCK EVERYTHING
Start a new game with the name 5TNEPO.

EASY DIFFICULTY (CHALLENGE MODE)
Lose two matches or tournaments in a row. You can change this in the Options.

AUTUMN PAGODA COURSE
Reach Beginner level in Challenge Mode.

GOLDEN DESERT COURSE
Reach Senior level in Challenge Mode.

OLIVE COAST COURSE
Reach Mid-Rank level in Challenge Mode.

5TH LOYALTY HEART
Defeat a character with a Super Win to get the 5th Loyalty Heart.

MANUAL REPLAY MODE
Reach Senior level in Challenge Mode.

JUICED: ELIMINATOR

ALL CARS AND TRACKS IN ARCADE MODE
Select Cheats from the Extras menu and enter PIES.

KINGDOM OF PARADISE

MOUNTAIN WIZARD SWORD
Select Download and get connected. Enter rkjulvj as a password and download the item.

SEIMA ANKLET

Select Download and get connected. Enter ydkvcex as a password and download the item.

SEIMA BRACELET

Select Download and get connected. Enter jticgek as a password and download the item.

SEIMA EAR ORNAMENT

Select Download and get connected. Enter lfiynvg as a password and download the item.

SEIMA HAIR ORNAMENT

Select Download and get connected. Enter otkciet as a password and download the item.

SEIMA NECKLACE

Select Download and get connected. Enter aietmaw as a password and download the item.

SEIMA RING

Select Download and get connected. Enter xktmvut as a password and download the item.

BYAKKO FREE STYLE & BYAKKO 6TH DAN, MU KATA

Select Download and get connected. Enter ptiuquc as a password and download the item.

GENBU FREE STYLE & GENBU 6TH DAN, MU KATA

Select Download and get connected. Enter zoeuiss as a password and download the item.

KIRIN FREE STYLE & KIRIN 6TH DAN, MU KATA

Select Download and get connected. Enter qucmtkb as a password and download the item.

SEIRYU FREE STYLE & SEIRYU 6TH DAN, MU KATA

Select Download and get connected. Enter kakeiti as a password and download the item.

SUZAKU FREE STYLE & SUZAKU 6TH DAN, MU KATA

Select Download and get connected. Enter myuicei as a password and download the item.

LEGO STAR WARS II: THE ORIGINAL TRILOGY

BEACH TROOPER

At Mos Eisley Canteena, select Enter Code and enter UCK868. You still need to select Characters and purchase this character for 20,000 studs.

BEN KENOBI (GHOST)

At Mos Eisley Canteena, select Enter Code and enter BEN917. You still need to select Characters and purchase this character for 1,100,000 studs.

BESPIN GUARD

At Mos Eisley Canteena, select Enter Code and enter VHY832. You still need to select Characters and purchase this character for 15,000 studs.

BIB FORTUNA

At Mos Eisley Canteena, select Enter Code and enter WTY721. You still need to select Characters and purchase this character for 16,000 studs.

BOBA FETT

At Mos Eisley Canteena, select Enter Code and enter HLP221. You still need to select Characters and purchase this character for 175,000 studs.

DEATH STAR TROOPER

At Mos Eisley Canteena, select Enter Code and enter BNC332. You still need to select Characters and purchase this character for 19,000 studs.

EWOK

At Mos Eisley Canteena, select Enter Code and enter TTT289. You still need to select Characters and purchase this character for 34,000 studs.

GAMORREAN GUARD

At Mos Eisley Canteena, select Enter Code and enter YZF999. You still need to select Characters and purchase this character for 40,000 studs.

GONK DROID

At Mos Eisley Canteena, select Enter Code and enter NFX582. You still need to select Characters and purchase this character for 1,550 studs.

GRAND MOFF TARKIN

At Mos Eisley Canteena, select Enter Code and enter SMG219. You still need to select Characters and purchase this character for 38,000 studs.

GREEDO

At Mos Eisley Canteena, select Enter Code and enter NAH118. You still need to select Characters and purchase this character for 60,000 studs.

HAN SOLO (HOOD)

At Mos Eisley Canteena, select Enter Code and enter YWM840. You still need to select Characters and purchase this character for 20,000 studs.

IG-88

At Mos Eisley Canteena, select Enter Code and enter NXL973. You still need to select Characters and purchase this character for 30,000 studs.

IMPERIAL GUARD

At Mos Eisley Canteena, select Enter Code and enter MMM111. You still need to select Characters and purchase this character for 45,000 studs.

IMPERIAL OFFICER

At Mos Eisley Canteena, select Enter Code and enter BBV889. You still need to select Characters and purchase this character for 28,000 studs.

IMPERIAL SHUTTLE PILOT

At Mos Eisley Canteena, select Enter Code and enter VAP664. You still need to select Characters and purchase this character for 29,000 studs.

IMPERIAL SPY

At Mos Eisley Canteena, select Enter Code and enter CVT125. You still need to select Characters and purchase this character for 13,500 studs.

JAWA

At Mos Eisley Canteena, select Enter Code and enter JAW499. You still need to select Characters and purchase this character for 24,000 studs.

LOBOT

At Mos Eisley Canteena, select Enter Code and enter UUB319. You still need to select Characters and purchase this character for 11,000 studs.

PALACE GUARD

At Mos Eisley Canteena, select Enter Code and enter SGE549. You still need to select Characters and purchase this character for 14,000 studs.

REBEL PILOT

At Mos Eisley Canteena, select Enter Code and enter CYG336. You still need to select Characters and purchase this character for 15,000 studs.

REBEL TROOPER (HOTH)

At Mos Eisley Canteena, select Enter Code and enter EKU849. You still need to select Characters and purchase this character for 16,000 studs.

SANDTROOPER

At Mos Eisley Canteena, select Enter Code and enter YDV451. You still need to select Characters and purchase this character for 14,000 studs.

SKIFF GUARD

At Mos Eisley Canteena, select Enter Code and enter GBU888. You still need to select Characters and purchase this character for 12,000 studs.

SNOWTROOPER
At Mos Eisley Canteena, select Enter Code and enter NYU989. You still need to select Characters and purchase this character for 16,000 studs.

STORMTROOPER
At Mos Eisley Canteena, select Enter Code and enter PTR345. You still need to select Characters and purchase this character for 10,000 studs.

THE EMPEROR
At Mos Eisley Canteena, select Enter Code and enter HHY382. You still need to select Characters and purchase this character for 275,000 studs.

TIE FIGHTER
At Mos Eisley Canteena, select Enter Code and enter HDY739. You still need to select Characters and purchase this item for 60,000 studs.

TIE FIGHTER PILOT
At Mos Eisley Canteena, select Enter Code and enter NNZ316. You still need to select Characters and purchase this character for 21,000 studs.

TIE INTERCEPTOR
At Mos Eisley Canteena, select Enter Code and enter QYA828. You still need to select Characters and purchase this item for 40,000 studs.

TUSKEN RAIDER
At Mos Eisley Canteena, select Enter Code and enter PEJ821. You still need to select Characters and purchase this character for 23,000 studs.

UGNAUGHT
At Mos Eisley Canteena, select Enter Code and enter UGN694. You still need to select Characters and purchase this character for 36,000 studs.

MAJOR LEAGUE BASEBALL 2K6

UNLOCK EVERYTHING
Select Enter Cheat Code from the My 2K6 menu and enter Derek Jeter. This does not unlock Topps 2K Stars.

TOPPS 2K STARS
Select Enter Cheat Code from the My 2K6 menu and enter Dream Team.

SUPER WALL CLIMB
Select Enter Cheat Code from the My 2K6 menu and enter Last Chance. Enable the cheats by selecting My Cheats or selecting Cheat Codes from the Options screen in-game.

SUPER PITCHES
Select Enter Cheat Code from the My 2K6 menu and enter Unhittable. Enable the cheats by selecting My Cheats or selecting Cheat Codes from the Options screen in-game.

ROCKET ARMS
Select Enter Cheat Code from the My 2K6 menu and enter Gotcha. Enable the cheats by selecting My Cheats or selecting Cheat Codes from the Options screen in-game.

BOUNCY BALL
Select Enter Cheat Code from the My 2K6 menu and enter Crazy Hops. Enable the cheats by selecting My Cheats or selecting Cheat Codes from the Options screen in-game.

MARVEL NEMESIS: RISE OF THE IMPERFECTS

BRIGADE
Finish story mode with the Thing.

IRON MAN
Finish story mode with Johnny Ohm.

SPIDER-MAN
Finish story mode with Venom.

VENOM
Finish story mode with Iron Man.

MARVEL ULTIMATE ALLIANCE

UNLOCK ALL SKINS
At the Team Menu, press Up, Down, Left, Right, Left, Right, Start.

UNLOCK ALL HERO POWERS
At the Team Menu, press Left, Right, Up, Down, Up, Down, Start.

ALL HEROES TO LEVEL 99
At the Team Menu, press Up, Left, Up, Left, Down, Right, Down, Right, Start.

UNLOCK ALL HEROES
At the Team Menu, press Up, Up, Down, Down, Left, Left, Left, Start.

UNLOCK DAREDEVIL
At the Team Menu, press Left, Left, Right, Right, Up, Down, Up, Down, Start.

UNLOCK SILVER SURFER
At the Team Menu, press Down, Left, Left, Up, Right, Up, Down, Left, Start.

GOD MODE
During gameplay, press Up, Down, Up, Down, Up, Left, Down, Right, Start.

TOUCH OF DEATH
During gameplay, press Left, Right, Down, Down, Right, Left, Start.

SUPER SPEED
During gameplay, press Up, Left, Up, Right, Down, Right, Start.

FILL MOMENTUM
During gameplay, press Left, Right, Right, Left, Up, Down, Down, Up, Start.

UNLOCK ALL COMICS
At the Review menu, press Left, Right, Right, Left, Up, Up, Right, Start.

UNLOCK ALL CONCEPT ART
At the Review menu, press Down, Down, Down, Right, Right, Left, Down, Start.

UNLOCK ALL CINEMATICS
At the Review menu, press Up, Left, Left, Up, Right, Right, Up, Start.

UNLOCK ALL LOAD SCREENS
At the Review menu, press Up, Down, Right, Left, Up, Up Down, Start.

UNLOCK ALL COURSES
At the Comic Missions menu, press Up, Right, Left, Down, Up, Right, Left, Down, Start.

MEDIEVIL: RESURRECTION

INVINCIBILITY & ALL WEAPONS
Pause the game, hold R and press Down, Up, ●, ▲, ●, ●, Down, Up, ●, ▲. Pause the game to access the Cheat menu.

METAL GEAR ACID

CARD NO.173—VIPER
Enter Viper as a password.

CARD NO.178—MIKA SLAYTON
Enter Mika as a password.

CARD NO.182—KAREN HOJO
Enter Karen as a password.

CARD NO.184—JEHUTY
Enter Jehuty as a password.

CARD NO.199—XM8
Enter Xmeight as a password.

CARD NO.200—YUKA KOSAKA
Enter Kobe as a password.

CARD NO.201—ASAKI YOSHIDA
Enter Umeda as a password.

CARD NO.203—ERI SHIBUYA
Enter Roppongi as a password.

METAL GEAR ACID 2

CARD NO. 046—STRAND
Enter nojiri as a password.

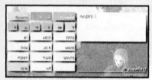

CARD NO. 099—GIJIN-SAN
Enter shinta as a password.

CARD NO. 119—REACTION BLOCK
Enter konami as a password.

CARD NO. 161—VIPER
Enter viper as a password.

CARD NO. 166—MIKA SLAYTON
Enter mika as a password.

CARD NO. 170—KAREN HOJO
Enter karen as a password.

CARD NO. 172—JEHUTY
Enter jehuty as a password.

CARD NO. 187—XM8
Enter xmeight as a password.

CARD NO. 188—MR. SIGINT
Enter signt as a password.

CARD NO. 197 SEA HARRIER
Enter shrrr as a password.

CARD NO. 203—DECOY OCTOPUS
Enter dcy as a password.

CARD NO. 212—ROGER MCCOY
Enter mccy as a password.

CARD NO. 281—REIKO HINOMOTO
Enter hnmt as a password.

CARD NO. 285—AYUMI KINOSHITA
Enter aym as a password.

CARD NO. 286—MEGURU ISHII
Enter mgr as a password.

CARD NO. 287—NATSUME SANO
Enter ntm as a password.

CARD NO. 288—MGS4
Enter nextgen as a password.

CARD NO. 289—EMMA'S PARROT
Enter ginormousj as a password.

CARD NO. 290—BANANA SKIN
Enter ronaldsiu as a password.

CARD NO. 292—POSSESSED ARM
Enter thespaniard as a password.

CARD NO. 293—SOLID EYE
Enter tobidacid as a password.

CARD NO. 294—SOLID SNAKE (MGS4)
Enter snake as a password.

CARD NO. 295—OTACON (MGS4)
Enter otacon as a password.

CARD NO. 296—GEKKO
Enter gekko as a password.

CARD NO. 297—METAL GEAR MK. II (MGS4)
Enter mk2 as a password.

CARD NO. 298—NO SMOKING
Enter smoking as a password.

MVP BASEBALL

ALL REWARDS

Select My MVP and create a player with the name Dan Carter.

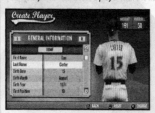 

MX VS. ATV UNLEASHED: ON THE EDGE

UNLOCK EVERYTHING

Select Cheat Codes from the Options screen and enter TOOLAZY.

1,000,000 POINTS

Select Cheat Codes from the Options screen and enter BROKEASAJOKE.

PRO PHYSICS

Select Cheat Codes from the Options screen and enter IAMTOOGOOD.

ALL GEAR

Select Cheat Codes from the Options screen and enter WARDROBE.

ALL BIKES

Select Cheat Codes from the Options screen and enter BRAPP.

50CC BIKE CLASS

Select Cheat Codes from the Options screen and enter MINIMOTO.

500CC BIKE CLASS

Select Cheat Codes from the Options screen and enter BIGBORE.

ALL ATVS

Select Cheat Codes from the Options screen and enter COUCHES.

ALL MACHINES

Select Cheat Codes from the Options screen and enter LEADFOOT.

ALL FREESTYLE TRACKS

Select Cheat Codes from the Options screen and enter HUCKIT.

ALL NATIONAL TRACKS

Select Cheat Codes from the Options screen and enter GOOUTSIDE.

ALL OPEN CLASS TRACKS

Select Cheat Codes from the Options screen and enter NOTMOTO.

ALL SUPERCROSS TRACKS

Select Cheat Codes from the Options screen and enter GOINSIDE.

ALL TRACKS

Select Cheat Codes from the Options screen and enter PITPASS.

NASCAR

ALL CHASE PLATES

Go to Fight to the Top mode. Next, edit the driver's first and last name so that it says ItsAll ForMe. Note that the code is case-sensitive.

$10,000,000

In Fight to the Top mode, enter your driver's name as GiveMe More.

10,000,000 FANS

In Fight to the Top mode, enter your driver's name as AllBow ToMe.

ALL CHASE PLATES

In Fight to the Top mode, enter your driver's name as ItsAll ForMe.

OLD SPICE TRACKS AND CARS

In Fight to the Top mode, enter your driver's name as KeepCool SmellGreat.

NBA BALLERS: REBOUND

VERSUS SCREEN CHEATS

You must enter the following codes at the Vs screen. The ● button corresponds to the first number in the code, the ▲ is the second number, and the ● button corresponds to the last number. Press the D-pad in any direction to enter the code. The name of the code will appear when entered correctly. Some of the codes will give you the wrong code name when entered.

EFFECT	CODE
Big Head	1 3 4
Pygmy	4 2 5
Alternate Gear	1 2 3
Show Shot Percentage	0 1 2
Expanded Move Set	5 1 2
Super Push	3 1 5
Super Block Ability	1 2 4
Great Handles	3 3 2
Unlimited Juice	7 6 3

EFFECT	CODE
Super Steals	2 1 5
Perfect Free Throws	3 2 7
Better Free Throws	3 1 7
Speedy Players	2 1 3
Alley-Oop Ability	7 2 5
Back-In Ability	1 2 2
Hotspot Ability	6 2 7
Pass 2 Friend Ability	5 3 6
Put Back Ability	3 1 3
Stunt Ability	3 7 4
2x Juice Replenish	4 3 1
Legal Goal Tending	7 5 6
Play As Afro Man	5 1 7
Play As Agent	5 5 7
Play As Business-A	5 3 7
Play As Business-B	5 2 7
Play As Coach	5 6 7
Play As Secretary	5 4 7
Super Back-Ins	2 3 5
Half House	3 6 7
Random Moves	3 0 0
Tournament Mode	0 1 1

PHRASE-OLOGY CODES

Select Phrase-ology from the Inside Stuff option and enter the following to unlock that bonus.

BONUS	PHRASE
All Players and Cinemas	NBA BALLERS TRUE PLAYA
Special Shoe #2	COLD STREAK
Special Shoe #3	LOST YA SHOES

CRIBS

Select Phrase-ology from the Inside Stuff option and enter the following to unlock player cribs.

CRIB	PHRASE
Allen Iverson's Recording Studio	THE ANSWER
Karl Malone's Devonshire Estate	ICE HOUSE
Kobe Bryant's Italian Estate	EURO CRIB
Ben Gordon's Yacht	NICE YACHT
Yao Ming's Childhood Grade School	PREP SCHOOL

NBA LIVE 06

1960S ALL-STAR TEAM
Earn all golds in Tier 1 of Superstar Challenge.

1970S ALL-STAR TEAM
Earn all golds in Tier 2 of Superstar Challenge.

1980S ALL-STAR TEAM
Earn all golds in Tier 3 of Superstar Challenge.

1990S ALL-STAR TEAM
Earn all golds in Tier 4 of Superstar Challenge.

ATLANTIC DIVISION VINTAGE JERSEYS
Earn silver in Tier 1 of Superstar Challenge.

NORTHWEST DIVISION VINTAGE JERSEYS
Earn silver in Tier 2 of Superstar Challenge.

NBA STREET SHOWDOWN

UNLIMITED TURBO
During a game, hold L + R and enter ⏺, ⏺, ▲, ▲.

NEOPETS PETPET ADVENTURE: THE WAND OF WISHING

START GAME WITH 5 CHOCOLATE TREATS
Enter treat4u as your Petpet's name. You can then rename your character. The chocolate treats are shaped according to the character you chose.

NFL STREET 2 UNLEASHED

Select Cheats and Codes from the Options menu and enter the following codes.

AFC EAST ALL-STARS
Enter EAASFSCT as a code.

AFC NORTH ALL-STARS
Enter NAOFRCTH as a code.

AFC SOUTH ALL-STARS
Enter SAOFUCTH as a code.

AFC WEST ALL-STARS
Enter WAEFSCT as a code.

NFC EAST ALL-STARS
Enter NNOFRCTH as a code.

NFC NORTH ALL-STARS
Enter NNAS66784 as a code.

NFC SOUTH ALL-STARS
Enter SNOFUCTH as a code.

NFC WEST ALL-STARS
Enter ENASFSCT as a code.

REEBOK TEAM
Enter Reebok as a code.

TEAM XZIBIT
Enter TeamXzibit as a code.

EA FIELD
Enter EAField as a code.

GRIDIRON FIELD
Enter GRIDIRONPRK as a code.

HUGE PLAYERS
Enter BIGsmash as a code.

BIG BALL
Enter BIGPig as a code.

MAX CATCH IN QUICK GAME
Enter MagnetHands as a code.

MAX SPEED IN QUICK GAME
Enter GottaBdshoes as a code.

MAX TACKLING IN QUICK GAME
Enter BlastTackle as a code.

DIFFICULT TO JUMP
Enter CementShoes as a code.

10X GAMEBREAKER
Enter XxGBCraZ as a code.

1X GAMEBREAKER
Enter IIxGBCraZ as a code.

NO FUMBLE MODE IN QUICK GAME
Enter GlueHands as a code.

FUMBLE MODE IN QUICK GAME
Enter GreasedPig as a code.

UNLIMITED TURBO IN QUICK GAME
Enter NozBoost as a code.

NO FIRST DOWNS
Enter NoChains as a code.

OUTRUN 2006: COAST 2 COAST

100% COMPLETE/UNLOCK EVERYTHING
Edit your license and change the name to ENTIRETY. Select Done, then back out of all menus.

1,000,000 OUTRUN MILES
Edit your license and change the name to MILESANDMILES. Select Done, then back out of all menus.

PAC-MAN WORLD 3

ALL LEVELS AND MAZES
At the Main menu, press Left, Right, Left, Right, ●, Up.

PINBALL HALL OF FAME

CUSTOM BALLS OPTION
Enter CKF as a code.

TILT OPTION
Enter BZZ as a code.

PAYOUT MODE
Enter WGR as a code.

ACES HIGH IN FREEPLAY
Enter UNO as a code.

CENTRAL PARK IN FREEPLAY
Enter NYC as a code.

LOVE MACHINE IN FREEPLAY
Enter HOT as a code.

PLAYBOY TABLE IN FREEPLAY
Enter HEF as a code.

STRIKES 'N SPARES IN FREEPLAY
Enter PBA as a code.

TEE'D OFF IN FREEPLAY
Enter PGA as a code.

XOLTEN IN FREEPLAY
Enter BIG as a code.

PIRATES OF THE CARIBBEAN: DEAD MAN'S CHEST

GOD MODE
During a game, press ▲, ●, ●, ▲, ▲, ■, ✕, ✕.

FULL HEALTH
During a game, press ▲, ●, ▲, ●, ▲, ●, ●, ✕.

UNLIMITED POWER MOVES
During a game, press ▲, ▲, ▲, ■, ■, ✕, ●, ●.

1-SHOT KILL
During a game, press ▲, ●, ●, ▲, ▲, ■, ■, ■.

ALL TREASURE LEVELS
During a game, press ●, ●, ▲, ▲, ▲, ▲, ✕, ✕.

KRAKEN BATTLE
During a game, press ●, ●, ▲, ▲, ▲, ▲, ■, ■.

THE SIMS 2

PERK CHEAT
At the Buy Perks screen, hold L + R + ■. Buy the Cheat Perk to get some money, skills, and more.

SPIDER-MAN 2

LEVEL WARP
Select Specials from the Options menu. Choose Cheats and enter WARPULON.

ALL MOVES
Select Specials from the Options menu. Choose Cheats and enter MYHERO.

INFINITE HEALTH
Select Specials from the Options menu. Choose Cheats and enter NERGETS.

INFINITE WEBBING
Select Specials from the Options menu. Choose Cheats and enter FILLMEUP.

ENEMIES BIG HEADS AND FEET
Select Specials from the Options menu. Choose Cheats and enter BAHLOONIE.

SPIDER-MAN BIG HEAD AND FEET
Select Specials from the Options menu. Choose Cheats and enter HEAVYHEAD.

TINY SPIDER-MAN
Select Specials from the Options menu. Choose Cheats and enter SPIDEYMAN.

MOVIE VIEWER
Select Specials from the Options menu. Choose Cheats and enter POPPYCORN.

STORYBOARD VIEWER
Select Specials from the Options menu. Choose Cheats and enter FRZFRAME.

PRODUCTION ART
Select Specials from the Options menu. Choose Cheats and enter SHUTT.

STAR WARS: BATTLEFRONT II

INFINITE AMMO
Pause the game and press Up, Down, Left, Down, Down, Left, Down, Down, Left, Down, Down, Down Left, Right.

INVINCIBILITY
Pause the game and press Up, Up, Up, Left, Down, Down, Down, Left, Up, Up, Up, Left, Right.

TIGER WOODS PGA TOUR

EMERALD DRAGON
Earn $1,000,000.

GREEK ISLES
Earn $1,500,000.

PARADISE COVER
Earn $2,000,000.

EA SPORTS FAVORITES
Earn $5,000,000

MEAN8TEEN
Earn $10,000,000.

FANTASY SPECIALS
Earn $15,000,000.

THE HUSTLER'S DREAM 18
Defeat The Hustler in Legend Tour.

TIGER'S DREAM 18
Defeat Tiger Woods in Legend Tour.

TOMB RAIDER: LEGEND

You must unlock the following cheats before you can use them.

BULLETPROOF
During a game, hold L and press ✕, R, ▲, R, ●, R.

DRAW ENEMY HEALTH
During a game, hold L and press ●, ●, ✕, R, R, ▲.

INFINITE ASSUALT RIFLE AMMO
During a game, hold L and press ✖, ◉, ✖, R, ◉, ▲.

INFINITE GRENADE LAUNCHER
During a game, hold L and press R, ▲, R, ◉, R, ◼.

INFINITE SHOTGUN AMMO
During a game, hold L and press R, ◉, ◼, R, ◼, ✖.

INFINITE SMG AMMO
During a game, hold L and press [CR}, ▲, R, R, ✖, ◉.

1-SHOT KILL
During a game, hold L and press ▲, ✖, ▲, ◼, R, ◉.

TEXTURELESS MODE
Hold L and press R, ✖, ◉, ✖, ▲, R.

WIELD EXCALIBUR
During a game, hold L and press ▲, ✖, ◉, R, ▲, R.

TONY HAWK'S UNDERGROUND 2 REMIX

PERFECT RAIL BALANCE
Select Cheat Codes from the Game Options and enter tightrope.

THPS1 TONY HAWK
Select Cheat Codes from the Game Options and enter birdman.

TWISTED METAL: HEAD-ON

Note that the following codes will not work for Multiplayer or Online modes.

HEALTH RECHARGED
Hold L + R and press ▲, ✖, ◼, ◉.

INFINITE AMMO
Hold L + R and press ▲, ▲, Down, Down, Left.

INVULNERABLE
Hold L + R and press Right, Left, Down, Up.

INFINITE WEAPONS
Hold L + R and press ▲, ▲, Down, Down.

KILLER WEAPONS
Hold L + R and press ✖, ✖, Up, Up.

MEGA GUNS
Hold L + R and press ✖, ▲, ✖, ▲

VIRTUA TENNIS: WORLD TOUR

KING & QUEEN
At the Main menu, hold L and press Up, Down, Up, Down, ◼, ▲, ◼.

ALL RACQUETS & CLOTHING
At the Main menu, hold L and press Right, Left, Right, Right, Up, Up, Up.

ALL STADIUMS
At the Main menu, hold L and press Up, Down, Left, Right, ◼, ◼, ◼.

BEGIN WORLD TOUR WITH $1,000,000
At the Main menu, hold L and press Up, Down, Left, Down, ▲, ▲, ▲.

$2000 A WEEK IN WORLD TOUR
At the Main menu, hold L and press Up, Down, Right, Down, ▲, ◼, ▲.

SEPIA MODE
At the Main menu, hold L and press Up, Down, Left, Right, Left, Left, Left.

WORLD CHAMPIONSHIP POKER 2: FEATURING HOWARD LEDERER

SKIP WEEK AND MONEY CHEATS
At the Career World map, hold R. Hold L and release R. Hold Up and release L. Hold L and release Up. Hold R and release L. While still holding R, press Up/Down to skip weeks and Right/Left for money.

WRC: FIA WORLD RALLY CHAMPIONSHIP

UNLOCK EVERYTHING
Create a new profile with the name PADLOCK.

EXTRA AVATARS
Create a new profile with the name UGLYMUGS.

GHOST CAR
Create a new profile with the name SPOOKY.

SUPERCHARGER
Create a new profile with the name MAXPOWER.

TIME TRIAL GHOST CARS
Create a new profile with the name AITRIAL.

BIRD CAMERA
Create a new profile with the name dovecam.

REVERSES CONTROLS
Create a new profile with the name REVERSE.

X-MEN LEGENDS II: RISE OF APOCALYPSE

ALL CHARACTERS
At the Team Management screen, press Right, Left, Left, Right, Up, Up, Up, Start.

LEVEL 99 CHARACTERS
At the Team Management screen, press Up, Down, Up, Down, Left, Up, Left, Right, Start.

ALL SKILLS
At the Team Management screen, press Left, Right, Left, Right, Down, Up, Start.

SUPER SPEED
Pause the game and press Up, Up, Up, Down, Up, Down, Start.

UNLIMITED XTREME POWER
Pause the game and press Left, Down, Right, Down, Up, Up, Down, Up Start.

100,000 TECHBITS
At Forge or Beast's equipment screen, press Up, Up, Up, Down, Right, Right, Start.

ALL CINEMATICS
At the Review Menu, press Left, Right, Right, Left, Down, Down, Left, Start.

ALL COMIC BOOKS
At the Review Menu, press Right, Left, Left, Right, Up, Up, Right, Start.

Nintendo Wii™

Games List

CALL OF DUTY 3

ALL CHAPTERS AND BONUS CONTENT
At the Chapter Select screen, hold Plus and press Right, Right, Left, Left, 2 Button, 2 Button.

MARVEL ULTIMATE ALLIANCE

UNLOCK ALL SKINS
At the Team menu, press Up, Down, Left, Right, Left, Right, Start.

UNLOCKS ALL HERO POWERS
At the Team menu, press Left, Right, Up, Down, Up, Down, Start.

ALL HEROES TO LEVEL 99
At the Team menu, press Up, Left, Up, Left, Down, Right, Down, Right, Start.

UNLOCK ALL HEROES
At the Team menu, press Up, Up, Down, Down, Left, Left, Left, Start.

UNLOCK DAREDEVIL
At the Team menu, press Left, Left, Right, Right, Up, Down, Up, Down, Start.

UNLOCK SILVER SURFER
At the Team menu, press Down, Left, Left, Up, Right, Up, Down, Left, Start.

GOD MODE
During gameplay, press Up, Down, Up, Down, Up, Left, Down, Right, Start.

TOUCH OF DEATH
During gameplay, press Left, Right, Down, Down, Right, Left, Start.

SUPER SPEED
During gameplay, press Up, Left, Up, Right, Down, Right, Start.

FILL MOMENTUM
During gameplay, press Left, Right, Right, Left, Up, Down, Down, Up, Start.

UNLOCK ALL COMICS
At the Review menu, press Left, Right, Right, Left, Up, Up, Right, Start.

UNLOCK ALL CONCEPT ART
At the Review menu, press Down, Down, Down, Right, Right, Left, Down, Start.

UNLOCK ALL CINEMATICS
At the Review menu, press Up, Left, Left, Up, Right, Right, Up, Start.

UNLOCK ALL LOAD SCREENS
At the Review menu, press Up, Down, Right, Left, Up, Up Down, Start.

UNLOCK ALL COURSES
At the Comic Missions menu, press Up, Right, Left, Down, Up, Right, Left, Down, Start.

NEED FOR SPEED CARBON

CASTROL CASH
At the Main menu, press Down, Up, Left, Down, Right, Up, Button 1, B. This gives you 10,000 extra cash.

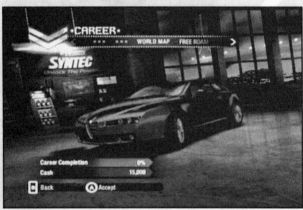

INFINITE CREW CHARGE
At the Main menu, press Down, Up, Up, Right, Left, Left, Right, Button 1.

INFINITE NITROUS
At the Main menu, press Left, Up, Left, Down, Left, Down, Right, Button 1.

INFINITE SPEEDBREAKER
At the Main menu, press Down, Right, Right, Left, Right, Up, Down, Button 1.

NEED FOR SPEED CARBON LOGO VINYLS
At the Main menu, press Right, Up, Down, Up, Down, Left, Right, Button 1.

NEED FOR SPEED CARBON SPECIAL LOGO VINYLS
At the Main menu, press Up, Up, Down, Down, Down, Down, Up, Button 1.

TONY HAWK'S DOWNHILL JAM

BOARDS

BOARD	COMPLETE EVENT
Street Issue	Street Issue Slalom (Tier 1)
Solar	Tourist Trap (Tier 1)
Chaos	Vista Point Race (Random)
Kuni	Hong Kong Race (Tier 2)
Red Rascal	San Francisco Elimination (Tier 3)
Cruiser	Grind Time (Tier 4)
Illuminate	Machu Pichu Top to Bottom Tricks (Tier 4)
Dark Sign	He-Man Club/Girl Power (Tier 5)
Spooky	Clearance Sale (Tier 6)
Black Icer	Precision Shopping Slalom (Tier 7)

BOARD	COMPLETE EVENT
Ripper	Del Centro Slalom (Tier 7)
Dispersion	Machu Picchu Top to Bottom Race (Tier 7)
Makonga	Mall Rats (Tier 8)
Goddess of Speed	The Hills Are Alive Tricks (Tier 9)
Dragon	Swiss Elimination (Tier 9)

OUTFITS

CHARACTER	OUTFIT	COMPLETE EVENT
Gunnar	High-G Armor	Gunnar's Threads (Tier 1)
Kyla	Shooting Star	Cuzco Challenge Race (Tier 2)
Tony	Business Camouflage	Mountain High Race (Random)
Budd	The Bohemian	Catacombs Slalom (Tier 2)
Tiffany	Baby Blue	Tourist Spot Slalom (Tier 2)
Ammon	Money Suit	Edinburgh Full Tricks (Tier 3)
Jynx	Black Tuesday	Road to Cuzco Race (Tier 3)
Jynx	Graveyard Casual	Cable Car Tricks (Random)
Crash	Bombs Away	Fallen Empire Race (Tier 4)
MacKenzie	Spitfire Squadron	Edinburgh Full Race (Tier 4)
Gunnar	Street Creds	Favela Rush (Tier 4)
Crash	Brace for Impact	Out of the Woods Race (Tier 5)
Kyla	Touchdown	Clear the Streets (Tier 5)
Tony	Mariachi Loco	Out of the Woods Tricks (Random)
MacKenzie	Killer Bee	High Street Slalom (Tier 6)
Ammon	Tommy T	Seaside Village Race (Tier 6)
Budd	Power of Chi	Rome Elimination (Tier 6)
Crash	Space Monkey	Lift Off (Tier 7)
Jynx	Funeral Fun	Del Centro Race (Tier 7)
Budd	Toys for Bob	Waterfront Race (Random)
MacKenzie	Street Combat	Parking Lot Shuffle (Tier 7)
Gunnar	Black Knight	Park It Anywhere (Tier 7)
Tiffany	Nero Style	Rome Burning (Tier 7)
Tiffany	Military Chic	Shopping Spree (Tier 8)
Ammon	Tan Suit	Saturday Matinee (Tier 9)
Tony	Downhill Jam	Hills Are Alive Race (Tier 9)
Kyla	Alpine Red	San Francisco Full Slalom (Tier 9)

SKATERS

SKATER	COMPLETE EVENT
Kevin Staab	Kevin's Challenge (Random)
MacKenzie	MacKenzie's Challenge (Tier 2)
Crash	Crash Test (Tier 3)
Armando Gnutbagh	Unknown Skater (Tier 10)

CHEAT CODES

Select Cheat Codes from the Options menu and enter the following cheats. Select Toggle Cheats to enable/disable them.

FREE BOOST
Enter OOTBAGHFOREVER.

ALWAYS SPECIAL
Enter POINTHOGGER.

UNLOCK MANUALS
Enter IMISSMANUALS.

PERFECT RAIL
Enter LIKETILTINGAPLATE.

PERFECT MANUAL
Enter TIGHTROPEWALKER.

PERFECT STATS
Enter IAMBOB.

EXTREME CAR CRASHES
Enter WATCHFORDOORS.

FIRST-PERSON SKATER
Enter FIRSTPERSONJAM.

SHADOW SKATER
Enter CHIMNEYSWEEP.

DEMON SKATER
Enter EVILCHIMNEYSWEEP.

MINI SKATER
Enter DOWNTHERABBITHOLE.

GIGANTO-SKATER
Enter IWANNABETALLTALL.

INVISIBLE BOARD
Enter LOOKMANOBOARD.

INVISIBLE SKATER
Enter NOWYOUSEEME.

PICASSO SKATER
Enter FOURLIGHTS.

CHIPMUNK VOICES
Enter HELLOHELIUM.

DISPLAY COORDINATES
Enter DISPLAYCOORDINATES.

LARGE BIRDS
Enter BIRDBIRDBIRDBIRD.

REALLY LARGE BIRDS
Enter BIRDBIRDBIRDBIRDBIRD.

TINY PEOPLE
Enter SHRINKTHEPEOPLE.

*There is no need to toggle on the following cheats. They take effect after entering them.

ALL EVENTS
Enter ADVENTURESOFKWANG.

ALL SKATERS
Enter IMINTERFACING.

ALL BOARDS/OUTFITS
Enter RAIDTHEWOODSHED.

ALL MOVIES
Enter FREEBOZZLER.

GAMECUBE™

Games List

1080° AVALANCHE

Select Enter An Avalanche Code from the Options screen and enter the following codes:

NOVICE AVALANCHE CHALLENGE
Enter JAS3IKRR.

HARD AVALANCHE CHALLENGE
Enter 2AUNIKFS.

EXPERT AVALANCHE CHALLENGE
Enter EATFIKRM.

EXTREME AVALANCHE CHALLENGE
Enter 9AVVIKNY.

ALIEN HOMINID

ALL LEVELS, MINI-GAMES, AND HATS
Select Player 1 Setup or Player 2 Setup and change the name to ROYGBIV.

HATS FOR 2-PLAYER GAME
Go to the Options screen and rename your alien one of the following names:

NAME	HAT	#
ABE	Top Hat	#11
APRIL	Blond Wig	#4
BEHEMOTH	Red Cap	#24
CLETUS	Hunting Hat	#3
DANDY	Flower Petal Hat	#13
GOODMAN	Black Curly Hair	#7
GRRL	Flowers	#10
PRINCESS	Tiara	#12
SUPERFLY	Afro	#6
TOMFULP	Brown Messy Hair	#2

ANIMAL CROSSING

TOM NOOK PASSWORDS
Talk to Tom Nook and select the Other Things option. Then, select Say Code and enter the following passwords. You will be able to enter only three at a time.

PASSWORD	ITEM
CbDahLBdaDh98d 9ub8ExzZKwu7Zl	Balloon Fight NES Game
1n5%N%8JUjE5fj lEcGr4%ync5eUp	Baseball NES Game
Crm%h4BNRyu98d 9uu8exzzZKwu7Zl	Clu Clu Land NES Game
bA5PC%8JUjE5fj ljcGr4%ync5EUp	DK Jr. Math NES Game
2n5@N%8JUjE5fj ljcGr4%ync5EUp	Donkey Kong NES Game
3%Q4fhMTRByAY3 O5yYAK9zNHxLd7	Excitebike NES Game
Crm%h4BNRbu98d 9un8exzzZKwo7Zl	Golf NES Game
bA5PC%8JUjE5fj 1EcGr4%ync5eup	Wario's Woods NES Game
Wn2&SAVAcgIC7N POudE2Tk8JHyUH	10,000 Bells from Project Hyrule
WB2&pARAcnOwnU jMCK%hTk8JHyrT	30,000 Bells from Project Hyrule
#SbaUIRmw#qwkY BK66q#LGscTY%2	? Block
IboOBCeHz3YbIC B5igPvQYsfMZMd	Block Flooring
1mWYg6lfB@&q75 8XzSNKpfWj76ts	Brick Block
4UT6T6L89ZnOW3 dw&%jtL3qjLZBf	Cannon
4UT6T948GZnOW3 dw#%jtLEqj5ZBf	Fire Flower
4UT6T6L89ZnOW3 dwU%jtL3qjLZBf	Flagpole
1mWYg6lfB@&q7z 8XzSNwpfij76ts	Green Pipe
BCQ4iZFK%i5xqo SnyrjcrwAeDMkQ	Luigi Trophy
QI6DLEnhm23CqH zrUHk3cXd#HOr9	Mushroom Mural
4UF6T948GZ3ZW3 dw#%jtL5qj5ZBf	Starman
1LhOwvrDA23fmt dsgnvzbCIBAsyd	Station Model 1

LETTER TO VILLAGER PASSWORDS

For the following codes, send the password to one of the animals living in your town. Only include the password in the body of the letter. Be sure to include a line break between the two lines of code.

PASSWORD	ITEM
rSbaUIRmwUgwkA 1K6tq#LMscTY%2	Coin
rSbaUIAmwUgwkY 1K6tq#LGscTY%2	Koopa Shell
ECzihy%rtHbHuk o3XlP3lslEql#K	Mario Trophy
#SbaUIRmw#gwkY Bh66qeLMscTY%2	Super Mushroom

ARMY MEN: AIR COMBAT - THE ELITE MISSIONS

UNLIMITED LIVES
During a game, press A, Y, X, Z, Down, Right, Up.

ATV QUAD POWER RACING 2

ALL RIDERS
Enter BUBBA as a profile name.

ALL VEHICLES
Enter GENERALLEE as a profile name.

ALL TRACKS
Enter ROADKILL as a profile name.

ALL CHAMPIONSHIPS
Enter REDROOSTER as a profile name.

ALL CHALLENGES
Enter DOUBLEBARREL as a profile name.

MAXED OUT SKILL LEVEL
Enter FIDDLERSELBOW as a profile name.

MAXED OUT STATS
Enter GINGHAM as a profile name.

AVATAR: THE LAST AIRBENDER

ALL TREASURE MAPS
Select Code Entry from the Extras screen and enter 37437.

1-HIT DISHONOR
Select Code Entry from the Extras screen and enter 54641.

DOUBLE DAMAGE
Select Code Entry from the Extras screen and enter 34743.

UNLIMITED COPPER
Select Code Entry from the Extras screen and enter 23637.

UNLIMITED CHI
Select Code Entry from the Extras screen and enter 24463.

UNLIMITED HEALTH
Select Code Entry from the Extras screen and enter 94677.

NEVERENDING STEALTH
Select Code Entry from the Extras screen and enter 53467.

CHARACTER CONCEPT ART GALLERY
Select Code Entry from the Extras screen and enter 97831.

BAD BOYS: MIAMI TAKEDOWN

CHEAT MODE
At the Title screen, press X, Up, B, Y, Right, Down.

BALDUR'S GATE: DARK ALLIANCE

ALL SPELLS
During gameplay, hold X + Right + L all the way + R halfway.

INVINCIBILITY AND LEVEL WARP
During gameplay, hold Y + Left + L all the way + R halfway and press START.

BATMAN BEGINS

GALLERY OF FEAR
Finish the game on any difficulty mode.

ALL MOVIES AND INTERVIEWS
Finish the game on any difficulty mode.

ALTERNATE COSTUMES
Finish the game on any difficulty mode.

PROTOTYPE BATMOBILE
Finish the game on any difficulty mode.

BATMAN: RISE OF SIN TZU

UNLIMITED HEALTH
At the Mode Select screen, hold L + R and press Up, Right, Up, Left, Down, Left, Down, Right.

ALL UPGRADES
At the Mode Select screen, hold L + R and press Down, Up, Down, Left, Down, Right, Up, Down.

ALL END GAME REWARDS
At the Mode Select screen, hold L + R and press Left, Down, Left, Right, Left, Left, Down, Right.

UNLIMITED COMBO METER
At the Mode Select screen, hold L + R and press Left, Right, Down, Up, Up, Down, Right, Left.

DARK KNIGHT DIFFICULTY
At the Mode Select screen, hold L + R and press Right, Up, Up, Right, Left, Down, Right, Up.

BEACH SPIKERS

UNIFORMS
In World Tour, name your player one of the following to unlock bonus outfits. The name disappears when entered correctly.

NAME	UNIFORMS
JUSTICE	105-106, Sunglasses 94
DAYTONA	107-108
FVIPERS	109-110, Face 51, Hair 75
ARAKATA	111-113, Face 52, Hair 76
PHANTA2	114-115, Face 53, Hair 77
OHTORII	116-117

BIG MUTHA TRUCKERS

ALL CHEATS
Enter CHEATINGMUTHATRUCKER as a code.

EVIL TRUCK
Enter VARLEY as a code.

FAST TRUCK
Enter GINGERBEER as a code.

$10 MILLION
Enter LOTSAMONEY as a code.

LEVEL SELECT
Enter LAZYPLAYER as a code.

UNLIMITED TIME
Enter PUBLICTRANSPORT as a code.

DISABLE DAMAGE
Enter 6WL as a code.

AUTOMATIC SAT NAV
Enter USETHEFORCE as a code.

DIPLOMATIC IMMUNITY
Enter VICTORS as a code.

SMALL PEDESTRIANS
Enter DAISHI as a code.

BONUS LEVELS
Enter JINGLEBELLS as a code in the Options screen.

BLOODRAYNE

CHEAT LIST
Select Cheat from the Options menu and enter the following to enable them. Pause the game to toggle the cheats.

CHEAT	CODE
Gratuitous Dismemberment	INSANEGIBSMODEGOOD
Fill Bloodlust	ANGRYXXXINSANEHOOKER
Enemy Freeze	DONTFARTONOSCAR
God Mode	TRIASSASSINDONTDIE
Juggy	JUGGYDANCESQUAD
Restore Health	LAMEYANKEEDONTFEED
Show Weapons	SHOWMEMYWEAPONS
Time Factor	NAKEDNASTYDISHWASHERDANCE

BRATZ: FOREVER DIAMONDZ

1000 BLINGZ
While in the Bratz Office, use the Cheat computer to enter SIZZLN.

2000 BLINGZ
While in the Bratz Office, use the Cheat computer to enter FLAUNT.

PET TREATS
While in the Bratz Office, use the Cheat computer to enter TREATZ.

GIFT SET A
While in the Bratz Office, use the Cheat computer to enter STYLIN.

GIFT SET B
While in the Bratz Office, use the Cheat computer to enter SKATIN.

GIFT SET C
While in the Bratz Office, use the Cheat computer to enter JEWELZ.

GIFT SET E
While in the Bratz Office, use the Cheat computer to enter DIMNDZ.

BRATZ: ROCK ANGELZ

CAMERON CHANGED
While in the Bratz Office, use the Cheat computer to enter STYLIN.

CHLOE CHANGED
While in the Bratz Office, use the Cheat computer to enter SPARKLE, FASHION, STRUT or FLAIR.

DYLAN CHANGED
While in the Bratz Office, use the Cheat computer to enter MEYGEN.

JADE CHANGED
While in the Bratz Office, use the Cheat computer to enter FUNKALISH, SLAMMIN or HOT.

LONDON BOY CHANGED
While in the Bratz Office, use the Cheat computer to enter BLINGZ.

PARIS BOY CHANGED
While in the Bratz Office, use the Cheat computer to enter ROCKIN.

SASHA CHANGED
While in the Bratz Office, use the Cheat computer to enter FUNKY, SCORCHIN, PRETTY or MODEL.

YASMIN CHANGED
While in the Bratz Office, use the Cheat computer to enter COOL, CRAZY or SASSY.

RECEIVE 1000 BLINGZ
While in the Bratz Office, use the Cheat computer to enter YASMIN.

RECEIVE 2000 BLINGZ
While in the Bratz Office, use the Cheat computer to enter PHOEBE.

RECEIVE 2100 BLINGZ
While in the Bratz Office, use the Cheat computer to enter DANCIN.

RECEIVE 3000 BLINGZ
While in the Bratz Office, use the Cheat computer to enter WAYFAB.

RECEIVE 6000 BLINGZ
While in the Bratz Office, use the Cheat computer to enter HOTTIE.

UNLOCKED RINGTONE 12
While in the Bratz Office, use the Cheat computer to enter BLAZIN.

UNLOCKED RINGTONE 15
While in the Bratz Office, use the Cheat computer to enter FIANNA.

UNLOCKED RINGTONE 16
While in the Bratz Office, use the Cheat computer to enter ANGELZ.

BUST-A-MOVE 3000

ANOTHER WORLD
At the Title screen, press Y, Left, Right, Y.

FUNGILA AND KATZE
At the Title screen, press Y, Right, Left, Y.

CABELA'S DANGEROUS HUNTS 2

DOUBLE HEALTH
Select the Codes option and enter Eye, Bolt, Skull, Hand, Boot.

HEALTH REGENERATES FASTER
Select the Codes option and enter Skull, Eye, Boot, Bolt, Hand.

DOUBLE DAMAGE
Select the Codes option and enter Hand, Boot, Skull, Eye, Bolt.

INFINITE AMMO
Select the Codes option and enter Bolt, Hand, Eye, Boot, Skull.

CALL OF DUTY: BIG RED ONE

ALL LEVELS
At the Chapter Select screen, hold L + R and press Up, Up, Down, Down, Left, Left, Right, Right, X, Right, X, Right, X.

CALL OF DUTY: FINEST HOUR

ALL CHEATS
Complete the game on Hard difficulty.

CARS

UNLOCK EVERYTHING
Select Cheat Codes from the Options screen and enter IF900HP.

ALL CHARACTERS
Select Cheat Codes from the Options screen and enter YAYCARS.

ALL CHARACTER SKINS
Select Cheat Codes from the Options screen and enter R4MONE.

ALL MINI-GAMES AND COURSES
Select Cheat Codes from the Options screen and enter MATTL66.

MATER'S COUNTDOWN CLEAN-UP MINI-GAME AND MATER'S SPEEDY CIRCUIT
Select Cheat Codes from the Options menu and enter TRGTEXC.

FAST START
Select Cheat Codes from the Options menu and enter IMSPEED.

INFINITE BOOST
Select Cheat Codes from the Options menu and enter VROOOOM.

ART
Select Cheat Codes from the Options menu and enter CONC3PT.

VIDEOS
Select Cheat Codes from the Options menu and enter WATCHIT.

CHICKEN LITTLE

INVINCIBILITY
Select Cheat Codes from the Extras menu and enter Baseball, Baseball, Baseball, Shirt.

BIG FEET
Select Cheat Codes from the Extras menu and enter Hat, Glove, Glove, Hat.

BIG HAIR
Select Cheat Codes from the Extras menu and enter Baseball, Bat, Bat, Baseball.

BIG HEAD
Select Cheat Codes from the Extras menu and enter Hat, Helmet, Helmet, Hat.

PAPER PANTS
Select Cheat Codes from the Extras menu and enter Bat, Bat, Hat, Hat.

SUNGLASSES
Select Cheat Codes from the Extras menu and enter Glove, Glove, Helmet, Helmet.

UNDERWEAR
Select Cheat Codes from the Extras menu and enter Hat, Hat, Shirt, Shirt.

THE CHRONICLES OF NARNIA: THE LION, THE WITCH AND THE WARDROBE

ENABLE CHEATS
At the Title screen, press A then hold L + R and press Down, Down, Right, Up. When entered correctly, the text turns green. Now you can enter the following:

LEVEL SELECT
At the wardrobe, hold L and press Up, Up, Right, Right, Up, Right, Down.

ALL BONUS LEVELS
At the Bonus Drawer, hold L and press Down, Down, Right, Right, Down, Right, Up.

LEVEL SKIP
During gameplay, hold L and press Down, Left, Down, Left, Down, Right, Down, Right, Up.

INVINCIBILITY
During gameplay, hold L and press Down, Up, Down, Right, Right.

RESTORE HEALTH
During gameplay, hold L and press Down, Left, Left, Right.

10,000 COINS
During gameplay, hold L and press Down, Left, Right, Down, Down.

ALL ABILITIES
During gameplay, hold L and press Down, Left, Right, Left, Up.

FILL COMBO METER
During gameplay, hold L and press Up, Up, Right, Up.

CRASH TAG TEAM RACING

FASTER VEHICLES
At the Main menu, hold L + R and press X, X, Y, Y.

1-HIT KO
At the Main menu, hold L + R and press A, X, X, A.

DISABLE HUD
At the Main menu, hold L + R and press A, B, Y, X.

CHICKEN HEADS
At the Main menu, hold L + R and press A, X, X, B.

JAPANESE CRASH
At the Main menu, hold L + R and press B, X, B, X.

DRIVE A BLOCK VEHICLE
At the Main menu, hold L + R and press X, X, Y, B.

CURIOUS GEORGE

CURIOUS GEORGE GOES APE
Pause the game, hold Z and press B, B, A, Y, B.

UNLIMITED BANANAS
Pause the game, hold Z and press A, X, X, Y, A.

ROLLERSKATES & FEZ HAT
Pause the game, hold Z and press X, A, A, A, B.

UPSIDE DOWN GRAVITY MODE
Pause the game, hold Z and press Y, Y, B, A, A.

DEF JAM: FIGHT FOR NY

Select Cheats from the Extras menu and enter the following:

100 REWARD POINTS
Enter NEWJACK, THESOURCE, CROOKLYN, DUCKETS, or GETSTUFF. You can only enter each code once.

UNLOCK SONG: "AFTERHOURS" BY NYNE
Enter LOYALTY.

UNLOCK SONG: "ANYTHING GOES" BY C-N-N
Enter MILITAIN.

UNLOCK SONG: "BUST" BY OUTKAST
Enter BIGBOI.

UNLOCK SONG: "BLINDSIDE" BY BAXTER
Enter CHOPPER.

UNLOCK SONG: "COMP" BY COMP
Enter CHOCOCITY.

UNLOCK SONG: "DRAGON HOUSE" BY CHIANG
Enter AKIRA.

UNLOCK SONG: "GET IT NOW" BY BLESS
Enter PLATINUMB.

UNLOCK SONG: "KOTO" BY CHIANG
Enter GHOSTSHELL.

UNLOCK SONG: "LIL' BRO" BY RIC-A-CHE
Enter GONBETRUBL.

UNLOCK SONG: "MAN UP" BY STICKY FINGAZ
Enter KIRKJONES.

UNLOCK SONG: "MOVE!" BY PUBLIC ENEMY
Enter RESPECT.

UNLOCK SONG: "O. G. ORIGINAL GANGSTER" BY ICE T
Enter POWER.

UNLOCK SONG: "POPPA LARGE" BY ULTRAMAGNETIC MC'S
Enter ULTRAMAG.

UNLOCK SONG: "SIEZE THE DAY" BY BLESS
Enter SIEZE.

UNLOCK SONG: "TAKE A LOOK AT MY LIFE" BY FAT JOE
Enter CARTAGENA.

UNLOCK SONG: "WALK WITH ME" BY JOE BUDDEN
Enter PUMP.

DEF JAM VENDETTA

ARII
At the Character Select screen, hold L + R + Z and press A, Y, B, X, Y.

CARLA
At the Character Select screen, hold L + R + Z and press A, Y, A (x3).

CHUKKLEZ
At the Character Select screen, hold L + R + Z and press Y, Y, B, A, X.

CRUZ
At the Character Select screen, hold L + R + Z and press X, B, A, A, X.

D-MOB
At the Character Select screen, hold L + R + Z and press Y, Y, B, Y, Y.

DAN G
At the Character Select screen, hold L + R + Z and press A, X, A, X, Y.

DEEBO
At the Character Select screen, hold L + R + Z and press X, X, A, A, B.

DEJA
At the Character Select screen, hold L + R + Z and press X, Y, X, X, A.

DMX
At the Character Select screen, hold L + R + Z and press X, A, X, B, Y.

DRAKE
At the Character Select screen, hold L + R + Z and press A, B, B, X, X.

FUNKMASTER FLEX
At the Character Select screen, hold L + R + Z and press X, B, X, X, Y.

HEADACHE
At the Character Select screen, hold L + R + Z and press B (x3), Y, X.

HOUSE
At the Character Select screen, hold L + R + Z and press B, A, B, X, A.

ICEBERG
At the Character Select screen, hold L + R + Z and press Y, B, X, Y, X.

LUDACRIS
At the Character Select screen, hold L + R + Z and press X (x3), Y, B.

MASA
At the Character Select screen, hold L + R + Z and press A, X, B, Y, Y.

METHOD MAN
At the Character Select screen, hold L + R + Z and press Y, X, A, B, X.

MOSES
At the Character Select screen, hold L + R + Z and press B, B, Y, Y, A.

N.O.R.E.
At the Character Select screen, hold L + R + Z and press X, Y, B, A, X.

NYNE
At the Character Select screen, hold L + R + Z and press Y, X, A, A, B.

OPAL
At the Character Select screen, hold L + R + Z and press X, X, Y, Y, B.

PEEWEE
At the Character Select screen, hold L + R + Z and press A, A, Y, B, Y.

PENNY
At the Character Select screen, hold L + R + Z and press A (x3), B, X.

POCKETS
At the Character Select screen, hold L + R + Z and press B, Y, X, Y, A.

RAZOR
At the Character Select screen, hold L + R + Z and press B, Y, B, X, A.

REDMAN
At the Character Select screen, hold L + R + Z and press X, X, B, Y, A.

RUFFNECK
At the Character Select screen, hold L + R + Z and press A, Y, A, B, X.

SCARFACE
At the Character Select screen, hold L + R + Z and press X, Y, A, B, Y.

SKETCH
At the Character Select screen, hold L + R + Z and press B, B, X, Y, A.

SNOWMAN
At the Character Select screen, hold L + R + Z and press B, B, A, A, X.

STEEL
At the Character Select screen, hold L + R + Z and press A, B, X, X, B.

T'AI
At the Character Select screen, hold L + R + Z and press X, X, Y, A, X.

ZAHEER
At the Character Select screen, hold L + R + Z and press B, B, Y, A, A.

ALTERNATE COSTUME, BRIGGS
At the Character Select screen, hold L + R + Z and press A, B, X, Y, X.

ALTERNATE COSTUME, MANNY
At the Character Select screen, hold L + R + Z and press X, Y, X, Y, X.

ALTERNATE COSTUME, PROOF
At the Character Select screen, hold L + R + Z and press A, Y, B, Y, X.

ALTERNATE COSTUME, RAZOR
At the Character Select screen, hold L + R + Z and press Y, X, A, B, B.

ALTERNATE COSTUME, RUFFNECK
At the Character Select screen, hold L + R + Z and press Y, X, B, A, Y.

ALTERNATE COSTUME, SPIDER
At the Character Select screen, hold L + R + Z and press X, X, Y, B, B.

ALTERNATE COSTUME, TANK
At the Character Select screen, hold L + R + Z and press B, Y, X, A, A.

DIGIMON RUMBLE ARENA 2

ONE-HIT KILLS
At the Title screen, press Right, Up, Left, Down, A, L + R.

EVOLVE ENERGY ITEM
At the Title screen, press Y, Right, Down, B, L, A, R, A, Y.

EVOLVE METER ALWAYS FULL
At the Title screen, press X, Right, A, Y, Left, B, L + R.

DONKEY KONGA

100M VINE CLIMB (1 OR 2 PLAYERS)
Collect 4800 coins to unlock this mini-game for purchase at DK Town.

BANANA JUGGLE (1 OR 2 PLAYERS)
Collect 5800 coins to unlock this mini-game for purchase at DK Town.

BASH K. ROOL (1 PLAYER)
Collect 5800 coins to unlock this mini-game for purchase at DK Town.

DRAGON BALL Z: SAGAS

ALL UPGRADES
Pause the game, select Controller and press Up, Left, Down, Right, Start, Start, Y, A, X, B.

INVINCIBILITY
Pause the game, select Controller and press Down, A, Up, Y, Start, Start, Right, Left, X, B.

PENDULUM MODE
Complete the game.

ENTER THE MATRIX

CHEAT MODE
After playing through the hacking system and unlocking CHEAT.EXE, you can use CHEAT.EXE to enter the following

EFFECT	CODE
All Guns	0034AFFF
Infinite Ammo	1DDF2556
Invisibility	FFFFFFF1
Infinite Focus	69E5D9E4
Infinite Health	7F4DF451
Speedy Logos	7867F443
Unlock Secret Level	13D2C77F
Fast Focus Restore	FFF0020A
Test Level	13D2C77F
Enemies Can't Hear You	4516DF45
Turbo Mode	FF00001A
Multiplayer Fight	D5C55D1E
Low Gravity	BB013FFF
Taxi Driving	312MF451

FAIRLY ODDPARENTS: BREAKIN' DA RULES

PASSWORDS

LEVEL	PASSWORD
2	Wanda, Vicky, Country Boy, Cosmo, Bronze Knee Cap
3	Wanda, Country Boy, Wanda, Crimson Chin, Crimson Chin
4	Bronze Knee Cap, Wanda, Country Boy, Bronze Knee Cap, Spatula Lady
5	Crimson Chin, Country Boy, Country Boy, Crimson Chin, Cosmo

FANTASTIC 4

BARGE ARENA & STAN LEE INTERVIEW #1
At the Main menu, press B, X, B, Down, Down, X, Up.

 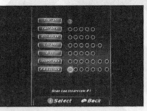

INFINITE COSMIC POWER
At the Main menu, press Up, B, B, B, Left, Right, X.

BONUS LEVEL
At the Main menu, press Right, Right, B, X, Left, Up, Down.

FIFA STREET 2

ALL STAGES
At the Main menu, hold L + Y and press Left, Up, Up, Right, Down, Down, Right, Down.

FIGHT NIGHT ROUND 2

ALL VENUES
At the Game Mode select, hold Left until you hear a bell.

SMALL FIGHTERS
At the Venue select, hold Up until you hear a bell.

FABOLOUS
Go into Create a Champ. Select New Boxer and enter getfab as his first name.

LI'L JOHN
Go into Create a Champ. Select New Boxer and enter Lijon as his first name.

LITTLE MAC
Go into Create a Champ. Select New Boxer and enter Macman as his first name.

FINDING NEMO

Enter the following at the Main menu. The word **"Cheat!"** will appear if entered correctly. Pause the game at the Level select to access the cheats.

LEVEL SELECT
Press Y (x3), B, B, X, B, Y, X, B, Y, B, Y, B, Y, X, Y, Y.

INVINCIBILITY
Press Y, B, B, X (x3), Y, Y, B (x3), X (x4), B, Y, X (x3), B,X, Y,X, X, B, X, X, Y, X, B, X (x3), Y.

CREDITS
Press Y, B, X, Y, Y, B, X, Y, B, X, Y, B, B, X, Y, B, X, Y, B, X, X, Y, B, X.

SECRET LEVEL
Press Y, B, X, X, B, Y, Y, B, X, X, B, Y, Y, X, B, Y, B, X, X, B, Y.

FIRE EMBLEM: PATH OF RADIANCE

FIRE EMBLEM: PATH OF RADIANCE ART
Complete the game.

FIRE EMBLEM ART
Connect a GBA to the GameCube with the Fire Emblem game.

FIRE EMBLEM: THE SACRED STONES ART
Connect a GBA to the GameCube with the Fire Emblem: The Sacred Stones game.

FREAKY FLYERS

ALL CHARACTERS, LEVELS, MINIGAMES AND SPECIALS
Enter ZENBU as your name.

FREEDOM FIGHTERS

CHEAT LIST

During the game, enter the following codes:

EFFECT	CODE
Invisibility	Y, A, X, B, B, Left
Infinite Ammo	Y, A, X, B, A, Right
Max Charisma	Y, A, X, B, A, Down
Heavy Machine Gun	Y, A, X, B, Y, Down
Nail Gun	Y, A, X, B, A, Left
Rocket Launcher	Y, A, X, B, Y, Left
Shotgun	Y, A, X, B, B, Up
Sniper Rifle	Y, A, X, B, Y, Right
Sub Machine Gun	Y, A, X, B, Y, Up
Ragdolls	Y, A, X, B, X, Up
Slow Motion	Y, A, X, B, B, Right
Fast Motion	Y, A, X, B, B, Down
Change Spawn Point	Y, A, X, B, A, Up

FREESTYLE METALX

Select Cheats from the Options and enter the following codes:

CHEAT	EFFECT
iwantitall	All Cheats
universe	All Levels and Events
johnnye	All Character Outfits
dudemaster	All Riders and Bikes
garageking	All Bike Parts
seeall	All Posters
fleximan	31 Trick Slots
sugardaddy	$1,000,000
hearall	All Songs
watchall	All Videos

FREESTYLE STREET SOCCER

Select Secrets from the Extras menu
and enter the following codes:

ALL GAME MODES
Enter GM2OPEN8.

ALL TEAMS
Enter A11T3AM5.

MAX SKILLS
Enter MAXSKILL.

INFINITE TURBO
Enter SPEEDY01.

ADDITIONAL ENVIRONMENTAL OBJECTS
Enter E06J3CT5.

THE STREETBALLERS TEAM
Enter 5Y104D9A.

MICRO SOCCER
Enter Z26BEXW8.

FROGGER: ANCIENT SHADOW

UNLOCK LEVELS
Select the Secret Code option and enter
the following to unlock various levels in
the game.

LEVEL	ENTER
Dr. Wani's Mansion Level 1 with Berry	Berry, Lily, Lumpy, Lily
Dr. Wani's Mansion Level 2 with Berry	Finnius, Frogger, Frogger, Wani

LEVEL	ENTER
Elder Ruins Level 1 with Berry	Lily, Lily, Wani, Wani

Elder Ruins Level 2 with Berry	Frogger, Berry, Finnius, Frogger
Doom's Temple Level 1 with Berry	Lily, Wani, Lily, Wani
Doom's Temple Level 2 with Berry	Frogger, Lily, Lily, Lily
Doom's Temple Level 3 with Berry	Frogger, Frogger, Frogger, Berry

Sealed Heart Level 1 with Berry	Lily, Lily, Wani, Lumpy
Sealed Heart Level 2 with Berry	Lily, Frogger, Frogger, Lumpy

UNLOCK LETTERS

Select the Secret Code option and enter the following to unlock various letters in the game.

LETTER	ENTER
WHCinc Letter with Hyacinth Flower Seed	Lumpy, Frogger, Frogger, Berry

Opart's Letter with Cosmos Flower Seed	Berry, Lumpy, Frogger, Lumpy

LETTER	ENTER
Secret Admirer Letter with Rose Flower Seed	Wani, Lily, Wani, Frogger

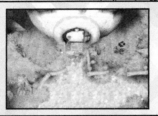

| Dr. Wani's Letter with Pansy Flower Seed | Lumpy, Berry, Lumpy, Finnius |

UNLOCK WIGS

Select the Secret Code option and enter the following to unlock various wigs in the game.

WIG	ENTER
Lobster Wig	Finnius, Wani, Lumpy, Frogger

| Bird Nest Wig | Lily, Lily, Lily, Lily |
| Masted Ship Wig | Lumpy, Lumpy, Lumpy, Lumpy |

| Skull Wig | Frogger, Lumpy, Lily, Frogger |

UNLOCK ARTWORK

Select the Secret Code option and enter the following to unlock various artwork pieces from the game.

ARTWORK	ENTER
Developer Picture 1	Wani, Frogger, Wani, Frogger

| Developer Picture 2 | Berry, Berry, Berry, Wani |
| Programmer Art 1 | Wani, Wani, Wani, Wani |

ARTWORK	ENTER
Programmer Art 2	Lumpy, Frogger, Berry, Lily
Programmer Art 3	Wani, Frogger, Lily, Finnius

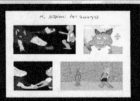

Additional Art 1	Frogger, Frogger, Frogger, Frogger

Additional Art 2	Finnius, Finnius, Finnius, Finnius
Additional Art 3	Berry, Berry, Berry, Berry

FUTURE TACTICS: THE UPRISING

UNLIMITED TURNS
During a game, press Up, Up, Down, Down, Left, Right, Left, Left, R, L.

BIG HEADS
During a game, press Up, Left, Down, Left, Down, Up, Up, Left.

DISCO MODE
During a game, press L, Left, L, Left, R, Right, R, Right.

LOW GRAVITY
During a game, press Up (x6), Down, Right, Up.

F-ZERO GX

SOUNDS OF BIG BLUE FOR PURCHASE
Select Customize and enter the shop. Press Z, Left, Right, Left, Z, Y, X, Z, Left, Right, Left, Right, Z, X, Z, X, Z. Select the Items option to find Sounds of Big Blue for sale.

SOUNDS OF MUTE CITY FOR PURCHASE
Select Customize and enter the shop. Press X (x3), Y, X (x3), Y, Z, Z, Left, Right, Left, Right, Left, Right. Select the Items option to find Sounds of Mute City for sale.

RUBY CUP CHAMPIONSHIP
Select Time Attack and choose Records. Select Ruby Cup, hold L and press R, A, Z, A, C-Up, C-Left, A, C-Down, R, Z.

SAPPHIRE CUP CHAMPIONSHIP
Select Time Attack and choose Records. Select Sapphire Cup, hold Z and press L, A, L, A, C-Up, L, C-Right, A, R, C-Up.

EMERALD CUP CHAMPIONSHIP
Select Time Attack and choose Records. Select Emerald Cup, hold R and press Z, A, C-Down, L, C-Left, A, Z, C-Left, L, A.

GLADIUS

1000 FREE DINARS
While at a League office, pause the game and press Right, Down, Left, Up, Left, Left, Left, Left, Y, Left.

EQUIP ANYTHING TO YOUR GLADIATORS
While at a League office, pause the game and press Right, Down, Left, Up, Left, Left, Left, Left, Y, Y, Y.

RAISE HP
While at a League office, pause the game and press Down, Right, Up, Left, Left, Left, Left, Left, Y, Up.

INSTANT EXPERIENCE
While at a League office, pause the game and press Right, Down, Left, Up, Left, Left, Left, Left, Y, Right.

DEFENSIVE AFFINITY UP
While at a League office, pause the game and press Down, Right, Up, Left, Left, Left, Left, Left, Y, Left.

OFFENSIVE AFFINITY UP
While at a League office, pause the game and press Down, Right, Up, Left, Left, Left, Left, Left, Y, Right.

LOWER LEVEL ENEMIES & RECRUITS
While at a League office, pause the game and press Right, Right, Right, Up, Up, Left, Left, Left, Left, Right, Down, Down, Down, Down, Up.

HARD MODE
While at a League office, pause the game and press Right, Right, Right, Up, Up, Left, Left, Left, Left, Right, Up, Up, Up, Up, Down.

FASTER TIMER
While at a League office, pause the game and press Right, Up, Left, Down, Left, Left, Left, Left, Down, Up.

NORMAL SPEED TIMER
While at a League office, pause the game and press Right, Up, Left, Down, Left, Left, Left, Left, Up, Down.

PULL BACK CAMERA
While at a League office, pause the game and press Up, Left, Down, Right, Left, Left, Left, Left, Up, Up, Up, Up.

TEAM BERSERK
While at a League office, pause the game and press Left, Down, Right, Up, Left, Left, Left, Left, Up, Right, Down, Left.

RANDOM ENCOUNTERS OFF
While at a League office, pause the game and press Right, Left, Up, Down, Left, Left, Left, Left, Y, Y, Y.

RANDOM ENCOUNTERS ON
While at a League office, pause the game and press Right, Left, Up, Down, Left, Left, Left, Left, A, A, A.

GO! GO! HYPERGRIND

Enter the following at the Cheat menu:

LEVEL SELECT
Enter OPENSESAME.

PLAY AS VERT
Enter LOOSETIGER.

PLAY AS VERT AND KEVIN
Enter BUTIEANDBEAST.

ALL FIGURES
Enter COOLDUDES.

ALL GEAR
Enter TONSOFJUNK.

ALL BOARD DESIGNS
Enter PRETTYBOARDS.

ALL BOARD ATTRIBUTES
Enter DECKCOLLECTOR.

ALL WHEELS
Enter NEEDMORESPEED.

ALL ILLUSTRATIONS
Enter NOTPICASSO.

ALL BONUSES
Enter PANDORASBOX.

DISABLE NEGATIVE REACTIONS
Enter REACTIONPROOF.

PERFECT BALANCE
Enter STABILIZER.

PERFECT LIP BALANCE
Enter LIPGRIPPER.

PERFECT MANUAL BALANCE
Enter MANUALMASTER.

PERFECT RAIL BALANCE
Enter PROGRINDER.

SPIN FASTER
Enter RUBBERNECKER.

REACTIONS WITHOUT PRESSING X
Enter AUTOREACTION.

ALL CHARACTER FMV SEQUENCES
Enter MOVIEFREAK.

GOBLIN COMMANDER: UNLEASH THE HORDE

During a game, hold R + L + Y + Down until a message appears in the upper-right corner of the screen. Re-enter the code to disable. Now enter the following codes. Again a message appears if entered correctly.

GOD MODE
Press R (x3), L (x3), R, L, Y, R.

AUTOMATIC WIN
Press R, R, L (x3), R, R, Y (x3).

ALL LEVEL ACCESS
Press Y (x3), L, R, L, L, R, L, R, R, L, R, L, L, R, L, R, L, L, R, L, L, R, L, R, R, Y (x3). Start up a Campaign to select a level.

DISABLE FOG OF WAR
Press R, L, R, R, L, L, Y, Y, L, R.

GAME SPEED X 1/2
Press L (x5), Y (x4), R.

GAME SPEED X 2
Press R (x5), L, Y, R (x3).

GOLD AND SOULS +1000
Press R, R, L, R, R, Y (x3), L, L.

GOLD +100
Press L, R (x4), L, Y, L (x3).

SOULS +100
Press R, L (x4), R, Y, R (x3).

GODZILLA: DESTROY ALL MONSTERS MELEE

CODES

At the Main menu, press and hold L, B, R, then release B, R, L. Enter the following codes:

EFFECT	CODE
All Cites	480148
All Monsters (except Orga)	696924
Godzilla 2K	225133
Gigan	616233
King Ghidorah	877467
Rodan	104332
Destoroyah	537084
Mecha King Ghidorah	557456
Mecha Godzilla	131008
11 Continues	760611
Throw All Buildings & Objects	756287
P2 Invisible	459113
All Players Invisible	316022
Player Indicators Always On	135984
Indestructible Buildings	112122
Turn Military On/Off	256806
Infinite Energy for P1	677251
Infinite Energy for P2	435976
No Freeze Tanks	841720
No Display	443253
No Energy (but stronger)	650867
No Health Power-ups	562142
No Mothra Power-ups	134615
No Energy Power-ups	413403
No Rage Power-ups	119702
P1 Always Rage	649640
P2 Always Rage	122224
P3 Always Rage	548053

EFFECT	CODE
P4 Always Rage	451242
P1 Damage-Proof	843901
P2 Damage-Proof	706149
P3 Damage-Proof	188522
P4 Damage-Proof	286552
All Players Damage-Proof	505634
Super Energy P1	677251
Super Energy P2	435976
Super Energy P3	603696
Super Energy P4	291680
Energy	650867
P1 4X Damage	511012
P2 4x Damage	815480
P3 4x Damage	212454
P4 4x Damage	286552
All Players 4x Damage	817683
P1 Small	986875
P2 Small	971934
P3 Small	895636
P4 Small	795735
All Players Small	174204
Regenerate Health	492877
Statistics Mode	097401
Black-and-White	567980
Technicolor	661334
View Credits	176542
Game Version	097401

GOLDENEYE: ROGUE AGENT

FULL HEALTH AND ARMOR
Pause the game and press R, R, R, L, R, R, L, R.

FULLY CHARGE EYE POWER
Pause the game and press L, R, L, L, L, R, R, L.

ALL EYE POWERS
Pause the game and press L, L, R, R, R, R, L, L.

ALL LEVELS
At the Extra screen, press Down, Right, Down, Right, Up, Down, Up, Left.

ALL SKINS IN MULTIPLAYER
At the Extra screen, press Down, Left, Up,
Left, Right, Down, Left, Up

NO EYE POWERS IN MULTIPLAYER
At the Extra screen, press Up, Up, Down, Left, Right, Right, Left, Down.

PAINTBALL
At the Extra screen, press Right, Left, Right, Left, Down, Down, Up, Up.

ONE -LIFE MODE
At the Extra screen, press Left, Down, Up, Right, Up, Right, Left, Down.

GROOVERIDER SLOT CAR THUNDER

UNLOCK EVERYTHING
Select Time Trial and enter MARK as your name. Return to the Main menu to find the Cheats option.

CREDITS
Select Time Trial and enter BGM as your name. Return to the Main menu to find the Cheats option.

THE HAUNTED MANSION

SKELETON ZEKE
At the Legal screen, hold A + B + X + Y. Release the buttons at the Title screen.

LEVEL SELECT
During a game, hold Right and press X, X, B, Y, Y, B, X, A.

INVINCIBILITY
During a game, hold Right and press B, X (x3), B, X, Y, A.

WEAPON UPGRADE
During a game, hold Right and press B, B, Y, Y, X (x3), A.

ICE AGE 2: THE MELTDOWN

ALL BONUSES
Pause the game and press Down, Left, Up, Down, Down, Left, Right, Right.

LEVEL SELECT
Pause the game and press Up, Right, Right, Left, Right, Right, Down, Down.

UNLIMITED PEBBLES
Pause the game and press Down, Down, Left, Up, Up, Right, Up, Down.

INFINITE ENERGY
Pause the game and press Down, Left, Right, Down, Down, Right, Left, Down.

INFINITE HEALTH
Pause the game and press Up, Right, Down, Up, Left, Down, Right, Left.

THE INCREDIBLE HULK: ULTIMATE DESTRUCTION

You must collect a specific comic in the game to activate each code. After collecting the appropriate comic, you can enter the following codes. If you don't have the comic and enter the code, you receive a message "That code cannot be activated... yet". Enter the cheats at the Code Input screen.

UNLOCKED: CABS GALORE
Select Code Input from the Extras menu and enter CABBIES.

UNLOCKED: GORILLA INVASION
Select Code Input from the Extras menu and enter kingkng.

UNLOCKED: MASS TRANSIT
Select Code Input from the Extras menu and enter TRANSIT.

UNLOCKED: 5000 SMASH POINTS
Select Code Input from the Extras menu and enter SMASH5.

UNLOCKED: 10000 SMASH POINTS
Select Code Input from the Extras menu and enter SMASH10.

UNLOCKED: 15000 SMASH POINTS
Select Code Input from the Extras menu and enter SMASH15.

UNLOCKED: AMERICAN FLAG SHORTS
Select Code Input from the Extras menu and enter AMERICA.

UNLOCKED: CANADIAN FLAG SHORTS
Select Code Input from the Extras menu and enter OCANADA.

UNLOCKED: FRENCH FLAG SHORTS
Select Code Input from the Extras menu and enter Drapeau.

UNLOCKED: GERMAN FLAG SHORTS
Select Code Input from the Extras menu and enter DEUTSCH.

UNLOCKED: ITALIAN FLAG SHORTS
Select Code Input from the Extras menu and enter MUTANDA.

UNLOCKED: JAPANESE FLAG SHORTS
Select Code Input from the Extras menu and enter FURAGGU.

UNLOCKED: SPANISH FLAG SHORTS
Select Code Input from the Extras menu and enter BANDERA.

UNLOCKED: UK FLAG SHORTS
Select Code Input from the Extras menu and enter FSHNCHP.

UNLOCKED: COW MISSILES
Select Code Input from the Extras menu and enter CHZGUN.

UNLOCKED: DOUBLE HULK'S DAMAGE
Select Code Input from the Extras menu and enter DESTROY.

UNLOCKED: DOUBLE POWER COLLECTABLES
Select Code Input from the Extras menu and enter BRINGIT.

UNLOCKED: BLACK AND WHITE
Select Code Input from the Extras menu and enter RETRO.

UNLOCKED: SEPIA
Select Code Input from the Extras menu and enter HISTORY.

UNLOCKED: ABOMINATION
Select Code Input from the Extras menu and enter VILLAIN.

UNLOCKED: GRAY HULK
Select Code Input from the Extras menu and enter CLASSIC.

UNLOCKED: JOE FIXIT SKIN
Select Code Input from the Extras menu and enter SUITFIT.

UNLOCKED: WILD TRAFFIC
Select Code Input from the Extras menu and enter FROGGIE.

UNLOCKED: LOW GRAVITY
Select Code Input from the Extras menu and enter PILLOWS.

THE INCREDIBLES

Pause the game, select Secrets and
enter the following codes:

RESTORE SOME HEALTH
Enter UUDDLRLRBAS.

BIG HEADS
Enter EINSTEINIUM.

SMALL HEADS
Enter DEEVOLVE.

1ONE-HIT KILLS
Enter KRONOS.

EYE LASER
Enter GAZERBEAM.

WEAKER BOMBS
Enter LABOMBE.

INFINITE INCREDI-POWER FOR ELASTIGIRL
Enter FLEXIBLE.

INFINITE INCREDI-POWER FOR MR. INCREDIBLE
Enter SHOWTIME.

INFINATE INCREDI-POWER TO MR INCREDIBLE OR ELASTAGIRL
Enter MCTRAVIS.

DESTROYS EVERYTHING
Enter SMARTBOMB.

FIRE TRAIL
Enter ATHLETESFOOT.

BATTLE MODE
Enter ROTAIDALG.

FASTER GAMEPLAY
Enter SASSMODE.

SLOW MOTION
Enter BWTHEMOVIE.

DIFFERENT COLORS
Enter DISCORULES.

BRIGHT COLORS
Enter EMODE.

INVERT HORIZONTAL CAMERA CONTROL
Enter INVERTCAMERAX.

INVERT VERTICAL CAMERA CONTROL
Enter INVERTCAMERAY.

TOGGLE HUD
Enter BHUD.

WATCH HEAVY IRON STUDIOS INTRO
Enter HI.

CREDITS
Enter YOURNAMEINLIGHTS.

DEACTIVATE ALL CODES
Enter THEDUDEABIDES.

THE INCREDIBLES: RISE OF THE UNDERMINER

BIG HEADS
Pause the game and access the menu. Choose the Secrets option and enter EGOPROBLEM. Re-enter the code to disable it.

MR. INCREDIBLE GAINS 1000 EXPERIENCE POINTS
Pause the game and access the menu. Choose the Secrets option and enter MRIPROF.

FROZONE GAINS 1000 EXPERIENCE POINTS
Pause the game and access the menu. Choose the Secrets option and enter FROZPROF.

MR. INCREDIBLE GAINS A SUPER-MOVE
Pause the game and access the menu. Choose the Secrets option and enter MRIBOOM.

FROZONE GAINS A SUPER-MOVE
Pause the game and access the menu. Choose the Secrets option and enter FROZBOOM.

SHOWS THE GAME CREDITS
Pause the game and access the menu. Choose the Secrets option and enter ROLLCALL.

TOUGHER GAME
Pause the game and access the menu. Choose the Secrets option and enter THISISTOOEASY. This code cuts damage caused to enemies in half, doubles damage inflicted to the Supers, allows no health recovery, and Experience Points are halved!

EASIER GAME
Pause the game and access the menu. Choose the Secrets option and enter THISISTOOHARD. This code doubles damage caused to enemies, halves damage inflicted to the Supers, and doubles the amount of health recovery and Experience Points!

ALL GALLERY ITEMS
Pause the game and access the menu. Choose the Secrets option and enter SHOWME.

DOUBLE EXPERIENCE POINTS
Pause the game and access the menu. Choose the Secrets option and enter MAXIMILLION.

JAMES BOND 007: EVERYTHING OR NOTHING

CHEATS
To enable the following codes, you must first earn the given number of Platinum, then pause the game and enter the corresponding code.

EFFECT	PLATINUM	CODE
Golden Gun	1	X, Y, A, X, Y
Improved Traction	3	X, A, A, B, Y
Improved Battery	5	X, B, B, A, X
Double Ammunition	7	X, X, A, X, Y
Double Damage	9	X, Y, Y, B, X
Full Ammunition	11	X, X, Y, B, B
Cloak	13	X, Y, A, Y, B
Full Battery	15	X, Y, Y, A, X
All Weapons	17	X, Y, A, A, X
Unlimited Battery	19	X, B, X, B, Y
Unlimited Ammo	23	X, A, B, A, Y
Slow Motion Driving	25	X, B, Y, A, Y
Platinum Gun	27	X, B, B, X, A

JIMMY NEUTRON BOY GENIUS

ALL KEY ITEMS
During a game, press R, R, L, A, B, B, A, R, L, R, Start, Down, A, Down.

JIMMY NEUTRON: JET FUSION

ALL MOVIES
During a game, press Z, L, R, R, B, X, X, B, R, R, L, L.

4-HIT COMBO
Pause the game, hold L + R and press A, B, A, Up.

JUDGE DREDD: DREDD VERSUS DEATH

UNLOCK EVERYTHING
Enter REBELLION as your user name.

LEGO STAR WARS: THE VIDEO GAME

*Pause the game and select Extras to toggle the following cheats on and off.

INVINCIBILITY
At Dexter's Diner, select Enter Code and enter 4PR28U.

BIG BLASTERS
At Dexter's Diner, select Enter Code and enter IG72X4.

CLASSIC BLASTERS
At Dexter's Diner, select Enter Code and enter L449HD.

SILLY BLASTERS
At Dexter's Diner, select Enter Code and enter NR37W1.

BRUSHES
At Dexter's Diner, select Enter Code and enter SHRUB1.

TEA CUPS
At Dexter's Diner, select Enter Code and enter PUCEAT.

MINIKIT DETECTOR
At Dexter's Diner, select Enter Code and enter LD116B.

MOUSTACHES
At Dexter's Diner, select Enter Code and enter RP924W.

PURPLE
At Dexter's Diner, select Enter Code and enter YD77GC.

SILHOUETTES
At Dexter's Diner, select Enter Code and enter MS999Q.

*The following codes make each character available for purchase from Dexter's Diner.

BATTLE DROID
At Dexter's Diner, select Enter Code and enter 987UYR.

BATTLE DROID (COMMANDER)
At Dexter's Diner, select Enter Code and enter EN11K5.

BATTLE DROID (GEONOSIS)
At Dexter's Diner, select Enter Code and enter LK42U6.

BATTLE DROID (SECURITY)
At Dexter's Diner, select Enter Code and enter KF999A.

BOBA FETT
At Dexter's Diner, select Enter Code and enter LA811Y.

CLONE
At Dexter's Diner, select Enter Code and enter F8B4L6.

CLONE (EPISODE III)
At Dexter's Diner, select Enter Code and enter ER33JN.

CLONE (EPISODE III, PILOT)
At Dexter's Diner, select Enter Code and enter BHU72T.

CLONE (EPISODE III, SWAMP)
At Dexter's Diner, select Enter Code and enter N3T6P8.

CLONE (EPISODE III, WALKER)
At Dexter's Diner, select Enter Code and enter RS6E25.

COUNT DOOKU
At Dexter's Diner, select Enter Code and enter 14PGMN.

DARTH MAUL
At Dexter's Diner, select Enter Code and enter H35TUX.

DARTH SIDIOUS
At Dexter's Diner, select Enter Code and enter A32CAM.

DISGUISED CLONE
At Dexter's Diner, select Enter Code and enter VR832U.

DROIDEKA
At Dexter's Diner, select Enter Code and enter DH382U.

GENERAL GRIEVOUS
At Dexter's Diner, select Enter Code and enter SF321Y.

GEONOSIAN
At Dexter's Diner, select Enter Code and enter 19D7NB.

GRIEVOUS' BODYGUARD
At Dexter's Diner, select Enter Code and enter ZTY392.

GONK DROID
At Dexter's Diner, select Enter Code and enter U63B2A.

JANGO FETT
At Dexter's Diner, select Enter Code and enter PL47NH.

KI-ADI MUNDI
At Dexter's Diner, select Enter Code and enter DP55MV.

KIT FISTO
At Dexter's Diner, select Enter Code and enter CBR954.

LUMINARA
At Dexter's Diner, select Enter Code and enter A725X4.

MACE WINDU (EPISODE III)
At Dexter's Diner, select Enter Code and enter MS952L.

PADMÉ
At Dexter's Diner, select Enter Code and enter 92UJ7D.

PK DROID
At Dexter's Diner, select Enter Code and enter R840JU.

PRINCESS LEIA
At Dexter's Diner, select Enter Code and enter BEQ82H.

REBEL TROOPER
At Dexter's Diner, select Enter Code and enter L54YUK.

ROYAL GUARD
At Dexter's Diner, select Enter Code and enter PP43JX.

SHAAK TI
At Dexter's Diner, select Enter Code and enter EUW862.

SUPER BATTLE DROID
At Dexter's Diner, select Enter Code and enter XZNR21.

LEGO STAR WARS II: THE ORIGINAL TRILOGY

BEACH TROOPER
At Mos Eisley Canteena, select Enter Code and enter UCK868. You must then select Characters and purchase this character for 20,000 studs.

BEN KENOBI (GHOST)
At Mos Eisley Canteena, select Enter Code and enter BEN917. You must then select Characters and purchase this character for 1,100,000 studs.

BESPIN GUARD
At Mos Eisley Canteena, select Enter Code and enter VHY832. You must then select Characters and purchase this character for 15,000 studs.

BIB FORTUNA
At Mos Eisley Canteena, select Enter Code and enter WTY721. You must then select Characters and purchase this character for 16,000 studs.

BOBA FETT
At Mos Eisley Canteena, select Enter Code and enter HLP221. You must then select Characters and purchase this character for 175,000 studs.

DEATH STAR TROOPER
At Mos Eisley Canteena, select Enter Code and enter BNC332. You must then select Characters and purchase this character for 19,000 studs.

EWOK
At Mos Eisley Canteena, select Enter Code and enter TTT289. You must then select Characters and purchase this character for 34,000 studs.

GAMORREAN GUARD
At Mos Eisley Canteena, select Enter Code and enter YZF999. You must then select Characters and purchase this character for 40,000 studs.

GONK DROID
At Mos Eisley Canteena, select Enter Code and enter NFX582. You must then select Characters and purchase this character for 1,550 studs.

GRAND MOFF TARKIN
At Mos Eisley Canteena, select Enter Code and enter SMG219. You must then select Characters and purchase this character for 38,000 studs.

GREEDO
At Mos Eisley Canteena, select Enter Code and enter NAH118. You must then select Characters and purchase this character for 60,000 studs.

HAN SOLO (HOOD)
At Mos Eisley Canteena, select Enter Code and enter YWM840. You must then select Characters and purchase this character for 20,000 studs.

IG-88
At Mos Eisley Canteena, select Enter Code and enter NXL973. You must then select Characters and purchase this character for 30,000 studs.

IMPERIAL GUARD
At Mos Eisley Canteena, select Enter Code and enter MMM111. You must then select Characters and purchase this character for 45,000 studs.

IMPERIAL OFFICER
At Mos Eisley Canteena, select Enter Code and enter BBV889. You must then select Characters and purchase this character for 28,000 studs.

IMPERIAL SHUTTLE PILOT
At Mos Eisley Canteena, select Enter Code and enter VAP664. You must then select Characters and purchase this character for 29,000 studs.

IMPERIAL SPY
At Mos Eisley Canteena, select Enter Code and enter CVT125. You must then select Characters and purchase this character for 13,500 studs.

JAWA
At Mos Eisley Canteena, select Enter Code and enter JAW499. You must then select Characters and purchase this character for 24,000 studs.

LOBOT
At Mos Eisley Canteena, select Enter Code and enter UUB319. You must then select Characters and purchase this character for 11,000 studs.

PALACE GUARD
At Mos Eisley Canteena, select Enter Code and enter SGE549. You must then select Characters and purchase this character for 14,000 studs.

REBEL PILOT
At Mos Eisley Canteena, select Enter Code and enter CYG336. You must then select Characters and purchase this character for 15,000 studs.

REBEL TROOPER (HOTH)
At Mos Eisley Canteena, select Enter Code and enter EKU849. You must then select Characters and purchase this character for 16,000 studs.

SANDTROOPER
At Mos Eisley Canteena, select Enter Code and enter YDV451. You must then select Characters and purchase this character for 14,000 studs.

SKIFF GUARD
At Mos Eisley Canteena, select Enter Code and enter GBU888. You must then select Characters and purchase this character for 12,000 studs.

SNOWTROOPER
At Mos Eisley Canteena, select Enter Code and enter NYU989. You must then select Characters and purchase this character for 16,000 studs.

STORMTROOPER
At Mos Eisley Canteena, select Enter Code and enter PTR345. You must then select Characters and purchase this character for 10,000 studs.

THE EMPEROR
At Mos Eisley Canteena, select Enter Code and enter HHY382. You must then select Characters and purchase this character for 275,000 studs.

TIE FIGHTER
At Mos Eisley Canteena, select Enter Code and enter HDY739. You must then select Characters and purchase this item for 60,000 studs.

TIE FIGHTER PILOT
At Mos Eisley Canteena, select Enter Code and enter NNZ316. You must then select Characters and purchase this character for 21,000 studs.

TIE INTERCEPTOR
At Mos Eisley Canteena, select Enter Code and enter QYA828. You must then select Characters and purchase this item for 40,000 studs.

TUSKEN RAIDER
At Mos Eisley Canteena, select Enter Code and enter PEJ821. You must then select Characters and purchase this character for 23,000 studs.

UGNAUGHT
At Mos Eisley Canteena, select Enter Code and enter UGN694. You must then select Characters and purchase this character for 36,000 studs.

THE LORD OF THE RINGS: THE RETURN OF THE KING

SHARE EXPERIENCE IN COOPERATIVE MODE
Pause the game, hold L + R and press X, A (x3).

SHARE HEALTH IN COOPERATIVE MODE
Pause the game, hold L + R and press Y, Up, A, A.

UNLIMITED RESPAWNS IN COOPERATIVE MODE
Pause the game, hold L + R and press X, B, Up, X.

Aragorn

1,000 EXPERIENCE
Pause the game, hold L + R and press Up, B, Y, A.

LEVEL 2 SKILLS
Pause the game, hold L + R and press X, Y, A, Y.

LEVEL 4 SKILLS
Pause the game, hold L + R and press Down, B, X, B.

LEVEL 6 SKILLS
Pause the game, hold L + R and press X, Y, B, B.

LEVEL 8 SKILLS
Pause the game, hold L + R and press Up, B, Y, Up.

RESTORE MISSILES
Pause the game, hold L + R and press Y, B, B, Y.

3 HIT COMBO
Pause the game, hold L + R and press B, Down, X, Up.

4 HIT COMBO
Pause the game, hole L + R and press Up, B, Y, X.

Faramir

1,000 EXPERIENCE
Pause the game, hold L + R and press B, Y, Up, B.

LEVEL 2 SKILLS
Pause the game, hold L + R and press A, B, A, Down.

LEVEL 4 SKILLS
Pause the game, hold L + R and press A, A, B, B.

LEVEL 6 SKILLS
Pause the game, hold L + R and press Y, A, Down, X.

LEVEL 8 SKILLS
Pause the game, hold L + R and press X, Down (x3).

RESTORE MISSILES
Pause the game, hold L + R and press Y, Up, A, A.

3 HIT COMBO
Pause the game, hold L + R and press B, Y, Up, Y.

4 HIT COMBO
Pause the game, hold L + R and press A, B, Up, A.

Frodo

1,000 EXPERIENCE
Pause the game, hold L + R and press X, Y, Up, X.

LEVEL 2 SKILLS
Pause the game, hold L + R and press Y, Up, Down, X.

LEVEL 4 SKILLS
Pause the game, hold L + R and press Y, Up, X, Down.

LEVEL 6 SKILLS
Pause the game, hold L + R and press Down, Down, A, Y.

LEVEL 8 SKILLS
Pause the game, hold L + R and press X, X, Down, Down.

RESTORE MISSILES
Pause the game, hold L + R and press Y (x3), X.

3 HIT COMBO
Pause the game, hold L + R and press B, Down, Y, B.

4 HIT COMBO
Pause the game, hold L + R and press Down, B, Down, X.

Gandalf

1,000 EXPERIENCE
Pause the game, hold L + R and press X, Y, Up, Down.

LEVEL 2 SKILLS
Pause the game, hold L + R and press Down, Y, A, Y.

LEVEL 4 SKILLS
Pause the game, hold L + R and press Y, Up, B, A.

LEVEL 6 SKILLS
Pause the game, hold L + R and press Y, Y, A, Up.

LEVEL 8 SKILLS
Pause the game, hold L + R and press X, B, Down, Down.

RESTORE MISSILES
Pause the game, hold L + R and press Y, X, A, B.

3 HIT COMBO
Pause the game, hold L + R and press Down, A, Y, Down.

4 HIT COMBO
Pause the game, hold L + R and press Down, Y, Up, X.

Gimli

1,000 EXPERIENCE
Pause the game, hold L + R and press X, X, Y, A.

LEVEL 2 SKILLS
Pause the game, hold L + R and press Up, X, B, B.

LEVEL 4 SKILLS
Pause the game, hold L + R and press Y, B, Down, Up.

LEVEL 6 SKILLS
Pause the game, hold L + R and press Down, Y, Down B.

LEVEL 8 SKILLS
Pause the game, hold L + R and press A, X, Down, B.

RESTORE MISSILES
Pause the game, hold L + R and press X (x3), A.

3 HIT COMBO
Pause the game, hold L + R and press Up, B, X, B.

4 HIT COMBO
Pause the game, hold L + R and press Y, B, Up, A.

Legolas

1,000 EXPERIENCE
Pause the game, hold L + R and press A, Y, Up, A.

LEVEL 2 SKILLS
Pause the game, hold L + R and press B, B, X, B.

LEVEL 4 SKILLS
Pause the game, hold L + R and press Down, Down, A, A.

LEVEL 6 SKILLS
Pause the game, hold L + R and press Down, X, Up, Down.

LEVEL 8 SKILLS
Pause the game, hold L + R and press B, Up, Up, Down.

RESTORE MISSILES
Pause the game, hold L + R and press Y (x3), X.

3 HIT COMBO
Pause the game, hold L + R and press Y (x3), Down.

4 HIT COMBO
Pause the game, hold L + R and press A, X, Y, B.

Merry

1,000 EXPERIENCE
Pause the game, hold L + R and press X, X, B, A.

LEVEL 2 SKILLS
Pause the game, hold L + R and press Down, Down, B, B.

LEVEL 4 SKILLS
Pause the game, hold L + R and press B, A, X, Down.

LEVEL 6 SKILLS
Pause the game, hold L + R and press Down, Down, B, Y.

LEVEL 8 SKILLS
Pause the game, hold L + R and press Down, Y, A, B.

RESTORE MISSILES
Pause the game, hold L + R and press B, X, X, Y.

3 HIT COMBO
Pause the game, hold L + R and press Y, A, Up, Y.

4 HIT COMBO
Pause the game, hold L + R and press Y, A, B, B.

Pippin

1,000 EXPERIENCE
Pause the game, hold L + R and press Y, A, B, A.

LEVEL 2 SKILLS
Pause the game, hold L + R and press Down, A, Down, Up.

LEVEL 4 SKILLS
Pause the game, hold L + R and press A, Down (x3).

LEVEL 6 SKILLS
Pause the game, hold L + R and press X, Y, X, Y.

LEVEL 8 SKILLS
Pause the game, hold L + R and press B, Up, Up, X.

RESTORE MISSILES
Pause the game, hold L + R and press Up, X, X, B.

3 HIT COMBO
Pause the game, hold L + R and press Up, Up, B, X.

4 HIT COMBO
Pause the game, hold L + R and press A, A, Down, X.

Sam

1,000 EXPERIENCE
Pause the game, hold L + R and press Y, A, Down, A.

LEVEL 2 SKILLS
Pause the game, hold L + R and press X, A, X, Y.

LEVEL 4 SKILLS
Pause the game, hold L + R and press Up, Down, B, A.

LEVEL 6 SKILLS
Pause the game, hold L + R and press Down, Down, Up, Up.

LEVEL 8 SKILLS
Pause the game, hold L + R and press X, X, Y, Y.

RESTORE MISSILES
Pause the game, hold L + R and press A, A, X, A.

3 HIT COMBO
Pause the game, hold L + R and press B, A, X, B.

4 HIT COMBO
Pause the game, hold L + R and press Up, Down, Y, Y.

You must complete the game before entering the following codes:

PERFECT MODE
Pause the game, hold L + R and press X, Down, Y, A.

ALL ATTACK UPGRADES
Pause the game, hold L + R and press Up, Down, Y, B.

INVINCIBILITY
Pause the game, hold L + R and press B, X, B, Up.

FULL HEALTH
Pause the game, hold L + R and press B, B, X, X.

UNLIMITED MISSILE WEAPONS
Pause the game, hold L + R and press B, B, Down, X.

ALWAYS DEVASTATING
Pause the game, hold L + R and press Y, Up, Y, Down.

TARGET INDICATOR
Pause the game, hold L + R and press Down, X, Up, B.

ALL INTERVIEWS
Pause the game, hold L + R and press A, B, A, Up.

THE LORD OF THE RINGS: THE TWO TOWERS

HEALTH
Pause the game, hold L + R and press Y, Down, A, Up.

ARROWS
Pause the game, hold L + R and press A, Down, Y, Up.

1000 UPGRADE POINTS
Pause the game, hold L + R and press A, Down (x3).

LEVEL 2 SKILLS
Pause the game, hold L + R and press X, Right, X, Right.

LEVEL 4 SKILLS
Pause the game, hold L + R and press Y, Up, Y, Up.

LEVEL 6 SKILLS
Pause the game, hold L + R and press B, Left, B, Left.

LEVEL 8 SKILLS
Pause the game, hold L + R and press A, A, Down, Down.

To access the following codes, you must first complete the game

ALWAYS DEVASTATING
Pause the game, hold L + R and press B, B, X, X.

SMALL ENEMIES
Pause the game, hold L + R and press Y, Y, A, A.

ALL UPGRADES
Pause the game, hold L + R and press Y, X, Y, X.

INVULNERABLE
Pause the game, hold L + R and press Y, B, A, X.

SLOW MOTION
Pause the game, hold L + R and press Y, X, A, B.

UNLIMITED MISSILE WEAPONS
Pause the game, hold L + R and press B, X, A, Y.

MADDEN NFL 2005

MADDEN CARD CODES

Select Madden Cards from the My Madden menu. Then, select Madden Codes and enter the following:

CODE	CARD	DESCRIPTION
P67E1I	TJ Duckett	Gold TJ Duckett
Z28X8K	3rd Down	For 1 Half, your opponent will only get 3 downs to get a first down
P66C4L	5th Down	For 1 Half, you will get 5 downs to get a first down
J33I8F	Bingo!	Your defensive interceptions increase by 75% for the game
B61A8M	Da Bomb	You will receive unlimited pass range for 1 Half
I76X3T	Da Boot	You will receive unlimited field goal range for 1 Half
M89S8G	Extra Credit	Awards 4 points for every interception and 3 points for every sack
V65J8P	First and Fifteen	Requires your opponent to get 15 yards to reach a first down for 1 Half
O72E9B	First and Five	Your first down yards to go will be set to 5 for 1 Half
R14B8Z	Fumblitis	Your opponent's fumbles will increase by 75% for the game
L96J7P	Human Plow	Your Broken Tackles will increases by 75% for the game
D57R5S	Lame Duck	Your opponent will throw a lob pass for 1 Half
X78P9Z	Mistake Free	You can't fumble or throw an interception for 1 Half
Y59R8R	Mr. Mobility	Your QB can't get sacked for 1 Half
D59K3Y	Super Dive	Your diving distance increases by 75% for the game
V34L6D	Tight Fit	Your opponent's uprights will be made very narrow for 1 Half
L48G1E	Unforced Errors	Your opponent will fumble every time he tries to juke for 1 Half

CODE	CARD
P74X8J	1958 Colts
G49P7W	1966 Packers
C24W2A	1968 Jets
G12N1I	1970 Browns
R79W6W	1972 Dolphins
R12D9B	1974 Steelers
P96Q8M	1976 Raiders
O18T2A	1977 Broncos
G97U5X	1978 Dolphins
K71K4E	1980 Raiders
Y27N9A	1981 Chargers
F56D6V	1982 Redskins
D23T8S	1983 Raiders
X23Z8H	1984 Dolphins
F92M8M	1985 Bears
K44F2Y	1986 Giants
F77R8H	1988 49ers

CODE	CARD
G95F2Q	1990 Eagles
I89F4I	1991 Lions
I44A1O	1992 Cowboys
Y66K3O	1993 Bills
G67F5X	Aloha Stadium
O85P6I	Super Bowl XL
P48Z4D	Super Bowl XLI
T67R1O	Super Bowl XLII
D58F1B	Super Bowl XXXIX

MADDEN NFL 06

Select Madden Cards from My Madden, then select Madden Codes and enter the following:

PASSWORD	CARD
6W5J6Z	#1 Rex Grossman Gold
6X7W2O	#2 Thomas Jones Gold
6Y5Z6H	#3 Brian Urlacher Gold
6Z9X5Y	#4 Olin Kreutz Gold
7A7Z2G	#5 Tommie Harris Gold
7C6U4H	#6 Carson Palmer Gold
7D1B2H	#7 Chad Johnson Gold
7D1X8K	#8 Rudi Johnson Gold
7D5W8J	#9 Brian Simmons Gold
7D8S6J	#10 J.P. Losman Gold
7E3G7Y	#11 Willis McGahee Gold
7F5B2Y	#12 Eric Moulds Gold
7H3B2Y	#13 Takeo Spikes Gold
7H9E8L	#14 Lawyer Milloy Gold
7J3Y7F	#15 Jake Plummer Gold
7J8F4J	#16 Ashley Lelie Gold
7K5C8V	#17 Al Wilson Gold
7L8C2W	#18 Champ Bailey Gold
1A2D9F	#19 John Lynch Gold
7O1J3F	#20 D.J. Williams Gold
7P5G3N	#21 Lee Suggs Gold
7Q2E45	#22 Kellen Winslow Jr. Gold
7Q6F4G	#23 Simeon Rice Gold
7Q6X4L	#24 Derrick Brooks Gold
7R7V2E	#25 Ronde Barber Gold
7S4C4D	#26 Anthony McFarland Gold
7T1G2Y	#27 Michael Clayton Gold
7T3V5K	#28 Anquan Boldin Gold
7T6B5N	#29 Larry Fitzgerald Gold
7U4M9B	#30 Bertrand Berry Gold
7U6B3L	#31 LaDainian Tomlinson Gold
8Q2J2R	#55 Donovan McNabb Bronze
8Q2J2X	#55 Donovan McNabb Gold
8V9Y3X	#62 Michael Vick Gold
8X2Y9G	#64 Alge Crumpler Gold
2W4P9T	#188 First and Fifteen Bronze
2W4P9G	#188 First and Fifteen Silver
2Y7L8B	#189 First and Five Bronze

PASSWORD	CARD
2Z2F4H	#190 Unforced Errors Bronze
2Z2F4G	#190 Unforced Errors Silver
3D3Q3P	#191 Extra Credit Bronze
3D8X6Z	#191 Extra Credit Gold
3D8X6T	#192 Tight Fit Bronze
3E9R4V	#193 5th Down Bronze
3E9R4I	#193 5th Down Silver
3F9G4J	#194 3rd Down Bronze
3F9G4O	#194 3rd Down Silver
3H3U7T	#194 3rd Down Gold
3H3U7F	#195 Human Plow Bronze
3H8M5U	#196 Super Dive Bronze
3J3S9Y	#197 Da Boot Bronze
3J3S9E	#197 Da Boot Silver
3T4E3Y	#208 Pocket Protectors Gold
3X1V2H	#210 QB on Target Gold
4D1V2Y	#217 Ouch Gold
4F9D2B	#220 Super Bowl XL Gold
4F9D2H	#221 Super Bowl XLI Gold
4I1V6T	#222 Super Bowl XLII Gold
4F3D7E	#223 Super Bowl XLIII Gold
4I1V6K	#224 Aloha Stadium Gold

MADDEN NFL 07

#199 GOLD LAME DUCK CHEAT CARD
In My Madden, select Madden Codes from Madden Cards and enter 5LAW00.

#200 GOLD MISTAKE FREE CHEAT CARD
In My Madden, select Madden Codes from Madden Cards and enter XL7SP1.

#210 GOLD QB ON TARGET CHEAT CARD
In My Madden, select Madden Codes from Madden Cards and enter WROA0R.

MAJOR LEAGUE BASEBALL 2K6

UNLOCK EVERYTHING
Select Enter Cheat Code from the My 2K6 menu and enter Derek Jeter.

TOPPS 2K STARS
Select Enter Cheat Code from the My 2K6 menu and enter Dream Team.

SUPER WALL CLIMB
Select Enter Cheat Code from the My 2K6 menu and enter Last Chance. Activate the cheat by selecting My Cheats or selecting Cheat Codes from the Options screen.

SUPER PITCHES
Select Enter Cheat Code from the My 2K6 menu and enter Unhittable. Activate the cheat by selecting My Cheats or selecting Cheat Codes from the Options screen.

ROCKET ARMS
Select Enter Cheat Code from the My 2K6 menu and enter Gotcha. Activate the cheat by selecting My Cheats or selecting Cheat Codes from the Options screen.

BOUNCY BALL
Select Enter Cheat Code from the My 2K6 menu and enter Crazy Hops. Activate the cheat by selecting My Cheats or selecting Cheat Codes from the Options screen.

MARIO GOLF: TOADSTOOL TOUR

At the Title screen, press Start + Z to access the Password screen. Enter the following to open the bonus tournaments.

TARGET BULLSEYE TOURNAMENT
Enter CEUFPXJ1.

HOLLYWOOD VIDEO TOURNAMENT
Enter BJGQBULZ.

CAMP HYRULE TOURNAMENT
Enter 0EKW5G7U.

BOWSER BADLANDS TOURNAMENT
Enter 9L3L9KHR.

BOWSER JR.'S JUMBO TOURNAMENT
Enter 2GPL67PN.

MARIO OPEN TOURNAMENT
Enter GGAA241H.

PEACH'S INVITATIONAL TOURNAMENT
Enter ELBUT3PX.

MARIO POWER TENNIS

EVENT MODE
At the Title screen, press Z + Start.

MARIO SUPERSTAR BASEBALL

STAR DASH MINI GAME
Complete Star difficulty on all mini-games.

BABY LUIGI
Complete Challenge Mode with Yoshi.

DIXIE KONG
Complete Challenge Mode with Donkey Kong.

HAMMER BRO
Complete Challenge Mode with Bowser.

MONTY MOLE
Complete Challenge Mode with Mario.

PETEY PIRANHA
Complete Challenge Mode with Wario.

TOADETTE
Complete Challenge Mode with Peach.

KOOPA CASTLE STADIUM
Complete Challenge Mode.

MARVEL NEMESIS: RISE OF THE IMPERFECTS

ALL FANTASTIC FOUR COMICS
Select Cheats from the Options screen and enter SAVAGELAND.

ALL TOMORROW PEOPLE COMICS
Select Cheats from the Options screen and enter NZONE.

ELEKTRA BONUS CARD
Select Cheats from the Options screen and enter THEHAND.

SOLARA BONUS CARD
Select Cheats from the Options screen and enter REIKO.

STORM BONUS CARD
Select Cheats from the Options screen and enter MONROE.

MEDAL OF HONOR: EUROPEAN ASSAULT

Pause the game, hold L + R and press Up, Y, Y, B, Up, A. You can now enter the following:

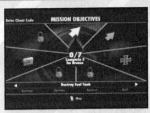

INVINCIBILITY
Press B, Y, Right, A, Z, R.

DISABLE SHELLSHOCK
Press Z, R, A, Y, Y, L.

FULL ADRENALINE
Press A, L, B, Z, L, Y.

HIDE HUD
Press A, Y, Right, A, Z, B.

KILL NEMESIS
Press L, Y, L, Z, L, Z.

PICK UP OSS DOCUMENT
Press Left, Y, B, A, Down, B.

PLAYER SUICIDE
Press L, Z, R, Up, A, Z.

UNLIMITED AMMO
Press Z, R, Up, A, B, A.

MEGA MAN ANNIVERSARY COLLECTION

Mega Man 2

VILLAIN DEFEAT PASSWORDS

Flash Man	A2, C1, C2, C5, D3, E1, E2, E3
Wood Man	A2, C2, C4, C5, D3, D4, E1, E2, E3
Air Man	A2, C2, C4, C5, D4, E1, E2, E3, E4
Metal Man	A4, B1, B3, C4, D1, D2, E1, E3, E4
Bubble Man	A4, B1, B3, C4, D2, D4, E1, E3, E4
Crash Man	A4, B1, B3, C4, D2, D3, D4, E1, E3
Heat Man	A1, B2, C1, C4, C5, D1, D3, E3, E5
Quick Man	A2, B1, B3, B5, C2, D1, D2, D4, E4

START GAME WITH FOUR E-TANKS
A5, B1, B3, C4, D2, D3, E1, E5

HALF OF GAME COMPLETE: AIR MAN, BUBBLE MAN, CRASH MAN, FLASH MAN, AND FOUR E-TANKS
A5, B2, C4, C5, D3, D4, D5, E4, E5

HALF OF GAME COMPLETE: HEAT MAN, METAL MAN, QUICK MAN, WOOD MAN, AND FOUR E-TANKS
A5, B1, B4, C1, C3, D2, E1, E2

ALL WEAPONS
A5, B2, B4, C1, C3, C5, D4, D5, E2

LONG JUMPS
Pause in the middle of a jump to reset Mega Man's downward velocity. Press START rapidly at the height of a jump to coast for long distances. This also makes most bullets fly through Mega Man without harm.

START WITH ALL BOSSES DEFEATED AT WILEY'S CASTLE
A1, B2, B4, C1, C5, D1, D3, E3, E5

START WITH ALL BOSSES DEFEATED AT WILEY'S CASTLE & 4 ENERGY TANKS
A5, B2, B4, C1, C3, C5, D4, D5, E2

Mega Man 3

ALL WEAPONS/ALL ITEMS/9 ETS/0 DOC ROBOTS
Blue: A3 B5 D3 F4
Red: A6

ALL WEAPONS/ALL ITEMS/9 ETS/DR. WILEY STAGE 1
Blue: A1 A3 B2 B5 D3 F4
Red: A6 E1

SPARK MAN DEFEATED
Red: C5, F4

SNAKE MAN DEFEATED
Red: C5, F6

NEEDLE MAN DEFEATED
Red: D3, E6

HARD MAN DEFEATED
Red: C4, E6

TOP MAN DEFEATED
Red: A3, C5

GEMINI MAN DEFEATED
Red: B5, C5

MAGNET MAN DEFEATED
Red: C5, F5

SHADOW MAN DEFEATED
Red: C5, D6

Mega Man 4

ALL WEAPONS AND ITEMS
A1, A4, B5, E2, F1, F3

BRIGHT MAN DEFEATED
A1, A4, B5, E2, F1, F3

DIVE MAN DEFEATED
A2, B4, B5, D2, E2, F3

DRILL MAN DEFEATED
A2, A4, B5, E2, E4, F3

PHARAOH MAN DEFEATED
A2, A5, B2, B4, D1, D3

RING MAN DEFEATED
A2, B3, B4, B5, D1, D3

SKULL MAN
A2, B4, B5, C4, D3, F2

TOAD MAN DEFEATED
A4, B1, B5, E2, E6, F3

Mega Man 5

ALL WEAPONS AND ITEMS
Blue: B4 D6 F1   Red: C1 D4 F6

CHARGE MAN DEFEATED
Red: C1, D4, F6   Blue: B4, D6, F1

CRYSTAL MAN DEFEATED
Red: A5, D2, E3   Blue: B1, B3, E5

DR. WILEY'S LAIR
Red: C1, D4, F6   Blue: B4, D6, F1

GRAVITY MAN DEFEATED
Red: A5, B1, F4   Blue: C4, E5, F1

GYRO MAN DEFEATED
Red: A5, B1, E3   Blue: B3, E5, F1

NAPALM MAN DEFEATED
Red: A5, C1, E3   Blue: B3, E2, E5

STAR MAN DEFEATED
Red: B1, B6, F4   Blue: C4, E6, F1

STONE MAN DEFEATED
Red: C1, E3, F6
Blue: B3, D6, E2

WAVE MAN DEFEATED
Red: B1, B6, D3   Blue: B3, E6, F1

EXTRA CONTINUES
Get the energy tank on the first level of Dr. Wiley's Castle. Then get killed, and Continue the game. You can do this until you have nine Continues.

M TANK & 1UP TRICK
If you have an M Tank, full energy, all weapons, pause the game, and use an M tank. All enemies will turn into 1Ups. This does not work on bosses!

Mega Man 6

ALL WEAPONS AND ITEMS
B6, D4, F2, F4, F6

Mega Man 7

ALL WEAPONS AND ITEMS
7251584228476137

FINAL STAGE
1415-5585-7823-6251

FINAL STAGE/ALL ITEMS/999 BOLTS/4 ENERGY TANKS/4 WEAPON TANKS
7853-5842-2245-7515

Mega Man 8

ANIMATION TEST
Choose Bonus Mode, hold down L + R, and press START.

MEGA MAN X COLLECTION

Mega Man X4

BLACK ZERO
At the Character Select screen, highlight Zero and hold R and press Right (x6). Release R, hold X and press Start. Continue holding X until the game starts.

ULTIMATE ARMOR FOR MEGA MAN X
At the Character Select screen, highlight Mega Man X and press X, X, Left (x6). Then hold L + Z and press Start. Continue holding L + Z until the game starts. Complete the level, then find the Leg power-up in the Jungle.

Mega Man X5

BLACK ZERO
At the Character Select screen, highlight Zero and press Down, Down, Up (x9).

ULTIMATE ARMOR FOR MEGA MAN X
At the Character Select screen, highlight Mega Man X and press Up, Up, Down (x9).

Mega Man X6

BLACK ZERO
At the Main menu, highlight Game Start and press L, L, L, R.

ULTIMATE ARMOR FOR MEGA MAN X
At the Main menu, highlight Game Start and press Left, Left, Left, Right.

MIDWAY ARCADE TREASURES 3

HYDRO THUNDER

ALL TRACKS AND BOATS
Get a high score and enter ?PB as your initials.

Offroad Thunder

CLIFFHANGER TRACK
Select Rally and press Right at the Choose Track screen, then press Right to access the Secret Code option. Press Right, Up, Left, to unlock the track.

CHIEFTAIN & GENERAL VEHICLES
Select Rally and press Right at the Choose Machine screen, then press Right to access the Secret Code option. Press Left (x3) to unlock Chieftain, or press Left (x3) again to unlock General.

DUST DEVIL & SILVER STREAK VEHICLES
Select Rally and press Right at the Choose Machine screen, then press Right to access the Secret Code option. Press Left, Up, Right to unlock Dust Devil, or press Left, Up, Right again to unlock Silver Streak.

HYENA & BAD OMEN VEHICLES
Select Rally and press Right at the Choose Machine screen, then press Right to access the Secret Code option. Press Right (x3) to unlock Hyena, or press Right (x3) again to unlock Bad Omen.

WILDCAT & THRASHER VEHICLES
Select Rally and press Right at the Choose Machine screen, then press Right to access the Secret Code option. Press Up (x3) to unlock Wildcat, or press Up (x3) again to unlock Thrasher.

SAN FRANCISCO: RUSH 2049

ACTIVATE CHEAT MENU
At the Main menu, highlight Options and press L + R + Y + X to enter the following cheats.

ALL CARS
At the Cheat menu, highlight All Cars and press A, A, X, X, L, L and then hold R and press Y. Release R, hold L and press A.

ALL TRACKS
At the Cheat menu, highlight All Tracks, hold A + Y and press R and then release A and Y. Hold Y + X and press L, then release Y and X. Press A, A, X, X, hold L + R and press Y.

ALL PARTS
At the Cheat menu, highlight All Parts, hold Y and press X, A, L, R. Release Y, hold X and press A. Release X and press Y, Y.

RESURRECT IN PLACE
At the Cheat menu, highlight Resurrect in Place and press R, R, L, L, A, Y, X.

FRAME SCALE
At the Cheat menu, highlight Frame Scale, hold L and then press A, A, X. Release L, hold R and press A, A, X.

TIRE SCALING
At the Cheat menu, highlight Tire Scaling and press Y, X, A, Y, X, A. Then hold R and press A.

FOG COLOR
At the Cheat menu, highlight Fog Color and hold L and press Y, release L, hold A and press Y, release A, hold X and press Y, release X, hold R and press Y.

CAR COLLISIONS
At the Cheat menu, highlight Car Collisions, hold L + R and press Y, X, A. Release L and R and press Y, X, A.

CONE MINES
At the Cheat menu, highlight Cone Mines, hold X and press R, L. Release X and press Y. Hold A and press Y, then release A and press Y.

CAR MINES
At the Cheat menu, highlight Car Mines, hold L + R + Y and press A, X. Release L, R and Y, then press A, X.

TRACK ORIENTATION
At the Cheat menu, highlight Track Orientation, hold L + R and press Y. Release L and R and press A, Y, X. Hold L + R and press Y.

AUTO ABORT
At the Cheat menu, highlight Auto Abort and press A, L, Y, R, X. Hold L + R and press A, Y.

SUPER SPEED
At the Cheat menu, highlight Super Speed, hold X + R and press L. Release X and R. Hold A and press Y, then release A and press A, A, A.

INVINCIBLE
At the Cheat menu, highlight Invincible, hold L + Y and press X, A. Release L + Y, then hold R and press A, Y, X.

INVISIBLE CAR
At the Cheat menu, highlight Invisible Car hold L and press Y and then release L. Hold R and press X, then release R and press A. Hold L + R and press Y. Release L and R and press X, X, X.

INVISIBLE TRACK
At the Cheat menu, highlight Invisible Track and press R, L, X, Y, A, A, Y, X. Hold L + R and press A.

BRAKES
At the Cheat menu, highlight Brakes and press X, X, X. Hold L + Y + A and then press R.

SUPER TIRES
At the Cheat Menu, highlight Super Tires, then hold R and press Y, Y, Y. Release R, then hold L and press A, A, X.

MASS
At the Cheat Menu, highlight Mass, then hold A and press Y, Y, X. Release A and press L, R.

SUICIDE MODE
At the Cheat Menu, highlight Suicide Mode, then hold X and press R, L, R, L. Release X, then hold Y and press R, L, R, L.

BATTLE PAINT SHOP
At the Cheat Menu, highlight Battle Paint Shop, then hold A and press L, R, L, R. Release A and press Y, Y, Y.

DEMOLITION BATTLE
At the Cheat Menu, highlight Demolition Battle, then hold L + A and press X, Y. Release L and A, then hold R + A and press X, Y.

RANDOM WEAPONS
At the Cheat Menu, highlight Random Weapons, then hold L + A and press Y, X. Release L and A, then hold R + A and press Y, X.

MONSTER HOUSE

FULL HEALTH
During a game, hold L + R and press A, A, A, Y.

REFILL SECONDARY WEAPON AMMO
During a game, hold L + R and press Y, Y, A, A.

ALL TOY MONKEYS AND ART GALLERY
During a game, hold L + R and press Y, X, Y, X, B, B, B, A.

MVP BASEBALL 2005

ALL STADIUMS, PLAYERS, UNIFORMS, & REWARDS
Create a player named Katie Roy.

RED SOX ST. PATRICK'S DAY UNIFORM
Create a player named Neverlose Sight.

BAD HITTER WITH THIN BAT
Create a player named Erik Kiss.

GOOD HITTER WITH BIG BAT
Create a player named Isaiah Paterson, Jacob Paterson or Keegan Paterson.

BIGGER BODY
Create a player named Kenny Lee.

NASCAR 2005: CHASE FOR THE CUP

ALL BONUSES
At the Edit Driver screen, enter Open Sesame as your name.

DALE EARNHARDT
At the Edit Driver screen, enter The Intimidator as your name.

$10,000,000
At the Edit Driver screen, enter Walmart NASCAR as your name.

LAKESHORE DRIVE TRACK
At the Edit Driver screen, enter Walmart Exclusive as your name.

DODGE EVENTS
At the Edit Driver screen, enter Dodge Stadium as your name.

MR CLEAN DRIVERS
At the Edit Driver screen, enter Mr.Clean Racing as your name.

MR. CLEAN PIT CREW
At the Edit Driver screen, enter Clean Crew as your name.

2,000,000 PRESTIGE POINTS/LEVEL 10 IN FIGHT TO THE TOP MODE
At the Edit Driver screen, enter You TheMan as your name.

NBA LIVE 2005

50,000 DYNASTY POINTS
Enter YISS55CZ0E as an NBA Live Code.

ALL CLASSICS HARDWOOD JERSEYS
Enter PRYI234N0B as an NBA Live Code.

ALL TEAM GEAR
Enter 1NVDR89ER2 as an NBA Live Code.

ALL SHOES
Enter FHM389HU80 as an NBA Live Code.

AIR UNLIMITED SHOES
Enter XVLJD9895V as an NBA Live Code.

HUARACHE 2K4 SHOES
Enter VNBA60230T as an NBA Live Code.

NIKE BG ROLLOUT SHOES
Enter 0984ADF90P as an NBA Live Code.

NIKE SHOX ELITE SHOES
Enter 2388HDFCBJ as an NBA Live Code.

ZOOM GENERATION LOW SHOES
Enter 234SDJF9W4 as an NBA Live Code.

ZOOM LEBRON JAMES II SHOES
Enter 1KENZO23XZ as an NBA Live Code.

ATLANTA HAWKS ALTERNATE UNIFORM
Enter HDI834NN9N as an NBA Live Code.

BOSTON CELTICS ALTERNATE UNIFORM
Enter XCV43MGMDS as an NBA Live Code.

DALLAS MAVERICKS ALTERNATE UNIFORM
Enter AAPSEUD09U as an NBA Live Code.

NEW ORLEANS HORNETS ALTERNATE UNIFORM
Enter JRE7H4D90F as a NBA Live Code.

NEW ORLEANS HORNETS ALTERNATE UNIFORM 2
Enter JRE7H4D9WH as a NBA Live Code.

SEATTLE SONICS ALTERNATE UNIFORM
Enter BHD87YY27Q as a NBA Live Code.

GOLDEN STATE WARRIORS ALTERNATE UNIFORM
Enter NAVNY29548 as an NBA Live Code.

NBA LIVE 06

EASTERN ALL-STARS 2005-06 AWAY JERSEYS
Select NBA Codes from My NBA Live and enter XCVB5387EQ.

EASTERN ALL-STARS 2005-06 HOME JERSEY
Select NBA Codes from My NBA Live and enter 234SDFGHMO.

WESTERN ALL-STARS 2005-06 AWAY JERSEY
Select NBA Codes from My NBA Live and enter 39N56B679J.

WESTERN ALL-STARS 2005-06 HOME JERSEY
Select NBA Codes from My NBA Live and enter 2J9UWABNP1.

BOSTON CELTICS 2005-06 ALTERNATE JERSEY
Select NBA Codes from My NBA Live and enter 193KSHU88J.

CLEVELAND CAVALIERS 2005-06 ALTERNATE JERSEY
Select NBA Codes from My NBA Live and enter 9922NVDKVT.

DENVER NUGGETS 2005-06 ALTERNATE JERSEYS
Select NBA Codes from My NBA Live and enter XWETJK72FC.

DETROIT PISTONS 2005-06 ALTERNATE JERSEY
Select NBA Codes from My NBA Live and enter JANTWIKBS6.

INDIANA PACERS 2005-06 ALTERNATE AWAY JERSEY
Select NBA Codes from My NBA Live and enter PSDF90PPJN.

INDIANA PACERS 2005-06 ALTERNATE HOME JERSEY
Select NBA Codes from My NBA Live and enter SDF786WSHW.

SACRAMENTO KINGS 2005-06 ALTERNATE JERSEY
Select NBA Codes from My NBA Live and enter 654NNBFDWA.

A3 GARNETT 3
Select NBA Codes from My NBA Live and enter DRI239CZ49.

JORDAN MELO V.5 WHITE & BLUE
Select NBA Codes from My NBA Live and enter 5223WERPII.

JORDAN MELO V.5 WHITE & YELLOW
Select NBA Codes from My NBA Live and enter ZXDR7362Q1.

JORDAN XIV BLACK & RED
Select NBA Codes from My NBA Live and enter 144FVNHM35.

JORDAN XIV WHITE & GREEN
Select NBA Codes from My NBA Live and enter 67YFH9839F.

JORDAN XIV WHITE & RED
Select NBA Codes from My NBA Live and enter 743HFDRAU8.

S. CARTER III LE
Select NBA Codes from My NBA Live and enter JZ3SCARTVY.

T-MAC 5 BLACK
Select NBA Codes from My NBA Live and enter 258SHQW95B.

T-MAC 5 WHITE
Select NBA Codes from My NBA Live and enter HGS83KP234P.

ANSWER DMX 10
Select NBA Codes from My NBA Live and
enter RBKAIUSAB7.

**ANSWER IX AND THE RBK
ANSWER IX VIDEO**
Select NBA Codes from My NBA Live and
enter AI9BUBBA7T.

**THE QUESTION & THE
MESSAGE FROM AI VIDEO**
Select NBA Codes from My NBA Live and
enter HOYAS3AI6L.

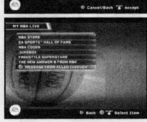

NBA STREET VOL. 2

Select the Pick Up Game option, hold L and enter the following when "Enter cheat
codes now" appears at the bottom of the screen.

UNLIMITED TURBO
Press B, B, Y, Y.

ABA BALL
Press X, B, X, B.

WNBA BALL
Press X, Y, Y, X.

NO DISPLAY BARS
Press B, X (x3).

ALL JERSEYS
Press X, Y, B, B.

ALL COURTS
Press B, Y, Y, B.

ST. LUNATICS TEAM & ALL STREET LEGENDS
Press X, Y, B, Y.

ALL NBA LEGENDS
Press X, Y, Y, B.

CLASSIC MICHAEL JORDAN
Press X, Y, X, X.

EXPLOSIVE RIMS
Press X (x3), Y.

SMALL PLAYERS
Press Y, Y, X, B.

BIG HEADS
Press X, B, B, X.

NO COUNTERS
Press Y, Y, X, X.

BALL TRAILS
Press Y, Y, Y, B.

ALL QUICKS
Press Y, X, Y, B.

EASY SHOTS
Press Y, X, B, Y.

HARD SHOTS
Press Y, B, X, Y.

NCAA FOOTBALL 2005

PENNANT CODES

Select My NCAA and choose Pennant Collection. Now you can enter the following Pennant Codes.

CODE NAME	ENTER
Cuffed Cheat	EA Sports
1st and 15	Thanks
Baylor Power-up	Sic Em
Blink (ball spotted short)	For
Boing (dropped passes)	Registering
Crossed the Line	Tiburon
Illinois Team Boost	Oskee Wow
Jumbalaya	Hike
Molasses Cheat	Home Field
QB Dud	Elite 11
Stiffed	NCAA
Take Your Time	Football
Texas Tech Team Boost	Fight
Thread the Needle	2005
Virginia Tech Team Boost	Tech Triumph
What a Hit	Blitz
2003 All-Americans	Fumble
Alabama All-Time	Roll Tide
Miami All-Time	Raising Cane
Michigan All-Time	Go Blue
Mississippi State All-Time	Hail State
Nebraska All-Time	Go Big Red
North Carolina All-Time	Rah Rah
Penn State All-Time	We Are
Clemson All-Time	Death Valley
Colorado All-Time	Glory
Kansas State All-Time	Victory
Oregon All-Time	Quack Attack
USC All-Time	Fight On
Washington All-Time	Bow Down
Arizona Mascot Team	Bear Down
Arkansas All-Time	WooPigSooie
Auburn All-Time	War Eagle
Badgers All-Time	U Rah Rah
Florida All-Time	Great To Be
Florida State All-Time	Uprising
Georgia All-Time	Hunker Down
Iowa All-Time	On Iowa
LSU All-Time	Geaux Tigers
Notre Dame All-Time	Golden Domer
Oklahoma All-Time	Boomer
Oklahoma State All-Time	Go Pokes
Pittsburgh All-Time	Lets Go Pitt
Purdue All-Time	Boiler Up
Syracuse All-Time	Orange Crush
Tennessee All-Time	Big Orange
Texas A&M All-Time	Gig Em

CODE NAME	ENTER
Texas All-Time	Hook Em
UCLA All-Time	Mighty
Ohio State All-Time	Killer Bucks
Ohio State All-Time	Killer Nuts
Virginia All-Time	Wahoos
Georgia Tech Mascot Team	Ramblinwreck
Iowa St. Mascot Team	Red And Gold
Kansas Mascot Team	Rock Chalk
Kentucky Mascot Team	On On UK
Michigan State Mascot Team	Go Green
Minnesota Mascot Team	Rah Rah Rah
Missouri Mascot Team	Mizzou Rah
NC State Mascot Team	Go Pack
Northwestern Mascot Team	Go Cats
Ole Miss Mascot Team	Hotty Totty
West Virginia Mascot Team	Hail WV
Wake Forest Mascot Team	Go Deacs Go
WSU Mascot Team	All Hail

NEED FOR SPEED CARBON

CASTROL CASH
At the Main menu, press Down, Up, Left, Down, Right, Up, X, B. This will provide access to 10,000 extra cash.

INFINITE CREW CHARGE
At the Main menu, press Down, Up, Up, Right, Left, Left, Right, X.

INFINITE NITROUS
At the Main menu, press Left, Up, Left, Down, Left, Down, Right, X.

INFINITE SPEEDBREAKER
At the Main menu, press Down, Right, Right, Left, Right, Up, Down, X.

NEED FOR SPEED CARBON LOGO VINYLS
At the Main menu, press Right, Up, Down, Up, Down, Left, Right, X.

NEED FOR SPEED CARBON SPECIAL LOGO VINYLS
At the Main menu, press Up, Up, Down, Down, Down, Down, Up, X.

NEED FOR SPEED MOST WANTED

BURGER KING CHALLENGE
At the Title screen, press Up, Down, Up, Down, Left, Right, Left, Right.

CASTROL SYNTEC VERSION OF FORD GT
At the Title screen, press Left, Right, Left, Right, Up, Down, Up, Down.

MARKER IN BACKROOM OF ONE-STOP SHOP
At the Title screen, press Up, Up, Down, Down, Left, Right, Up, Down.

NEED FOR SPEED UNDERGROUND 2

$200 IN CAREER MODE
At the Title screen, press Up, Up, Up, Left, R, R, R, Down.

$1000 IN CAREER MODE
At the Title screen, press Left, Left, Right, X, X, Right, L, R.

HUMMER H2 CAPONE
At the Title screen, press Up, Left, Up, Up, Down, Left, Down, Left.

BEST BUY VINYL
At the Title screen, press Up, Down, Up, Down, Down, Up, Right, Left.

BURGER KING VINYL
At the Title screen, press Up, Up, Up, Up, Down, Up, Up, Left.

PERFORMANCE LEVEL 1
At the Title screen, press L, R, L, R, Left, Left, Right, Up.

PERFORMANCE LEVEL 2
At the Title screen, press R, R, L, R, Left, Right, Up, Down.

VISUAL LEVEL 1
At the Title screen, press R, R, Up, Down, L, L, Up, Down.

VISUAL LEVEL 2
At the Title screen, press L, R, Up, Down, L, Up, Up, Down.

NFL STREET 2

Select Cheats from the Options screen and enter the following:

FUMBLE MODE
Enter GreasedPig as a code.

MAX CATCHING
Enter MagnetHands as a code.

NO FIRST DOWNS
Enter NoChains as a code.

NO FUMBLES MODE
Enter GlueHands as a code.

UNLIMITED TURBO
Enter NozBoost as a code.

EA FIELD
Enter EAField as a code.

GRIDIRON PARK
Enter GRIDIRONPRK as a code.

AFC EAST ALL-STARS
Enter EAASFSCT as a code.

AFC NORTH ALL-STARS
Enter NAOFRCTH as a code.

AFC SOUTH ALL-STARS
Enter SAOFUCTH as a code.

AFC WEST ALL-STARS
Enter WAEFSCT as a code.

NFC EAST ALL-STARS
Enter NNOFRCTH as a code.

NFC NORTH ALL-STARS
Enter NNAS66784 as a code.

NFC SOUTH ALL-STARS
Enter SNOFUCTH as a code.

NFC WEST ALL-STARS
Enter ENASFSCT as a code.

REEBOK TEAM
Enter Reebo as a code.

TEAM XZIBIT
Enter TeamXzibit as a code.

OVER THE HEDGE

COMPLETE LEVELS
Pause the game, hold L + R and press Y, X, Y, X, X, B.

ALL MINI-GAMES
Pause the game, hold L + R and press Y, X, Y, Y, B, B.

ALL MOVES
Pause the game, hold L + R and press Y, X, Y, B, B, X.

EXTRA DAMAGE
Pause the game, hold L + R and press Y, X, Y, X, Y, B.

MORE HP FROM FOOD
Pause the game, hold L + R and press Y, X, Y, X, B, Y.

ALWAYS POWER PROJECTILE
Pause the game, hold L + R and press Y, X, Y, X, B, X.

BONUS COMIC 14
Pause the game, hold L + R and press Y, X, B, B, X, Y.

BONUS COMIC 15
Pause the game, hold L + R and press Y, Y, B, X, B, X.

PAC-MAN WORLD 3

ALL LEVELS AND MAZE GAMES
At the Main menu, press Left, Right, Left, Right, X, Up to unlock all levels and the 3D maze mini-games.

PETER JACKSON'S KING KONG: THE OFFICIAL GAME OF THE MOVIE

At the Main menu, hold L + R and press Down, X, Up, Y, Down, Down, Up, Up. Release L + R to access the Cheat option. The Cheat option is also located on the pause menu.

GOD MODE
Select Cheat and enter 8wonder

ALL CHAPTERS
Select Cheat and enter KKst0ry.

AMMO 999
Select Cheat and enter KK 999 mun.

MACHINE GUN
Select Cheat and enter KKcapone.

REVOLVER
Select Cheat and enter KKtigun.

SNIPER RIFLE
Select Cheat and enter KKsn1per.

INFINITE SPEARS
Select Cheat and enter lance 1nf.

1-HIT KILLS
Select Cheat and enter GrosBras.

EXTRAS
Select Cheat and enter KKmuseum.

PIKMIN 2

TITLE SCREEN

At the Title screen, press the following for a variety of options.

Press R to make the Pikmin form the word NINTENDO.

Press L to go back to PIKMIN 2.

Press X to get a beetle.

Use the C-Stick to move the beetle around.

Press L to dispose of the Beetle.

Press Y to get a Chappie.

Use the C-Stick to move the Chappie around.

Press Z to eat the Pikmin.

Press L to dispose of the Chappie.

PRINCE OF PERSIA: THE SANDS OF TIME

CLASSIC PRINCE OF PERSIA PASSWORDS

LEVEL	PASSWORD
2	KIEJSC
3	VNNNPC
4	IYVPTC
5	RWSWWC
6	GONWUC
7	DEFNUC
8	SVZMSC
9	DBJRPC
10	MZFYSC
11	BRAYQC
12	UUGTPC
Jafar	LRARUC

PRINCE OF PERSIA: THE TWO THRONES

BABY TOY HAMMER WEAPON
Pause the game and press Left, Left, Right, Right, A, Y, Y, A, Up, Down.

CHAINSAW WEAPON
Pause the game and press Up, Up, Down, Down, Left, Right, Left, Right, A, Y, A, Y.

SWORDFISH WEAPON
Pause the game and press Up, Down, Up, Down, Left, Right, Left, Right, A, Y, A, Y.

TELEPHONE OF SORROW WEAPON
Pause the game and press Right, Left, Right, Left, Down, Down, Up, Up, A, Y, A, A, Y, Y.

RAMPAGE: TOTAL DESTRUCTION

ALL MONSTERS AND CITIES
At the Main menu, press R + L to access the Cheat menu and enter 141421.

ALL LEVELS
At the Main menu, press R + L to access the Cheat menu and enter 271828.

INVULNERABLE TO ATTACKS
At the Main menu, press R + L to access the Cheat menu and enter 986960.

ALL SPECIAL ABILITIES
At the Main menu, press R + L to access the Cheat menu and enter 011235.

CPU VS CPU DEMO
At the Main menu, press R + L to access the Cheat menu and enter 082864. This unlocks all of the monsters.

FAST CPU VS CPU DEMO
At the Main menu, press R + L to access the Cheat menu and enter 874098. This unlocks all of the monsters.

ONE HIT DESTROYS BUILDINGS
At the Main menu, press R + L to access the Cheat menu and enter 071767.

OPENING MOVIE
At the Main menu, press R + L to access the Cheat menu and enter 667300.

ENDING MOVIE
At the Main menu, press R + L to access the Cheat menu and enter 667301.

CREDITS
At the Main menu, press R + L to access the Cheat menu and enter 667302.

VERSION INFORMATION
At the Main menu, press R + L to access the Cheat menu and enter 314159.

DISABLE CHEATS
At the Main menu, press R + L to access the Cheat menu and enter 000000.

RAVE MASTER

REINA
At the Title screen, press Up, Up, Down, Down, Left, Right, Left, Right, B, A.

ROBOTS

BIG HEAD
Pause the game and press Up, Down, Down, Up, Right, Right, Left, Right.

INVINCIBLE
Pause the game and press Up, Right, Down, Up, Left, Down, Right, Left.

UNLIMITED SCRAP
Pause the game and press Down, Down, Left, Up, Up, Right, Up, Down.

ROGUE OPS

LEVEL SKIP
Pause the game and press R, X, R, Y, R, Left, R, Right, R, L, L, X, L, Y, L, Left, L, Right, X.

While playing the level you want to complete, pause the game and enter the following code that corresponds to that level.

LEVEL	CODE
Training	Left, Right, Right, Left, Y, X, L, R, Y, Y, X
Bank	L, R, X, Y, Left, L, Left, Left, X, Y, X
Carmen	L, R, Right, Left, Left, R, L, X (x3), L
Forsythe	R, R, Right (x3), R, L, X, L, X, L
Installation K	L, R, X, X, Left, R, R, X, X, L, X
La Casa	L, R, Right, Left, Left, R, L, X (x3), L
Magyar	L, Y, Y, Left, Left, R, L, Right, X, Right, Right
Mod	L, R, Right, L, Left, Y, L, Y, Right, Right, Left
Museum	R, R, Right (x3), R, L, X, L, X, L
Reliance	L, R, Right, Left, L, R, Right, X, Y, X, Y
Silo	L, R, Right, Left, Left, R, Y, L, X (x3)

UNLIMITED HEALTH
Pause the game and press Left, Right, Right, Left, Left, Right, Right, Left, Left, Right, Right, Left, X, X.

UNLIMITED SPY CAM
Pause the game and press Left, Left, Right, Right, L, L, R, R, X, X, Y, Y.

UNLIMITED TOC
Pause the game and press Y, Y, X, X, Left, Right, Right, Left, R, L, R.

BIG FEET
Pause the game and press Right (x3), Left, Right, Left, Right, Left (x3).

SKELETON MODE
Pause the game and press Left (x3), Right, Left, Right, Left, Right (x3).

BIG GUN
Pause the game and press X (x4), Y, Y.

HALF DAMAGE
Pause the game and press X, X, Y, Y, Left, Left, Right, Right, Y, Y, X, X.

NO BULLET DAMAGE
Pause the game and press Left, Right, Right, Left, X, Y, Y, X.

ONE-HIT KILLS
Pause the game and press Y, Left, Right, Right, Left, Y, R, L, Y, X, X.

EXPLOSIVE CROSSBOW
Pause the game and press Left, Right, Right, Left, X, Y, R, L, X, Y, Left, Right.

EXPLOSIVE SNIPER
Pause the game and press R, L, Right, Right, Left, Left, Right, Right, L, R, X, Y.

MISSILE CROSSBOW
Pause the game and press Right, Right, Left, Left, R, R, L, L, Y, Y, X, X.

MISSILE SNIPER
Pause the game and press X, Left, Right, R, L, Right, X, L, L, R, Left, Left.

UNLIMITED BULLETS
Pause the game and press X, Y, X, Y, X, Y, X, Y, Left, Y, X, Y, X, Y, X, Y, X.

SAMURAI JACK: THE SHADOW OF AKU

CRYSTAL SWORD
During a game, press the Analog-stick Down + C-stick Up, A, X, B, Y.

SCALER

FULL HEALTH
Pause the game, select audio from the Options menu and press R, L, R, L, Y, Y, X, X, R, X.

200,000 KLOKKIES
Pause the game, select audio from the Options menu and press L, L, R, R, Y, X, Y.

INFINITE ELECTRIC BOMBS
Pause the game, select audio from the Options menu and press R, R, L, L, Y, Y, X.

SCOOBY-DOO! NIGHT OF 100 FRIGHTS

ALL POWER-UPS
Pause the game, hold L + R, and press X, B, X, B, X, B, B, B, X, X, B, X, X, X.

ALL WARP GATES
Pause the game, hold L + R, and press B, B, X, B, B, X, B, X (x3).

ALL MOVIES
Pause the game, hold L + R, and press B (x3), X (x3), B, X, B.

ALTERNATE CREDITS
Pause the game, hold L + R, and press B, X, X, B, X, B.

HOLIDAYS
January 1
July 4
October 31
December 25

SHREK 2

BONUS GAMES
Pause the game and select Scrapbook. Press Left, Up, A, X, Left, Up, A, X, Left, Up, A, X, Y, X, Y, X, Y, X. Exit the level and select Bonus to access the games.

CHAPTER SELECT
Pause the game and select Scrapbook. Press Left, Up, A, X, Left, Up, A, X, Left, Up, A, X, Up 5 (x5). Exit the level and select Chapter Select to change chapters.

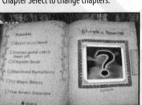

FULL HEALTH
Pause the game and select Scrapbook. Press Left, Up, A, X, Left, Up, A, X, Left, Up, A, X, Up, Right, Down, Left, Up.

1,000 COINS
Pause the game and select Scrapbook. Press Left, Up, A, X, Left, Up, A, X, Left, Up, A, X (x6).

SHREK SUPERSLAM

ALL CHARACTERS AND LEVELS
At the Title screen, press L, R, X, B.

ALL CHALLENGES
At the Title screen, press Y, Y, Y, X, X, X, Y, B, X, B, B, B, Up, Down, Left, Right, L, R.

ALL STORY MODE CHAPTERS
At the Title screen, press Y, B, R, X.

ALL MEDALS AND TROPHIES
At the Title screen, press R, L, Y, B.

SUPER SPEED MODIFIER
At the Title screen, press L, L, R, R, L, R, L, R, B, X, Y, Y.

PIZZA ONE
At the Title screen, press Up, Up, Y, Y, Right, Right, X, X, Down, Down, L, R, Left, Left, B, B, L, R.

PIZZA TWO
At the Title screen, press X, X, B, B, R, R, Left, Left, L, L.

PIZZA THREE
At the Title screen, press Down, Down, Right, X, Up, Y, Left, B, L, L.

SLAMMAGEDDON
At the Title screen, press Up, Up, Down, Down, Left, Right, Left, Right, Y, B, B, L, R.

THE SIMPSONS: HIT & RUN

Select the Options from the Main menu, hold L + R and enter the following:

RED BRICK CAR
Enter B, B, Y, X.

FAST CARS
Enter X, X, X, X.

FASTER CARS
Enter Y, Y, Y, Y.

ONE-HIT WRECK
Enter Y, Y, X, X.

USE HORN TO JUMP IN CAR
Enter X, X, X, Y.

SHOW SPEED
Enter Y, Y, B, X.

CHANGE CAMERA
Enter B, B, B, A.

GRID
Enter B, A, B, Y.

TRIPPY
Enter Y, B, Y, B.

CREDITS DIALOG
Enter A, X, X, Y.

HOLIDAY DECORATED LIVING ROOM
Change the date of your system to Thanksgiving, Halloween, or Christmas for a new look.

THE SIMPSONS: ROAD RAGE

NEW YEAR'S KRUSTY
At the Options screen, hold L + R and press B, B, X, Y. Or, set the GameCube date to January 1.

HALLOWEEN BART
At the Options screen, hold L + R and press B, B, X, A. Or, set the GameCube date to October 31.

THANKSGIVING MARGE
At the Options screen, hold L + R and press B, B, X, X. Or, set the GameCube date to Thanksgiving.

CHRISTMAS APU
At the Options screen, hold L + R and press B, B, X, B. Or, set the GameCube date to December 25.

FLAT CHARACTERS
At the Options screen, hold L + R and press X (x4).

NO MAP
At the Options screen, hold L + R and press Y, B, B, X.

HORIZONTAL SPLIT SCREEN, MULTIPLAYER MODE
At the Options screen, hold L + R and press Y (x4).

NIGHT
At the Options screen, hold L + R and press A (x4).

ALTERNATE CAMERA VIEWS
At the Options screen, hold L + R and press B (x4).

MORE CAMERA OPTIONS
At the Options screen, hold L + R and press B, A (x3).

COLLISION LINES
At the Options screen, hold L + R and press B, B, A, A.

SMITHERS IN MR. BURNS'S LIMOUSINE
At the Options screen, hold L + R and press B, B, Y, Y.

NUCLEAR BUS
At the Options screen, hold L + R and press B, B, Y, A.

RED BRICK CAR
At the Options screen, hold L + R and press B, B, Y, X.

SPECIAL MOVES
At the Options screen, hold L1 + R1 and press A, B, B, A.

| Road Rage Roll | Hold Gas + Brake + Handbrake in air |
| Speed Boost | Hold Gas + Handbrake, then release Handbrake. |

TIME TRIAL
At the Options screen, hold L + R and press X, B, Y, A.

SLOW MOTION
At the Options screen, hold L + R and press A, X, B, Y.

DISABLE CODES
At the Options screen, hold L + R and press START (x4).

THE SIMS

At the Main menu, press L + R to enter the following codes:

PLAY THE SIMS MODE, ALL 2-PLAYER GAMES, OBJECTS, AND SKINS
Enter MIDAS. Select Get A Life and start a new game. Join Roxy in the hot tub, pause the game and quit.

ALL OBJECTS COST ZERO SIMOLEANS
Enter FREEALL.

PARTY MOTEL, 2-PLAYER GAME
Enter PARTY M.

PLAY THE SIMS MODE
Enter SIMS.

FIRST-PERSON VIEW
Enter FISH EYE. Press X to toggle the view.

THE SIMS 2: PETS

CHEAT GNOME
During a game, press L, L, R, A, A, Up.

CAT AND DOG CODES
Select New Key from Game Options and enter the following codes for the corresponding cat or dog.

PET	CODE
Bandit Mask Cats	EEGJ2YRQZZAIZ9QHA64
Bandit Mask Dogs	EEGJ2YRQZQARQ9QHA64
Black Dot Cats	EEGJ2YRZQQ1IQ9QHA64
Black Dot Dogs	EEGJ2YRQZZ1IQ9QHA64
Black Smiley Cats	EEGJ2YRQQZ1RQ9QHA64
Black Smiley Dogs	EEGJ2YRQZQARQ9QHA64
Blue Bones Cats	EEGJ2YRQZZARQ9QHA64
Blue Bones Dogs	EEGJ2YRZZZ1IZ9QHA64
Blue Camouflage Cats	EEGJ2YRZZQ1IQ9QHA64
Blue Camouflage Dogs	EEGJ2YRZZZ1RQ9QHA64
Blue Cats	EEGJ2YRQZZAIQ9QHA64
Blue Dogs	EEGJ2YRQQQ1IZ9QHA64
Blue Star Cats	EEGJ2YRQQZ1IZ9QHA64
Blue Star Dogs	EEGJ2YRQZQ1IQ9QHA64
Deep Red Cats	EEGJ2YRQQQAIQ9QHA64
Deep Red Dogs	EEGJ2YRQZQ1RQ9QHA64
Goofy Cats	EEGJ2YRQZQ1IZ9QHA64
Goofy Dogs	EEGJ2YRZZZARQ9QHA64
Green Cats	EEGJ2YRZQQAIZ9QHA64
Green Dogs	EEGJ2YRQZQAIQ9QHA64
Green Flower Cats	EEGJ2YRQZQZAIQ9QHA64
Green Flower Dogs	EEGJ2YRQZZ1RQ9QHA64
Light Green Cats	EEGJ2YRZZQ1RQ9QHA64
Light Green Dogs	EEGJ2YRQZQQ1RQ9QHA64
Navy Hearts Cats	EEGJ2YRZQZ1IQ9QHA64
Navy Hearts Dogs	EEGJ2YRQQZ1IQ9QHA64
Neon Green Cats	EEGJ2YRZZQAIQ9QHA64
Neon Green Dogs	EEGJ2YRQQQAIQ9QHA64
Neon Yellow Cats	EEGJ2YRZZQARQ9QHA64
Neon Yellow Dogs	EEGJ2YRQQQAIZ9QHA64
Orange Diagonal Cats	EEGJ2YRQQZAIQ9QHA64
Orange Diagonal Dogs	EEGJ2YRQZQ1IZ9QHA64
Panda Cats	EEGJ2YRQZQAIZ9QHA6
Pink Cats	EEGJ2YRQZZ1IZ9QHA64
Pink Dogs	EEGJ2YRZRQZ1RQ9QHA64
Pink Vertical Stripe Cats	EEGJ2YRQQQARQ9QHA6
Pink Vertical Stripe Dogs	EEGJ2YRZZZAIQ9QHA64
Purple Cats	EEGJ2YRQQZARQ9QHA64

PET	CODE
Purple Dogs	EEGJ2YRQQZAIZ9QHA64
Star Cats	EEGJ2YRZQZARQ9QHA6
Star Dogs	EEGJ2YRZQZAIZ9QHA64
White Paws Cats	EEGJ2YRQQQ1RQ9QHA64
White Paws Dogs	EEGJ2YRZQQ1IZ9QHA64
White Zebra Stripe Cats	EEGJ2YRZZZ1IZ9QHA6
White Zebra Stripe Dogs	EEGJ2YRZZZ1IQ9QHA64
Zebra Stripes Dogs	EEGJ2YRZZZQAIZ9QHA64

THE SIMS: BUSTIN' OUT

Pause the game to enter the following codes. You must enter the Enable Cheats code first. After entering another code, select the gnome to access it.

ENABLE CHEATS
Press Down, L, Z, R, Left, X. When entered correctly, a gnome appears in front of your house.

FILL ALL MOTIVES
Press L, R, Y, Down, Down, X.

UNLOCK ALL LOCATIONS
Press Down, Z, R, L, Z.

UNLOCK ALL OBJECTS
Press Down, Z, Up, Y, R.

UNLOCK ALL SKINS
Press L, Y, A, R, Left.

UNLOCK ALL SOCIAL OPTIONS
Press L, R, Down, Down, Y.

SONIC ADVENTURE DX DIRECTOR'S CUT

Note that you must first unlock these mini-games with emblems.

Sonic Chaos

LEVEL SELECT
At the Title screen, press Up (x4), Right, Left, Right, Left, Start.

INSTANT CHAOS EMERALDS
At the Character Select screen, press Up, Down, Up, Down, B, A, B, A, B, A.

SOUND TEST
At the Title screen, press Down, Down, Up, Up, Left, Right, Left, Right, B, A.

Sonic Labyrinth

LEVEL SELECT
At the title screen, press Up, Up, Right (x3), Down (x6), Left (x6).

Sonic Spinball

LEVEL SELECT
At the Sound Test option, play the sounds in the following order: 0, 2, 1, 5, 6, 6.

NO GRAVITY
At the Sound Test option, play the sounds in the following order: 0, 9, 0, 1, 6, 8.

FAST BACKGROUND MUSIC
At the Sound Test option, play the sounds in the following order: 0, 4, 2, 5, 5, 7.

ZOOMED IN
At the Sound Test option, play the sounds in the following order: 0, 2, 1, 1, 6, 6.

SONIC GEMS COLLECTION

Sonic CD

STAGE SELECT
At the Title screen, press Up, Down, Down, Left, Right, A.

HIGH SCORES
At the Title screen, press Right, Right, Up, Up, Down, A.

SOUND TEST
At the Title screen, press Down, Down, Down, Left, Right, A.

Sonic R

SAME CHARACTER SELECT
When selecting your character in Multiplayer mode, hold L and press A or X. This will enable you to choose the same character as the other player.

Sonic Spinball

Enter the following codes by accessing the Options screen and entering them using the SFX option. The screen will shake to confirm that the code is entered correctly.

SKIP BOSS
Choose Sound Effects from the Options screen and play the following tracks in order: 00, 02, 01, 05, 06, 06. During a boss battle pause the game, hold A + B + Start and press Down.

ANTI-GRAVITY SONIC
Choose Sound Effects from the Options screen and play the following tracks in order: 00, 09, 00, 01, 06, 08. Pause the game and press A + B + Start.

FAST MUSIC
Choose Sound Effects from the Options screen and play the following tracks in order: 00, 04, 02, 05, 05, 07.

Tails Skypatrol

SOUND AND STAGE TEST
At the Title screen, hold Up + A and press Start.

Vectorman 2

LEVEL SELECT AND SOUND TEST
Pause the game and press Up, Right, B, A, B, Down, Left, B, Down.

NEW WEAPONS
Pause the game and press X, B, Left, Left, Down, B, Down.

EXTRA LIFE
Pause the game and press Right, Up, A, B, Down, Up, A, Down, Up, A.

REFILL LIFE METER
Pause the game and press A, B, A, B, Left, Up, Up.

MAP COORDINATES
Pause the game and press A, B, Left, Left.

Vectorman

CHEAT MENU
At the Options screen, press B, A, A, B, Down, B, A, A, B.

REFILL LIFE METER
Pause the game and press B, A, Right, B, X, B, Down, B, A, Right, B.

SLOW MOTION
Pause the game and press Down, Right, B, X, Up, Left, B.

TAXI MODE
Pause the game and press X, B, Left, Left, B, X, B, A.

ALL ITEMS AND LEVEL SELECT
Enter the password ADE7 AA2A 51A6 6D12.

SONIC HEROES

METAL CHARACTERS, 2-PLAYER MODE
Select a level in 2-Player mode, then press and hold A + Y.

SONIC MEGA COLLECTION

BLUE SPHERE
Play Sonic 1 and Sonic 3D 20 times each.

THE COMIX ZONE
At the Manuals screen, press Z, Z, Z, Up, Up, Up, Down, Down, Down, L, R, Z.

FLICKY
Play Dr. Robotnik's Mean Bean Machine 20 times.

RISTAR
Play every game 20 times.

SONIC 2 AND KNUCKLES
Play Sonic 2 and Sonic Spinball 20 times each.

SONIC 3 AND KNUCKLES
Play Sonic 3 and Sonic and Knuckles 20 times each.

SONIC THE HEDGEHOG

LEVEL SELECT
At the Title screen, press Up, Down, Left, Right.

DEBUG MODE
At the Title screen, press Up, X, Down, X, Left, X, Right. Hold B, then hold START until level loads. Press A for Debug Mode.

SONIC THE HEDGEHOG 2

LEVEL SELECT
Select Sound Test from the Options menu and play the following sounds in order: 19, 65, 9, and 17. Hold X and press START. At the Title screen, hold B and press START.

DEBUG MODE
After enabling the Level Select code, use the Sound Test to play the following sounds in order: 1, 9, 9, 2, 1, 1, 2, 4. Select the desired level, then hold B + START until the level loads.

SONIC THE HEDGEHOG 3

LEVEL SELECT
After the Sega logo fades and as Sonic appears, press Up, Up, Down, Down, Up (x4). At the Title screen, press Up to access the Level Select.

DEBUG MODE
With the Level Select code enabled, hold B and press Start.

SONIC SPINBALL

LEVEL SELECT
At the Options menu, press B, Down, A, Down, X, Down, B, A, Up, B, X, Up, A, X, Up.

FLICKY

LEVEL SELECT
Start a game and hold Up + A + X + Start. When Round 1 appears, release the buttons.

RISTAR
Enter the following as passwords:

PASSWORD	EFFECT
ILOVEU	Level Select
MUSEUM	Bosses Only
SUPERB	Very Hard Difficulty
DOFEEL	Time Attack
MAGURO	Different Sounds
MIEMIE	Hidden Items
XXXXXX	Disable Codes

SPARTAN: TOTAL WARRIOR

ALL LEVELS IN SINGLE MISSION REPLAY
At the Main menu, highlight Extras and press Left (x11), Right (x7), Y.

SPAWN: ARMAGEDDON

LEVEL SELECT
Pause the game and press Up, Down, Left, Right, Left, Left, Right, Right.

UNLIMITED HEALTH
Pause the game and press Up, Down, Left, Right, Right, Left, Down, Up.

UNLIMITED NECROPLASM
Pause the game and press Up, Down, Left, Right, Down, Left, Up, Right.

ALL WEAPONS
Pause the game and press Up, Down, Left, Right, Left, Right, Left, Left.

UNLIMITED AMMUNITION
Pause the game and press Up, Down, Left, Right, Up, Left, Down, Right.

NO BLOOD
Pause the game and press Up, Down, Left, Right, Up (x4).

UNLOCK ENCYCLOPEDIA
Pause the game and press Up, Down, Left, Right, Left, Right, Up, Down.

ALL COMICS
Pause the game and press Up, Down, Left, Right, Right, Left, Left, Up.

SPEED KINGS

Enter the following as your Handle:

COMPLETE DRIVING TEST
Enter .TEST9.

ALL MEETS WON
Enter .MEET6.

RESPECT POINTS
Enter .Resp ##. Replace ## with the desired amount of respect.

MASTER CHEAT
Enter borkbork as a name.

SPIDER-MAN 2

TREYARCH PASSWORD
Start a New Game and enter HCRAYERT as your name. This code starts the game at 44% complete, 201,000 Hero Points, some upgrades and more.

SPONGEBOB SQUAREPANTS: BATTLE FOR BIKINI BOTTOM

You must enter the following codes quickly.

RESTORE HEALTH
Pause the game, hold L + R and press X (x4), Y, X, Y, X, Y (x4).

EXPERT MODE
Pause the game, hold L + R and press X (x3), Y, Y, X (x3), Y, X, Y (x3), X, Y, Y.

EARN 1,000 SHINY OBJECTS
Pause the game, hold L + R and press Y, X, X, Y, Y, Y, X, X, Y.

EARN 10 GOLD SPATULAS
Pause the game, hold L + R and press X, Y, Y, X, X, Y, Y, X.

BUBBLE BOWL POWER-UP
Pause the game, hold L + R and press X, Y, X, Y, X, X, Y, Y. Press X to use the power-up.

CRUISE BUBBLE POWER-UP
Pause the game, hold L + R and press Y, X, Y, X, Y, Y, Y, X, X. Press L to use the power-up.

INCREASE VALUE OF SHINY OBJECTS
Pause the game, hold L + R and press Y, X, Y, X, X, Y, X (x3), Y (x4), X, X, Y.

MODIFIED CRUISE BUBBLE CONTROLS
Pause the game, hold L + R and press X (x4), Y, Y, X, X, Y, X, Y, Y.

VILLAGERS GIVE SHINY OBJECTS WHEN HIT
Pause the game, hold L + R and press Y (x5), X, Y, X, X, Y, X, Y.

VILLAGERS RESTORE HEALTH WHEN NEAR
Pause the game, hold L + R and press Y (x5), X, Y, X (x3), Y, Y.

NO PANTS
Pause the game, hold L + R and press X (x4), Y, X, X, Y, X, Y, Y, X.

BIG PLANKTON
Pause the game, hold L + R and press Y (x4), X, Y, X, Y, X (x4).

SMALL CHARACTERS
Pause the game, hold L + R and press Y (x4), X, Y, X, Y (x5).

SMALL VILLAGERS
Pause the game, hold L + R and press Y (x5), X, Y, X, Y, X, Y, X.

SPONGEBOB BREAKS APART WHEN DEFEATED

Pause the game, hold L + R and press X (x4), Y, Y, X, Y, X (x3), Y.

INVERT LEFT/RIGHT CAMERA CONTROLS

Pause the game, hold L + R and press Y, Y, X (x4), Y, Y.

INVERT UP/DOWN CAMERA CONTROLS

Pause the game, hold L + R and press Y, X (x6), Y.

SPONGEBOB SQUAREPANTS: CREATURE FROM THE KRUSTY KRAB

30,000 EXTRA ZS

Select Cheat Codes from the Extras menu and enter ROCFISH.

PUNK SPONGEBOB IN DIESEL DREAMING

Select Cheat Codes from the Extras menu and enter SPONGE. Select Activate Bonus Items to unlock this bonus item.

HOT ROD SKIN IN DIESEL DREAMING

Select Cheat Codes from the Extras menu and enter HOTROD. Select Activate Bonus Items to unlock this bonus item.

PATRICK TUX IN STARFISHMAN TO THE RESCUE

Select Cheat Codes from the Extras menu and enter PATRICK. Select Activate Bonus Items to unlock this bonus item.

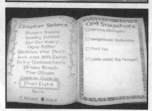

SPONGEBOB PLANKTON IN SUPER-SIZED PATTY

Select Cheat Codes from the Extras menu and enter PANTS. Select Activate Bonus Items to unlock this bonus item.

PATRICK LASER COLOR IN ROCKET RODEO

Select Cheat Codes from the Extras menu and enter ROCKET. Select Activate Bonus Items to unlock this bonus item.

PATRICK ROCKET SKIN COLOR IN ROCKET RODEO

Select Cheat Codes from the Extras menu and enter SPACE. Select Activate Bonus Items to unlock this bonus item.

PLANKTON EYE LASER COLOR IN REVENGE OF THE GIANT PLANKTON MONSTER

Select Cheat Codes from the Extras menu and enter LASER. Select Activate Bonus Items to unlock this bonus item.

HOVERCRAFT VEHICLE SKIN IN HYPNOTIC HIGHWAY— PLANKTON

Select Cheat Codes from the Extras menu and enter HOVER. Select Activate Bonus Items to unlock this bonus item.

SPONGEBOB SQUAREPANTS: LIGHTS, CAMERA, PANTS!

SILVER STORY MODE
Select Rewards from the Bonuses menu, then choose Codes and enter 486739.

ALL ACTION FIGURES
Select Rewards from the Bonuses menu, then choose Codes and enter 977548.

HOOK, LINE & CHEDDAR GAME
Select Rewards from the Bonuses menu, then choose Codes and enter 893634.

SPYHUNTER

SALIVA: THE SPY HUNTER THEME MOVIE
Enter the Agent name as GUNN. After the name disappears, enter your name and select System Options at the next screen to access the movie.

EARLY TEST ANIMATIC MOVIE
Enter the Agent name as WOODY. After the name disappears, enter your name and select System Options at the next screen to access the movie.

SSX 3

Select Options from the Main menu. Choose Cheat Codes from the Options menu and enter the following codes to unlock each character. To access the characters, go to the Lodge and select Rider Details. Then select Cheat Characters to find them.

BRODI
Enter zenmaster.

BUNNY SAN
Enter wheresyourtail.

CANHUCK
Enter greatwhitenorth.

CHURCHILL
Enter tankengine.

CUDMORE
Enter milkemdaisy.

EDDIE
Enter worm.

GUTLESS
Enter boneyardreject.

HIRO
Enter slicksuit.

JJ
Enter potty.

JURGEN
Enter brokenleg.

LUTHER
Enter bronco.

MARTY
Enter back2future.

NORTH WEST LEGEND
Enter callhimgeorge.

SNOWBALLS
Enter betyouveneverseen.

STRETCH
Enter windmilldunk.

SVELTE LUTHER
Enter notsosvelte.

UNKNOWN RIDER
Enter finallymadeitin.

PEAK 1 CLOTHES
Enter shoppingspree.

ALL PEAKS
Enter biggerthank7.

ALL ARTWORK
Enter naturalconcept.

ALL BOARDS
Enter graphicdelight.

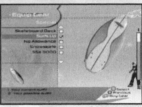

ALL VIDEOS
Enter myeyesaredim.

ALL PLAYLIST SONGS
Enter djsuperstar.

ALL TOYS
Enter nogluerequired.

ALL TRADING CARDS
Enter gotitgotitneedit.

ALL POSTERS
Enter postnobills.

SSX ON TOUR

NEW THREADS
Select Cheats from the Extras menu and enter FLYTHREADS.

THE WORLD IS YOURS
Select Cheats from the Extras menu and enter BACKSTAGEPASS.

SHOW TIME (ALL MOVIES)
Select Cheats from the Extras menu and enter THEBIGPICTURE.

BLING BLING (INFINITE CASH)
Select Cheats from the Extras menu and enter LOOTSNOOT.

FULL BOOST, FULL TIME
Select Cheats from the Extras menu and enter ZOOMJUICE.

MONSTERS ARE LOOSE (MONSTER TRICKS)
Select Cheats from the Extras menu and enter JACKALOPESTYLE.

SNOWBALL FIGHT
Select Cheats from the Extras menu and enter LETSPARTY.

FEEL THE POWER (STAT BOOST)
Select Cheats from the Extras menu and enter POWERPLAY.

CHARACTERS ARE LOOSE
Select Cheats from the Extras menu and enter ROADIEROUNDUP.

UNLOCK CONRAD
Select Cheats from the Extras menu and enter BIGPARTYTIME.

UNLOCK MITCH KOOBSKI
Select Cheats from the Extras menu and enter MOREFUNTHANONE.

UNLOCK NIGEL
Select Cheats from the Extras menu and enter THREEISACROWD.

UNLOCK SKI PATROL
Select Cheats from the Extras menu and enter FOURSOME.

STAR WARS BOUNTY HUNTER

Enter the following at the Code Setup screen:

CHAPTER CODES

CHAPTER	CODE
1	SEEHOWTHEYRUN
2	CITYPLANET
3	LOCKDOWN
4	DUGSOPLENTY
5	BANTHAPOODOO
6	MANDALORIANWAY

LEVEL CODES

LEVEL	CODE
1	BEAST PIT
2	GIMMEMYJETPACK
3	CONVEYORAMA
4	BIGCITYNIGHTS
5	IEATNERFMEAT
6	VOTE4TRELL
7	LOCKUP
8	WHAT A RIOT
9	SHAFTED
10	BIGMOSQUITOS
11	ONEDEADDUG
12	WISHIHADMYSHIP
13	MOS GAMOS
14	TUSKENS R US
15	BIG BAD DRAGON
16	MONTROSSISBAD
17	VOSAISBADDER
18	JANGOISBADDEST

ALL CONCEPT ART
Enter R ARTISTS ROCK.

ALL TGC CARDS
Enter GO FISH.

STAR WARS - JEDI KNIGHT II: JEDI OUTCAST

Select Cheats from the Extras menu and
enter the following:

6 LEVELS
Enter **CHERRY**.

ALL LEVELS
Enter DINGO.

UNLIMITED FORCE
Enter SCOOTER.

INFINITE AMMO
Enter BISCUIT.

INVINCIBILITY IN JEDI ARENA
Enter BUBBLE.

ALL HIDDEN CHARACTERS
Enter PEEPS.

ALZOC III
Enter DEMO.

LIGHTSABER
Enter FUDGE.

ALL MOVIES
Enter FLICKY.

STAR WARS ROGUE SQUADRON III: REBEL STRIKE

Select Passcodes from the Options screen and enter the following. When there are
two passcodes, enter the first one and choose Enter Code and then enter the second
one and choose Enter Code.

UNLIMITED LIVES
Enter IIOUAOYE, then enter WIMPIAM!.

ACE MODE
Enter YNMSFY?P, then enter YOUDAMAN.

LEVEL SELECT (COOPERATIVE MODE)
Enter SWGRCQPL, then enter UCHEATED.

ALL SINGLE-PLAYER MISSIONS
Enter HYWSC!WS, then enter NONGAMER.

ALL SINGLE-PLAYER MISSIONS & BONUS MISSIONS
Enter EEQQ?YPL, then enter CHE!ATER.

BEGGAR'S CANYON RACE (COOPERATIVE MODE)
Enter FRLL!CSF, then enter FARMBOY?.

ASTEROID FIELD MISSION (COOPERATIVE MODE)
Enter RWALPIGC, then enter NOWAYOUT.

DEATH STAR ESCAPE MISSION (COOPERATIVE MODE)
Enter YFCEDFRH, then enter DSAGAIN?.

ENDURANCE MISSION (COOPERATIVE MODE)
Enter WPX?FGC!, then enter EXCERSIZ.

ALL SHIPS (VERSUS MODE)
Enter W!WSTPQB, then enter FREEPLAY.

MILLENNIUM FALCON
Enter QZCRPTG!, then enter HANSRIDE.

NABOO STARFIGHTER
Enter RTWCVBSH, then enter BFNAGAIN.

SLAVE I
Enter TGBCWLPN, then enter ZZBOUNTY.

TIE BOMBER
Enter JASDJWFA, then enter !DABOMB!.

TIE HUNTER
Enter FRRVBMJK, then enter LOOKOUT!.

TIE FIGHTER (COOPERATIVE MODE)
Enter MCKEMAKD, then enter ONESHOT!.

TIE ADVANCE IN COOPERATIVE
Enter VDX?WK!H, then enter ANOKSHIP.

RUDY'S CAR
Enter AXCBPRHK, then enter WHATTHE?.

CREDITS
Enter LOOKMOM!. This option is available in the Special Features menu.

STAR WARS ARCADE GAME
Enter RTJPFC!G, then enter TIMEWARP.

EMPIRE STRIKES BACK ARCADE GAME
Enter !H!F?HXS, then enter KOOLSTUF.

DOCUMENTARY
Enter THEDUDES.

ART GALLERY
Enter !KOOLART.

MUSIC HALL
Enter HARKHARK.

BLACK & WHITE
Enter NOCOLOR?.

STREET HOOPS

Select Cheats from Game Settings and enter the following:

CLOWN UNIFORMS
Press R, Y, R, R.

COWBOY UNIFORMS
Press Y, Y, X, Y.

ELVIS UNIFORMS
Press Y, L, Y, R, Y, Y, X, Y.

KUNG FU UNIFORMS
Press R, R, L, Y.

PIMP UNIFORMS
Press R, X, L, L.

TUXEDO UNIFORMS
Press Y, X, R, Y.

TOMMY TALLARICO UNIFORMS
Press L (x3), R, Y, R, R, X.

ALL COURTS
Press L, L, X, L, Y, R, R, X.

ALL PLAYERS
Press Y, Y, R, L, Y, Y, X, Y.

BLOCK PARTY
Press Y, R, L, Y.

POWER GAME
Press R, L, L, Y.

BLACK BALL
Press L, R, L, L.

AND1 BALL
Press X, L, X, X, L, Y, R, L.

ABA BALL
Press Y, Y, R, X.

GLOBE BALL
Enter R, Y, R, R, L, X, Y, X.

NORMAL BALL
Press R, X, X, L.

$10,000,000
Press R, Y, R, Y, L, L, X, Y.

STREET RACING SYNDICATE

At the Main menu, press Up, Down, Left, Right. This will bring up the code entry screen. Enter the following codes:

MAZDA RX-8
Enter RENESIS.

TOYOTA SUPRA 3.0L RZ
Enter SICKJZA.

MITSUBISHI ECLIPSE GS-T
Enter IGOTGST.

TOYOTA CELICA GT-S
Enter MYTCGTS.

SUBARU IMPREZA S202 STI
Enter SICKGDB.

POLICE CAR
Enter GOTPOPO.

PAC MAN VINYL
Enter GORETRO.

FREE CAR REPAIR
Enter FIXITUP. Your first car repair is free.

GET WARNING FOR FIRST 3 BUSTS
Enter LETMEGO. The first three times you are pulled over, you get a warning.

STRIKE FORCE BOWLING

ALL LEVELS
Name your bowler !LEVELS!.

ALL BOWLERS
Name your bowler !BOWLER!.

TAK: THE GREAT JUJU CHALLENGE

BONUS SOUND EFFECTS
In Juju's Potions, select Universal Card and enter the following numbers for Bugs, Crystals and Fruit: 20, 17, 5.

BONUS SOUND EFFECTS 2
In Juju's Potions, select Universal Card and enter the following numbers for Bugs, Crystals and Fruit: 50, 84, 92.

BONUS MUSIC TRACK 1
In Juju's Potions, select Universal Card and enter the following numbers for Bugs, Crystals and Fruit: 67, 8, 20.

BONUS MUSIC TRACK 2
In Juju's Potions, select Universal Card and enter the following numbers for Bugs, Crystals and Fruit: 6, 18, 3.

MAGIC PARTICLES
In Juju's Potions, select Universal Card and enter the following numbers for Bugs, Crystals and Fruit: 24, 40, 11.

MORE MAGIC PARTICLES
In Juju's Potions, select Universal Card and enter the following numbers for Bugs, Crystals and Fruit: 48, 57, 57.

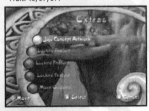

VIEW JUJU CONCEPT ART
In Juju's Potions, select Universal Card and enter the following numbers for Bugs, Crystals and Fruit: Art 33, 22, 28.

VIEW VEHICLE ART
In Juju's Potions, select Universal Card and enter the following numbers for Bugs, Crystals and Fruit: 11, 55, 44.

VIEW WORLD ART
In Juju's Potions, select Universal Card and enter the following numbers for Bugs, Crystals and Fruit: 83, 49, 34.

TAK 2: THE STAFF OF DREAMS

BALLOON HEAD SHOWDOWN MINI GAME
Select Universal Card from Juju Potions and enter the following numbers for bugs, crystals and fruit: 48, 62, 19.

BARREL BLITZ MINI GAME
Select Universal Card from Juju Potions and enter the following numbers for bugs, crystals and fruit: 1, 105, 81.

CATAPULT CHAOS MINI GAME
Select Universal Card from Juju Potions and enter the following numbers for bugs, crystals and fruit: 103, 33, 20.

CHICKEN TENNIS MINI GAME

Select Universal Card from Juju Potions and enter the following numbers for bugs, crystals and fruit: 202, 17, 203.

CHUCKIN' CHICKENS MINI GAME

Select Universal Card from Juju Potions and enter the following numbers for bugs, crystals and fruit: 18, 71, 50.

DART TOOM DODGEM MINI GAME

Select Universal Card from Juju Potions and enter the following numbers for bugs, crystals and fruit: 83, 43, 142.

DINKY SNOWBOARD BIG AIR MINI GAME

Select Universal Card from Juju Potions and enter the following numbers for bugs, crystals and fruit: 233, 127, 204.

FLEA FLYER MINI GAME

Select Universal Card from Juju Potions and enter the following numbers for bugs, crystals and fruit: 22, 6, 17.

FROG DERBY MINI GAME

Select Universal Card from Juju Potions and enter the following numbers for bugs, crystals and fruit: 281, 62, 149.

GLIDE RIDE MINI GAME

Select Universal Card from Juju Potions and enter the following numbers for bugs, crystals and fruit: 131, 61, 179.

GLOOMLEAF ARENA MINI GAME

Select Universal Card from Juju Potions and enter the following numbers for bugs, crystals and fruit: 68, 13, 8.

KRASH KOURSE MINI GAME

Select Universal Card from Juju Potions and enter the following numbers for bugs, crystals and fruit: 5, 41, 41.

VINE CLIMB MINI GAME

Select Universal Card from Juju Potions and enter the following numbers for bugs, crystals and fruit: 8, 1, 3.

FAUNA IN MULTIPLAYER

Select Universal Card from Juju Potions and enter the following numbers for bugs, crystals and fruit: 44, 13, 0.

JB IN MULTIPLAYER

Select Universal Card from Juju Potions and enter the following numbers for bugs, crystals and fruit: 16, 19, 38.

LOK IN MULTIPLAYER

Select Universal Card from Juju Potions and enter the following numbers for bugs, crystals and fruit: 2, 2, 5.

SKELETON JUJU SPIRIT IN MULTIPLAYER

Select Universal Card from Juju Potions and enter the following numbers for bugs, crystals and fruit: 55, 171, 35.

TAK'S FEATHER COLOR

Select Universal Card from Juju Potions and enter the following numbers for bugs, crystals and fruit: 4, 9, 23.

BETTER MANA MAGNET

Select Universal Card from Juju Potions and enter the following numbers for bugs, crystals and fruit: 3, 27, 31.

TAK 1 GAME CINEMATIC SEQUENCE

Select Universal Card from Juju Potions and enter the following numbers for bugs, crystals and fruit: 30, 21, 88.

CONCEPT ART

Select Universal Card from Juju Potions and enter the following numbers for bugs, crystals and fruit: 30, 37, 51.

PICTURES OF THE TAK SUIT

Select Universal Card from Juju Potions and enter the following numbers for bugs, crystals and fruit: 11, 4, 17.

SOUND EFFECTS SET ONE
Select Universal Card from Juju Potions and enter the following numbers for bugs, crystals and fruit: 4, 55, 36.

VIEW COMMERICIALS
Select Universal Card from Juju Potions and enter the following numbers for bugs, crystals and fruit: 6, 16, 6.

TAK AND THE POWER OF JUJU

Pause the game and enter the following codes:

ALL EXTRAS AND CHEATS
Enter Left, Right, B, B, X, X, Left, Right.

100 FEATHERS
Enter B, Y, X, B, Y, X, B, Y.

ALL MOONSTONES
Enter Y, Y, B, B, X, X, Left, Right.

ALL PLANTS
Enter B, Y, X, Left, Up, Right, Down, Down.

ALL JUJU POWER-UPS
Enter Up, Right, Left, Down, Y, X, B, Down.

ALL YORBELS
Enter Up, Y, Left, B, Right, X, Down, Up.

TEENAGE MUTANT NINJA TURTLES 2: BATTLE NEXUS

Select Password from the Options menu and enter the following. Hold L while selecting a turtle to get his New Nexus Turtle outfit.

EFFECT	PASSWORD
Challenge Code Abyss	SDSDRLD
Challenge Code Endurance	MRMDRMD
Challenge Code Fatal Blow	LRSRDRD
Challenge Code Lose Shuriken	RLMRDSL
Challenge Code Nightmare	SLSDRDL
Challenge Code Poison	DRSLLSR
Challenge Code Super-Tough	RDSRMRL
Cheat Code All-You-Can-Throw Shuriken	RSRLRSM
Cheat Code Health	DSRDMRM
Cheat Code Mighty Turtle	LSDRRDR
Cheat Code Pizza Paradise	MRLMRMR
Cheat Code Self Recovery	DRMSRLR
Cheat Code Squeaking	MLDSRDM
Cheat Code Super Defense Power	LDRMRLM
Cheat Code Super Offense Power	SDLSRLL

EFFECT	PASSWORD
Cheat Code Toddling	SSSMRDD
New Nexus Turtle outfit for Donatello	DSLRDRM
New Nexus Turtle outfit for Leonardo	LMRMDRD
New Nexus Turtle outfit for Michelangelo	MLMRDRM
New Nexus Turtle outfit for Raphael	RMSRMDR
Playmates added to Bonus Materials	SRMLDDR

TEENAGE MUTANT NINJA TURTLES 3: MUTANT NIGHTMARE

INVINCIBILITY
Select Passwords from the Options screen and enter MDLDSSLR.

HEALTH POWER-UPS BECOME SUSHI
Select Passwords from the Options screen and enter SLLMRSLD.

NO HEALTH POWER-UPS
Select Passwords from the Options screen and enter DMLDMRLD.

ONE HIT DEFEATS TURTLE
Select Passwords from the Options screen and enter LDMSLRDD.

MAX OUGI
Select Passwords from the Options screen and enter RRDMLSDL.

UNLIMITED SHURIKEN
Select Passwords from the Options screen and enter LMDRRMSR.

NO SHURIKEN
Select Passwords from the Options screen and enter LLMSRDMS.

DONATELLO'S LEVEL 2 DINO ARMOR SCROLL
Select Passwords from the Options screen and enter MSSRDLMR.

DONATELLO'S LEVEL 3 DINO ARMOR SCROLL
Select Passwords from the Options screen and enter DLRLDMSR.

LEO'S LEVEL 2 DINO ARMOR SCROLL
Select Passwords from the Options screen and enter RLDMRMSD.

LEO'S LEVEL 3 DINO ARMOR SCROLL
Select Passwords from the Options screen and enter MLMSRRDS.

MICHELANGELO'S LEVEL 2 DINO ARMOR SCROLL
Select Passwords from the Options screen and enter SRDMMLRS.

MICHELANGELO'S LEVEL 3 DINO ARMOR SCROLL
Select Passwords from the Options screen and enter LSMRRDSL.

RAPHAEL'S LEVEL 2 DINO ARMOR SCROLL
Select Passwords from the Options screen and enter DRMDLLRS.

RAPHAEL'S LEVEL 3 DINO ARMOR SCROLL
Select Passwords from the Options screen and enter SMRDRSLD.

DOUBLE ENEMY ATTACK
Select Passwords from the Options screen and enter MSRLSMML.

DOUBLE ENEMY DEFENSE
Select Passwords from the Options screen and enter SLRMLSSM.

TIGER WOODS PGA TOUR 06

ALL GOLFERS
Select Password from the Options screen and enter WOOGLIN.

ALL CLUBS
Select Password from the Options screen and enter CLUB11.

LEVEL 2 NIKE ITEMS
Select Password from the Options screen and enter JUSTDOIT.

ALL COURSES
Select Password from the Options screen and enter ITSINTHEHOLE.

TIGER WOODS IN HAT & TIE
Select Password from the Options screen and enter GOLDENAGE.

TIGER WOODS IN STRIPED PANTS
Select Password from the Options screen and enter TECHNICOLOR.

TIGER WOODS IN OLD GOLF OUTFIT
Select Password from the Options screen and enter OLDSKOOL.

TIGER WOODS IN A DIFFERENT OLD GOLF OUTFIT
Select Password from the Options screen and enter THROWBACK.

ARNOLD PALMER
Select Password from the Options screen and enter ARNIESARMY.

BEN HOGAN
Select Password from the Options screen and enter THEHAWK.

JACK NICKLAUS
Select Password from the Options screen and enter GOLDENBEAR.

OLD TOM MORRIS
Select Password from the Options screen and enter FEATHERIE.

TOMMY BLACK
Select Password from the Options screen
and enter IDONTHAVEAPROBLEM.

WESLEY ROUNDER
Select Password from the Options screen
and enter POCKETPAIR.

TONY HAWK'S AMERICAN WASTELAND

ALWAYS SPECIAL
Select Cheat Codes from the Options screen and enter uronfire. Pause the game and select
Cheats from the Game Options to unlock the cheat.

PERFECT RAIL
Select Cheat Codes from the Options screen and enter grindxpert. Pause the game and select
Cheats from the Game Options to unlock the cheat.

PERFECT SKITCH
Select Cheat Codes from the Options screen and enter h!tchar!de. Pause the game and select
Cheats from the Game Options to unlock the cheat.

PERFECT MANUAL
Select Cheat Codes from the Options and enter 2wheels!. Pause the game and select Cheats
from the Game Options to unlock the cheat.

MOON GRAVITY
Select Cheat Codes from the Options screen and enter 2them00n. Pause the game and select
Cheats from the Game Options to unlock the cheat.

MAT HOFFMAN
Select Cheat Codes from the Options screen and enter the_condor.

JASON ELLIS
Select Cheat Codes from the Options screen and enter sirius-dj.

TONY HAWK'S UNDERGROUND

Select Cheat Codes from the Options
menu and enter the following. You
must turn on some cheats by pausing
the game and selecting Cheats from the
Options menu.

PLAY AS T.H.U.D.
Enter NOOO!!.

PERFECT RAIL
Enter letitslide.

PERFECT SKITCH
Enter rearrider.

PERFECT MANUAL
Enter keepitsteady.

MOON GRAVITY
Enter getitup.

TONY HAWK'S UNDERGROUND 2

ALWAYS SPECIAL
Select Cheat Codes from the Game Options and enter likepaulie. Select Cheats from the Game Options to toggle the code on and off.

PERFECT RAIL
Select Cheat Codes from the Game Options and enter straightedge. Select Cheats from the Game Options to toggle the code on and off.

TRUE CRIME: NEW YORK CITY

DOUBLE DAMAGE
At the City Map screen, hold L + R and press A, A, B, A, A, A.

MILLIONAIRE
At the City Map screen, hold L + R and press B, B, Y, B, Y, B.

SUPER COP
At the City Map screen, hold L + R and press Y, A, Y, A, Y, Y.

ULTRA EASY MODE
At the City Map screen, hold L + R and press A, B, A, A, Y, A.

UNLIMITED AMMO
At the City Map screen, hold L + R and press A, B, A, B, B, Y.

UNLIMITED ENDURANCE
At the City Map screen, hold L + R and press A, B, A, B, A, A.

STREET RACES OPEN
At the City Map screen, hold L + R and press Y, Y, A, A, Y.

FIGHTS OPEN
At the City Map screen, hold L + R and press B, B, A, A, B.

GHETTO CITY
At the City Map screen, hold L + R and press A, B, A, Y, Y, Y.

ZOMBIEFIED
At the City Map screen, hold L + R and press A, Y, B, A, B, A.

NEW OUTFIT IN PUMA STORE
At the City Map screen, hold L + R and press Y, A, A, B.

RED GONE WILD
At the City Map screen, hold L + R and press Y, A, A, B, A, B.

ALL MUSIC
At the City Map screen, hold L + R and press A, B, A, B.

TRUE CRIME: STREETS OF LA

VARIOUS CODES
At the City Map in a Destination Driving mission, input the following combos (use the D-Pad to input directions):

CODE	EFFECT
R, L, Up, Right, Left, Down, Z, Z, A, Y, X, Y	Play as Snoop Dog
Up, Right, Down, Left, Up, A	All Bonuses
Up, Left, Down, Left, Up, A	All Upgrades
Up, Down, Up, Down, A	All Combat Moves
Left, Right, Left, Right, A	All Driving Maneuvers
Right, Left, Right, Left, A	All Gun Upgrades
Up, Right, Down, Left, Up, A	Impound Garage Cars
Down, Down, Down, A	Extra Car Mass
Up, Up, Up, A	Lesser Car Mass
Hold Up and press A, A, A	Boost

LICENSE PLATE CHEATS

Create a License Plate using the following codes. Then highlight OK, hold L + R and press A. Nick will look like the corresponding character.

FATT	George
B1G1	The Chief
ROSA	Rosie
HURT M3	Rosie in Lingerie
FUZZ	Policeman Johnson
5WAT	SWAT Officer
M1K3	Commando
TFAN	Gangsta_Alt
HARA	Asian Worker
MNKY	Street Punk
MRFU	Jimmy Fu
PHAM	Triad Butcher
BRUZ	Dirty Morales
HAWG	Bartender
BOOB	Lola Gees
TATS	Tattoo Concubines
P1MP	Pimp
BOOZ	Bum
J1MM	Sewer Ghoul
JASS	Donkey

TY THE TASMANIAN TIGER 3: NIGHT OF THE QUINKAN

100,000 OPALS
During a game, press Start, Start, Y, Start, Start, Y, X, A, X, A.

ALL CHASSIS
During a game, press Start, Start, Y, Start, Start, Y, X, B, X, B.

THE URBZ: SIMS IN THE CITY

CHEAT GNOME
During a game, press Down, L, Z, R, X, Left. Now you can enter the following cheats.

ACQUIRE SKILL OBJECT
During a game, find the Gnome and press Down, Z, Up, Y, R.

ALL POWER SOCIALS
During a game, find the Gnome and press B, Left, X, R, L, A.

POWER SOCIALS
During a game, find the Gnome and press B, Left, X, R, L.

MAX ARTISTIC SKILL
During a game, find the Gnome and press R, Y, Up, Z, Down.

MAX MENTAL SKILL
During a game, find the Gnome and press Down, X, Left, R, Down.

MAX PHYSICAL SKILL
During a game, find the Gnome and press R, Z, Down, Y, Y.

ULTIMATE SPIDER-MAN

ALL CHARACTERS
Pause the game and select Controller Setup from the Options menu. Press Right, Down, Right, Down, Left, Up, Left, Right.

ALL COVERS
Pause the game and select Controller Setup from the Options menu. Press Left, Left, Right, Left, Up, Left, Left, Down.

ALL CONCEPT ART
Pause the game and select Controller Setup from the Options menu. Press Down, Down, Down, Up, Down, Up, Left, Left.

ALL LANDMARKS
Pause the game and select Controller Setup from the Options menu. Press Up, Right, Down, Left, Down, Up, Right, Left.

THE URBZ: SIMS IN THE CITY

CHEAT GNOME
During a game, press Down, L, Z, R, X, Left. Now, go find the gnome and enter the following cheats. Select the gnome to access the cheats.

MAX PHYSICAL SKILL
Press R, Z, Down, Y, Y.

MAX ARTISTIC SKILL
Press R, Y, Up Z, Down.

MAX MENTAL SKILL
Press Down, X, Left, R, Down.

ALL POWERSOCIAL ITEMS
Press B, Left, X, R, L, A.

SKILL OBJECTS
Press Down, Z, Up, Y, R.

PHOTO
At the credits screen, press Up, Down, A, Up, Down, A.

WAVE RACE: BLUE STORM

PASSWORD SCREEN
At the Options menu press X + Z + Start.

DOLPHIN
Enter DLPHNMOD as a password. This will disable the save feature.

WRECKLESS

GOLD RATING ON ALL MISSIONS
Highlight Unlimited Time, hold L + R + Right and press Z.

WWE CRUSH HOUR

ALL VEHICLES AND LEVEL SELECT
At the player select, press Y, Z, X, L.

KEVIN NASH
At the player select, press L, X, Z, Y.

WWE DAY OF RECKONING 2

Secrets & Unlockables

There are several hidden extras available in Day of Reckoning 2. Some items require that you complete certain Shows in Story Mode, while completing a specific number of matches in Exhibition Mode unlocks other extras. The specific requirements needed to earn each reward are listed below.

Bonus Attribute Points

REWARD	REQUIREMENT
Increase Create a Superstar Experience to 800	Finish Show 16
Increase Create a Superstar Experience to 1100	Finish Show 21
Increase Create a Superstar Experience to 1400	Finish Show 32
Increase Create a Superstar Experience to 1700	Finish Show 43

Bonus Arenas

REWARD	REQUIREMENT
Backlash Arena	Finish Show 08
Vengeance Arena	Finish Show 12
Summerslam Arena	Finish Show 16
Unforgiven Arena	Finish Show 20
No Mercy Arena	Finish Show 21
Survivor Series	Finish Show 26
Armageddon Arena	Finish Show 33
Royal Rumble	Finish Show 37
No Way Out Arena	Finish Show 40
Wrestlemania	Finish Show 43

Legendary Superstars

REWARD	REQUIREMENT
The Rock	Finish Show 20
Steve Austin	Defeat the computer in Exhibition's Single Match Mode 5 times
Mankind	Defeat the computer in Exhibition's Single Match Mode 10 times
Hulk Hogan	Finish Show 43
Bret Hart	Defeat the computer in Exhibition's Single Match Mode 20 times

X-MEN LEGENDS II: RISE OF APOCALYPSE

ALL CHARACTERS
At the Team Management screen, press Right, Left, Left, Right, Up, Up, Up, Start.

ALL SKINS
At the Team Management screen, press Down, Up, Left, Right, Up, Up, Start.

ALL SKILLS
At the Team Management screen, press Left, Right, Left, Right, Down, Up, Start.

LEVEL 99
At the Team Management screen, press Up, Down, Up, Down, Left, Up, Left, Right, Start.

GOD MODE
Pause the game and press Down, Up, Down, Up, Right, Down, Right, Left, Start.

MOVE FASTER
Pause the game and press Up, Up, Up, Down, Up, Down, Start.

UNLIMITED XTREME TOKENS
Pause the game and press Left, Down, Right, Down, Up, Up, Down, Up, Start.

TOUCH OF DEATH
During a game, press Left, Left, Right, Left, Right, Up, Start.

100,000 TECH-BITS
At Forge or Beast's store, press Up, Up, Up, Down, Right, Right, Start.

ALL DANGER ROOM COURSES
At the Danger Room Course menu, press Right, Right, Left, Left, Up, Down, Up, Down, Start.

ALL COMICS
Select Review from the Main menu and press Right, Left, Left, Right, Up, Up, Right, Start.

ALL CUTSCENES
Select Review from the Main menu and press Left, Right, Right, Left, Down, Down, Left, Start.

ALL CONCEPTS
Select Review from the Main menu and press Left, Right, Left, Right, Up, Up, Down, Start.

ALL SCREENS
Select Review from the Main menu and press Right, Left, Right, Left, Up, Up, Down, Start.

X-MEN: THE OFFICIAL GAME

DANGER ROOM ICEMAN
At the Cerebro Files menu, press Right, Right, Left, Left, Down, Up, Down, Up, Start.

DANGER ROOM NIGHTCRAWLER
At the Cerebro Files menu, press Up, Up, Down, Down, Left, Right, Left, Right, Start.

DANGER ROOM WOLVERINE
At the Cerebro Files menu, press Down, Down, Up, Up, Right, Left, Right, Left, Start.

X2: WOLVERINE'S REVENGE

LEVEL SELECT & ALL CHALLENGES
At the Main menu, press B, A, B, Y, B, A, L, R, Z.

ALL CEREBRO FILES AND MOVIES
At the Main menu, press B, A, B, Y (x3), R, R, Z.

ALL COSTUMES
At the Main menu, press B, A, B, Y (x3), L, L, Z.

CHEATS
At the Main menu, press B, B, A, A, Y, Y, A, A, L, L, R, R, Z. Pause the game to find the cheats.

ALL MOVIES
At the main menu, press B, A, B, Y, Y, Y, R, R, Z.

XGRA: EXTREME-G RACING ASSOCIATION

ALL LEVELS OF RACING
Enter FREEPLAY at the Cheat menu.

ALL TRACKS
Enter WIBBLE at the Cheat menu.

O2 LIVERIED
Enter UCANDO at the Cheat menu.

MESSAGE IN CREDITS
Enter MUNCHKIN, EDDROOLZ, or EDDIEPOO at the Cheat menu.

YU-GI-OH: FALSEBOUND KINGDOM

GOLD COINS
On an empty piece of land and during a mission, press Up, Up, Down, Down, Left, Right, Left, Right, B, A.

ZAPPER

INFINITE LIVES
Pause the game, hold L and press Up, Up, Up, Left, Left, Right, Left, Right.

INFINITE SHIELDS
Pause the game, hold L and press Up, Down, Up, Left, Right, Down, Up.

ZOIDS: BATTLE LEGENDS

ENERGY LIGER
Select Config and play the following voices: 004, 044, 019, 066, 034.

LIGER ZERO PHOENIX
Select Config and play the following voices: 021, 001, 018, 006, 023.

MEGASAURER IN VS MODE
Select Config and play the following voices: 000, 007, 077, 041, 054.

Games List

ACE COMBAT ADVANCE

COMPLETE GAME WITH ALL PLANES & LEVELS OPEN
Select Enter Code and enter QF9B9F59.

ACTION MAN: ROBOT ATAK

ADVENTURE LEVEL 2
Select Password from the Main menu and enter REDWOLF.

ADVENTURE LEVEL 3
Select Password from the Main menu and enter FLYNT.

ADVENTURE LEVEL 4
Select Password from the Main menu and enter MOTHER.

ADVENTURE LEVEL 5
Select Password from the Main menu and enter MOTOX.

ADVENTURE LEVEL 6
Select Password from the Main menu and enter TEMPLE.

ADVENTURE LEVEL 7
Select Password from the Main menu and enter ACTION.

ADVENTURE LEVEL 8
Select Password from the Main menu and enter BEACH.

ADVENTURE LEVEL 9
Select Password from the Main menu and enter JURA.

ADVENTURE LEVEL 10
Select Password from the Main menu and enter AIR.

ADVENTURE LEVEL 11
Select Password from the Main menu and enter SURF.

ADVENTURE LEVEL 12
Select Password from the Main menu and enter SEWERS.

ADVENTURE LEVEL 13
Select Password from the Main menu and enter TUNNEL.

ADVENTURE LEVEL 14
Select Password from the Main menu and enter LABO.

ADVENTURE LEVEL 15
Select Password from the Main menu and enter KONGO.

ADVENTURE LEVEL 16
Select Password from the Main menu and enter BASIC.

ADVENTURE LEVEL 17
Select Password from the Main menu and enter ROCKET.

ADVANCED MODE
Select Password from the Main menu and enter JUNGLE.

ADVANCED LEVEL 2
Select Password from the Main menu and enter AZTEC.

ADVANCED LEVEL 3
Select Password from the Main menu and enter SPIDER.

ADVANCED LEVEL 4
Select Password from the Main menu and enter DIRT.

ADVANCED LEVEL 5
Select Password from the Main menu and enter CROCO.

ADVANCED LEVEL 6
Select Password from the Main menu and enter QUEEN.

ADVANCED LEVEL 7
Select Password from the Main menu and enter BOW.

ADVANCED LEVEL 8
Select Password from the Main menu and enter LAVA.

ADVANCED LEVEL 9
Select Password from the Main menu and enter ROCKS.

ADVANCED LEVEL 10
Select Password from the Main menu and enter VOLCANO.

ADVANCED LEVEL 11
Select Password from the Main menu and enter TRAPS.

ADVANCED LEVEL 12
Select Password from the Main menu and enter DINO.

ADVANCED LEVEL 13
Select Password from the Main menu and enter SHORE.

ADVANCED LEVEL 14
Select Password from the Main menu and enter RAPTOR.

ADVANCED LEVEL 15
Select Password from the Main menu and enter BATS.

ADVANCED LEVEL 16
Select Password from the Main menu and enter TREX.

ADVANCED LEVEL 17
Select Password from the Main menu and enter BIRD.

ADVANCED LEVEL 18
Select Password from the Main menu and enter ATTACK.

ADVANCED LEVEL 19
Select Password from the Main menu and enter SHELL.

ADVANCED LEVEL 20
Select Password from the Main menu and
enter PATROL.

ADVANCED LEVEL 21
Select Password from the Main menu and
enter WIND.

ADVANCED LEVEL 22
Select Password from the Main menu and
enter RATS.

ADVANCED LEVEL 23
Select Password from the Main menu and enter SECRET.

ADVANCED LEVEL 24
Select Password from the Main menu and enter WATER.

ADVANCED LEVEL 25
Select Password from the Main menu and enter VAPOR.

ADVANCED LEVEL 26
Select Password from the Main menu and enter MORAN.

ADVANCED LEVEL 27
Select Password from the Main menu and enter LIANA.

ADVANCED LEVEL 28
Select Password from the Main menu and enter BACK.

ADVANCED LEVEL 29
Select Password from the Main menu and enter CLOCK.

ADVANCED LEVEL 30
Select Password from the Main menu and enter UNITY.

ADVANCED LEVEL 31
Select Password from the Main menu and enter FINAL.

ADVANCED LEVEL 32
Select Password from the Main menu and enter DOCTORX.

TIME ATTACK MODE
Select Password from the Main menu and
enter HURRY.

TIME ATTACK 2
Select Password from the Main menu and
enter RUINS.

TIME ATTACK 3
Select Password from the Main menu and
enter VENOM.

TIME ATTACK 4
Select Password from the Main menu and enter STORM.

TIME ATTACK 5
Select Password from the Main menu and enter BAYOU.

TIME ATTACK 6
Select Password from the Main menu and enter EGGS.

TIME ATTACK 7
Select Password from the Main menu and enter ARROW.

TIME ATTACK 8
Select Password from the Main menu and enter RACE.

TIME ATTACK 9
Select Password from the Main menu and
enter SLOPE.

TIME ATTACK 10
Select Password from the Main menu and
enter HASTE.

TIME ATTACK 11
Select Password from the Main menu and
enter PITFALL.

TIME ATTACK 12
Select Password from the Main menu and enter DESCENT.

TIME ATTACK 13
Select Password from the Main menu and enter RUN.

TIME ATTACK 14
Select Password from the Main menu and enter CLAWS.

TIME ATTACK 15
Select Password from the Main menu and enter STONES.

TIME ATTACK 16
Select Password from the Main menu and enter WAOW.

TIME ATTACK 17
Select Password from the Main menu and enter AERO.

TIME ATTACK 18
Select Password from the Main menu and enter BREEZE.

TIME ATTACK 19
Select Password from the Main menu and enter RUSH.

TIME ATTACK 20
Select Password from the Main menu and enter CLOUDS.

TIME ATTACK 21
Select Password from the Main menu and enter GUST.

TIME ATTACK 22
Select Password from the Main menu and enter STINK.

TIME ATTACK 23
Select Password from the Main menu and enter BASE.

TIME ATTACK 24
Select Password from the Main menu and enter DANGER.

TIME ATTACK 25
Select Password from the Main menu and enter STEAM.

TIME ATTACK 26
Select Password from the Main menu and enter RESCUE.

TIME ATTACK 27
Select Password from the Main menu and enter MONKEY.

TIME ATTACK 28
Select Password from the Main menu and enter CHAMBER.

TIME ATTACK 29
Select Password from the Main menu and enter BANANA.

TIME ATTACK 30
Select Password from the Main menu and enter FORCE.

TIME ATTACK 31
Select Password from the Main menu and enter TELE.

TIME ATTACK 32
Select Password from the Main menu and enter BOSS.

GAME COMPLETE
Select Password from the Main menu and enter MAXIM.

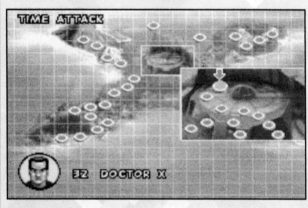

AGGRESSIVE INLINE

ALL SKATERS
At the Title screen, press L, L, B, B, R, R, L, R.

LEVEL SELECT
At the Title screen, press Up, Down, Up, Down, Left, Right, B, R.

ALIENATORS: EVOLUTION CONTINUES

LEVEL 2
Enter MDKMZKCC as a password.

LEVEL 3
Enter BHSZSKTC as a password.

LEVEL 4
Enter ZKTSHKMC as a password.

LEVEL 5
Enter JLPFDKHB as a password.

LEVEL 6
Enter HMDBRKCB as a password.

LEVEL 7
Enter GLDKLKZB as a password.

LEVEL 8
Enter GLPKLKRB as a password.

LEVEL 9
Enter GLDJBKKF as a password.

LEVEL 10
Enter GLPJBKFF as a password.

LEVEL 11
Enter GLPKBKRF as a password.

LEVEL 12
Enter GLPKBKRF as a password.

LEVEL 13
Enter GLDJLKHD as a password.

UNLIMITED AMMO
Enter RBJPXCKC as a password.

ANIMAL SNAP: RESCUE THEM 2 BY 2

BLOCK BLASTER MINI-GAME
At the Main menu, hold L and press Up, Down, Left, Right, Right, Left, Down, Up.

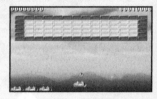

ANIMANIACS: LIGHTS, CAMERA, ACTION!

SKIP LEVEL
Pause the game and press L, L, R, R, Down, Down.

DISABLE TIME
Pause the game and press L, R, Left, Left, Up, Up.

KINGSIZE PICKUPS
Pause the game and press Right, Right, Right, Left, Left, Left, R, L.

PASSWORDS

LEVEL	PASSWORD
1	Wakko, Wakko, Wakko, Wakko, Wakko
2	Dot, Yakko, Brain, Wakko, Pinky
3	Yakko, Dot, Wakko, Wakko, Brain
4	Pinky, Yakko, Yakko, Dot, Brain
5	Pinky, Pinky, Yakko, Wakko, Wakko
6	Brain, Dot, Brain, Pinky, Yakko
7	Brain, Pinky, Wakko, Pinky, Brain
8	Brain Pinky, Pinky, Wakko, Wakko
9	Dot, Dot, Yakko, Pinky, Wakko
10	Brain, Dot, Brain, Yakko, Wakko
11	Wakko, Yakko, Pinky, Dot, Dot
12	Pinky, Pinky, Brain, Dot, Wakko
13	Yakko, Wakko, Pinky, Wakko, Brain
14	Pinky, Wakko, Brain, Wakko, Yakko
15	Dot, Pinky, Wakko, Wakko, Yakko

AROUND THE WORLD IN 80 DAYS

PASSWORDS

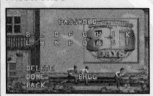 

LEVEL	PASSWORD
Day 1 - London	BHGG
Day 3 - Paris	CLGG
Day 18 - Train	DCHJ
Day 20 - Turkey	FSHJ
Day 25 - India	GKMN
Day 25 - Wanted in India	HLSN
Day 40 - China	JMBJ
Day 61 - San Francisco	KNQN
Day 61 - Train to New York	MQGG
Day 61 - Wild West	LPGG
Old Foe	NRGG
Ending	PSGG

ATV QUAD POWER RACING

ALL ATVS AND TRACKS
Enter the following as a password: Frog, Frog, Helmet, Speed Burst, Tire.

BACKTRACK

ALL WEAPONS
During gameplay press SELECT, then press L, Right, B, L, R, Left. Now enter WEAP as a password.

AUTO AMMO
During a game press SELECT, then press L, Right, B, L, R, Left. Now enter AMMO as a password.

INVINCIBILITY
During a game press SELECT, then press L, Right, B, L, R, Left. Now enter GOD as a password.

BACKYARD BASEBALL 2006

SAMMY SOSA
In a season, enter BABYBEAR as a coach's name.

DONTRELLE WILLIS
In a season, enter BIGFISH as a coach's name.

BANJO PILOT

GRUNTY
Defeat Grunty in the Broomstick battle race. Then you can purchase Grunty from Cheato.

HUMBA WUMBA
Defeat Humba Wumba in the Jiggu battle race. Then you can purchase Humba Wumba from Cheato.

JOLLY
Defeat Jolly in the Pumpkin battle race. Then you can purchase Jolly from Cheato.

KLUNGO
Defeat Klungo in the Skull battle race. Then you can purchase Klungo from Cheato.

BARBIE IN THE 12 DANCING PRINCESSES

EASY PASSWORDS

LEVEL	PASSWORD
2-a	Cat, Cat, Slippers, Prince
2-b	Cat, Old Lady, Bird, Monkey
3-a	Old Lady, Slippers, Slippers, Slippers
3-b	Blonde Girl, Blonde Girl, Monkey, Blonde Girl
4-a	Old Lady, Brunette Girl, Cat, Brunette Girl
4-b	Monkey, Prince, Blonde Girl, Bird
5-a	Old Lady, Bird, Slippers, Monkey
5-b	Brunette Girl, Bird, Blonde Girl, Old Lady
6-a	Prince, Monkey, Blonde, Old Lady
6-b	Brunette Girl, Cat, Old Lady, Slippers
7-a	Blonde Girl, Brunette Girl, Prince, Old Lady
7-b	Monkey, Cat, Blonde Girl, Old Lady
8	Blonde Girl, Blonde Girl, Prince, Brunette Girl

BATTLE B-DAMAN: FIRE SPIRITS!

2,000 B-DABUCKS
Enter HEY TOMMI! at the parts shop with a Bronze Pass.

3,000 B-DABUCKS
Enter B-DAFIRING at the parts shop with a Bronze Pass.

CHEESY MOUSE B-DAMAN
Enter HARD TEETH at the parts shop with a Bronze Pass.

SABER BARREL & SHIELD STAND
Enter SHOOT IT!! at the parts shop with a Bronze Pass.

BERSERK OGRE B-DAMAN SET
Enter MONGREL FANG! at the parts shop with a Silver Pass.

BLOOD SHARK B-DAMAN SET
Enter A BLOODY BODY at the parts shop with a Silver Pass.

GAOTIGER B-DAMAN SET
Enter GLEAMING FANG at the parts shop with a Silver Pass.

KOKURYU-OH B-DAMAN SET
Enter SHADOWY ARMOR at the parts shop with a Silver Pass.

OAK RAVEN
Enter GUST OF WIND! at the parts shop with a Silver Pass.

OHRYU-OH B-DAMAN SET
Enter GOLDEN ARMOR! at the parts shop with a Silver Pass.

SABER MAGAZINE
Enter TONS OF BALLS at the parts shop with a Silver Pass.

VENOM STING B-DAMAN SET
Enter VENOMOUS TAIL at the parts shop with a Silver Pass.

YOKUSAIMARU B-DAMAN SET
Enter YOKUSAIMARU! at the parts shop with a Silver Pass.

ASSAULT BEAST & STORM CHIMERA
Enter FEROCIOUS WOLF! at the parts shop with a Gold Pass.

BLITZ EAGLE
Enter THE SWIFT WINGS at the parts shop with a Gold Pass.

CHROME HARRIER
Enter STRONG RED GALE at the parts shop with a Gold Pass.

CRIMSON SABER
Enter THE RAZING FIRE at the parts shop with a Gold Pass.

LABYRINTH
Enter REVIVAL OF EVIL at the parts shop with a Gold Pass.

MEGA DIABROS
Enter DEVILISH FIGURE at the parts shop with a Gold Pass.

REVOLVER HEAVEN
Enter LET'S B-DAFIRE! at the parts shop with a Gold Pass.

STREAM PEGASUS
Enter GIFT FROM ATLUS at the parts shop with a Gold Pass.

BIONICLE: TALES OF THE TOHUNGA

EVERYTHING BUT THE MINI-GAMES
Enter B9RBRN as a name.

GALI MINI-GAME
Enter 9MA268 as a name.

KOPAKA MINI-GAME
Enter V33673 as a name.

LEWA MINI-GAME
Enter 3LT154 as a name.

ONUA MINI-GAME
Enter 8MR472 as a name.

POHATU MINI-GAME
Enter 5MG834 as a name.

TAHU MINI-GAME
Enter 4CR487 as a name.

BLACKTHORNE

INFINITE HEALTH
At the Title screen, press Left, Right, Down, Up, B, B, Down.

INVISIBLE
At the Title screen, press B, Down, Right, Down, Up, Up, Left, B, Up.

FALLING WON'T KILL YOU
At the Title screen, press B, B, Up, Left, Down, Right, Right, Up.

BLADES OF THUNDER

LEVEL 1 ON EASY
Enter the password 4265.

LEVEL 2 ON EASY
Enter the password 7332.

LEVEL 3 ON EASY
Enter the password 6578.

LEVEL 4 ON EASY
Enter the password 7213.

LEVEL 5 ON EASY
Enter the password 8234.

LEVEL 6 ON EASY
Enter the password 9322.

LEVEL 7 ON EASY
Enter the password 1279.

LEVEL 8 ON EASY
Enter the password 5682.

LEVEL 9 ON EASY
Enter the password 3211.

LEVEL 1 ON MEDIUM
Enter the password 6932.

LEVEL 2 ON MEDIUM
Enter the password 3682.

LEVEL 3 ON MEDIUM
Enter the password 5892.

LEVEL 4 ON MEDIUM
Enter the password 4468.

LEVEL 5 ON MEDIUM
Enter the password 1127.

LEVEL 6 ON MEDIUM
Enter the password 9902.

LEVEL 7 ON MEDIUM
Enter the password 2332.

LEVEL 8 ON MEDIUM
Enter the password 8658.

LEVEL 9 ON MEDIUM
Enter the password 7745.

LEVEL 1 ON HARD
Enter the password 1979.

LEVEL 2 ON HARD
Enter the password 2034.

LEVEL 3 ON HARD
Enter the password 7809.

LEVEL 4 ON HARD
Enter the password 6776.

LEVEL 5 ON HARD
Enter the password 9054.

LEVEL 6 ON HARD
Enter the password 4311.

LEVEL 7 ON HARD
Enter the password 8282.

LEVEL 8 ON HARD
Enter the password 2468.

LEVEL 9 ON HARD
Enter the password 1410.

BUFFY THE VAMPIRE SLAYER: WRATH OF THE DARKHUL KING

9 OF EVERYTHING
At the Title screen, press Up, Down, Up, Down, B, A.

INFINITE LIVES
At the Title screen, press L, L, L, R, R, R, Right, Right.

INVINCIBLE
At the Title screen, press B, B, A, A, L, R, Down, Up.

BUTT UGLY MARTIANS: B.K.M. BATTLES

UNLIMITED LIVES
Enter KMIORMAO as a password.

MAX DEFENSE, FIREPOWER, & RESTORATION PICKUPS
Enter ALWMAA15 as a password.

2 DEFENSE UPGRADES
Enter JT2DU 4MP as a password.

2 EXTRA LIVES
Enter 2ELFM PLS as a password.

2 WEAPON UPGRADES
Enter GMACO EWU as a password.

4 DEFENSE UPGRADES
Enter DUATO U4M as a password.

4 EXTRA LIVES
Enter IAGAW 4EL as a password.

4 WEAPON UPGRADES
Enter IAGAW 4WU as a password.

START AT MECHTROPOLIS
Select Resume Game and enter IWTSOWN2.

START AT AQUATICA
Select Resume Game and enter TMTWN3PD.

START AT ARBOREA
Select Resume Game and enter IIALTSMO4.

START AT SILICON CITY
Select Resume Game and enter IOTJOWN5.

START AT MAGMA
Select Resume Game and enter FILGSOW6.

START AT KOO FOO SHIP
Select Resume Game and enter IWTSOWN7.

CAR BATTLER JOE

BIG BANG
At the Main menu, select Battle League. When the game asks "Use which machine," choose password and enter HAMA!333.

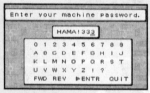

BLUE GALPE EV
At the Main menu, select Battle League. When the game asks "Use which machine," choose password and enter SHISYO!!.

CASEY'S WHLS
At the Main menu, select Battle League. When the game asks "Use which machine," choose password and enter !KOKICHI.

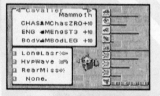

CAVALIER
At the Main menu, select Battle League. When the game asks "Use which machine," choose password and enter CUREWAND.

COPA ZONE23
At the Main menu, select Battle League. When the game asks "Use which machine," choose password and enter CDMACAPA.

EMP FORCE X

At the Main menu, select Battle League. When the game asks "Use which machine," choose password and enter EMPIRE!!.

ISSUE X

At the Main menu, select Battle League. When the game asks "Use which machine," choose password and enter 8998981!.

JOE JIM ZERO

At the Main menu, select Battle League. When the game asks "Use which machine," choose password and enter Todoroki.

LONG VALLEY

At the Main menu, select Battle League. When the game asks "Use which machine," choose password and enter NAGOYADB.

MATSU K MK4

At the Main menu, select Battle League. When the game asks "Use which machine," choose password and enter MR!HURRY.

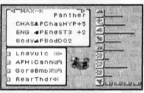

MAX-K

At the Main menu, select Battle League. When the game asks "Use which machine," choose password and enter GANKOMAX.

MEGA M

At the Main menu, select Battle League. When the game asks "Use which machine," choose password and enter M!M!M!M!.

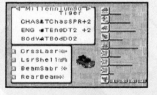

MILLENNIUM90

At the Main menu, select Battle League. When the game asks "Use which machine," choose password and enter 90!60!92.

MRIN'S DREAM
At the Main menu, select Battle League. When the game asks "Use which machine," choose password and enter MARRON!!.

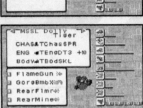

MSSL DOLLY
At the Main menu, select Battle League. When the game asks "Use which machine," choose password and enter KINNIKU!.

PISTON GH
At the Main menu, select Battle League. When the game asks "Use which machine," choose password and enter GO!HOME!.

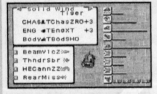

SOLID WIND
At the Main menu, select Battle League. When the game asks "Use which machine," choose password and enter RED!GUNS.

TAKAH'S LSR
At the Main menu, select Battle League. When the game asks "Use which machine," choose password and enter TK000056.

WNN SPECIAL
At the Main menu, select Battle League. When the game asks "Use which machine," choose password and enter BOM!BOM!.

CARS

ALL LEVELS & 90 BOLTS
At the Title screen, press Up, Up, Down, Down, Left, Right, Left, Right, B, A.

ALL CARS
At the Title screen, press Right, Down, Right, B.

ALL CAR COLORS
At the Title screen, press Up, Up, Left, Right, Right, Left, Down, Down.

RADIATOR CAP SECRET CIRCUIT
At the Title screen, press Left, Left, Right, Right, B, B, A.

ALL SCREENSHOTS AT THE DRIVE-IN
At the Title screen, press Left, Down, Right, A.

CARTOON NETWORK SPEEDWAY

UNLOCK EVERYTHING
Enter 96981951 as a password.

ALL FIVE CHAMPIONSHIPS COMPLETE
Enter 34711154 as a password.

START AT FARM FROLICS
Enter 12761357 as a password.

START AT DOWN ON THE FARM
Enter 25731079 as a password.

START AT MURIEL
Enter 25731079 as a password.

START AT EDOPOLIS
Enter 38611791 as a password.

START AT JOHNNY 2X4
Enter 52681314 as a password.

START AT SCARY SPEEDWAY
Enter 68851752 as a password.

START AT DESERT DRIVE
Enter 81821475 as a password.

START AT LITTLE SUZY
Enter 81821475 as a password.

START AT HOT ROD JOHNNY
Enter 84891097 as a password.

START AT SWANKY
Enter 98761719 as a password.

START AT ALPINE ANTICS
Enter 98761719 as a password.

ACME AXEL AWARD TROPHY
Enter 50000050 as a password.

CARTOON SPEEDWAY TROPHY
Enter 10000010 as a password.

FENDER BENDER FRENZY TROPHY
Enter 32000010 as a password.

CASTLEVANIA: ARIA OF SORROW

NO ITEMS
Start a new game with the name NOUSE to use no items in the game.

NO SOULS
Start a new game with the name NOSOUL to use no souls in the game.

CLASSIC NES SERIES: PAC-MAN

PAC-ATTACK PUZZLE MODE

STAGE	PASSWORD
1	STR
2	HNM
3	KST
4	TRT
5	MYX
6	KHL
7	RTS
8	SKB

STAGE	PASSWORD
9	HNT
10	SRY
11	YSK
12	RCF
13	HSM
14	PWW
15	MTN
16	TKY
17	RGH

CT SPECIAL FORCES 3: NAVY OPS

LEVEL PASSWORDS

LEVEL #	ENTER
Level 1-2	5073
Level 2-1	1427
Level 2-2	2438
Level 2-3	7961
Level 2-4	8721
Level 3-1	5986
Level 3-2	2157
Level 3-3	4796
Level 3-4	3496
Level 3-5	1592
Level 3-6	4168
Level 3-7	1364
Level 4-1	7596
Level 4-2	9108
Level 4-3	6124
Level 4-4	7234
Level 4-5	6820
Level 5-1	2394
Level 5-2	4256
Level 5-3	0842

CURIOUS GEORGE

PASSWORDS

LEVEL	PASSWORD
2	TNTDBHNQ
3	TNTDBHBQ
6	PSTDHHSS
8	TNSDBHAG

DANNY PHANTOM: THE ULTIMATE ENEMY

BOSS RUSH MODE
  Select Password from the Options menu and enter Rush.

EASY AND HARD DIFFICULTY
  Select Password from the Options menu and enter Vlad.

DASH'S HAUNTED LOCKER MINI-GAME
  Select Password from the Options menu and enter Dash.

HINDIN' GHOST SEEK MINI-GAME
Select Password from the Options menu and enter Seek.

LEVITATION MINI-GAME
Select Password from the Options menu and enter Jazz.

SAM'S X-RAY ECTO DETECTOR MINI-GAME
Select Password from the Options menu and enter Ecto.

DAREDEVIL: THE MAN WITHOUT FEAR

UNLOCK EVERYTHING
Enter the password 41TK1S6ZNGV.

DARK ARENA

ALL CHEATS
Enter S_X_N as a password. This cheat unlocks Map, Invincibility, All Weapons, All Keys, Unlimited Ammo, and Level Skip.

INVINCIBILITY
Enter HLGNDSBR as a password.

ALL WEAPONS
Enter THRBLDNS as a password.

UNLIMITED AMMO
Enter NDCRSDRT as a password.

ALL KEYS
Enter KNGHTSFR as a password.

MAP
Enter LMSPLLNG as a password.

LEVEL SKIP
Enter NFTRWLLH as a password. Then pause the game, go to the map, and press SELECT to skip to the next level.

SOUND EFFECTS
Enter CRSDR as a password. At the Game Options screen, switch the Sound FX off and then back on to hear a random sound effect.

PASSWORDS

LEVEL	EASY	MEDIUM	HARD
2	CRSDRPLS	VWHTSRGH	LDNHGHNT
3	TKMWTHYB	TCRSDRLR	DBYFTHND
4	TTLLSFRT	DFRLMWTH	CSSRCNHT

LEVEL	EASY	MEDIUM	HARD
5	STCRSTRD	LLYRMGHT	HNSWLLSN
6	NTLVMLNW	WRMRCHNG	TSTRSTLR
7	NTTRDTNY	TLNDFRFR	STNDRDSW
8	RQSTMWTN	MHMNNCNS	LLRSCRSS
9	GTSTNDBY	YWHLLRTR	LNDTBTTL
10	YRSDTFGH	NFRCHRSN	SRCNHRDS
11	TWTHYVRS	DMSSKWLL	WFLLWRWR
12	THYRCLLN	TKRRVNGN	RRKNGNWR
13	GHVTBTHR	PGNFRMTF	DNTFGHTW
14	HLYLNDHS	STWCHRST	CRRYSGNF
15	TBFRFGHT	NSRCMNGW	CRSSWRLR
End	GDFGHTBL	THSWRDSH	DSFNGLND

CHEAT MODE

Enter NRYRDDS as a password. This enables you to enter the following passwords. Note that the previous passwords *won't work*.

EFFECT	PASSWORD
All Cheats	ALL
Invincibility	HEALTH
All Weapons	WEAPONS

Unlimited Ammo	AMMO
All Keys	KEYS
Map	MAPS

Level Skip	SKIP

EFFECT	PASSWORD
Sound Effects	SFX TEST

Disable Cheat Mode	PWORD

PASSWORDS

Use the following passwords in Cheat Mode.

LEVEL	EASY	NORMAL	HARD
2	A	AA	AAA
3	B	BB	BBB
4	C	CC	CCC
5	D	DD	DDD
6	E	EE	EEE
7	F	FF	FFF
8	G	GG	GGG
9	H	HH	HHH
10	I	II	III
11	J	JJ	JJJ
12	K	KK	KKK
13	L	LL	LLL
14	M	MM	MMM
15	N	NN	NNN
End	O	OO	OOO

DAVE MIRRA FREESTYLE BMX 3

METAL AND FLASH
At the Title screen, press R, R, L, L, B, B, L, R.

DESERT STRIKE ADVANCE

10 LIVES
Enter BS9JS27 as a password.

LEVEL PASSWORDS

LEVEL	PASSWORD
2	3ZJMZT7
3	K32L82R
4	JR8P8M8
End	F9N5CJ8

DEXTER'S LAB CHESS CHALLENGE

PASSWORDS

LEVEL	PASSWORD
2	CSHJMQNS HQJSJJBP
3	CSHJMQNS TTHRDGDN
4	CSHJMQNS KPHHDKFN
5	CSHJMQNS QGPFCLMH
6	CSHJMQNS HSJSDGBF
7	CSHJMQNS TKHQNGBN
8	CSHJMQNS FNHHDJFS
9	CSHJMQNS QQPFMNMG
10	CSHJMQNS HSJJJBGNF
11	CSHJMQNS SKRGNBBN
12	CSHJMQNS TRJQHGQM
13	CSHJMQNS SQTKMNMQ
14	CSHJMQNS RSKJLGNK
15	CSHJMQNS QPMCFFFK
16	CSHJMQNS RRDQRGGM
17	CSHJMQNS GRGFFQSR
18	CSHJMQNS RSRJLLNK
19	CSHJMQNS QMRCFFPH
20	CSHJMQNS QRDLMGGL
21	CSHJMQNS BMGFFRSM
22	CSHJMQNS QBSFDSRF
23	CSHJMQNS SMRCHFPC
24	CSHJMQNS QHBLMGJN
25	CSHJMQNS BMQDFHQM
26	CSHJMQNS GLRPKGHP
27	CSHJMQNS GFLMPSKD
28	CSHJMQNS QKLMMQJN
29	CSHJMQNS BLRNKHQM
30	CSHJMQNS BLRNKHHM

DEXTER'S LABORATORY DEESASTER STRIKES

DEXTER-ROO
Pause the game and press LLRR LLRL RRRR LLLR.

EXTRA LIFE
Pause the game and press LLRR LRLL LRLL RRLL.

INVINCIBILITY
Pause the game and press LLLR RRRR LRRR RLL.

LESS DAMAGE
Pause the game and press LRRR RLLL RLLL LLLR.

FASTER DEXTER
Pause the game and press LRRR RLRL RRLL RLRR.

STRONGER DEXTER
Pause the game and press LLRR RLLR LLRR LRLR.

FASTER ENEMIES
Pause the game and press LRRR RRLL LLRR RRLL.

MORE AMMO
Pause the game and press LRRR LLRR LLLL RLLR.

LOW GRAVITY
Pause the game and press LLRR RRRR LLRR LLLR.

REVERSED CONTROLS
Pause the game and press LRRR RRRL RLLR RLLL.

SKIP A LEVEL
Pause the game and press LLLR RLRR RLRL RRRL.

SLOWER ENEMIES
Pause the game and press LLRR RLRR RLLR RLLR.

STRONGER ENEMIES
Pause the game and press LLRR RRLR RRLL LLLL.

WEAK ENEMIES
Pause the game and press LLRR LRRL LLLR RLLL.

SLIPPERY FLOOR
Pause the game and press LLRR RLRR RLLR RLLR.

DINOTOPIA

LEVEL SELECT
At the Title screen press Up, Up, Down, Down, Left, Right, A, Left, Right, B, Start. Select Credits and allow them to finish to access the Level Select option.

DISNEY'S EXTREME SKATE ADVENTURE

PETER PAN
At the Main menu, press L, R, L, R, L, L, Start.

DISNEY'S HOME ON THE RANGE

LEVEL PASSWORDS

LEVEL #	ENTER
Level 1	DVHB
Level 2	VCFK
Level 3	BQMF
Level 4	HFKM
Level 5	DMCV
Level 6	BBKD
Level 7	KNLC
Level 8	BDJR
Level 9	BDRN
Level 10	PSBH
Level 11	QRNN
Level 12	MMKN
Level 13	PSFH
Level 14	DBVJ

DK: KING OF SWING

ATTACK BATTLE 3
At the Title screen, press Up + L + A + B to access a password screen. Enter 65942922.

CLIMBING RACE 5
At the Title screen, press Up + L + A + B to access a password screen. Enter 55860327.

OBSTACLE RACE 4
At the Title screen, press Up + L + A + B to access a password screen. Enter 35805225.

UNLOCK TIME ATTACK
Complete the game as DK.

UNLOCK DIDDY MODE
Collect 24 medals as DK.

UNLOCK BUBBLES
Complete Diddy Mode with 24 Medals.

UNLOCK KREMLING
Collect 6 gold medals in Jungle Jam.

UNLOCK KING K. ROOL
Collect 12 gold medals in Jungle Jam.

DONKEY KONG COUNTRY 2: DIDDY KONG'S QUEST

ALL LEVELS
Select Cheats from the Options menu and enter freedom.

START WITH 15 LIVES
Select Cheats from the Options menu and enter helpme.

START WITH 55 LIVES
Select Cheats from the Options menu and enter weakling.

START WITH 10 BANANA COINS
Select Cheats from the Options menu and enter richman.

START WITH 50 BANANA COINS
Select Cheats from the Options menu and enter wellrich.

NO DK OR HALFWAY BARRELS
Select Cheats from the Options menu and enter rockard.

MUSIC PLAYER
Select Cheats from the Options menu and enter onetime.

CREDITS
Select Cheats from the Options menu and enter kredits.

DORA THE EXPLORER: SUPER SPIES

RAINFOREST 2 PASSWORD
Select Continue and enter Arrow up, Plus sign, Triangle, Star, Plus sign, Triangle, Frown.

DRAGON BALL GT: TRANSFORMATION

REFILL ENERGY
During a game, press Down, Up, Right, Right, Right, Left, Right, Left, B.

REFILL HEALTH
During a game, press Down, Up, Left, Left, Up, Right, Down, B.

PICCOLO
At the Main menu, press Left, Right, Left Right, Up, Up, Down, B.

SUPER BABY VEGETA
At the Main menu, press Left, Right, Left Right, Down, Down, Up, B.

SUPER SAIYAN 4 GOKU
At the Main menu, press Left, Right, Left Right, Down, Down, Down, B.

SUPER SAIYAN KID GOKU
At the Main menu, press Left, Right, Left Right, Up, Up, Up, B.

SUPER SAIYAN VEGETA
At the Main menu, press Left, Right, Left Right, Up, Down, Down, B.

DUAL BLADES

IMPOSSIBLE DIFFICULTY
At the Options screen, highlight Difficulty
and press Left (x4), Right, Right, Left,
Right, B.

DUKE NUKEM ADVANCE

GOD MODE, FULL WEAPONS, INFINITE AMMO, AND NO CLIPPING
Pause the game, hold L, and press Left, Up, A, Up, Left, A, START, SELECT.

E.T.: THE EXTRA-TERRESTRIAL

PASSWORDS

LEVEL	PASSWORD
2	Up, Up, A, Down, Down, B, R, L
3	Left, Up, Right, Down, L, A, R, B
4	A, Left, B, Right, L, Up, R, Down
5	L, R, R, L, A, Up, B, Left
6	L, Left, R, Right, A, A, B, A
7	B, R, B, L, A, Up, B, Up
8	Up, Up, A, Down, Down, Left, A, B
9	Right, B, B, Left, Up, R, R, L
10	Left, Left, A, L, Right, Right, B, R

EXTREME GHOSTBUSTERS

LEVEL PASSWORDS

LEVEL	PASSWORD
The Hall	HGBNL14VJ
Corridor	5PMDTF/K2
Office	21QSR9JTS
Big Building Boss	8G20S86SC
Racing 2	30J82JBMB
The Main Aisle	BNKN34SMW
The Crypt	V8JNNVGLC
Closer to the Underworld	MD*XN7KTJ
Racing 3	VD*PJKFTS
In the Wings	MDZ9KK/T8
Ethereal Ball	MD2TK4XTK
On Stage	WS0PJ6LTC
Broadway Star Theater Boss	VS31JL9TW
Racing 4	LDK9K6HTC
Don't Forget the Guide	WSJPJLZIV
Carnivorous and Hungry	WSFKP6WT3
The Final Confrontation	MS29P7JTW
Final Boss	VSFPPMHT8
End	LXK8KKFTL

FAIRLY ODDPARENTS: BREAKIN' DA RULES

CHEAT MODE
Enter X3YSV3!P as a password.

FINAL FANTASY I & II: DAWN OF SOULS

FF I TILE GAME
During a game of Final Fantasy I and after you get the ship, hold A and press B about 55 times.

FF II CONCENTRATION GAME
After obtaining the Snowcraft, hold B and press A about 20 times.

FINDING NEMO

LEVEL SELECT AND GALLERY
Enter the password M6HM.

PASSWORDS

LEVEL	PASSWORD
1	IH5I
2	HZ5I
3	ZZ5I
4	806I
5	7KPI
6	8JPI
7	3N6J
8	MP3K
9	L67K
10	45ZK
11	3NGH
12	4PHC

FIRE PRO WRESTLING 2

ALL WRESTLERS
Edit a wrestler using the following information, then save the wrestler.

Nick Name: ALL
Last Name: WRESTLER
First Name: CLEAR
Exchange: Off
Middle: NONE

UNLOCK WRESTLERS
Select Talent Search from Manager of the Ring mode. Then select the following Fighting Style and Region to open each wrestler.

WRESTLER	FIGHTING STYLE	REGION
Dick Murdoch	Strong	America
D-Von and Bubba Ray Dudley	Any	America
Dynamite Kid	Showmen	Europe
Gary Albright	King Road	America
Goldberg	Strong	America
Great Muta	Lucha	Mexico
Hiroshi Tanahashi	Strong	Japan
Mike Modest	Showmen	America
Roland Bock	Stoic	Anywhere
Royce Gracie	Stoic	Anywhere
Salman Hashmikov	Strong	Europe
Stacy Kiebler	Showman	America
Tajiri	Showman	Mexico
Takehiro Murahama	Lucha	Japan
William Regal	Any	Europe

FROGGER'S ADVENTURES 2: THE LOST WAND

UNLOCK MAGICIAN'S REALM
At the Main menu, press Up, Up, Down, Down, Left, Right, Left, Right, B, A.

GALIDOR: DEFENDERS OF THE OUTER DIMENSION

INVINCIBILITY
At the Title screen, hold R + L and press A, B, A, A, B.

GOLDEN SUN 2

RENAME CHARACTERS
When prompted to enter a new name for Felix, press SELECT (x3). Now enter a new name for Felix to enter a new name for Jenna, Sheba, and Picard. Press Up, Down, Up, Down, Left, Right, Left, Right, Up, Right, Down, Left, Up, SELECT to enter new names for Garet, Ivan, and Mia (if playing a non-linked game). A sound chimes when the code is entered correctly.

GRADIUS GALAXIES

SLOWER
Pause the game and press Left, Right, Up, Down, Left, Left, Right, Start.

ALL WEAPONS
Pause the game and press Up, Up, Down, Down, L, R, L, R, B, A.

SELF-DESTRUCT
Pause the game and press Up, Up, Down, Down, Left, Right, Left, Right, B, A, Start.

GRAND THEFT AUTO

CHEAT MODE/COORDINATES
During a game, press A + B + Start.

ALL WEAPONS
After entering the Cheat Mode code, press
Left, Right, Up, Down, A, A.

RESTORE ARMOR
After entering the Cheat Mode code, press
Left, Right, Up, Down, A, L.

15,000 DOLLARS
After entering the Cheat Mode code, press
Left, Right, Up, Down, L, L.

RESTORE HEALTH
After entering the Cheat Mode code, press Left, Right, Up, Down, B, B.

LOWER WANTED LEVEL
After entering the Cheat Mode code, press Left, Right, Up, Down, A, R.

RAISE WANTED LEVEL
After entering the Cheat Mode code, press Left, Right, Up, Down, R, A.

TOGGLE BETWEEN 0 STARS AND 6 STARS
After entering the Cheat Mode code, press Left, Right, Up, Down, R, R.

TOGGLE GANG HOSTILITY
After entering the Cheat Mode code, press Left, Right, Up, Down, B, R.

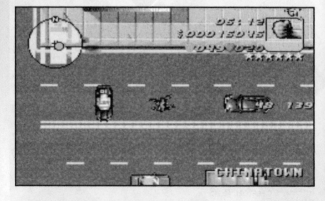

HARLEM GLOBETROTTERS: WORLD TOUR

PASSWORDS

TEAMS DEFEATED	PASSWORD
2	XCTXJK
3	XNSXHD
4	XYRXGT
5	X7QXFL
6	XHQXXG
7	XSPXWD
8	XZNXVS
10	X4LX9L
11	XDLXRH
12	XPKXQJ
13	XZJXPM
14	X8HXNQ
15	XTGX3H

HOT WHEELS VELOCITY X

PASSWORDS

LEVEL	PASSWORD
02	143-24-813
03	141-38-985
04	249-48-723
05	294-16-277
06	457-51-438
07	112-86-545
08	447-65-112
09	368-54-466
10	718-59-438
11	363-95-545
12	373-65-848
13	171-49-211
14	373-59-216
15	373-62-927
16	718-42-276
17	358-59-355
18	478-68-254
19	573-77-683
20	188-58-352
21	766-46-341
22	187-98-394
23	188-12-234
24	786-84-747
25	466-59-979
26	477-58-369
27	447-62-191
28	614-81-432
29	641-18-239
30	399-68-584
31	662-84-635
32	476-63-843
33	616-67-341

LEVEL	PASSWORD
34	384-97-475
35	363-13-298
36	521-71-135
37	543-17-658
38	782-57-387

ICE AGE

LEVEL SELECT
Enter NTTTTT as a password.

ART GALLERY
Enter MFKRPH as a password.

LEVEL PASSWORDS

LEVEL	PASSWORD
2	PBBQBB
3	QBCQBB
4	SBFQBB
5	DBKQBB
6	NBTQBB
7	PCTQBB
8	RFTQBB
9	CKTQBB
10	MTTQBB

THE INCREDIBLE HULK

STAGE SKIP
Pause the game and press Down, Right, Down, Right, Left, Left, Left, Up.

THE INCREDIBLES

PASSWORDS

LEVEL	PASSWORD
1-1-1	MSW5
1-1-2	BK8V
1-2-1	69NN
1-3-1	GFVY
1-3-2	V34K
2-1-1	94HR
2-1-2	ZWLG
2-1-3	SP??
2-2-1	KDY3
2-3-1	Y27F
2-3-2	6!2N
2-3-3	BHBV

LEVEL	PASSWORD
2-4-1	MQR5
2-4-2	3YTK
2-4-3	?6DS
2-5-2	6?SR
2-5-3	SNJ5
3-1-1	MNW9
3-2-1	BF8Z
3-2-2	65NS
3-2-3	YVKK
3-2-4	KGTY
3-3-1	SDR6
3-4-1	Z3ZB
3-5-1	9?5M
3-5-2	FC73
3-5-3	NL2?
3-6-1	VXBG
3-6-2	YWKJ
3-6-3	GJQZ
3-7-1	KHP2
3-7-2	313K
4-1-1	?!JT
4-2-1	ML17
4-3-1	YXFC
4-4-1	GHV1
4-5-1	VW4C
4-6-1	YX!F

THE INCREDIBLES: RISE OF THE UNDERMINER

TUTORIAL
Enter XL9ZMD as a password.

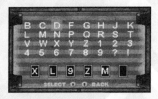

GIANT ROBOT FACTORY 1
Enter G!G1DK as a password.

GIANT ROBOT FACTORY 2
Enter DXY6FK as a password.

GIANT ROBOT FACTORY 3
Enter BBT7FK as a password.

BLIZZARD BACKDOOR 1
Enter ZPGVFK as a password.

BLIZZARD BACKDOOR 2
Enter B94GFK as a password.

BLIZZARD BACKDOOR 3
Enter J2B?FK as a password.

STAGE CORRUPTORATOR 1
Enter QF1XFK as a password.

STAGE CORRUPTORATOR 2
Enter SW3!FK as a password.

STAGE CORRUPTORATOR 3
Enter QQ?7DK as a password.

UNDERMINER
Enter 24NCGK as a password.

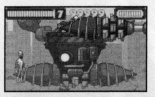

THE INVINCIBLE IRON MAN

LEVEL SELECT
At the Title screen, press Select, Up, B, A, Right, Up.

INVINCIBILITY
At the Title screen, press Right, Up, Left, A, Right, Select.

STRONGER CLOSE-RANGE
At the Title screen, press Up, Down, Left, Right, B.

UNLIMITED SUPER-BLASTS
At the Title screen, press B, A, Left, Down, Up, Right.

IRIDION II

EASY PASSWORDS

LEVEL	PASSWORD
2	SBJS5
3	9CRT5
4	T3KG3
5	93PNV
6	95FN3
7	5MYCX
8	6C3L5
9	PW3NX
10	649QV
11	NFK2V
12	5DS2V
13	!GDV5
14	T7H8X
15	!9ROX
End	4RC8!

ADVANCED PASSWORDS

LEVEL	PASSWORD
2	9PTBY
3	TYHLY
4	9VDBW
5	SLZGW
6	TDZQ4
7	5M!H6
8	N59G6
9	558GY
10	54!H4
11	PCGZW
12	NPH74
13	9GF46
14	SOL46
15	9!H84

COMPLETE GAME, UNLOCK ARCADE, AND CHALLENGE
Enter 4RC8! as a password.

CHANGE SHIP COLORS
Enter !SH1P2! as a password.

ROTATING SATELLITES
Enter !R0T8! as a password.

ENABLE MICRO SHIP MODE
Enter !M1CR0! as a password.

SHOW SECRETS
Enter !S3CR3TS! as a password.

CPU LOAD PERCENTAGE
Enter !L04D! as a password.

NUMBER OF OBJECTS ON-SCREEN
Enter !0BJS! as a password.

JUKEBOX
Enter !G4X! or CH4LL as a password.

I SPY CHALLENGER

UNLOCK LEVEL CODES
Pause the game, select Code, then enter the corresponding button presses to unlock various levels.

LEVEL	ENTER
Level 2 (Easy)	Up, Up, Left
Level 5 (Easy)	Down, Down, Left
Level 10 (Easy)	Left, Left, Left
Level 15 (Easy)	Right, Right, Left
Level 20 (Easy)	Left, Right, Left
Level 2 (Medium)	Up, Up, Right
Level 5 (Medium)	Down, Down, Right
Level 10 (Medium)	Left, Left, Right
Level 15 (Medium)	Right, Right, Right
Level 20 (Medium)	Right, Left, Right
Level 2 (Hard)	Up, Up, Down
Level 5 (Hard)	Down, Down, Down
Level 10 (Hard)	Left, Left, Down
Level 15 (Hard)	Right, Right, Down
Level 20 (Hard)	Up, Down, Up
Level 2 (Expert)	Up, Up, Up
Level 5 (Expert)	Down, Down, Up
Level 10 (Expert)	Left, Left, Up
Level 15 (Expert)	Right, Right, Up
Level 20 (Expert)	Down, Up, Down

JACKIE CHAN ADVENTURES: LEGEND OF THE DARK HAND

ALL STAGES AND SCROLLS
At the Title screen, hold R and press B, A, Left, Down, Up, Right.

JAMES BOND 007: NIGHTFIRE

LEVEL SELECT
Pause the game and press R, Left, L, Right, Up, Select, R.

UNLIMITED HEALTH
Pause the game and press R, Left, L, Right, Up, Select, Left.

500 BULLETS
Pause the game and press R, Left, L, Right, Up, Select, Right.

HIGH-PITCHED VOICES
Pause the game and press R, Left, L, Right, Up, Select, L.

JAZZ JACKRABBIT

500 CREDITS
Pause the game and press Right, Left, Right, Left, L, R, Up, Up, R, R, L, L.

1000 CREDITS
Pause the game and press Up, Down, Up, Down, Left, Right, L, R, L, R, R, L.

5000 CREDITS
Pause the game and press Up, Right, Down, Left, L, L, Right, Left, R, R, L, L.

JIMMY NEUTRON: BOY GENIUS

LEVEL PASSWORDS

LEVEL	EASY	HARD
Asteroids	WM5DR5H3MCLB	2040YL61TT0T
Yokian Moon	KVZQG3Q50LZG	GGP6WCC273-3
Yolkus	51867F7MJ5YP	2H?-!L81TT0K
Yokian Palace	MMS-KXBVC4FS	+R6H!L91TT0F
Dungeon	N?+94T1?DJXW	456NSDWBWM?F
Poutra	939BSYT41N0Z	XZ16F2F8NS$!
King Goobot	BD5VVRDF3GXV	GRZB87HNYFR2
End	3L!VPH26V7$8	+CLT3LD1TTSF

Congratulations! You have freed the parents from the clutches of the evil Yokians! Now you're one big happy family again. Good Job!

JUSTICE LEAGUE HEROES: THE FLASH

ALL HEROES
At the Title screen, hold B and press Up, Down, Left, Right, Right, Left, Down, Up, Select.

ALL POWERS
At the Title screen, hold B and press Down, Down, Down, Down, Left, Right, Up, Down, Select.

LIVES
At the Title screen, hold B and press Up, Down, Up, Up, Down, Down, Up, Down, Select.

BIG FLASH
At the Title screen, hold B and press Left, Up, Right, Down, Left, Up, Right, Down, Select.

SMALL FLASH
At the Title screen, hold B and press Down, Down, Down, Left, Up, Up, Up, Right, Select.

BIG BAD GUYS
At the Title screen, hold B and press Up, Up, Down, Down, Left, Right, Left, Right, Select.

SMALL BAD GUYS
At the Title screen, hold B and press Down, Down, Up, Up, Right, Left, Right, Left, Select.

JUSTICE LEAGUE: INJUSTICE FOR ALL

CAN'T BE HIT
Pause the game, press Select and then unpause the game.

KIEN

QUEST II
Enter KA10LVQ1M as a password.

QUEST III
Enter KB18LVQ2L as a password.

QUEST IV
Enter KC30LVQ3G as a password.

QUEST V
Enter KD70LVQ4S as a password.

KONAMI COLLECTOR'S SERIES: ARCADE ADVANCED

FROGGER: ADVANCED
At the Frogger Title screen, press Up, Up, Down, Down, Left, Right, Left, Right, B, A, Start.

SCRAMBLE: ADVANCED
At the Scramble Title screen, press Up, Up, Down, Down, Left, Right, Left, Right, B, A, Start.

TIME PILOT: RAPID FIRE AND NEW STAGE
At the Time Pilot Title screen, press Up, Up, Down, Down, Left, Right, Left, Right, B, A, Start.

GYRUSS: ADVANCED
At the Gyruss Title screen, press Up, Up, Down, Down, Left, Right, Left, Right, B, A, Start.

YIE-AR KUNG FU: ALL FIGHTERS IN MULTIPLAYER
At the Yie Ar Kung Fu Title screen, press Up, Up, Down, Down, Left, Right, Left, Right, B, A, Start.

RUSH N' ATTACK: 2 EXTRA LIVES AND 2 NEW STAGES
At the Rush N' Attack Title screen, press Up, Up, Down, Down, Left, Right, Left, Right, B, A, Start.

KONG: KING OF ATLANTIS

LEVEL PASSWORDS
Enter the following passwords to unlock certain levels in the game.

LEVEL	PASSWORD
Level 1-2	FJLJBDG
Level 1-3	GGJJJBF
Level 1-4	BFBGLJG
Level 2-1	LDBMLMD
Level 2-2	GMLLDDD

LEVEL	PASSWORD
Level 2-3	LDFMLJD
Level 2-4	DGDDGML
Level 3-1	GMMMDFB
Level 3-2	MPFDMLB
Level 3-3	FMJBFFP
Level 3-4	LFGPMGB
Level 4-1	GPPMBGB
Level 4-2	DLBGDPP
Level 4-3	LGFPPJB

THE LAND BEFORE TIME

PASSWORDS

LEVEL	PASSWORD
2	Spike, Cera, Littlefoot, Golden Tree Star
3	Golden Tree Star, Spike, Ducky, Littlefoot
4	Golden Tree Star, Golden Tree Star, Cera, Spike
5	Ducky, Cera, Golden Tree Star, Cera

LEGO KNIGHT'S KINGDOM

STORY 100% COMPLETE
Enter YZZVZYZ as a password.

LEGO STAR WARS

SHEEP MODE
Pause the game and press L, R, L, Down, Up, R, R, Right, Left, Down, Right, Right, Select.

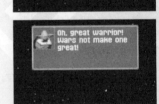

YODA SAYS
Pause the game and press Down, L, R, Select.

WATCH CUTSCENES
Pause the game and press Down, Up, R, L, R, R, R, Down, Down, Up, Down, Down, Select.

REPAIR BOT
Pause the game and press Down, Down, Down, Down, L, Right, Down, Right, L.

TEMPORARY SPEED BOOST
Pause the game and press Right, Right, Down, Up, Right, L.

PLAY AS BATTLE DROID
At the start screen, press Start, Start, Left, Down, Down, Down, Down, Right.

PLAY AS A DROIDEKA
Pause the game and press Start, Start, Down, Right, Left, Down, Right, Left.

PLAY AS A REPAIR DROID
Pause the game and press Start, Start, Up, Up, Up, Down, Down, Down.

PLAY AS BLUE GUNGAN
Pause the game and press Start, Start, Down, Left, Right, Down, Left, Right.

PLAY AS C-3PO
Pause the game and press Start, Start, Left, Down, Right, Up, Right, Right.

PLAY AS DROID ON HOVERSLED
Pause the game and press Start, Start, Down, Up, Down, Up, Down, Up.

PLAY AS GENERAL GRIEVOUS
Pause the game and press Start, Start, Down, Down, Down, Down, Down, Down.

PLAY AS WINGED GUY
Pause the game and press Start, Start, Right, Down, Right, Down, Left, Up.

PLAY AS R2-D2
Pause the game and press Start, Start, Up (x6).

PLAY AS R4-P17
Pause the game and press Start, Start, Up, Down, Up, Down, Up, Down.

POWERFUL BLASTERS
Pause the game and press Down, Down, Left, Right, Down, L.

A FEW LEGO PIECES
Pause the game and press L, L, L, Right, Left, R, R, R.

BLACK SABER
Pause the game and press L, L, R, Start.

BLUE SABER
Pause the game and press R, R, R, Start.

GREEN SABER
Pause the game and press R, L, R, Start.

PURPLE SABER
Pause the game and press L, R, L, Start.

RED SABER
Pause the game and press L, R, R, Start.

YELLOW SABER
Pause the game and press R, R, L, Start.

LEGO STAR WARS II: THE ORIGINAL TRILOGY

ALDERAAN
At Mos Eisley Cantina, enter 27000 as a code.

BUBBLE BLASTER
At Mos Eisley Cantina, enter 80873 as a code.

CARBONITE CHAMBER
At Mos Eisley Cantina, enter 08433 as a code.

DANCING GIRL
At Mos Eisley Cantina, enter 70546 as a code.

DEATH STAR
At Mos Eisley Cantina, enter 52577 as a code.

DEATH STAR 2
At Mos Eisley Cantina, enter 52583 as a code.

DEATH STAR HANGER
At Mos Eisley Cantina, enter 80500 as a code.

DEATH STAR SUBSECTOR 1
At Mos Eisley Cantina, enter 51999 as a code.

EMPEROR'S LAIR
At Mos Eisley Cantina, enter 20876 as a code.

EWOK VILLAGE
At Mos Eisley Cantina, enter 31299 as a code.

JEDI SPIRIT
At Mos Eisley Cantina, enter 75046 as a code.

MILLENIUM FALCON
At Mos Eisley Cantina, enter 89910 as a code.

MOS EISELY
At Mos Eisley Cantina, enter 82434 as a code.

MOS EISLEY CANTINA
At Mos Eisley Cantina, enter 13197 as a code.

OBI WAN'S HOUSE
At Mos Eisley Cantina, enter 40214 as a code.

SENSOR BALCONY
At Mos Eisley Cantina, enter 61806 as a code.

SITH MODE
At Mos Eisley Cantina, enter 11340 as a code.

THE DARK CAVE
At Mos Eisley Cantina, enter 50250 as a code.

TRASH COMPACTOR
At Mos Eisley Cantina, enter 11911 as a code.

WAMPA CAVE
At Mos Eisley Cantina, enter 42352 as a code.

YODA'S HUT
At Mos Eisley Cantina, enter 06881 as a code.

LILO AND STITCH

LEVEL PASSWORDS

LEVEL	PASSWORD
Beach	Stitch, Stitch, Stitch, Stitch, Stitch, Stitch, Stitch
Mothership	UFO, Scrump, Stitch, Rocket, UFO, Stitch, UFO
Space Cruiser	Lilo, Rocket, Stitch, Rocket, Rocket, Scrump, Stitch
Junkyard Planet	UFO, Rocket, Stitch, Rocket, Rocket, Scrump, Stitch

LEVEL	PASSWORD
Escape!	Stitch, Scrump, UFO, Gun, Rocket, Scrump, UFO
Rescue	Flower, Scrump, UFO, Gun, Gun, Gun, UFO
Final Challenge	Lilo, Pineapple, Flower, Pineapple, Gun, Gun, Stitch
End	Pineapple, Pineapple, Pineapple, Pineapple, Stitch, Stitch, Stitch

MADAGASCAR: OPERATION PENGUIN

CHRISTMAS
During gameplay, press Select, Up, L, Left, R, Right, L, Down, R.

MATCHBOX CROSS TOWN HEROES

PASSWORDS

```
       Enter Password
                        ▲
    C     B     C      T
                        ▼
  Ⓑ Cancel          OK  Ⓐ
```

LEVEL	PASSWORD
2	CBCT
3	QBKL
4	CBCL
5	QBVJ
6	QBDJ
End	QBVN

MEDAL OF HONOR: UNDERGROUND

INVULNERABILITY
Enter MODEDEDIEU as a password.

PASSWORDS

LEVEL	EASY	MEDIUM	HARD
1	TRILINGUE	IRRADIER	DOSSARD
2	SQUAME	FRIMAS	CUBIQUE
3	REVOLER	ESCARGOT	CHEMIN
4	FAUCON	DEVOIR	BLONDEUR
5	UNANIME	COALISER	BLESSER
6	ROULIS	BASQUE	AVOCAT
7	RELAVER	ROBUSTE	AFFINER
8	POUSSIN	SOYEUX	LAINE
9	PANOPLIE	TERRER	MESCLUN
10	NIMBER	VOULOIR	NORME
11	NIAIS	COUVERT	ORNER
12	KARMA	VOYANCE	PENNE
13	INCISER	PIGISTE	QUELQUE
14	GADOUE	NOMMER	REPOSE
15	FUSETTE	JETER	SALIFIER
16	EXCUSER	ENJAMBER	TROPIQUE
17	ENRICHIR	MORPHE	VOTATION

MEGA MAN BATTLE NETWORK 4

BATTLE CHIP CHALLENGE CODES
If you've been exploring everything, you should have acquired six NaviCodes. This chart lists them all, plus a special seventh code that gives you a shot at acquiring Chip #229, the HubStyle NaviChip!

NAME	NAVICODE
LAN	NG75-H5RF-R0MN-440N-2QX[c]-X341
MAYL	8NT8-JZFL-3Q9D-7RPX-T[d]CH-JX51
DEX	FD[s]3-3JW1-PS[s]V-[d]01[d]-[h]6R[c]-1J32
CHAU	93[c]5-WXNH-9MWT-[s]VX8-DY7M-88H0
KAI	M[s]SP-3[h][d]C-6KGQ-[h]9FM-X0N[h]-M[d]P1
MARY	CX4[s]-1GA9-5JKL-S[c]GD-3L5B-90Z1
LAN	5[s]4H-B81R-[s]KKZ-P15X-ZS5B-[c]XK0

MEGA MAN BATTLE NETWORK 5: TEAM PROTOMAN & MEGA MAN BATTLE NETWORK 5: TEAM COLONEL

To compress the following Navi Customizer Programs, you must highlight that program and enter the appropriate code.

COMPRESS AIRSHOES
Highlight AirShoes, hold Right and press B, L, B, A, B, L, B, B, A, A.

COMPRESS ATTACKMAX
Highlight AttackMAX, hold Right and press L, L, L, R, R, B, A, R, B, L.

COMPRESS BATTERYMODE
Highlight BatteryMode, hold Right and press A, A, B, R, A, B, R, L, L, R.

COMPRESS BEATSUPPORT
Highlight BeatSupport, hold Right and press A, B, B, R, A, A, B, R, B, R.

COMPRESS BODYPACK
Highlight BodyPack, hold Right and press B, A, R, A, B, R, L, R, R, A.

COMPRESS BUGSTOPPER
Highlight Bugstopper, hold Right and press B, A, B, L, A, B, R, L, R, B.

COMPRESS BUSTERPACK
Highlight BusterPack, hold Right and press L, L, R, A, R, L, B, L, A, R.

COMPRESS CHARGEMAX
Highlight ChargeMAX, hold Right and press A, L, A, A, R, B, R, B, A, R.

COMPRESS COLLECT
Highlight Collect, hold Right and press B, R, A, L, A, R, B, A, A, B.

COMPRESS CUSTOM +1
Highlight Custom, hold Right and press A, A, R, L, B, A, B, A, L, B.

COMPRESS CUSTOM2
Highlight Custom, hold Right and press B, A, R, L, L, R, A, L, B, R.

COMPRESS DANDYISM
Highlight Dandyism, hold Right and press R, R, B, B, R, B, R, B, A, A.

COMPRESS FIRST BARRIER
Highlight Barrier, hold Right and press R, L, A, B, B, A, R, A, L, R.

COMPRESS FLOATSHOES
Highlight FloatShoes, hold Right and press A, L, L, B, R, L, A, A, A, L.

COMPRESS GIGAFOLDER1
Highlight GigaFolder, hold Right and press R, R, L, B, L, L, A, R, B, L.

COMPRESS GIGAVIRUS
Highlight GigaVirus, hold Right and press B, B, R, A, L, B, L, A, R, R.

COMPRESS HUMOURSENSE
Highlight HumourSense, hold Right and press A, B, L, A, R, A, B, L, R, L.

COMPRESS I'M FISH
Highlight I'm Fish, hold Right and press B, A, B, A, L, R, A, R, A, A.

COMPRESS THE JUNGLELAND
Highlight JungleLand, hold Right and press L, R, L, A, B, L, B, B, L, A.

COMPRESS KAWARIMIMAGIC
Highlight KawarimiMagic, hold Right and press R, B, B, A, R, B, R, A, R, B.

COMPRESS MEGAFOLDER 1
Highlight MegaFolder, hold Right and press B, B, A, B, B, R, R, L, A, R.

COMPRESS MEGAVIRUS
Highlight MegaVirus, hold Right and press A, A, B, L, A, R, B, L, A, A.

COMPRESS MILLIONARE
Highlight Millionare, hold Right and press R, L, R, A, R, R, L, L, L, R.

COMPRESS THE OIL BODY
Highlight Oil Body, hold Right and press L, B, R, A, R, L, A, B, L, B.

COMPRESS RAPIDMAX
Highlight RapidMAX, hold Right and press R, A, R, L, L, R, R, A, B, A.

COMPRESS THE REFLECT PROGRAM
Highlight Program, hold Right and press L, L, R, B, L, L, A, A, L, B.

COMPRESS RUSHSUPPORT
Highlight RushSupport, hold Right and press R, B, L, R, B, R, L, L, R, L.

COMPRESS SAITOBATCH
Highlight SaitoBatch, hold Right and press A, L, R, A, B, L, R, A, L, R.

COMPRESS SELFRECOVERY
Highlight SelfRecovery, hold Right and press R, L, R, L, R, B, B, R, A, B.

COMPRESS SHIELD
Highlight Shield, hold Right and press A, B, A, R, A, L, R, B, B, A.

COMPRESS SHINOBIDASH
Highlight ShinobiDash, hold Right and press R, L, L, A, L, L, B, A, B, B.

COMPRESS SUPERARMOUR
Highlight SuperArmour, hold Right and press R, A, B, R, A, L, L, R, B, A.

COMPRESS TANGOSUPPORT
Highlight TangoSupport, hold Right and press L, B, L, A, B, L, A, B, A, L.

COMPRESS UNDERSHIRT
Highlight UnderShirt, hold Right and press A, R, B, B, R, L, R, A, L, A.

ANTI ELEC * NUMBERMAN CODE
Once the Numberman Machine is in Higsby's shop, use it and enter 35607360.

ANTI FIRE * NUMBERMAN CODE
Once the Numberman Machine is in Higsby's shop, use it and enter 73877466.

ANTI NAVI V NUMBERMAN CODE
Once the Numberman Machine is in Higsby's shop, use it and enter 05068930.

ANTI SWORD R NUMBERMAN CODE
Once the Numberman Machine is in Higsby's shop, use it and enter 10386794.

ANTI WATER * NUMBERMAN CODE
Once the Numberman Machine is in Higsby's shop, use it and enter 25465278.

ANTI WOOD * NUMBERMAN CODE
Once the Numberman Machine is in Higsby's shop, use it and enter 10133670.

ATTACK MAX (YELLOW NCP) NUMBERMAN CODE
Once the Numberman Machine is in Higsby's shop, use it and enter 63231870.

BEATSUPPORT NCP NUMBERMAN CODE
Once the Numberman Machine is in Higsby's shop, use it and enter 79877132.

BODY PACK NUMBERMAN CODE
Once the Numberman Machine is in Higsby's shop, use it and enter 30112002.

BUSTERPACK NCP NUMBERMAN CODE
Once the Numberman Machine is in Higsby's shop, use it and enter 80246758.

CHARGE MAX (WHITE NCP) NUMBERMAN CODE
Once the Numberman Machine is in Higsby's shop, use it and enter 87412146.

CUSTOM 2 NUMBERMAN CODE
Once the Numberman Machine is in Higsby's shop, use it and enter 15595587.

CUSTOM BOLT 3 G NUMBERMAN CODE
Once the Numberman Machine is in Higsby's shop, use it and enter 07765623.

DARK INVIS * NUMBERMAN CODE
Once the Numberman Machine is in Higsby's shop, use it and enter 68799876.

DJANGOSP D NUMBERMAN CODE
Once the Numberman Machine is in Higsby's shop, use it and enter 91098051.

FULL ENERGY NUMBERMAN CODE
Once the Numberman Machine is in Higsby's shop, use it and enter 12118790.

FULL ENERGY NUMBERMAN CODE
Once the Numberman Machine is in Higsby's shop, use it and enter 90914896.

GUN DEL SOL 3 O NUMBERMAN CODE
Once the Numberman Machine is in Higsby's shop, use it and enter 35321321.

HP +200 (PINK NCP) NUMBERMAN CODE
Once the Numberman Machine is in Higsby's shop, use it and enter 90630807.

HP+300 (WHITE NCP) NUMBERMAN CODE
Once the Numberman Machine is in Higsby's shop, use it and enter 13926561.

HP+400 (PINK NCP) NUMBERMAN CODE
Once the Numberman Machine is in Higsby's shop, use it and enter 03419893.

HP+400 NCP NUMBERMAN CODE
Once the Numberman Machine is in Higsby's shop, use it and enter 45654128.

HP+50 NCP NUMBERMAN CODE
Once the Numberman Machine is in Higsby's shop, use it and enter 31084443.

HP+500 (WHITE NCP) NUMBERMAN CODE
Once the Numberman Machine is in Higsby's shop, use it and enter 72846472.

LOCK ENEMY NUMBERMAN CODE
Once the Numberman Machine is in Higsby's shop, use it and enter 29789661.

RAPID MAX (PINK NCP) NUMBERMAN CODE
Once the Numberman Machine is in Higsby's shop, use it and enter 36695497.

RECOVERY-300 Y NUMBERMAN CODE
Once the Numberman Machine is in Higsby's shop, use it and enter 18746897.

RUSHSUPPORT NCP NUMBERMAN CODE
Once the Numberman Machine is in Higsby's shop, use it and enter 09609807.

SHINOBI DASH NUMBERMAN CODE
Once the Numberman Machine is in Higsby's shop, use it and enter 64892292.

SOULTIME +1 (YELLOW NCP) NUMBERMAN CODE
Once the Numberman Machine is in Higsby's shop, use it and enter 28256341.

SPIN BLUE NUMBERMAN CODE
Once the Numberman Machine is in Higsby's shop, use it and enter 12541883.

SPIN GREEN NUMBERMAN CODE
Once the Numberman Machine is in Higsby's shop, use it and enter 78987728.

SPIN RED NUMBERMAN CODE
Once the Numberman Machine is in Higsby's shop, use it and enter 30356451.

STATIC S NUMBERMAN CODE
Once the Numberman Machine is in Higsby's shop, use it and enter 48958798.

TANGOSUPPORT NCP NUMBERMAN CODE
Once the Numberman Machine is in Higsby's shop, use it and enter 54288793.

UNLOCKER NUMBERMAN CODE
Once the Numberman Machine is in Higsby's shop, use it and enter 64664560.

UNLOCKER NUMBERMAN CODE
Once the Numberman Machine is in Higsby's shop, use it and enter 28706568.

UNLOCKER NUMBERMAN CODE
Once the Numberman Machine is in Higsby's shop, use it and enter 73978713.

UNTRAP NUMBERMAN CODE
Once the Numberman Machine is in Higsby's shop, use it and enter 00798216.

MONSTER FORCE

RESTART LEVEL
Pause the game, hold L + R and press A.

FINISH LEVEL
During a game, hold L + R + A and press Up.

PLAY AS MINA OR DREW
At the Character Select screen, hold L + R + B and press Right.

MORTAL KOMBAT: DEADLY ALLIANCE

25,000 KOINS
Enter KWIKKASH as your name.

MUPPET PINBALL MAYHEM

ANIMAL MACHINE
At the Options screen, select Credits. Then press Left, Right, Right, Up, R, Down, Down, L.

MUPPETS: ON WITH THE SHOW!

ALL MINI-GAMES
Enter the password J09J4.

MEDIUM DIFFICULTY
Enter the password G07n0.

HARD DIFFICULTY
Enter the password H08L2.

NANCY DREW: HAUNTED MANSION

LEVEL PASSWORDS

LEVEL	PASSWORD
2	Ox, Horse, Tiger, Sheep
3	Rooster, Pig, Rabbit, Dragon
4	Rat, Dog, Monkey, Snake
5	Sheep, Tiger, Horse, Ox
6	Dragon, Rabbit, Pig, Rooster
7	Snake, Monkey, Dog, Rat

NICKTOONS RACING

ALL CHARACTERS, TRACKS, CUPS AND DIFFICULTIES
At the Main menu, hold R and press Start, Select, L, Select, Start.

NICKTOONS UNITE!

LEVEL 2: FENTON LAB
Select Continue and enter JAZMINE.

LEVEL 3: VLAD'S CHATEAU
Select Continue and enter PAULINA.

LEVEL 4: BIKINI BOTTOM
Select Continue and enter SKULKER.

LEVEL 5: CHUM BUCKET
Select Continue and enter PATRICK.

LEVEL 6: PLANKTON
Select Continue and enter MERMAID.

LEVEL 7: TIMMY'S HOME
Select Continue and enter SCALLOP.

LEVEL 8: DIMMSDALE DUMP
Select Continue and enter BABYSIT.

LEVEL 9: CROCKER'S LOCKER ROOM
Select Continue and enter GODDARD.

LEVEL 10: JIMMY'S LAB
Select Continue and enter ESTEVEZ.

LEVEL 11: SUBTERRANEAN CAVES
Select Continue and enter LIBERTY.

LEVEL 12: PROF CALAMITOUS' LAB
Select Continue and enter SKYLARK.

OPERATION ARMORED LIBERTY

MISSION PASSWORDS

MISSION	PASSWORD
2	BKFSZW
3	DFFSKZ
4	SKXSZP
5	QKFSZB
6	XKFSJZ
7	BKFJZC
8	DYFSZJ
9	VKFSZQ
10	SKFSPZ

PAC-MAN COLLECTION

APPENDIX FOR PAC-ATTACK
At the Main menu, select Pac-Attack. Then highlight Puzzle, hold Right, and press A.

PAC ATTACK PASSWORDS

LEVEL	PASSWORD
1	STR
2	HNM
3	KST
4	TRT
5	MYX

LEVEL	PASSWORD
6	KHL
7	RTS
8	SKB
9	HNT
10	SRY
11	YSK
12	RCF
13	HSM
14	PWW
15	MTN
16	TKY
17	RGH
18	TNS
19	YKM
20	MWS
21	KTY
22	TYK
23	SMM
24	NFL
25	SRT
26	KKT
27	MDD
28	CWD
29	DRC
30	WHT
31	FLT
32	SKM
33	QTN
34	SMN
35	TGR
36	WKR
37	YYP
38	SLS
39	THD
40	RMN
41	CNK
42	FRB
43	MLR
44	FRP
45	SDB
46	BQJ
47	VSM
48	RDY
49	XPL
50	WLC
51	TMF
52	QNS
53	GWR
54	PLT
55	KRW
56	HRC
57	RPN
58	CNT
59	BTT

LEVEL	PASSWORD	
60	TMP	
61	MNS	
62	SWD	
63	LDM	
64	YST	
65	QTM	
66	BRP	
67	MRS	
68	PPS	
69	SWT	
70	WTM	
71	FST	
72	SLW	
73	XWF	
74	RGJ	
75	SNC	
76	BKP	
77	CRN	
78	XNT	
79	RNT	
80	BSK	
81	JWK	
82	GSN	
83	MMT	
84	DNK	
85	HPN	
86	DCR	
87	BNS	
88	SDC	
89	MRH	
90	BTF	
91	NSM	
92	QYZ	
93	KTT	
94	FGS	
96	YLW	
97	PNN	
98	SPR	
99	CHB	
100	LST	

THE PINBALL OF THE DEAD

BOSS MODE
Enter D0NTN33DM0N3Y as a password.

PIRATES OF THE CARIBBEAN: THE CURSE OF THE BLACK PEARL

UNLIMITED LIVES
Enter 1MM0RT4L as a password.

UNLIMITED CANNONBALLS AND BULLETS
Enter BVLL1TZ as a password.

START WITH TRIPLE CANNONS, SABER, AND PISTOL
Enter G00D13S as a password.

SOLDIERS AND PIRATES BECOME SHEEP
Enter SH33P as a password.

SMARTER AI
Enter G3N1VS as a password.

CREDITS
Enter CR3D1TS as a password.

BABY
Enter L1TTLVN

PIRATES OF THE CARIBBEAN: DEAD MAN'S CHEST

1,000 GOLD
Pause the game, press Select and then press A, L, Select, R, Right, Right.

INVINCIBILITY
Pause the game, press Select and then press R, L, Up, Up, Left, Right.

RESTORE HEALTH
Pause the game, press Select and then press Select, R, A, L, Left, Right.

ALL SHIP UPGRADES
Pause the game, press Select and then press Right, Left, Left, Down, Up, Select.

BEST JACK UPGRADES
Pause the game, press Select and then press Right, L, Down, A, Left, Select.

RESTORE GROG/FOOD
Pause the game, press Select and then press A, Select, Left, Down, Right, Up.

UNLOCK RUMORS
Pause the game, press Select and then press A, L, Select, A, Right, Up.

MAGIC WIND
Pause the game, press Select and then press Up, R, Down, Left, Left, Right.

POWER RANGERS: SPACE PATROL DELTA

EPISODE 1 ON EASY
Enter ZZB as a password.

EPISODE 2A ON EASY
Enter ZVC as a password.

EPISODE 2B ON EASY
Enter QZB as a password.

EPISODE 3A ON EASY
Enter QVC as a password.

EPISODE 3B ON EASY
Enter !0G as a password.

EPISODE 4A ON EASY
Enter !XH as a password.

EPISODE 4B ON EASY
Enter R0G as a password.

EPISODE 5A ON EASY
Enter Z2B as a password.

EPISODE 5B ON EASY
Enter V6C as a password.

EPISODE 6A ON EASY
Enter L6C as a password.

EPISODE 6B ON EASY
Enter !4G as a password.

EPISODE 7A ON EASY
Enter R4G as a password.

EPISODE 7B ON EASY
Enter M8H as a password.

EPISODE 8A ON EASY
Enter 0BF as a password.

EPISODE 8B ON EASY
Enter SGD as a password.

FINAL BATTLE ON EASY
Enter SBF as a password.

RACING GEARS ADVANCE

You can enter up to three codes at a time. Note that entering a wrong code resets the codes.

AAA
After selecting the Circuit, hold R and press A, L, B, Right, Right, Up, A. This code eliminates damage.

ARMAGEDDON
After selecting the Circuit, hold R and press B, B, L, Right, Left, Down. This unlocks unlimited ammo.

BLINDSPOT
After selecting the Circuit, hold R and press Right, A, B, B, Left. With this code activated, all opponents become invisible.

CASHCROP
After selecting the Circuit, hold R and press Right, L, Up, A, Left, B. This makes dollar signs worth more.

ENDURANCE
After selecting the Circuit, hold R and press Left, B, A, Right, L, L, Down. This makes the race five laps long.

EQUALIZER
After selecting the Circuit, hold R and press Up, Up, B, Down, A.

HAMBURGER
After selecting the Circuit, hold R and press A, A, L, Left, Right, Up. This code unlocks weapons from the start of the race.

SPRINT
After selecting the Circuit, hold R and press Down, Up, B, Left, Right, A. This makes the race one lap long.

TAXMAN
After selecting the Circuit, hold R and press L, A, B, L, Down, Down. This makes dollar signs worth less.

WUSSY
After selecting the Circuit, hold R and press B, A, B, B, L. This code eliminates weapons.

R-TYPE III: THE THIRD LIGHTNING

PASSWORDS

LEVEL	PASSWORD
2	5bdgb
3	5hhlq
4	5mglt
5	5rflx
6	5wdl0

RAINBOW SIX: ROGUE SPEAR

LEVEL SKIP
Pause the game and press L, R, Down, Down.

RAMPAGE PUZZLE ATTACK

LEVEL PASSWORDS

LEVEL	PASSWORD
Tokyo 1-1	GQGGHKGBHF

Tokyo 1-2	LLMLMPLQMT
Tokyo 1-3	GJJBHKGBHF
Tokyo 1-4	BDFGCFBGCK
Tokyo 1-5	GSBBHKGBHF
Delhi 2-1	LPRQMPLQMT
Delhi 2-2	QKNLRTQLRP
Delhi 2-3	BFKGCFBGCK
Delhi 2-4	QBGLRTQLRP
Delhi 2-5	LQCQMPLQMT

Helsinki 3-1	GLSBHKGBHF
Helsinki 3-2	BGPGCFBGCK
Helsinki 3-3	GBLBHKGBHF

LEVEL	PASSWORD
Helsinki 3-4	LQHQMPLQMT
Helsinki 3-5	QLDLRTQLRP
Paris 4-1	BKTGCFBGCK
Paris 4-2	LMLRMPLQMT
Paris 4-3	GJHCHKGBHF
Paris 4-4	BDDHCFBGCK
Paris 4-5	GSKCHKGBHF
Hollywood 5-1	LPQRMPLQMT
Hollywood 5-2	QKMMRTQLRP
Hollywood 5-3	BFJHCFBGCK
Hollywood 5-4	QBPMRTQLRP
Hollywood 5-5	LQBRMPLQMT
Washington D.C. 6-1	GLRCHKGBHF

RAZOR FREESTYLE SCOOTER

LEVEL PASSWORDS

Enter the following passwords to start with the indicated level complete.

LEVEL	PASSWORD
Aircraft Carrier	VDY3ZJ6LJVCQBF
Circus	ZBF4GJ5VJVCQBF
Construction Site	QHY4LJ2LHZCQBF
Scooter Park	SBY5VJ4BJVCQBF
Shopping Mall	QLY67J3BJVCQBF
Sports Stadium	7JY4GJZBJVCQBF

RESCUE HEROES: BILLY BLAZES

LEVEL SELECT
Turn on the GBA. Then at the Way Forward logo, hold L + R + Up + Start.

RIPPING FRIENDS

LEVEL SELECT
Select Password and press Right, L, Up, Down, B, Left, Left, Right, Left.

RIVER CITY RANSOM EX

Select the status menu and change your name to one of the following.

MAX STATS
DAMAX

$999999.99
PLAYA

CUSTOM CHAR
XTRA0

CUSTOM SELF
XTRA1

CUSTOM MOVE
XTRA2

CLEAR SAVE
ERAZE

TECHNIQUES 1
FUZZY. This group includes Mach Punch, Dragon Kick, Acro Circus, Grand Slam, Javelin Man, Slick Trick, Nitro Port, Twin Kick, Deadly Shot, Top Spin, Helicopter, Torpedo.

TECHNIQUES 2
WUZZY. This group includes Slap Happy, Pulper, Headbutt, Kickstand, Big Bang, Wheel Throw, Glide Chop, Head Bomb, Chain Chump, Jet Kick, Shuriken, Flip Throw.

TECHNIQUES 3
WAZZA. This group includes Boomerang, Charge It, Bat Fang, Flying Kick, Speed Drop, Bomb Blow, Killer Kick, Bike Kick, Slam Punk, Dragon Knee, God Fist, Hyperguard.

TECHNIQUES 4
BEAR*. This group includes PhoenixWing, Inlines, Springlines, Rocketeers, Air Merc's Narcishoes, Magic Pants, Pandora Box, Skaterz, Custom Fit.

ROAD RASH: JAILBREAK

ALL CHARACTERS AT LEVEL 4 & ALL RACES
Press Select at the Player Select screen and enter ALAKAZAMM.

ALL RACES
Press Select at the Player Select screen and enter KEEPOUT.

ALL RACES IN COP PATROL
Press Select at the Player Select screen and enter FELONY.

SURVIVAL
Press Select at the Player Select screen and enter MENACE.

ACE LEVEL 2
Press Select at the Player Select screen and enter SWING.

ACE LEVEL 3
Press Select at the Player Select screen and enter FLUSH.

ACE LEVEL 4
Press Select at the Player Select screen and enter BRUISE.

FAT HOAGIE
Press Select at the Player Select screen and enter EDGY.

FAT HOAGIE LEVEL 2
Press Select at the Player Select screen and enter SLAP.

FAT HOAGIE LEVEL 3
Press Select at the Player Select screen and enter FURIOUS.

FAT HOAGIE LEVEL 4
Press Select at the Player Select screen and enter HEADACHE.

HURL LEVEL 1
Press Select at the Player Select screen and enter HOWDY.

HURL LEVEL 2
Press Select at the Player Select screen and enter PULSE.

HURL LEVEL 3
Press Select at the Player Select screen and enter STRIDER.

HURL LEVEL 4
Press Select at the Player Select screen and enter BEATNIK.

LULU LEVEL 2
Press Select at the Player Select screen and enter BLOW.

LULU LEVEL 3
Press Select at the Player Select screen and enter SCOURGE.

LULU LEVEL 4
Press Select at the Player Select screen and enter QUICKEN.

TINY LEVEL 2
Press Select at the Player Select screen and enter AXLE.

TINY LEVEL 3
Press Select at the Player Select screen and enter WHEEL.

TINY LEVEL 4
Press Select at the Player Select screen and enter PROPER.

ROAD TRIP: SHIFTING GEARS

DRAGON PARTS
Complete the Angel Cup. Select Change Name from the Options menu and enter DRAGON.

ROCK 'EM SOCK 'EM ROBOTS

TITLE FIGHT PASSWORDS
Select Passwords from the Select Game Mode screen and enter one of the following.

TITLE FIGHT	PASSWORD
Black Bruiser	LSTL2B
Blue Bomber	B5T32J
Brown Bully	J[]T7KH
Green Grappler	NMTZKQ
Orange Oppressor	2XT9KN
Pink Pummeller	6QT1KK
Purple Pyro	O2TX2T

TITLE FIGHT	PASSWORD
Silver Stretcher	GZTV2K
Yellow Yahoo	W8T52Q
End	3CTNKS

RUGRATS: I GOTTA GO PARTY

GO TO LEVEL 2
Enter CBKBBB as a password.

GO TO LEVEL 3
Enter RBHBNB as a password.

GO TO LEVEL 4
Enter SNFBBC as a password.

GO TO LEVEL 5
Enter TNHHBG as a password.

GO TO LEVEL 6
Enter VNFTNG as a password.

GO TO LEVEL 7
Enter XNHTFC as a password.

GO TO LEVEL 8
Enter ZNFTRJ as a password.

SECRET AGENT BARBIE: ROYAL JEWELS MISSION

ALL SECRETS
Enter TTTTTS as a password.

ENGLAND—THE ROYAL TOWER
Enter BBBBCG as a password.

ENGLAND—STREET CHASE
Enter DBBFCM as a password.

CHINA—CITY STREETS
Enter FBBFFQ as a password.

CHINA—SECRET HIDEOUT
Enter GBBPFH as a password.

CHINA—GOLDEN CITY
Enter HBBPKN as a password.

CHINA—THE PALACE
Enter JCBPKQ as a password.

ITALY—OPERA HOUSE
Enter KCBTKC as a password.

ITALY—CANAL CHASE
Enter LCGTKJ as a password.

ITALY—FASHION DISTRICT
Enter MCHTKL as a password.

ITALY—SCUBA SEARCH
Enter NCHTTC as a password.

MEXICO—SUNNY CITY
Enter PCRTTN as a password.

SEGA ARCADE GALLERY

CREDITS AND TIME CHEAT

Select one of the games, then hold L + R + Select and press Up to access the Show Credits
option. Select this and press Left, Right, Left, Right. When the second credit screen appears, press Up, Down. At the third screen, press A. You should get an audible confirmation that the code worked. This cheat gives you 5 Credits in After Burner, Infinite Credits in Space Harrier, and Infinite Time in OutRun and Super Hang-On.

SEGA SMASH PACK

ECCO THE DOLPHIN

Pause the game with Ecco facing the screen and press Right, B, R, B, R, Down, R, Up. This
unlocks Stage Select, Sound Select, and Unlimited Lives.

GOLDEN AXE

Select arcade mode and hold Down/Left + B and press START at the Character Select screen.
This unlocks Level Select.

GOLDEN AXE

Select arcade mode and hold Down/Left + A + R. Release the buttons and press Start to gain
Nine Continues.

SONIC SPINBALL

At the Options screen, press A, Down, B, Down, R, Down, A, B, Up, A, R, Up, B, R, Up. This
unlocks Level Select. The following commands will start you at that level.

LEVEL	COMMAND
2 Lava Powerhouse	Hold A and press START
3 The Machine	Hold B and press START
4 Showdown	Hold R and press START

SONIC SPINBALL

At the Options screen, press A, Up, R, Up, L, Up, A, R, Down, A, L, Down, R, L, Down. This
unlocks the game's Credits.

SERIOUS SAM ADVANCE

EASY PASSWORDS

LEVEL	PASSWORD
Amon Thule, Subterranean Palace of the Pharaohs	HEXMODE
Baths of Diocletian	NEED
Caesar's Palace	WAFTY
Gladiator Training School	COINAGE
Praetorian Fort	NORTHERN
Pyramid Entrance Maze	BADDUN
Slave Compound	BOBBINS
Slave Quarters	TOAST
The Forum of Mars	GAMES
The Temple of Herkat Lower	MNIP
Tomb Of Ramses	MEGAMUNT

NORMAL PASSWORDS

LEVEL	PASSWORD
Amon Thule, Subterranean Palace of the Pharaohs	OPEE
Baths OF Diocletian	OWL
Caesar's Palace	MOOPAY
Gladiator Training School	FRYUP
Praetorian Fort	FILLY
Pyramid Entrance Maze	BETTERER
Slave Compound	PILCH
Slave Quarters	BEVIL
The Forum Of Mars	DUCKAROO
The Temple of Herkat Lower	KIPPAGE
Tomb of Ramses	HORSE

HARD PASSWORDS

LEVEL	PASSWORD
Amon Thule, Subterranean Palace of the Pharaohs	WOLF
Baths OF Diocletian	LIMO
Caesar's Palace	MOCKNEY
Gladiator Training School	MADEUP
Praetorian Fort	MIRROR
Pyramid Entrance Maze	CHIPPER
Slave Compound	FORREST
Slave Quarters	BEAK
The Forum Of Mars	FOZZER
The Temple of Herkat Lower	TITHES
Tomb of Ramses	EYE

SHAMAN KING: LEGACY OF THE SPIRITS, SOARING HAWK

SPIRIT OF FIRE
At the Title screen, press Right, Right, L, Left + R, Down, R, Right, B.

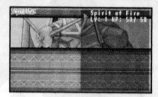

SHAMAN KING: LEGACY OF THE SPIRITS, SPRINTING WOLF

SPIRIT OF FIRE
At the Title screen, press Right, Right, L, Left + R, Down, R, Right, B.

SHINING SOUL

2 EXTRA HERBS
Enter your name as Shining.

2 VALUING SCROLLS
Enter your name as Force.

HEALING DROP
Enter your name as Soul.

MONKEY DOLL
Enter your name as AiAi.

PAINTER'S SOUL
Enter your name as Salamander.

JUDO UNIFORM FOR DRAGONUTE
Select the Dragonute and enter your name as Segata.

LEAF BRIEFS FOR ARCHER
Select the Archer and enter your name as NomuNomu.

SHINING SOUL II

DREAM HAT
Enter Nindri as your name.

GENOME RING
Enter Genomes as your name.

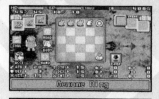

ATLUS RING
Enter Vjum as your name.

POWER GLOVES
Enter VJxSS as your name.

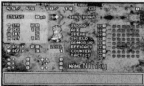

STR +5
Enter Ninky as your name.

DEX +5
Enter Yoshi as your name.

VIT +5
Enter Taicho as your name.

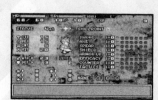

INT +5, RTH +30
Enter Dengeki as your name.

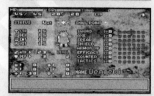

RDK +30
Enter Montaka as your name.

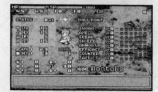

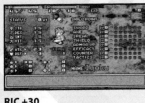

RFR +30
Enter Iyoku as your name.

RIC +30
Enter Mizupin as your name.

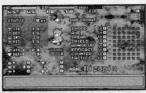

RPO +30
Enter Hachi as your name.

SPIDER-MAN 2

INVINCIBILITY
At the Title screen, press Up, Down, Right, A.

LEVEL SELECT
After completing the game, start a new game with the name FLUWDEAR.

SPONGEBOB SQUAREPANTS: REVENGE OF THE FLYING DUTCHMAN

DEBUG MODE
Enter the password D3BVG-M0D3.

SPORTS ILLUSTRATED FOR KIDS BASEBALL

ALL-STARS
Select Season, then choose Cheat Code from the Season menu. Enter the following codes to unlock these all-stars.

ENTER	ALL-STAR
BAMSTAR	Riley Waters
BESTBUYSTR	Michael Quince
EBRULES	Nateo Geeoni
GAMESTOP	Keith Fisher
GOCIRCUIT	Mark Modesto
SIKPOWER	Tecumseh Brown
SIKSTAR	Eddie Penn
TARGETPLYR	George Stocks

SPORTS ILLUSTRATED FOR KIDS FOOTBALL

ALL-STARS

Select Season, then choose Cheat Code from the Season menu. Enter the following codes to unlock these all-stars.

CHEAT CODE	ALLSTAR
BAMPLYR	Mac Marshall
BESTBUYPWR	Wayne Selby
CIRCUITFUN	Mark Haruf
EBPLAYER	Eddie Brown
RZONESTAR	Hal Church
SIKPOWER	Rob Lewis
SIKSTAR	Sandy Sanders
TARGETSTAR	Ryan Hunter
TOUCHDOWN	Sammy Rivera

SPYRO ORANGE: THE CORTEX CONSPIRACY

100 GEMS

At the Mode menu, press L + R, then enter V1S10NS.

ORANGE GAME

At the Mode menu, press L + R, then enter SP4RX.

PURPLE GAME

At the Mode menu, press L + R, then enter PORT4L.

ORANGE SPYRO

At the Mode menu, press L + R, then enter SPYR0.

SHEEP MODE

At the Mode menu, press L + R, then enter SH33P.

SHEEP FLAME MODE

At the Mode menu, press L + R, then enter B41S0KV.

CRASH PARTY USA MINI-GAME

Start up your Game Boy Advance and hold L + R.

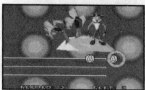

SPYRO: SEASON OF FLAME

BLUE SPYRO

At the Title screen, press Up, Up, Up, Up, Down, Left, Right, Down, B.

ALL PORTALS

At the Title screen, press Up, Left, Up, Right, Up, Down, Up, Down, B.

ALL WORLDS IN ATLAS

At the Title screen, press Left, Right, Up, Up, Right, Left, Right, Up, B.

ATLAS WARPING

At the Title screen, press Down, Up, Left, Left, Up, Left, Left, Right, B.

INFINITE LIVES
At the Title screen, press Left, Right, Left, Right (x3), Up, Down, B.

INFINITE SHIELD FOR AGENT 9
At the Title screen, press Left, Down, Up, Right, Left, Up, Up, Left, B.

INFINITE AMMO
At the Title screen, press Right, Left, Up, Down, Right, Down, Up, Right, B.

NEVER DROWN
At the Title screen, press Down, Up, Right, Left, Right, Up, Right, Left, B.

ALL BREATH TYPES
At the Title screen, press Right, Down, Up, Right, Left, Up, Right, Down, B.

SUPER CHARGE
At the Title screen, press Left, Left, Down, Up, Up, Right, Left, Left, B.

DRAGON DRAUGHTS MINI-GAME
At the Title screen, press Right, Up, Down, Down, Down, Right, Up, Down, B.

STAR WARS: EPISODE 2 ATTACK OF THE CLONES

LEVEL PASSWORDS

LEVEL	APPRENTICE	PADAWAN	KNIGHT
2	BLDBGP	BHDBGJ	BJDGGM
3	BMFBHN	BHFBHJ	BJFGHM
4	BMGBDN	BHGBDJ	BJGGDM
5	BMHBFN	BHHBFJ	BJHGFM
6	BMKBCN	BGKBCK	BJKGCM
7	BMLBSN	BGLBSK	BJLGSM
8	BMMGTS	BGMBTK	BJMGTM
9	BMNGQS	BGNBQK	BJNGQM
10	BMPGRS	BGPBRK	BJPGRM
11	BLQGNT	BGQBNK	BGQGNP

STAR WARS EPISODE 2: THE NEW DROID ARMY

After correctly entering the following passwords, you should receive an Invalid Password message.

LEVEL SELECT
Enter 2D4 as a password. Use L and R to select a level.

200 HEALTH AND 200 FORCE
Enter 8!T as a password.

ALL FORCE ABILITIES
Enter FRC as a password.

LUKE SKYWALKER
Enter SKY as a password.

OVERHEAD MAP
Enter CQL as a password.

CHANGE CONTROLS
Enter BTW as a password.

DISABLE SHADOW
Enter !B4 as a password.

BLACK SHADOWS
Enter SK8 as a password.

REDUCE RESOLUTION
Enter GFX as a password.

TOGGLE LANGUAGE OPTION
Enter LNG as a password. Select Language from the Options screen.

PASSWORDS
After correctly entering the following passwords, you should receive a password accepted message.

LEVEL	PASSWORD
Droids at Speeder	D31
Mos Espa	QK1
Xelric Draw	BKT
Womp Rat Cave	FKW
Xelric Draw	C3P
Xelric Draw	CYD
Mos Espa	AK?
Hutt's Assassins	A3W
Mos Espa	AY4
Dune Sea	KK4
Moisture Farms	M34
Moisture Farms	MYW
Jundland Wastes	TKP
Jundland Wastes	T3H
Jundland Wastes	TYQ
Jabba's Dungeon	J38
Jabba's Dungeon	JY1
Jabba's Dungeon	J?T
Jabba's Dungeon	J7J
High City	7KQ
High City	73D
High City (Interior)	7YP
High City (Interior)	7?W
Underlevels	!3C
Underlevels	!YL
Bentho's Nightclub	H3D
Core Bay	6K7
Core Bay	63L
Jedi Temple	532
Jedi Archives	4KX
Jedi Archives	438
Droid Factory Outskirts	XK1
Production Facility 1	23X
Production Facility 1	2Y7
Production Facility 2	3K2
Production Facility 2	334
Cortosis Processing Plant	WKP
Dual Duel!	W3H
Dual Duel!	WYQ
Droid Factory Core	?KH
Droid Factory Core	?3P

LEVEL	PASSWORD
Duel with Vandalor	8K7
Race the Bombs	831
Ending	Y3W

STAR WARS: FLIGHT OF THE FALCON

PASSWORDS

LEVEL	PASSWORD
Episode IV	TGHK
Episode V	8TV2
Episode VI	TSB2
Bonus	RRV2
All Levels and Bonus	4?6C

STAR WARS: JEDI POWER BATTLES

DARTH MAUL PASSWORDS

LEVEL	PASSWORD
2	VCJ0D2J
3	VCJ0G*J
4	VCJ0JKK
5	VCJ0LTK
6	VCJ0N2K
7	VCJ0Q1K
8	VCJ0SFK
9	VCJ0VPK
10	VCJ0XYK

MACE WINDU PASSWORDS

LEVEL	PASSWORD
8	VC1FCFH
9	VCJGCPH
10	VC1GCYH

OBI-WAN PASSWORDS

LEVEL	PASSWORD
2	WDJ3B6F
3	XDJ3BFG
4	FDJ3BFG
5	GBJ3BPF
6	0BJ3B6F
7	1FJ3BYH
8	2FJ3B6H
9	3FJ3BFJ
10	4FJ3BPJ

STAR X

UNLIMITED SMART BOMBS
Enter GSBOOM as a password.

INVINCIBILITY
Enter GSHARD as a password.

FULL WEAPONS
Enter GSMAX as a password.

LEVEL PASSWORDS

LEVEL	PASSWORD
Aquess, Part 2	IGIFCDLC
Aquess, Orbit	2EA3QD01
Egaon, Part 1	NGK3QD0S
Egaon, Part 2	YGA5QSON
Egaon, Orbit	JGIXASPT
Birmen, Part 1	FECXEQ51
Birmen, Part 2	ECMXUQXL
Birmen, Orbit	IIC3ADC0
Wolf X2, Part 1	ZLI3CQQB
Wolf X2, Part 2	MJC3CQA1
Wolf X2, Orbit	EJI3QDC4
Hades, Part1	BLCXQFVG
Hades, Part 2	YLMZAQVR
Hades, Orbit	2JAXABFQ
Tritopia, Part 1	MLI5ABES
Tritopia, Part 2	JTBFABRW
Tritopia, Orbit	QRLFADTM
SILICON, Part 1	NTBFABBW
Silicon, Part 2	MTLNAQAL
Silicon, Moon	ZSBPABEU

STREET FIGHTER ALPHA 3

ALL FIGHTERS
At the Title screen, press Left, Right, Down, Right, L, L, A, L, L, B, R, A, Up.

ALL MODES
At the Title screen, press A, Up, A, L, R, Right, L, Right, A, Down, Right. Then press L, Right, A, R, Up,L, Right, B, A, Up, Right, Down, Right.

PLAY AS SUPER BISON
At the Character Select screen, hold Start and select Bison.

PLAY AS SHIN AKUMA
At the Character Select screen, hold Start and select Akuma.

ALTERNATE COSTUMES
At the Character Select screen, press L or R.

FINAL BATTLE
At the Speed Select screen, hold A + B.

SUPER COLLAPSE 2

PUZZLE MODE PASSWORDS

PUZZLE	PASSWORD
2	G6CLG
3	69MR3
4	F6DHM
5	2XNSX

PUZZLE	PASSWORD
6	RQCJD
7	DL4NX
8	TCLV5
9	G5DYR
10	GDXSV
11	FVH4M
12	7TD4K
13	F6GS4

THAT'S SO RAVEN 2: SUPERNATURAL STYLE

COSTUME MODE
At the Title screen, press Left, Right, Up, Down, B, B, B, Up, Down.

UNLIMITED ENERGY MODE
At the Title screen, press B, B, L, R, Up, Down, Up, Left, Right.

TOM AND JERRY: THE MAGIC RING

LEVEL PASSWORDS	ENTER
Level 1-1 as Jerry	1236
Level 1-2 as Jerry	6878
Level 1-3 as Jerry	5121
Level 1-4 as Jerry	2753
Level 1-5 as Jerry	7616
Level 2 as Jerry	7531
Level 3 as Jerry	8358
Level 4-1 as Jerry	1176
Level 4-2 as Jerry	6718
Level 4-3 as Jerry	5261
Level 5 as Jerry	8251
Level 6 as Jerry	2761
Level 7-1 as Jerry	2856
Level 7-2 as Jerry	5228
Level 1-1 as Tom	5488
Level 1-2 as Tom	4121
Level 1-3 as Tom	1353
Level 1-4 as Tom	8246
Level 1-5 as Tom	3868
Level 2 as Tom	3783
Level 3 as Tom	5423
Level 4-1 as Tom	5348
Level 4-2 as Tom	4281
Level 4-3 as Tom	1413
Level 5 as Tom	5126
Level 6 as Tom	8238
Level 7-1 as Tom	8143
Level 7-2 as Tom	1456

TONY HAWK'S UNDERGROUND

SKIP TUTORIAL
At the Main menu, hold R and press Left, Down, Start, Start, Right, Up, Up, L, Down.

TONY HAWK'S UNDERGROUND 2

TENNIS SHOOTER MINI-GAME
After unlocking Bam's character on the map, talk to him. Knock down the rollerbladers, then go back. He'll give you the Tennis Shooter mini-game. After completing three levels, save your game to access Tennis Shooter at any time from the Main menu.

TOP GUN: COMBAT ZONES

LEVEL 2—PACIFIC OCEAN ON EASY
Enter 9799 as a password.

LEVEL 3—NORTHERN SIBERIA ON EASY
Enter 8457 as a password.

LEVEL 4—BERING STRAIT ON EASY
Enter 6767 as a password.

LEVEL 5—NORTH SEA ON EASY
Enter 6891 as a password.

LEVEL 6—EASTERN EUROPE ON EASY
Enter 2468 as a password.

LEVEL 7—ARABIAN PENINSULA ON EASY
Enter 4479 as a password.

LEVEL 8—SOUTHEAST ASIA ON EASY
Enter 3232 as a password.

LEVEL 9—MONGOLIAN DESERT ON EASY
Enter 1295 as a password.

LEVEL 10—ARCTIC CIRCLE ON EASY
Enter 7783 as a password.

LEVEL 11—SOUTH AMERICA ON EASY
Enter 8226 as a password.

LEVEL 12—GULF OF MEXICO ON EASY
Enter 7453 as a password.

LEVEL 2—PACIFIC OCEAN ON NORMAL
Enter 7294 as a password.

LEVEL 3—NORTHERN SIBERIA ON NORMAL
Enter 4947 as a password.

LEVEL 4—BERING STRAIT ON NORMAL
Enter 1599 as a password.

LEVEL 5—NORTH SEA ON NORMAL
Enter 9145 as a password.

LEVEL 6—EASTERN EUROPE ON NORMAL
Enter 8813 as a password.

LEVEL 7—ARABIAN PENINSULA ON NORMAL
Enter 9915 as a password.

LEVEL 8—SOUTHEAST ASIA ON NORMAL
Enter 8212 as a password.

LEVEL 9—MONGOLIAN DESERT ON NORMAL
Enter 9215 as a password.

LEVEL 10—ARCTIC CIRCLE ON NORMAL
Enter 4518 as a password.

LEVEL 11—SOUTH AMERICA ON NORMAL
Enter 2121 as a password.

LEVEL 12—GULF OF MEXICO ON NORMAL
Enter 4211 as a password.

LEVEL 2—PACIFIC OCEAN ON HARD
Enter 3468 as a password.

LEVEL 3—NORTHERN SIBERIA ON HARD
Enter 2345 as a password.

LEVEL 4—BERING STRAIT ON HARD
Enter 8791 as a password.

LEVEL 5—NORTH SEA ON HARD
Enter 6642 as a password.

LEVEL 6—EASTERN EUROPE ON HARD
Enter 2918 as a password.

LEVEL 7—ARABIAN PENINSULA ON HARD
Enter 5748 as a password.

LEVEL 8—SOUTHEAST ASIA ON HARD
Enter 5367 as a password.

LEVEL 9—MONGOLIAN DESERT ON HARD
Enter 3783 as a password.

LEVEL 10—ARCTIC CIRCLE ON HARD
Enter 9818 as a password.

LEVEL 11—SOUTH AMERICA ON HARD
Enter 9319 as a password.

LEVEL 12—GULF OF MEXICO ON HARD
Enter 6161 as a password.

TOP GUN: FIRESTORM ADVANCE

PASSWORDS

LEVEL	PASSWORD
2	Jet, Missile, Jet, Jet
3	Top View Car, Side View Car, Tank, Missile
4	Boat, Missile, Boat, Missile
5	Boat, Top View Car, Jet, Missile Man
6	AA Gun, Top View Car, Boat, Top View Car
7	Side View Car, Side View Car, Missile, Jet
8	Paratrooper, AA Gun, Paratrooper, AA Gun
9	Missile Man, AA Gun, Jet, Tank
10	Missile, Missile, Top View Car, Paratrooper
11	Top View Car, AA Gun, AA Gun, Boat
12	Missile, Side View Car, Tank, Paratrooper

TREASURE PLANET

PASSWORDS

LEVEL	PASSWORD
1	MUSHROOM
2	TRUMPET
3	CLOUDY
4	RABBIT
5	SUNSHINE
6	SPIDER
7	APRON
8	RAINBOW
9	GOOSE
10	ENGLAND

LEVEL	PASSWORD
11	MOUNTAIN
12	CAPTAIN
13	SNOWMAN
14	WITCHES
15	MONKEY
16	PRINCESS
17	WINDOW
18	COCONUT
19	FOOTBALL
20	CONCRETE
21	ELEPHANT
22	PHANTOM
23	DRAGON

TRON 2.0: KILLER APP

ALL MINI-GAMES
At the Title screen, press Left, Left, Left, Left, Up, Right, Down, Down, Select.

ULTIMATE ARCADE GAMES

ALL GAMES
At the Main menu press L, L, L, L, R, L, R, Left, Up, Right, Down, Left, Up, Right, Down, R, L, R, L, Select.

URBAN YETI

UNLOCK EVERYTHING
Enter TONYGOLD as a password.

DISCUS TOURNAMENT
Enter PINGPONG as a password.

LAZY SEWER O' FUN
Enter YETIRAFT as a password.

SOUP KITCHEN MANAGER
Enter HAMSTEAK as a password.

YETI CHICKEN RANCHER
Enter PROVIDER as a password.

START AT LEVEL 1
Enter BUZZWORD as a password.

START AT LEVEL 2
Enter FOREWORD as a password.

START AT LEVEL 3
Enter COOKBOOK as a password.

START AT LEVEL 4
Enter FEEDBAGS as a password.

START AT LEVEL 5
Enter HAMSTEAK as a password.

START AT LEVEL 6
Enter DAYBREAK as a password.

START AT LEVEL 7
Enter SUNLIGHT as a password.

START AT LEVEL 8
Enter NITETIME as a password.

START AT LEVEL 9
Enter EASTSIDE as a password.

START AT LEVEL 10
Enter BEATDOWN as a password.

START AT LEVEL 11
Enter VENGEFUL as a password.

START AT LEVEL 12
Enter FRISBEES as a password.

START AT LEVEL 13
Enter ICESKATE as a password.

START AT LEVEL 14
Enter PINGPONG as a password.

START AT LEVEL 15
Enter DOWNTOWN as a password.

START AT LEVEL 16
Enter CITYMAPS as a password.

START AT LEVEL 17
Enter DUMPSTER as a password.

START AT LEVEL 18
Enter WATERWAY as a password.

START AT LEVEL 19
Enter TIRETUBE as a password.

START AT LEVEL 20
Enter YETIRAFT as a password.

START AT LEVEL 21
Enter SUBURBIA as a password.

START AT LEVEL 22
Enter HOUSETOP as a password.

START AT LEVEL 23
Enter CITIZENS as a password.

START AT LEVEL 24
Enter CHICKENS as a password.

START AT LEVEL 25
Enter SONGBIRD as a password.

START AT LEVEL 26
Enter PROVIDER as a password.

STRANGE COLORS AND SOUND
Enter BSWSBSWS as a password

THE URBZ: SIMS IN THE CITY

CLUB XIZZLE
Upon gaining access to Club Xizzle, enter with the password bucket.

THE URBZ: SIMS IN THE CITY

CLUB XIZZLE
Once you gain access to Club Xizzle, enter with the password "bucket."

V.I.P.

PASSWORDS

LEVEL	PASSWORD
2	AWJW
3	Q4KT
4	PSLQ
5	TQWN
6	S3NK
7	AM3H
8	QKP1

WARIO LAND 4

KARAOKE MODE
At the Sound Room, highlight Exit and hold SELECT + START + Up + L + R.

WILD THORNBERRYS: THE MOVIE

LEVEL SELECT
Enter HB5F as a password.

WINNIE THE POOH'S RUMBLY TUMBLY ADVENTURE

GAME COMPLETED
Enter 3013736 as a password.

EEYORE'S FIRST AREA
Enter 9744991 as a password.

EEYORE'S SECOND AREA
Enter 9301241 as a password.

EEYORE'S THIRD AREA
Enter 3220311 as a password.

EEYORE'S AREA COMPLETE
Enter 3412121 as a password.

PIGLET'S FIRST AREA
Enter 5735172 as a password.

PIGLET'S SECOND AREA
Enter 7045732 as a password.

PIGLET'S THIRD AREA
Enter 1156612 as a password.

PIGLET'S AREA COMPLETE
Enter 1348422 as a password.

POOH'S FIRST AREA
Enter 1937986 as a password.

POOH'S SECOND AREA
Enter 1388596 as a password.

POOH'S THIRD AREA
Enter 5399476 as a password.

ROO'S FIRST AREA
Enter 3412773 as a password.

ROO'S SECOND AREA
Enter 9999053 as a password.

ROO'S THIRD AREA
Enter 5505553 as a password.

ROO'S AREA COMPLETE
Enter 3011033 as a password.

TIGGER'S FIRST AREA
Enter 7847570 as a password.

TIGGER'S SECOND AREA
Enter 5560830 as a password.

TIGGER'S THIRD AREA
Enter 3834540 as a password.

TIGGER'S FOURTH AREA
Enter 9172120 as a password.

TIGGER'S AREA COMPLETE
Enter 1749510 as a password.

WOLFENSTEIN 3D

GOD MODE
Pause the game, hold L + R, and press A, A, B, A (x5).

ALL WEAPONS, ALL KEYS, FULL AMMO, AND FULL HEALTH
Pause the game, hold L + R, and press A, B, B, A (x5).

LEVEL SKIP
Pause the game, hold L + R, and press A, B, A, A, B, B, B, A.

SKIP TO BOSS
Pause the game, hold L + R, and press A, B, A, A, B, B, A, A.

WORLD CHAMPIONSHIP POKER

10 MILLION DOLLAR
Enter the following as a password: 7 Hearts, King Spades, 2 Hearts, Queen Clubs, 9 Hearts, Jack Hearts.

WORMS WORLD PARTY

ALL WEAPONS
During gameplay, open the Weapon Select menu. Highlight Skip Go and press A. Return to the Weapon Select screen, hold L + Down + B, and press SELECT (x4).

X2: WOLVERINE'S REVENGE

Enter the following codes at the Slot select:

100 LIVES
Hold L, press Right (7x).

ALL POWER-UPS
Hold L, press Right, Left, Right, Left, Right, Left, Right.

INFINITE DOUBLE JUMP
Hold L, press Select, Left, Up, Down, Down, Up, Down.

INVINCIBILITY
Hold L, press Down, Up, Down, Down, Up, Down, Select.

REGENERATE WITH CLAWS EXTENDED
Hold L, press Right, Up, Down, Right, Left, Select, Select.

XXX

INFINITE HEALTH AND AMMUNITION
After completing Level 12, select Extras to find Infinite Health and Ammunition.

YOSHI TOPSY-TURVY

CHALLENGE MODE & CHALLENGE 1
Defeat Bowser for the second time in Story Mode.

CHALLENGES 2, 3, 4
Complete the Egg Gallery in Story Mode.

FINAL CHALLENGE
Earn all Golds in Story Mode.

YU-GI-OH! 7 TRIALS TO GLORY: WORLD CHAMPIONSHIP TOURNAMENT 2005

PURPLE TITLE SCREEN
Completing the game changes the Title screen from blue to purple. To switch it back, press Up, Up, Down, Down, Left, Right, Left, Right, B, A at the Title screen.

CREDITS
Defeat the game, then press Up, Up, Down, Down, Left, Right, Left, Right, B, A.

CARD PASSWORDS
At the password machine, press R and enter the following.

CARD	PASSWORD
30,000-Year White Turtle	11714098
7 Colored Fish	23771716
7 Completed	86198326
A Hero Emerges	21597117
Acid Trap Hole	41356845
Air Eater	08353769
Alligator's Sword	64428736
Alligator's Sword Dragon	03366982
Alpha The Magnet Warrior	99785935
Amazon Archer	91869203
Amazon of the Seas	17968114
Amphibian Beast	67371383
Amphibious Bugroth	40173854
Ancient Brain	42431843
Ancient Elf	93221206
Ancient Lizard Warrior	43230671
Anti Raigeki	42364257
Aqua Chorus	95132338
Aqua Dragon	86164529
Archfiend Soldier	49881766
Arma Knight	36151751
Armaill	53153481
Armed Ninja	09076207
Armored Lizard	15480588

CARD	PASSWORD
Armored Rat	16246527
Armored Starfish	17535588
Armored Zombie	20277860
Axe of Despair	40619825
Axe Raider	48305365
Baby Dragon	88819587
Banisher of the Light	61528025
Baron of the Fiend Sword	86325596
Barrel Dragon	81480460
Barrel Dragon	81480460
Barrel Lily	67841515
Barrel Rock	10476868
Beaver Warrior	32452818
Beta The Magnet Warrior	39256679
Bite Shoes	50122883
Black Luster Soldier—Envoy of the Beginning	72989439
Black Pendant	65169794
Bladefly	28470714
Blast Sphere	26302522
Blast Sphere	26302522
Blue Eyes Toon Dragon	53183600
Blue Eyes White Dragon	89631139
Boneheimer	98456117
Book of SecretArts	91595718
Bottom Dweller	81386177
Catapult Turtle	95727991
Celtic Guardian	91152256
Ceremonial Bell	20228463
Change of Heart	04031928
Chaos Emperor Dragon—EotE	82301904
Crass Clown	93889755
Curse of the Masked Beast	94377247
Cyber Falcon	30655537
Cyber Harpie	80316585
Cyber Jar	34124316
Cyber Shield	63224564
Cyber Soldier of Darkworld	75559356
Cyber-Stein	69015963
Cyber-Tech Alligator	48766543
D.D. Warrior Lady	07572887
Dark Artist	72520073
Dark Illusion Ritual	41426869
Dark-Eyes Illusionist	38247752
Darkfire Soldier #1	05388481
Darkfire Soldier #2	78861134
Des Koala	69579761
Destroyer Golem	73481154
Dissolverock	40826495
Dragonic Attack	32437102
Dunames Dark Witch	12493482
Durnames Dark Witch	12493482
Eatgaboon	42578427
Exile of the Wicked	26725158

CARD	PASSWORD
Exodia the Forbidden One	33396948
Fiend Reflection #2	02863439
Final Destiny	18591904
Firegrass	53293545
Flame Champion	42599677
Flash Assailant	96890582
Flower Wolf	95952802
Flying Kamakiri #1	84834865
Flying Kamakiri #2	03134241
Gaia the Fierce Knight	06368038
Gamma The Magnet Warrior	11549357
Garnecia Elefantis	49888191
Gemini Elf	69140098
Giant Flea	41762634
Giant Rat	97017120
Gift of the Mystical Elf	98299011
Graverobber's Retribution	33737664
Great White	13429800
Harpie Lady	76812113
Headless Knight	05434080
Humanoid Worm Drake	05600127
Hyosube	02118022
Hyozanryu	62397231
Illusion Wall	13945283
Iron Blacksmith Kotetsu	73431236
Jellyfish	14851496
Jinzo	77585513
Jinzo	77585513
Jowgen the Spiritualist	41855169
Karate Man	23289281
Kojikocy	01184620
Kuriboh	40640057
La Jinn	97590747
Lady of Faith	17358176
Lady Panther	38480590
Last Day of Witch	90330453
Lava Battleguard	20394040
Left Arm of the Forbidden One	07902349
Left Leg of the Forbidden One	44519536
Little Chimera	68658728
Luminous Spark	81777047
Mad Dog of Darkness	79182538
Mad Sword Beast	79870141
Magic Swordsman Neo	50930991
Magical Scientist	34206604
Magician of Faith	31560081
Malevolent Nuzzler	99597615
Man Eating Treasure Chest	13723605
Manga Ryu Ran	38369349
Marauding Captain	02460565
Mask of Darkness	28933734
Mechanicalchaser	07359741
Melchid the Four-Face Beast	86569121

CARD	PASSWORD
Metal Guardian	68339286
Millennium Shield	32012841
Milus Radiant	07489323
Monster Reborn	83764718
Mother Grizzly	57839750
Mystic Plasma Zone	18161786
Mystic Tomato	83011277
Offerings to the Doomed	19230407
Ooguchi	58861941
Overdrive	02311603
Pendulum Machine	24433920
Pinch Hopper	26185991
Pot of Greed	55144522
Red-Eyes Black Dragon	74677422
Red-Eyes Black Metal Dragon	64335804
Reflect Bounder	02851070
Relinquished	64631466
Relinquished	64631466
Restructer Revolution	99518961
Right Arm of the Forbidden One	70903634
Right Leg of the Forbidden One	08124921
Robbin' Zombie	83258273
Rogue Doll	91939608
Ryu Ran	02964201
Ryu-Kishin Powered	24611934
Shining Abyss	87303357
Shining Angel	95956346
Shining Friendship	82085619
Silver Fang	90357090
Sinister Serpent	08131171
Skull Mark Ladybug	64306248
Skull Servant	32274490
Slate Warrior	78636495
Slot Machine	03797883
Soul of Purity and Light	77527210
Soul Release	05758500
Spear Dragon	31553716
Spike Bot	87511987
Spirit of Flames	13522325
St. Joan	21175632
Sword of Deep-Seated	98495314
Swords of Revealing Light	72302403
Tainted Wisdom	28725004
Talwar Demon	11761845
The 13th Grave	00032864
The All-Seeing White Tiger	32269855
The Bistro Butcher	71107816
The Earl of Demise	66989694
The Gross Ghost of Fled Dreams	68049471
The Portrait's Secret	32541773
The Shallow Grave	43434803
The Unhappy Maiden	51275027
Thousand Eyes Idol	27125110

CARD	PASSWORD
Thousand Eyes Relinquished	63519819
Time Seal	85316708
Tornado Bird	71283180
Total Defense Shogun	75372290
Tribe Infecting Virus	33184167
Turtle Tiger	37313348
Two-Headed King Rex	94119974
UFO Turtle	60806437
Ultimate Offering	80604091
Ushi Oni	48649353
Vorse Raider	14898066
Water Omotics	02483611
Wingweaver	31447217
Yata-Garusa	03078576

ZOIDS: LEGACY

CYCLOPES TYPE ONE/TWO, DIABLO TIGER DATA, & ZOID CORES TO BUILD THEM

Complete the game. Then at the Title screen, press L, L, R, R, Up, Down, Up, Down, Left, Left, R, R, Right, Right, Left, Up, Start.

GILVADER, KING GOJULA ZI DATA, & ZOID CORES TO BUILD THEM

Complete the game. Then at the Title screen, press R, R, L, L, Down, Up, Down, Up, Right, Right, L, L, Left, Left, Right, Down, Start.

NINTENDO DS™

Games List

ADVANCE WARS: DUAL STRIKE

Advance Wars Map

Select Map from the Design Room menu and immediately press and hold L + R. This reveals a map that spells out Advance Wars.

Advance Warpaper

Insert Advance Wars into the GBA slot of your Nintendo DS. Start Advance Wars: Dual Strike. Select Battle maps and purchase Advance Warpaper. Select Display from the Design Room and choose Classic 1.

Hachi's Land

Insert Advance Wars into the GBA slot of your Nintendo DS. Start Advance Wars: Dual Strike. Select Battle Maps and purchase Hachi's Land for 1.

Nell's Land

Insert Advance Wars into the GBA slot of your Nintendo DS. Start Advance Wars: Dual Strike. Select Battle Maps and purchase Nell's Land for 1.

Advance Warpaper 2

Insert Advance Wars 2: Black Hole Rising into the GBA slot of your Nintendo DS. Start Advance Wars: Dual Strike. Select Battle maps and purchase Advance Warpaper 2. Select Display from the Design Room and choose Classic 2.

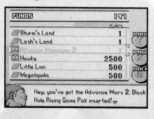

Lash's Land
Insert Advance Wars 2: Black Hole Rising into the GBA slot of your Nintendo DS. Start Advance Wars: Dual Strike. Select Battle Maps and purchase Lash's Land for 1.

Strum's Land
Insert Advance Wars 2: Black Hole Rising into the GBA slot of your Nintendo DS. Start Advance Wars: Dual Strike. Select Battle Maps and purchase Strum's Land for 1.

ALEX RIDER: STORMBREAKER

10,000 SPY POINTS
Select Password from the Main menu and enter 5204025.

EVERYTHING HALF PRICE AT SHOP
Select Password from the Main menu and enter 4298359.

PURCHASE BLACK BELT
Select Password from the Main menu and enter JESSICA PARKER.

DISK 6 AVAILABLE AFTER COMPLETING GAME
Select Password from the Main menu and enter 6943059.

PURCHASE FUGU
Select Password from the Main menu and enter RENATO CELANI.

PURCHASE M16 BADGE
Select Password from the Main menu and enter VICTORIA PARR.

PURCHASE SUNGLASSES
Select Password from the Main menu and enter SARYL HIRSCH.

HARD LEVEL
Select Password from the Main menu and enter 9785711.

GALLERY
Select Password from the Main menu and enter 9603717.

OUTFIT CHANGE
Select Password from the Main menu and enter 6894098.

ANIMANIACS: LIGHTS, CAMERA, ACTION!

SKIP LEVEL
Pause the game and press L, L, R, R, Down, Down.

DISABLE TIME
Pause the game and press L, R, Left, Left, Up, Up.

KINGSIZE PICK-UPS
Pause the game and press Right, Right, Right, Left, Left, Left, R, L.

PASSWORDS

LEVEL	PASSWORD
1	Wakko, Wakko, Wakko, Wakko, Wakko
2	Dot, Yakko, Brain, Wakko, Pinky
3	Yakko, Dot, Wakko, Wakko, Brain
4	Pinky, Yakko, Yakko, Dot, Brain
5	Pinky, Pinky, Yakko, Wakko, Wakko
6	Brain, Dot, Brain, Pinky, Yakko
7	Brain, Pinky, Wakko, Pinky, Brain
8	Brain Pinky, Pinky, Wakko, Wakko
9	Dot, Dot, Yakko, Pinky, Wakko
10	Brain, Dot, Brain, Yakko, Wakko
11	Akko, Yakko, Pinky, Dot, Dot

LEVEL	PASSWORD
12	Pinky, Pinky, Brain, Dot, Wakko
13	Yakko, Wakko, Pinky, Wakko, Brain
14	Pinky, Wakko, Brain, Wakko, Yakko
15	Dot, Pinky, Wakko, Wakko, Yakko

ASPHALT URBAN GT

MONEY FOR NOTHING
Buy the Chevrolet 2005 Corvette C6 for $45,000. Then go to your garage and sell it for $45,500.

ATV: QUAD FRENZY

FLY MODE
At the Title screen, press A + Y + X.

BIG MUTHA TRUCKERS

EVIL BOB TRUCK
At the Title screen, press X, L, R, R, A, B, Y, Y, R.

BRAIN AGE: TRAIN YOUR BRAIN IN MINUTES A DAY

BRAIN AGE CHECK SELECTION MENU
At the Daily Training Menu, hold Select while choosing Brain Age Check.

TOP 3 LISTS
At the Daily Training Menu, hold Select while choosing Graph.

BUBBLE BOBBLE REVOLUTION

BONUS LEVELS IN CLASSIC MODE
At the Classic Mode Title screen, press L, R, L, R, L, R, Right, Select. Touch the door at Level 20.

POWER UP! MODE IN CLASSIC VERSION
At the Classic Mode Title screen, press Select, R, L, Left, Right, R, Select, Right.

SUPER BUBBLE BOBBLE IN CLASSIC VERSION
You must first defeat the boss with two players. Then at the Classic Mode Title screen, press Left, R, Left, Select, Left, L, Left, Select.

BUST-A-MOVE DS

DARK WORLD
Complete the game then press A Left Right A at the Title screen.

SOUND TEST
At the Main menu, press Select, A, B, Left, Right, A, Select, Right.

CARS

SECRET MUSIC TRACK FOR RAMONE'S STYLE
At the Title screen, press Up, Down, Up, Down, A, B, X, Y.

EVERYTHING EXCEPT HIDDEN MUSIC
At the Title screen, press Up, Up, Down, Down, Left, Right, Left, Right, B, A, B.

CASTLEVANIA: DAWN OF SORROW

POTION
Complete Boss Rush Mode.

RPG
Complete Boss Rush Mode in less than 5 minutes.

DEATH'S ROBE
Complete Boss Rush Mode in less than 6 minutes.

TERROR BEAR
Complete Boss Rush Mode in less than 7 minutes.

NUNCHAKUS
Complete Boss Rush Mode in less than 8 minutes.

THE CHRONICLES OF NARNIA: THE LION, THE WITCH AND THE WARDROBE

RESTORE HEALTH
At the Main menu, press Left, Right, Up, Down, A (x4).

INVINCIBILITY
At the Main menu, press A, Y, X, B, Up, Up, Down, Down.

ARMOR
At the Main menu, press A, X, Y, B, Up, Up, Up, Down.

EXTRA MONEY
At the Main menu, press Up, X, Up, X, Down, B, Down, B.

ALL BLESSINGS
At the Main menu, press Left, Up, A, B, Right, Down, X, Y.

MAXIMUM ATTRIBUTES
At the Main menu, press Left, B, Up, Y, Down, X, Right, A.

MAX SKILLS
At the Main menu, press A, Left, Right, B, Down, Up, X, X.

STRONGER ATTACKS
At the Main menu, press A, Up, B, Down, X, X, Y, Y.

DRAGON QUEST HEROES: ROCKET SLIME

KNIGHTRO TANK IN MULTIPLAYER
While inside the church, press Y, L, L, Y, R, R, Y, Up, Down, Select.

THE NEMESIS TANK IN MULTIPLAYER
While inside the church, press Y, R, R, up, L, L, Y, Down, Down, Down, Y, Select.

FEEL THE MAGIC: XY/XX

RECORD YOUR VOICE ON TITLE SCREEN

At the Title screen, hold Down + Y to record your voice into the microphone. It will now play back whatever you recorded at random intervals while the title music plays. If you want to play it back immediately, press Down + X. Pressing Down/Left + X will play it back slowly, while pressing Down/Right + X will speed it up.

HARD MODE

Defeat the game on Normal difficulty.

HELL MODE

Defeat the game on Hard difficulty.

KIRBY: CANVAS CURSE

JUMP GAME

Defeat the game with all five characters, then select the game file to get Jump Game next to the Options on the Main menu.

LEGO STAR WARS II: THE ORIGINAL TRILOGY

10 STUDS

At the Mos Eisley cantina, enter 4PR28U.

OBI WAN GHOST

At the Mos Eisley cantina, enter BEN917.

MADDEN NFL 2005

THREE DOWNS FOR OPPONENT

Touch the spot in the middle of the Main menu and enter SHORTTIME.

FIVE DOWNS

Touch the spot in the middle of the Main menu and enter LONGTIME.

HARDER HITS

Touch the spot in the middle of the Main menu and enter SMASHMOUTH.

MORE FUMBLES

Touch the spot in the middle of the Main menu and enter SUPERSLICK.

MORE INTERCEPTIONS

Touch the spot in the middle of the Main menu and enter BADPASS.

MORE SACKS

Touch the spot in the middle of the Main menu and enter SAD SACK.

MEGAMAN BATTLE NETWORK 5: DOUBLE TEAM

NUMBERMAN CODES

When the Numberman machine is available in Higsby's Shop, enter the following codes.

CODE	ENTER
Area Steal *	99428938
Dark Recovery *	91182599
DoroTsunamiBall *	78234329
Leaders Raid L	01285874
Lord of Chaos X	39285712
MagmaSeed *	29387483

CODE	ENTER
NumberBall *	64836563
P. Battle Pack 1	22323856
P. Battle Pack 2	66426428
P.Attack+3	76820385
P.Chip+50	48582829
P.HP+100	28475692
P.HP+50	53891756
Super Kitakaze *	29486933
Sword *	12495783
TP Chip	85375720
Tsunami Hole *	19283746
Unlocker	15733751

NUMBERMAN NAVI CUSTOMIZER PROGRAM
Enter the following codes in the Numberman Lotto Number.

CODE	ENTER
Attack Max Yellow	63231870
Beat Blue	79877132
BodyPack Green	30112002
BustPack Blue	80246758
Charge Max White	87412146
HP+200 Pink	90630807
HP+300 Pink	48785625
HP+300 White	13926561
HP+400 Pink	03419893
HP+400 Yellow	45654128
HP+500 Pink	50906652
HP+500 White	72846472
Mega Folder 2 Green	97513648
Rush Yellow	09609807
SoulT+1 Yellow	28256341
Speed Max Pink	36695497
Spin Blue	12541883
Spin Green	78987728
Spin Red	30356451
Tango Green	54288793

METROID PRIME PINBALL

PHAZON MINES
Complete Omega Pirate in Multi Mission Mode.

PHENDRANA DRIFTS
Complete Thardus in Multi Mission Mode.

NEW SUPER MARIO BROS.

PLAY AS LUIGI IN SINGLE-PLAYER MODE
At the Select a File screen, press and hold L + R while selecting a saved game.

SECRET CHALLENGE MODE
While on the map, pause the game and press L, R, L, R, X, X, Y, Y.

NINTENDOGS

FEED DOG A LIGHT BULB

When the light bulb appears above your dog, grab it and drag it to his/her mouth.

PAC-PIX

BUTTERFLY HIDDEN GESTURE

Select Sketchbook from the Gallery and draw a figure eight. The drawing should fly upwards.

CHERRIES HIDDEN GESTURE

Select Sketchbook from the Gallery and draw a pair of cherries starting with one of the circles.

POGO STICK HIDDEN GESTURE

Select Sketchbook from the Gallery and draw a "P." It will then bounce off the screen.

RAIN CLOUD HIDDEN GESTURE

Select Sketchbook from the Gallery and draw a cloud. It will turn blue and rain will fall from the drawing.

SNAKE HIDDEN GESTURE

Select Sketchbook from the Gallery and draw a squiggly line. It will turn green and slither away.

 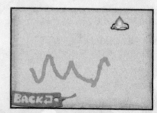

TREBLE CLEF HIDDEN GESTURE

Select Sketchbook from the Gallery and draw a treble clef.

SHOOT ARROWS AT PAC-MAN

After you earn the Arrow gesture in Chapter 4, select Sketchbook from the Gallery. Then draw an arrow facing Pac-Man.

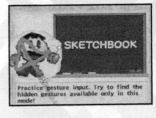

Practice gesture input. Try to find the hidden gestures available only in this mode!

PING PALS

50 COINS

Select Credits and let them finish playing.

HOLIDAY ITEMS

Set the date on your Nintendo DS to the following dates to gain access to special Holiday Items.

DATE	ITEM	COST
February 14	Valentine (Boy)	300 Coins
February 14	Valentine (Girl)	200 Coins
February 21	Vessel Top	700 Coins
March 17	Snowflake	250 Coins
October 31	Bat Treats	400 Coins
October 31	Jack Hat	4000 Coins
October 31	Succubus	321 Coins
December 25	Elf Skirt	300 Coins
December 25	Jolly Suit	300 Coins
December 25	Merry Cap	10 Coins
Birthday	Birthday (Boy)	5 Coins
Birthday	Birthday (Girl)	5 Coins

SHANTAE BACKGROUND

Touch the Ping Pals logo exactly at midnight.

PIRATES OF THE CARIBBEAN: DEAD MAN'S CHEST

10 GOLD
During a game, press Right, X, X, Right, Left.

INVINCIBILITY
During a game, press Up, Down, Left, Right (x5), Left, Right, Up, Down, Left, Right, Up (x5), Left.

UNLIMITED POWER
During a game, press Up, Up, Down, Down, Left, Right, Left, Right, L, R.

RESTORE HEALTH
During a game, press Y, Y, Select, Left, Right, Left, Right, Left.

RESTORE SAVVY
During a game, press X, X, Select, Up, Down, Up, Down, Up.

GHOST FORM MODE
During a game, press Y, X, Y, X, Y, X.

SEASICKNESS MODE
During a game, press X, X, Y, X, X, Y.

SILLY WEAPONS
During a game, press Y, Y, X, Y (x3).

AXE
During a game, press Left, L, L, Down, Down, Left, Up, Up, Down, Down.

BLUNDERBUSS
During a game, press Down, L, L, Down (x3).

CHICKEN
During a game, press Right, L, L, Up, Down, Down.

EXECUTIONER AXE
During a game, press Right, L, L, Up, Down, Up, Right, Right, Left(x2).

PIG
During a game, press Right, R, R, Down, Up, Up.

PISTOL
During a game, press Down, L, L, Down, Down, Right.

RIFLE
During a game, press Left, L, L, Up (x3).

FAST MUSIC
During a game, press Y, Select, Y (x4).

SLOW MUSIC
During a game, press Y, Select, X (x4).

DISABLE CHEATS
During a game, press X (x6).

PUYO POP FEVER

ALL CHARACTERS & CUTSCENES
Select Gallery from the Options menu, highlight Cutscene Viewer, press and hold X, then press Up, Down, Left, Right.

RIDGE RACER DS

00-AGENT CAR
Finish more than 10 races in Multiplayer.

CADDY CAR
Finish more than 10 races in Multiplayer.

GALAGA '88 CAR
Finish more than 10 races in Multiplayer.

MARIO RACING CAR
Finish more than 10 races in Multiplayer.

POOKA CAR
Finish more than 10 races in Multiplayer.

RED SHIRT RAGE CAR
Finish more than 10 races in Multiplayer.

SHY GUY CAR
Finish more than 10 races in Multiplayer.

GALAGA PAC JAM SONG
Unlock the Pooka car.

MUSHROOM KINGDOM II SONG
Unlock the DK Team Racing car.

THE RUB RABBITS!

BOXING GLOVES
Start the game with Sonic Battle in the GBA slot of your Nintendo DS.

FIST GLOVES
Start the game with Chu Chu Rocket in the GBA slot of your Nintendo DS.

HAND PUPPETS
Start the game with Sonic Advance 3 in the GBA slot of your Nintendo DS.

PINK GLOVES
Start the game with Sonic Advance 1 or 2 in the GBA slot of your Nintendo DS.

WHITE GLOVES
Start the game with Puyo Pop in the GBA slot of your Nintendo DS.

SHREK SUPERSLAM

ALTERNATE OUTFIT FOR SHREK
Start the game with the GBA version of Shrek SuperSlam in the GBA slot.

THE SIMS 2

MONGOO MONKEY FOR THE CASINO
Start the game with Sims 2 in the GBA slot of your Nintendo DS.

SPIDER-MAN 2

ALL SPECIAL MOVES
Load the game with Spider-Man: Mysterio's Menace for Game Boy Advance in the Nintendo DS.

STAR WARS EPISODE III: REVENGE OF THE SITH

MASTER DIFFICULTY
Defeat the game.

ANAKIN'S STARFIGHTER
Beat the Anakin bot in Multiplayer mode.

DARTH VADER'S TIE FIGHTER
Defeat Darth Vader bot in Multiplayer mode.

GENERAL GREVIOUS'S STARFIGHTER
Defeat General Grevious bot in Multiplayer mode.

MILLENIUM FALCON
Defeat the Solo bot in Multiplayer mode.

SLAVE I
Defeat Fett bot in Multiplayer mode.

X-WING
Defeat Luke bot in multiplayer.

SUPER PRINCESS PEACH

MINI-GAME
At the Title screen, hold R and press Start.

TEENAGE MUTANT NINJA TURTLES 3: MUTANT NIGHTMARE

EASTER EGG CRYSTALS
Select Input Password from the Options menu and enter SRDSLLMS.

JACK-O-LANTERN CRYSTALS
Select Input Password from the Options menu and enter DRSSMRLD.

SANTA CRYSTALS
Select Input Password from the Options menu and enter LLDMSRMD.

PIZZA LIFE ICONS
Select Input Password from the Options menu and enter DDRMLRDS.

COWABUNGA
At the Title screen, press U, U, D, D, L, R, L, R, B, A.

TIGER WOODS PGA TOUR 2005

EMERALD DRAGON
Earn $1,000,000.

GREEK ISLES
Earn $1,500,000.

PARADISE COVER
Earn $2,000,000.

EA SPORTS FAVORITES
Earn $5,000,000

MEAN8TEEN
Earn $10,000,000.

FANTASY SPECIALS
Earn $15,000,000.

LEGEND COMPILATION 1
Defeat Hogan in Legend Tour.

LEGEND COMPILATION 2
Defeat Gary Player in Legend Tour.

LEGEND COMPILATION 3
Defeat Ballesteros in Legend Tour.

LEGEND COMPILATION 4
Defeat Palmer in Legend Tour.

LEGEND COMPILATION 5
Defeat Nicklaus in Legend Tour.

THE HUSTLER'S DREAM 18
Defeat The Hustler in Legend Tour.

TIGER'S DREAM 18
Defeat Tiger Woods in Legend Tour.

TOM CLANCY'S SPLINTER CELL CHAOS THEORY

UNLIMITED AMMO/GADGETS
Defeat the game.

CHARACTER SKINS
Defeat the game.

TONY HAWK'S DOWNHILL JAM

ALWAYS SNOWSKATE
Select Buy Stuff from the Skateshop. Choose Enter Code and enter SNOWSK8T.

MIRRORED MAPS
Select Buy Stuff from the Skateshop. Choose Enter Code and enter MIRRORBALL.

ABOMINABLE SNOWMAN OUTFIT
Select Buy Stuff from the Skateshop. Choose Enter Code and enter BIGSNOWMAN.

ZOMBIE SKATER OUTFIT
Select Buy Stuff from the Skateshop. Choose Enter Code and enter ZOMBIEALIVE.

TRAUMA CENTER: UNDER THE KNIFE

X1: KYRIAKI MISSION
Defeat the game. Find the X Missions under Challenge Mode.

X2: DEFTERA MISSION
Defeat X1: Kyriaki Mission. Find the X Missions under Challenge Mode.

X3: TRITI MISSION
Defeat X2: Deftera Mission. Find the X Missions under Challenge Mode.

X4: TETARTI MISSION
Defeat X3: Triti Mission. Find the X Missions under Challenge Mode.

X5: PEMPTI MISSION
Defeat X4: Tetarti Mission. Find the X Missions under Challenge Mode.

X6: PARAKEVI MISSION
Defeat X5: Pempti Mission. Find the X Missions under Challenge Mode.

X7: SAVATO MISSION
Defeat X6: Parakevi Mission. Find the X Missions under Challenge Mode.

THE URBZ: SIMS IN THE CITY

CLUB XIZZLE
After gaining access to Club Xizzle, enter with the password bucket.

YU-GI-OH! NIGHTMARE TROUBADOUR

CREDITS
Unlock the Password Machine by defeating the Expert Cup. Enter the Duel Shop and select the Slot Machine, then enter 00000375.

SOUND TEST
Unlock the Password Machine by defeating the Expert Cup. Enter the Duel Shop and select the Slot Machine, then enter 57300000.

ZOO KEEPER

GEKIMUZU DIFFICULTY
Earn a high score in all 4 modes.

MODE	HIGH SCORE
Zoo Keeper	200000
Tokoton 100	800000
Quest Mode	10000
Time Attack	600000

XBOX 360™

Games List

AMPED 3

ALL SLEDS
Select Cheat Codes from the Options menu and press Right Trigger, X, Left Trigger, Down, Right, Left Bumper, Left Trigger, Right Trigger, Y, X.

ALL GEAR
Select Cheat Codes from the Options menu and press Y, Down, Up, Left, Right, Left Bumper, Right, Right Trigger, Right Trigger, Right Bumper.

ALL TRICKS
Select Cheat Codes from the Options menu and press Left Bumper, Right Trigger, Y, Up, Down, X, Left Trigger, Left, Right Bumper, Right Trigger.

ALL LEVELS
Select Cheat Codes from the Options menu and press X, Y, Up, Left, Left Bumper, Left Bumper, Right Trigger, X, Y, Left Trigger.

ALL CONFIGS
Select Cheat Codes from the Options menu and press Down, X, Right, Left Bumper, Right, Right Bumper, X, Right Trigger, Left Trigger, Y.

SUPER SPINS
Select Cheat Codes from the Options menu and press X (x4), Y (x3), X.

AWESOME METER ALWAYS FULL
Select Cheat Codes from the Options menu and press Up, Right Trigger, X, Y, Left Bumper, X, Down, Left Bumper, Right Trigger, Right Bumper.

ALL AWESOMENESS
Select Cheat Codes from the Options menu and press Right Bumper, Right Bumper, Down, Left, Up, Right Trigger, X, Right Bumper, X, X.

ALL BUILD LICENSES
Select Cheat Codes from the Options menu and press Left, Right Trigger, Left Bumper, Right Trigger, X, X, Y, Down, Up, X.

ALL BUILD OBJECTS
Select Cheat Codes from the Options menu and press Left Trigger, Right Trigger, Up, Up, Right Bumper, Left, Right, X, Y, Left Bumper.

ALL CHALLENGES
Select Cheat Codes from the Options menu and press Right, Left Bumper, Left Trigger, X, Left, Right Bumper, Right Trigger, Y, Left Trigger, X.

LOUD SPEAKERS
Select Cheat Codes from the Options menu and press Y, Right Trigger, Right Trigger, Left Bumper, Down, Down, Left, Left, Right, Left Bumper.

LOW GRAVITY BOARDERS
Select Cheat Codes from the Options menu and press Right Trigger, Down, Down, Up, X, Left Bumper, Y, Right Trigger, Y, Down.

NO AI
Select Cheat Codes from the Options menu and press X, X, Left Bumper, Down, Right, Right, Up, Y, Y, Left Trigger.

ALL MUSIC
Select Cheat Codes from the Options menu and press Up, Left, Right Trigger, Right Bumper, Right Trigger, Up, Down, Left, Y, Left Trigger.

BATTLEFIELD 2: MODERN COMBAT

ALL WEAPONS
During a game, hold Right Bumper + Left Bumper and quickly press Right, Right, Down, Up, Left, Left.

BLAZING ANGELS: SQUADRONS OF WWII

ALL MISSIONS, MEDALS, & PLANES
At the Main menu hold Left Trigger + Right Trigger and press X, Left Bumper, Right Bumper, Y, Y, Right Bumper, Left Bumper, X.

GOD MODE
Pause the game, hold Left Trigger and press X, Y, Y, X. Release Left Trigger, hold Right Trigger and press Y, X, X, Y. Re-enter the code to disable it.

INCREASED DAMAGE
Pause the game, hold Left Trigger and press Left Bumper, Left Bumper, Right Bumper, Right Bumper. Release Left Trigger, hold Right Trigger and press Right Bumper, Right Bumper, Left Bumper, Left Bumper. Re-enter the code to disable it.

CALL OF DUTY 2

ALL LEVELS
At the Mission Select screen, hold Left Bumper + Right Bumper and press Left, Left, Right, Right, Y, Y.

CALL OF DUTY 3

ALL CHAPTERS AND BONUS CONTENT
At the Chapter Select screen, hold Back and press Right, Right, Left, Left, X, X.

CARS

UNLOCK EVERYTHING
Select Cheat Codes from the Options menu and enter IF900HP.

ALL CHARACTERS
Select Cheat Codes from the Options menu and enter YAYCARS.

ALL CHARACTER SKINS
Select Cheat Codes from the Options menu and enter R4MONE.

ALL MINI-GAMES AND COURSES
Select Cheat Codes from the Options menu and enter MATTL66.

MATER'S COUNTDOWN CLEAN-UP MINI-GAME & MATER'S SPEEDY CIRCUIT
Select Cheat Codes from the Options menu and enter TRGTEXC.

FAST START
Select Cheat Codes from the Options menu and enter IMSPEED.

INFINITE BOOST
Select Cheat Codes from the Options menu and enter VROOOOM.

ART
Select Cheat Codes from the Options menu and enter CONC3PT.

VIDEOS
Select Cheat Codes from the Options menu and enter WATCHIT.

CONDEMNED: CRIMINAL ORIGINS

ALL LEVELS
Enter ShovelFighter as a profile name.

FAR CRY INSTINCTS PREDATOR

EVOLUTION GAME
Select the Cheat Menu option from the Main menu or the pause menu and enter GiveMeItAll.

HEAL
Select the Cheat Menu option from the Main menu or the pause menu and enter ImJackCarver.

INFINITE ADRENALINE
Select the Cheat Menu option from the Main menu or the pause menu and enter Bloodlust.

INFINITE AMMO
Select the Cheat Menu option from the Main menu or the pause menu and enter UnleashHell.

ENABLE EVOLUTIONS
Select the Cheat Menu option from the Main menu or the pause menu and enter FeralAttack.

ALL MAPS
Select the Cheat Menu option from the Main menu or the pause menu and enter GiveMeTheMaps.

FIGHT NIGHT ROUND 3

ALL VENUES
Create a champ with a first name of NEWVIEW.

FROGGER

BIG FROGGER
At the One/Two-Player screen, press Up, Up, Down, Down, Left, Right, Left, Right, B, A.

FULL AUTO

ALL TRACKS, VEHICLES, & WEAPONS
Create a new profile with the name magicman.

THE GODFATHER: THE GAME

FULL AMMO
Pause the game and press Y, Left, Y, Right, X, Right Thumbstick.

FULL HEALTH
Pause the game and press Left, X, Right, Y, Right, Left Thumbstick.

UNLOCK ENTIRE FILM ARCHIVE
After loading a game and before joining the family, press Y, X, Y, X, X, Left Thumbstick.
Select Film Archive to view the films.

LEGO STAR WARS II: THE ORIGINAL TRILOGY

BEACH TROOPER
At Mos Eisley Canteena, select Enter Code and enter UCK868. You must still select Characters
and purchase this character for 20,000 studs.

BEN KENOBI (GHOST)
At Mos Eisley Canteena, select Enter Code and enter BEN917. You must still select Characters
and purchase this character for 1,100,000 studs.

BESPIN GUARD
At Mos Eisley Canteena, select Enter Code and enter VHY832. You must still select Characters
and purchase this character for 15,000 studs.

BIB FORTUNA
At Mos Eisley Canteena, select Enter Code and enter WTY721. You must still select Characters
and purchase this character for 16,000 studs.

BOBA FETT
At Mos Eisley Canteena, select Enter Code and enter HLP221. You must still select Characters and purchase this character for 175,000 studs.

DEATH STAR TROOPER
At Mos Eisley Canteena, select Enter Code and enter BNC332. You must still select Characters and purchase this character for 19,000 studs.

EWOK
At Mos Eisley Canteena, select Enter Code and enter TTT289. You must still select Characters and purchase this character for 34,000 studs.

GAMORREAN GUARD
At Mos Eisley Canteena, select Enter Code and enter YZF999. You must still select Characters and purchase this character for 40,000 studs.

GONK DROID
At Mos Eisley Canteena, select Enter Code and enter NFX582. You must still select Characters and purchase this character for 1,550 studs.

GRAND MOFF TARKIN
At Mos Eisley Canteena, select Enter Code and enter SMG219. You must still select Characters and purchase this character for 38,000 studs.

GREEDO
At Mos Eisley Canteena, select Enter Code and enter NAH118. You must still select Characters and purchase this character for 60,000 studs.

HAN SOLO (HOOD)
At Mos Eisley Canteena, select Enter Code and enter YWM840. You must still select Characters and purchase this character for 20,000 studs.

IG-88
At Mos Eisley Canteena, select Enter Code and enter NXL973. You must still select Characters and purchase this character for 30,000 studs.

IMPERIAL GUARD
At Mos Eisley Canteena, select Enter Code and enter MMM111. You must still select Characters and purchase this character for 45,000 studs.

IMPERIAL OFFICER
At Mos Eisley Canteena, select Enter Code and enter BBV889. You must still select Characters and purchase this character for 28,000 studs.

IMPERIAL SHUTTLE PILOT
At Mos Eisley Canteena, select Enter Code and enter VAP664. You must still select Characters and purchase this character for 29,000 studs.

IMPERIAL SPY
At Mos Eisley Canteena, select Enter Code and enter CVT125. You must still select Characters and purchase this character for 13,500 studs.

JAWA
At Mos Eisley Canteena, select Enter Code and enter JAW499. You must still select Characters and purchase this character for 24,000 studs.

LOBOT
At Mos Eisley Canteena, select Enter Code and enter UUB319. You must still select Characters and purchase this character for 11,000 studs.

PALACE GUARD
At Mos Eisley Canteena, select Enter Code and enter SGE549. You must still select Characters and purchase this character for 14,000 studs.

REBEL PILOT
At Mos Eisley Canteena, select Enter Code and enter CYG336. You must still select Characters and purchase this character for 15,000 studs.

REBEL TROOPER (HOTH)
At Mos Eisley Canteena, select Enter Code and enter EKU849. You must still select Characters and purchase this character for 16,000 studs.

SANDTROOPER
At Mos Eisley Canteena, select Enter Code and enter YDV451. You must still select Characters and purchase this character for 14,000 studs.

SKIFF GUARD
At Mos Eisley Canteena, select Enter Code and enter GBU888. You must still select Characters and purchase this character for 12,000 studs.

SNOWTROOPER
At Mos Eisley Canteena, select Enter Code and enter NYU989. You must still select Characters and purchase this character for 16,000 studs.

STORMTROOPER
At Mos Eisley Canteena, select Enter Code and enter PTR345. You must still select Characters and purchase this character for 10,000 studs.

THE EMPEROR
At Mos Eisley Canteena, select Enter Code and enter HHY382. You must still select Characters and purchase this character for 275,000 studs.

TIE FIGHTER
At Mos Eisley Canteena, select Enter Code and enter HDY739. You must still select Characters and purchase this item for 60,000 studs.

TIE FIGHTER PILOT
At Mos Eisley Canteena, select Enter Code and enter NNZ316. You must still select Characters and purchase this character for 21,000 studs.

TIE INTERCEPTOR
At Mos Eisley Canteena, select Enter Code and enter QYA828. You must still select Characters and purchase this item for 40,000 studs.

TUSKEN RAIDER
At Mos Eisley Canteena, select Enter Code and enter PEJ821. You must still select Characters and purchase this character for 23,000 studs.

UGNAUGHT
At Mos Eisley Canteena, select Enter Code and enter UGN694. You must still select Characters and purchase this character for 36,000 studs.

MAJOR LEAGUE BASEBALL 2K6

UNLOCK EVERYTHING
Select Enter Cheat Code from the My 2K6 menu and enter Derek Jeter.

TOPPS 2K STARS
Select Enter Cheat Code from the My 2K6 menu and enter Dream Team.

SUPER WALL CLIMB
Select Enter Cheat Code from the My 2K6 menu and enter Last Chance. Enable the cheats by selecting My Cheats or selecting Cheat Codes from the in-game Options screen.

SUPER PITCHES
Select Enter Cheat Code from the My 2K6 menu and enter Unhittable. Enable the cheats by selecting My Cheats or selecting Cheat Codes from the in-game Options screen.

ROCKET ARMS
Select Enter Cheat Code from the My 2K6 menu and enter Gotcha. Enable the cheats by selecting My Cheats or selecting Cheat Codes from the in-game Options screen.

BOUNCY BALL
Select Enter Cheat Code from the My 2K6 menu and enter Crazy Hops. Enable the cheats by selecting My Cheats or selecting Cheat Codes from the in-game Options.

MARVEL ULTIMATE ALLIANCE

UNLOCK ALL SKINS
At the Team menu, press Up, Down, Left, Right, Left, Right, Start.

UNLOCKS ALL HERO POWERS
At the Team menu, press Left, Right, Up, Down, Up, Down, Start.

ALL HEROES TO LEVEL 99
At the Team menu, press Up, Left, Up, Left, Down, Right, Down, Right, Start.

UNLOCK ALL HEROES
At the Team menu, press Up, Up, Down, Down, Left, Left, Left, Start.

UNLOCK DAREDEVIL
At the Team menu, press Left, Left, Right, Right, Up, Down, Up, Down, Start.

UNLOCK SILVER SURFER
At the Team menu, press Down, Left, Left, Up, Right, Up, Down, Left, Start.

GOD MODE
During gameplay, press Up, Down, Up, Down, Up, Left, Down, Right, Start.

TOUCH OF DEATH
During gameplay, press Left, Right, Down, Down, Right, Left, Start.

SUPER SPEED
During gameplay, press Up, Left, Up, Right, Down, Right, Start.

FILL MOMENTUM
During gameplay, press Left, Right, Right, Left, Up, Down, Down, Up, Start.

UNLOCK ALL COMICS
At the Review menu, press Left, Right, Right, Left, Up, Up, Right, Start.

UNLOCK ALL CONCEPT ART
At the Review menu, press Down, Down, Down, Right, Right, Left, Down, Start.

UNLOCK ALL CINEMATICS
At the Review menu, press Up, Left, Left, Up, Right, Right, Up, Start.

UNLOCK ALL LOAD SCREENS
At the Review menu, press Up, Down, Right, Left, Up, Up Down, Start.

UNLOCK ALL COURSES
At the Comic Missions menu, press Up, Right, Left, Down, Up, Right, Left, Down, Start.

MOTOGP 06

USA EXTREME BIKE
At the Game Mode screen, press Right, Up, B, B, A, B, Up, B, B, A.

NBA 2K6

CELEBRITY STREET OPTION
Select Codes from the Features menu and enter ballers.

2KSPORTS TEAM
Select Codes from the Features menu and enter 2ksports.

2K6 TEAM
Select Codes from the Features menu and enter nba2k6.

VC TEAM
Select Codes from the Features menu and enter vcteam.

NIKE SHOX MTX SHOES
Select Codes from the Features menu and enter crazylift.

NIKE ZOOM 20-5-5 SHOES
Select Codes from the Features menu and enter lebronsummerkicks.

NIKE ZOOM KOBE 1 SHOES
Select Codes from the Features menu and enter kobe.

NIKE ZOOM LEBRON III ALL-STAR COLORWAY SHOES
Select Codes from the Features menu and enter lb allstar.

NIKE ZOOM LEBRON III BLACK/CRIMSON SHOES
Select Codes from the Features menu and enter lb crimsonblack.

NIKE ZOOM LEBRON III SPECIAL BIRTHDAY EDITION SHOES
Select Codes from the Features menu and enter lb bday.

NIKE ZOOM LEBRON III WHITE/GOLD SHOES
Select Codes from the Features menu and enter lb whitegold.

NIKE UP TEMPO PRO SHOES
Select Codes from the Features menu and enter anklebreakers.

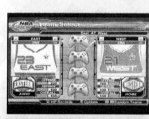

2006 ALL-STAR UNIFORMS
Select Codes from the Features menu and enter fanfavorites.

ST. PATRICK'S DAY UNIFORMS
Select Codes from the Features menu and enter gogreen.

BULLS RETRO UNIFORM
Select Codes from the Features menu and enter chi retro.

CAVALIERS ALTERNATE UNIFORM
Select Codes from the Features menu and enter cle 2nd.

CELTICS ALTERNATE UNIFORM
Select Codes from the Features menu and enter bos 2nd.

CLIPPERS RETRO UNIFORM
Select Codes from the Features menu and enter lac retro.

GRIZZLIES RETRO UNIFORM
Select Codes from the Features menu and enter mem retro.

HEAT RETRO UNIFORM
Select Codes from the Features menu and enter mia retro.

HORNETS RETRO UNIFORM
Select Codes from the Features menu and enter no retro.

KINGS ALTERNATE UNIFORM
Select Codes from the Features menu and enter sac 2nd.

KNICKS RETRO UNIFORM
Select Codes from the Features menu and enter ny retro.

MAGIC RETRO UNIFORM
Select Codes from the Features menu and enter orl retro.

NETS RETRO UNIFORM
Select Codes from the Features menu and enter nj retro.

NUGGETS ALTERNATE UNIFORM
Select Codes from the Features menu and enter den 2nd.

2005-06 PACERS UNIFORM
Select Codes from the Features menu and enter 31andonly.

PISTONS ALTERNATE UNIFORM
Select Codes from the Features menu and enter det 2nd.

ROCKETS RETRO UNIFORM
Select Codes from the Features menu and enter hou retro.

SONICS RETRO UNIFORM
Select Codes from the Features menu and enter sea retro.

SUNS RETRO UNIFORM
Select Codes from the Features menu and enter phx retro.

WIZARDS RETRO UNIFORM
Select Codes from the Features menu and enter was retro.

+10 BONUS FOR DEFENSIVE AWARENESS
Find the PowerBar vending machine in The Crib. Select Enter Code and enter lockdown.

+10 BONUS FOR OFFENSIVE AWARENESS
Find the PowerBar vending machine in The Crib. Select Enter Code and enter getaclue.

MAX DURABILITY
Find the PowerBar vending machine in The Crib. Select Enter Code and enter noinjury.

UNLIMITED STAMINA
Find the PowerBar vending machine in The Crib. Select Enter Code and enter nrgmax.

POWERBAR TATTOO
Find the PowerBar vending machine in The Crib. Select Enter Code and enter pbink.
You can now use it in the game's Create Player feature.

NBA 2K7

MAX DURABILITY
Select Codes from the Features menu and enter ironman.

UNLIMITED STAMINA
Select Codes from the Features menu and enter norest.

+10 DEFFENSIVE AWARENESS
Select Codes from the Features menu and enter getstops.

+10 OFFENSIVE AWARENESS
Select Codes from the Features menu and enter inthezone.

TOPPS 2K SPORTS ALL-STARS
Select Codes from the Features menu and enter topps2ksports.

ABA BALL
Select Codes from the Features menu and enter payrespect.

NBA LIVE 06

EASTERN ALL-STARS 2005-06 AWAY JERSEYS
Select NBA Codes from My NBA Live and enter XCVB5387EQ.

EASTERN ALL-STARS 2005-06 HOME JERSEY
Select NBA Codes from My NBA Live and enter 234SDFGHMO.

WESTERN ALL-STARS 2005-06 AWAY JERSEY
Select NBA Codes from My NBA Live and enter 39N56B679J.

WESTERN ALL-STARS 2005-06 HOME JERSEY
Select NBA Codes from My NBA Live and enter 2J9UWABNP1.

BOSTON CELTICS 2005-06 ALTERNATE JERSEY
Select NBA Codes from My NBA Live and enter 193KSHU88J.

CLEVELAND CAVALIERS 2005-06 ALTERNATE JERSEY
Select NBA Codes from My NBA Live and enter 9922NVDKVT.

DENVER NUGGETS 2005-06 ALTERNATE JERSEYS
Select NBA Codes from My NBA Live and enter XWETJK72FC.

DETROIT PISTONS 2005-06 ALTERNATE JERSEY
Select NBA Codes from My NBA Live and enter JANTWIKBS6.

INDIANA PACERS 2005-06 ALTERNATE AWAY JERSEY
Select NBA Codes from My NBA Live and enter PSDF90PPJN.

INDIANA PACERS 2005-06 ALTERNATE HOME JERSEY
Select NBA Codes from My NBA Live and enter SDF786WSHW.

SACRAMENTO KINGS 2005-06 ALTERNATE JERSEY
Select NBA Codes from My NBA Live and enter 654NNBFDWA.

A3 GARNETT 3
Select NBA Codes from My NBA Live and enter DRI239CZ49.

JORDAN MELO V.5 WHITE & BLUE
Select NBA Codes from My NBA Live and enter 5223WERPII.

JORDAN MELO V.5 WHITE & YELLOW
Select NBA Codes from My NBA Live and enter ZXDR7362Q1.

JORDAN XIV BLACK & RED
Select NBA Codes from My NBA Live and enter 144FVNHM35.

JORDAN XIV WHITE & GREEN
Select NBA Codes from My NBA Live and enter 67YFH9839F.

JORDAN XIV WHITE & RED
Select NBA Codes from My NBA Live and enter 743HFDRAU8.

S. CARTER III LE
Select NBA Codes from My NBA Live and enter JZ3SCARTVY.

T-MAC 5 BLACK
Select NBA Codes from My NBA Live and enter 258SHQW95B.

T-MAC 5 WHITE
Select NBA Codes from My NBA Live and enter HGS83KP234P.

ANSWER DMX 10
Select NBA Codes from My NBA Live and enter RBKAIUSAB7.

ANSWER IX & THE RBK ANSWER IX VIDEO
Select NBA Codes from My NBA Live and enter AI9BUBBA7T.

THE QUESTION & THE MESSAGE FROM ALLEN IVERSON VIDEO
Select NBA Codes from My NBA Live and enter HOYAS3AI6L.

NBA LIVE 07

ADIDAS ARTILLERY II BLACK AND THE RBK ANSWER 9 VIDEO
Select NBA Codes from My NBA Live and enter 99B6356HAN.

ADIDAS ARTILLERY II
Select NBA Codes and enter NTGNFUE87H.

ADIDAS BTB LOW AND THE MESSAGE FROM ALLEN IVERSON VIDEO
Select NBA Codes and enter 7FB3KS9JQ0.

ADIDAS C-BILLUPS
Select NBA Codes and enter BV6877HB9N.

ADIDAS C-BILLUPS BLACK
Select NBA Codes and enter 85NVLDMWS5.

ADIDAS CAMPUS LT
Select NBA Codes and enter CLT2983NC8.

ADIDAS CRAZY 8
Select NBA Codes and enter CC98KKL814.

ADIDAS EQUIPMENT B-BALL
Select NBA Codes and enter 22OIUJKMDR.

ADIDAS GARNETT BOUNCE
Select NBA Codes and enter HYIOUHCAAN.

ADIDAS GARNETT BOUNCE BLACK
Select NBA Codes and enter KDZ2MQL17W.

ADIDAS GIL-ZERO
Select NBA Codes and enter 23DN1PPOG4.

ADIDAS GIL-ZERO BLACK
Select NBA Codes and enter QQQ3JCUYQ7.

ADIDAS GIL-ZERO MID
Select NBA Codes and enter 1GSJC8JWRL.

ADIDAS GIL-ZERO MID BLACK
Select NBA Codes and enter 369V6RVU3G.

ADIDAS STEALTH
Select NBA Codes and enter FE454DFJCC.

ADIDAS T-MAC 6
Select NBA Codes and enter MCJK843NNC.

ADIDAS T-MAC 6 WHITE
Select NBA Codes and enter 84GF7EJG8V.

CHARLOTTE BOBCATS 2006-07 ALTERNATE JERSEY
Select NBA Codes and enter WEDX671H7S.

UTAH JAZZ 2006-07 ALTERNATE JERSEY
Select NBA Codes and enter VCBI89FK83.

NEW JERSEY NETS 2006-07 ALTERNATE JERSEY
Select NBA Codes and enter D4SAA98U5H.

WASHINGTON WIZARDS 2006-07 ALTERNATE JERSEY
Select NBA Codes and enter QV93NLKXQC.

EASTERN ALL-STARS 2006-07 AWAY JERSEY
Select NBA Codes and enter WOCNW4KL7L.

EASTERN ALL-STARS 2006-07 HOME JERSEY
Select NBA Codes and enter 5654ND43N6.

WESTERN ALL-STARS 2006-07 AWAY JERSEY
Select NBA Codes and enter XX93BVL20U.

WESTERN ALL-STARS 2006-07 HOME JERSEY
Select NBA Codes and enter 993NSKL199.

NCAA FOOTBALL 07

#16 BAYLOR
Select Pennant Collection from My NCAA, then press SELECT and enter Sic Em.

#16 NIKE SPEED TD
Select Pennant Collection from My NCAA, then press SELECT and enter Light Speed.

#63 ILLINOIS
Select Pennant Collection from My NCAA, then press SELECT and enter Oskee Wow.

#160 TEXAS TECH
Select Pennant Collection from My NCAA, then press SELECT and enter Fight.

#200 FIRST AND FIFTEEN
Select Pennant Collection from My NCAA, then press SELECT and enter Thanks.

#201 BLINK
Select Pennant Collection from My NCAA, then press SELECT and enter For.

#202 BOING
Select Pennant Collection from My NCAA, then press SELECT and enter Registering.

#204 BUTTER FINGERS
Select Pennant Collection from My NCAA, then press SELECT and enter With EA.

#205 CROSSED THE LINE
Select Pennant Collection from My NCAA, then press SELECT and enter Tiburon.

#206 CUFFED
Select Pennant Collection from My NCAA, then press SELECT and enter EA Sports.

#207 EXTRA CREDIT
Select Pennant Collection from My NCAA, then press SELECT and enter Touchdown.

#208 HELIUM
Select Pennant Collection from My NCAA, then press SELECT and enter In The Zone.

#209 HURRICANE
Select Pennant Collection from My NCAA, then press SELECT and enter Turnover.

#210 INSTANT FREEPLAY
Select Pennant Collection from My NCAA, then press SELECT and enter Impact.

#211 JUMBALAYA
Select Pennant Collection from My NCAA, then press SELECT and enter Heisman.

#212 MOLASSES
Select Pennant Collection from My NCAA, then press SELECT and enter Game Time.

#213 NIKE FREE
Select Pennant Collection from My NCAA, then press SELECT and enter Break Free.

#214 NIKE MAGNIGRIP
Select Pennant Collection from My NCAA, then press SELECT and enter Hand Picked.

#215 NIKE PRO
Select Pennant Collection from My NCAA, then press SELECT and enter No Sweat.

#219 QB DUD
Select Pennant Collection from My NCAA, then press SELECT and enter Elite 11.

#221 STEEL TOE
Select Pennant Collection from My NCAA, then press SELECT and enter Gridiron.

#222 STIFFED
Select Pennant Collection from My NCAA, then press SELECT and enter NCAA.

#223 SUPER DIVE
Select Pennant Collection from My NCAA, then press SELECT and enter Upset.

#224 TAKE YOUR TIME
Select Pennant Collection from My NCAA, then press SELECT and enter Football.

#225 THREAD & NEEDLE
Select Pennant Collection from My NCAA, then press SELECT and enter 06.

#226 TOUGH AS NAILS
Select Pennant Collection from My NCAA, then press SELECT and enter Offense.

#227 TRIP
Select Pennant Collection from My NCAA, then press SELECT and enter Defense.

#228 WHAT A HIT
Select Pennant Collection from My NCAA, then press SELECT and enter Blitz.

#229 KICKER HEX
Select Pennant Collection from My NCAA, then press SELECT and enter Sideline.

#273 2004 ALL-AMERICANS
Select Pennant Collection from My NCAA, then press SELECT and enter Fumble.

#274 ALL-ALABAMA
Select Pennant Collection from My NCAA, then press SELECT and enter Roll Tide.

#276 ALL-ARKANSAS
Select Pennant Collection from My NCAA, then press SELECT and enter Woopigsooie.

#277 ALL-AUBURN
Select Pennant Collection from My NCAA, then press SELECT and enter War Eagle.

#278 ALL-CLEMSON
Select Pennant Collection from My NCAA, then press SELECT and enter Death Valley.

#279 ALL-COLORADO
Select Pennant Collection from My NCAA, then press SELECT and enter Glory.

#280 ALL-FLORIDA
Select Pennant Collection from My NCAA, then press SELECT and enter Great To Be.

#281 ALL-FSU
Select Pennant Collection from My NCAA, then press SELECT and enter Uprising.

#282 ALL-GEORGIA
Select Pennant Collection from My NCAA, then press SELECT and enter Hunker Down.

#283 ALL-IOWA
Select Pennant Collection from My NCAA, then press SELECT and enter On Iowa.

#284 ALL-KANSAS STATE
Select Pennant Collection from My NCAA, then press SELECT and enter Victory.

#285 ALL-LSU
Select Pennant Collection from My NCAA, then press SELECT and enter Geaux Tigers.

#286 ALL-MIAMI
Select Pennant Collection from My NCAA, then press SELECT and enter Raising Cane.

#287 ALL-MICHIGAN
Select Pennant Collection from My NCAA, then press SELECT and enter Go Blue.

#288 ALL-MISSISSIPPI STATE
Select Pennant Collection from My NCAA, then press SELECT and enter Hail State.

#289 ALL-NEBRASKA
Select Pennant Collection from My NCAA, then press SELECT and enter Go Big Red.

#290 ALL-NORTH CAROLINA
Select Pennant Collection from My NCAA, then press SELECT and enter Rah Rah.

#291 ALL-NOTRE DAME
Select Pennant Collection from My NCAA, then press SELECT and enter Golden Domer.

#292 ALL-OHIO STATE
Select Pennant Collection from My NCAA, then press SELECT and enter Killer Nuts.

#293 ALL-OKLAHOMA
Select Pennant Collection from My NCAA, then press SELECT and enter Boomer.

#294 ALL-OKLAHOMA STATE
Select Pennant Collection from My NCAA, then press SELECT and enter Go Pokes.

#295 ALL-OREGON
Select Pennant Collection from My NCAA, then press SELECT and enter Quack Attack.

#296 ALL-PENN STATE
Select Pennant Collection from My NCAA, then press SELECT and enter We Are.

#297 ALL-PITTSBURGH
Select Pennant Collection from My NCAA, then press SELECT and enter Lets Go Pitt.

#298 ALL-PURDUE
Select Pennant Collection from My NCAA, then press SELECT and enter Boiler Up.

#299 ALL-SYRACUSE
Select Pennant Collection from My NCAA, then press SELECT and enter Orange Crush.

#300 ALL-TENNESSEE
Select Pennant Collection from My NCAA, then press SELECT and enter Big Orange.

#301 ALL-TEXAS
Select Pennant Collection from My NCAA, then press SELECT and enter Hook Em.

#302 ALL-TEXAS A&M
Select Pennant Collection from My NCAA, then press SELECT and enter Gig Em.

#303 ALL-UCLA
Select Pennant Collection from My NCAA, then press SELECT and enter MIGHTY.

#304 ALL-USC
Select Pennant Collection from My NCAA, then press SELECT and enter Fight On.

#305 ALL-VIRGINIA
Select Pennant Collection from My NCAA, then press SELECT and enter Wahoos.

#306 ALL-VIRGINIA TECH
Select Pennant Collection from My NCAA, then press SELECT and enter Tech Triumph.

#307 ALL-WASHINGTON
Select Pennant Collection from My NCAA, then press SELECT and enter Bow Down.

#308 ALL-WISCONSIN
Select Pennant Collection from My NCAA, then press SELECT and enter U Rah Rah.

#311 ARK MASCOT
Select Pennant Collection from My NCAA, then press SELECT and enter Bear Down.

#329 GT MASCOT
Select Pennant Collection from My NCAA, then press SELECT and enter RamblinWreck.

#333 ISU MASCOT
Select Pennant Collection from My NCAA, then press SELECT and enter Red And Gold.

#335 KU MASCOT
Select Pennant Collection from My NCAA, then press SELECT and enter Rock Chalk.

#341 MINN MASCOT
Select Pennant Collection from My NCAA, then press SELECT and enter Rah Rah Rah.

#344 MIZZOU MASCOT
Select Pennant Collection from My NCAA, then press SELECT and enter Mizzou Rah.

#346 MSU MASCOT
Select Pennant Collection from My NCAA, then press SELECT and enter Go Green.

#349 NCSU MASCOT
Select Pennant Collection from My NCAA, then press SELECT and enter Go Pack.

#352 NU MASCOT
Select Pennant Collection from My NCAA, then press SELECT and enter Go Cats.

#360 S CAR MASCOT
Select Pennant Collection from My NCAA, then press SELECT and enter Go Carolina.

#371 UK MASCOT
Select Pennant Collection from My NCAA, then press SELECT and enter On On UK.

#382 WAKE FOREST
Select Pennant Collection from My NCAA, then press SELECT and enter Go Deacs Go.

#385 WSU MASCOT
Select Pennant Collection from My NCAA, then press SELECT and enter All Hail.

#386 WVU MASCOT
Select Pennant Collection from My NCAA, then press SELECT and enter Hail WV.

NEED FOR SPEED CARBON

CASTROL CASH
At the Main menu, press Down, Up, Left, Down, Right, Up, X, B. This will give you 10,000 extra cash.

INFINITE CREW CHARGE
At the Main menu, press Down, Up, Up, Right, Left, Left, Right, X.

INFINITE NITROUS
At the Main menu, press Left, Up, Left, Down, Left, Down, Right, X.

INFINITE SPEEDBREAKER
At the Main menu, press Down, Right, Right, Left, Right, Up, Down, X.

NEED FOR SPEED CARBON LOGO VINYLS
At the Main menu, press Right, Up, Down, Up, Down, Left, Right, X.

NEED FOR SPEED CARBON SPECIAL LOGO VINYLS
At the Main menu, press Up, Up, Down, Down, Down, Down, Up, X.

NEED FOR SPEED MOST WANTED

BURGER KING CHALLENGE
At the Title screen, press Up, Down, Up, Down, Left, Right, Left, Right.

CASTROL SYNTEC VERSION OF THE FORD GT
At the Title screen, press Left, Right, Left, Right, Up, Down, Up, Down.

MARKER FOR BACKROOM OF THE ONE-STOP SHOP
At the Title screen, press Up, Up, Down, Down, Left, Right, Up, Down.

JUNKMAN ENGINE
At the Title screen, press Up, Up, Down, Down, Left, Right, Up, Down.

PORSCHE CAYMAN
At the Title screen, press L, R, R, R, Right, Left, Right, Down.

NHL 2K6

CHEAT MODE
Select Manage Profiles from the Options menu. Create a new profile with the name Turco813.

PETER JACKSON'S KING KONG: THE OFFICIAL GAME OF THE MOVIE

At the Main menu hold Left Bumper + Right Bumper + Left Trigger + Right Trigger and press Down, Up, Y, X, Down, Down, Y, Y. Release the buttons to access the Cheat option. The Cheat option is also available on the pause menu. Note that you cannot record your scores using cheat codes.

GOD MODE
Select Cheat and enter 8wonder.

ALL CHAPTERS
Select Cheat and enter KKst0ry.

AMMO 999
Select Cheat and enter KK 999 mun.

MACHINE GUN
Select Cheat and enter KKcapone.

REVOLVER
Select Cheat and enter KKtigun.

SNIPER RIFLE
Select Cheat and enter KKsn1per.

INFINITE SPEARS
Select Cheat and enter lance 1nf.

1-HIT KILLS
Select Cheat and enter GrosBras.

EXTRAS
Select Cheat and enter KKmuseum.

QUAKE 4

ALL WEAPONS, FULL ARMOR, HEALTH & AMMO
Press the Back button to access the Objectives, then press Up, Up, Down, Down, Left, Right, Left, Right, B, A.

FULL AMMO
Press the Back button to access the Objectives, then press B, A, RT, LB, Left, Right, Left.

FULL HEALTH
Press the Back button to access the Objectives, then press B, A, B, A, Up, Up, Down, RT.

SAINTS ROW

Pause the game and select Dial from your phone. Enter the following codes and then press Call. Select Cheats to enable the first set of codes, the ones that start with "#." You cannot earn achievements if using these cheats. Note that vehicles are delivered to your garage.

CODE NAME	DIAL
Give Cash	#MONEY

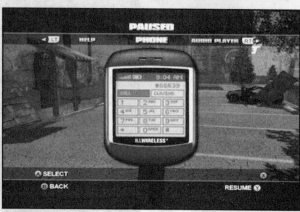

Full Health	#FULLHEALTH
Repair Car	#778
Infinite Ammo	#AMMO
Infinite Sprint	#SPRINT
No Cop Notoriety	#NOCOPS
No Gang Notoriety	#NOGANGS
Evil Cars	#EVILCARS
Clear Skies	#SUNNY
Wrath of God	#10
44	#SHEPHERD
12 Gauge	#12GAUGE
Ambulance	#AMBULANCE
Anchor	#ANCHOR
Ant	#ANT
Aqua	#A7UA

CODE NAME	DIAL
AR40	#AR40XTND
AS12	#AS12RIOT
Baron	#BARON
Baseball Bat	#BASEBALL
Betsy	#BETSY
Bulldog	#BULLDOG
Cavallaro	#CAVALLARO
Compton	#COMPTON
Cosmos	#COSMOS
Destiny	#DESTINY
Justice	#JUSTICE
FBI	#FBI
Ferdelance	#FERDELANCE
Gdhc	#GDHC50
Grenade	#GRENADE
Gunslinger	#GUNSLINGER
Halberd	#HALBERD
Hammerhead	#HAMMERHEAD
Hannibal	#42664225
Hollywood	#HOLLYWOOD
Jackrabbit	#JACKRABBIT
The Job	#THEJOB
K6	#K6KRUKOV
Keystone	#KEYSTONE
Knife	#KNIFE
Komodo	#KOMODO
La Fuerza	#LAFUER9A
Mag	#MAG
McManus	#MACMANUS
Mockingbird	#MOCKINGBIRD
Molotov	#MOLOTOV
Nelson	#635766
Newman	#NEWMAN
Nightstick	#NIGHTSTICK
Nordberg	#NORDBERG
NR4	#NR4
Pimp Cane	#PIMPCANE
Pipebomb	#PIPEBOMB
Quasar	#7UASAR
Quota	#7UOTA
Rattler	#RATTLER
Reaper	#REAPER
RPG	#ROCKET
Shogun	#SHOGUN
SKR7	#SKRSPREE
T3K	#T3KURBAN
Taxi	#TAXI
Titan	#TITAN
Tombstone	#TOMBSTONE
Traxxmaster	#TRAXXMASTER
VICE9	#Vice9
Vortex	#VORTEX
Voxel	#VOXEL

CODE NAME	DIAL
Zenith	#9ENITH
Zimos	#9IMOS
Zircon	#9IRCON
GameStop	#42637867
Chicken Ned	5552445 (select Homies from your Phone to access Chicken Ned)

For the following codes, select the Phone Book to call.

CODE NAME	DIAL
EagleLine Yellow	5550180174

Big Willy's Cab	5558198415
Brown Baggers	5553765
Crash Landing	5556278
The Dead Cow	5556238
Emergency	911
Eye for an Eye	5555966
Freckle Bitch's	5556328
Grounds for Divorce	5559473
Impression	5553248
Legal Lee's	5559467
Lik-a-Chick	5553863
On the Fence	5557296
On the Rag	5555926
On Thin Ice	5552564
Rim Jobs	5553493
Stock$	5552626
Suicide Hotline	5554876837
TNA Taxis	5554558008

TIGER WOODS PGA TOUR 06

ALL GOLFERS
Select Password from the Options menu and enter itsinthegame.

ALL CLUBS
Select Password from the Options menu and enter clubs11.

GOLD COLLECTION EA SPORTS BALL
Select Password from the Options menu and enter golfisfun.

NICKLAUS ITEMS
Select Password from the Options menu and enter goldenbear.

ALL COURSES
Select Password from the Options menu and enter eyecandy.

VIJAY SINGH
Select Password from the Options menu and enter victory.

TOMB RAIDER: LEGEND

You must unlock the following codes in the game before using them.

BULLETPROOF
During a game, hold Left Trigger and press A, Right Trigger, Y, Right Trigger, X, Left Bumper.

DRAIN ENEMY HEALTH
During a game, hold Left Trigger and press X, B, A, Left Bumper, Right Trigger, Y.

INFINITE ASSAULT RIFLE AMMO
During a game, hold Left Bumper and press A, B, A, Left Trigger, X, Y.

INFINITE GRENADE LAUNCHER AMMO
During a game, hold Left Bumper and press Left Trigger, Y, Right Trigger, B, Left Trigger, X.

INFINITE SHOTGUN AMMO
During a game, hold Left Bumper and press Right Trigger, B, X, Left Trigger, X, A.

INFINITE SMG AMMO
During a game, hold Left Bumper and press B, Y, Left Trigger, Right Trigger, A, B.

EXCALIBUR
During a game, hold Left Bumper and press Y, A, B, Right Trigger, Y, Left Trigger.

SOUL REAVER
During a game, hold Left Bumper and press A, Right Trigger, B, Right Trigger, Left Trigger, X.

1-SHOT KILL
During a game, hold Left Trigger and press Y, A, Y, X, Left Bumper, B.

TEXTURELESS MODE
During a game, hold Left Trigger and press Left Bumper, A, B, A, Y, Right Trigger.

TOM CLANCY'S GHOST RECON ADVANCED WARFIGHTER

ALL MISSIONS
At the Mission Select screen, hold Back +
Left Trigger + Right Trigger and press Y,
Right Bumper, Y, Right Bumper, X.

FULL HEALTH
Pause the game, hold Back + Left Trigger
+ Right Trigger and press Left Bumper, Left
Bumper, Right Bumper, X, Right Bumper, Y.

INVINCIBLE
Pause the game, hold Back + Left Trigger + Right Trigger and press Y, Y, X, Right Bumper, X,
Left Bumper.

TEAM INVINCIBLE
Pause the game, hold Back + Left Trigger + Right Trigger and press X, X, Y, Right Bumper, Y,
Left Bumper.

UNLIMITED AMMO
Pause the game, hold Back + Left Trigger
+ Right Trigger and press Right Bumper,
Right Bumper, Left Bumper, X, Left
Bumper, Y.

TONY HAWK'S AMERICAN WASTELAND

ALWAYS SPECIAL
Select Cheat Codes from the Options menu
and enter uronfire. Pause the game and
select Cheats from the Game Options to
enable the code.

PERFECT RAIL
Select Cheat Codes from the Options menu
and enter grindxpert. Pause the game and
select Cheats from the Game Options to
enable the code.

PERFECT SKITCH
Select Cheat Codes from the Options menu and enter h!tchar!de. Pause the game and select Cheats from the Game Options to enable the code.

PERFECT MANUAL
Select Cheat Codes from the Options menu and enter 2wheels!. Pause the game and select Cheats from the Game Options to enable the code.

MOON GRAVITY
Select Cheat Codes from the Options menu and enter 2them00n. Pause the game and select Cheats from the Game Options to enable the code.

MAT HOFFMAN
Select Cheat Codes from the Options menu and enter the_condor.

TONY HAWK'S PROJECT 8

SPONSOR ITEMS
As you progress through Career mode and move up the rankings, you gain sponsors. Each sponsor comes with its own Create-a-Skater item.

RANK	CAS ITEM UNLOCKED
Rank 040	Adio Kenny V2 Shoes
Rank 050	Quiksilver_Hoody_3
Rank 060	Birdhouse Tony Hawk Deck
Rank 080	Vans No Skool Gothic Shoes
Rank 100	Volcom Scallero Jacket
Rank 110	eS Square One Shoes
Rank 120	Almost Watch What You Say Deck
Rank 140	DVS Adage Shoe
Rank 150	Element Illuminate Deck
Rank 160	Etnies Sheckler White Lavender Shoes
Complete Skateshop Goal	Stereo Soundwave Deck

SKATERS
You must unlock all of the skaters, except for Tony Hawk, by completing challenges in the Career Mode. They are playable in Free Skate and 2-Player modes.

SKATER	HOW TO UNLOCK
Tony Hawk	Always unlocked
Lyn-z Adams Hawkins	Complete Pro Challenge
Bob Burquist	Complete Pro Challenge
Dustin Dollin	Complete Pro Challenge
Nyjah Huston	Complete Pro Challenge
Bam Margera	Complete Pro Challenge
Rodney Mullen	Complete Pro Challenge
Paul Rodriguez	Complete Pro Challenge
Ryan Sheckler	Complete Pro Challenge
Daewon Song	Complete Pro Challenge
Mike Vallely	Complete Pro Challenge
Stevie Willams	Complete Pro Challenge
Travis Barker	Complete Pro Challenge
Kevin Staab	Complete Pro Challenge
Zombie	Complete Pro Challenge
Christaian Hosoi	Rank #1
Jason Lee	Complete Final Tony Hawk Goal

SKATER	HOW TO UNLOCK
Photographer	Unlock Shops
Security Guard	Unlock School
Bum	Unlock Car Factory
Beaver Mascot	Unlock High School
Real Estate Agent	Unlock Downtown
Filmer	Unlock High School
Skate Jam Kid	Rank #4
Dad	Rank #1
Colonel	All Gaps
Nerd	Complete School Spirit Goal

CHEAT CODES

Select Cheat Codes from the Options menu to enter the following codes. You can access some of these codes from the Options menu.

CODE	WHAT IT UNLOCKS
plus44	Travis Barker
hohohosoi	Christian Hosoi

XBOX 360™ ACHIEVEMENTS

Games List

BLITZ: THE LEAGUE

ACHIEVEMENTS

NAME	GOAL/REQUIREMENT	POINT VALUE
High Roller	Earn $150,000 in one Campaign Mode game.	15
Whale	Earn $250,000 in one Campaign Mode game.	25
Bombs Away	Win a game by only passing the ball.	13
Ground Attack	Win a game by only running the ball.	17
Underdog	Defeat the Nightmare in Hard Difficulty in Quickplay when using the Grizzlies or Hammerheads.	15
Butterfingaz	Defeat the computer in bonus Quick Play game of Butterfingaz.	10
Domination	Defeat the computer in a bonus Quick Play game of Domination.	10

NAME	GOAL/REQUIREMENT	POINT VALUE
Special Teamer	Return a punt or a kickoff for a touchdown in a Campaign Mode game.	25
Shutout	Complete one shutout game in Campaign Mode.	10
Juiced	Train both Rookie and Veteran up to an A+ rating during Campaign Mode.	15
Top Dog	Defeat an online opponent with your Campaign Mode custom team.	6
Custom Pain	Defeat 10 online opponents with your Campaign Mode custom team.	14
Air Supremacy	Gain 400 passing yards in any Campaign Mode game.	20
Groundhog	Gain 200 rushing yards in any Campaign Mode game.	35
Sticky Fingers	Gain 200 receiving yards in any Campaign Mode game.	20
Ownage	Win 10 games online.	20
Pwnage	Win 25 games online.	50
Mexico'd	Knock Mexico out of the game with a game-ending injury (Quickplay or Campaign Mode).	11
Headhunter	Knock Julius Williams out of the game (Quickplay or Campaign).	10
Shutdown	Hold an opposing team to under 100 combined (pass/rush) in a Campaign Mode game.	10
Buffet Victory	Win a Quick Play game with every team.	30
Fast Learner	Complete every Training Camp task.	10
Playmaker	Score a 90+ yard touchdown in Campaign mode.	5
Romo	Cause 3 or more injuries to your opponent in a single Campaign Mode game.	25
Gunslinger	Throw at least 6 TD passes in a single game in Campaign Mode.	6
Scrubs Champ	Defeat Division 3 in Campaign Mode.	25
Division 2 Champ	Defeat Division 2 in Campaign Mode.	70
The End	Defeat Campaign Mode.	150
Rushing Champ	Win the rushing title with your rookie (any division in Campaign Mode).	15
Passing Champ	Win the passing title with your rookie (any division in Campaign Mode).	15
Receiving Champ	Win the receiving title with your rookie (any division in Campaign Mode).	15
LT's Pride	Get 20 sacks with a veteran in one Division Season.	25
Thief	Force 7 turnovers with your veteran in a Division Season in Campaign Mode.	15
L33T	Win every game in Campaign Mode.	50
Arsenal	Score 19 points in a quarter in Campaign Mode.	9
Greatest Show	Score 24 points in a quarter in Campaign Mode.	15
Manvalanche	Get 12 sacks in one Campaign Mode game.	15
Bling Bling	Buy every piece of bonus equipment that's unlocked after you Defeat Campaign Mode.	25
Deep Pockets	Earn $500,000 dollars online.	10
Mad Bank	Earn $1,000,000 dollars online.	20
ROFL Waffle	Lost 5 games in a row online.	0

NAME	GOAL/REQUIREMENT	POINT VALUE
Blind	Threw 5+ interceptions in one game	0
O RLY?	Lost by more than 24 pts in Campaign Mode	0
Weak Sauce	Lost to Arizona in game 1 of Campaign Mode	0
Burning Sensation	You feel itchy down below. Did you pick something up from your last opponent	69

CALL OF DUTY 3

ACHIEVEMENTS

NAME	GOAL/REQUIREMENT	POINT VALUE
Basic Training	Complete the basic training in the beginning of Saint Lo.	5
American Infantryman	Complete two missions as an American soldier.	20
British Commando	Complete two missions as a British soldier.	20
Canadian Highlander	Complete two missions as a Canadian soldier.	10
Polish Tanker	Complete two missions as a Polish soldier.	15
Won the War	Complete the Single-Player Campaign on any difficulty setting.	80
Hot Potato	Pick up and return 5 live grenades.	25
Rifleman	Complete a mission by firing only bolt action rifles. Melee attacks don't count.	15
Assault Trooper	Complete a mission by firing only assault rifles. Melee attacks don't count.	15
Battlefield Scavenger	Complete a mission by firing only German weapons. Melee attacks don't count.	15
Still Ticking	Complete a mission without dying or using checkpoints.	30
Allergic to Bullets	Avoid getting hit more than 30 times during a mission.	25
Conservationist	Complete a mission using less than 300 rounds of ammunition.	20
Close Quarter Combatant	Complete a mission without firing a round. Player can make use of melee attacks and hand grenades.	100
Grizzled Veteran	Complete the Single-Player Campaign on Veteran difficulty.	150
Supply Officer	Supply ammunition to at least 20 friendly soldiers in a single ranked match (Multiplayer).	15
Doc	Revive 10 of your teammates in a ranked match without getting a team kill (Multiplayer).	30
A War Hero	Capture the final objective in the game mode War. Must be a ranked match (Multiplayer).	30
Victory Medal	Be the player with the highest score and on the winning team in a ranked match (Multiplayer).	30
Lieutenant	Receive 200 total points in ranked matches (Multiplayer).	20
Captain	Receive 2000 total points in ranked matches (Multiplayer).	40
Major	Receive 8000 total points in ranked matches (Multiplayer).	60
Colonel	Receive 20000 total points in ranked matches (Multiplayer).	80

NAME	GOAL/REQUIREMENT	POINT VALUE
General	Receive 40000 total points in ranked matches (Multiplayer).	120
Purple Heart	For perserverence despite grevious injuries.	5
EXTREME!	Found a big jump and caught some air.	25

THE ELDER SCROLLS IV: OBLIVION

ACHIEVEMENTS

NAME	GOAL/REQUIREMENT	POINT VALUE
Escaped the Imperial Sewers	Escaped the Imperial Sewers, Main Quest Beginning.	50
Closed an Oblivion Gate	Closed an Oblivion Gate, Main Quest.	50
Located the Shrine of Dagon	Located the Shrine of Dagon, Main Quest.	50
Delivered Daedric Artifact	Delivered Daedric Artifact, Main Quest.	50
Destroyed the Great Gate	Destroyed the Great Gate, Main Quest.	50
Champion of Cyrodiil	Completed the Main Questline.	110
Murderer, Dark Brotherhood	Join the Dark Brotherhood.	10
Slayer, Dark Brotherhood	Reached Slayer rank in the Dark Brotherhood.	10
Eliminator, Dark Brotherhood	Reached Eliminator rank in the Dark Brotherhood.	10
Assassin, Dark Brotherhood	Reached Assassin rank in the Dark Brotherhood.	10
Silencer, Dark Brotherhood	Reached Silencer rank in the Dark Brotherhood.	10
Speaker, Dark Brotherhood	Reached Speaker rank in the Dark Brotherhood.	10
Listener, Dark Brotherhood	Completed the Dark Brotherhood Questline.	50
Pit Dog, Arena	Joined the Arena in the Imperial City.	10
Brawler, Arena	Reached Brawler rank in the Arena.	10
Bloodletter, Arena	Reached Bloodletter rank in the Arena.	10
Myrmidon, Arena	Reached Myrmidon rank in the Arena.	10
Warrior, Arena	Reached Warrior rank in the Arena.	10
Gladiator, Arena	Reached Gladiator rank in the Arena.	10
Hero, Arena	Reached Hero rank in the Arena.	10
Champion, Arena	Reached Champion rank in the Arena.	10
Grand Champion, Arena	Completed the Arena Questline.	50
Pickpocket, Thieves Guild	Joined the Thieves Guild.	10
Footpad, Thieves Guild	Reached Footpad rank in the Thieves Guild.	10
Bandit, Thieves Guild	Reached Bandit rank in the Thieves Guild.	10
Prowler, Thieves Guild	Reached Prowler rank in the Thieves Guild.	10
Cat Burglar, Thieves Guild	Reached Cat Burglar rank in the Thieves Guild.	10
Shadowfoot, Thieves Guild	Reached Shadowfoot rank in the Thieves Guild.	10
Master Thief, Thieves Guild	Reached Master Thief rank in the Thieves Guild.	10
Guildmaster, Thieves Guild	Completed the Thieves Guild Questline.	50
Associate, Mages Guild	Joined the Mages Guild.	10
Apprentice, Mages Guild	Reached Apprentice rank in the Mages Guild.	10
Journeyman, Mages Guild	Reached Journeyman rank in the Mages Guild.	10
Evoker, Mages Guild	Reached Evoker rank in the Mages Guild.	10
Conjurer, Mages Guild	Reached Conjurer rank in the Mages Guild.	10

NAME	GOAL/REQUIREMENT	POINT VALUE
Magician, Mages Guild	Reached Magician rank in the Mages Guild.	10
Warlock, Mages Guild	Reached Warlock rank in the Mages Guild.	10
Wizard, Mages Guild	Reached Wizard rank in the Mages Guild.	10
Master-Wizard, Mages Guild	Reached Master-Wizard rank in the Mages Guild.	10
Arch-Mage, Mages Guild	Completed the Mages Guild Questline.	50
Associate, Fighters Guild	Joined the Fighters Guild.	10
Apprentice, Fighters Guild	Reached Apprentice rank in the Fighters Guild.	10
Journeyman, Fighters Guild	Reached Journeyman rank in the Fighters Guild.	10
Swordsman, Fighters Guild	Reached Swordsman rank in the Fighters Guild.	10
Protector, Fighters Guild	Reached Protector rank in the Fighters Guild.	10
Defender, Fighters Guild	Reached Defender rank in the Fighters Guild.	10
Warder, Fighters Guild	Reached Warder rank in the Fighters Guild.	10
Guardian, Fighters Guild	Reached Guardian rank in the Fighters Guild.	10
Champion, Fighters Guild	Reached Champion rank in the Fighters Guild.	10
Master, Fighters Guild	Completed the Fighters Guild Questline.	50

ENCHANTED ARMS

ACHIEVEMENTS

NAME	GOAL/REQUIREMENT	POINT VALUE
First Match	Battle against Yuki at the betting Golem Battle.	25
In the Dungeon	Defeat Fire Golem in the Sealed Ward.	25
Out of Control	Defeat Queen of Ice in the Sealed Ward.	75
Great Forest	Defeat Amazonia at Military Path.	25
The Great Sea	Defeat Aqua Jelly at Ragau Coast Wharf.	25
Tragedy	Defeat Cerberus at the Magic Lab.	25
Zeal	Defeat Prof. Kou at the Magic Lab.	75
Unfathomable Enemy	Defeat Minotaur in the Abandoned Mine.	25
Betrayal	Defeat Giggling Man in the Abandoned Mine.	25
Enmity	Defeat Ooka in the Abandoned Mine.	25
Conclusion	Defeat Ooka at the London Castle.	25
Gurdian	Defeat Poseidon at the Inferno Temple.	25
Purgatory	Defeat Emperor of Fire at the Inferno Temple.	75
De ja vu	Defeat Sphinx in the White Flower Field.	25
Rescue	Defeat Oboro at the Ninja Hideout.	25
Change of Heart	Defeat Sayaka in the Iwato Village.	25
Attack	Defeat Oboro in the Iwato Village.	25
Suspicious Movement	Defeat Tokimune Bodygurads at the Kyoto Castle.	25
Immobile	Defeat Saisho at the Temple of Trials.	75
Guardian	Defeat Odin in the Sage's Tower.)	25
Subordinates of Ice	Beat Siren in the Sage's Tower.	25
Riddle	Defeat the mysterious man in the Graveyard Town.	25

NAME	GOAL/REQUIREMENT	POINT VALUE
Resolve	Defeat Touya at the Ice Palace.	25
Close	Defeat the Queen of Ice at the Ice Palace.	75
Grand Finale	Happy Ending.	150

F.E.A.R.

ACHIEVEMENTS

NAME	GOAL/REQUIREMENT	POINT VALUE
Survivalist	Complete the Campaign on any difficulty without dying.	150
Fearsome	Complete the Campaign on Extreme difficulty.	100
No Juice	Complete the Campaign on any difficulty without using any boosters.	65
Real Time	Complete the Campaign on any difficulty without using SlowMo.	65
Fearless Flagman	Successfully capture 50 flags in ranked CTF or SlowMo CTF games.	75
MP 1000	Participate in 1000 ranked Multiplayer games of any type.	75
Multiplayer Victory	Win any ranked Deathmatch, SlowMo Deathmatch, or Elimination Multiplayer game.	75
Fearless	Win the Campaign on any difficulty except Low.	35
Explorer	Find every Health Booster and Reflex Booster in the Single-player Campaign.	35
Exterminator	Kill every enemy in the Campaign.	35
Ammo Hog	Win the Campaign using less than 500 rounds of ammo.	35
No Fear	Win every Instant Action map on Extreme difficulty.	35
Demolitions Expert	Kill 200 enemies with the N6A3, AT-S or M77 in any ranked Multiplayer games.	35
Dead Eye	Kill 150 enemies with Headshots in any ranked Multiplayer games.	35
Initiation	Complete Interval 2 in the Campaign.	5
Water Treatment Facility	Complete Interval 3 in the Campaign.	5
Armacham	Complete Interval 7 in the Campaign.	5
Slums	Complete Interval 8 in the Campaign.	5
Secret Facility	Complete Interval 10 in the Campaign.	5
Intel	Gather every phone message and lap top in the Campaign.	5
Explosives Expert	Kill 3 or more enemies with a single N6A3, AT-S or M77 in the Campaign or Instant Action.	5
Environmentalist	Kill 10 enemies with barrels, fire extinguishers or fuse boxes in the Campaign or Instant Action.	5
Slow Jo	Kill 5 enemies with one SlowMo use in the Campaign or Instant Action.	5
Medic!	Use 50 Medkits in the Campaign or Instant Action.	5
Bullet Sponge	Use 50 armor vests in the Campaign or Instant Action.	5
Feared	Complete every Instant Action map on any difficulty except Low.	5

NAME	GOAL/REQUIREMENT	POINT VALUE
Team Victory	Win 5 each of ranked CTF, SlowMo CTF, TDM, SlowMo TDM, and Team Elimination games in Multiplayer.	5
MP 100	Participate in 100 rank Multiplayer games of any type.	5
Assaulter	Kill 50 enemies with the G2A2 in any ranked Multiplayer games.	5
Sub-Jugator	Kill 50 enemies with the RPL in any ranked Multiplayer games.	5
Dual Machinist	Kill 50 enemies with the SM15 in any ranked Multiplayer games.	5
Repeating Offender	Kill 50 enemies with the MP-50 in any ranked Multiplayer games.	5
PumpShotty Ownage	Kill 50 enemies with the VK-12 in any ranked Multiplayer games.	5
Grenadier	Kill 50 enemies with the N6A3 in any ranked Multiplayer games.	5
Rocketman	Kill 50 enemies with the MOD-3 in any ranked Multiplayer games.	5
Perforator	Kill 50 enemies with the 10mm HV Penetrator in any ranked Multiplayer games.	5
Pistoleer	Kill 50 enemies with the AT-14 in any ranked Multiplayer games.	5
Disintegrator	Kill 50 enemies with the Type-7 in any ranked Multiplayer games.	5
Trap Layer	Kill 50 enemies with the AT-S in any ranked Multiplayer games.	5
Sapper	Kill 50 enemies with the M77 in any ranked Multiplayer games.	5
Sniper	Kill 50 enemies with the ASP in any ranked Multiplayer games.	5
Brawler	Kill 50 enemies with Punches or Rifle Butts in any ranked Multiplayer games.	5
Black Belt	Kill 50 enemies with Round House Kicks, Flying Kicks, or Slide Tackles in any ranked MP games.	5
Belly Gunner	Kill 50 enemies with the turret in any ranked Multiplayer games.	5
Afraid	Finished a Multiplayer game with a negative score.	0
Vermin Badge	You killed 5 rats and crows.	0
Suicide King	Killed yourself 5 times	0

FIGHT NIGHT ROUND 3

ACHIEVEMENTS

NAME	GOAL/REQUIREMENT	POINT VALUE
Burger King Achievement	Win the BK Invitational Fight.	100
Dodge Achievement	Win the Dodge sponsored fight.	100
EA SPORTS Achievement	Win any EA SPORTS sponsored fight.	150
ESPN FNF Achievement	Win any ESPN Friday Night Fight event.	150
ESPN PPV Achievement	Win any ESPN Pay Per View fight event.	150
ESPN WNF Achievement	Win any ESPN Wednesday Night Fight event.	150
Everlast Achievement	Win the Everlast sponsored fight	100
Under Armour Achievement	Win the Under Armour sponsored fight.	100

FINAL FANTASY XI

ACHIEVEMENTS

NAME	GOAL/REQUIREMENT	POINT VALUE
Bard Lv.75	Level up the Bard job up to its maximum level.	30
Beastmaster Lv.75	Level up the Beastmaster job up to its maximum level.	30
Black Mage Lv.75	Level up the Black Mage job up to its maximum level.	30
Blue Mage Lv.75	Level up the Blue Mage job up to its maximum level.	30
Corsair Lv.75	Level up the Corsair job up to its maximum level.	30
Dark Knight Lv.75	Level up the Dark Knight job up to its maximum level.	30
Dragoon Lv.75	Level up the Dragoon job up to its maximum level.	30
Monk Lv.75	Level up the Monk job up to its maximum level.	30
Ninja Lv.75	Level up the Ninja job up to its maximum level.	30
Paladin Lv.75	Level up the Paladin job up to its maximum level.	30
Puppetmaster Lv.75	Level up the Puppetmaster job up to its maximum level.	30
Ranger Lv.75	Level up the Ranger job up to its maximum level.	30
Red Mage Lv.75	Level up the Red Mage job up to its maximum level.	30
Samurai Lv.75	Level up the Samurai job up to its maximum level.	30
Summoner Lv.75	Level up the Summoner job up to its maximum level.	30
Thief Lv.75	Level up the Thief job up to its maximum level.	30
Warrior Lv.75	Level up the Warrior job up to its maximum level.	30
White Mage Lv.75	Level up the White Mage job up to its maximum level.	30
Bastokan Rank 10	Complete all the missions available for Bastok	30
San d'Orian Rank 10	Complete all the missions available for San d'Oria	30
Windurstian Rank 10	Complete all the missions available for Windurst	30
Synthesis Skill 100	Achieved 100 in a synthesis skill or fishing.	50
Relic Weapon	Obtained the relic weapon.	40
Chains of Promathia complete	Complete all the missions from the Chains of Promathia expansion pack.	40
Rise of the Zilart complete	Complete all the missions from the Rise of the Zilart expansion pack.	40
Treasures of Aht Urhgan complete	Complete all missions from the Treasures of Aht Urhgan expansion pack.	40
Breaker of the Chains	Earned the title "Breaker of the Chains."	30
Apollyon Ravager	Earned the title "Apollyon Ravager."	20
Temenos Liberator	Earn the title "Temenos Liberator".	20

NAME	GOAL/REQUIREMENT	POINT VALUE
Top Assault/Merc Rank	Earned the Top Assault / Merc Rank.	30
Dynamis-Tavnazia interloper	Clear Dynamis-Tavnazia.	30
Dynamis-Xarcabard interloper	Clear Dynamis-Xarcabard	30

GEARS OF WAR

CAMPAIGN ACHIEVEMENTS

CAMPAIGN ACHIEVEMENTS	TYPE	DIFFICULTY	POINTS	DESCRIPTION

Game Completion on Casual

Prison Breakout	Campaign	Easy	10	Complete the Tutorial (on any difficulty)
Completed Act 1 on Casual	Campaign	Easy	10	Complete Act 1 on Casual Difficulty
Completed Act 2 on Casual	Campaign	Easy	10	Complete Act 2 on Casual Difficulty
Completed Act 3 on Casual	Campaign	Easy	10	Complete Act 3 on Casual Difficulty
Completed Act 4 on Casual	Campaign	Easy	10	Complete Act 4 on Casual Difficulty
Completed Act 5 on Casual	Campaign	Easy	10	Complete Act 5 on Casual Difficulty
Mercenary (unlocks Gamer Pic)	Campaign	Easy	10	Complete all Acts on Casual Difficulty

Game Completion on Hardcore

Completed Act 1 on Hardcore	Campaign	Medium	20	Complete Act 1 on Hardcore Difficulty
Completed Act 2 on Hardcore	Campaign	Medium	20	Complete Act 2 on Hardcore Difficulty
Completed Act 3 on Hardcore	Campaign	Medium	20	Complete Act 3 on Hardcore Difficulty
Completed Act 4 on Hardcore	Campaign	Medium	20	Complete Act 4 on Hardcore Difficulty
Completed Act 5 on Hardcore	Campaign	Medium	20	Complete Act 5 on Hardcore Difficulty
Soldier (unlocks Gamer Pic)	Campaign	Medium	20	Complete all Acts on Hardcore Difficulty

Game Completion on Insane

Completed Act 1 on Insane	Campaign	Hard	30	Complete Act 1 on Insane Difficulty
Completed Act 2 on Insane	Campaign	Hard	30	Complete Act 2 on Insane Difficulty
Completed Act 3 on Insane	Campaign	Hard	30	Complete Act 3 on Insane Difficulty
Completed Act 4 on Insane	Campaign	Hard	30	Complete Act 4 on Insane Difficulty
Completed Act 5 on Insane	Campaign	Hard	30	Complete Act 5 on Insane Difficulty
Commando (unlocks Gamer Pic)	Campaign	Hard	30	Complete all Acts on Insane Difficulty

COG Tags

Time to Remember	Campaign	Easy	10	Recover 10 COG Tags (on any difficulty)
Honor Bound	Campaign	Medium	20	Recover 20 COG Tags (on any difficulty)

CAMPAIGN ACHIEVEMENTS	TYPE	DIFFICULTY	POINTS	DESCRIPTION
For the Fallen	Campaign	Hard	30	Recover 30 COG Tags (on any difficulty)

Killing Bosses

	TYPE	DIFFICULTY	POINTS	DESCRIPTION
My Love for You is Like a Truck	Campaign	Hard	30	Defeat a Berserker on Hardcore Difficulty
Broken Fingers	Campaign	Hard	30	Defeat a Corpser on Hardcore Difficulty
A Dish Best Served Cold	Campaign	Hard	30	Defeat General RAAM on Hardcore Difficulty

Game Skills

	TYPE	DIFFICULTY	POINTS	DESCRIPTION
Zen and the Art of Reloading	Campaign	Easy	10	Perform 25 Perfect Active Reloads (on any difficulty)
Zen and the Art Part 2	Campaign	Medium	20	Perform 5 Perfect Active Reloads in a row (on any difficulty)
Clusterluck	Campaign	Medium	20	Kill 3 enemies at once 10 different times (on any difficulty)

CO-OP ACHIEVEMENTS

CO-OP SPECIFIC ACHIEVEMENTS	TYPE	DIFFICULTY	POINTS	DESCRIPTION
Dom-curious	Co-op	Easy	10	Complete 1 chapter as Dominic Santiago on any difficulty
Domination	Co-op	Medium	20	Complete 10 chapters as Dominic Santiago on any difficulty
I Can't Quit You Dom	Co-op	Hard	30	Complete all Acts in Co-Op on any difficulty

VERSUS ACHIEVEMENTS

VERSUS ACHIEVEMENTS	TYPE	DIFFICULTY	POINTS	DESCRIPTION
Don't You Die on Me	Versus	Easy	10	Revive 100 teammates in Ranked Matches
A Series of Tubes	Versus	Medium	20	Host 50 complete Ranked Matches

Weapon Mastery

	TYPE	DIFFICULTY	POINTS	DESCRIPTION
Fall Down Go Boom	Versus	Easy	10	Kill 100 enemies in Ranked Matches with the Boomshot
Pistolero	Versus	Medium	20	Kill 100 enemies in Ranked Matches with a Pistol
The Nuge	Versus	Medium	20	Kill 100 enemies in Ranked Matches with the Torquebow
I Spy With My Little Eye	Versus	Medium	20	Kill 100 enemies in Ranked Matches with the Longshot
Don't Hurt 'Em	Versus	Medium	20	Kill 100 enemies in Ranked Matches with the Hammer of Dawn

Humiliation Mastery

	TYPE	DIFFICULTY	POINTS	DESCRIPTION
It's a Massacre	Versus	Easy	10	Kill 100 enemies in Ranked Matches with the Chainsaw
Curb Appeal	Versus	Medium	20	Kill 100 enemies in Ranked Matches with the Curb Stomp
Capital Punishment	Versus	Medium	20	Kill 100 enemies in Ranked Matches with an Execution

VERSUS ACHIEVEMENTS	TYPE	DIFFICULTY	POINTS	DESCRIPTION
Crackdown	Versus	Medium	20	Kill 100 enemies in Ranked Matches with Melee
Is it a Spider?	Versus	Medium	20	Kill 100 enemies in Ranked Matches with Grenade Tag
The Money Shot	Versus	Medium	20	Kill 100 enemies in Ranked Matches with a Head Shot

VERSUS SUCCESS

VERSUS ACHIEVEMENTS	TYPE	DIFFICULTY	POINTS	DESCRIPTION
Always Remember Your First	Versus	Easy	10	Finish playing a Versus Ranked Match
Don't Hate the Player	Versus	Easy	10	Finish with the highest points in a Ranked Match
Mix it Up	Versus	Medium	20	Win a Ranked Match in every Versus game type
Can't Touch Us	Versus	Medium	20	Win 10 Ranked Matches without losing a Round
Around the World	Versus	Hard	30	Win a Ranked Match on every Versus map
Seriously...(unlocks Gamer Pic)	Versus	Hard	50	Kill 10,000 people in Versus Ranked Match total

LEGO STAR WARS II: THE ORIGINAL TRILOGY

ACHIEVEMENTS

NAME	GOAL/REQUIREMENT	POINT VALUE
Secret Plans Level Complete	Complete the first level of the game—Secret Plans.	20
Episode IV Complete	Complete all six levels in this Episode in Story Mode.	50
Episode V Complete	Complete all six levels in this Episode in Story Mode.	50
Episode VI Complete	Complete all six levels in this Episode in Story Mode.	50
LEGO City Complete	Complete the LEGO City level.	50
Bounty Hunter Missions Complete	Complete all of the 10 Bounty Hunter Missions.	40
Game 20% Complete	Complete 20% of the game.	20
Game 40% Complete	Complete 40% of the game.	40
Game 60% Complete	Complete 60% of the game.	60
Game 80% Complete	Complete 80% of the game.	80
Game 100% Complete	Complete everything in the game!	180
Secret Plans—Undefeated	Complete this level without dying. No Extras should be turned on.	20
Jundland Wastes—Undefeated.	Complete this level without dying. No Extras should be turned on.	20
Mos Eisley—Undefeated.	Complete this level without dying. No Extras should be turned on.	20
Rescue the Princess—Undefeated	Complete this level without dying. No Extras should be turned on.	20
Death Star Escape—Undefeated	Complete this level without dying. No Extras should be turned on.	20
Rebel Attack—Undefeated	Complete this level without dying. No Extras should be turned on.	20
Hoth Battle—Undefeated	Complete this level without dying. No Extras should be turned on.	20

NAME	GOAL/REQUIREMENT	POINT VALUE
Echo Base—Undefeated	Complete this level without dying. No Extras should be turned on.	20
Facon Flight—Undefeated	Complete this level without dying. No Extras should be turned on.	20
Dagobah—Undefeated	Complete this level without dying. No Extras should be turned on.	20
Cloud City Trap—Undefeated	Complete this level without dying. No Extras should be turned on.	20
Bespin—Undefeated	Complete this level without dying. No Extras should be turned on.	20
Jabba's Palace—Undefeated	Complete this level without dying. No Extras should be turned on.	20
Carkoon—Undefeated.	Complete this level without dying. No Extras should be turned on.	20
Speeder Showdown—Undefeated	Complete this level without dying. No Extras should be turned on.	20
Endor—Undefeated.	Complete this level without dying. No Extras should be turned on.	20
Jedi Destiny—Undefeated.	Complete this level without dying. No Extras should be turned on.	20
Death Star II—Undefeated	Complete this level without dying. No Extras should be turned on	20

MARVEL ULTIMATE ALLIANCE

ACHIEVEMENTS

NAME	GOAL/REQUIREMENT	POINT VALUE
Mandarin's Downfall	The evil Mandarin was crushed by the forces of good.	45
Mephisto's Defeat	Mephisto was struck down.	45
The Trickster	Loki was defeated.	45
The Power Cosmic	The mighty Galactus was toppled.	45
Doomed Ending	Dr. Doom was utterly defeated.	45
Scarlet Swashbuckler	Daredevil was unlocked as a playable hero.	30
Wakandan Royalty	Black Panther was unlocked as a playable hero.	30
Agent of S.H.I.E.L.D.	Nick Fury was unlocked as a playable hero.	30
Surfs Up	Silver Surfer was unlocked as a playable hero.	30
Dragon Slayer	Fin Fang Foom was defeated.	15
Blue Screen of Death	M.O.D.O.K was defeated.	15
Underwater Battle	Tigershark and Attuma were defeated.	15
Swimming with the Fish	The mighty Kraken was defeated.	15
Defeated Grey Gargoyle	Grey Gargoyle was defeated.	15
Game Over	Arcade was defeated.	15
Son of a Devil	Blackheart was defeated.	15
The Executioner's Blade	Executioner and Enchantress were defeated.	15
Giant Relief	Ymir fell to the forces of good.	15
Warrior's Path	Gladiator was defeated.	15
Deathbird's Defeat	Deathbird was crushed.	15
Titanic Victory	Titannus was defeated.	15
Golden Age of Comics	Attained gold on all comic missions.	30
The Ultimate Super Hero	Defeated 4000 enemies.	50
Marvel Geek	Answered 15 trivia questions correctly.	5
Comic God	Answered 20 trivia questions correctly in a row.	15

NAME	GOAL/REQUIREMENT	POINT VALUE
Marvel Master	Answered 150 trivia questions correctly.	10
I have a friend	Completed a level with at least 1 other player.	5
Super Hero Team	Completed 25 levels with at least 1 other player.	15
Excelsior!	Beat Marvel: Ultimate Alliance in Hard Mode.	50
Fall to Death	Threw 5 enemies off a ledge.	10
Scared of Heights	Threw 50 enemies off a ledge	20
Widowmaker	Threw 500 enemies off a ledge.	30
Battle Tested	Won 1 Arcade mode level.	5
Battle Hardened	Won 20 Arcade mode levels.	15
Mad Skillz	Won 3 Arcade mode levels consecutively.	10
Teh Mast3r	Won 15 Arcade mode levels consecutively.	25
The Destroyer	Won 100 Arcade mode (Competitive) games.	25
Teamwork	Completed 1 level with 3 other players.	5
Ultimate Team Alliance	Completed 25 levels with 3 other players.	15
Fledging superhero	Defeated 10 enemies.	5
Legendary Superhero	Defeated 100 enemies.	15
Pugilist	Performed 5 finishing moves.	5
Melee Master	Performed 50 finishing moves.	15
Touch of Death	Performed 200 finishing moves.	30
Good Samaritan	Completed Skrull Cityscape level without defeating a single enemy.	20
Dressed for Success	Unlocked ALL outfits for EVERY hero.	45

THE OUTFIT

MEDAL OPPORTUNITIES—SINGLE-PLAYER

NAME	GOAL/REQUIREMENT	POINT VALUE
Air Defense	Shoot down at least 5 Nazi Stukas (Mission 1: Beyond the Beachhead).	15
Combat Aid	Protect at least five of the Allied paratroopers (Mission 1: Beyond the Beachhead).	10
Troop Car Destroyed	Destroy the Axis troop car (Mission 2: Into the Fray).	15
Searchlights Destroyed	Destroy all Nazi spotlights in the mission (Mission 2: Into the Fray).	10
Destroy the Nazi convoy	Convoy Ambush (Mission 3: Yo Adrienne).	20
Propaganda Destroyed	Destroy the Nazi propaganda statues (Mission 3: Yo Adrienne).	15
Tank Crew Rescue	Protect the Allied tank crew (Mission 4: Mortain).	15
Reinforcement Rescue	Protect the Allied paratroops from Nazi Stukas (Mission 4: Mortain).	20
Allied Rescue	Protect the Allied soldiers at the armory (Mission 5: Assault on Rochereau).	15
Panther Tank Capture	Secure the Nazi Panther (Mission 5: Assault on Rochereau; must locate Allied engineers to activate this medal).	20
Transport Ship Destruction	Destroy the offshore transports (Mission 6: See the Light).	20
Submarine Destruction	Destroy the Nazi submarines (Mission 6: See the Light).	20
Train Destroyed	Destroy the Armored train (Mission 7: Sole Survivors).	25

NAME	GOAL/REQUIREMENT	POINT VALUE
POW Savior	Protect the Wehrmacht POWs (Mission 7: Sole Survivors).	25
Fuel Depot Destroyed	Destroy the Nazi fuel barrels (Mission 8: Vengeance).	20
Allied Savior	Protect the Allied emplacements from Nazi Panzers/Panther (Mission 8: Vengeance).	20
Howitzer Defense	Protect the Allied emplacements from Nazi Stukas (Mission 9: Crossing Over).	20
Tank Column Destroyed	Destroy Nazi tank column (Mission 9: Crossing Over).	20
Prototype Jet Destroyed	Destroy Nazi prototype jet (Mission 10: Iron Zeppelin).	25
V1 Rockets Destroyed	Destroy the Nazi V1 rockets (Mission 10: Iron Zeppelin).	20
AA Guns Destroyed	Destroy all the Nazi Flak guns (Mission 11: The Gates of Hell).	20
Bunker Defense	Protect the Wehrmacht bunker from Nazi SS (Mission 11: The Gates of Hell).	25
Radar Tower Destroyed	Destroy the Nazi radar tower (Mission 12: The Fortress).	20
Airfield Saved	Defeat the Nazi counterattack at the airfield (Mission 12: The Fortress).	25
Game Completion Award	Complete the Single-Player Campaign.	30

MEDAL OPPORTUNITIES—MULTIPLAYER

NAME	GOAL/REQUIREMENT	POINT VALUE
Wounded in Action	Awarded for an average lifetime shorter than 30 seconds in Ranked Quick Match games.	20
Master of Capturing	Must capture more than 10 objectives in a single Ranked Quick Match game.	20
Great Score	Must achieve a score greater than 350 in a single Ranked Quick Match game.	30
Lightning Victory	Must achieve victory in less than two minutes in any Ranked Quick Match game.	30
Prisoner of War	Awarded when your total number of losses exceeds 200 in Ranked Quick Match games.	20
Victories Keep Piling Up	Awarded for winning 500 Ranked Quick Match games.	75
Persistence Counts	Must die 1000 times in Ranked Quick Match games.	20
Infantry Killer	Achieve 1000 infantry kills in Ranked Quick Match games.	25
Vehicle Killer	Get 200 vehicle kills in Ranked Quick Match games.	25
Emplacement Killer	Attain 250 emplacement kills in Ranked Quick Match games.	25
Great Shooting	Achieve accuracy greater than 40% in a single Ranked Quick Match game.	25
Marksman	Attain accuracy greater than 25% over your Ranked Quick Match game career.	50
Feared	Achieve more than 15 enemy player kills in a single Ranked Quick Match game.	25
Clear Winner	Awarded for victories totaling 1000 Command Points in Ranked Quick Match games.	35
Guns Blazing	Complete an average score of over 18 per minute of play in Ranked Quick Match games.	45
Focused Fire	Must kill enemy players at a rate of 1.7 or greater per minute of play in Ranked Quick Match games.	40

PHANTASY STAR UNIVERSE

ACHIEVEMENTS

NAME	GOAL/REQUIREMENT	POINT VALUE
De Ragan Slayer	Defeat the Chapter 3 boss.	100
Onmagoug Slayer	Defeat the Chapter 5 boss.	100
Adahna Degahna Slayer	Defeat the Chapter 7 boss.	100
De Ragnus Slayer	Defeat the Chapter 8 boss.	100
Magas Maggahna Slayer	Defeat the Chapter 9 boss.	100
Dimmagolus Slayer	Defeat the Chapter 11 boss.	100
Dulk Fakis Slayer	Defeat the Chapter 12 boss.	200
Dulk Fakis 2 Slayer	Defeat the last boss	200

PREY

ACHIEVEMENTS

NAME	GOAL/REQUIREMENT	POINT VALUE
1: Last Call	Last Call completed.	10
2: Escape Velocity	Escape Velocity completed.	10
3:	Downward Spiral completed.	10
4: Rites of Passage	Rites of Passage completed.	10
5: Second Chances	Second Chances completed.	15
6: All Fall Down	All Fall Down completed.	15
7: Crash Landing	Crash Landing completed.	15
8: Sacrifices	Sacrifices completed.	20
9: There Are Others	There Are Others completed.	20
10: Guiding Fires	Guiding Fires completed.	20
11: The Old Tribes	The Old Tribes completed.	25
12: Hidden Agenda	Hidden Agenda completed.	25
13: Jen	Jen completed.	25
14: The Dark Harvest	The Dark Harvester completed.	30
15: Following Her	Following Her completed.	30
16: The Complex	The Complex completed.	30
17: Ascent	Ascent completed.	40
18: Center of Gravity	Center of Gravity completed	40
19:	Resolutions completed.	40
20: Oath of Vengeance	Oath of Vengeance completed.	50
21: Facing the Enemy	Facing the Enemy completed.	50
22: Mother's Embrace	Mother's Embrace finished.	60
Saviour	Completed game on Normal difficulty.	65
Galactic Hero	Completed game on Cherokee difficulty.	65
Young Blood	Reached 50 kills total in Deathmatch.	10
Brave Star	Reached 125 kills total in Deathmatch.	15
Ultimate Warrior	Reached 500 kills total in Deathmatch.	50
Team member	Reached 50 kills total in team Deathmatch.	10
Team player	Reached 125 kills total in team Deathmatch.	15
Team leader	Reached 250 kills total in team Deathmatch.	20
Sharpshooter	Reached 25 Sniper kills in Deathmatch and Team Deathmatch.	10
Invisible Assassin	Reached 25 kills in Deathmatch and Team Deathmatch using spirit form.	10
Mechanic	Reached 25 kills in Deathmatch and Team Deathmatch using the wrench.	10
Rifle Ranger	Reached 25 kills in Deathmatch and Team Deathmatch using the rifle.	10

NAME	GOAL/REQUIREMENT	POINT VALUE
Crawler King	Reached 25 kills in Deathmatch and Team Deathmatch using Crawler grenades.	10
Machine Gun Tommy	Reached 25 kills in Deathmatch and Team Deathmatch using the Auto-Cannon.	10
Launcher Lord	Reached 25 kills in Deathmatch and Team Deathmatch using the Crawler Launcher.	10
Soul Sucker	Reached 25 kills in Deathmatch and Team Deathmatch using the Leech Gun.	10
Toxic Overlord	Reached 25 kills in Deathmatch and Team Deathmatch using the Acid Sprayer.	10
Rank 1	Won a ranked match.	20
Ten Ranked Matches	Play ten ranked matches.	20
Black Jack	$250 won on Black Jack.	10
Poker Face	$250 won on Draw Poker.	10
Retro Gamer	Scored over 15,000 on Runeman.	10

SAINTS ROW

ACHIEVEMENTS

NAME	GOAL/REQUIREMENT	POINT VALUE
Colombian Made	Take over Los Carnales territory.	40
Regicide	Take over Vice Kings territory.	40
Road Warrior	Take over Westside Rollerz territory.	40
Ruler of Stilwater	Help the 3rd Streets Saints take over Stilwater.	160
Thug	Reach a TrueSkill rank of Thug in any multiplayer mode.	10
Killa	Reach a TrueSkill rank of Killa in any multiplayer mode.	20
Gangsta	Reach a TrueSkill rank of Gangster in any multiplayer mode.	40
Kingpin	Reach a TrueSkill rank of Kingpin in any multiplayer mode.	80
Penny Pincher	Earn $1,000,000 in the city of Stilwater.	10
Grifter	Earn $200,000 in Insurance Fraud.	10
Shopaholic	Acquire 100 clothing and jewelry items for your single-player wardrobe.	10
Coupon Clipper	Purchase 100 clothing and jewelry items for your multiplayer wardrobe.	10
Leader of the Pack	Acquire all 7 Homies.	10
Getting Up	Tag all tag locations hidden throughout Stilwater.	10
Grease Monkey	Own a total of 50 cars.	10
Racket Lord	Complete all activities in Stilwater.	160
Contract Killer	Complete all of the Hitman locations.	10
Demo Demon	Complete all levels of Demolition Derby.	10
Fast and Furious	Complete all of the Hijacking locations and levels.	10
Fluffer	Complete all of the Escort locations and levels.	10
Pimp	Complete all of the Snatch locations and levels.	10
Pusher	Complete all of the Drug Trafficking locations and levels.	10
Scavenger	Complete all of the Chop Shop locations.	10
Tuner	Complete all of the Racing locations and levels.	10

NAME	GOAL/REQUIREMENT	POINT VALUE
Vandal	Complete all of the Mayhem locations and levels.	10
Bulletproof	Complete Co-op level Turbulence at the highest difficulty level.	10
Errand Boy	Complete Co-op level Mob Rule at the highest difficulty level.	10
Canonized	Join the 3rd Street Saints.	10
Reclamationist	Retake Saints Row.	10
Audiophile	Collected all 60 CDs hidden throughout Stilwater.	10
Dominator	Won 10 ranked matches in a row.	10
Jumped the Shark	Withdrew a total of $200,000 from the Loan Office.	10
Professional Thief	Stole 30 boxes and delivered them successfully.	10
Scourge of the Air	Destroyed 50 helicopters.	10
Stilwater PD Award	Killed 50 Stilwater residents with only melee attacks.	10
Addicted to tha Row	Played Saints Row for a total of 20 hours.	20
Chain Gang	Dropped off a total of 500 chains in the Big Ass Chains multiplayer mode in ranked matches.	20
Marathon Runner	Traveled 26.2 miles on foot	20
Negotiator	Took 50 Hostages.	20
Tourist	Drove 500 miles in the city of Stilwater.	20
Pimp Killer	Killed the Pimp in Protect Tha Pimp 50 times in ranked matches.	20
Clocktower Camper	Head shot and killed a total of 100 enemies with a Sniper Rifle in ranked matches.	10
Xzibitionist	Got your team car to level 4 in the Blinged Out Ride mode a total of 50 times in ranked matches.	20

SONIC THE HEDGEHOG

ACHIEVEMENTS

NAME	GOAL/REQUIREMENT	POINT VALUE
Sonic Episode: Cleared	Clear Sonic Episode!	30
Shadow Episode: Cleared	Clear Shadow Episode!	30
Silver Episode: Cleared	Clear Silver Episode!	30
One to Reach the End	End the last hidden story.	20
Sonic Episode: Completed	Clear unlocked Sonic difficult level mission.	40
Shadow Episode: Completed	Clear unlocked Shadow difficult level mission.	40
Silver Episode: Completed	Clear unlocked Silver difficult level mission.	40
Shadow Episode: Mastered	Clear all unlocked Shadow ACT Missions with Rank S.	60
Sonic Episode: Mastered	Clear all unlocked Sonic ACT Missions with Rank S.	60
Silver Episode: Mastered	Clear all unlocked Silver ACT Missions with Rank S.	60
Nights of Kronos	Unlock the complete ending to the last hidden story.	60
Legend of Soleanna	Overcome all trials and accomplish a great feat.	100
Silver Medalist	Collect all the Silver Medals scattered around Soleanna...	50

NAME	GOAL/REQUIREMENT	POINT VALUE
Gold Medalist	Collect all the Soleanna legendary Gold Medals...	50
Blue Phantom	Obtain the all moves.	20
Ultimate Life Form	Resurrect the ultimate power from the lost memory.	20
Psychic Soldier	Obtain all the power to save the future world.	20
Soleanna's Hero	Solve all Soleannans' problems.	40
Elite Agent	Complete all the tasks given as agent.	40
Silver The Liberator	Solve all the mysteries in Soleanna.	40
Soleanna's blue wind	Solve all the problems swiftly.	50
Dark Hero	Meet all the requests with magnificent skill.	50
Silver the Savior	Reveal all the secrets with your ultimate power.	50

SUPERMAN RETURNS

ACHIEVEMENTS

NAME	GOAL/REQUIREMENT	POINT VALUE
Hero of Metropolis	Complete All Metro Events and Mini-Games	200
Armageddon Averted	Complete Level 01: Meteor Storm	30
Mr. What's-his-name	Complete All Mini-Games	50
You Am Bizarro!	Complete The Bizarro Mini-Game	20
Super Sonic	Finished All Fast Flyer Mini-Games	20
Mr. Whiskers	Find All Kittens	50
Souped-Up Superman	Obtain All 15 Power-Ups	30
Frequent Flyer	Travel For 10,000 Miles	30
Roadside Assistance	Pick Up 100 Cars Throughout The Game	30
The Greatest Day	Play A Total Of 12 Hours	30
Heavy Lifting	Lift 10,000 Tons Throughout The Game	30
Warworld	Visited and Dominated Warworld	50
Twisted	Saved Metropolis from the rampaging tornado	100
The Mongul Hordes	Vanquished Mongul once again	100
Me aM savE yOU!	By you is Bizarro not undefeated!	100
Metallo Mastered	Stopped Metallo in the name of justice	100
Versatile Fighter	Perform 99 fighting combos.	30
Not that Super	Entered a cheat code in a desperate plea for help.	0

TOMB RAIDER: LEGEND

ACHIEVEMENTS

NAME	GOAL/REQUIREMENT	POINT VALUE
Collected 15 Silver Rewards	Collected 15 Silver Rewards.	25
Collected 30 Silver Rewards	Collected 30 Silver Rewards.	35
Collected 35 Bronze Rewards	Collected 35 Bronze Rewards.	15
Collected 5 Bronze Rewards	Collected 5 Bronze Rewards.	10
Collected 5 Gold Rewards	Collected 5 Gold Rewards.	50
Collected 60 Bronze Rewards	Collected 60 Bronze Rewards.	20
Complete the Adventure	Complete the Tomb Raider: Legend adventure at Explorer or Adventurer difficulty.	125

NAME	GOAL/REQUIREMENT	POINT VALUE
Complete the Hard Adventure	Complete the Tomb Raider: Legend adventure with the difficulty level set to "Tomb Raider."	175
Completed All Time Trials	Complete all levels while in time trial mode.	50
Completed Bolivia	Complete the level "Bolivia—Tiwanaku."	50
Completed Bolivia Time Trial	Complete the Bolivia Level while in Time Trial mode.	10
Completed England	Complete the level "England—King Arthur's Tomb?"	75
Completed England Time Trial	Complete the England Level while in Time Trial mode.	10
Completed Ghana	Complete the level "Ghana—Pursuing James Rutland."	50
Completed Ghana Time Trial	Complete the Ghana Level while in Time Trial mode.	10
Completed Kazakhstan	Complete the level "Kazakhstan—Project Carbonek."	75
Completed Kazakhstan Time Trial	Complete the Kazakhstan Level while in Time Trial mode.	10
Completed Nepal	Complete the level "Nepal—The Ghalali Key."	75
Completed Nepal Time Trial	Complete the Nepal Level while in Time Trial mode.	10
Completed Peru	Complete the level "Peru—Return to Paraiso."	50
Completed Peru Time Trial	Complete the Peru Level while in Time Trial mode.	10
Completed Tokyo	Complete the Level "Tokyo—Meeting with Takamoto."	50
Completed Tokyo Time Trial	Complete the Tokyo Level while in Time Trial mode	10

TONY HAWK'S PROJECT 8

ACHIEVEMENTS

NAME	GOAL/REQUIREMENT	POINT VALUE
Training Complete	You completed the training, go put what you learned into practice.	10
Outta the Houses	You escaped the suburban life, explore the world.	10
School Unlocked	Unlocked the School.	10
Slums Unlocked	Unlocked the Slums.	10
Skate Park Unlocked	You made your way to the skate park. Enjoy yourself.	10
Funpark Unlocked	Unlocked the Funpark.	10
Factory Unlocked	Go shred the factory, you deserve it.	10
First Sick Goal	Congratulations, you completed a goal at Sick difficulty	5
All Pro Challenges Completed	You stepped up to the challenge. You did everything the pro's challenged you to do.	20
Sick Chalk Challenges	Incredible, you beat all the goals at Sick difficulty	30
Sick Classic Goals	All classic goals at Sick? That's amazing.	30
Hit 50% of the Gaps	Wow! 50 percent of the gaps found… Keep going you're halfway there.	20
Hit All of the Gaps	You've skated the world and found every gap. Congratulations!	35

NAME	GOAL/REQUIREMENT	POINT VALUE
Scored Over 1,000,000 Points!	That's a nice highs core run, but you can do better right?	10
Nice Combo!	Well done, you landed over a 500,000 point combo.	20
Played Xbox Live	Play an online game.	10
50 games Online	Finish 50 games online.	15
100 games Online	Finish 100 games online.	20
You Made It into Project 8	Congratulations you cracked the top 8, can you get higher?	50
You Made It to Spot 4!	Congratulations you cracked the top 4, can you get to number 1?	75
Ranked Number 1!	You did it. You are the number one skater on Project 8.	100
Secret Area Found	You found your first secret area. Don't tell anyone.	5
Manual Master	You've manualed for 140,000 feet!	20
Hang Time	14,000 seconds of air time.	20
The Daily Grind	You've managed to grind for 140,000 total feet	20
Beat a Developer	Win a skate session against a member of the Project 8 development team, or someone who already has.	50
Suburbia Classic Beaten at Sick	Amazing. You got Sick on the Suburbia classic goal.	15
Main St Classic Beaten at Sick	Amazing. You got Sick on the Main St classic goal.	15
Capitol Classic Beaten at Sick	Capitol Classic beaten at Sick.	15
School Classic Beaten at Sick	Amazing. You got Sick on the School classic goal.	15
Slums Classic Beaten at Sick	Amazing. You got Sick on the Slums classic goal.	15
Skate Classic Beaten at Sick	Amazing. You got Sick on the Skate Park classic goal.	15
Fun Park Classic Beaten at Sick	Amazing. You got Sick on the Fun Park classic goal.	15
Factory Classic Beaten at Sick	Amazing. You got Sick on the Factory classic goal.	15
Full Stats	You got every stat maxed. How long did that take you?	50
Mullen Pro Challenge	Find Rodney and beat his challenge.	10
Vallely Pro Challenge	Find Mike V and beat his challenge.	10
Song Pro Challenge	Find Daewon and beat his challenge.	10
Burnquist Pro Challenge	Find Bob and beat his challenge.	10
Sheckler Pro Challenge	Find Ryan and beat his challenge.	10
Margera Pro Challenge	Find Bam and beat his challenge.	10
Nyjah & Lyn-Z Pro Challenge	Find Nyjah and Lyn-Z and beat their challenge.	10
Williams & Dollin Pro Challenge	Find Stevie and Dustin and beat their challenge.	10
P-Rod Pro Challenge	Find P-Rod and beat his challenge.	10
Shhhh it's a secret	You found all the secret areas, nice going Sherlock.	25
That combo was sick!	Wow you landed a combo over 5,000,000 points.	35
Sick Highscore Run	That's a huge high score.	20
Impressing the locals	Congratulations, you got 1000 Stokens.	25
Break 15 bones in one bail	Man that hurt.	10

VIVA PIÑATA

ACHIEVEMENTS

NAME	GOAL/REQUIREMENT	POINT VALUE
Challenger	Successfully completed 5 Factory requests.	20
Master Challenger	Successfully completed 20 Factory requests.	20
Romancer	Become Master Romancer for 5 species.	20
Master Romancer	Become Master Romancer for 20 species.	20
Collector	Made 5 species resident.	20
Master Collector	Made 50 species resident.	20
Longevity	Played the game for 10 hours (real time).	20
Garden Value	Garden worth 25,000 chocolate coins.	20
Garden Value Master	Garden worth 100,000 chocolate coins.	20
Piñata Value	One Piñata worth 5,000 chocolate coins.	20
Piñata Value Master	One Piñata worth 10,000 chocolate coins.	20
Green Fingers	Grown 5 plants to maturity.	20
Master Green Fingers	Grown 25 plants to maturity.	20
Wealthy	Player has 25,000 chocolate coins.	20
Label Designer	Made a Custom Label.	20
Piñata Name Caller	Named a Piñata.	20
Helper Name Caller	Named a Helper.	20
Talent	Player has reached Level 10.	20
Master Talent	Player has reached Level 50.	20
Wealth Master	Player has 100,000 chocolate coins.	20
Land Owner	Garden Size increased Once.	20
Sprinkling	Employed a sprinkling.	20
Gatherling	Employed a Gatherling.	20
Super Shovel	All the Shovel Head upgrades.	20
Weedling	Employed a Weedling.	20
Harvester	Collected produce from a Buzzlegum, Moozipan, or Goobaa.	20
Watchling	Employed a Watchling.	20
Generosity	Player turned the Beggar into a Trader.	20
Sour Tower	Tower of Sour has 2 pieces.	20
Taffly Fertilizer	Player has made fertilizer with the Taffly.	20
Evolver	Evolved 2 species.	20
Master Land Owner	Garden size at maximum.	20
Variants	Made 5 variant Piñatas.	20
Pigxie Prize	Cross romancing a Swanana and a Rashberry.	20
Shovel Strength	All the Shovel Handle upgrades.	20
Watering Can Do	All the Watering Can upgrades.	20
Diggerling	Employed a Diggerling.	20
Master Sour Tower	Tower of Sour has 6 pieces.	20
Cluckles Hatches Egg	Player has hatched an egg using the Cluckles.	20
Horticulturist	Full bonus growth for 5 plants.	20
Macaracoon Gift	Player has been brought a Romance Sweet by a Macaracoon.	20
Variants Master	Made 20 variant Pinatas	20
Crowla Delay	Player has distracted Dastardos with the Crowla.	20
Longevity Master	Played the game for 50 hours (real time).	20
Sherbat Dance	Player has distracted Dastardos with the Sherbat.	20

NAME	GOAL/REQUIREMENT	POINT VALUE
Master Evolver	Evolved 8 species.	20
Cocoadile Tears	Player has attained full bonus growth for a plant using the Cocodile Tears.	20
Master Horticulturist	Full bonus growth for 25 plants.	20
Mallowolf Howl	Player has used the Mallowolf to scare off Ruffians.	20
Chewnicorn Healing	Player has healed a Piñata with the Chewnicorn's power.	20

WWE SMACKDOWN VS. RAW 2007

ACHIEVEMENTS

NAME	GOAL/REQUIREMENT	POINT VALUE
Season Mode Jobber	Complete Season Mode on Easy or Normal difficulty.	50
Season Mode Veteran	Complete Season Mode on Hard difficulty.	100
Season Mode Legend	Complete Season Mode on Legend difficulty.	100
New Hire	Complete one full year of General Manager mode.	50
Employee of the year	Win the General Manager of the year trophy.	100
Royal Rumble Rookie	Win a 10 Man Exhibition Royal Rumble as the #1 entrant on any difficulty setting.	10
Royal Rumble Jobber	Win a 15 Man Exhibition Royal Rumble as the #1 entrant on any difficulty.	10
Royal Rumble Veteran	Win a 20 Man Exhibition Royal Rumble as the #1 entrant on Hard difficulty.	20
Royal Rumble Pro	Win a 25 Man Exhibition Royal Rumble as the #1 entrant on Hard difficulty.	20
Royal Rumble Legend	Win a 30 Man Exhibition Royal Rumble as the #1 entrant on Legend difficulty.	20
In Ring Journeyman	Win at least one match using every Superstar on the roster on any difficulty setting.	10
In Ring Technician	Defeat every Superstar on the roster by pin or submission at least once on Hard difficulty.	10
Complete Domination!	Defeat every Superstar on the roster at least once on Legend difficulty.	20
Championship Gold!	Unlock every WWE Championship title.	30
Those Who Paved The Way	Unlock every WWE Legend.	20
Way Past Jobber	Win 50 matches on any difficulty setting.	20
Seasoned Vet	Win 100 matches on any difficulty setting.	50
Online Rising Star	Win 20 matches online.	10
Online Veteran	Win 50 matches online.	30
Online Blue Chipper	Win 20 consecutive online matches.	40
Certified Online Superstar	Win 50 consecutive online matches.	70
A Fighting Online Champion	Defend your created Championship 20 times online.	60
Let It Reign!	Defend your created Championship 50 times online.	100
With Friends Like These…	Create an original stable of Superstars in Create-A-Stable mode.	5
Crown Us The Champ!	Create a Tag Team Championship in Create-A-Championship mode.	10

NAME	GOAL/REQUIREMENT	POINT VALUE
Self Anointed Champion	Create a singles Championship in Create-A-Championship mode.	10
Curtain Call	Create an original entrance in Create-An-Entrance mode.	5
Let The Creative Juices Flow	Create one original Superstar using the Create-A-Superstar mode.	5
Mr. PPV	Create an original PPV event in Create-A-PPV mode.	5

X-MEN: THE OFFICIAL GAME

ACHIEVEMENTS

NAME	GOAL/REQUIREMENT	POINT VALUE
Danger Room	This Danger Room Challenge for Iceman is unlocked by completing Act 1 of the game.	20
Danger Room	This Danger Room Challenge for Nightcrawler is unlocked by completing Act 2 of the game.	20
Danger Room	This Danger Room Challenge for Wolverine is unlocked by completing Act 3 of the game.	30
Xavier Institute	This Achievement is awarded when Nightcrawler's training mission is completed.	0
Xavier Institute	This Achievement is awarded when Iceman's training mission is completed.	0
Xavier Institute	This Achievement is awarded when Wolverine's training mission is completed.	0
Evolution	This Achievement is awarded when Iceman has been upgraded with all available mutations.	125
Evolution	This Achievement is awarded when Nightcrawler has been upgraded with all available mutations.	125
Evolution	This Achievement is awarded when Wolverine has been upgraded with all available mutations.	120
Champion	This Achievement is awarded to those who collect all Sentinel Tech as Iceman.	70
Champion	This Achievement is awarded to those who collect all Sentinel Tech as Nightcrawler.	70
Champion	This Achievement is awarded to those who collect all Sentinel Tech as Wolverine.	110
Secret Identity	This Achievement is awarded to those who collect all Weapon X Files as Iceman.	70
Secret Identity	This Achievement is awarded to those who collect all Weapon X Files as Nightcrawler.	80
Secret Identity	This Achievement is awarded to those who collect all Weapon X Files as Wolverine.	110
X-Men	This Achievement is awarded when the player profile accumulates 950 achievement score.	50

XBOX®

Games List

50 CENT: BULLETPROOF

BULLETPROOF CHEAT
Pause the game and select Codes from the Options menu. Enter ny'sfinestyo to become invincible.

ALL WEAPONS
Pause the game and select Codes from the Options menu. Enter gotthemrachets.

INFINITE AMMO
Pause the game and select Codes from the Options menu. Enter grizzspecial.

MIKE MODE
Pause the game and select Codes from the Options menu. Enter the hub is broken to receive better guns.

BLOODHOUND COUNTERKILL
Pause the game and select Codes from the Options menu. Enter gunrunner.

EMPTY'N CLIPS COUNTERKILL
Pause the game and select Codes from the Options menu. Enter workout.

GUILLOTINE COUNTERKILL
Pause the game and select Codes from the Options menu. Enter gettingdropped.

G'D UP COUNTERKILL
Pause the game and select Codes from the Options menu. Enter gooddieyoung.

WANKSTA COUNTERKILL
Pause the game and select Codes from the Options menu. Enter aintgotnothin.

TRACK ACTION 26
Pause the game and select Codes from the Options menu. Enter orangejuice.

ALL MUSIC
Pause the game and select Codes from the Options menu. Enter graballthat50.

BULLETPROOF EXCLUSIVES
Pause the game and select Codes from the Options menu. Enter 50bpexclusives. This unlocks the following music tracks: "I'm A Rider," "Maybe We Crazy," and "Pimp Pt2."

SO SEDUCTIVE SONG UNLOCKED
Pause the game and select Codes from the Options menu. Enter killa1.

ALL MOVIES
Pause the game and select Codes from the Options menu. Enter HookMeUp50.

SO SEDUCTIVE VIDEO
Pause the game and select Codes from the Options menu. Enter yayoshome.

MY BUDDY VIDEO
Pause the game and select Codes from the Options menu. Enter sayhellotomylittlefriend.

ADVENT RISING

CHEAT MENU
Pause the game and press Up, Up, Down, Down, Left, Right, Left, Right, White, Black, X.

AEON FLUX

BOMBER JACKET OUTFIT
Select Enter Cheat from the Extras menu and enter JULIET ALPHA CHARLIE KILO ECHO TANGO. Look for the outfit under Outfits in the Extras menu.

FAME OUTFIT
Select Enter Cheat from the Extras menu and enter GOLF ROMEO ALPHA YANKEE. Look for the outfit under Outfits in the Extras menu.

MULTIPLE OUTFITS
Select Enter Cheat from the Extras menu and enter CHARLIE LIMA OSCAR TANGO HOTEL ECHO SIERRA. Look for the outfits under Outfits in the Extras menu. The outfits include the following: Freya, Monican Freya, Hostess Judy, Una, and Fashion Una.

MRS. GOODCHILD OUTFIT
Select Enter Cheat from the Extras menu and enter WHISKEY HOTEL INDIA TANGO ECHO. Look for the outfit under Outfits in the Extras menu.

REVELATION OUTFIT
Select Enter Cheat from the Extras menu and enter ALPHA ROMEO MIKE SIERRA. Look for the outfit under Outfits in the Extras menu.

SEEDS OUTFIT
Select Enter Cheat from the Extras menu and enter MIKE OSCAR VICTOR INDIA ECHO. Look for the outfit under Outfits in the Extras menu.

WAR OUTFIT
Select Enter Cheat from the Extras menu and enter BRAVO LIMA UNIFORM ROMEO. Look for the outfit under Outfits in the Extras menu.

ALL REPLAY EPISODES
Select Enter Cheat from the Extras menu and enter BRAVO ALPHA YANKEE OSCAR UNIFORM. Then select Replay Episode from the Extras menu to view the episodes.

ALL SLIDESHOWS
Select Enter Cheat from the Extras menu and enter PAPA INDIA XRAY ECHO SIERRA. Then select Slideshows from the Extras menu to view the slideshows.

ACTION MOVIE CHEAT
Select Enter Cheat from the Extras menu and enter BRAVO ALPHA GOLF MIKE ALPHA NOVEMBER. Or, enter UNIFORM KILO GOLF ALPHA MIKE ECHO ROMEO. Pause the game and select Cheats to access the code.

GOD MODE
Select Enter Cheat from the Extras menu and enter TANGO ROMEO INDIA ROMEO OSCAR XRAY. Pause the game and select Cheats to access God Mode.

FREE FATALITIES CHEAT
Select Enter Cheat from the Extras menu and enter CHARLIE UNIFORM TANGO INDIA OSCAR NOVEMBER ECHO. Pause the game and select Cheats to access the code.

ONE-STRIKE KILLS
Select Enter Cheat from the Extras menu and enter BRAVO UNIFORM CHARLIE KILO FOXTROT SIERRA TANGO. Pause the game and select Cheats to access the code.

RESTORE HEALTH
Select Enter Cheat from the Extras menu and enter HOTEL ECHO ALPHA LIMA MIKE ECHO. Pause the game and select Cheats to access the code.

UNLIMITED AMMO
Select Enter Cheat from the Extras menu and enter FOXTROT UNIFORM GOLF. Pause the game and select Cheats to access the code.

UNLIMITED HEALTH
Select Enter Cheat from the Extras menu and enter CHARLIE LIMA OSCAR NOVEMBER ECHO. Pause the game and select Cheats to access the code.

UNLIMITED POWER STRIKES
Select Enter Cheat from the Extras menu and enter LIMA CHARLIE VICTOR GOLF. Pause the game and select Cheats to access the code.

ALIEN HOMINID

ALL LEVELS, MINI-GAMES, AND HATS
Select Player 1 Setup or Player 2 Setup and change the name to ROYGBIV.

HATS FOR 2-PLAYER GAME
Go to the Options menu and rename your alien one of the following:

ABE	Top Hat	#11
APRIL	Blond Wig	#4
BEHEMOTH	Red Cap	#24
CLETUS	Hunting Hat	#3
DANDY	Flower Petal Hat	#13
GOODMAN	Black Curly Hair	#7
GRRL	Flowers	#10
PRINCESS	Tiara	#12
SUPERFLY	Afro	#6
TOMFULP	Brown Messy Hair	#2

AND 1 STREETBALL

GLOBAL UNLOCK
Select Cheat Codes from the Options menu and enter B, B, A, A, X, Y, X, Y. This unlocks all Bonus Stuff

ALL CHARACTERS
Select Cheat Codes from the Options menu and enter B, X, X, Y, B, X, A, A.

ALL BREAKDOWNS
Select Cheat Codes from the Options menu and enter A, A, Y, X, X, B, Y, B.

CHATTERBOX UNLOCK
Select Cheat Codes from the Options menu and enter B, X, Y, X, B, A, X, B.

SIDE GAMES
Select Cheat Codes from the Options menu and enter Y, X, B, A, A, Y, Y, X.

DJ GREEN LANTERN
Select Cheat Codes from the Options menu and enter Y, Y, B, A, X, A, B, Y.

PLAY AS FLASH
Select Cheat Codes from the Options menu and enter B, A, A, Y, A, B, B, X.

PLAY AS SHANE
Select Cheat Codes from the Options menu and enter X, A, B, A, B, Y, B, A.

PLAY AS SKIP TO MY LOU
Select Cheat Codes from the Options menu and enter Y, A, Y, X, B, A, Y, X.

HAMILTONS
Select Cheat Codes from the Options menu and enter Y, B, X, X, B, Y, A, Y. This gives you $1,000,000.

ALWAYS ON FIRE
Select Cheat Codes from the Options menu and enter X, B, A, B, X, A, X, Y.

IBALL MOVES
Select Cheat Codes from the Options menu and enter A, B, B, A, X, Y, A, X.

LIKE WATER
Select Cheat Codes from the Options menu and enter X, A, Y, X, A, Y, B, B.

THE OG WAY
Select Cheat Codes from the Options menu and enter B, Y, X, X, Y, B, A, X.

SHOT TIMING TEXT
Select Cheat Codes from the Options menu and enter B, X, Y, Y, X, X, Y, B.

ARMED AND DANGEROUS

Pause the game, select Cheats from the Options menu and enter the following codes.

ANY LEVEL
Press Y, White, Black, L, A, R, R, Y.

INVINCIBLE
Press X (x3), R, A, L, L, Y.

GOD MODE
Press Y, A, B, X, B, A, A, L.

FILL HEALTH BAR
Press X, R, A, Y, Black, B, A, R.

FILL AMMO
Press Black, B, A, R, R, A, L, Black.

INFINITE AMMO
Press A, L, L, Black, B, White, L, L.

TOPSY TURVY
Press Y, A, B, B, A, B, White, White.

BIG HEADS
Press L, Black, B, White, White, B, Black, L.

BIG HANDS
Press R, White, X, L, White, R, R, Y.

BIG BOOTS
Press R, White, Y, A, L, B, White, X.

VIEW ANY MOVIE
Press A, Y, A, Y, Black, R, A, Y.

AVATAR: THE LAST AIRBENDER

ALL TREASURE MAPS
Select Code Entry from the Extras menu and enter 37437.

1 HIT DISHONOR
Select Code Entry from the Extras menu and enter 54641.

DOUBLE DAMAGE
Select Code Entry from the Extras menu and enter 34743.

UNLIMITED COPPER
Select Code Entry from the Extras menu and enter 23637.

UNLIMITED CHI
Select Code Entry from the Extras menu and enter 24463.

UNLIMITED HEALTH
Select Code Entry from the Extras menu and enter 94677.

NEVERENDING STEALTH
Select Code Entry from the Extras menu and enter 53467.

CHARACTER CONCEPT ART GALLERY
Select Code Entry from the Extras menu and enter 97831.

BACKYARD WRESTLING: DON'T TRY THIS AT HOME

UNLOCK EVERYTHING
At the Main menu, hold L and press A, X, Y, B, A, X, Y, B.

Create a wrestler with the following names to activate that cheat.

BIG HANDS
Enter okendall as a name.

BIG FEET
Enter tpiperi as a name.

BIG HEAD
Enter rtaylor as a name.

BIG HANDS, FEET AND HEAD
Enter tho as a name.

HALO
Enter jgintu as a name.

CARTOON CHARACTER
Enter pstapley as a name.

GHOST
Enter pjefferies as a name.

GREYSCALE
Enter ksimeonov as a name.

WIRE FRAME
Enter ewilliams as a name.

TOON BACKGROUNDS
Enter mstapley as a name.

TOON BACKGROUNDS
Enter mbilodeau as a name.

FIRST PERSON CAMERA
Enter edma as a name.

BALDUR'S GATE: DARK ALLIANCE II

INVULNERABILITY & LEVEL WARP
During a game, hold L + R + A + B + X + Y and press Start.

LEVEL 10
During a game, hold L + R + A + B + X + Y and press White Button.

THE BARD'S TALE

During a game, hold L + R and enter the following:

EVERYTHING ON (SILVER AND ADDERSTONES)
Up, Up, Down, Down, Left, Right, Left, Right

FULL HEALTH AND MANA
Left, Left, Right, Right, Up, Down, Up, Down

CAN'T BE HURT
Right, Left, Right, Left, Up, Down, Up, Down

CAN'T BE STRUCK
Left, Right, Left, Right, Up, Down, Up, Down

DAMAGE X100
Up, Down, Up, Down, Left, Right, Left, Right

BATTLEFIELD 2: MODERN COMBAT

ALL WEAPONS
During gameplay, hold Black + White and press Right, Right, Down, Up, Left, Left.

BLAZING ANGELS: SQUADRONS OF WWII

ALL MISSIONS, MEDALS, & PLANES
At the Main menu, hold Left Trigger + Right Trigger and press X, White, Black, Y, Y, Black, White, X.

GOD MODE
Pause the game, hold Left Trigger and press X, Y, Y, X. Release Left Trigger, hold Right Trigger and press Y, X, X, Y. Re-enter the code to disable it.

DAMAGE INCREASED
Pause the game, hold Left Trigger and press White, White, Black. Release Left Trigger, hold Right Trigger and press Black, Black, White. Re-enter the code to disable it.

BRATZ: FOREVER DIAMONDZ

1000 BLINGZ
While in the Bratz Office, use the Cheat computer to enter SIZZLN.

2000 BLINGZ
While in the Bratz Office, use the Cheat computer to enter FLAUNT.

PET TREATS
While in the Bratz Office, use the Cheat computer to enter TREATZ.

GIFT SET A
While in the Bratz Office, use the Cheat computer to enter STYLIN.

GIFT SET B
While in the Bratz Office, use the Cheat computer to enter SKATIN.

GIFT SET C
While in the Bratz Office, use the Cheat computer to enter JEWELZ.

GIFT SET E
While in the Bratz Office, use the Cheat computer to enter DIMNDZ.

CABELA'S DANGEROUS HUNTS 2

DOUBLE HEALTH
Select Codes and enter Eye, Bolt, Skull, Hand, Boot.

HEALTH REGENERATES FASTER
Select Codes and enter Skull, Eye, Boot, Bolt, Hand.

DOUBLE DAMAGE
Select Codes and enter Hand, Boot, Skull, Eye, Bolt.

INFINITE AMMO
Select Codes and enter Bolt, Hand, Eye, Boot, Skull.

CALL OF DUTY 2: BIG RED ONE

LEVEL SELECT
At the Chapter Select screen, hold Left Trigger + Right Trigger and press Up, Up, Down, Down, Left, Left, Right, Right, X, Right, X, Right, X.

CALL OF DUTY 3

ALL CHAPTERS AND BONUS CONTENT
At the Chapter Select screen, hold Back and press Right, Right, Left, Left, X, X.

CAPCOM CLASSICS COLLECTION

ALL LOCKS OPENED
At the Title screen, press Left Trigger, Right Trigger, Up on Right Thumbstick, Down on Right Thumbstick, Left Trigger, Right Trigger, Up on Left Thumbstick, Down on Left Thumbstick, Left Trigger, Right Trigger, Up, Down.

CARS

UNLOCK EVERYTHING
Select Cheat Codes from the Options menu and enter IF900HP.

ALL CHARACTERS
Select Cheat Codes from the Options menu and enter YAYCARS.

ALL CHARACTER SKINS
Select Cheat Codes from the Options menu and enter R4MONE.

ALL MINI-GAMES AND COURSES
Select Cheat Codes from the Options menu and enter MATTL66.

MATER'S COUNTDOWN CLEAN-UP MINI-GAME & MATER'S SPEEDY CIRCUIT
Select Cheat Codes from the Options menu and enter TRGTEXC.

FAST START
Select Cheat Codes from the Options menu and enter IMSPEED.

INFINITE BOOST
Select Cheat Codes from the Options menu and enter VROOOOM.

ART
Select Cheat Codes from the Options menu and enter CONC3PT.

VIDEOS
Select Cheat Codes from the Options menu and enter WATCHIT.

CHICKEN LITTLE

INVINCIBILITY
Select Cheat Codes from the Extras menu and enter Baseball, Baseball, Baseball, Shirt.

BIG FEET
Select Cheat Codes from the Extras menu and enter Hat, Glove, Glove, Hat.

BIG HAIR
Select Cheat Codes from the Extras menu and enter Baseball, Bat, Bat, Baseball.

BIG HEAD
Select Cheat Codes from the Extras menu and enter Hat, Helmet, Helmet, Hat.

PAPER PANTS
Select Cheat Codes from the Extras menu and enter Bat, Bat, Hat, Hat.

SUNGLASSES
Select Cheat Codes from the Extras menu and enter Glove, Glove, Helmet, Helmet.

UNDERWEAR
Select Cheat Codes from the Extras menu and enter Hat, Hat, Shirt, Shirt.

THE CHRONICLES OF NARNIA: THE LION, THE WITCH AND THE WARDROBE

ENABLE CHEATS
At the Title screen, press A and hold Left Trigger + Right Trigger and press Down, Down, Right, Up. The text should turn green when entered correctly. When this occurs, you can enter the following codes.

LEVEL SELECT
At the wardrobe, hold Left Trigger and press Up, Up, Right, Right, Up, Right, Down.

ALL BONUS LEVELS
At the Bonus Drawer, hold Left Trigger and press Down, Down, Right, Right, Down, Right, Up.

LEVEL SKIP
During gameplay, hold Left Trigger and press Down, Left, Down, Left, Down, Right, Down, Right, Up.

INVINCIBILITY
During gameplay, hold Left Trigger and press Down, Up, Down, Right, Right.

RESTORE HEALTH
During gameplay, hold Left Trigger and press Down, Left, Left, Right.

10,000 COINS
During gameplay, hold Left Trigger and press Down, Left, Right, Down, Down.

ALL ABILITIES
During gameplay, hold Left Trigger and press Down, Left, Left, Up.

FILL COMBO METER
During gameplay, hold Left Trigger and press Up, Up, Right, Up.

COLD FEAR

THE ART OF COLD FEAR
Check the bonus menu to find 13 art galleries, which are unlocked as you progress through the game. The conditions for each gallery are as follows:

GALLERY	CONDITION
The Origins	Find Lieutenant Lansing.
Clip	Reach the radio room onboard the "Spirit of the East."
Mutants	Free Anna.
The Whaler	Escort Anna to the radio room.
The Heroes	Find the unlocking code.
The ExoCels	Find the medicine cabinet on the oil rig.
Publicity	Find Anischenko's eye.
The Platform	Disable the magnetic jammer.
Creatures—1	Find the antidote.
Modeling	Find Dr. Kamsky's laptop.
Creatures—2	Find the C4 charges.
Characters	Find the chopper.
Final	Complete the game.

COLD WAR

INVULNERABILITY
Pause the game and press X, White, Y, Black, Left.

WIN CURRENT LEVEL
Pause the game and press X, White, Y, Black, X.

ALL ITEMS, GADGETS, & TECH POINTS
Pause the game and press X, White, Y, Black, Y.

COMMANDOS STRIKE FORCE

MISSION SELECT
Enter TRUCO as a profile name.

UNLIMITED AMMO
Pause the game, hold Left Trigger + Right Trigger and press A, Y, A, B, X, Y.

CONSTANTINE

BIG DEMON HEADS
Press Back to get to the Journal and press Black, Left, Right, Left, Left, Right, Left, Black.

BIG WEAPON MODE
Press Back to get to the Journal and press Left, X, X, X, Y, Y, Y.

INFINITE AMMO
Press Back to get to the Journal and press Left, Right, Left, X, Y, X, X, Y, Y, X, Y, X, X, Y, Y.

INFINITE SPELL SOUL ENERGY
Press Back to get to the Journal and press Left, Right, Right, Left, Left, Right, Right, Left, Y, Y.

RAPID FIRE SHOTGUN
Press Back to get to the Journal and press White, Left, Black, Left, Y, X, Y, X.

SHOOT LARGE FIREBALLS
Press Back to get to the Journal and press Y, Y, Y, Left, Right, Right, Left, Left, Right.

EXPLOSIVE HOLY BOMBS
Press Back to get to the Journal and press Right, Left, X, Y, X, Y, Left, Right.

CRASH TAG TEAM RACING

FASTER VEHICLES
At the Main menu, hold Left Trigger + Right Trigger and press B, B, Y, Y.

CHICKEN HEADS
At the Main menu, hold Left Trigger + Right Trigger and press A, B, B, X.

ONE-HIT KO
At the Main menu, hold Left Trigger + Right Trigger and press A, B, B, A.

JAPANESE CRASH
At the Main menu, hold Left Trigger + Right Trigger and press X, B, X, B.

DISABLE HUD
At the Main menu, hold Left Trigger + Right Trigger and press A, X, Y, B.

DRIVE A BLOCK VEHICLE
At the Main menu, hold Left Trigger + Right Trigger and press B, B, Y, X.

CRIMSON SKIES: HIGH ROAD TO REVENGE

GOD MODE
During a game, press Y, A, X, B, Black.

ALL PLANES
During a game, press Y, X, B, Y, Black.

$5,000
During a game, press A, Y, A, Y, Black.

SUPER PRIMARY WEAPON
During a game, press B, X, A, B, Black.

10 TOKENS
During a game, press X, B, X, B, Black.

ULTRA HARD DIFFICULTY
During a game, press X, B, A, X, Black.

DANCE DANCE REVOLUTION ULTRAMIX 2

ALL SONGS
With a controller in port four, select Credits from the Options menu. Then press Up, Up, Down, Down, Left, Right, Left, Right, B, A, Up, Up, Down, Down, Left, Right, Left, Right, A, B.

KONSENTO:03 AND MAID-ZUKIN CHARACTERS
With a controller in port four, select Dancers from the Options menu. Then press and hold X + Y for five seconds.

DANCE DANCE REVOLUTION ULTRAMIX 3

ALL SONGS
Select Credits from the Options menu and play the Credits mini-game, then press the opposite of what the game indicates. (For example, press Up when it says Down and so on. Or, if it says Left + Right, press Up + Down.) You'll hear applause when the code is entered correctly.

THE DA VINCI CODE

GOD MODE
Select Codes from the Options menu and enter VITRUVIAN MAN.

EXTRA HEALTH
Select Codes from the Options menu and enter SACRED FEMININE.

MISSION SELECT
Select Codes from the Options menu and enter CLOS LUCE 1519.

1-HIT FIST KILL
Select Codes from the Options menu and enter PHILLIPS EXETER.

ONE-HIT WEAPON KILL
Select Codes from the Options menu and enter ROYAL HOLLOWAY.

ALL VISUAL DATABASE
Select Codes from the Options menu and enter APOCRYPHA.

ALL VISUAL DATABASE & CONCEPT ART
Select Codes from the Options menu and enter ET IN ARCADIA EGO.

DEAD OR ALIVE 3

EIN AND RANDOM SELECT
Finish Story Mode with all 16 characters. Use Hayate in Survival Mode or Mode. Enter EIN as your name.

DEAD TO RIGHTS

CHAPTER SELECT
At the Main menu, press Up, Down, Up, Down, Left, Right, Left, Right, Y, X, X. Select Chapters at the bottom of the menu to select a destination.

DEF JAM: FIGHT FOR NY

Select Cheats from the Extras menu and enter the following.

100 REWARD POINTS
Enter NEWJACK, THESOURCE, CROOKLYN, DUCKETS, or GETSTUFF. You can only enter each code once.

UNLOCK SONG: "AFTERHOURS" BY NYNE
Enter LOYALTY.

UNLOCK SONG: "ANYTHING GOES" BY C-N-N
Enter MILITAIN.

UNLOCK SONG: "BUST" BY OUTKAST
Enter BIGBOI.

UNLOCK SONG: "BLINDSIDE" BY BAXTER
Enter CHOPPER.

UNLOCK SONG: "COMP" BY COMP
Enter CHOCOCITY.

UNLOCK SONG: "DRAGON HOUSE" BY CHIANG
Enter AKIRA.

UNLOCK SONG: "GET IT NOW" BY BLESS
Enter PLATINUMB.

UNLOCK SONG: "KOTO" BY CHIANG
Enter GHOSTSHELL.

UNLOCK SONG: "LIL' BRO" BY RIC-A-CHE
Enter GONBETRUBL.

UNLOCK SONG: "MAN UP" BY STICKY FINGAZ
Enter KIRKJONES.

UNLOCK SONG: "MOVE!" BY PUBLIC ENEMY
Enter RESPECT.

UNLOCK SONG: "O. G. ORIGINAL GANGSTER" BY ICE T
Enter POWER.

UNLOCK SONG: "POPPA LARGE" BY ULTRAMAGNETIC MC'S
Enter ULTRAMAG.

UNLOCK SONG: "SIEZE THE DAY" BY BLESS
Enter SIEZE.

UNLOCK SONG: "TAKE A LOOK AT MY LIFE" BY FAT JOE
Enter CARTAGENA.

UNLOCK SONG: "WALK WITH ME" BY JOE BUDDEN
Enter PUMP.

DESTROY ALL HUMANS!

AMMO-A-PLENTY
Pause the game, hold Left Trigger and press Left, Y, White, Right, Black, X. This gives you unlimited ammo.

BULLETPROOF CRYPTO
Pause the game, hold Left Trigger and press X, Y, Left, Left, Y, X. This makes you invincible.

DEEP THINKER
Pause the game, hold Left Trigger and press Black, White, Y, Right, White, Y. This gives you unlimited concentration.

AWARE LIKE A FOX
Pause the game, hold Left Trigger and press Right, Right, X, White, Black, Right, White. This maxes out the alert meter.

NOBODY LOVES YOU
Pause the game, hold Left Trigger and press White, Right, White, Black, X, Right. This resets the alert meter.

FIND KEY TO ORTHOPOX'S LAB
On the Mothership, hold Left Trigger and press X, Y, Left, Left, Y, X. This gives you access to the Upgrades at Pox's Lab.

MMMM BRAINS!
On the Mothership, hold Left Trigger and press Black, Black, White, White, Left, Right, Left, Right, White, Black. This gives you extra DNA.

DESTROY ALL HUMANS! 2

SALAD DAYS WITH POX & CRYPTO MOVIE
Pause the game and select Archives. Hold Left Thumbstick and press A, X, Y, B, X, B, Y, A, A.

DIGIMON RUMBLE ARENA 2

1-HIT KILLS
At the Title screen, press Right, Up, Left, Down, A, Left Trigger + Right Trigger.

EVOLVE ENERGY ITEM
At the Title screen, press Y, Right, Down, B, Left Trigger, A, Right Trigger, A, Y.

EVOLVE METER ALWAYS FULL
At the Title screen, press X, Right, A, Y, Left, B, Left Trigger + Right Trigger.

DOOM 3: THE COLLECTOR'S EDITION

GOD MODE
During a game, hold Left Trigger and press X, Y, B, A.

SKIP LEVEL
During a game, hold Left Trigger and press B, A, X, Y.

TEMPORARY INVINCIBILITY
During a game, hold Left Trigger and press X, X, X, X.

INVISIBILITY
During a game, hold Left Trigger and press X, X, Y, Y.

WEAPONS AND AMMO
During a game, hold Left Trigger and press B, B, B, B.

ALL KEYS, ALL WEAPONS AND FULL AMMO
During a game, hold Left Trigger and press A, B, A, B.

BERSERK MODE
During a game, hold Left Trigger and press X, X, X, Y.

END LEVEL
During a game, hold Left Trigger and press A, A, B, B.

CHAINSAW
During a game, hold Left Trigger and press B, B, A, A.

LIGHT AMPLIFICATION GOGGLES
During a game, hold Left Trigger and press Y, Y, Y, X.

RADIATION SUIT
During a game, hold Left Trigger and press X, Y, Y, Y.

SHOW ALL MAP
During a game, hold Left Trigger and press Y, Y, Y, Y.

DRAGON BALL Z: SAGAS

ALL UPGRADES
Pause the game, select Controller and press Up, Left, Down, Right, Back, Start, Y, X, A, B.

INVINCIBILITY
Pause the game, select Controller and press Down, A, Up, Y, Back, Start, Right, X, Left, B.

DRIV3R

At the Main menu, enter the following cheats. Then select Cheats from the Options menu to toggle them on and off.

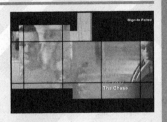

ALL MISSIONS
Enter X, X, Y, Y, R, R, L.

ALL WEAPONS
Enter L, L, X, Y, Y, R, R.

UNLIMITED AMMO
Enter R, R, L, L, X, Y, Y.

INVINCIBILITY (TAKE A RIDE)
Enter X, Y, L, R, L, R, R.

IMMUNITY
Enter X, Y, R, R, L, L, Y.

ALL VEHICLES
Enter X, X, Y, Y, L, R, L.

DRIVER: PARALLEL LINES

ALL VEHICLES
Pause the game, select Cheat from the Settings menu and enter CARSHOW.

ALL WEAPONS
Pause the game, select Cheat from the Settings menu and enter GUNRANGE.

INDESTRUCTIBLE CARS
Pause the game, select Cheat from the Settings menu and enter ROLLBAR. Enable the cheat from the Cheats page.

INFINITE AMMO
Pause the game, select Cheat from the Settings menu and enter GUNBELT. Enable the cheat from the Cheats page.

INFINITE NITRO
Pause the game, select Cheat from the Settings menu and enter ZOOMZOOM. Enable the cheat from the Cheats page.

INVINCIBILITY
Pause the game, select Cheat from the Settings menu and enter IRONMAN. Enable the cheat from the Cheats page.

WEAK COP CARS
Pause the game, select Cheat from the Settings menu and enter KEYSTONE. Enable the cheat from the Cheats page.

ZERO COST
Pause the game, select Cheat from the Settings menu and enter TOOLEDUP. Enable the cheat from the Cheats page. Also, upgrades won't cost anything!

DUNGEONS AND DRAGONS HEROES

During a game, hold L and press A + Y. Now you can enter the following:

CODE	ENTER
Invincibility	PELOR
Nightmare Difficulty Setting	MPS LABS
Unlimited Mystical Will	OBADHAI
10,000 Experience Points	DSP633
500,000 Gold	KNE637
Dexterity Up 10	YAN or ZXE053
Constitution Up 10	N STINE

CODE	ENTER
10 Anti-Venom	SPINRAD
10 Berserk Brew	THOMAS
10 Fash Freeze	ESKO
10 Fire Bomb	WEBER
10 Fire Flask	BROPHY
10 Firey Oil	EHOFF
10 Globe Potion	WRight
10 Insect Plague	DERISO
10 Keys	KEIDEL
10 Keys	SNODGRASS
10 Large Healing Potions	THOMPSON
10 Large Will Potions	GEE
10 Medium Potions of Will	LU
10 Potions of Haste	UHL
10 Pyrokins	SMITH
10 Rod of Destruction	AUSTIN
10 Rod of Fire	DELUCIA
10 Rod of Miracles	JARMAN
10 Rod of Missiles	MILLER
10 Rod of Reflection	WHITTAKE
10 Rod of Shadows	DINOLT
10 Thrown Axe of Ruin	RAMERO
10 Thrown Daggers of Stunning	BELL
10 Thrown Daggers	MOREL
10 Thrown Halcyon Hammer	PRASAD
10 Thrown Hammer	BRATHWAI
10 Thrown Viper Axe	FRAZIER
10 Thrown Viper Axe	HOWARD
10 Thuderstone	ELSON
10 Tome of Lessons	PAQUIN
10 Tome of the Apprentice	BILGER
10 Tome of the Teacher	MEFFORD
10 Tomes of the Master	SPANBURG
10 Warp Stones	HOPPENST
10 Holy Water	CRAWLEY
View Concept Art	CONCEPTS
View Credits	CREDITS
Disable Cheats	UNBUFF

EA SPORTS ARENA FOOTBALL

BIG BALL
While at the line of scrimmage, press Left
Trigger + Y, Up, Up.

SMALL BALL
While at the line of scrimmage, press Left
Trigger + Y, Down, Down.

NORMAL SIZE BALL
While at the line of scrimmage, press Left Trigger + Y, Up, Down.

MAX STATS IN QUICK PLAY
Load a profile with the name IronMen. This will maximize all players' stats in Quick Play.

FANTASTIC 4

BARGE ARENA AND STAN LEE INTERVIEW #1
At the Main menu, press X, B, X, Down, Down, B, Up.

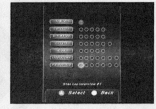

INFINITE COSMIC POWER
At the Main menu, press Up, X, X, X, Left, Right, B.

BONUS LEVEL
At the Main menu, press Right, Right, X, B, Left, Up, Down.

FAR CRY INSTINCTS

SECRET MESSAGE IN MAP MAKER
Select Map Maker, hold Left Trigger + Right Trigger + Y + B + X + Left Thumbstick + Right Thumbstick and press A.

ALL MAPS
Pause the game, select Cheat menu and enter TheWorldIsMine.

100 HEALTH POINTS
Pause the game, select Cheat menu and enter GiveMeHealth.

INFINITE AMMO
Pause the game, select Cheat menu and enter BulletsofHell.

INFINITE ADRENALINE
Pause the game, select Cheat menu and enter VitruviAnRush.

FERAL ATTACK ABILITY
Pause the game, select Cheat menu and enter PunchMeHard.

DISABLE AUTO AIM
Pause the game, select Cheat menu and enter NotForSissies.

FAR CRY: INSTINCTS—EVOLUTION

ALL MAPS
Enter GiveMeTheMaps at the Cheats menu.

FERAL ATTACKS (EARLY LEVELS)
Enter FeralAttack at the Cheats menu.

RESTORE HEALTH
Enter ImJackCarver at the Cheats menu.

INFINITE AMMO
Enter UnleashHell at the Cheats menu.

INFINITE ADRENALINE
Enter BloodLust at the cheats menu.

FIFA STREET 2

ALL VENUES
At the Main menu, hold Left Trigger + Y and press Left, Up, Up, Right, Down, Down, Right, Down.

FIGHT NIGHT ROUND 2

ALL VENUES
At the Game Mode Select screen, hold Left until you hear a bell.

SMALL FIGHTERS
At the Main menu, hold Up until you hear a bell. Select Play Now to get small fighters.

FABOLOUS
Select CAB and enter getfab as his first name. Save and delete.

LIL JOHN
Select CAB and enter Lijon as his first name. Save and delete.

FINDING NEMO

Enter the following at the Main menu. The word "Cheat!" will appear if entered correctly. Pause the game at the level select to access the cheats.

LEVEL SELECT
Press Y (x3), X, X, B, X, Y, B, X, Y, X, Y, X, Y, B, Y, Y.

INVINCIBILITY
Press Y, X, X, B (x3), Y, Y, X (x3), B (x4), X, Y, B (x3), X, B, Y, B, B, X, B, B, Y, B, X, B (x3), Y.

CREDITS
Press Y, X, B, Y, Y, X, B, Y, X, B, Y, X, X, B, Y, X, B, Y, X, B, B, Y, X, B.

SECRET LEVEL
Press Y, X, B, B, X, Y, Y, X, B, B, X, Y, Y, B, X, Y, X, B, B, X, Y.

FLATOUT 2

ALL CARS AND 1,000,000 CREDITS
Select Enter Code from Extras and enter GIEVEPIX.

1,000,000 CREDITS
Select Enter Code from the Extras and enter GIVECASH.

PIMPSTER CAR
Select Enter Code from Extras and enter RUTTO.

FLATMOBILE CAR
Select Enter Code from Extras and enter
WOTKINS.

MOB CAR
Select Enter Code from the Extras and enter
BIGTRUCK.

SCHOOL BUS
Select Enter Code from Extras and enter
GIEVCARPLZ.

ROCKET CAR
Select Enter Code from Extras and enter
KALJAKOPPA.

TRUCK
Select Enter Code from the Extras and enter
ELPUEBLO.

FORZA MOTORSPORT

START CAREER WITH 900,000,000 CREDITS
Start a new profile with the name tEAm4za.

ALL CARS
Start a new profile with the name nOsLiW.

FROGGER: ANCIENT SHADOW

UNLOCK LEVELS
To unlock various levels, select Cheat Codes and enter the following:

LEVEL	ENTER
Level 4-1	Lily, Lumpy, Frogger, Finnius
Level 4-2	Wani, Frogger, Lily, Berry
Level 5-1	Wani, Wani, Berry, Frogger
Level 5-2	Frogger, Finnius, Lily, Lily
Level 6-1	Wani, Lily, Lily, Frogger
Level 6-2	Lily, Lily, Wani, Lily
Level 6-3	Berry, Frogger, Lily, Lily
Level 7-1	Lumpy, Wani, Frogger, Frogger
Level 7-2	Lumpy, Frogger, Lily, Berry

UNLOCK LETTERS
To unlock various letters, select Cheat Codes and enter the following:

LEVEL	ENTER
Hyacinth Letter	Berry, Frogger, Lumpy, Berry
Cosmos Letter	Lumpy, Frogger, Frogger, Lumpy
Rose Letter	Frogger, Wani, Berry, Lumpy
Pansy Letter	Finnius, Lumpy, Lily, Wani

UNLOCK WIGS

To unlock various wigs, select Cheat Codes and enter the following:

LEVEL	ENTER
Lobster Wig	Finnius, Wani, Lumpy, Frogger
Bird Nest Wig	Lily, Lily, Lily, Lily
Sail Boat Wig	Lumpy, Lumpy, Lumpy, Lumpy
Skull Wig	Frogger, Lumpy, Lily, Frogger

UNLOCK ARTWORK

To unlock different kinds of artwork, select Cheat Codes and enter the following:

LEVEL	ENTER
Programmer Art 1	Wani, Wani, Wani, Wani
Programmer Art 2	Lumpy, Frogger, Berry, Lily
Programmer Art 3	Wani, Frogger, Lily, Finnius
Additional Art 1	Frogger, Frogger, Frogger, Frogger
Additional Art 2	Finnius, Finnius, Finnius, Finnius
Additional Art 3	Berry, Berry, Berry, Berry

DEVELOPER PICTURE 1

Select Cheat Codes and enter Wani, Frogger, Wani, Frogger.

DEVELOPER PICTURE 2

Select Cheat Codes and enter Berry, Berry, Berry, Wani.

FULL SPECTRUM WARRIOR

INFINITE AMMO

Select Cheat Codes from the Extra Content and enter MERCENARIES. Create a new profile and start a game.

BIG HEAD MODE

Select Cheat Codes from the Extra Content and enter NICKWEST. Create a new profile and start a game.

US ARMY VERSION

Select Cheat Codes from the Extra Content and enter HA2P1PY9TUR5TLE. Create a new profile and start a game.

AUTHENTIC MODE

Select Cheat Codes from the Extra Content and enter SWEDISHARMY. Create a new profile and start a game.

FULL SPECTRUM WARRIOR: TEN HAMMERS

ALL LEVELS

Enter FULLSPECTRUMPWNAGE at the Cheat menu.

FUTURAMA

FULL HEALTH

During the game, hold L, and press A. Hold R, and press X, Y. Release R, and press A. Hold R, then press X, Y, B, A, Black. Release R, then press Y. Hold R, then press Back.

INVINCIBILITY

During the game, hold L, and press A. Hold R, and press X, Y. Release R, and press A. Hold R, then press X, Y, B, A, Black, Y, Back.

FULL CHARGE

During the game, hold L, and press A. Hold R, and press X, Y. Release R, and press A. Hold R, then press X, Y, B, A, Black. Release R, then press X. Hold R, then press Back.

INFINITE AMMO

During the game, hold L, and press A. Hold R, and press X, Y. Release R, and press A. Hold R, then press X, Y, B, A, Black. Release R, then press B. Hold R, then press Back.

UNLIMITED LIVES

During the game, hold L, and press A. Hold R, and press X, Y. Release R, and press A. Hold R, then press X, Y, B, A, Black. Release R, then press A. Hold R, then press Back.

ALL EXTRAS

During the game, hold L, and press A. Hold R, and press X, Y. Release R, and press A. Hold R, then press X, Y, B, A, Black, B, Back.

FUTURE TACTICS: THE UPRISING

LEVEL SKIP
At the Game Select screen, press Left Trigger, X, Right Trigger, Right Trigger, Black, X, Left Trigger, Right Trigger, Black.

UNLIMITED TURNS AND MOVEMENT
During a game, press Up, Up, Down, Down, Left, Right, Left, Left, Right Trigger, Left Trigger.

BIG HEADS
During a game, press Up, Left, Down, Left, Down, Up, Up, Left.

DISCO MODE
During a game, press Left Trigger, Left, Left Trigger, Left, Right Trigger, Right, Right Trigger, Right.

LOW GRAVITY
During a game, press Up (x6), Down, Right, Up.

GOBLIN COMMANDER: UNLEASH THE HORDE

During a game, hold Right Trigger + Left Trigger + Y + Down until a message appears on the right side of the screen. Re-enter the code to disable it. Now you can enter the following codes. Note that a message appears when the code is entered correctly.

GOD MODE
Press Right Trigger (x3), Left Trigger (x3), Right Trigger, Left Trigger, Y, Right Trigger.

AUTOMATIC WIN
Press Right Trigger, Right Trigger, Left Trigger (x3), Right Trigger, Right Trigger, Y (x3).

ALL LEVEL ACCESS
Press Y (x3), Left Trigger, Right Trigger, Left Trigger, Left Trigger, Right Trigger, Left Trigger, Right Trigger, Right Trigger, Left Trigger, Right Trigger, Left Trigger, Left Trigger, Right Trigger, Left Trigger, Right Trigger, Left Trigger, Left Trigger, Right Trigger, Left Trigger, Left Trigger, Right Trigger, Left Trigger, Right Trigger, Right Trigger, Y (x3). Start up a Campaign to select a level.

DISABLE FOG OF WAR
Press Right Trigger, Left Trigger, Right Trigger, Right Trigger, Left Trigger, Left Trigger, Y, Y, Left Trigger, Right Trigger.

GAME SPEED X1/2
Press Left Trigger (x5), Y (x4), Right Trigger.

GAME SPEED X2
Press Right Trigger (x5), Left Trigger, Y, Right Trigger (x3).

GOLD AND SOULS +1000
Press Right Trigger, Right Trigger, Left Trigger, Right Trigger, Right Trigger, Y (x3), Left Trigger, Left Trigger.

GOLD +100
Press Left Trigger, Right Trigger (x4), Left Trigger, Y, Left Trigger (x3).

SOULS +100
Press Right Trigger, Left Trigger (x4), Right Trigger, Y, Right Trigger (x3).

THE GODFATHER

$5,000
Pause the game and press X, Y, X, X, Y, Left Thumbstick.

FULL AMMO
Pause the game and press Y, Left, Y, Right, X, Right Thumbstick.

FULL HEALTH
Pause the game and press Left, X, Right, Y, Right, Left Thumbstick.

UNLOCK ENTIRE FILM ARCHIVE
After loading a game and before joining the family, press Y, X, Y, X, X, Left Thumbstick. Select Film Archive to view films.

GODZILLA: SAVE THE EARTH

CHEAT MENU
At the Main menu, press and hold Left Trigger, B, Right Trigger in that order, then release B, Right Trigger, Left Trigger. Now you can enter the following cheats:

ALL CITIES
Enter 659996.

ALL MONSTERS
Enter 525955.

UNLOCK CHALLENGES
Enter 975013.

HEALTH REGENERATES
Enter 536117.

ENERGY DOESN'T REGENERATE
Enter 122574.

INDESTRUCTIBLE BUILDINGS
Enter 812304.

100,000 POINTS
Enter 532459.

150,000 POINTS
Enter 667596.

200,000 POINTS
Enter 750330.

PLAYER 1: 4X DAMAGE
Enter 259565.

PLAYER 1: INFINITE ENERGY
Enter 819342.

PLAYER 1: INVISIBLE
Enter 531470.

PLAYER 1: INVULNERABLE
Enter 338592.

PLAYER 2: 4X DAMAGE
Enter 927281.

PLAYER 2: INFINITE ENERGY
Enter 324511.

PLAYER 2: INVISIBLE
Enter 118699.

PLAYER 2: INVULNERABLE
Enter 259333.

PLAYER 3: 4X DAMAGE
Enter 500494.

PLAYER 3: INFINITE ENERGY
Enter 651417.

PLAYER 3: INVISIBLE
Enter 507215.

PLAYER 3: INVULNERABLE
Enter 953598.

PLAYER 4: 4X DAMAGE
Enter 988551.

PLAYER 4: INFINITE ENERGY
Enter 456719.

PLAYER 4: INVISIBLE
Enter 198690.

PLAYER 4: INVULNERABLE
Enter 485542.

GALLERY
Enter 294206.

GODZILLA FINAL WARS
Enter 409014.

GOLDENEYE: ROGUE AGENT

ALL LEVELS AND MULTIPLAYER POWER-UPS/MODIFIERS
At the Extras menu, press Down, Right, Down, Right, Up, Down, Up, Left.

ALL SKINS IN MULTIPLAYER
At the Extras menu, press Down, Left, Up, Left, Right, Down, Left, Up.

PAINTBALL MODE
At the Extras menu, press Right, Left, Right, Left, Down, Down, Up, Up.

ONE LIFE MODE
At the Extras menu, press Left, Down, Up, Right, Up, Right, Left, Down.

FULL HEALTH AND ARMOR
Pause the game and press Right Trigger, Right Trigger, Black, White, Black, Right Trigger, Left Trigger, Black.

RECHARGE GOLDENEYE
Pause the game and press Left Trigger, Right Trigger, Left Trigger, White, White, Black, Right Trigger, White.

ALL EYE POWERS
Pause the game and press Left Trigger, Left Trigger, Black, Black, Right Trigger, Black, Left Trigger, White.

GRAND THEFT AUTO: THE TRILOGY

GRAND THEFT AUTO 3

BETTER VEHICLE HANDLING
Press Right Trigger, Left Trigger, Black, Left Trigger, Left, Right Trigger, Right Trigger, Y while *outside* your vehicle. This code makes all vehicles handle better. When entered correctly, press the Left Thumbstick to cause the vehicle to hop.

VEHICLE HEALTH
Press Black, Black, Left Trigger, Right Trigger, Left, Down, Right, Up, Left, Down, Right, Up while *inside* a vehicle. The car will remain damaged, but it will stop smoking and retain its perfect "health" status.

EXPLODE ALL VEHICLES
Press White, Black, Left Trigger, Right Trigger, White, Black, Y, X, B, Y, White, Left Trigger.

RHINO
Press B (x6), Right Trigger, White, Left Trigger, Y, B, Y.

INVISIBLE CAR CHASSIS
Press Left Trigger, Left Trigger, X, Black, Y, Left Trigger, Y.

FLYING VEHICLES
Press Right, Black, B, Right Trigger, White, Down, Left Trigger, Right Trigger.

FOGGY
Press Left Trigger, White, Right Trigger, Black, Black, Right Trigger, White, A.

CLOUDY
Press Left Trigger, White, Right Trigger, Black, Black, Right Trigger, White, X.

RAIN
Press Left Trigger, White, Right Trigger, Black, Black, Right Trigger, White, B.

NORMAL WEATHER
Press Left Trigger, White, Right Trigger, Black, Black, Right Trigger, White, Y.

PEDESTRIANS RIOT
Press Down, Up, Left, Up, A, Right Trigger, Black, White, Left Trigger. Please note that this code is irreversible, so do NOT enter the code and save your game.

PEDESTRIANS OUT TO GET YOU
Press Down, Up, Left, Up, A, Right Trigger, Black, Left Trigger, White. Please note that this code is irreversible, so do NOT enter the code and save your game.

PEDESTRIANS PACKING HEAT
Press Black, Right Trigger, Y, A, White, Left Trigger, Up, Down. Please note that this code is irreversible, so do NOT enter the code and save your game.

WANTED LEVEL INCREASE
Press Black, Black, Left Trigger, Black, Left, Right, Left, Right, Left to increase your Wanted Level by two each time the code is entered.

WANTED LEVEL DECREASE
Press Black, Black, Left Trigger, Black, Up, Down, Up, Down, Up, Down to decrease your Wanted Level.

WEAPON CHEAT
Press Black, Black, Left Trigger, Black, Left, Down, Right, Up, Left, Down, Right, Up. Continue to enter the code until the maximum ammo capacity of 9999 is reached for each weapon. When a weapon reaches its maximum ammo capacity, its ammunition supply becomes infinite.

CHANGE CHARACTER MODEL
Press Right, Down, Left, Up, Left Trigger, White, Up, Left, Down, Right. Please note that this code is irreversible, so do NOT enter the code and save your game.

HEALTH CHEAT
Press Black, Black, Left Trigger, Right Trigger, Left, Down, Right, Up, Left, Down, Right, Up.

ARMOR CHEAT
Press Black, Black, Left Trigger, White, Left, Down, Right, Up, Left, Down, Right, Up.

MONEY CHEAT ($250,000)
Press Black, Black, Left Trigger, Left Trigger, Left, Down, Right, Up, Left, Down, Right, Up.

INCREASED GORE FACTOR
Press X, Left Trigger, B, Down, Left Trigger, Right Trigger, Y, Right, Left Trigger, A to make victims lose body parts.

SLOW MOTION
Press Y, Up, Right, Down, X, Right Trigger, Black. Enter this cheat three times for even more slowdown.

FASTER GAMEPLAY
Press Y, Up, Right, Down, X, Left Trigger, White. Enter this cheat three times for even faster gameplay.

INCREASE TIME
Press B (x3), X (x5), Left Trigger, Y, B, Y. Enter this cheat a second time to return to "normal" time.

GRAND THEFT AUTO: VICE CITY

Enter the following cheats during gameplay. Note that some of these codes may affect your gameplay, so don't save your game unless you want the code to stay in effect.

HEALTH CHEAT
Press Right Trigger, Black, Left Trigger, B, Left, Down, Right, Up, Left, Down, Right, Up.

ARMOR CHEAT
Press Right Trigger, Black, Left Trigger, A, Left, Down, Right, Up, Left, Down, Right, Up.

LOW GRAVITY
Press Right, Black, B, Right Trigger, White, Down, Left Trigger, Right Trigger.

BETTER DRIVING
Press Y, Right Trigger, Right Trigger, Left, Right Trigger, Left Trigger, Black, Left Trigger. Press the Left Thumbstick to jump.

SUICIDE
Press Right, White, Down, Right Trigger, Left, Left, Right Trigger, Left Trigger, White, Left Trigger.

WANTED LEVEL UP 2 STARS
Press Right Trigger, Right Trigger, B, Black, Left, Right, Left, Right, Left, Right.

WANTED LEVEL DOWN 2 STARS
Press Right Trigger, Right Trigger, B, Black, Up, Down, Up, Down, Up, Down.

SLOW MOTION
Press Y, Up, Right, Down, X, Black, Right Trigger.

SPEED UP TIME
Press B, B, Left Trigger, X, Left Trigger, X, X, X, Left Trigger, Y, B, Y.

BLACK CARS
Press B, White, Up, Right Trigger, Left, A, Right Trigger, Left Trigger, Left, B.

PINK CARS
Press B, Left Trigger, Down, White, Left, A, Right Trigger, Left Trigger, Right, B.

CHANGE WHEELS
Press Right Trigger, A, Y, Right, Black, X, Up, Down, X.

CAR SPEED X2
Press Right Trigger, Black, Left Trigger, L, Left, Down, Right, Up, Left, Down, Right, Up.

CARS FLOAT
Press Right, Black, B, Right Trigger, White, X, Right Trigger, Black.

ALL CARS EXPLODE
Press Black, White, Right Trigger, Left Trigger, White, Black, X, Y, B, Y, White, Left Trigger.

ROBOCOPS
Press B, Left Trigger, Down, White, Left, A, Right Trigger, Left Trigger, Right, A.

CARS DON'T STOP
Press Black, B, Right Trigger, White, Left, Right Trigger, Left Trigger, Black, White.

PEDESTRIANS RIOT
Press Down, Left, Up, Left, A, Black, Right Trigger, White, Left Trigger.

PEDESTRIANS ATTACK
Press Down, Up (x3), A, Black, Right Trigger, White, White.

ARMED PEDESTRIANS
Press Black, Right Trigger, A, Y, A, Y, Up, Down.

WOMEN WITH GUNS
Press Right, Left Trigger, B, White, Left, A, Right Trigger, Left Trigger, Left Trigger, A.

WOMEN FOLLOW YOU
Press B, A, Left Trigger, Left Trigger, Black, A, A, B, Y.

MEDIA LEVEL METER
Press Black, B, Up, Left Trigger, Right, Right Trigger, Right, Up, X, Y.

The following codes provide one weapon for each weapon class:

WEAPONS SET 1
Press Black, Black, Right Trigger, Black, Left Trigger, Black, Left, Down, Right, Up, Left Down, Right, Up.

WEAPONS SET 2
Press Right Trigger, Black, Left Trigger, Black, Left, Down, Right, Up, Left, Down, Down, Left.

WEAPONS SET 3
Press Right Trigger, Black, Left Trigger, Black, Left, Down, Right, Up, Left, Down, Down, Down.

CLEAR WEATHER
Press Black, A, Left Trigger, Left Trigger, White, White, White, Down.

SUNNY
Press Black, A, Left Trigger, Left Trigger, White (x3), Y.

OVERCAST
Press Black, A, Left Trigger, Left Trigger, White (x3), X.

RAIN
Press Black, A, Left Trigger, Left Trigger, White (x3), B.

FOG
Press Black, A, Left Trigger, Left Trigger, White (x3), A.

RED LEATHER
Press Right, Right, Left, Up, Left Trigger, White, Left, Up, Down, Right.

CANDY SUXXX
Press B, Black, Down, Right Trigger, Left, Right, Right Trigger, Left Trigger, A, White.

HILARY KING
Press Right Trigger, B, Black, Left Trigger, Right, Right Trigger, Left Trigger, A, Black.

KEN ROSENBERG
Press Right, Left Trigger, Up, White, Left Trigger, Right, Right Trigger, Left Trigger, A, R.

LANCE VANCE
Press B, White, Left, A, Right Trigger, Left Trigger, A, Left Trigger.

LOVE FIST 1
Press Down, Left Trigger, Down, White, Left, A, Right Trigger, Left Trigger, A, A.

LOVE FIST 2
Press Right Trigger, White, Black, Left Trigger, Right, Black, Left, A, X, Left Trigger.

MERCEDES
Press Black, Left Trigger, Up, Left Trigger, Right, Right Trigger, Right, Up, B, Y.

PHIL CASSADY
Press Right, Right Trigger, Up, Black, Left Trigger, Right, Right Trigger, Left Trigger, Right, B.

RICARDO DIAZ
Press Left Trigger, White, Right Trigger, Black, Down, Left Trigger, Black, White.

SONNY FORELLI
Press B, Left Trigger, B, White, Left, A, Right Trigger, Left Trigger, A, A.

BLOODRING BANGER
Press Up, Right, Right, Left Trigger, Right, Up, X, White.

BLOODRING BANGER
Press Down, Right Trigger, B, White, White, A, Right Trigger, Left Trigger, Left, Left.

CADDY
Press B, Left Trigger, Up, Right Trigger, White, A, Right Trigger, Left Trigger, B, A.

HOTRING RACER 1
Press Black, Left Trigger, B, Right, Left Trigger, Right Trigger, Right, Up, B, Black.

HOTRING RACER 2
Press Right Trigger, B, Black, Right, Left Trigger, White, A, A, X, Right Trigger.

LOVE FIST LIMO
Press Black, Up, White, Left, Left, Right Trigger, Left Trigger, B, Right.

RHINO TANK
Press B, B, Left Trigger, B (x3), Left Trigger, White, Right Trigger, Y, B, Y.

ROMERO'S HEARSE
Press Down, Black, Down, Right Trigger, White, Left, Right Trigger, Left Trigger, Left, Right.

SABRE TURBO
Press Right, White, Down, White, White, A, Right Trigger, Left Trigger, B, Left.

TRASHMASTER
Press B, Right Trigger, B, Right Trigger, Left, Left, Right Trigger, Left Trigger, B, Right.

GRAND THEFT AUTO: SAN ANDREAS

During gameplay, enter the following cheats:

FULL HEALTH, FULL ARMOR, & $250,000
Press Right Trigger, Black, Left Trigger, A, Left , Down, Right, Up, Left, Down, Right, Up.

INFINITE HEALTH
Press Down, A, Right, Left, Right, Right Trigger, Right, Down, Up, Y.

INFINITE AMMO
Press Left Trigger, Right Trigger, X, Right Trigger, Left, Black, Right Trigger, Left, X, Down, Left Trigger, Left Trigger.

INFINITE LUNG CAPACITY
Press Down, Left, Left Trigger, Down, Down, Black, Down, White, Down.

MAX RESPECT
Press Left Trigger, Right Trigger, Y, Down, Black, A, Left Trigger, Up, White, White, Left Trigger, Left Trigger.

MAX SEX APPEAL
Press B, Y, Y, Up, B, Right Trigger, White, Up, Y, Left Trigger, Left Trigger, Left Trigger

MAX VEHICLE STATS
Press X, White, A, Right Trigger, White, White, Left, Right Trigger, Right, Left Trigger, Left Trigger, Left Trigger.

0 FAT AND 0 MUSCLE
Press Y, Up, Up, Left, Right, X, B, Right.

MAXIMUM MUSCLES
Press Y, Up, Up, Left, Right, X, B, Left.

MAXIMUM FAT
Press Y, Up, Up, Left, Right, X, B, Down.

BIG JUMPS
Press Up, Up, Y, Y, Up, Up, Left, Right, X, Black, Black.

BIG BUNNY HOPS ON BMX
Press Y, X, B, B, X, B, B, Left Trigger, White, White, Right Trigger, Black

SUICIDE
Press Right, White, Down, Right Trigger, Left, Left, Right Trigger, Left Trigger, White, Left Trigger.

MIDNIGHT
Press X, Left Trigger, Right Trigger, Right, A, Up, Left Trigger, Left, Left.

FASTER GAMEPLAY
Press Y, Up, Right, Down, White, Left Trigger, X.

SLOWER GAMEPLAY
Press Y, Up, Right, Down, X, Black, Right Trigger.

FASTER TIME
Press B, B, Left Trigger, X, Left Trigger, X, X, X, Left Trigger, Y, B, Y.

JUNK CARS
Press White, Right, Left Trigger, Up, A, Left Trigger, White, Black, Right Trigger, Left Trigger, Left Trigger, Left Trigger.

FARM VEHICLES
Press Left Trigger, Left Trigger, Right Trigger, Right Trigger White, Left Trigger, Black, Down, Left, Up.

BLACK CARS
Press B, White, Up, Right Trigger, Left, A, Right Trigger, Left Trigger, Left, B.

PINK CARS
Press B, Left Trigger, Down, White, Left, A, Right Trigger, Left Trigger, Right, B.

FAST CARS
Press Up, Left Trigger, Right Trigger, Up, Right, Up, A, White, A, Left Trigger.

NITROUS FOR ALL CARS
Press Left, Y, Right Trigger, Left Trigger, Up, X, Y, Down, B, White, Left Trigger, Left Trigger.

NITROUS FOR TAXIS & HOP
Press Up, A, Y, A, Y, A, X, Black, Right.

INVISIBLE VEHICLES
Press Y, Left Trigger, Y, Black, X, Left Trigger, Left Trigger.

INVINCIBLE VEHICLE
Press Left Trigger, White, White, Up, Down, Down, Up, Right Trigger, Black, Black.

DRIVE-BY WHILE DRIVING
Press Up, Up, X, White, Right, A, Right Trigger, Down, Black, B.

GREEN STOPLIGHTS
Press Right, Right Trigger, Up, White, White, Left, Right Trigger, Left Trigger, Right Trigger, Right Trigger.

AGGRESSIVE DRIVERS
Press Right, Black, Up, Up, Black, B, X, Black, Left Trigger, Right, Down, Left Trigger.

AGGRESSIVE TRAFFIC
Press Black, B, Right Trigger, White, Left, Right Trigger, Left Trigger, Black, White.

LESS TRAFFIC
Press A, Down, Up, Black, Down, Y, Left Trigger, Y, Left.

FASTER CARS
Press Right, Right Trigger, Up, White, White, Left, Right Trigger, Left Trigger, Right Trigger, Right Trigger.

BETTER HANDLING CARS
Press Y, Right Trigger, Right Trigger, Left, Right Trigger, Left Trigger, Black, Left Trigger.

FLOATING CARS
Press Right, Black, B, Right Trigger, White, X, Right Trigger, Black.

FLYING CARS
Press X, Down, White, Up, Left Trigger, B, Up, A, Left.

EXPLODING CARS
Press Black, White, Right Trigger, Left Trigger, White, Black, X, Y, B, Y, White, Left Trigger.

FLYING BOATS
Press Black, B, Up, Left Trigger, Right, Right Trigger, Right, Up, X, Y.

PEDESTRIANS ATTACK
Press Down, Up, Up, Up, A, Black, Right Trigger, White, White.

PEDESTRIANS ATTACK WITH GUNS
Press A, Left Trigger, Up, X, Down, A, White, Y, Down, Right Trigger, Left Trigger, Left Trigger.

PEDESTRIANS ATTACK EACH OTHER
Press Down, Left, Up, Left, A, Black, Right Trigger, White, Left Trigger.

PEDESTRIANS CARRY WEAPONS
Press Black, Right Trigger, A, Y, A, Y, Up, Down.

ELVIS IS EVERYWHERE
Press Left Trigger, B, Y, Left Trigger, Left Trigger, X, White, Up, Down, Left.

ATTRACT LADIES OF THE NIGHT
Press X, Right, X, X, White, A, Y, A, Y.

LADIES OF THE NIGHT PAY YOU
Press Right, White, White, Down, White, Up, Up, White, Black.

MULTIPLE UNLOCKABLES
When this code is entered, CJ turns into a Clown, civilians appear in fast food apparel and as clowns, there are BF Injections, HotDogs and so on. Press Y, Y, Left Trigger, X, X, B, X, Down, B.

PEOPLE IN SWIMSUITS
Press Up, Up, Down, Down, X, B, Left Trigger, Right Trigger, Y, Down.

GANGS
Press White, Up, Right Trigger, Right Trigger, Left, Right Trigger, Right Trigger, Black, Right, Down.

DECREASE WANTED LEVEL
Press Right Trigger, Right Trigger, B, Black, Up, Down, Up, Down, Up, Down.

INCREASE WANTED LEVEL
Press Right Trigger, Right Trigger, B, Black, Right, Left, Right, Left, Right, Left.

CLEAR WEATHER
Press Black, A, Left Trigger, Left Trigger, White, White, White, X.

NIGHT
Press Black, A, Left Trigger, Left Trigger, White, White, White, Y.

SUNNY WEATHER
Press Black, A, Left Trigger, Left Trigger, White, White, White, Down.

ORANGE SKY
Press Left, Left, White, Right Trigger, Right, X, X, Left Trigger, White, A.

FOGGY WEATHER
Press Black, A, Left Trigger, Left Trigger, White, White, White, A.

CLOUDY WEATHER
Press White, Down, Down, Left, X, Left, Black, X, A, Right Trigger, Left Trigger, Left Trigger.

OVERCAST
Press Black, A, Left Trigger, Left Trigger, White, White, White, X.

SAND STORM
Press Up, Down, Left Trigger, Left Trigger, White, White, Left Trigger, White, Right Trigger, Black.

RAINY WEATHER
Press Black, A, Left Trigger, Left Trigger, White, White, White, B.

HITMAN RANK
Press Down, X, A, Left, Right Trigger, Black, Left, Down, Down, Left Trigger, Left Trigger, Left Trigger.

WEAPONS SET 1
Press Right Trigger, Black, Left Trigger, Black, Left, Down, Right, Up, Left, Down, Right, Up.

WEAPONS SET 2
Press Right Trigger, Black, Left Trigger, Black, Left, Down, Right, Up, Left, Down, Down, Left.

WEAPONS SET 3
Press Right Trigger, Black, Left Trigger, Black, Left, Down, Right, Up, Left , Down, Down, Down.

PARACHUTE
Press Left, Right, Left Trigger, White, Right Trigger, Black, Black, Up, Down, Right, Left Trigger.

JETPACK
Press Left, Right, Left Trigger, White, Right Trigger, Black, Up, Down, Left, Right.

BLOODRING BANGER
Press Down, Right Trigger, B, White, White, A, Right Trigger, Left Trigger, Left, Left.

CADDY
Press B, Left Trigger, Up, Right Trigger, White, A, Right Trigger, Left Trigger, B, A.

DOZER
Press Black, Left Trigger, Left Trigger, Right, Right, Up, Up, A, Left Trigger, Left.

HOTRING RACER 1
Press Right Trigger, B, Black, Right, Left Trigger, White, A, A, X, Right Trigger.

HOTRING RACER 2
Press Black, Left Trigger, B, Right, Left Trigger, Right Trigger, Right, Up, B, Black.

HUNTER
Press B, A, Left Trigger, B, B, Left Trigger, B, Right Trigger, Black, White, Left Trigger, Left Trigger.

HYDRA
Press Y, Y, X, B, A, Left Trigger, Left Trigger, Down, Up.

MONSTER
Press Right, Up, Right Trigger, Right Trigger, Right Trigger, Down, Y, Y, A, B, Left Trigger, Left Trigger.

QUADBIKE
Press Left, Left, Down, Down, Up, Up, X, B, Y, Right Trigger, Black.

RANCHER
Press Up, Right, Right, Left Trigger, Right, Up, X, White.

RHINO
Press B, B, Left Trigger, B, B, B, Left Trigger, White, Right Trigger, Y, B, Y.

ROMERO
Press Down, Black, Down, Right Trigger, White, Left, Right Trigger, Left Trigger, Left, Right.

STRETCH
Press Black, Up, White, Left, Left, Right Trigger, Left Trigger, B, Right.

STUNTPLANE
Press B, Up, Left Trigger, White, Down, Right Trigger, Left Trigger, Left Trigger, Left, Left, A, Y.

TANKER
Press Right Trigger, Up, Left, Right, Black, Up, Right, X, Right, White, Left Trigger, Left Trigger.

TRASHMASTER
Press B, Right Trigger, B, Right Trigger, Left, Left, Right Trigger, Left Trigger, B, Right.

VORTEX
Press Y, Y, X, B, A, Left Trigger, White, Down, Down.

GREG HASTINGS' TOURNAMENT PAINTBALL

FLYING
During a game, hold Black + X + Right Trigger and press Up, Up, Down, Down, Right, Left, Down, Up.

GUN METAL

ALL MISSIONS
At the Mission Select screen, press Left Thumbstick, Black, Right Trigger, Right Thumbstick, White, Left Trigger.

MISSION SKIP
During a mission, press Left Thumbstick, White, White, Down, Right Thumbstick, White.

ALTERNATE MUSIC
At the Title screen, press Left Thumbstick, Left Thumbstick, Right Thumbstick, Right Thumbstick, Left Trigger, Right Trigger.

JOKE MISSION BREIFINGS
During Missions 1, 3, 6, 8, 9 or 14, press Left Trigger, Left Trigger, Right Trigger, Right Trigger, Left Thumbstick, Right Thumbstick.

HEROES OF THE PACIFIC

Note that the following cheats will disable game saving.

CHEAT MENU
At the Main menu, press Y, Left Trigger, Left on D-pad, Right Trigger, Right on D-pad, White.

UPGRADE PLANES
At the Main menu, press Left Trigger, Left on the Right Thumbstick, Right Trigger, Right on the Right Thumbstick, White, Y.

ALL PLANES AND MISSIONS
At the Main menu, press Up on the Right Thumbstick, Down on the Right Thumbstick, White, Black, Left on the Right Thumbstick, Right on the Right Thumbstick.

JAPANESE PLANES
At the Main menu, press White, Black, Left Trigger, Right Trigger, Up on the Right Thumbstick, Left on the Right Thumbstick.

HITMAN: CONTRACTS

ALL LEVELS
At the Main menu, press X, Y, B, Left, Up, Right, L, R.

COMPLETE LEVEL
During a game, press R, L, Up, Down, X, A, Left Thumbstick, B, A, B, A.

HITMAN 2: SILENT ASSASSIN

LEVEL SELECT
At the Main menu, press R, L, Up, Down, Y, B.

COMPLETE LEVEL
During gameplay, press R, L, Up, Down, A, X, press Left Analog Stick, B, A, B, A.

ALL WEAPONS
During gameplay, press R, L, Up, Down, A, Up, X, A.

INVINCIBILTY
During gameplay, press R, L, Up, Down, A, R, L, Black, Whi te.

FULL HEAL
During gameplay, press R, L, Up, Down, A, Up, Down.

TOGGLE LETHAL CHARGE
During gameplay, press L, R, Up, Down, A, Black, Black.

GRAVITY
During gameplay, press R, L, Up, Down, A, L, L.

SLOW MOTION
During gameplay, press R, L, Up, Down, A, Up, L.

MEGAFORCE
During gameplay, press R, L, Up, Down, A, R, R.

TOGGLE BOMB MODE
During gameplay, press R, L, Up, Down, A, Up, White.

TOGGLE PUNCH MODE
During gameplay, press R, L, Up, Down, A, Up, Up.

TOGGLE NAILGUN MODE
During gameplay, press R, L, Up, Down A, White, White.

HULK

CHEAT CODES

Select Code Input from the Options, then enter the following and press Accept. Turn on the cheats by selecting Cheats from the Special Features menu.

DESCRIPTION	CODE INPUT
Invulnerability	GMMSKIN
Regenerator	FLSHWND
Unlimited Continues	GRNCHTR
Double Hulk HP	HLTHDSE
Double Enemies HP	BRNGITN
Half Enemies HP	MMMYHLP
Reset High Score	NMBTHIH
Full Rage Meter	ANGMNGT
Puzzle Solved	BRCESTN
Wicked Punch	FSTOFRY
Unlock All Levels	TRUBLVR

UNIVERSAL UNLOCK CODES

Enter the following at the special terminals, called "Universal Code Input," that are found throughout the levels. You will find this bonus material in the Special Features menu.

DESCRIPTION	CODE INPUT
Play as Gray Hulk	JANITOR
Desert Battle Art	FIFTEEN
Hulk Movie FMV Art	NANOMED
Hulk Transformed ART	SANFRAN
Hulk vs. Hulk Dogs Art	PITBULL

HUNTER: THE RECKONING REDEEMER

Enter the following codes during game play:

GOD MODE
Press R, R, A, A, Up, Down, Up, Down.

MAX HEALTH
Press B, B, White, White, White.

SUPER SPEED
Press Y, B, Y, B, Up, Up, Down, Down.

UNLIMITED AMMO
Press X, X, X, X, Up, Down, Up, Down.

MAX AMMO FOR CURRENT WEAPON
Press A, B, White, Black, B.

WEAPONS INFLICT MAX DAMAGE
Press B, B, B, B, Up, Down, Up, Down.

ALL WEAPONS
Press A, A, A, A, Up, Down, Up, Down.

HEAVY WEAPONS
Press B, A, A, B, A, B, A, Black, White.

ALL EDGES
Press Y, Y, Y, Y, Up, Down, Up, Down.

MEGA-MELEE DAMAGE
Press X, X, Y, Y, Up, Down, Up, Down.

NIGHTMARE DIFFICULTY
Press Black, Black, Up, Up, Down, Down.

NO CONVICTION COST FOR EDGES
Press L, L, A, A, Up, Down, Up, Down.

99 CONVICTION
Press Y, Y, Y , Y, Up , Down , Up , Down.

PROGRESS TO NEXT LEVEL
Press Black, L, Black, L, Up, Down, Up, Down.

ALL SPECIAL FEATURES AND CHARACTERS
Press X, B, X, B, Up, Up, Down, Down.

ALL SECRETS
Press X, B, X, B, Up, Up, Down, Down.

ICE AGE 2: THE MELTDOWN

INFINITE PEBBLES
Pause the game and press Down, Down, Left, Up, Up, Right, Up, Down.

INFINITE ENERGY
Pause the game and press Down, Left, Right, Down, Down, Right, Left, Down.

INFINITE HEALTH
Pause the game and press Up, Right, Down, Up, Left, Down, Right, Left.

IHRA DRAG RACING: SPORTSMAN EDITION

$999,999
Select Season and enter Loaded as your profile name.

ROCKET CARS
Select Season and enter HotRodz as your profile name.

ALL BONUSES
Select Season and enter IWantIt as your profile name.

ALL ITEMS IN TROPHY ROOM
Select Season and enter FilMeUp as your profile name.

THE INCREDIBLE HULK: ULTIMATE DESTRUCTION

You must first collect a specific comic in the game to activate each code. After collecting the appropriate comic, you can enter the following. If you don't have the comic and enter the code, you get the following message: "That code cannot be activated...yet". You can access the cheats on the Code Input screen.

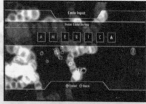

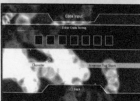

UNLOCKED: CABS GALORE
Select Code Input from the Extras menu and enter CABBIES.

UNLOCKED: GORILLA INVASION
Select Code Input from the Extras menu and enter KINGKNG.

UNLOCKED: MASS TRANSIT
Select Code Input from the Extras menu and enter TRANSIT.

UNLOCKED: 5000 SMASH POINTS
Select Code Input from the Extras menu and enter SMASH5.

UNLOCKED: 10000 SMASH POINTS
Select Code Input from the Extras menu and enter SMASH10.

UNLOCKED: 15000 SMASH POINTS
Select Code Input from the Extras menu and enter SMASH15.

UNLOCKED: AMERICAN FLAG SHORTS
Select Code Input from the Extras menu and enter AMERICA.

UNLOCKED: CANADIAN FLAG SHORTS
Select Code Input from the Extras menu and enter OCANADA.

UNLOCKED: FRENCH FLAG SHORTS
Select Code Input from the Extras menu and enter Drapeau.

UNLOCKED: GERMAN FLAG SHORTS
Select Code Input from the Extras menu and enter DEUTSCH.

UNLOCKED: ITALIAN FLAG SHORTS
Select Code Input from the Extras menu and enter MUTANDA.

UNLOCKED: JAPANESE FLAG SHORTS
Select Code Input from the Extras menu and enter FURAGGU.

UNLOCKED: SPANISH FLAG SHORTS
Select Code Input from the Extras menu and enter BANDERA.

UNLOCKED: UK FLAG SHORTS
Select Code Input from the Extras menu and enter FSHNCHP.

UNLOCKED: COW MISSILES
Select Code Input from the Extras menu and enter CHZGUN.

UNLOCKED: DOUBLE HULK'S DAMAGE
Select Code Input from the Extras menu and enter DESTROY.

UNLOCKED: DOUBLE POWER COLLECTABLES
Select Code Input from the Extras menu and enter BRINGIT.

UNLOCKED: BLACK AND WHITE
Select Code Input from the Extras menu and enter RETRO.

UNLOCKED: SEPIA
Select Code Input from the Extras menu and enter HISTORY.

UNLOCKED: ABOMINATION
Select Code Input from the Extras menu and enter VILLAIN.

UNLOCKED: GRAY HULK
Select Code Input from the Extras menu and enter CLASSIC.

UNLOCKED: JOE FIXIT SKIN
Select Code Input from the Extras menu and enter SUITFIT.

UNLOCKED: WILD TRAFFIC
Select Code Input from the Extras menu and enter FROGGIE.

UNLOCKED: LOW GRAVITY
Select Code Input from the Extras menu and enter PILLOWS.

THE INCREDIBLES: RISE OF THE UNDERMINER

BIG HEADS
Pause the game and press B to access the Options screen. Choose Secrets and enter EGOPROBLEM. Re-enter the code to disable it.

MR. INCREDIBLE GAINS 1000 EXPERIENCE POINTS
Pause the game and press B to access the Options screen. Choose Secrets and enter MRIPROF.

FROZONE GAINS 1000 EXPERIENCE POINTS
Pause the game and press B to access the Options screen. Choose Secrets and enter FROZPROF.

MR. INCREDIBLE GAINS A SUPER-MOVE
Pause the game and press B to access the Options screen. Choose Secrets and enter MRIBOOM.

FROZONE GAINS A SUPER-MOVE
Pause the game and press B to access the Options screen. Choose Secrets and enter FROZBOOM.

SHOWS THE GAME CREDITS
Pause the game and press B to access the Options screen. Choose Secrets and enter ROLLCALL.

TOUGHER GAME
Pause the game and press B to access the Options screen. Choose Secrets and enter THISISTOOEASY. This code cuts damage done to enemies in half, doubles damage caused to the Supers, there is no health recovery, and Experience Points are halved.

EASIER GAME
Pause the game and press B to access the Options screen. Choose Secrets and enter THISISTOOHARD. This code causes double damage to enemies, halves damage done to the Supers, and doubles the amount of health recovery and Experience Points!

ALL GALLERY ITEMS
Pause the game and press B to access the Options screen. Choose Secrets and enter SHOWME.

DOUBLE EXPERIENCE POINTS
Pause the game and press B to access the Options screen. Choose Secrets and enter MAXIMILLION.

JAMES BOND 007: EVERYTHING OR NOTHING

CHEATS
To access the following codes, you must first earn the given number of Platinum. Upon doing so, pause the game and enter the corresponding code.

EFFECT	PLATINUM	CODE
Golden Gun	1	B, Y, A, B, Y
Improved Traction	3	B, A, A, X, Y
Improved Battery	5	B, X, X, A, B
Double Ammunition	7	B, B, A, B, Y
Double Damage	9	B, Y, Y, X, B
Full Ammunition	11	B, B, Y, X, X
Cloak	13	B, Y, A, Y, X
Full Battery	15	B, Y, Y, A, B
All Weapons	17	B, Y, A, A, B
Unlimited Battery	19	B, X, B, X, Y
Unlimited Ammo	23	B, A, X, A, Y
Slow Motion Driving	25	B, X, Y, A, Y
Platinum Gun	27	B, X, X, B, A

JAWS UNLEASHED

LEVEL SELECT AT BEGINNING
Start a new game with shaaark as your profile name.

1,000,000 UPGRADE POINTS
Start a new game with blooood as your profile name.

JUICED

ARCADE/CUSTOM MODE UNLOCKED
Select Cheats from the Extras menu and enter PINT.

JUSTICE LEAGUE HEROES

ALL COSTUMES
Pause the game, hold Left Trigger + Right Trigger and press Down, Left, Up, Right.

UNLIMITED ENERGY
Pause the game, hold Left Trigger + Right Trigger and press Down, Down, Right, Right, Up, Up, Left, Left.

20 SHIELDS
Pause the game, hold Left Trigger + Right Trigger and press Up, Up, Down, Down.

L.A. RUSH

$5,000
During a game, press Up, Down, Left, Right, B, Left, A, Up.

UNLIMITED N20
During a game, press Up, Down, Left, Right, X, Up, Down, B, Up.

ALL CARS IN GARAGE PIMPED
During a game, press Up, Down, Left, Right, B, X, A, Y, Up, Down, Left, Right.

DISABLE POLICE
During a game, press Up, Down, Left, Right, A, X, Right, Y, Left.

FAST TRAFFIC
During a game, press Up, Down, Left, Right, X, Right, B, Left.

NO CATCH UP
Use C-VHARD as a profile name.

SLOWER OPPONENTS
Use C-EASY as a profile name.

LEGACY OF KAIN: BLOOD OMEN 2

BEGIN GAME WITH SOUL REAVER AND IRON ARMOR
At the Main menu press White, Black, L, R, X, B, Y.

LEGACY OF KAIN: DEFIANCE

INVINCIBILITY
Pause the game and press Up, Down, Right, Down, R, Black, Down, Y, L.

ALL POWER-UPS
Pause the game and press Left, Left, Up, Up, L, Black, B, Down, Y.

ALL COMBO MOVES
Pause the game and press Right, Down, Up, Down, Down, R, Y, B, Down.

FULL HEALTH, TK, AND REAVER CHARGE
Pause the game and press Left, Right, Left, Right, R, L, B, Y, Down.

UNLIMITED REAVER CHARGE AND BALANCE EMBLEM
Pause the game and press Down, Down, Up, Left, R, Black, Down, Y, B.

ALL DARK CHRONICLES
Pause the game and press R, Down, Black, L, Right, Black, Y, Down, L.

ALL BONUSES
Pause the game and press Black, Down, White, R, Left, White, Down, L, Y.

TUBE REAVER
Pause the game and press Up, Down, Left, Right, Black, White, Y, Down, B.

CARTOON CHARACTER
Pause the game and press Up, Down, Up, Down, R, Black, Down, B, Y.

NO TEXTURES
Pause the game and press L, Down, Black, Right, Black, Up, Y, L, Down.

LEGENDS OF WRESTLING

ALL WRESTLERS
At the Main menu, press Up, Up, Down, Down, Left, Right, Left, Right, Y, Y, X.

LEGO STAR WARS: THE VIDEO GAME

Pause the game and select Extras to toggle these cheats on and off.

INVINCIBILITY
At Dexter's Diner, select Enter Code and enter 4PR28U.

BIG BLASTERS
At Dexter's Diner, select Enter Code and enter IG72X4.

CLASSIC BLASTERS
At Dexter's Diner, select Enter Code and enter L449HD.

SILLY BLASTERS
At Dexter's Diner, select Enter Code and enter NR37W1.

BRUSHES
At Dexter's Diner, select Enter Code and enter SHRUB1.

TEA CUPS
At Dexter's Diner, select Enter Code and enter PUCEAT.

MINIKIT DETECTOR
At Dexter's Diner, select Enter Code and enter LD116B.

MOUSTACHES
At Dexter's Diner, select Enter Code and enter RP924W.

PURPLE
At Depxter's Diner, select Enter Code and enter YD77GC.

SILHOUETTES
At Dexter's Diner, select Enter Code and enter MS999Q.

The following codes make each character available for purchase from Dexter's Diner.

BATTLE DROID
At Dexter's Diner, select Enter Code and enter 987UYR.

BATTLE DROID (COMMANDER)
At Dexter's Diner, select Enter Code and enter EN11K5.

BATTLE DROID (GEONOSIS)
At Dexter's Diner, select Enter Code and enter LK42U6.

BATTLE DROID (SECURITY)
At Dexter's Diner, select Enter Code and enter KF999A.

BOBA FETT
At Dexter's Diner, select Enter Code and enter LA811Y.

CLONE
At Dexter's Diner, select Enter Code and enter F8B4L6.

CLONE (EPISODE III)
At Dexter's Diner, select Enter Code and enter ER33JN.

CLONE (EPISODE III, PILOT)
At Dexter's Diner, select Enter Code and enter BHU72T.

CLONE (EPISODE III, SWAMP)
At Dexter's Diner, select Enter Code and enter N3T6P8.

CLONE (EPISODE III, WALKER)
At Dexter's Diner, select Enter Code and enter RS6E25.

COUNT DOOKU
At Dexter's Diner, select Enter Code and enter 14PGMN.

DARTH MAUL
At Dexter's Diner, select Enter Code and enter H35TUX.

DARTH SIDIOUS
At Dexter's Diner, select Enter Code and enter A32CAM.

DISGUISED CLONE
At Dexter's Diner, select Enter Code and enter VR832U.

DROIDEKA
At Dexter's Diner, select Enter Code and enter DH382U.

GENERAL GRIEVOUS
At Dexter's Diner, select Enter Code and enter SF321Y.

GEONOSIAN
At Dexter's Diner, select Enter Code and enter 19D7NB.

GRIEVOUS' BODYGUARD
At Dexter's Diner, select Enter Code and enter ZTY392.

GONK DROID
At Dexter's Diner, select Enter Code and enter U63B2A.

JANGO FETT
At Dexter's Diner, select Enter Code and enter PL47NH.

KI-ADI MUNDI
At Dexter's Diner, select Enter Code and enter DP55MV.

LUMINARA
At Dexter's Diner, select Enter Code and enter A725X4.

MACE WINDU (EPISODE III)
At Dexter's Diner, select Enter Code and enter MS952L.

PADMÉ
At Dexter's Diner, select Enter Code and enter 92UJ7D.

PK DROID
At Dexter's Diner, select Enter Code and enter R840JU.

PRINCESS LEIA
At Dexter's Diner, select Enter Code and enter BEQ82H.

REBEL TROOPER
At Dexter's Diner, select Enter Code and enter L54YUK.

ROYAL GUARD
At Dexter's Diner, select Enter Code and enter PP43JX.

SHAAK TI
At Dexter's Diner, select Enter Code and enter EUW862.

SUPER BATTLE DROID
At Dexter's Diner, select Enter Code and enter XZNR21.

LEGO STAR WARS II: THE ORIGINAL TRILOGY

BEACH TROOPER
At Mos Eisley Canteena, select Enter Code and enter UCK868. You still need to select Characters and purchase this character for 20,000 studs.

BEN KENOBI (GHOST)
At Mos Eisley Canteena, select Enter Code and enter BEN917. You still need to select Characters and purchase this character for 1,100,000 studs.

BESPIN GUARD

At Mos Eisley Canteena, select Enter Code and enter VHY832. You still need to select Characters and purchase this character for 15,000 studs.

BIB FORTUNA

At Mos Eisley Canteena, select Enter Code and enter WTY721. You still need to select Characters and purchase this character for 16,000 studs.

BOBA FETT

At Mos Eisley Canteena, select Enter Code and enter HLP221. You still need to select Characters and purchase this character for 175,000 studs.

DEATH STAR TROOPER

At Mos Eisley Canteena, select Enter Code and enter BNC332. You still need to select Characters and purchase this character for 19,000 studs.

EWOK

At Mos Eisley Canteena, select Enter Code and enter TTT289. You still need to select Characters and purchase this character for 34,000 studs.

GAMORREAN GUARD

At Mos Eisley Canteena, select Enter Code and enter YZF999. You still need to select Characters and purchase this character for 40,000 studs. Gonk Droid

At Mos Eisley Canteena, select Enter Code and enter NFX582. You still need to select Characters and purchase this character for 1,550 studs.

GRAND MOFF TARKIN

At Mos Eisley Canteena, select Enter Code and enter SMG219. You still need to select Characters and purchase this character for 38,000 studs.

GREEDO

At Mos Eisley Canteena, select Enter Code and enter NAH118. You still need to select Characters and purchase this character for 60,000 studs.

HAN SOLO (HOOD)

At Mos Eisley Canteena, select Enter Code and enter YWM840. You still need to select Characters and purchase this character for 20,000 studs.

IG-88

At Mos Eisley Canteena, select Enter Code and enter NXL973. You still need to select Characters and purchase this character for 30,000 studs.

IMPERIAL GUARD

At Mos Eisley Canteena, select Enter Code and enter MMM111. You still need to select Characters and purchase this character for 45,000 studs.

IMPERIAL OFFICER

At Mos Eisley Canteena, select Enter Code and enter BBV889. You still need to select Characters and purchase this character for 28,000 studs.

IMPERIAL SHUTTLE PILOT

At Mos Eisley Canteena, select Enter Code and enter VAP664. You still need to select Characters and purchase this character for 29,000 studs.

IMPERIAL SPY

At Mos Eisley Canteena, select Enter Code and enter CVT125. You still need to select Characters and purchase this character for 13,500 studs.

JAWA

At Mos Eisley Canteena, select Enter Code and enter JAW499. You still need to select Characters and purchase this character for 24,000 studs.

LOBOT

At Mos Eisley Canteena, select Enter Code and enter UUB319. You still need to select Characters and purchase this character for 11,000 studs.

PALACE GUARD
At Mos Eisley Canteena, select Enter Code and enter SGE549. You still need to select Characters and purchase this character for 14,000 studs.

REBEL PILOT
At Mos Eisley Canteena, select Enter Code and enter CYG336. You still need to select Characters and purchase this character for 15,000 studs.

REBEL TROOPER (HOTH)
At Mos Eisley Canteena, select Enter Code and enter EKU849. You still need to select Characters and purchase this character for 16,000 studs.

SANDTROOPER
At Mos Eisley Canteena, select Enter Code and enter YDV451. You still need to select Characters and purchase this character for 14,000 studs.

SKIFF GUARD
At Mos Eisley Canteena, select Enter Code and enter GBU888. You still need to select Characters and purchase this character for 12,000 studs.

SNOWTROOPER
At Mos Eisley Canteena, select Enter Code and enter NYU989. You still need to select Characters and purchase this character for 16,000 studs.

STROMTROOPER
At Mos Eisley Canteena, select Enter Code and enter PTR345. You still need to select Characters and purchase this character for 10,000 studs.

THE EMPEROR
At Mos Eisley Canteena, select Enter Code and enter HHY382. You still need to select Characters and purchase this character for 275,000 studs. TIE Fighter

At Mos Eisley Canteena, select Enter Code and enter HDY739. You still need to select Characters and purchase this character for 60,000 studs.

TIE FIGHTER PILOT
At Mos Eisley Canteena, select Enter Code and enter NNZ316. You still need to select Characters and purchase this character for 21,000 studs.

TIE INTERCEPTOR
At Mos Eisley Canteena, select Enter Code and enter QYA828. You still need to select Characters and purchase this character for 40,000 studs.

TUSKEN RAIDER
At Mos Eisley Canteena, select Enter Code and enter PEJ821. You still need to select Characters and purchase this character for 23,000 studs.

UGNAUGHT
At Mos Eisley Canteena, select Enter Code and enter UGN694. You still need to select Characters and purchase this character for 36,000 studs.

MADDEN NFL 06

Select Madden Cards from My Madden, then select Madden Codes and enter the following:

PASSWORD	CARD
6W5J6Z	#1 Rex Grossman Gold
6X7W2O	#2 Thomas Jones Gold
6Y5Z6H	#3 Brian Urlacher Gold
6Z9X5Y	#4 Olin Kreutz Gold
7A7Z2G	#5 Tommie Harris Gold
7C6U4H	#6 Carson Palmer Gold
7D1B2H	#7 Chad Johnson Gold
7D1X8K	#8 Rudi Johnson Gold
7D5W8J	#9 Brian Simmons Gold
7D8S6J	#10 J.P. Losman Gold
7E3G7Y	#11 Willis McGahee Gold

PASSWORD	CARD
7F5B2Y	#12 Eric Moulds Gold
7H3B2Y	#13 Takeo Spikes Gold
7H9E8L	#14 Lawyer Milloy Gold
7J3Y7F	#15 Jake Plummer Gold
7J8F4J	#16 Ashley Lelie Gold
7K5C8V	#17 Al Wilson Gold
7L8C2W	#18 Champ Bailey Gold
1A2D9F	#19 John Lynch Gold
70I1J3F	#20 D.J. Williams Gold
7P5G3N	#21 Lee Suggs Gold
7Q2E45	#22 Kellen Winslow Jr. Gold
7Q6F4G	#23 Simeon Rice Gold
7Q6X4L	#24 Derrick Brooks Gold
7R7V2E	#25 Ronde Barber Gold
7S4C4D	#26 Anthony McFarland Gold
7T1G2Y	#27 Michael Clayton Gold
7T3V5K	#28 Anquan Boldin Gold
7T6B5N	#29 Larry Fitzgerald Gold
7U4M9B	#30 Bertrand Berry Gold
7U6B3L	#31 LaDainian Tomlinson Gold
8Q2J2R	#55 Donovan McNabb Bronze
8Q2J2X	#55 Donovan McNabb Gold
8V9Y3X	#62 Michael Vick Gold
8X2Y9G	#64 Alge Crumpler Gold
2W4P9T	#188 First and Fifteen Bronze
2W4P9G	#188 First and Fifteen Silver
2Y7L8B	#189 First and Five Bronze
2Z2F4H	#190 Unforced Errors Bronze
2Z2F4G	#190 Unforced Errors Silver
3D3Q3P	#191 Extra Credit Bronze
3D8X6Z	#191 Extra Credit Gold
3D8X6T	#192 Tight Fit Bronze
3E9R4V	#193 5th Down Bronze
3E9R4I	#193 5th Down Silver
3F9G4J	#194 3rd Down Bronze
3F9G4O	#194 3rd Down Silver
3H3U7T	#194 3rd Down Gold
3H3U7F	#195 Human Plow Bronze
3H8M5U	#196 Super Dive Bronze
3J3S9Y	#197 Da Boot Bronze
3J3S9E	#197 Da Boot Silver
3T4E3Y	#208 Pocket Protectors Gold
3X1V2H	#210 QB on Target Gold
4D1V2Y	#217 Ouch Gold
4F9D2B	#220 Super Bowl XL Gold
4F9D2H	#221 Super Bowl XLI Gold
4I1V6T	#222 Super Bowl XLII Gold
4F3D7E	#223 Super Bowl XLIII Gold
4I1V6K	#224 Aloha Stadium Gold

MADDEN NFL 07

#199 GOLD LAME DUCK CHEAT CARD
In My Madden, select Madden Codes from Madden Cards. Enter 5LAWO0.

#200 GOLD MISTAKE FREE CHEAT CARD
In My Madden, select Madden Codes from Madden Cards. Enter XL7SP1.

#210 GOLD QB ON TARGET CHEAT CARD
In My Madden, select Madden Codes from Madden Cards. ENTER WROA0R.

MAGIC: THE GATHERING—BATTLEGROUNDS

ALL QUESTS
At the Quest Select screen, press Left Trigger + Right Trigger, Down, Up, press the Left Thumbstick, White, Up, Right, Left, Down, Left Trigger + Right Trigger.

SECRET LEVEL
At the Arena Select screen, press Left Trigger + Right Trigger, Left, Up, X, Up, Right, Y, Left Trigger + Right Trigger.

ALL DUELISTS
At the Character Select screen, press Left Trigger + Right Trigger, Down, Up, X, White, Up, X, Black, Up, X, Left Trigger + Right Trigger.

MAJOR LEAGUE BASEBALL 2K6

UNLOCK EVERYTHING
Select Enter Cheat Code from the My 2K6 menu and enter Derek Jeter.

TOPPS 2K STARS
Select Enter Cheat Code from the My 2K6 menu and enter Dream Team.

SUPER WALL CLIMB
Select Enter Cheat Code from the My 2K6 menu and enter Last Chance. Enable the cheats by selecting My Cheats or selecting Cheat Codes from the Options screen in-game.

SUPER PITCHES
Select Enter Cheat Code from the My 2K6 menu and enter Unhittable. Enable the cheats by selecting My Cheats or selecting Cheat Codes from the Options screen in-game.

ROCKET ARMS
Select Enter Cheat Code from the My 2K6 menu and enter Gotcha. Enable the cheats by selecting My Cheats or selecting Cheat Codes from the Options screen in-game.

BOUNCY BALL
Select Enter Cheat Code from the My 2K6 menu and enter Crazy Hops. Enable the cheats by selecting My Cheats or selecting Cheat Codes from the Options screen in-game.

MANHUNT

CHEAT CODES
The following codes cannot be used until they are unlocked. To unlock them, you must earn a five-star rating (which is only possible on Hardcore mode) in each pair of two consecutive scenes. After unlocking the codes, enter them at the Title screen.

EFFECT	CODE
Runner	White, White, L, White, Left, Right, Left, Right (Scenes 01 and 02)
Silence	R, L, White, L, Right, Left (x3) (Scenes 03 and 04)
Regenerate	White, Right, B, White, Black, Down, B, Left (Scenes 05 and 06)
Helium Hunters	R, R, Y, B, X, Black, L, Down (Scenes 07 and 08)
Fully Equipped	R, White, L, Black, Down, Up, Left, Up (Scenes 09 and 10)
Super Punch	L, Y (x3), B (x3), R (Scenes 11 and 12)
Rabbit Skin	Left, R, R, Y, R, R, X, L (Scenes 13 and 14)
Monkey Skin	X, X, White, Down, Y, X, B, Down (Scenes 15 and 16)
Invisibility	X (x3), Down, X, Down, B, Up (Scenes 17 and 18)
Piggsy Skin	Up, Down, Left, Left, R, White, L, L (Scenes 19 and 20)

GOD MODE
After defeating the game on Fetish mode, press Down, Down, B, Up, X, Y, X, White, Up, Up, L, Y,

MARC ECKO'S GETTING UP: CONTENTS UNDER PRESSURE

ALL LEVELS
Select Codes from the Options menu and enter IPULATOR.

INFINITE HEALTH
Select Codes from the Options menu and enter MARCUSECKOS.

MAX HEALTH
Select Codes from the Options menu and enter BABYLONTRUST.

INFINITE SKILLS
Select Codes from the Options menu and enter FLIPTHESCRIPT.

MAX SKILLS
Select Codes from the Options menu and enter VANCEDALLISTER.

ALL COMBAT UPGRADES
Select Codes from the Options menu and enter DOGTAGS.

ALL CHARACTERS IN VERSUS MODE
Select Codes from the Options menu and enter STATEYOURNAME.

ALL VERSUS ARENAS
Select Codes from the Options menu and enter WORKBITCH.

ALL ART
Select Codes from the Options menu and enter SIRULLY.

ALL BLACK BOOK
Select Codes from the Options menu and enter SHARDSOFGLASS.

ALL IPOD
Select Codes from the Options menu and enter GRANDMACELIA.

ALL LEGENDS
Select Codes from the Options menu and enter NINESIX.

ALL MOVIES
Select Codes from the Options menu and enter DEXTERCROWLEY.

MARVEL NEMESIS: RISE OF THE IMPERFECTS

UNLOCKS ALL FANTASTIC FOUR COMICS
Select Cheats from the Options menu and enter SAVAGELAND.

UNLOCKS ALL TOMORROW PEOPLE COMICS
Select Cheats from the Options menu and enter NZONE.

ELEKTRA BONUS CARD
Select Cheats from the Options menu and enter THEHAND.

SOLARA BONUS CARD
Select Cheats from the Options menu and enter REIKO.

STORM BONUS CARD
Select Cheats from the Options menu and enter MONROE.

MARVEL ULTIMATE ALLIANCE

UNLOCK ALL SKINS
At the Team Menu, press Up, Down, Left, Right, Left, Right, Start.

UNLOCKS ALL HERO POWERS
At the Team Menu, press Left, Right, Up, Down, Up, Down, Start.

ALL HEROES TO LEVEL 99
At the Team Menu, press Up, Left, Up, Left, Down, Right, Down, Right, Start.

UNLOCK ALL HEROES
At the Team Menu, press Up, Up, Down, Down, Left, Left, Left, Start.

UNLOCK DAREDEVIL
At the Team Menu, press Left, Left, Right, Right, Up, Down, Up, Down, Start.

UNLOCK SILVER SURFER
At the Team Menu, press Down, Left, Left, Up, Right, Up, Down, Left, Start.

GOD MODE
During gameplay, press Up, Down, Up, Down, Up, Left, Down, Right, Start.

TOUCH OF DEATH
During gameplay, press Left, Right, Down, Down, Right, Left, Start.

SUPER SPEED
During gameplay, press Up, Left, Up, Right, Down, Right, Start.

FILL MOMENTUM
During gameplay, press Left, Right, Right, Left, Up, Down, Down, Up, Start.

UNLOCK ALL COMICS
At the Review menu, press Left, Right, Right, Left, Up, Up, Right, Start.

UNLOCK ALL CONCEPT ART
At the Review menu, press Down, Down, Down, Right, Right, Left, Down, Start.

UNLOCK ALL CINEMATICS
At the Review menu, press Up, Left, Left, Up, Right, Right, Up, Start.

UNLOCK ALL LOAD SCREENS
At the Review menu, press Up, Down, Right, Left, Up, Up Down, Start.

UNLOCK ALL COURSES
At the Comic Missions menu, press Up, Right, Left, Down, Up, Right, Left, Down, Start.

MAX PAYNE 2: THE FALL OF MAX PAYNE

ALL GAME MODES & CHAPTERS
During a game, press X (x3), A, Left, Right, Left, Right, X (x3), A, Left, Right, Left, Right. Return to the Main menu and select New Game.

MEDAL OF HONOR: EUROPEAN ASSAULT

Pause the game, hold Left Trigger + Right Trigger and press Down, A, X, Black, A. You can now enter the following:

DISABLE SHELLSHOCK
Press X, Y, A, B, Left Trigger, X.

INFINITE HEALTH
Press White, Black, Y, White, Left Trigger, Left Trigger.

HIDE HUD
Press Black, Left Trigger, Black, Right Trigger, Up, Y.

KILL NEMESIS
Press Right, Left, Right Trigger, Left Trigger, X, Y.

PICKUP OSS DOCUMENT
Press A, B, Right Trigger, White, Black, Left Trigger.

SUICIDE (SINGLE PLAYER ONLY)
Press B, Right Trigger, White, Y, Left Trigger, White.

UNLIMITED AMMO
Press L, Y, B, Up, A, A.

MIDNIGHT CLUB 3: DUB EDITION REMIX

ALL CITIES AND RACES IN ARCADE MODE
Select Cheat Codes from the Options menu and enter urbansprawl, roadtrip or crosscountry.

NO DAMAGE
Select Cheat Codes from the Options menu and enter ontheroad.

ARGO SPECIAL MOVE
Select Cheat Codes from the Options menu and enter dfens.

ROAR SPECIAL MOVE
Select Cheat Codes from the Options menu and enter Rjnr.

ZONE SPECIAL MOVE
Select Cheat Codes from the Options menu and enter allin.

ADD $1 TO CAREER MONEY
Select Cheat Codes from the Options menu and enter kubmir.

SUBTRACT $1 OF CAREER MONEY
Select Cheat Codes from the Options menu and enter rimbuk.

BUNNY HEAD
Select Cheat Codes from the Options menu and enter getheadl.

CHROME HEAD
Select Cheat Codes from the Options menu and enter haveyouseenthisboy.

FLAMING HEAD
Select Cheat Codes from the Options menu and enter trythisathome.

SNOWMAN HEAD
Select Cheat Codes from the Options menu and enter getheadm.

PUMPKIN HEAD
Select Cheat Codes from the Options menu and enter getheadk.

YELLOW SMILE HEAD
Select Cheat Codes from the Options menu and enter getheadj.

MIDWAY ARCADE TREASURES 3

HYDRO THUNDER

ALL TRACKS AND BOATS
Get a high score and enter ?PB as your initials.

OFFROAD THUNDER

CLIFFHANGER TRACK
Select Rally and press Right at the Choose Track screen to bring up the Secret Code option. Press Right, Up, Left, to unlock the Cliffhanger track.

CHIEFTAIN & GENERAL VEHICLES
Select Rally and press Right at the Choose Machine screen to bring up the Secret Code option. Press Left (x3) to unlock Chieftain. Press Left (x3) again to unlock General.

DUST DEVIL & SILVER STREAK VEHICLES
Select Rally and press Right at the Choose Machine screen to bring up the Secret Code option.
Press Left, Up, Right to unlock Dust Devil. Press Left, Up, Right again to unlock Silver Streak.

HYENA & BAD OMEN VEHICLES
Select Rally and press Right at the Choose Machine screen to bring up the Secret Code option.
Press Right (x3) to unlock Hyena. Press Right (x3) again to unlock Bad Omen.

WILDCAT & THRASHER VEHICLES
Select Rally and press Right at the Choose Machine screen to bring up the Secret Code option.
Press Up (x3) to unlock Wildcat. Press Up (x3) again to unlock Thrasher.

MLB SLUGFEST 2006

ATLANTIS
Hit a Homer in AT&T Park.

COLISEUM
Hit a Homer in Fenway.

EMPIRE
Hit a Homer in Yankee Stadium.

FORBIDDEN CITY
Hit Homer in PetCo Park.

MONUMENT STADIUM
Hit homer in Citizens Bank Park.

ROCKET PARK
Hit a Homer in Minute Maid Park.

TEAM BOBBLE HEAD
Hit 10 homers in one game.

TEAM CASEY
Hit a Triple in Wrigley Field.

TEAM DOLPHINS
Hit a homer in Atlantis.

TEAM EAGLES
Walk 3 times in one game.

TEAM EVIL CLOWNS
Hit a homer in Empire Park with the Yankees.

TEAM GLADIATOR
Hit homer in The Coliseum.

TEAM HORSE
Steal 5 bases in one game.

TEAM LIONS
Hit a homer with the Tigers in Comerica Park.

TEAM MARTIANS
Hit a Triple in Rocket Park.

TEAM MINTAUR
Hit a homer in The Forbidden City.

TEAM PINTO
Hit an inside-the-park homer in Busch Stadium.

TEAM RODEO CLOWN
Perform a double play.

MLB SLUGFEST: LOADED

CHEATS
At the Match-Up screen, press X, Y, and B to enter the following codes, then press the appropriate direction. For example, for 16" Softball press X (x2), Y (x4), B (x2), then press Down.

CODE	ENTER
Bone Bat	0-0-1 Up
Blade Bat	0-0-2 Up
Ice Bat	0-0-3 Up
Log Bat	0-0-4 Up
Spike Bat	0-0-5 Up
Whiffle Bat	0-0-4 Right
Max Batting	3-0-0 Left
Max Power	0-3-0 Left
Max Speed	0-0-3 Left
Unlimited Turbo	4-4-4 Down
Extra Time After Plays	1-2-3 Left
Little League Mode	1-0-1 Down
16" Softball	2-4-2 Down
Rubber Bball	2-4-2 Up
Tiny Head	2-0-0 Left
Big Head	2-0-0 Right

CODE	ENTER
Alien Team	2-3-1 Down
Bobblehead Team	1-3-3 Down
Casey team	2-3-3 Down
Dolphin Team	1-0-2 Down
Dwarf Team	1-0-3 Down
Eagle Team	2-1-2 Right
Evil Clown Team	2-1-1 Down
Gladiator Team	1-1-3 Down
Horse Team	2-1-1 Right
Lion Team	2-2-0 Right
Minotaur Team	1-1-0 Down
Napalitano Team	2-3-2 Down
Olshan Team	2-2-2 Down
Pinto Team	2-1-0 Right
Rivera Team	2-2-2 Up
Rodeo Clown Team	1-3-2 Down
Scorpion Team	1-1-2 Down
Terry Fitzgerald Team	3-3-3 Right
Todd McFarlane Team	2-2-2 Right
Atlantis Stadium	3-2-1 Left
Coliseum Stadium	3-3-3 Up
Empire Park Stadium	3-2-1 Right
Forbidden City Stadium	3-3-3 Left
Midway Park Stadium	3-2-1 Down
Monument Stadium	3-3-3 Down
Rocket Park Stadium	3-2-1 Up

MORTAL KOMBAT: ARMAGEDDON

BLAZE CHARACTER
While in The Krypt, select the "?" and press Y, X, Left, Right Trigger, Left, B.

DAEGON CHARACTER
While in The Krypt, select the "?" and press Right Trigger, Right Trigger, Y, Down, Down, X.

MEAT CHARACTER
While in The Krypt, select the "?" and press Up, X, X, B, B, Up.

TAVEN CHARACTER
While in The Krypt, select the "?" and press White, Left, Right Trigger, Up, B, Down.

DRAHMIN'S ALTERNATE COSTUME
While in The Krypt, select the "?" and press White, Right, A, White, Up, Up.

FROST'S ALTERNATE COSTUME
While in The Krypt, select the "?" and press Down, White, Right Trigger, Right Trigger, B, White.

NITARA'S ALTERNATE COSTUME
While in The Krypt, select the "?" and press Down, Right Trigger, Up, Right Trigger, Right Trigger, Right.

SHANG TSUNG'S ALTERNATE COSTUME
While in The Krypt, select the "?" and press Right Trigger, Left, Up, B, Up, White.

FALLING CLIFFS ARENA
While in The Krypt, select the "?" and press White, B, X, A, B, Y.

KRIMSON FOREST ARENA
While in The Krypt, select the "?" and press B, Right Trigger, Up, X, B, Down.

NETHERSHIP INTERIOR ARENA
While in The Krypt, select the "?" and press Right Trigger, Left, Left, Down, Right Trigger, X.

THE PYRAMID OF ARGUS ARENA
While in The Krypt, select the "?" and press Right Trigger, Right Trigger, X, A, White, Up.

REIKO'S WAR ROOM ARENA
While in The Krypt, select the "?" and press White, Y, Right Trigger, Up, A, A.

SHINNOK'S SPIRE ARENA
While in The Krypt, select the "?" and press Left, Left, B, Up, Y, White.

ARMAGEDDON PROMO MOVIE
While in The Krypt, select the "?" and press Up, Up, Down, Up, Right Trigger, A.

CYRAX FATALITY BLOOPER MOVIE
While in The Krypt, select the "?" and press Right, Right Trigger, White, Down, Up, Right Trigger.

MOTOR GAMEPLAY MOVIE
While in The Krypt, select the "?" and press Y, Up, White, Right Trigger, Right Trigger, White.

BLAZE BOSS SKETCH KONCEPT ART
While in The Krypt, select the "?" and press Right Trigger, Y, White, White, Right Trigger, X.

COLOR STUDY FOR OPENING MOVIE 3 KONCEPT ART
While in The Krypt, select the "?" and press Y, Left, Left, A, Down, B.

FIREWELL SKETCH 3 KONCEPT ART
While in The Krypt, select the "?" and press Up, X, Right Trigger, White, B, Right Trigger.

GAUNTLET TRAP SKETCH KONCEPT ART
While in The Krypt, select the "?" and press B, White, Y, Down, B, Left.

HERO SKETCHES 1 KONCEPT ART
While in The Krypt, select the "?" and press Up, A, White, Down, White, A.

MILEENA'S CAR SKETCH KONCEPT ART
While in The Krypt, select the "?" and press White, Right, Up, Right Trigger, Y, Up.

SCORPION THROW SKETCH KONCEPT ART
While in The Krypt, select the "?" and press Right Trigger, Left, Up, B, White, Right Trigger.

SEKTOR'S 2-HAND PULSE BLADE SKETCH KONCEPT ART
While in The Krypt, select the "?" and press White, Right Trigger, Left, A, Up, Right Trigger.

ARMORY FIGHT TUNE
While in The Krypt, select the "?" and press A, X, Left, Y, X, A.

LIN KUEI PALACE TUNE
While in The Krypt, select the "?" and press White, Left, B, A, White, Right.

PYRAMID OF ARGUS TUNE
While in The Krypt, select the "?" and press Down, Left, White, White, Up, Right Trigger.

TEKUNIN WARSHIP TUNE
While in The Krypt, select the "?" and press Up, B, Right Trigger, Right Trigger, Right Trigger, A.

MOTOCROSS MANIA 3

ALL TRACKS
At the Main menu, press Up, Left, Down, Right, Up, Left, Down, Left, Left, X.

ALL RIDERS & BIKES
At the Main menu, press Up, Left, Down, Right, Up, Left, Down, Up, X.

ALL BIKE UPGRADES
At the Main menu, press Up, Left, Down, Right, Up, Down, Down, Left, Down, X.

ALL WEAPONS & ARMOR
At the Main menu, press Up, Left, Down, Right, Up, Left, Down, Left, Down, X.

FREESTYLE
At the Main menu, press Up, Left, Down, Right, Up, Left, Down, Left, Left, X. Go to another menu and back out to access Freestyle.

MVP 06 NCAA BASEBALL

ALL CHALLENGE ITEMS
In Dynasty Mode, create a player with the name Dee Jay Randall.

LEVEL 1 CHALLENGE ITEMS
In Dynasty Mode, create a player with the name Peter Trenouth.

ALL LEVEL 2 CHALLENGE ITEMS
In Dynasty Mode, create a player with the name Trey Smith.

ALL LEVEL 3 CHALLENGE ITEMS
In Dynasty Mode, create a player with the name Chris Chung.

ALL LEVEL 4 CHALLENGE ITEMS
In Dynasty Mode, create a player with the name Federico Rahal.

BIG BAT
In Dynasty Mode, create a player with the name Chris Deas.

SHORT PLAYER WITH BIG BAT
In Dynasty Mode, create a player with the name Alan Blouin.

THICK BAT
In Dynasty Mode, create a player with the name Melissa Shim.

LARGE PLAYER WITH THIN BAT
In Dynasty Mode, create a player with the name Neale Genereux.

SHORT PLAYER WITH THIN BAT
In Dynasty Mode, create a player with the name Julia Kwan.

SUPER HITTER
In Dynasty Mode, create a player with the name Tim Regel.

MVP BASEBALL 2005

ALL STADIUMS, PLAYERS, UNIFORMS AND REWARDS
Create a player named Katie Roy.

GOOD HITTER WITH BIG BAT
Create a player named Isaiah Paterson, Jacob Paterson, or Keegan Paterson.

BONE-SCALING CHEAT
Create a player named Kenny Lee.

MX UNLEASHED

Select Cheat Codes from the Options menu, then highlight the desired cheat and press X to access a keyboard. Enter the following codes.

SUPERCROSS TRACKS
Enter STUpERCROSS.

NATIONAL TRACKS
Enter ECONATION.

FREESTYLE TRACKS
Enter BUSTBIG.

PRO PHYSICS
Enter SWAPPIN.

EXPERT AI
Enter OBTGOFAST.

MACHINES
Enter MINIGAMES.

50CC BIKES
Enter SQUIRRELDOG.

500CC BIKES
Enter BIGDOGS.

CAREER COMPLETION
Enter CLAPPEDOUT.

AI BOWLING
Enter WRECKINGBALL.

MX vs. ATV UNLEASHED

UNLOCK EVERYTHING
Select Cheat Codes from the Options menu and enter TOOLAZY.

1,000,000 POINTS
Select Cheat Codes from the Options menu and enter BROKEASAJOKE. After entering the code, press Done multiple times for more points.

ALL PRO RIDERS
Select Cheat Codes from the Options menu and enter WANNABE.

ALL GEAR
Select Cheat Codes from the Options menu and enter WARDROBE.

50CC BIKE CLASS
Select Cheat Codes from the Options menu and enter MINIMOTO.

ALL MACHINES
Select Cheat Codes from the Options menu and enter LEADFOOT.

ALL FREESTYLE TRACKS
Select Cheat Codes from the Options menu and enter HUCKIT.

NARC

ALL DRUGS
During a game, press R, L, R, L, R, L, Left Thumbstick.

ALL WEAPONS
During a game, press R, L, R, L, R, L, Right Thimbstick.

INVINCIBILITY
During a game, press R, L, R, L, R, L, A.

SHOW HIDDEN STASHES
During a game, press R, L, R, L, R, L, Left.

UNLIMITED AMMO FOR CURRENT WEAPON
During a game, press R, L, R, L, R, L, Down.

THE REFINERY
During a game, press R, L, R, L, R, L, X.

NASCAR 06: TOTAL TEAM CONTROL

UNLOCK EVERYTHING
In Fight to the Top mode, select Edit Driver. Enter Gimme Gimme as the first and last names.

$10,000,000
In Fight to the Top mode, select Edit Driver. Enter Walmart Money as the first and last names.

MAX FAN LEVEL
In Fight to the Top mode, select Edit Driver. Enter Super Star as the first and last names.

MAX PRESTIGE
In Fight to the Top mode, select Edit Driver. Enter MeMyself AndI as the first and last names.

MAX TEAM PRESTIGE
In Fight to the Top mode, select Edit Driver. Enter All ForOne as the first and last names.

WALMART TRACKS AND CARS
In Fight to the Top mode, select Edit Driver. Enter Walmart Exclusive as the first and last names.

OLD SPICE TRACKS AND CARS
In Fight to the Top mode, select Edit Driver. Enter KeepCool SmellGreat as the first and last names.

DALE EARNHARDT SR.
In Fight to the Top mode, select Edit Driver. Enter The Intimidator as the first and last names.

NASCAR 07

$10,000,000
In Fight to the Top mode, enter your name as GiveMe More.

10,000,000 FANS
In Fight to the Top mode, enter your name as AllBow ToMe.

PRESTIGE LEVEL 10 WITH 2,000,000 POINTS
In Fight to the Top mode, enter your name as Outta MyWay.

100% TEAM PRESTIGE
In Fight to the Top mode, enter your name as MoMoney BlingBling.

ALL CHASE PLATES
In Fight to the Top mode, enter your name as ItsAll ForMe.

OLD SPICE TRACKS AND CARS
In Fight to the Top mode, enter your name as KeepCool SmellGreat.

WALMART TRACK AND CARS
In Fight to the Top mode, enter your name as Walmart EveryDay.

NASCAR 2005: CHASE FOR THE CUP

DALE EARNHARDT
At the Edit Driver screen, enter The Intimidator as your name.

$10,000,000
At the Edit Driver screen, enter Walmart NASCAR as your name.

2,000,000 PRESTIGE POINTS
At the Edit Driver screen, enter You TheMan as your name.

EXCLUSIVE TRACK
At the Edit Driver screen, enter Walmart Exclusive as your name.

ALL THUNDER PLATES
At the Edit Driver screen, enter Open Sesame as your name.

NBA 2K6

CELEBRITY STREET OPTION
Select Codes from the Features menu and enter ballers.

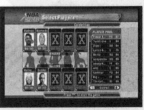

2KSPORTS TEAM
Select Codes from the Features menu and enter 2ksports.

2K6 TEAM
Select Codes from the Features menu and enter nba2k6.

VC TEAM
Select Codes from the Features menu and enter vcteam.

NIKE SHOX MTX SHOES
Select Codes from the Features menu and enter crazylift.

NIKE ZOOM 20-5-5 SHOES
Select Codes from the Features menu and enter lebronsummerkicks.

NIKE ZOOM KOBE 1 SHOES
Select Codes from the Features menu and enter kobe.

NIKE ZOOM LEBRON III ALL-STAR COLORWAY SHOES
Select Codes from the Features menu and enter lb allstar.

NIKE ZOOM LEBRON III BLACK/CRIMSON SHOES
Select Codes from the Features menu and enter lb crimsonblack.

NIKE ZOOM LEBRON III SPECIAL BIRTHDAY EDITION SHOES
Select Codes from the Features menu and enter lb bday.

NIKE ZOOM LEBRON III WHITE/GOLD SHOES
Select Codes from the Features menu and enter lb whitegold.

NIKE UP TEMPO PRO SHOES
Select Codes from the Features menu and enter anklebreakers.

ALTERNATE UNIFORMS
To access various uniforms, select Codes from the Features menu and enter the following to unlock the different uniforms.

UNIFORM	ENTER
2006 All-Star	fanfavorites
St. Patrick's Day	gogreen
Bulls Retro	chi retro
Cavaliers Alternate	cle 2nd
Celtics Alternate	bos 2nd
Clippers Retro	lac retro
Grizzlies Retro	mem retro
Heat Retro	mia retro
Hornets Retro	no retro
Kings Alternate	sac 2nd
Knicks Retro	ny retro
Magic Retro	orl retro
Nets Retro	nj retro
Nuggets Alternate	den 2nd
2005-06 Pacers	31andonly
Pistons Alternate	det 2nd
Rockets Retro	hou retro
Sonics Retro	sea retro
Suns Retro	phx retro
Wizards Retro	was retro

+10 BONUS FOR DEFENSIVE AWARENESS
Find the PowerBar vending machine in The Crib. Choose Enter Code and enter lockdown.

+10 BONUS FOR OFFENSIVE AWARENESS
Find the PowerBar vending machine in The Crib. Choose Enter Code and enter getaclue.

MAX DURABILITY
Find the PowerBar vending machine in The Crib. Choose Enter Code and enter noinjury.

UNLIMITED STAMINA
Find the PowerBar vending machine in The Crib. Choose Enter Code and enter nrgmax.

POWERBAR TATTOO
Find the PowerBar vending machine in The Crib. Choose Enter Code and enter pbink. You can now use this feature in the game's Create Player feature.

ALL ITEMS IN THE CRIB
Find the PowerBar vending machine in The Crib. Choose Enter Code and enter criball.

NBA 2K7

MAX DURABILITY
Select Codes from the Features menu and enter ironman.

UNLIMITED STAMINA
Select Codes from the Features menu and enter norest.

+10 DEFFENSIVE AWARENESS
Select Codes from the Features menu and enter getstops.

+10 OFFENSIVE AWARENESS
Select Codes from the Features menu and enter inthezone.

TOPPS 2K SPORTS ALL-STARS
Select Codes from the Features menu and enter topps2ksports.

ABA BALL
Select Codes from the Features menu and enter payrespect.

NBA BALLERS

VERSUS SCREEN CHEATS

You can enter the following codes at the Vs screen. The X button corresponds to the first number in the code, the Y is the second number, and the B button corresponds to the last number. Press the D-pad in any direction to enter the code.

CODE	ENTER
Tournament Mode	0 1 1
Big Head	1 3 4
Baby Ballers	4 2 3
Kid Ballers	4 3 3
Young Ballers	4 4 3
Paper Ballers	3 5 4
Alternate Gear	1 2 3
Expanded Move Set	5 1 2
Super Push	3 1 5
Super Block Ability	1 2 4
Great Handles	3 3 2
Unlimited Juice	7 6 3
Super Steals	2 1 5
Perfect Free Throws	3 2 7
Speedy Players	2 1 3
Better Free Throws	3 1 7
Fire Ability	7 2 2
Hotspot Ability	6 2 7
Back-In Ability	1 2 2
2x Juice Replenish	4 3 1
Stunt Ability	3 7 4
Pass 2 Friend Ability	5 3 6
Alley-Oop Ability	7 2 5
Put Back Ability	3 1 3
Legal Goal Tending	7 5 6
Show Shot Percentage	0 1 2
R2R Mode	0 0 8
Play as Coach	5 6 7
Play as Agent	5 5 7
Play as Secretary	5 4 7
Play as BiznezMan-A	5 3 7
Play as BiznezMan-B	5 2 7
Play as Afro Man	5 1 7
Super Back-Ins	2 3 5
Half House	3 6 7
Random Moves	3 0 0
Pygmy	4 2 5

PHRASE-OLOGY CODES/ALTERNATE GEAR

Select Phrase-ology from the Inside Stuff option and enter the following codes to unlock the Alternate Gear for the corresponding player.

PLAYER	PHRASE
Allan Houston	KNICKER BOCKER PLEASE
Allen Iverson	KILLER CROSSOVER
Alonzo Mourning	ZO
Amare Stoudemire	RISING SUN
Antoine Walker	BALL HAWK
Baron Davis	STYLIN' & PROFILIN'

PLAYER	PHRASE
Ben Wallace	RADIO CONTROLLED CARS
Bill Russell	CELTICS DYNASTY
Bill Walton	TOWERS OF POWER
Carmelo Anthony	NEW TO THE GAME
Chris Webber	24 SECONDS
Clyde Drexler	CLYDE THE GLIDE
Darko Milicic	NBA FASTBREAK
Darryl Dawkins	RIM WRECKER
Dejaun Wagner	NBA HANGTIME
Dikembe Mutumbo	IN THE PAINT
Dominique Wilkins	DUNK FEST
Eddie Jones	BALLER UPRISING
Elton Brand	REBOUND
Manu Ginobili	MANU
Gary Payton	GLOVE IS IN LA
George Gervin	THE ICE MAN COMETH
Grant Hill	GONE GOLD WITH IT
Isiah Thomas	TRUE BALLER
Jalen Rose	BRING IT
Jason Kidd	PASS THE ROCK
Jason Terry	BALL ABOVE ALL
Jason Williams	GIVE AND GO
Jerry Stackhouse	STOP DROP AND ROLL
John Stockton	COURT VISION
Julius Irving	ONE ON ONE
Karl Malone	SPECIAL DELIVERY
Kenyon Martin	TO THE HOLE
Kevin Garnett	BOSS HOSS
Kevin McHale	HOLLA BACK
Kobe Bryant	JAPANESE STEAK
Larry Bird	HOOSIER
Latrell Sprewell	SPREE
Lebron James	KING JAMES
Magic Johnson	LAKER LEGENDS
Michael Finley	STUDENT OF THE GAME
Mike Bibby	DREAMS & SCHEMES
Moses Malone	LOST FREESTYLE FILES
Nate "Tiny" Archibald	NATE THE SKATE
Nene Hilario	RAGS TO RICHES
Oscar Robertson	AINT NO THING
Pau Gasol	POW POW POW
Paul Pierce	CELTICS SUPREME
Pete Maravich	PISTOL PETE
Rashard Lewis	FAST FORWARD
Rasheed Wallace	BRING Down THE HOUSE
Ray Allen	ALL STAR
Reggie Miller	FROM DownTOWN
Richard Hamilton	RIP
Robert Parish	THE CHIEF
Scottie Pippen	PLAYMAKER
Shaquille O'Neal	DIESEL RULES THE PAINT
Shawn Marion	MAKE YOUR MARK
Stephon Marbury	PLATINUM PLAYA

PLAYER	PHRASE
Steve Francis	ANKLE BREAKER
Steve Francis	RISING STAR
Steve Nash	HAIR CANADA
Tim Duncan	MAKE IT TAKE IT
Tony Parker	RUN AND SHOOT
Tracy McGrady	LIVING LIKE A BALLER
Vince Carter	CHECK MY CRIB
Wally Szczerbiak	WORLD
Walt Frazier	PENETRATE AND PERPETRATE
Wes Unseld	OLD SCHOOL
Willis Reed	HALL OF FAME
Wilt Chamberlain	WILT THE STILT
Yao Ming	CENTER OF ATTENTION

CRIBS
Select Phrase-ology from the Inside Stuff option and enter the following to unlock player cribs.

CRIB	PHRASE
Allen Iverson's Recording Studio	THE ANSWER
Karl Malone's Devonshire Estate	ICE HOUSE
Kobe Bryant's Italian Estate	EURO CRIB
Scottie Pippen's Yacht	NICE YACHT
Yao Ming's Childhood Grade School	PREP SCHOOL

OTHER PHRASE-OLOGY CODES
Select Phrase-ology from the Inside Stuff option and enter the following to unlock that bonus.

BONUS	PHRASE
All Players, Alternate Gear, and Cinemas	NBA BALLERS TRUE PLAYA
Special Movie #1	JUICE HOUSE
Special Movie #2	NBA SHOWTIME
Special Movie #3	NBA BALLERS RULES
Special Movie #4	HATCHET MAN
Special Movie #5	SLAM IT
Special Shoe #2	COLD STREAK
Special Shoe #3	LOST YA SHOES

NBA BALLERS: PHENOM

VERSUS SCREEN CHEATS
You can enter the following codes at the Vs screen. The X button corresponds to the first number in the code, the Y is the second number, and the B button corresponds to the last number. Press the D-pad in any direction to enter the code.

CODE NAME	ENTER
Tournament Mode	0 1 1
Big Head	1 3 4
Baby Ballers	4 2 3
Kid Ballers	4 3 3
2D Ballers	3 5 4
Speedy Players	2 1 3
Unlimited Juice	7 6 3
House meter half full at start	3 6 7
Super block ability	1-2-4
Show Shot Percentage	0 1 2
Alternate Gear	1 2 3

NBA LIVE 06

EASTERN ALL-STARS 2005-06 AWAY JERSEYS
Select NBA Codes from My NBA Live and enter XCVB5387EQ.

EASTERN ALL-STARS 2005-06 HOME JERSEY
Select NBA Codes from My NBA Live and enter 234SDFGHMO.

WESTERN ALL-STARS 2005-06 AWAY JERSEY
Select NBA Codes from My NBA Live and enter 39N56B679J.

WESTERN ALL-STARS 2005-06 HOME JERSEY
Select NBA Codes from My NBA Live and enter 2J9UWABNP1.

BOSTON CELTICS 2005-06 ALTERNATE JERSEY
Select NBA Codes from My NBA Live and enter 193KSHU88J.

CLEVELAND CAVALIERS 2005-06 ALTERNATE JERSEY
Select NBA Codes from My NBA Live and enter 9922NVDKVT.

DENVER NUGGETS 2005-06 ALTERNATE JERSEYS
Select NBA Codes from My NBA Live and enter XWETJK72FC.

DETROIT PISTONS 2005-06 ALTERNATE JERSEY
Select NBA Codes from My NBA Live and enter JANTWIKBS6.

INDIANA PACERS 2005-06 ALTERNATE AWAY JERSEY
Select NBA Codes from My NBA Live and enter PSDF90PPJN.

INDIANA PACERS 2005-06 ALTERNATE HOME JERSEY
Select NBA Codes from My NBA Live and enter SDF786WSHW.

SACRAMENTO KINGS 2005-06 ALTERNATE JERSEY
Select NBA Codes from My NBA Live and enter 654NNBFDWA.

A3 GARNETT 3
Select NBA Codes from My NBA Live and enter DRI239CZ49.

 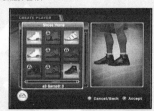

JORDAN MELO V.5 WHITE & BLUE
Select NBA Codes from My NBA Live and enter 5223WERPII.

JORDAN MELO V.5 WHITE & YELLOW
Select NBA Codes from My NBA Live and enter ZXDR7362Q1.

JORDAN XIV BLACK & RED
Select NBA Codes from My NBA Live and enter 144FVNHM35.

JORDAN XIV WHITE & GREEN
Select NBA Codes from My NBA Live and
enter 67YFH9839F.

JORDAN XIV WHITE & RED
Select NBA Codes from My NBA Live and
enter 743HFDRAU8.

S. CARTER III LE
Select NBA Codes from My NBA Live and
enter JZ3SCARTVY.

T-MAC 5 BLACK
Select NBA Codes from My NBA Live and enter 258SHQW95B.

T-MAC 5 WHITE
Select NBA Codes from My NBA Live and enter HGS83KP234P.

ANSWER DMX 10
Select NBA Codes from My NBA Live and enter RBKAIUSAB7.

ANSWER IX & THE RBK ANSWER IX VIDEO
Select NBA Codes from My NBA Live and enter AI9BUBBA7T.

THE QUESTION & THE MESSAGE FROM ALLEN IVERSON VIDEO
Select NBA Codes from My NBA Live and enter HOYAS3AI6L.

NBA LIVE 07

ADIDAS ARTILLERY II BLACK & THE RBK ANSWER 9 VIDEO
Select NBA Codes from My NBA Live and enter 99B6356HAN.

ADIDAS ARTILLERY II
Select NBA Codes and enter NTGNFUE87H.

ADIDAS BTB LOW AND THE MESSAGE FROM ALLEN IVERSON VIDEO
Select NBA Codes and enter 7FB3KS9JQ0.

ADIDAS C-BILLUPS
Select NBA Codes and enter BV6877HB9N.

ADIDAS C-BILLUPS BLACK
Select NBA Codes and enter 85NVLDMWS5.

ADIDAS CAMPUS LT
Select NBA Codes and enter CLT2983NC8.

ADIDAS CRAZY 8
Select NBA Codes and enter CC98KKL814.

ADIDAS EQUIPMENT B-BALL
Select NBA Codes and enter 220IUJKMDR.

ADIDAS GARNETT BOUNCE
Select NBA Codes and enter HYIOUHCAAN.

ADIDAS GARNETT BOUNCE BLACK
Select NBA Codes and enter KDZ2MQL17W.

ADIDAS GIL-ZERO
Select NBA Codes and enter 23DN1PPOG4.

ADIDAS GIL-ZERO BLACK
Select NBA Codes and enter QQQ3JCUYQ7.

ADIDAS GIL-ZERO MID
Select NBA Codes and enter 1GSJC8JWRL.

ADIDAS GIL-ZERO MID BLACK
Select NBA Codes and enter 369V6RVU3G.

ADIDAS STEALTH
Select NBA Codes and enter FE454DFJCC.

ADIDAS T-MAC 6
Select NBA Codes and enter MCJK843NNC.

ADIDAS T-MAC 6 WHITE
Select NBA Codes and enter 84GF7EJG8V.

CHARLOTTE BOBCATS 2006-07 ALTERNATE JERSEY
Select NBA Codes and enter WEDX671H7S.

UTAH JAZZ 2006-07 ALTERNATE JERSEY
Select NBA Codes and enter VCBI89FK83.

NEW JERSEY NETS 2006-07 ALTERNATE JERSEY
Select NBA Codes and enter D4SAA98U5H.

WASHINGTON WIZARDS 2006-07 ALTERNATE JERSEY
Select NBA Codes and enter QV93NLKXQC.

EASTERN ALL-STARS 2006-07 AWAY JERSEY
Select NBA Codes and enter WOCNW4KL7L.

EASTERN ALL-STARS 2006-07 HOME JERSEY
Select NBA Codes and enter 5654ND43N6.

WESTERN ALL-STARS 2006-07 AWAY JERSEY
Select NBA Codes and enter XX93BVL20U.

WESTERN ALL-STARS 2006-07 HOME JERSEY
Select NBA Codes and enter 993NSKL199.

NBA STREET VOL. 2

Select Pick Up Game, hold Left Trigger and enter the following codes when "Enter cheat codes now" appears at the bottom of the screen:

CODE NAME	ENTER
Unlimited Turbo	X, X, Y, Y
ABA Ball	B, X, B, X
WNBA Ball	B, Y, Y, B.
No Display Bars	X, B (x3)
All Jerseys	B, Y, X, X
All Courts	X, Y, Y, X
St. Lunatics Team & All Street Legends	X, Y, B, Y
All NBA Legends	B, Y, Y, X
Classic Michael Jordan	B, Y, B, B
Explosive Rims	B (x3), Y
Small Players	Y, Y, B, X
Big Heads	B, X, X, B
No Counters	Y, Y, B, B
Ball Trails	Y, Y, Y, X
All Quicks	Y, B, Y, X
Easy Shots	Y, B, X, Y
Hard Shots	Y, X, B, Y

NCAA FOOTBALL 06

PENNANT CODES
Select Pennant Collection from My NCAA, then press Select to enter the following codes.

CODE NAME	ENTER
#16 Baylor	Sic Em
#63 Illinois	Oskee Wow
#160 Texas Tech	Fight
#200 First and Fifteen	Thanks
#201 Blink	For
#202 Boing	Registering
#204 Butter Fingers	With EA
#205 Crossed the Line	Tiburon
#206 Cuffed	EA Sports
#207 Extra Credit	Touchdown
#208 Helium	In The Zone
#209 Hurricane	Turnover
#210 Instant Freeplay	Impact
#211 Jumbalaya	Heisman

CODE NAME	ENTER
#212 Molasses	Game Time
#213 Nike Free	Break Free
#214 Nike Magnigrip	Hand Picked
#215 Nike Pro	No Sweat
#216 Nike Speed TD	Light Speed
#219 QB Dud	Elite 11
#222 Stiffed	NCAA
#224 Take Your Time	Football
#225 Thread & Needle	06
#226 Tough as Nails	Offense
#227 Trip	Defense
#228 What a Hit!	Blitz
#229 Kicker Hex	Sideline
#273 2004 All-Americans	Fumble
#274 All-Alabama	Roll Tide
#276 All-Arkansas	Woopigsooie
#277 All-Auburn	War Eagle
#278 All-Clemson	Death Valley
#279 All-Colorado	Glory
#280 All-Florida	Great To Be
#281 All-FSU	Uprising
#282 All-Georgia	Hunker Down
#283 All-Iowa	On Iowa
#284 All-Kansas State	Victory
#285 All-LSU	Geaux Tigers
#286 All-Miami	Raising Cane
#287 All-Michigan	Go Blue
#288 All-Mississippi State	Hail State
#289 All-Nebraska	Go Big Red
#290 All-North Carolina	Rah Rah
#291 All-Notre Dame	Golden Domer
#292 All-Ohio State	Killer Nuts
#293 All-Oklahoma	Boomer
#294 All-Oklahoma State	Go Pokes
#295 All-Oregon	Quack Attack
#296 All-Penn State	We Are
#297 All-Pittsburgh	Lets Go Pitt
#298 All-Purdue	Boiler Up
#299 All-Syracuse	Orange Crush
#300 All-Tennessee	Big Orange
#301 All-Texas	Hook Em
#302 All-Texas A&M	Gig Em
#303 All-UCLA	Mighty
#304 All-USC	Fight On
#305 All-Virginia	Wahoos
#306 All-Virginia Tech	Tech Triumph
#307 All-Washington	Bow Down
#308 All-Wisconsin	U Rah Rah
#311 Ark Mascot	Bear Down
#333 ISU Mascot	Red And Gold
#335 KU Mascot	Rock Chalk
#346 Michigan State Mascot	Go Green
#341 Minn Mascot	Rah Rah Rah

CODE NAME	ENTER
#342 Miss Mascot	Hotty Totty
#344 Mizzou Mascot	Mizzou Rah
#349 NCSU Mascot	Go Pack
#352 NU Mascot	Go Cats
#371 UK Mascot	On On UK
#382 Wake Mascot	Go Deacs Go
#385 WSU Mascot	All Hail
#386 WVU Mascot	Hail WV

NCAA FOOTBALL 07

PENNANT CODES
Select Pennant Collection from My NCAA, then press Select to enter the following codes.

CODE NAME	ENTER
#16 Baylor	Sic Em
#16 Nike Speed TD	Light Speed
#63 Illinois	Oskee Wow
#160 Texas Tech	Fight
#200 First and Fifteen	Thanks
#201 Blink	For
#202 Boing	Registering
#204 Butter Fingers	With EA
#205 Crossed the Line	Tiburon
#206 Cuffed	EA Sports
#207 Extra Credit	Touchdown
#208 Helium	In The Zone
#209 Hurricane	Turnover
#210 Instant Freeplay	Impact
#211 Jumbalaya	Heisman
#212 Molasses	Game Time
#213 Nike Free	Break Free
#214 Nike Magnigrip	Hand Picked
#215 Nike Pro	No Sweat
#219 QB Dud	Elite 11
#221 Steel Toe	Gridiron
#222 Stiffed	NCAA
#223 Super Dive	Upset
#224 Take Your Time	Football
#225 Thread & Needle	06
#226 Tough As Nails	Offense
#227 Trip	Defense
#228 What a Hit	Blitz
#229 Kicker Hex	Sideline
#273 2004 All-Americans	Fumble
#274 All-Alabama	Roll Tide
#276 All-Arkansas	Woopigsooie
#277 All-Auburn	War Eagle
#278 All-Clemson	Death Valley
#279 All-Colorado	Glory
#280 All-Florida	Great To Be
#281 All-FSU	Uprising
#282 All-Georgia	Hunker Down

CODE NAME	ENTER
#283 All-Iowa	On Iowa
#284 All-Kansas State	Victory
#285 All-LSU	Geaux Tigers
#286 All-Miami	Raising Cane
#287 All-Michigan	Go Blue
#288 All-Mississippi State	Hail State
#289 All-Nebraska	Go Big Red
#290 All-North Carolina	Rah Rah
#291 All-Notre Dame	Golden Domer
#292 All-Ohio State	Killer Nuts
#293 All-Oklahoma	Boomer
#294 All-Oklahoma State	Go Pokes
#295 All-Oregon	Quack Attack
#296 All-Penn State	We Are
#297 All-Pittsburgh	Lets Go Pitt
#298 All-Purdue	Boiler Up
#299 All-Syracuse	Orange Crush
#300 All-Tennessee	Big Orange
#301 All-Texas	Hook Em
#302 All-Texas A&M	Gig Em
#303 All-UCLA	MIGHTY
#304 All-USC	Fight On
#305 All-Virginia	Wahoos
#306 All-Virginia Tech	Tech Triumph
#307 All-Washington	Bow Down
#308 All-Wisconsin	U Rah Rah
#311 Ark Mascot	Bear Down
#329 GT Mascot	RamblinWreck
#333 ISU Mascot	Red And Gold
#335 KU Mascot	Rock Chalk
#341 Minn Mascot	Rah Rah Rah
#344 Mizzou Mascot	Mizzou Rah
#346 MSU Mascot	Go Green
#349 NCSU Mascot	Go Pack
#352 NU Mascot	Go Cats
#360 S Car Mascot	Go Carolina
#371 UK Mascot	On On UK
#382 Wake Forest	Go Deacs Go
#385 WSU Mascot	All Hail
#386 WVU Mascot	Hail WV

NCAA MARCH MADNESS 06

ALL TEAMS
Select My NCAA, then Cheat Codes from the lounge. Enter PSDF9078VT.

AIR JORDAN III SHOES
Select My NCAA, then Cheat Codes from the lounge. Enter 39N56BXC4S.

FIRST AIR JORDANS
Select My NCAA, then Cheat Codes from the lounge. Enter 2J9UWAS44L.

NEED FOR SPEED CARBON

CASTROL CASH
At the Main menu, press Down, Up, Left, Down, Right, Up, X, B. This will give you 10,000 extra cash.

INFINITE CREW CHARGE
At the Main menu, press Down, Up, Up, Right, Left, Left, Right, X.

INFINITE NITROUS
At the Main menu, press Left, Up, Left, Down, Left, Down, Right, X.

INFINITE SPEEDBREAKER
At the Main menu, press Down, Right, Right, Left, Right, Up, Down, X.

NEED FOR SPEED CARBON LOGO VINYLS
At the Main menu, press Right, Up, Down, Up, Down, Left, Right, X.

NEED FOR SPEED CARBON SPECIAL LOGO VINYLS
At the main menu, press Up, Up, Down, Down, Down, Down, Up, X.

NEED FOR SPEED MOST WANTED

BURGER KING CHALLENGE
At the Title screen, press Up, Down, Up, Down, Left, Right, Left, Right.

CASTROL SYNTEC VERSION OF THE FORD GT
At the Title screen, press Left, Right, Left, Right, Up, Down, Up, Down.

MARKER FOR BACKROOM OF ONE-STOP SHOP
At the Title screen, press Up, Up, Down, Down, Left, Right, Up, Down.

PORSCHE CAYMAN
At the Title screen, press Left Trigger, Right Trigger, Right Trigger, Right Trigger, Right, Left, Right, Down.

NEED FOR SPEED UNDERGROUND 2

ALL CIRCUIT TRACKS
At the Main menu, press Down, Right Trigger, Right Trigger, Right Trigger, Black, Black, Black, X.

BEST BUY VINYL
At the Main menu, press Up, Down, Up, Down, Down, Up, Right, Left.

BURGER KING VINYL
At the Main menu, press Up, Up, Up, Up, Down, Up, Up, Left.

H2 CAPONE
At the Main menu, press Up, Left, Up, Up, Down, Left, Down, Left.

NISSIAN SKYLINE
At the Main menu, press Down, Down, Left Trigger, White, Left Trigger, White, Left Trigger, Down.

LEVEL 1 PERFORMANCE PARTS
At the Main menu, press Left Trigger, Right Trigger, Left Trigger, Right Trigger, Left, Left, Right, Up.

LEVEL 2 PERFORMANCE PARTS
At the Main menu, press Right Trigger, Right Trigger, Left Trigger, Right Trigger, Left, Right, Up, Down.

LEVEL 1 VISUAL PARTS
At the Main menu, press Right Trigger, Right Trigger, Up, Down, Left Trigger, Left Trigger, Up, Down.

LEVEL 2 VISUAL PARTS
At the Main menu, press Left Trigger, Right Trigger, Up, Down, Left Trigger, Up, Up, Down.

NFL HEAD COACH

CLOWN
Name your coach Red Nose.

JOHN MADDEN
Name your coach John Madden.

SANTA CLAUS
Name your coach Merry Christmas.

SUPER BOWL ALWAYS AT HOMETOWN
Name your coach Hometown Hero.

NFL STREET 2

FUMBLE MODE IN QUICK GAME
Enter GreasedPig as a code.

MAX CATCH IN QUICK GAME
Enter MagnetHands as a code.

NO CHAINS MODE IN QUICK GAME
Enter NoChains as a code.

NO FUMBLE MODE IN QUICK GAME
Enter GlueHands as a code.

UNLIMITED TURBO IN QUICK GAME
Enter NozBoost as a code.

EA FIELD
Enter EAField as a code.

AFC EAST ALL-STARS
Enter EAASFSCT as a code.

AFC NORTH ALL-STARS
Enter NAOFRCTH as a code.

AFC SOUTH ALL-STARS
Enter SAOFUCTH as a code.

AFC WEST ALL-STARS
Enter WAEFSCT as a code.

NFC EAST ALL-STARS
Enter NNOFRCTH as a code.

NFC NORTH ALL-STARS
Enter NNAS66784 as a code.

NFC SOUTH ALL-STARS
Enter SNOFUCTH as a code.

NFC WEST ALL-STARS
Enter ENASFSCT as a code.

TEAM REEBOK
Enter Reebok as a code.

TEAM XZIBIT
Enter TeamXzibit as a code.

NHL 2K6

UNLOCK EVERYTHING
Select Manage Profiles from the Options menu. Create a New Profile with the name Turco813.

NIGHTCASTER

TEMPORARY INVINCIBILITY
Pause the game, hold Left Trigger + Right Trigger and press Left, Left, Up, Down.

NINJA GAIDEN

ORIGINAL BLUE NINJA COSTUME
Highlight New Game and press Left Trigger + Right Trigger, then press the A button.

ODDWORLD STRANGER'S WRATH

CHEAT MODE
During a game, insert a controller in port 2. Remove the controller and press X, X, Y, Y, B, B, A, A on controller 1.

INVINCIBILITY
After entering the Cheat Mode code, press X, Y, A, B, X, Y.

$1000
After entering the Cheat Mode code, press Left Thumbstick, Left Thumbstick, Right Thumbstick, Right Thumbstick, Left Thumbstick, Left Thumbstick, Right Thumbstick, Right Thumbstick. You can repeat this code multiple times.

OUTLAW GOLF 2

ALL GOLFERS, COURSES, OUTFITS, EVENTS AND CLUBS
Enter your name as I Have No Time.

BIG HEAD MODE
During a game, hold L and press B, A, B, Y, Back.

OUTLAW TENNIS

UNLOCK EVERYTHING
Create a profile with the name Cut To The Chase. Hold Left Trigger + Right Trigger while you save the profile.

OUTLAW VOLLEYBALL

ALL CHARACTERS AND COSTUMES
Select exhibition, then at the character select, hold L and press Left, White, Right, White.

ALL COURTS
Select exhibition, then at the Court select, hold L, and press Up, Down, Up, Down, Left, Left, Right, Right.

MAXIMUM STATS IN EXHIBITION
Select exhibition, then at the character select, hold R, and press Left, White, Right, White.

BIG HEADS
During the game, hold L and quickly press B, A, B, Y during gameplay.

BIG CHESTS
Hold L and quickly press B, Up, Up, B, Y during gameplay.

MINES IN EXHIBITION
During the game, hold L and press A, B, B, Y, A + X.

OUTRUN 2

Select OutRun Challenge and go to the Gallery screen. Choose Enter Code and input the following.

ALL CARS
Enter DREAMING.

ALL MISSION STAGES
Enter THEJOURNEY.

BONUS TRACKS
Enter TIMELESS.

REVERSE TRACKS
Enter DESREVER.

ALL MUSIC
Enter RADIOSEGA.

ORIGINAL OUTRUN
Enter NINETEEN86.

ALL CARDS
Enter BIRTHDAY.

OUTRUN 2006: COAST 2 COAST

100% COMPLETE/UNLOCK EVERYTHING
Edit your license and change the name to ENTIRETY. Select Done, then back out of all menus.

1000000 OUTRUN MILES
Edit your license and change the name to MILESANDMILES. Select Done, then back out of all menus.

OVER THE HEDGE

COMPLETE LEVELS
Pause the game, hold Left Trigger + Right Trigger and press Y, B, Y, B, B, X.

ALL MINIGAMES
Pause the game, hold Left Trigger + Right Trigger and press Y, B, Y, Y, X, X.

ALL MOVES
Pause the game, hold Left Trigger + Right Trigger and press Y, B, Y, X, X, B.

EXTRA DAMAGE
Pause the game, hold Left Trigger + Right Trigger and press Y, B, Y, B, Y, X.

MORE HP FROM FOOD
Pause the game, hold Left Trigger + Right Trigger and press Y, B, Y, B, X, Y.

ALWAYS POWER PROJECTILE
Pause the game, hold Left Trigger + Right Trigger and press Y, B, Y, B, X, B.

BONUS COMIC 14
Pause the game, hold Left Trigger + Right Trigger and press Y, B, X, X, B, Y.

BONUS COMIC 15
Pause the game, hold Left Trigger + Right Trigger and press Y, Y, X, B, X, B.

PAC-MAN WORLD 3

ALL LEVELS & MAZE GAMES
At the main menu, press Left, Right, Left, Right, B, Up.

PAINKILLER: HELL WARS

GOD MODE
During a game, hold White + L and press B.

TOGGLE DEMON MODE
During a game, hold White + L and press X.

PANZER DRAGOON ORTA

ORIGINAL PANZER DRAGOON CODES
The following codes are for the original Panzer Dragoon. Unlock it first by defeating the game or playing for five hours. After doing so, enter the following codes at the Main menu of the original Panzer Dragoon.

INVINCIBLE
Press Left Trigger, Left Trigger, Right Trigger, Right Trigger, Up, Down, Left, Right.

STAGE SELECT
Press Up, Up, Down, Down, Left, Right, Left, Right, X, Y, White.

PLAY STAGE 0
Press Up, Up, Up, Down, Down, Down, Left, Right, Left, Right, Left, Right, Left Trigger, Right Trigger.

ROLLING MODE
Press Up, Right, Down, Left, Up, Right, Down, Left, Up, Right, Down, Left, Up, Right, Down, Left.

WIZARD MODE (FASTER GAMEPLAY)
Press Left Trigger, Right Trigger, Left Trigger, Right Trigger, Up, Down, Up, Down, Left, Right.

WATCH ENDING
Press Up, Up, Down, Up, Right, Right, Left, Right, Down, Down, Up, Down, Left, Left, Right, Left.

PARIAH

ALL AMMO
Select Cheat Codes from the Settings menu and press Down, Up, Down, Y.

GOD MODE
Select Cheat Codes from the Settings menu and press Up, Left Trigger, X, Left Trigger.

ALL SINGLE-PLAYER LEVELS
Select Cheat Codes from the Settings menu and press Y, Down, Right Trigger, Down.

LOCATION STATUS
Select Cheat Codes from the Settings menu and press X, Right, Left Trigger, Left.

BEST BUY MULTIPLAYER LEVEL
Select Cheat Codes from the Settings menu and press Left Trigger, Black, White, Right Trigger.

EB MULTIPLAYER LEVEL
Select Cheat Codes from the Settings menu and press White, Y, X, Black.

GAMESTOP MULTIPLAYER LEVEL
Select Cheat Codes from the Settings menu and press Left, Left Trigger, X, Left.

TOYS 'R' US MULTIPLAYER LEVEL
Select Cheat Codes from the Settings menu and press Left, Up, White, Black.

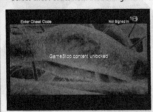 

PETER JACKSON'S KING KONG: THE OFFICIAL GAME OF THE MOVIE

At the Main menu, hold Left Trigger + Right Trigger and press Down, X, Up, Y, Down, Down, Up, Up. Release Left Trigger + Right Trigger to get the Cheat option on the menu. The Cheat option is also available on the pause menu.

GOD MODE
Select Cheat and enter 8wonder

ALL CHAPTERS
Select Cheat and enter KKst0ry.

AMMO 999
Select Cheat and enter KK 999 mun.

MACHINE GUN
Select Cheat and enter KKcapone.

REVOLVER
Select Cheat and enter KKtigun.

SNIPER RIFLE
Select Cheat and enter KKsn1per.

INFINITE SPEARS
Select Cheat and enter lance 1nf.

1-HIT KILLS
Select Cheat and enter GrosBras.

EXTRAS
Select Cheat and enter KKmuseum.

PIRATES OF THE CARIBBEAN

100,000 GOLD
During a game, press A, X, Y, B, Y, B, X, B, B, A.

GOD MODE
During a game, press A, Y, X, X, Y, Y, B, Y, X, A.

50 SKILL POINTS
During a game, press A, B, Y, X, Y, B, B, Y, B, A.

RESET REPUTATION
During a game, press A, X, Y, X, Y, B, B, Y, B, A.

POWERDROME

TACHE TEPLAN XSU-K0CC RACER
At the Vehicle Select screen, hold Right Trigger + Left Trigger and press Black, White, X, X, Y. Release Right Trigger and Left Trigger.

PRINCE OF PERSIA: THE SANDS OF TIME

CLASSIC PRINCE OF PERSIA ROOM
Start a new game. Then while on the balcony, press Left Thumbstick, A, X, Y, B, Y, A, X, B.

CLASSIC PASSWORDS

LEVEL	PASSWORD
Level 2	KIEJSC
Level 3	VNNNPC
Level 4	IYVPTC

LEVEL	PASSWORD
Level 5	RWSWWC
Level 6	GONWUC
Level 7	DEFNUC
Level 8	SVZMSC
Level 9	DBJRPC
Level 10	MZFYSC
Level 11	BRAYQC
Level 12	UUGTPC
Battle with Jafar	LRARUC

PRINCE OF PERSIA: THE TWO THRONES

BABY TOY HAMMER WEAPON
Pause the game and press Left, Left, Right, Right, Y, X, X, Y, Up, Down.

CHAINSAW WEAPON
Pause the game and press Up, Up, Down, Down, Left, Right, Left, Right, Y, X, Y, X.

SWORDFISH WEAPON
Pause the game and press Up, Down, Up, Down, Left, Right, Y, X, Y, X.

TELEPHONE OF SORROW WEAPON
Pause the game and press Right, Left, Right, Left, Down, Down, Up, Up, Y, X, Y, Y, X, X].

PRISONER OF WAR

Select Passwords from the Main menu and enter the following codes:

ALL CHAPTERS
Enter GER1ENG5.

DEFAULT CHAPTERS
Enter DEFAULTM.

INFORMED OF ALL EVENTS
Enter ALLTIMES.

INFORMED OF CORE CURRENT EVENTS
Enter CORETIMES.

ALL SECRETS
Enter FARLEYMYDOG.

FIRST-PERSON MODE
Enter BOSTON.

TOP DOWN MODE
Enter FOXY.

UNLIMITED GOODIES
Enter DINO.

GUARD SIZE
Enter MUFFIN.

GUARD PERCEPTION
Enter QUINCY.

DEFIANCE
Enter Fatty.

GAME CREATION DATE AND TIME
Enter DT.

PROJECT GOTHAM RACING

ALL CARS AND COURSES
Enter your name as Nosliw.

PSI-OPS: THE MINDGATE CONSPIRACY

Highlight Extra Content and press R. Now you can enter the following cheats. Select Mission Select to access the cheats.

Unlocked All Powers Cheat

ALL POWERS
Enter 537893.

BULLET RESISTANT
Enter 548975.

NO HEAD
Enter 987978.

SUPER PSI
Enter 456456.

UNLIMITED AMMO
Enter 978945.

ARCADE MODE
Enter 05051979.

COOPERATIVE PLAY MODE
Enter 07041979.

DARK MODE
Enter 465486.

SURVIVAL EXTRA MISSION
Enter 7734206.

AURA POOL EXTRA MISSION
Enter 659785.

BOTTOMLESS PIT EXTRA MISSION
Enter 154897.

BOUNCY BOUNCY EXTRA MISSION
Enter 568789.

FLOOR OF DEATH EXTRA MISSION
Enter 05120926.

GASOLINE EXTRA MISSION
Enter 9442662.

GEARSHIFT EXTRA MISSION
Enter 154684.

GNOMOTRON EXTRA MISSION
Enter 456878.

PANIC ROOM EXTRA MISSION
Enter 76635766.

PSI POOL EXTRA MISSION
Enter 565485.

STOPLIGHTS EXTRA MISSION
Enter 945678.

TIP THE IDOL EXTRA MISSION
Enter 428584.

TK ALLEY EXTRA MISSION
Enter 090702.

UP AND OVER EXTRA MISSION
Enter 020615.

CRISPY SOLDIER SKIN
Enter 454566.

DOCKWORKER SKIN
Enter 364654.

EDGAR BARRETT SKIN
Enter 497878.

EDGAR BARRET (TRAINING 1) SKIN
Enter 196001.

EDGAR BARRET (TRAINING 2) SKIN
Enter 196002.

EDGAR BARRET (TRAINING 3) SKIN
Enter 196003.

EDGAR BARRET (TRAINING 5) SKIN
Enter 196005.

EDGAR BARRET (TRAINING 6) SKIN
Enter 196006.

THE GENERAL (DEFAULT) SKIN
Enter 459797.

THE GENERAL (CLOWN) SKIN
Enter 431644.

JACK SKIN
Enter 698798.

JOV LEONOV SKIN
Enter 468987.

KOMIKO JONES SKIN
Enter 978798.

LABCOAT SKIN
Enter 998789.

MARLENA KESSLER SKIN
Enter 489788.

MARLENA KESSLER (BIKINI) SKIN
Enter 135454.

MARLENA KESSLER (LEATHER) SKIN
Enter 136876.

MARLENA KESSLER (SARANAE)
Enter 65496873.

MP1 SKIN
Enter 321646.

MP2 SKIN
Enter 698799.

MP3 SKIN
Enter 654659.

NICK SCRYER (STEALTH) SKIN
Enter 456498.

NICK SCRYER (TRAINING)SKIN
Enter 564689.

NICK SCRYER (URBAN) SKIN
Enter 484646.

NICK SCRYER (WASTELAND) SKIN
Enter 975466.

SARA BLAKE SKIN
Enter 135488.

SARA BLAKE (PSI) SKIN
Enter 468799.

SARA BLAKE (SUICIDE)
Enter 231644.

SCORPION SKIN
Enter 546546.

TONYA SKIN
Enter 678999.

UN SOLDIER SKIN
Enter 365498.

WEI LU SKIN
Enter 231324.

WEI LU (DRAGON) SKIN
Enter 978789.

WEI LU (TRANQUILITY) SKIN
Enter 654654.

PSYCHONAUTS

ALL POWERS
During a game, hold Left Trigger + Right Trigger and press B, B, Y, White, Left Thumbstick, Y.

9999 LIVES
During a game, hold Left Trigger + Right Trigger and press Left Thumbstick, White, White, B, A, Right Thumbstick.

9999 AMMO (BLAST, CONFUSION)
During a game, hold Left Trigger + Right Trigger and press Right Thumbstick, A, Left Thumbstick, Left Thumbstick, Y, B.

GLOBAL ITEMS (NO PSI-BALL COLORIZER, NO DREAM FLUFFS)
During a game, hold Left Trigger + Right Trigger and press Right Thumbstick, B, White, White, Left Thumbstick, Y.

ALL POWERS UPGRADED (MAX RANK)
During a game, hold Left Trigger + Right Trigger and press Left Thumbstick, Right Thumbstick, Left Thumbstick, White, B, White.

9999 ARROWHEADS
During a game, hold Left Trigger + Right Trigger and press A, Right Thumbstick, Right Thumbstick, White, Y, X.

INVINCIBILITY
During a game, hold Left Trigger + Right Trigger and press B, White, B, B, Y, Black.

WEIRD TEXT
During a game, hold Left Trigger + Right Trigger and press White, A, click Left Thumbstick, White, White, B.

RALLISPORT CHALLENGE 2

CARS & TRACKS SET 1
Select Credits from the Options menu and press Down, Left, Down, Right, Up, Up.

CARS &TRACKS SET 2
Select Credits from the Options menu and press Left, Left, Down, Down, Right, Right.

CARS & TRACKS SET 3
Select Credits from the Options menu and press Down, Down, Left, Left, Up, Down.

CARS & TRACKS SET 4
Select Credits from the Options menu and press Right, Down, Right, Down, Left, Up.

CARS & TRACKS SET 5
Select Credits from the Options menu and press Left, Left, Right, Right, Down, Left.

CARS & TRACKS SET 6
Select Credits from the Options menu and press Right, Up, Up, Up, Down, Left.

CARS & TRACKS SET 7
Select Credits from the Options menu and press Left, Left, Left, Up, Up, Right.

CARS & TRACKS SET 8
Select Credits from the Options menu and press Right, Up, Left, Up, Down, Right.

CARS & TRACKS SET 9
Select Credits from the Options menu and press Down, Up, Down, Left, Left, Down.

CARS & TRACKS SET 10
Select Credits from the Options menu and press Up, Up, Down, Down, Left, Right.

ROBOTECH: INVASION

Select Extras from the Options menu to enter the following codes.

INVINCIBILITY
Enter supercyc.

UNLIMITED AMMO
Enter trgrhpy.

1-HIT KILLS
Enter dustyayres.

ALL LEVELS
Enter reclamation.

LANCER'S MULTIPLAYER SKIN
Enter yllwfllw.

SCOTT BERNARD'S MULTIPLAYER SKIN
Enter ltntcmdr.

RAND'S MULTIPLAYER SKIN
Enter kidgloves.

ROOK'S MULTIPLAYER SKIN
Enter blueangls.

ROBOTS

BIG HEAD FOR RODNEY
Pause the game and press Up, Down, Down, Up, Right, Right, Left, Right.

UNLIMITED HEALTH
Pause the game and press Up, Right, Down, Up, Left, Down, Right, Left.

UNLIMITED SCRAP
Pause the game and press Down, Down, Left, Up, Up, Right, Up, Down.

ROGUE OPS

BIG FEET
Pause the game and press Right (x3), Left, Right, Left, Right, Left (x3).

SKELETON
Pause the game and press Left (x3), Right, Left, Right, Left, Right (x3).

BIG GUN
Pause the game and press X (x4), Y, Y.

UNLIMITED HEALTH
Pause the game and press Left, Right, Right, Left, Left, Right, Right, Left, Left, Right, Right, Left, X, X.

UNLIMITED BULLETS
Pause the game and press X, Y, X, Y, X, Y, X, Y, Left, Y, X, Y, X, Y, X, Y, X.

UNLIMITED SPY CAM
Pause the game and press Left, Left, Right, Right, White, White, Black, Black, X, X, Y, Y.

UNLIMITED TOC
Pause the game and press Y, Y, X, X, Left, Right, Right, Left, Black, White, Black.

HALF DAMAGE
Pause the game and press X, X, Y, Y, Left, Left, Right, Right, Y, Y, X, X.

NO BULLET DAMAGE
Pause the game and press Left, Right, Right, Left, X, Y, Y, X.

1-HIT KILLS
Pause the game and press Y, Left, Right, Right, Left, Y, Black, White, Y, X, X.

EXPLOSIVE CROSSBOW
Pause the game and press Left, Right, Right, Left, X, Y, Black, White, X, Y, Left, Right.

MISSILE CROSSBOW
Pause the game and press Right, Right, Left, Left, Black, Black, White, White, Y, Y, X, X.

EXPLOSIVE SNIPER
Pause the game and press Black, White, Right, Right, Left, Left, Right, Right, White, Black, X, Y.

MISSILE SNIPER
Pause the game and press X, Left, Right, Black, White, Right, X, White, White, Black, Left, Left.

COMPLETE LEVEL
While in the level you want to complete, pause the game and enter the following code that corresponds with that level.

LEVEL NAME	CODE
Bank	White, Black, X, Y, Left, White, Left, Left, X, Y, X
Carmen	White, Black, Right, Left, Left, Black, White, X (x3), White
Forsythe	Black, Black, Right (x3), Black, White, X, White, X, White
Installation K	White, Black, X, X, Left, Black, Black, X, X, L1, X
La Casa	White, Black, Right, Left, Left, Black, White, X (x3), White
Magyar	White, Y, Y, Left, Left, Black, White, Right, X, Right, Right
Mod	White, Black, Right, White, Left, Y, White, Y, Right, Right, Left
Museum	Black, Black, Right (x3), Black, White, X, White, X, White
Reliance	White, Black, Right, Left, White, Black, Right, X, Y, X, Y
Silo	White, Black, Right, Left, Left, Black, Y, White, X (x3)
Training	Left, Right, Right, Left, Y, X, White, Black, Y, Y, X

ROGUE TROOPER

INFINITE HEALTH
At the Extra menu, press Left, Right, Up, Down, Left Thumbstick, X.

INFINITE SUPPLIES
At the Extra menu, press Back, R, L, Back, Right Thumbstick, L.

LOW GRAVITY RAGDOLL
At the Extra menu, press X, X, X, B, B, B, Up, Down.

EXTREME RAGDOLL
At the Extra menu, press Up, Up, Up, Black, Black, Black, Up.

HIPPY BLOOD
At the Extra menu, press White, Right, B, Down, R, Back.

RUGBY LEAGUE 2

UNLOCK EVERYTHING
Create a player with the name Darren Unlockyer.

BIG HANDS
Create a player with the name Jumbo Mittens.

BIG HEADS
Create a player with the name Planetoid.

SMALL HEADS
Create a player with the name micro noggin.

BIG MUSCLES
Create a player with the name Dale P Pugh.

FAT PLAYERS
Create a player with the name Cakemaster 3000.

SKINNY PLAYERS
Create a player with the name Crash Diet.

TIRE IN BODY
Create a player with the name Junkinthetrunk.

TOGGLE MATRIX KICKING OFF
Create a player with the name There is no spoon.

SCALER

FULL HEALTH
Pause the game, select Audio from the Options menu and press Right Trigger, Left Trigger, Right Trigger, Left Trigger, Y, Y, X, X, Right Trigger, X.

200,000 KLOKKIES
Pause the game, select Audio from the Options menu and press Left Trigger, Left Trigger, Right Trigger, Right Trigger, Y, X, Y.

INFINITE ELECTRIC BOMBS
Pause the game, select Audio from the Options menu and press Right Trigger, Right Trigger, Left Trigger, Left Trigger, Y, Y, X.

SCARFACE: THE WORLD IS YOURS

After entering the following cheats, highlight the cheat and press A to "DO IT."

MAX AMMO
Pause the game, select Cheats and enter AMMO.

REFILL HEALTH
Pause the game, select Cheats and enter MEDIK.

FILL BALLS METER
Pause the game, select Cheats and enter FPATCH.

KILL TONY
Pause the game, select Cheats and enter KILTONY.

DECREASE COP HEAT
Pause the game, select Cheats and enter FLYSTRT.

INCREASE COP HEAT
Pause the game, select Cheats and enter DONUT.

DECREASE GANG HEAT
Pause the game, select Cheats and enter NOBALLS.

INCREASE GANG HEAT
Pause the game, select Cheats and enter GOBALLS.

REPAIR TONY'S VEHICLE
Pause the game, select Cheats and enter TBURGLR.

SPAWN ARIEL MK III
Pause the game, select Cheats and enter OLDFAST.

SPAWN BACINARI
Pause the game, select Cheats and enter 666999.

SPAWN BODOG STAMPEDE
Pause the game, select Cheats and enter BUMMER.

SPAWN BULLDOZER
Pause the game, select Cheats and enter DOZER.

SPAWN ODIN VH88
Pause the game, select Cheats and enter DUMPER.

BLACK SUIT TONY
Pause the game, select Cheats and enter BLACK.

BLUE PINSTRIPE SUIT TONY WITH SHADES
Pause the game, select Cheats and enter BLUESH.

GRAY SUIT TONY
Pause the game, select Cheats and enter GRAY.

GRAY SUIT TONY WITH SHADES
Pause the game, select Cheats and enter GRAYSH.

HAWAIIAN SHIRT TONY
Pause the game, select Cheats and enter HAWAII.

HAWAIIAN SHIRT TONY WITH SHADES
Pause the game, select Cheats and enter HAWAIIG.

SANDY SHIRT TONY
Pause the game, select Cheats and enter SANDY.

SANDY SHIRT TONY WITH SHADES
Pause the game, select Cheats and enter SANDYSH.

WHITE SUIT TONY
Pause the game, select Cheats and enter WHITE.

WHITE SUIT TONY WITH SHADES
Pause the game, select Cheats and enter WHITESH.

CHANGE TIME OF DAY
Pause the game, select Cheats and enter MARTHA.

TOGGLE LIGHTNING
Pause the game, select Cheats and enter SHAZAAM.

TOGGLE RAIN
Pause the game, select Cheats and enter RAINY.

BREAL "THE WORLD IS YOURS" MUSIC TRACK
Pause the game, select Cheats and enter TUNEME.

SECRET WEAPONS OVER NORMANDY

ALL PLANES, ENVIRONMENTS, GALLERY, & MISSIONS
At the Main menu, press Y, Y, Y, X, X, X, Left Trigger, Right Trigger, Black, Black, White White.

ALL ENVIRONMENTS IN INSTANT ACTION
At the Main menu, press Up, Down, Left, Right, Left Trigger, Right Trigger, Left Trigger, Right Trigger.

INVINCIBILITY
At the Main menu, press Up, Down, Left, Right, Left, Left, Right, Right, Left Trigger, Left Trigger, Right Trigger, Right Trigger, White, Black.

UNLIMITED AMMUNITION
At the Main menu, press Up, Right, Down, Left, Up, Right, Down, Left, Left Trigger, Right Trigger.

BIG HEADS
At the Main menu, press Right, Up, Left, Down, Right, Up, Left, Down, Right, Left Trigger, Right Trigger, Left Trigger, Right Trigger.

SERIOUS SAM

CHEATS
At the Main menu, click and hold the Left Thumbstick and press Black, White, Y.

SERIOUS SAM II

CHEATS LIST
At the main menu, hold R and press White, Black, X, White, Black, X, White, Black, X, X.

SHADOW OPS: RED MERCURY

UNLIMITED AMMO
During a game, select Cheats from the menu and enter packmule.

ALL SINGLE PLAYER LEVELS
During a game, select Cheats from the menu and enter happycamper.

ALL COOPERATIVE LEVELS
During a game, select Cheats from the menu and enter wanderlust.

ALL MOVIES
During a game, select Cheats from the menu and enter filmcritic.

SHATTERED UNION

SKIP CURRENT WEEK IN CAMPAIGN MODE
At the US Map, press Start for the Options. Then select Cheat Menu and press X, Y, X, B, A.

WIN CIVIL WAR IN CAMPAIGN MODE
At the US Map, press Start for the Options. Then select Cheat Menu and press X, B, A, B, Y.

$100,000
At the US Map, press Start for the Options. Then select Cheat Menu and press X, X, A, A, Y.

ARCADIA PLAINS
At the US Map, press Start for the Options. Then select Cheat Menu and press B, X, X, X, A.

ARIZONA TERRITORY
At the US Map, press Start for the Options. Then select Cheat Menu and press B, X, X, A, X.

CAROLINAS
At the US Map, press Start for the Options. Then select Cheat Menu and press B, X, Y, X, A.

CENTRAL CASCADES
At the US Map, press Start for the Options. Then select Cheat Menu and press B, X, X, X, Y.

CENTRAL HEARTLAND
At the US Map, press Start for the Options. Then select Cheat Menu and press B, X, X, B, Y.

CUMBERLANDS
At the US Map, press Start for the Options. Then select Cheat Menu and press B, X, Y, X, Y.

DAKOTAS
At the US Map, press Start for the Options. Then select Cheat Menu and press B, X, X, B, X.

EASTERN SHENANDOAH
At the US Map, press Start for the Options. Then select Cheat Menu and press B, X, Y, Y, B.

FLORIDA
At the US Map, press Start for the Options. Then select Cheat Menu and press B, X, Y, X, B.

GREAT BASIN
At the US Map, press Start for the Options. Then select Cheat Menu and press B, X, X, Y, A.

GREAT LAKES
At the US Map, press Start for the Options. Then select Cheat Menu and press B, X, X, B, A.

GREAT PLAINS
At the US Map, press Start for the Options. Then select Cheat Menu and press B, X, X, B, B.

MISSISSIPPI DELTA
At the US Map, press Start for the Options. Then select Cheat Menu and press B, X, Y, X, X.

NEW MEXICO
At the US Map, press Start for the Options. Then select Cheat Menu and press B, X, X, Y, B.

NEW YORK
At the US Map, press Start for the Options. Then select Cheat Menu and press B, X, Y, Y, Y.

NORTHERN CALIFORNIA
At the US Map, press Start for the Options. Then select Cheat Menu and press B, X, X, Y, X.

NORTHERN CASCADES
At the US Map, press Start for the Options. Then select Cheat Menu and press B, X, X, X, B.

NORTHERN NEW ENGLAND
At the US Map, press Start for the Options. Then select Cheat Menu and press B, X, Y, Y, A.

NORTHERN TEXAS
At the US Map, press Start for the Options. Then select Cheat Menu and press B, X, X, A, A.

OHIO VALLEY
At the US Map, press Start for the Options. Then select Cheat Menu and press B, X, Y, Y, X.

OKLAHOMA GRASSLANDS
At the US Map, press Start for the Options. Then select Cheat Menu and press B, X, X, A, Y.

SOUTHEASTERN CASCADES
At the US Map, press Start for the Options. Then select Cheat Menu and press B, X, X, X, X.

SOUTHERN CALIFORNIA
At the US Map, press Start for the Options. Then select Cheat Menu and press B, X, X, Y, Y.

SOUTHERN TEXAS
At the US Map, press Start for the Options. Then select Cheat Menu and press B, X, X, A, B.

SHREK 2

BONUS GAMES
Pause the game and select Scrapbook. Press Left, Up, A, B, Left, Up, A, B, Left, Up, A, B, X, B, X, B, X, B. Exit the level and select Bonus to access the games.

CHAPTER SELECT
Pause the game and select Scrapbook. Press Left, Up, A, B, Left, Up, A, B, Left, Up, A, B, Up (x5). Exit the level and choose Chapter Select to change chapters.

FULL HEALTH
Pause the game and select Scrapbook. Press Left, A, B, Circle, Left, A, B, Circle, Left, A, B, Up, Right, Down, Left, Up.

1,000 COINS
Pause the game and select Scrapbook. Press Left, Up, A, B, Left, Up, A, B, Left, Up, A, B (x6).

SHREK SUPERSLAM

ALL CHALLENGES
At the Title screen, press Y, Y, Y, B, B, B, Y, X, B, X, X, X, X, Up, Down, Left, Right, Left Trigger, Right Trigger.

SUPER SPEED MODIFIER
At the Title screen, press Left Trigger, Left Trigger, Right Trigger, Right Trigger, Left Trigger, Right Trigger, Left Trigger, Right Trigger, X, B, Y, Y.

PIZZA ONE
At the Title screen, press Up, Up, Y, Y, Right, Right, B, B, Down, Down, Left Trigger, Right Trigger, Left, Left, X, X, Left Trigger, Right Trigger.

PIZZA TWO
At the Title screen, press B, B, X, X, Right Trigger, Right Trigger, Left, Left, Left Trigger, Left Trigger.

PIZZA THREE
At the Title screen, press Down, Down, Right, B, Up, Y, Left, X, Left Trigger, Left Trigger.

SLAMMAGEDDON
At the Title screen, press Up, Up, Down, Down, Left, Right, Left, Right, Y, X, X, Left Trigger, Right Trigger.

SID MEIER'S PIRATES!

FOOD NEVER DWINDLES
Name your character Sweet Tooth.

INVINCIBLE SHIP
Name your character Bloody Bones Baz.

JEFF BRIGGS AS ABBOTT
Name your character Firaxis.

SNAPPY DRESSER
Name your character Bonus Frag.

BEST SHIP AND FULL CREW
Name your character D.Gackey.

FLEET IS TWICE AS FAST
Name your character Sprinkler.

HIGHEST MORALE
Name your character B.Caudizzle.

DUELING INVINCIBILITY
Name your character Dragon Ma.

SID MEIER AS MYSTERIOUS STRANGER
Name your character Max Remington.

THE SIMS 2

During gameplay, press Left Trigger, Right Trigger, Up on D-pad, A, Black. Now you can enter the following cheats.

ALL LOCATIONS
Press B, White, Left, B, Up, B.

ALL CLOTHES
Press X, Black, Down, Right, X.

ALL OBJECTS
Press White, B, Down, Left, Up.

ALL RECIPES
Press Black, X, Up, Down, Right, A.

MAX ALL MOTIVES
Press Up, B, Up, Right, White.

§10,000
Press Right Trigger, Left Trigger, Black, Right, Left.

CHANGES SIMS'S SKILL
Press Y, B, X, Black, D-pad Left.

JUMP AHEAD SIX HOURS
Press B, X, Left Trigger, Up, Down.

REMOVE MESSAGES
Press Right, Up, Right, Down, Right, Up, Down, Right.

THE SIMS BUSTIN' OUT

Pause the game to enter the following codes. Note that you must enter the "Enable Cheats" code first. After entering another code, select the gnome to access it.

ENABLE CHEATS
Press Right Trigger, Left Trigger, Down, Black, Left, B. A gnome appears in your yard when the code is entered correctly.

GIVE MONEY
Press Left Trigger, Black, Right, X, Left. Select the gnome to receive money.

UNLOCK ALL LOCATIONS
Press Black, Down, Right Trigger, Left Trigger, Down, Y.

UNLOCK ALL OBJECTS
Press Black, Up, Y, Down, Right Trigger.

UNLOCK ALL SOCIAL OPTIONS
Press Left Trigger, Right Trigger, A, Down, Black.

SONIC HEROES

METAL CHARACTERS IN 2-PLAYER
After selecting a level in 2-Player mode, hold A + Y.

SONIC MEGA COLLECTION PLUS

COMIX ZONE

INVINCIBILITY
Select the Jukebox from the Options screen and play the following tracks in order: 3, 12, 17, 2, 2, 10, 2, 7, 7, 11.

STAGE SELECT
Select the Jukebox from the Options screen and play the following tracks in order: 14, 15, 18, 5, 13, 1, 3, 18, 15, 6.

DR. ROBOTNIK'S MEAN BEAN MACHINE

EASY PASSWORDS
Continue a game with the following passwords.

LEVEL	PASSWORD
2	Red Bean, Red Bean, Red Bean, Has Bean
3	Clear Bean, Purple Bean, Clear Bean, Green Bean
4	Red Bean, Clear Bean, Has Bean, Yellow Bean
5	Clear Bean, Blue Bean, Blue Bean, Purple Bean
6	Clear Bean, Red Bean, Clear Bean, Purple Bean
7	Purple Bean, Yellow Bean, Red Bean, Blue Bean
8	Yellow Bean, Green Bean, Purple Bean, Has Bean
9	Yellow Bean, Purple Bean, Has Bean, Blue Bean
10	Red Bean, Yellow Bean, Clear Bean, Has Bean
11	Green Bean, Purple Bean, Blue Bean, Clear Bean
12	Red Bean, Has Bean, Has Bean, Yellow Bean
13	Yellow Bean, Has Bean, Blue Bean, Blue Bean

NORMAL PASSWORDS

LEVEL	PASSWORD
2	Has Bean, Clear Bean, Yellow Bean, Yellow Bean
3	Blue Bean, Clear Bean, Red Bean, Yellow Bean
4	Yellow Bean, Blue Bean, Clear Bean, Purple Bean
5	Has Bean, Green Bean, Blue Bean, Yellow Bean
6	Green Bean, Purple Bean, Purple Bean, Yellow Bean
7	Purple Bean, Blue Bean, Green Bean, Has Bean
8	Green Bean, Has Bean, Clear Bean, Yellow Bean
9	Blue Bean, Purple Bean, Has Bean, Has Bean
10	Has Bean, Red Bean, Yellow Bean, Clear Bean
11	Clear Bean, Red Bean, Red Bean, Blue Bean
12	Green Bean, Green Bean, Clear Bean, Yellow Bean
13	Purple Bean, Yellow Bean, Has Bean, Clear Bean

HARD PASSWORDS

LEVEL	PASSWORD
2	Green Bean, Clear Bean, Yellow Bean, Yellow Bean
3	Yellow Bean, Clear Bean, Purple Bean, Clear Bean
4	Blue Bean, Green Bean, Clear Bean, Blue Bean
5	Red Bean, Purple Bean, Green Bean, Green Bean
6	Yellow Bean, Yellow Bean, Clear Bean, Green Bean
7	Purple Bean, Clear Bean, Blue Bean, Blue Bean
8	Clear Bean, Yellow Bean, Has Bean, Yellow Bean
9	Purple Bean, Blue Bean, Blue Bean, Green Bean
10	Clear Bean, Green Bean, Red Bean, Yellow Bean
11	Blue Bean, Yellow Bean, Yellow Bean, Has Bean
12	Green Bean, Clear Bean, Clear Bean, Blue bean
13	Has Bean, Clear Bean, Purple Bean, Has Bean

HARDEST PASSWORDS

LEVEL	PASSWORD
2	Blue Bean, Blue Bean, Green Bean, Yellow Bean
3	Green Bean, Yellow Bean, Green Bean, Clear Bean
4	Purple Bean, Purple Bean, Red Bean, Has Bean
5	Green Bean, Red Bean, Purple Bean, Blue Bean
6	Blue Bean, Purple Bean, Green Bean, Yellow Bean
7	Blue Bean, Purple Bean, Green Bean, Has Bean
8	Clear Bean, Purple Bean, Has Bean, Yellow Bean
9	Purple Bean, Green Bean, Has Bean, Clear Bean
10	Green Bean, Blue Bean, Yellow Bean, Has Bean
11	Green Bean, Purple Bean, Has Bean, Red Bean
12	Red Bean, Green Bean, Has Bean, Blue Bean
13	Red Bean, Red Bean, Clear Bean, Yellow Bean

RISTAR

LEVEL SELECT
Enter ILOVEU as a password.

FIGHT ONLY BOSSES
Enter MUSEUM as a password.

TIME ATTACK
Enter DOFEEL as a password.

TONE DEAF SOUNDS
Enter MAGURO as a password.

TRUE SIGHT
Enter MIEMIE as a password.

SUPER HARD
Enter SUPER as a password.

VERY HARD
Enter SUPERB as a password.

CANCEL CODES
Enter XXXXXX as a password.

SPARTAN: TOTAL WARRIOR

ALL MISSIONS IN SINGLE MISSION REPLAY
At the Main menu, highlight Extras and press Left (x11), Right (x7), X.

SPAWN ARMAGEDDON

UNLIMITED HEALTH AND NECROPLASM
Pause the game and press Up, Down, Left, Right, Right, Left, Down, Up.

UNLIMITED NECROPLASM
Pause the game and press Up, Down, Left, Right, Down, Left, Up, Right.

LEVEL SELECT
Pause the game and press Up, Down, Left, Right, Left, Left, Right, Right.

ALL WEAPONS
Pause the game and press Up, Down, Left, Right, Left, Right, Left, Left.

UNLIMITED AMMUNITION
Pause the game and press Up, Down, Left, Right, Up, Left, Down, Right.

NO BLOOD
Pause the game and press Up, Down, Left, Right, Up (x4).

ALL COMICS
Pause the game and press Up, Down, Left, Right, Right, Left, Left, Up.

ENCYCLOPEDIA
Pause the game and press Up, Down, Left, Right, Left, Right, Up, Down.

SPEED KINGS

Enter the following as your Handle:

LAP TIMES – UNLOCK GRAND PRIX
Enter .LAPT18.

COMPLETE DRIVING TEST
Enter .TEST9.

ALL MEETS WON
Enter .MEET6.

RESPECT POINTS
Enter .Resp ##. Replace ## with the desired amount of respect.

MASTER CHEAT
Enter borkbork as a name.

SPIDER-MAN 2

TREYARCH PASSWORD
Start a New Game and enter HCRAYERT as your name. This starts the game at 44% complete, 201,000 Hero Points, some upgrades and more.

SPIKEOUT: BATTLE STREET

EASY MODE
Die twice and continue the game to unlock a new Easy Mode option.

SPONGEBOB SQUAREPANTS: BATTLE FOR BIKINI BOTTOM

You must enter the codes very quickly.

RESTORE HEALTH
Pause the game, hold Left Trigger + Right Trigger and press X, X, X, X, Y, X, Y, X, Y, Y, Y, Y.

EXPERT MODE
Pause the game, hold Left Trigger + Right Trigger and press X, X, X, Y, Y, X, X, X, Y, X, Y, Y, Y, Y, X, Y.

EARN 1,000 SHINY OBJECTS
Pause the game, hold Left Trigger + Right Trigger and press Y, X, X, Y, Y, X, X, Y.

EARN 10 GOLD SPATULAS
Pause the game, hold Left Trigger + Right Trigger and press X, Y, Y, X, X, Y, Y, X.

BUBBLE BOWL POWER-UP
Pause the game, hold Left Trigger + Right Trigger and press X, Y, X, Y, X, X, Y, Y. Press X to use.

CRUISE BUBBLE POWER-UP
Pause the game, hold Left Trigger + Right Trigger and press X, X, Y, X, Y, Y, X, X. Press Left Trigger to use.

INCREASE VALUE OF SHINY OBJECTS
Pause the game, hold Left Trigger + Right Trigger and press Y, X, Y, X, X, Y, X, X, X, Y, Y, Y, Y, X, X, Y.

MODIFIED CRUISE BUBBLE CONTROLS
Pause the game, hold Left Trigger + Right Trigger and press X, X, X, X, Y, Y, X, Y, X, X, Y, X, Y, Y.

VILLAGERS GIVE SHINY OBJECTS WHEN HIT
Pause the game, hold Left Trigger + Right Trigger and press Y, Y, Y, Y, Y, Y, X, Y, X, X, Y, X, Y.

VILLAGERS RESTORE HEALTH WHEN NEAR
Pause the game, hold Left Trigger + Right Trigger and press Y, Y, Y, Y, Y, X, Y, X, X, X, Y, Y.

NO PANTS
Pause the game, hold Left Trigger + Right Trigger and press X, X, X, X, Y, X, X, X, Y, X, Y, Y, X.

BIG PLANKTON
Pause the game, hold Left Trigger + Right Trigger and press Y, Y, Y, Y, X, Y, X, Y, X, Y, X, X, X, X.

SMALL CHARACTERS
Pause the game, hold Left Trigger + Right Trigger and press Y, Y, Y, Y, X, Y, X, Y, X, Y, Y, Y, Y.

SMALL VILLAGERS
Pause the game, hold Left Trigger + Right Trigger and press Y, Y, Y, Y, Y, X, Y, X, Y, X, Y, X.

SPONGEBOB BREAKS APART WHEN DEFEATED
Pause the game, hold Left Trigger + Right Trigger and press X, X, X, X, Y, Y, X, Y, X, X, X, X.

INVERT LEFT/RIGHT CAMERA CONTROLS
Pause the game, hold Left Trigger + Right Trigger and press Y, Y, X, X, X, X, Y, Y.

INVERT UP/DOWN CAMERA CONTROLS
Pause the game, hold Left Trigger + Right Trigger and press Y, X, X, X, X, X, X, Y.

SPONGEBOB SQUAREPANTS: THE MOVIE

ALL HEALTH
Pause the game, hold L + R and press Y, Y, Y, Y, X, Y, X, Y.

ALL TASKS
Pause the game, hold L + R and press Y, X, Y, Y, X, Y, X, X.

ALL MOVES
Pause the game, hold L + R and press X, X, Y, X, Y, Y, X, X.

ALL MOVES TO MACHO
Pause the game, hold L + R and press X, X, Y, X, Y, Y, X, Y.

SONGEBOB CAVEMAN COSTUME
Pause the game, hold L + R and press X, X, X, X, Y, X, X, X.

SPONGEBOB RIPPED SHORTS COSTUME
Pause the game, hold L + R and press X, X, X, X, Y, X, X, Y.

PATRICK CAVEMAN COSTUME
Pause the game, hold L + R and press X, X, X, X, Y, X, Y, Y.

PATRICK GOOFY GOOBER COSTUME
Pause the game, hold L + R and press X, X, X, X, Y, X, Y, X.

SPONGEBOB SQUAREPANTS: LIGHTS, CAMERA, PANTS!

SILVER STORY MODE
Select Rewards from the Bonuses menu, then select Codes and enter 486739.

ALL ACTION FIGURES
Select Rewards from the Bonuses menu, then select Codes and enter 977548.

HOOK, LINE & CHEDDAR GAME
Select Rewards from the Bonuses menu, then select Codes and enter 893634.

SPY HUNTER: NOWHERE TO RUN

SPY HUNTER ARCADE
Activate the machine when you come across it in the safe house on Level 7, "Cleaning Up."

SPY VS SPY

ALL CLASSIC MAPS
Enter RETROSPY at the password screen.

ALL STORY MODE LEVELS
Enter ANTONIO at the password screen.

ALL LEVELS FOR SINGLE-PLAYER MODERN MODE
Enter PROHIAS at the password screen.

ALL MULTIPLAYER MAPS
Enter MADMAG at the password screen.

ALL OUTFITS
Enter DISGUISE at the password screen.

ALL WEAPONS
Enter WRKBENCH at the password screen.

INVULNERABILITY
Enter ARMOR at the password screen.

SUPER DAMAGE
Enter BIGGUNZ at the password screen.

PERMANENT FAIRY IN MODERN MODE
Enter FAIRY at the password screen.

NO DROPPED ITEMS WHEN KILLED
Enter NODROP at the password screen.

INVISIBLE HUD
Enter BLINK at the password screen.

ALL MOVIES
Enter SPYFLIX at the password screen.

CONCEPT ART
Enter SPYPICS at the password screen.

SSX ON TOUR

NEW THREADS
Select Cheats from the Extras menu and enter FLYTHREADS.

THE WORLD IS YOURS
Select Cheats from the Extras menu and enter
BACKSTAGEPASS.

SHOW TIME (ALL MOVIES)
Select Cheats from the Extras menu and enter
THEBIGPICTURE.

BLING BLING (INFINITE CASH)
Select Cheats from the Extras menu and enter
LOOTSNOOT.

FULL BOOST, FULL TIME
Select Cheats from the Extras menu and enter ZOOMJUICE.

MONSTERS ARE LOOSE (MONSTER TRICKS)
Select Cheats from the Extras menu and enter JACKALOPESTYLE.

SNOWBALL FIGHT
Select Cheats from the Extras menu and enter LETSPARTY.

FEEL THE POWER (STAT BOOST)
Select Cheats from the Extras menu and enter POWERPLAY.

CHARACTERS ARE LOOSE
Select Cheats from the Extras menu and enter ROADIEROUNDUp.

UNLOCK CONRAD
Select Cheats from the Extras menu and enter BIGPARTYTIME.

UNLOCK MITCH KOOBSKI
Select Cheats from the Extras menu and enter MOREFUNTHANONE.

UNLOCK NIGEL
Select Cheats from the Extras menu and enter THREEISACROWD.

UNLOCK SKI PATROL
Select Cheats from the Extras menu and enter FOURSOME.

STAR WARS: BATTLEFRONT II

INFINITE AMMO
Pause the game and press Up, Down, Left, Down, Down, Left, Down, Down, Left, Down, Down, Down, Left, Right.

INVINCIBILITY
Pause the game and press Up, Up, Up, Left, Down, Down, Down, Left, Up, Up, Up, Left, Right.

NO HUD
Pause the game and press Up, Up, Up, Up, Left, Up, Up, Down, Left, Down, Up, Up, Left, Right. Re-enter the code to enable HUD again.

ALTERNATE SOLDIERS
Pause the game and press Down, Down, Down, Up, Up, Left, Down, Down, Down, Down, Down, Left, Up, Up, Up, Left.

ALTERNATE SOUNDS
Pause the game and press Up, Up, Up, Left, Up, Down, Up, Up, Left, Down, Down, Down, Left, Up, Down, Down, Left, Right.

FUNNY MESSAGES WHEN REBELS DEFEATED
Pause the game and press Up, Down, Left, Down, Left, Right.

STAR WARS EPISODE III: REVENGE OF THE SITH

INFINITE FORCE
Select Codes from the Settings menu and enter KAIBURR.

INFINITE HEALTH
Select Codes from the Settings menu and enter XUCPHRA.

QUICK HEALTH & FORCE RESTORATION
Select Codes from the Settings menu and enter BELSAVIS.

ALL STORY, BONUS & CO-OP MISSIONS, & DUELISTS
Select Codes from the Settings menu and enter 021282.

ALL STORY MISSIONS
Select Codes from the Settings menu and enter KORRIBAN.

ALL BONUS MISSIONS
Select Codes from the Settings menu and enter NARSHADDAA.

ALL DUEL ARENAS
Select Codes from the Settings menu and enter TANTIVIEV.

ALL DUELISTS
Select Codes from the Settings menu and enter ZABRAK.

ALL POWERS & MOVES
Select Codes from the Settings menu and enter JAINA.

SUPER LIGHTSABER MODE
Select Codes from the Settings menu and enter SUPERSABERS.

TINY DROID MODE
Select Codes from the Settings menu and enter 071779.

ALL REPLAY MOVIES
Select Codes from the Settings menu and enter COMLINK.

ALL CONCEPT ART
Select Codes from the Settings menu and enter AAYLASECURA.

STAR WARS KNIGHTS OF THE OLD REPUBLIC II: THE SITH LORDS

CHANGE VOICES
Add a controller to the controller port 4 and press Black or White to raise and lower character voices.

STATE OF EMERGENCY

INVULNERABLE
During gameplay, press White, L, Black, R, A.

UNLIMITED AMMO
During gameplay, press White, L, Black, R, Y.

COMPLETE CURRENT MISSION

LEVEL SKIP
At the Title screen, press Right Trigger, Left Trigger, Start + Down.

99 OF ALL ITEMS
During gameplay, go to Equipment and press Right Trigger, Left Trigger, Right.

STREET HOOPS

Select Cheats from Game Settings and enter the following.

BRICK CITY CLOTHING
Press R, Black, R, L, Y, X, R, L.

CLOWN UNIFORM
Press X, L, X, Y.

COWBOY UNIFORM
Press Y, White, White, R.

ELVIS UNIFORMS
Press Y, Black, White, Black, Black, White, L, Black.

KUNG FU UNIFORM
Press Y, Y, X, L.

PIMP UNIFORMS
Press R, X, Y, Black.

SANTA UNIFORM
Press White, Black, White, Black.

TUXEDO UNIFORM
Press Black, Black, Y, X.

NORMAL BALL
Press R, X, X, L.

ABA BALL
Press Y, White, X, White.

COURT SELECT BALL
Press Y, X, Y, L, Y, X, X.

BLACK BALL
Press White, White, Y, Black.

THEFT MODE (EASIER STEALS)
Press R, X (x3), R, Black, Y, White.

BLOCK PARTY (EASIER BLOCKS)
Press R, Y, Black, White.

POWER GAME
Press White, Y, Black, Y.

FAST CLOCK
Press Y, Y, Y, X, X, X, L, Black.

PERFECT FIELD GOALS
Press Y, Y, Y, X, X, X, R, White.

STREET RACING SYNDICATE

At the Main menu, press Up, Down, Left, Right. This will bring up the code entry screen. Enter the following.

MAZDA RX-8
Enter RENESIS.

TOYOTA SUPRA 3.0L RZ
Enter SICKJZA.

MITSUBISHI ECLIPSE GS-T
Enter IGOTGST.

TOYOTA CELICA GT-S
Enter MYTCGTS.

SUBARU IMPREZA S202 STI
Enter SICKGDB.

POLICE CAR
Enter GOTPOPO.

PAC MAN VINYL
Enter GORETRO.

FREE CAR REPAIR
Enter FIXITUP. Your first car repair is free.

GET WARNING FOR FIRST 3 BUSTS
Enter LETMEGO. The first three times you are pulled over, you get a warning.

STOLEN

LEVEL SKIP
At the Title screen, press Right Trigger, Left Trigger, Start + Down.

99 OF ALL ITEMS
During gameplay, go to Equipment and press Right Trigger, Left Trigger, Right.

STRIKE FORCE BOWLING

ALL LEVELS
Name your bowler !LEVELS!.

ALL BOWLERS
Name your bowler !BOWLER!.

THE SUFFERING: TIES THAT BIND

REFILL HEALTH
During a game, hold L + R + X and press Down (x3), A, Up, Up, Down, Up, A.

ALL WEAPONS AND ITEMS
During a game, hold Left Trigger + Right Trigger + X and press Down, Up, Down, Left, Right, Left, A, Up, Left, Down, Right, Up, Right, Down, Left, A, Down (x3), A, A.

SHOTGUN
During a game, hold Left Trigger + Right Trigger + X and press Left (x3), Down (x3).

FULL AMMUNITION FOR EQUIPPED GUN
During a game, hold Left Trigger + Right Trigger + X and press Right, Right, Down, Up, Left, Right, Left, Left, A.

SUICIDE
During gameplay, hold Left Trigger + Right Trigger + X and press Down, Down, Down, Down.

SHOTGUN AND AMMO
During gameplay, hold Left Trigger + Right Trigger + X and press Left, Left, Left, Down, Down, Down.

MOLOTOV COCKTAILS
During gameplay, hold Left Trigger + Right Trigger + X and press Down, Down, Down, Up, Up, Up.

FULL FLASHLIGHT
During gameplay, hold Left Trigger + Right Trigger + X and press Up, Left, Down, Right, Up, Right, Down, Left, A.

FULL AMMO CURRENT THROWN
During gameplay, hold Left Trigger + Right Trigger + X and press Left, Left, Up, Down, Right, Left, Right, Right, A.

FULL INSANITY
During gameplay, hold Left Trigger + Right Trigger + X and press Right, Right, Right, A, Left, Left, Right, Left, A.

FULL HEALTH
During gameplay, hold Left Trigger + Right Trigger + X and press Down, Down, Down, A, Up, Up, Down, Up, A.

ARSENAL
During gameplay, hold Left Trigger + Right Trigger + X and press Down, Right, Up, Left, Down, A, Left, Left, Right, Right, A, Down, Up, Left, Right, A.

INVINCIBILITY
During gameplay, hold Left Trigger + Right Trigger + X and press Down, Up, Down, Up.

MINUS 50 REP
During gameplay, hold Left Trigger + Right Trigger + X and press Left, Left, Down, Up.

PLUS 50 REP
During gameplay, hold Left Trigger + Right Trigger + X and press Up, Up, Right, Up.

FULL BLOOD
During gameplay, hold Left Trigger + Right Trigger + X and press Up, Down, Left, Right.

ZERO BLOOD
During gameplay, hold Left Trigger + Right Trigger + X and press Down, Up, Right, Left.

SHRAPNEL
During gameplay, hold Left Trigger + Right Trigger + X and press Right, Right, Right, Left, Left, Left.

MAX EVIL REP
During gameplay, hold Left Trigger + Right Trigger + X and press Left, Down, Left, Down, Left, Down, A.

MAX GOOD REP
During gameplay, hold Left Trigger + Right Trigger + X and press Up, Right, Up, Right, Up, Right, A.

FULL BOTTLES
During gameplay, hold Left Trigger + Right Trigger + X and press Right, Right, Up, Up, A, Left, Right, A, Right, Up, Right, A.

SUPER BAD DUDE
During gameplay, hold Left Trigger + Right Trigger + X and press Down, Up, Down, Left, Right, Left, A, Up, Left, Down, Right, Up, Right, Down, Left, A, Down, Down, Down, A, A.

PROJECTOR STATE
During gameplay, hold Left Trigger + Right Trigger + X and press Up, A, Left, A, Down, A, Right, A.

DREAM STATE
During gameplay, hold Left Trigger + Right Trigger + X and press Left, Left, A, Right, Right, A, Up, Up, A, Down, Down, A.

ALL NOTES
During gameplay, hold Left Trigger + Right Trigger + X and press Right, Left, Up, Left, A, Right, Down, Right.

ALL MAPS
During gameplay, hold Left Trigger + Right Trigger + X and press Left, Right, Down, Right, A, Left, Up, Left.

SUPERMAN: THE MAN OF STEEL

ALL LEVELS AND BONUSES
Pause the game and press R, Black, Y, Black, L, White.

UNLIMITED HEALTH
Pause the game and press Black, White, L, X, L, White.

X-RAY GRAPHICS
Pause the game and press L, L, R, L, Y, X, White, Black, Black, White.

FREEZE GRAPHICS
Pause the game and press R, L, Black, White, L, Y, Y, Black, R, White.

SVC CHAOS: SNK VS. CAPCOM

DAN
Highlight Dhalsim and hold R.

DEMITRI
Highlight Chun-Li and hold R.

GEESE
Highlight Kyo and hold R.

GOENITZ
Highlight Ryo and hold R.

MARS PEOPLE
Highlight Terry and hold R.

SHIN GOUKI
Highlight Balrog and hold R.

SHIN MR.KARATE
Highlight Kasumi and hold R.

VIOLENT KEN
Highlight Vega and hold R.

WILD IORI
Highlight Kim and hold R.

ZERO
Highlight Ryu and hold R.

SWAT: GLOBAL STRIKE TEAM

ALL MISSIONS
Pause the game and press Up, L, Down, R, Left, L, Right, R, Up.

INVINCIBILITY
Pause the game and press Up, Down, Left, Right, Left, Right, White, Black.

UNLIMITED AMMO
Pause the game and press Left, Right, Up, Down, Up, Down, Black, White.

TAK: THE GREAT JUJU CHALLENGE

BONUS SOUND EFFECTS
In Juju's Potions, select Universal Card and enter the following numbers for Bugs, Crystals and Fruits: 20, 17, 5.

BONUS SOUND EFFECTS 2
In Juju's Potions, select Universal Card and enter the following numbers for Bugs, Crystals and Fruits: 50, 84, 92.

BONUS MUSIC TRACK 1
In Juju's Potions, select Universal Card and enter the following numbers for Bugs, Crystals and Fruits: 67, 8, 20.

BONUS MUSIC TRACK 2
In Juju's Potions, select Universal Card and enter the following numbers for Bugs, Crystals and Fruits: 6, 18, 3.

MAGIC PARTICLES
In Juju's Potions, select Universal Card and enter the following numbers for Bugs, Crystals and Fruits: 24, 40, 11.

MORE MAGIC PARTICLES
In Juju's Potions, select Universal Card and enter the following numbers for Bugs, Crystals and Fruits: 48, 57, 57.

VIEW JUJU CONCEPT ART
In Juju's Potions, select Universal Card and enter the following numbers for Bugs, Crystals and Fruits: Art 33, 22, 28.

VIEW VEHICLE ART
In Juju's Potions, select Universal Card and enter the following numbers for Bugs, Crystals and Fruits: 11, 55, 44.

VIEW WORLD ART
In Juju's Potions, select Universal Card and enter the following numbers for Bugs, Crystals and Fruits: 83, 49, 34.

TAK 2: THE STAFF OF DREAMS

BALLOON HEAD SHOWDOWN MINI-GAME
Select Universal Card from Juju Potions and enter the following numbers for Bugs, Crystals and Fruit: 48, 62, 19.

BARREL BLITZ MINI-GAME
Select Universal Card from Juju Potions and enter the following numbers for Bugs, Crystals and Fruit: 1, 105, 81.

CATAPULT CHAOS MINI-GAME
Select Universal Card from Juju Potions and enter the following numbers for Bugs, Crystals and Fruit: 103, 33, 20.

CHICKEN TENNIS MINI-GAME
Select Universal Card from Juju Potions and enter the following numbers for Bugs, Crystals and Fruit: 202, 17, 203.

CHUCKIN' CHICKENS MINI-GAME
Select Universal Card from Juju Potions and enter the following numbers for Bugs, Crystals and Fruit: 18, 71, 50.

DART TOOM DODGEM MINI-GAME
Select Universal Card from Juju Potions and enter the following numbers for Bugs, Crystals and Fruit: 83, 43, 142.

DINKY SNOWBOARD BIG AIR MINI-GAME
Select Universal Card from Juju Potions and enter the following numbers for Bugs, Crystals and Fruit: 233, 127, 204.

FLEA FLYER MINI-GAME
Select Universal Card from Juju Potions and enter the following numbers for Bugs, Crystals and Fruit: 22, 6, 17.

FROG DERBY MINI-GAME
Select Universal Card from Juju Potions and enter the following numbers for Bugs, Crystals and Fruit: 281, 62, 149.

GLIDE RIDE MINI-GAME
Select Universal Card from Juju Potions and enter the following numbers for Bugs, Crystals and Fruit: 131, 61, 179.

GLOOMLEAF ARENA MINI-GAME
Select Universal Card from Juju Potions and enter the following numbers for Bugs, Crystals and Fruit: 68, 13, 8.

KRASH KOURSE MINI-GAME
Select Universal Card from Juju Potions and enter the following numbers for Bugs, Crystals and Fruit: 5, 41, 41.

VINE CLIMB MINI-GAME
Select Universal Card from Juju Potions and enter the following numbers for Bugs, Crystals and Fruit: 8, 1, 3.

FAUNA IN MULTIPLAYER
Select Universal Card from Juju Potions and enter the following numbers for Bugs, Crystals and Fruit: 44, 13, 0.

JB IN MULTIPLAYER
Select Universal Card from Juju Potions and enter the following numbers for Bugs, Crystals and Fruit: 16, 19, 38.

LOK IN MULTIPLAYER
Select Universal Card from Juju Potions and enter the following numbers for Bugs, Crystals and Fruit: 2, 2, 5.

SKELETON JUJU SPIRIT IN MULTIPLAYER
Select Universal Card from Juju Potions and enter the following numbers for Bugs, Crystals and Fruit: 55, 171, 35.

TAK'S FEATHER COLOR
Select Universal Card from Juju Potions and enter the following numbers for Bugs, Crystals and Fruit: 4, 9, 23.

BETTER MANA MAGNET
Select Universal Card from Juju Potions and enter the following numbers for Bugs, Crystals and Fruit: 3, 27, 31.

TAK 1 GAME CINEMATIC SEQUENCE
Select Universal Card from Juju Potions and enter the following numbers for Bugs, Crystals and Fruit: 30, 21, 88.

CONCEPT ART
Select Universal Card from Juju Potions and enter the following numbers for Bugs, Crystals and Fruit: 30, 37, 51.

PICTURES OF THE TAK SUIT
Select Universal Card from Juju Potions and enter the following numbers for Bugs, Crystals and Fruit: 11, 4, 17.

SOUND EFFECTS SET ONE
Select Universal Card from Juju Potions and enter the following numbers for Bugs, Crystals and Fruit: 4, 55, 36.

VIEW COMMERICIALS
Select Universal Card from Juju Potions and enter the following numbers for Bugs, Crystals and Fruit: 6, 16, 6.

TAZ WANTED

ALL LEVELS
At the Start Game screen, select Marvin the Martian and enter #OP.

ALL BONUS GAMES
At the Start Game screen, select Daffy Duck and enter ?BN.

2-PLAYER BOSS GAMES
At the Start Game screen, select Big red and enter *JC.

ART GALLERY
At the Start Game screen, select Tweety and enter .RT.

DISABLE WHACK IN THE BOXES
At the Start Game screen, select Taz and enter !WB.

TEENAGE MUTANT NINJA TURTLES 2: BATTLE NEXUS

PASSWORDS

Select Password from the Options menu and enter the following. Hold Left Trigger while selecting a turtle to get his New Nexus Turtle outfit.

NAME	PASSWORD
Challenge Code Abyss	SDSDRLD
Challenge Code Endurance	MRMDRMD
Challenge Code Fatal Blow	LRSRDRD
Challenge Code Lose Shuriken	RLMRDSL
Challenge Code Nightmare	SLSDRDL
Challenge Code Poison	DRSLLSR
Challenge Code Super-Tough	RDSRMRL
Cheat Code All-You-Can-Throw Shuriken	RSRLRSM
Cheat Code Health	DSRDMRM
Cheat Code Mighty Turtle	LSDRRDR
Cheat Code Pizza Paradise	MRLMRMR
Cheat Code Self Recovery	DRMSRLR
Cheat Code Squeaking	MLDSRDM
Cheat Code Super Defense Power	LDRMRLM
Cheat Code Super Offense Power	SDLSRLL
Cheat Code Toddling	SSSMRDD
New Nexus Turtle outfit for Donatello	DSLRDRM
New Nexus Turtle outfit for Leonardo	LMRMDRD
New Nexus Turtle outfit for Michelangelo	MLMRDRM
New Nexus Turtle outfit for Raphael	RMSRMDR

TEENAGE MUTANT NINJA TURTLES 3: MUTANT NIGHTMARE

INVINCIBILITY
Select Passwords from the Options menu and enter MDLDSSLR.

HEALTH POWER-UPS TURN INTO SUSHI
Select Passwords from the Options menu and enter SLLMRSLD.

NO HEALTH POWER-UPS
SELECT PASSWORDS FROM THE OPTIONS MENU AND ENTER DMLDMRLD.

1-HIT DEFEATS TURTLE
Select Passwords from the Options menu and enter LDMSLRDD.

MAX OUGI
Select Passwords from the Options menu and enter RRDMLSDL.

UNLIMITED SHURIKEN
Select Passwords from the Options menu and enter LMDRRMSR.

NO SHURIKEN
Select Passwords from the Options menu and enter LLMSRDMS.

DOUBLE ENEMY ATTACK
Select Passwords from the Options menu and enter MSRLSMML.

DOUBLE ENEMY DEFENSE
Select Passwords from the Options menu and enter SLRMLSSM.

TENCHU: RETURN FROM DARKNESS

PLAY AS TESSHU
At the Title screen, hold White + Black and press Up, Right, Left, Down. Release White + Black and press Left Trigger, Right Trigger.

ALL MISSIONS
At the mission select, press White, White, Left Trigger, Right Trigger, Right, X, L-Click, R-Click.

ALL LAYOUTS
At the mission select, press R-Click, L-Click, Left Trigger, Right Trigger, White, Black.

SCORE
Pause the game and press Right, Right, Right, Left.

RESTORE HEALTH
Pause the game and press Up, Down, Up, Down, X, X, X.

INCREASE POWER
Pause the game, hold Right Trigger + White Button and press Up, Down, Up, Down. Release Right Trigger + White Button and press X, X, X.

FILL THE KUJI METER
Pause the game, hold Right Trigger + Left Triggers and press Left, Left, Left, Right, X.

UNLOCK NEW ABILITY
Pause the game, hold Right Trigger + Black Button and press Up, Up, Down, Down. Release Right Trigger + Black Button and press X, X, Left Trigger, Right Trigger.

ONE KANJI
Pause the game and press Left, Left, Left, Right, X.

ALL ITEMS
At the item select, hold Right Trigger + Left Trigger and press Up, Down, Up, Down, X, X, X, Left, Right, Left, Right, X, X, X.

10 OF EACH AVAILABLE ITEM
At the item select, hold Right Trigger + Left Trigger and press Up, Left, Down, Right, X, X, X.

MAX CAPACITY
At the item select, hold Right Trigger + Left Trigger + White Button and press Up, Up, Down, Down, Left, Right, Left, Right. Release the White Button and press X, X, X.

B-SIDE LANGUAGE
At the Title screen, hold Left Trigger + Right Trigger and press Down, X, X, Up, X, X, Left, X, X, Right, X, X. Enable B-Side Language in the Sound Options.

TERMINATOR 3: RISE OF THE MACHINES

Select Cheats from the Options menu and enter the following:

EFFECT	CODE
Unlimited Continues	B,B,B,X,B,A,Y,A
Invincibility	Y,X,B,B,A,A,B,X
Unlimited Ammunition	X,A,Y,Y,Y,A,X,B
All Weapons - Future	A,A,A,X,B,X,B,B
Terminator HP's 50 More in Every Fight	A,Y,A,Y
Terminator HP's 50 Less in Every Fight	B,Y,A,A
T-X HP's 50 More in Every Fight	B,X,X,X,B,A,Y,A
T-X HP's 50 Less in Every Fight	B,B,X,X,X,B,A,Y
Unlock All Levels	X,Y,Y,X,B,A,A,B
Unlock All Exclusive Movies	B,B,B,A,X,Y,X,Y
Unlock All in Game Movies	B,B,B,X,B,Y,B,B

CENTEPIDE

Press A, B, B, B, X, Y, B, A. You can find it in Special Features/Atari Games menu.

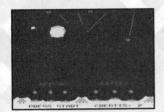

MISSILE COMMAND
Press A, B, B, B, X, Y, A, B. You can find it in Special Features/Atari Games menu.

TERMINATOR 3: THE REDEMPTION

LEVEL SELECT
Select Credits and press B + Black + Y.

INVINCIBILITY
Select Credits and press B + Black + R.

ALL UPGRADES
Select Credits and press B + Y + L.

TIGER WOODS PGA TOUR 2005

Select Passwords from the Options menu and enter the following:

ALL GOLFERS AND COURSES
Enter THEGIANTOYSTER.

ALL COURSES
Enter THEWORLDISYOURS.

ALL ACCESSORIES
Enter TIGERMOBILE.

THE ROOF IN THE SKILLZONE GAME MODE
Enter NIGHTGOLFER.

JUSTIN TIMBERLAKE
Enter THETENNESSEEKID.

ARNOLD PALMER
Enter THEKING.

BEN HOGAN
Enter PUREGOLF.

SEVE BALLESTEROS
Enter THEMAGICIAN.

JACK NICKLAUS
Enter GOLDENBEAR.

GARY PLAYER
Enter BLACKKNIGHT.

TIFFANY "TIFF" WILLIAMSON
Enter RICHGIRL.

JEB "SHOOTER" MCGRAW
Enter SIXSHOOTER.

HUNTER "STEELHEAD" ELMORE
Enter GREENCOLLAR.

ALASTAIR" CAPTAIN" MCFADDEN
Enter NICESOCKS.

BEV "BOOMER" BUOUCHIER
Enter THEBEEHIVE.

ADRIANA "SUGAR" DULCE
Enter SOSWEET.

APHRODITE PAPADAPOLUS
Enter TEMPTING.

BILLY "BEAR" HIGHTOWER
Enter TOOTALL.

KENDRA "SPIKE" LOVETTE
Enter ENGLISHPUNK.

DION "DOUBLE D" DOUGLAS
Enter DDDOUGLAS.

RAQUEL "ROCKY" ROGERS
Enter DOUBLER.

BUNJIRO "BUD" TANAKA
Enter INTHEFAMILY.

CEASAR "THE EMPEROR" ROSADO
Enter LANDOWNER.

REGINALD "REG" WEATHERS
Enter REGGIE.

THE HUSTLER
Enter ALTEREGO.

SUNDAY TIGER WOODS
Enter NEWLEGEND.

ADIDAS ITEMS
Enter 91treSTR.

CALLAWAY ITEMS
Enter cgTR78qw.

CLEVELAND ITEMS
Enter CL45etUB.

MAXFLI ITEMS
Enter FDGH597i.

NIKE ITEMS
Enter YJHk342B.

ODYSSEY ITEMS
Enter kjnMR3qv.

PING ITEMS
Enter R453DrTe.

PRECEPT ITEMS
Enter BRi3498Z.

TAG ITEMS
Enter cDsa2fgY.

TOURSTAGE ITEMS
Enter TS345329.

TIGER WOODS PGA TOUR 06

ALL GOLFERS
Select Password from the Options menu and enter WOOGLIN.

ALL CLUBS
Select Password from the Options menu and enter CLUB11.

LEVEL 2 NIKE ITEMS
Select Password from the Options menu and enter JUSTDOIT.

ALL COURSES
Select Password from the Options menu and enter ITSINTHEHOLE.

TIGER WOODS IN HAT AND TIE
Select Password from the Options menu and enter GOLDENAGE.

TIGER WOODS IN STRIPED PANTS
Select Password from the Options menu and enter TECHNICOLOR.

TIGER WOODS IN OLD GOLF OUTFIT
Select Password from the Options menu and enter OLDSKOOL.

TIGER WOODS IN ALTERNATE OLD GOLF OUTFIT
Select Password from the Options menu and enter THROWBACK.

ARNOLD PALMER
Select Password from the Options menu and enter ARNIESARMY.

BEN HOGAN
Select Password from the Options menu and enter THEHAWK.

JACK NICKLAUS
Select Password from the Options menu and enter GOLDENBEAR.

OLD TOM MORRIS
Select Password from the Options menu and enter FEATHERIE.

TOMMY BLACK
Select Password from the Options menu and enter IDONTHAVEAPROBLEM.

WESLEY ROUNDER
Select Password from the Options menu and enter POCKETPAIR.

TIGER WOODS PGA TOUR 07

NIKE ITEMS
Select the Password option and enter JUSTDOIT.

TIM BURTON'S THE NIGHTMARE BEFORE CHRISTMAS: OOGIE'S REVENGE

PUMPKIN KING & SANTA JACK COSTUMES
During gameplay, press Down, Up, Right, Left, Left Thumbstick, Right Thumbstick.

TOM CLANCY'S RAINBOW SIX 3: BLACK ARROW

GOD MODE
During gameplay, press Up, Up, Down, Down, Left, Right, Left, Right, B, A.

WALL OF FAME MAP
At the Main menu, press Left Thumbstick, Left Thumbstick, Right Thumbstick, Right Thumbstick, X, Y, B, A, B, A.

LASER TRAILS
During gameplay, press Up, Down, Up, Down, Right Thumbstick, Right Thumbstick. This makes your team's shots red and the enemies' shots blue.

ALL MAPS
At the Main menu, press Left, Left, Right, Right, A, B, Left Thumbstick, Left Thumbstick.

CREDITS LEVEL
At the Main menu, press Left Thumbstick, Left Thumbstick, Right Thumbstick, Right Thumbstick, X, Y, B, A, B, A.

TOM CLANCY'S SPLINTER CELL CHAOS THEORY

ALL MISSIONS
Enter COOPA22COOL as your profile name.

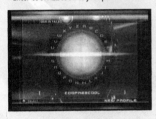

TOMB RAIDER: LEGEND

You must unlock the following codes in the game before using them.

BULLETPROOF
During gameplay, hold Left Trigger and press A, Right Trigger, Y, Right Trigger, X, Black.

DRAIN ENEMY HEALTH
During gameplay, hold Left Trigger and press X, B, A, Black, Right Trigger, Y.

INFINITE ASSAULT RIFLE AMMO
During gameplay, hold Black and press A, B, A, Left Trigger, X, Y.

INFINITE GRENADE LAUNCHER AMMO
During gameplay, hold Black and press Left Trigger, Y, Right Trigger, B, Left Trigger, X.

INFINITE SHOTGUN AMMO
During gameplay, hold Black and press Right Trigger, B, X, Left Trigger, X, A.

INFINITE SMG AMMO
During gameplay, hold Black and press B, Y, Left Trigger, Right Trigger, A, B.

EXCALIBUR
During gameplay, hold Black and press Y, A, B, Right Trigger, Y, Left Trigger.

SOUL REAVER
During gameplay, hold Black and press A, Right Trigger, B, Right Trigger, Left Trigger, X.

NO TEXTURE MODE
During gameplay, hold Left Trigger and press Black, A, B, A, Y, Right Trigger.

TONY HAWK'S AMERICAN WASTELAND

ALWAYS SPECIAL
Select Cheat Codes from the Options menu and enter uronfire. Pause the game and select Cheats from the Game Options to enable the cheat.

PERFECT RAIL
Select Cheat Codes from the Options menu and enter grindxpert. Pause the game and select Cheats from the Game Options to enable the cheat.

PERFECT SKITCH
Select Cheat Codes from the Options menu and enter h!tchar!de. Pause the game and select Cheats from the Game Options to enable the cheat.

PERFECT MANUAL
Select Cheat Codes from the Options menu and enter 2wheels!. Pause the game and select Cheats from the Game Options to enable the cheat.

MOON GRAVITY
Select Cheat Codes from the Options menu and enter 2them00n. Pause the game and select Cheats from the Game Options to enable the cheat.

MAT HOFFMAN
Select Cheat Codes from the Options screen and enter the_condor.

JASON ELLIS
Select Cheat Codes from the Options menu and enter sirius-dj.

TONY HAWK'S PROJECT 8

SPONSOR ITEMS
As you progress through Career mode and move up the rankings, you gain sponsors and each comes with its own Create-a-Skater item.

RANK	ITEM UNLOCKED
Rank 040	Adio Kenny V2 Shoes
Rank 050	Quiksilver_Hoody_3
Rank 060	Birdhouse Tony Hawk Deck
Rank 080	Vans No Skool Gothic Shoes
Rank 100	Volcom Scallero Jacket
Rank 110	eS Square One Shoes
Rank 120	Almost Watch What You Say Deck
Rank 140	DVS Adage Shoe
Rank 150	Element Illuminate Deck
Rank 160	Etnies Sheckler White Lavender Shoes
Complete Skateshop Goal	Stereo Soundwave Deck

SKATERS
You must unlock all of the skaters, except for Tony Hawk, by completing challenges in the Career Mode. They are useable in Free Skate and 2-Player modes.

SKATER	HOW TO UNLOCK
Tony Hawk	Always unlocked
Lyn-z Adams Hawkins	Complete Pro Challenge
Bob Burquist	Complete Pro Challenge
Dustin Dollin	Complete Pro Challenge
Nyjah Huston	Complete Pro Challenge
Bam Margera	Complete Pro Challenge
Rodney Mullen	Complete Pro Challenge
Paul Rodriguez	Complete Pro Challenge
Ryan Sheckler	Complete Pro Challenge
Daewon Song	Complete Pro Challenge
Mike Vallely	Complete Pro Challenge
Stevie Willams	Complete Pro Challenge
Travis Barker	Complete Pro Challenge
Kevin Staab	Complete Pro Challenge
Zombie	Complete Pro Challenge
Christaian Hosoi	Animal Chin Challenge
Jason Lee	Complete Final Tony Hawk Goal
Photographer	Unlock Shops
Security Guard	Unlock School
Bum	Unlock Car Factory
Beaver Mascot	Unlock High School
Real Estate Agent	Unlock Downtown

SKATER	HOW TO UNLOCK
Filmer	Unlock High School
Skate Jam Kid	Rank #4
Dad	Rank #1
Colonel	All Gaps
Nerd	Complete School Spirit Goal

CHEAT CODES

Select Cheat Codes from the Options menu and enter the following codes. You can access some of the codes in game from the Options menu.

ENTER	WHAT IT DOES
plus44	Unlocks Travis Barker
hohohosoi	Unlocks Christian Hosoi
notmono	Unlocks Jason Lee
mixitup	Unlocks Kevin Staab
strangefellows	Unlocks Dad & Skater Jam Kid
themedia	Unlocks Photog Girl & Filmer
militarymen	Unlocks Colonel & Security Guard
jammypack	Unlocks Always Special
balancegalore	Unlocks Perfect Rail
frontandback	Unlocks Perect Manual
shellshock	Unlocks Unlimited Focus
shescaresme	Unlocks Big Realtor
birdhouse	Unlocks Inkblot deck
allthebest	Full Stats
needaride	All Decks unlocked and free, except for Inkblot Deck and Gamestop Deck
yougotitall	All specials unlocked and in player's special list and set as owned in skate shop
enterandwin	Unlocks bum
wearelosers	Unlocks nerd
manineedadate	Unlocks mascot
suckstobedead	Unlocks zombie
sellsellsell	Unlocks skinny real estate agent
newshound	Unlocks anchor man
badverybad	Unlocks twin

TONY HAWK'S UNDERGROUND

Select Cheat Codes from the Options menu and enter the following codes. Pause the game and select Cheats from the Options menu to toggle the cheats on and off.

PERFECT RAIL
Enter **letitslide**.

PERFECT SKITCH
Enter **rearrider**.

PERFECT MANUAL
Enter **keepitsteady**.

MOON GRAVITY
Enter **getitup**.

TONY HAWK'S UNDERGROUND 2

Select Cheat Codes from the Game Options menu and enter the following. To access the cheats, pause the game and select Cheats to turn them on.

NATAS KAUPAS
Enter bedizzy.

NIGEL BEAVERHOPUSEN
Enter skullet.

PAULIE RYAN
Enter 4wheeler.

PHIL MARGERA
Enter notvito.

ALL LEVELS
Enter accesspass.

ALWAYS SPECIAL CHEAT
Enter likepaulie.

PERFECT RAIL CHEAT
Enter straightedge.

ALL MOVIES
Enter frontrowseat.

TOTAL OVERDOSE: A GUNSLINGER'S TALE IN MEXICO

CHEAT MODE
Hold Left Trigger + Right Trigger + White + Black + Left Thumbstick + Right Thumbstick for a few seconds. Now enter any of the following cheats.

RESTORE HEALTH
Press A, X, B, Y.

ALL LOCO MOVES
Press B, B, White, Black.

MAXIMUM REWINDING
Press Right Trigger, Black, White, A.

ALL WEAPONS
Press Y, Left Trigger, Black, X.

TRUE CRIME: NEW YORK CITY

DOUBLE DAMAGE
At the City Map screen, hold Left Trigger + Right Trigger and press A, A, X, A, A, A.

MILLIONAIRE
At the City Map screen, hold Left Trigger + Right Trigger and press X, X, Y, X, Y, X.

SUPER COP
At the City Map screen, hold Left Trigger + Right Trigger and press Y, A, Y, A, Y, Y.

ULTRA EASY MODE
At the City Map screen, hold Left Trigger + Right Trigger and press B, X, A, A, Y, B.

UNLIMITED AMMO
At the City Map screen, hold Left Trigger + Right Trigger and press B, X, A, X, X, Y.

UNLIMITED ENDURANCE
At the City Map screen, hold Left Trigger + Right Trigger and press B, X, A, X, A, B.

STREET RACES OPEN
At the City Map screen, hold Left Trigger + Right Trigger and press Y, Y, A, A, Y.

FIGHTS OPEN
At the City Map screen, hold Left Trigger + Right Trigger and press X, X, B, B, X.

GHETTO CITY
At the City Map screen, hold Left Trigger + Right Trigger and press A, X, A, Y, Y, Y.

ZOMBIEFIED
At the City Map screen, hold Left Trigger + Right Trigger and press B, Y, X, A, X, A.

NEW OUTFIT IN PUMA STORE
At the City Map screen, hold Left Trigger + Right Trigger and press Y, A, B, X.

RED GONE WILD
At the City Map screen, hold Left Trigger + Right Trigger and press Y, A, A, X, A, X.

ALL MUSIC
At the City Map screen, hold Left Trigger + Right Trigger and press B, X, B, X.

TY THE TASMANIAN TIGER 2: BUSH RESCUE

ALL BUNYIP KEYS
During a game, press Start, Y, Start, Start, Y, X, B, X, A.

ALL FIRST-LEVEL RANGS
During a game, press Start, Y, Start, Start, Y, B, X, B, X.

ALL SECOND-LEVEL RANGS
During a game, press Start, Y, Start, Start, Y, X, B, X, Y.

GET 100,000 OPALS
During a game, press Start, Y, Start, Start, Y, B, A, B, A.

CHEAT GNOME
During a game, press Left + Y + Down + A + X. Now you can enter the following cheats.

MAX ARTISTIC
Press Y, Down, Black, A, B.

MAX MENTAL
Press Left Trigger, B, A, Black, Down.

MAX PHYSTICAL
Press Left Trigger, Right Trigger, A, Down, Black.

ACQUIRE SKILL
Press Left Trigger, Black, Right, X, Left.

POWER SOCIAL
Press Down, Black, Right, X, Left.

TEAM PHOTO
At the Credits screen, press Up, Down, X, Up, Down.

TY THE TASMANIAN TIGER 3: NIGHT OF THE QUINKAN

100,000 OPALS
During a game, press Start, Start, Y, Start, Start, Y, B, A, B, A.

ALL RINGS
During a game, press Start, Start, Y, Start, Start, Y, B, X, B, X.

ULTIMATE SPIDER-MAN

ALL CHARACTERS
Pause the game and select Controller Setup from the Options menu. Press Right, Down, Right, Down, Left, Up, Left, Right.

ALL COVERS
Pause the game and select Controller Setup from the Options menu. Press Left, Left, Right, Left, Up, Left, Left, Down.

ALL CONCEPT ART
Pause the game and select Controller Setup from the Options menu. Press Down, Down, Down, Up, Down, Up, Left, Left.

ALL LANDMARKS
Pause the game and select Controller Setup from the Options menu. Press Up, Right, Down, Left, Down, Up, Right, Left.

UNREAL CHAMPIONSHIP 2: THE LIANDRI CONFLICT

AT THE MAIN MENU, PRESS UP, UP, DOWN, DOWN, Y, DOWN, UP, Y. THIS UNLOCKS THE CHEAT MENU.

Pause the game, hold L + R and press White. This menu is not available in System Link or Xbox Live modes. You can advance through Story Mode using cheats, but you won't be able to record statistics such as your Best Time. The Cheat menu contains the following: Infinite Health, Infinite Ammo, Infinite Adrenaline, Lock-on Stuns, Bot Adrenaline, and Give Me a Point.

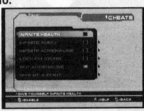

HIDDEN COUP DE GRACE MOVES

A stunned enemy can be finished in a single stroke (regardless of his or her health) if you can pull off a Coup de Grace move.

To perform the hidden Coup de Grace:

1. Stun an enemy

2. Lock on (if not already done)

3. Switch to melee weapon (if not already armed)

4. Ignore the onscreen button combo and perform the hidden Coup de Grace button combo for your combatant before the stun expires

ANUBIS HIDDEN COUP DE GRACE COMBO
X, Y, Up, A, Right Trigger

ARCLITE HIDDEN COUP DE GRACE COMBO
X, Y, Right, A, A, A, Left

BROCK HIDDEN COUP DE GRACE COMBO
X, Y, Right, Left, A, A

DEVASTATION HIDDEN COUP DE GRACE COMBO
X, Y, Up, Left, Down, Right, Left Trigger

GORGE HIDDEN COUP DE GRACE COMBO
X, Y, Right, A, Left Trigger +Right Trigger, A

LAUREN HIDDEN COUP DE GRACE COMBO
X, Y, Left, Right, Right Trigger

MALCOLM HIDDEN COUP DE GRACE COMBO
X, Y, Down, Up, A, Left Trigger

RAIDEN HIDDEN COUP DE GRACE COMBO
X, Y, Up, Down, Down, Down, A

RAPTOR HIDDEN COUP DE GRACE COMBO
X, Y, Down, Left, Up, Right, Right Trigger

SAPPHIRE HIDDEN COUP DE GRACE COMBO
X, Y, Up, Down, Left Trigger, A

SELKET HIDDEN COUP DE GRACE COMBO
X, Y, Down, A, A, Left Trigger + Right Trigger

SOBEK HIDDEN COUP DE GRACE COMBO
X, Y, Right Trigger, Up, Down, Down

SZALOR HIDDEN COUP DE GRACE COMBO
X, Y, Left Trigger + Right Trigger, Down, Up

TORGR HIDDEN COUP DE GRACE COMBO
X, Y, Left Trigger, Right Trigger, Down, Down, Up

URBAN CHAOS: RIOT RESPONSE

At the Main menu, press Up, Up, Down, Down, Y, Down, Up, Y. This opens the Cheat screen. Select Add Cheat and enter the following.

ALL LEVELS & EMERGENCIES
Enter KEYTOTHECITY.

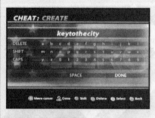

TERROR MODE
Enter BURNERSREVENGE. This unlocks the Terror Difficulty.

ASSUALT RIFLE MK. 3 WITH INFINITE SHELLS
Enter ULTIMATEPOWER.

MINI-GUN
Enter MINIFUN.

PISTOL MK. 4
Enter ZEROTOLERANCE.

ENHANCED STUN GUN
Enter FRYINGTIME.

BURNING BULLETS
Enter BURNINGBULLET.

DISCO CHEAT
Enter DANCINGFEET.

HEADLESS CHEAT
Enter KEEPYOURHEAD.

SQUEAKY VOICES
Enter WHATWASTHAT.

VAN HELSING

BONUS MOVIE 1
During a game, press Up, Down, Up, Down, Left, Left, Right, Right, Left Trigger, Left Thumbstick, Right Thumbstick, Right Trigger.

BONUS MOVIE 2
During a game, press Up, Right, Down, Left, Up, Left, Down, Right, Up, Right Trigger, Black, Right Thumbstick.

BONUS MOVIE 3
During a game, press Left Trigger, White, Black, Right Trigger, Black, White, Left Trigger, Up, Up, Down, Down, Back.

BONUS MOVIE 4
During a game, press Back, Left Thumbstick, Right Thumbstick, Back, Right Thumbstick, Left Thumbstick, Back, Left, Left, Up, Right, Right.

BONUS MOVIE 5
During a game, press White, Black, Left Trigger, Right Trigger, Back, Back, Left Trigger, Left Trigger, Black, Black, Left Thumbstick, Right Thumbstick.

BONUS MOVIE 6
During a game, press Black, Right Trigger, Black, Right Trigger, Left Trigger, White, Left Trigger, White, Left, Right, Back, Back.

BONUS MOVIE 7
During a game, press Left Thumbstick, Left, Right Thumbstick, Right, White, Up, Black, Down, Left Trigger, Left, Right Trigger, Right.

VIETCONG: PURPLE HAZE

GOD MODE
During a game, press L + R + A + Down.

ALL LEVELS
Highlight options and hold L + R + Black + White.

WARPATH

ALL AMMO
Select Cheat Codes from the Options menu and press Down, Up, Down, Y. You can also enter this code during a game by pausing the game and selecting Cheat Codes from the Settings menu.

GOD MODE
Select Cheat Codes from the Options menu and enter Up, Left Trigger, X, Left Trigger. You can also enter this code during a game, by pausing the game and selecting Cheat Codes from the Settings menu.

WIN CURRENT MATCH
Select Cheat Codes from the Options menu and enter Left Trigger, Left Trigger, Left Trigger, Y. You can also enter this code during a game, by pausing the game and selecting Cheat Codes from the Settings menu.

LOSE CURRENT MATCH
Select Cheat Codes from the Options menu and enter Left Trigger, Left Trigger, Left Trigger, A. You can also enter this code during a game by pausing the game and selecting Cheat Codes from the Settings menu.

SINGLE PLAYER
Select Cheat Codes from the Options menu and enter Y, Down, Right Trigger, Down. You can also enter this code during a game by pausing the game and selecting Cheat Codes from the Settings menu.

LOCATION STAT
Select Cheat Codes from the Options menu and enter X, Right, Left Trigger, Left. You can also enter this code during a game by pausing the game and selecting Cheat Codes from the Settings menu.

THE WARRIORS

100% COMPLETE
During gameplay, press Right Trigger, Back, X, Down, Left Trigger, Right.

99 CREDITS IN ARMIES OF THE NIGHT
During the Armies of the Night mini-game, press Up, Up, Down, Down, Left, Right.

$200, FLASH, & SPRAY PAINT
During gameplay, press Black, Left Thumbstick, Right Trigger, A, Down, R.

INFINITE HEALTH
During gameplay, press Up, Y, White, Back, A, Left Trigger, Down, X, Left, A, Right Trigger, Back.

INFINITE RAGE
During gameplay, press X, B, Y, Back, A, Left.

INFINITE SPRINT
During gameplay, press Down, X, Left, A, R, Back.

COMPLETE MISSION
During gameplay, press Down, X, A, Back, Back, Left.

BAT
During gameplay, press X, Left Thumbstick, Down, Down, Right Trigger, Right Trigger.

UNBREAKABLE BAT
During gameplay, press White, White, B, Up, B, Back.

BRASS KNUCKLES
During gameplay, press B, B, B, R, Back, Y.

KNIFE
During gameplay, press Down, Down, Back, Up, Up, White.

MACHETE
During gameplay, press Right Trigger, A, Black, Black, Back, Left Thumbstick.

PIPE
During gameplay, press Left Thumbstick, B, Back, Up, Right Trigger, Right.

STEEL-TOE BOOTS
During gameplay, press Click Right Thumbstick, Click Left Thumbstick, Black, White, Left Trigger, Right Trigger.

BUM ADVICE UPGRADE
During gameplay, press B, B, Down, Click Left Thumbstick, Left Trigger, B.

COMBAT STAMINA UPGRADE
During gameplay, press A, Right Trigger, Down, X, Up, A.

FLASH CAPACITY UPGRADE
During gameplay, press Left Trigger, A, Click Left Thumbstick, Right Trigger, Right Trigger, B.

FLASH UPGRADE
During gameplay, press Down, Left, Up, Up, X, Right.

SPRINT STAMINA UPGRADE
During gameplay, press Left Trigger, Back, Back, Back, Back, Y.

CUFF DROPS
During gameplay, press Up, A, Up, Back, White, Right Trigger.

CUFF KEY DROPS
During gameplay, press Left, A, A, Click Left Thumbstick, Right Trigger, Down.

UNCUFF SELF
During gameplay, press Y, Y, Y, Back, Y, Black.

LOSE THE POLICE
During gameplay, press Up, Back, A, Y, Y, B.

HOBO ALLIANCE
During gameplay, press Black, Black, Right Trigger, Black, Right Trigger, Up.

WEAPONS DEALER
During gameplay, press Right, Black, B, A, Back, X.

WHACKED!

Enter the following as a profile name in Gameshow mode:

UBER MODE
Enter UBERHUNGARIAN.

ALL ARENAS, WEAPONS, WEAPON SETS, AND FMVS
Enter AROUNDDAWORLD.

ALL WEAPONS AND FMVS
Enter TIMEFORCHAOS.

ALL CHARACTERS, FOOD PRODUCTS, BURGERS, AND FMVS
Enter FOODFIGHT.

ALL CHARACTERS AND FMVS
Enter DOUBLEDOUBLE.

WHITEOUT

ALL CHARACTERS
At the Main menu, hold R + L and press Down (x4).

ALL TRACKS, SNOWMOBILES, AND RIDERS
At the Main menu, hold R + L and press Right (x4).

ALL COURSES
At the Main menu, hold R + L and press Up (x4).

ALL PARTS
At the Main menu, hold R + L and press Left (x4).

WITHOUT WARNING

LEVEL SKIP AND LEVEL SELECT
At the Main menu, press X, Y, B, Left Trigger, Left, Up, Right, Right Trigger. Pause the game to access both options.

WORLD RACING 2

The following codes are case sensitive. You can enter them as many times as you want while creating a profile.

100 SPEEDBUCKS
Create a new profile with the name EC.

1,000 SPEEDBUCKS
Create a new profile with the name Visa.

10,000 SPEEDBUCKS
Create a new profile with the name MASTERCARD.

100,000 SPEEDBUCKS
Create a new profile with the name AmEx.

X-MEN LEGENDS II: RISE OF APOCALYPSE

ALL CHARACTERS
At the Team Management screen, press Right, Left, Left, Right, Up, Up, Up, Start.

ALL SKINS
At the Team Management screen, press Down, Up, Left, Right, Up, Up, Start.

ALL SKILLS
At the Team Management screen, press Left, Right, Left, Right, Down, Up, Start.

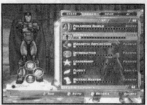

LEVEL 99
At the Team Management screen, press Up, Down, Up, Down, Left, Up, Left, Right, Start.

GOD MODE
Pause the game and press Down, Up, Down, Up, Right, Down, Right, Left, Start.

MOVE FASTER
Pause the game and press Up, Up, Up, Down, Up, Down, Start.

UNLIMITED XTREME TOKENS
Pause the game and press Left, Down, Right, Down, Up, Up, Down, Up, Start.

TOUCH OF DEATH
During a game, press Left, Left, Right, Left, Right, Up, Start.

100,000 TECH-BITS
At Forge or Beast's store, press Up, Up, Up, Down, Right, Right, Start.

ALL DANGER ROOM COURSES
At the Danger Room Course menu, press Right, Right, Left, Left, Up, Down, Up, Down, Start.

ALL COMICS
Select Review from the Main menu and press Right, Left, Left, Right, Up, Up, Right, Start.

ALL CINEMATICS
Select Review from the Main menu and press Left, Right, Right, Left, Down, Down, Left, Start.

ALL CONCEPTS
Select Review from the Main menu and press Left, Right, Left, Right, Up, Up, Down, Start.

ALL SCREENS
Select Review from the Main menu and press Right, Left, Right, Left, Up, Up, Down, Start.